MW00591046

THE SOCIALIST SYSTEM

USE

THE SOCIALIST SYSTEM

THE POLITICAL ECONOMY
OF COMMUNISM

János Kornai

PRINCETON UNIVERSITY PRESS   PRINCETON, NEW JERSEY

Copyright © 1992 by János Kornai
Published by Princeton University Press, 41 William Street, Princeton,
New Jersey 08540

All Rights Reserved

ISBN 0-691-04298-5
      0-691-00393-9 (pbk.)

Library of Congress Cataloging-in-Publication Data

Kornai, János.
    The socialist system : the political economy of communism / János
Kornai.
      p.   cm.
    Includes bibliographical references and index.
    ISBN 0-691-04298-5
    ISBN 0-691-00393-9 (pbk.)
    1. Communism. I. Title.
HX73.K6715   1992
335.43—dc20   91-37866
                                                        CIP

This book has been composed in Times Roman.

Princeton University Press books are printed on acid-free paper, and meet the guidelines
for permanence and durability of the Committee on Production Guidelines for Book
Longevity of the Council on Library Resources

Printed in the United States of America

10 9 8 7 6 5 4 3 2 1

10 9 8 7 6 5 4 3 2 1
(Pbk.)

For my first reader, Zsuzsa

———————————————————————————————

Contents

Figures

Tables

Preface _____

P.1 Purpose

WRITING and publishing this book is a risky business. When I began writing it, the Berlin Wall was still standing, several leaders of the Czechoslovak opposition were still in prison, and governmental power in the countries of Eastern Europe was still in the exclusive hands of the Communist party. Now, as I write this introduction in the spring of 1991, new parliaments brought about by the first free elections have been operating in those countries for several months, and governments qualified to carry out the governmental tasks of the postsocialist transition have formed. Who would dare forecast what the situation will be when this book appears, or when a reader picks it up some years later? But even though the socialist world is creaking at every joint, the purpose of this book remains to arrive at statements of a generalized nature about this system.

Let me quote from the introduction to Simon Schama's excellent book on the French revolution (1989): "Chou Enlai, the Chinese prime minister, when asked what he thought of the significance of the French revolution, is said to have replied, 'It's still too early to say.' After two hundred years it may still be too early (or too late) to say." That ironically ambiguous comment of Schama's is what I would like to latch onto: it is too early, or possibly too late, after the passage of two hundred years, for a social researcher to comment on a great event.

Be that as it may, the author of this book does not intend to wait. I accept all the risks and drawbacks of proximity to the events: the beginning of the period in 1917 is only seven to eight decades ago, and every day in the present brings a new development. I may fail to appreciate the proportions, overrate some features of the system, and underrate others for want of a historical perspective of several centuries. I may be subject to prejudice even though my aim is objectiveness. Nevertheless, I feel an inner compulsion, which I cannot and do not want to resist, to express what I have to say. Before attempting to state objectively the useful purpose I hope this book can serve, I would like to recount frankly my personal motives for writing it, which inseparably entails evaluation of my own previous work.

All I have written about the socialist system hitherto has appeared in the dismembered form of monographs and articles in academic journals. However important the subject of any particular study may have been in itself—on the distorted strategy of growth, the chronic shortage, or the failure of the reform—and however thorough an analysis it attempted to make, each has dealt with some part of the operation of the system.[1] Now I would like this message of mine, expressed so far in separate writings, to develop into a more comprehensive synthesis. This book sums up the main arguments in much of my previous work. It contains equally the main inferences that can be considered to be products of my own deliberations and those that I have adopted from others.

In compiling the book, I have endeavored to point out who the original pioneers of each idea were, and in addition to guide the reader toward the works that provide a summary of each subject area. My own thinking has been affected by a very large number of authors, and this is apparent, for instance, in the references given. However, I would like here to emphasize particularly four names, those of Marx, Schumpeter, Keynes, and Hayek, since they have exerted the greatest influence on my ideas and on the method of approach to the problems employed in this book. I may be reproached on the grounds that these four giants among thinkers represent widely different political principles and philosophies of science. That is true, and I can add, without listing the names, that I have attempted also to utilize a great deal from the neoclassical theory of economics, for instance, or the results of the present-day Western institutionalist approach to the social sciences. Those who condemn this multiplicity of inspirations may go so far as to call the book's approach eclectic. But I would hope that there will be some who pass a more favorable judgment upon it, some who approve of my attempt at a synthesis between the partly conflicting and partly complementary approaches that have come from several different directions.

My previous work, too, was critical of the socialist system. It did not follow the example of those who sought to explain the problems in terms of the personalities of top leaders, or possibly the mistakes made by the leading organizations or the planners. My writings suggested that the system itself produces insoluble internal conflicts and renders its own forms of operation dysfunctional. But my analyses were confined largely to the economic sphere, and at most alluded to the role of the political sphere. This book crosses that boundary. Discussion of the role of the political power structure and communist ideology can occupy in this book the place they deserve according to my analysis. No doubt the reader will sense that the arguments on the power structure or property relations and the summarizing verdicts on the system's performance contained in this book, on which I have worked for several years, are not

---

[1]The introduction to my most comprehensive book so far, *Economics of Shortage,* states emphatically that the discussion does *not* cover the entire subject of the political economy of socialism.

based on improvised impressions or inspired by the latest news but are, in fact, the foundations of a carefully assembled theoretical edifice.

Of course, I know that nowadays this book does not constitute a "courageous act"; one almost needs a modicum of bravery today to write about the socialist system in a tone of scientific dispassion that avoids harshly critical epithets, to convey that the system was able for a long time to operate in a comparatively stable way and reproduce itself. But it is not for the sake of bravery that I include in the analysis the political subjects with which my earlier writings did not deal. I do so because discussion of them is fundamentally important to an understanding of the political economy of socialism.

Finally, I must add a personal note. I am sixty-three years old. My generation has the ability and the duty to give testimony on its observations. There are some who give their accounts in memoir or historiographical form. I am sticking to my own literary form: professional analysis. We were adults when we entered the period of socialism, and we lived under it for four decades; those younger than us have less experience of it to offer. Those of my age may still have enough years of active life ahead in which we can thoroughly analyze all we have lived through. But we are certainly not young enough to reassure ourselves that we can wait until the silt of our turbulent personal experiences has settled. And that brings me back to the thought with which I began this introduction: I have no time to lose; I must write and publish this book *now*.

After revealing my subjective motives, I would like to say a few introductory words on what this book has to offer the reader. The development and the break-up and decline of the socialist system amount to the most important political and economic phenomena of the twentieth century. At the height of this system's power and extent, a third of humanity lived under it. But the system did not merely influence its own subjects, past and present. It had a deep effect on those living outside the socialist world as well. Millions feared they would come under the sway of the Communist parties, or that war would break out and they would have to encounter the military might of the socialist countries. In several parts of the world this was not merely a hypothetical danger but a very real peril: truly bloody wars arose between socialism's adherents and opponents, within or between certain countries. The existence and destiny of the socialist order influenced the world outlook of many people, particularly members of the intelligentsia; that applies equally to those attracted by communist ideology, and to the contrary, those whose thinking became imbued with anticommunism. The consequences of the socialist system's existence were experienced even by those who sought to withdraw themselves from the struggles between the world political forces or the ideologies, and declared themselves apolitical. For they could not close their eyes or ears to the sights and sounds of the Cold War, and, willingly or not, they paid the horrific price of the arms race. On that basis I believe it is worth the while of everyone, friends and foes of socialism alike, to become acquainted with the nature of this system.

Within the wide sphere of potential interest, I count mainly on four groups of readers, and within those groups on both university students and those who have completed their formal education.

First of all, this book has been written for the citizens of countries that belonged to the socialist system until the recent past and have now taken the path to democracy, free enterprise, and the market economy. An analysis of the old system is needed not just as a memento, but as an aid to understanding the present and the future.

I would like my book to reach those who still live under the socialist system today. It is not that I overestimate its power to influence or that of the written word of any kind, but I think the book may assist them in methodically examining their social environment, in clarifying their ideas, and ultimately in their struggle to change their destiny.

I hope my work will be used by those outside the socialist countries, past and present, for whom, nonetheless, a knowledge of the socialist system is a professional requirement. A great many professional areas can be listed here, from academic economists and political scientists specializing in the comparison of systems, and historians of recent history, by way of the professional advisers to banks and business people, to governmental specialists, diplomats, and journalists.

Finally, there is a motive that may persuade people to study the socialist system even though it falls outside their stricter sphere of professional interest. For the socialist and capitalist worlds are not direct opposites in all respects; there are phenomena found, to varying degrees and with varying frequencies, in both systems. Let me mention just a few economic ones. Both the highly developed and the developing capitalist economies show more than one tendency one can describe (in Marxist parlance) as "germs of socialism." There too one finds excessive centralization, a propensity for the bureaucracy to overspend, and bargaining between superiors and subordinates in hierarchical organizations. There too one encounters shortage phenomena, particularly in sectors subsidized by the state. There too one observes cases of paternalistic authorities intent on deciding on the citizen's behalf. There too experiments are made with central planning and price control. There too it occurs that large firms on the brink of insolvency are rescued from their financial predicament. I need not continue. The socialist system presents such phenomena in their ultimate form, which makes it a particularly instructive environment for studying them. A medical researcher studying a disease finds it worth examining in the "pure, laboratory form" in which it is fully developed. He or she is then able in the future to keep a sharp watch for even the milder initial symptoms of it.

Information on the past and present of the socialist countries is flowing as never before, with hundreds of books and tens of thousands of articles appearing. This work is intended to help readers to orient themselves in this flow of information. I want to make it easier for people to survey and impose order on the flood of knowledge available to them. A great many people these days are recounting the history of the socialist system (or a particular country or period of it), which is most useful. I neither can nor want to compete with such accounts. My purpose is to promote discipline in these analyses by addressing the problems in the field within a tight structure. Since this book sets out to provide a survey, summary, and synthesis, I hope it will be useful as a textbook as well.[2]

I certainly hope the book will be able to say something new to the sophisticated expert who has specialized in this field. Nevertheless, I did not set out to address myself exclusively to that important, but small, group of readers. I wanted to write a comprehensive book. I would like to feel that a student of economics or politics, or perhaps an economic consultant, diplomat, or journalist about to visit Eastern Europe or the Soviet Union for the first time and wanting to read just one book on the subject, could find here the vital information needed for orientation.[3]

An author who nowadays sets about writing a concise account of the micro or macroeconomics of the capitalist system, perhaps for use as a textbook as well, has the security of knowing that a range of similar syntheses have been written already. That is not the case with this book's efforts at synthesis in a subject that has been treated in a comprehensive

---

[2]I am aware that these purposes may on first sight seem contradictory. As far as I can judge, the book does not fit the customary classification, which draws a sharp line between the comparatively easy to read introductory text written for the undergraduate and the highly technical advanced graduate text, and between a book aimed at a wider circle of educated readers and a monograph written for specialists. Unfortunately, my limited capacity permitted me to write only one comprehensive book, and I have tried to do it in a simple style. I am sure that open-minded graduate students or researchers will not push it aside with a pout just for not finding mathematical models in it. I am fully convinced that as long as they are interested in the subject, a book of this kind will certainly be of some use to them.

[3]Because of the comprehensive nature of the book, exhaustive discussion of certain questions is prevented by limitations of space. Guidance for readers interested in the details is provided in the references given in the footnotes. These are one-sided from a linguistic point of view, since they are almost entirely confined to works that have appeared in English.

As a rule, reference is made to a work published in another language only where it has been the source of an idea or piece of data that features in this book, or where it has played a special part in the history of the system and is not available in English.

way in only a few, not at all recent, works.[4] The reader should therefore
be prepared to find a number of shortcomings in it. Some problems have
not been explored at all; many debates are still inconclusive. The archives
are just beginning to open, and light is now being shed on many cases
of statistical falsification. If a tenth book on the political economy of
the socialist countries is written a good many years from now, it will
certainly be a better grounded book than this. But in the meantime,
someone has to make a start on the work of synthesizing.

P.2   Classical Socialism, Reform, and Postsocialist Transition

The first half of the book deals mainly with the system termed here
"classical socialism." Its characteristics are expounded more precisely
later in the book, and here I would rather confine myself to conveying
that this is the political structure and economy that developed in the
Soviet Union under Stalin and in China under Mao Zedong, the system
that emerged in the smaller socialist countries of Eastern Europe and in
several Asian, African, and Latin American countries.

Here one must return to the problem raised at the very beginning of
the preface in connection with the quotation from Schama: the question
of distance from the phenomenon. The first half of the book provides a
theoretical summary of the main features of a more-or-less closed period
of history. Except in a few countries, the classical system is a thing of
the past. To that extent there is a little distance at least from which to
gain a perspective sufficient to analyze it.

Nonetheless, the period of its existence is still too close for it to be
marked as the subject matter of history. Though superseded, the classical
socialist system still affects the world today in a thousand ways. These
effects are referred to emphatically in the second part of the book. An
understanding of the classical system is essential for finding one's way
around the complex phenomena of the process of reform and the postsocialist transition. The examination of the classical system presents the
operation of socialist society in a theoretical "pure form," before it has
become "tainted" by other systems. Once this system has been understood, the political and theoretical conclusions almost drop into one's
lap.

The second half of the book deals with the processes of reform, like
the changes that started in Hungary under Kádár in 1968 or in the Soviet
Union under Gorbachev in 1985. The reform was designed to renew the
socialist system, which at times surges forward and at times stagnates.

---

[4]Special mention must be made of the pioneer work of P. Wiles (1962).

A number of favorable changes take place: the political and ideological erosion begins; it becomes possible for private entrepreneurship to appear, although the constraints upon it are strict. Numerous earlier, but hitherto submerged, problems come to the surface, however, and new difficulties arise out of the ambivalent situation caused by the conflict between the reform and the resistance to it. The book's ultimate conclusion on the reforms is a negative one: the system is incapable of stepping away from its own shadow. No partial alteration of the system can produce a lasting breakthrough. For that a change of system is required.

The final political conclusion of the book is easy to sum up. Stalinist classical socialism is repressive and inefficient, but it constitutes a coherent system. When it starts reforming itself, that coherence slackens and its internal contradictions strengthen. In spite of generating a whole series of favorable changes, reform is doomed to fail: the socialist system is unable to renew itself internally so as to prove viable in the long run. So the time for really revolutionary changes does come in the end, eliminating the socialist system and leading society toward a capitalist market economy.

I feel the time has arrived for a comprehensive description and a positive analysis of socialism in both its classical and its reform phases. I do not dare at present, however, to undertake the writing of a similar positive analysis of a synthesizing nature on the subject of the postsocialist transition.[5] In part 3, where reform within the socialist system is analyzed, references are made repeatedly to the legacy socialism hands down to the postsocialist period. But I go no further: the reader should not expect an analysis of the postsocialist transition.[6] Those who aim exclusively at quickly learning something about the transition and its present state should not go near this book. But those who really want to understand the transition following socialism, with all its difficulties and immanent, unsolved problems, will find it worthwhile studying it. Transition, as the word itself clearly suggests, sets out from somewhere in a certain direction. Well, the point of departure is the socialist system,

[5]My book *The Road to a Free Economy* (1990) deals in detail with several basic problems to do with the postsocialist transition, from a normative point of view. It sums up my economic policy proposals on the economic policy actions to be taken. But that is a different task from making a synthetic positive analysis covering a process that has only just started and is largely still to come. I feel that the time has not yet arrived for the latter.

[6]Although the book does not give a positive analysis of the postsocialist transition, I would like to assist the reader—both instructors teaching the subject and students as well—in surveying the literature on it. That is the purpose of complementing the references at the end of the book with an appendix containing a selected bibliography of literature in English on the problems of the postsocialist transition. Several of these works are not referred to in the text of the book and thus are not included in the list of references.

which will have a lasting influence on the society wishing to depart; it is there in all the institutions and in the thinking and reflexes of the people.

There will certainly be some readers who would like to come closer to the present state of affairs, and they may be tempted to start reading at chapter 16. I can understand their impatience, but even so I advise them not to grudge the effort to study the classical, prereform system, for that is the only route to a thorough understanding of the problems, crises, and vicissitudes met with by the socialist reforms, and then of the state of affairs and the problems as the postsocialist transition begins.

There are tumultuous changes still taking place in the socialist and postsocialist systems as this book goes to press, and the future course of events cannot be forecast in detail. I have tried to ensure that the book's main argument will stand its ground regardless of what specific political and economic events take place in these countries. Readers will not find it hard to tell robust statements of a general nature from illustrative observations tied to a particular time and place. Although the latter include many relatively new pieces of data and quotations from 1988–91, I have not tried to give "up-to-date" illustrations of all propositions in the book.

P.3 Acknowledgments

I began preparatory research for this book in 1983. I spent these years of research alternately in the East and West, and this too inspired me to attain a better understanding of the anatomy of the socialist system by comparative means.

Since 1984, I have regularly taught a course on the political economy of socialism at Harvard University. The lecture notes for it appeared in 1986 in duplicated form, and they can be considered the first written precursor of this book. The task of presenting this subject to critically minded and well-prepared students was an extremely forceful inspiration to me.

The audience for the series of lectures, which was repeated over several years and reworked each time it commenced again, was an international community. Among the audience there were many Western students with no knowledge of socialism whatever, but sitting among them were a Chinese student who had been deported to the countryside for years under Mao, and visiting Polish researchers with inside experience of the witches' coven of the socialist economy. Also among them were more than one conservative young man, anticommunist to the point of prejudice, as well as naive members of the "New Left," quite unaware of the grave absurdities of the socialist systems. That multiplicity spurred me to try and make it plain to them all how I see the main attributes of the system. I am grateful for their attentiveness, their interesting questions, and their thought-provoking examination papers. They were the subjects of a teaching experiment whose result is this book.

I am most grateful to all the institutions that assisted me while I was working on this book by providing a thought-provoking environment and favorable conditions for research: the Hungarian Academy of Sciences' Institute of Economics, the Department of Economics at Harvard University, and the World Institute for Development Economics Research at the United Nations University. Special mention must be made of Dr. Lal Jayawardena, director of WIDER, and his staff for their most effective assistance. I am also indebted to the foundations that gave generous financial support to my research: the Sloan Foundation, the Ford Foundation, the McDonnell Foundation, and Hungary's National Scientific Research Foundation.

My thanks go to my wife, Zsuzsa Dániel, not only for her encouragement and self-sacrificing support, but for the constant opportunity she gave me to discuss the problems that arose as the book was being written, and for the useful comments she contributed as the first to read the freshly completed drafts and manuscripts.

Of my colleagues, I must mention first, and with the greatest appreciation, Mária Kovács. Her dedicated, intellectually exacting, patient, and effective cooperation and attention to every detail were an inestimable help to me. I am extremely grateful to Carla Krüger for her devoted work, stimulating remarks, and the high standard and wide range of the contribution she made, and to Judit Rimler, for her very efficient help in the compilation of the statistical tables.

I wrote the bulk of the manuscript in Hungarian. The translation was made by Brian McLean, with the unsparing help of Julianna Parti. As far as I, the author of this book whose mother tongue is Hungarian, can judge, the translation expresses to the full what I have set out to say. I am really grateful to both of them for their precise and unswerving work and their efforts to cope with not only translating the original draft but the repeated floods of corrections as well.

Among my other colleagues, I must mention particularly the collaboration of János Árvay, Attila Chikán, Mariann Dicker, Piroska Gerencsér, Zsuzsa Kapitány, János Köllő, Goohon Kwon, Aladár Madarász, Péter Mihályi, László Muraközy, József Pálfi, Jane Prokop, Yingyi Qian, István Salgó, Judit Schulmann, Anna Seleny, György Such, Iván Szegvári, István János Tóth, Jane Trahan, Ágnes Vészi, and Chenggang Xu in gathering data, compiling notes, tables, and references, or performing other editorial tasks. I am grateful for the assistance I received from them and from many others not mentioned here by name. My thanks are due to Ilona Fazekas, Ann Flack, and Liisa Roponen for the conscientious way they tackled the arduous task of typing.

Numerous colleagues read earlier and later versions of the manuscript. Let me mention particularly those who gave me very valuable assistance by making detailed comments: Tamás Bauer, John P. Burkett, Timothy J. Colton, Ellen Commisso, Ed A. Hewett, Mihály Laki, Ed Lim, Frederic L. Pryor, András Simonovits, Robert C. Stuart, and Martin Weitzman. Of course, the author is responsible for the errors that remain in the book in spite of the many useful critical comments I received from my colleagues and the early readers of the manuscript.

Finally, I express my gratitude for the swift publication of the book to the two publishers, Princeton University Press and Oxford University Press. I am especially indebted, for their enthusiasm, encouragement, and careful editing, to Jack Repcheck, Anita O'Brien, Karen Fortgang (*bookworks*), Jane Low, and Andrew Schuler.

Cambridge, Massachusetts, and Budapest
April 1991

Part One

POINTS OF DEPARTURE

1

The Subject and Method

ONE of this chapter's objects is to explain the title of the book. It is worth making clear from the outset not only what the book deals with and what methods it uses to do so, but what the examination does not include.

1.1 Specific Lines of Historical Development and General Features

Let me begin describing the book's subject matter by taking an example: present-day China. Many researchers are studying it, and every one of them feels how difficult it is to know and understand so vast, stratified, and complex a country. Here I shall mention just a few of its attributes.

1. The Communist party has been in power in China for more than four decades. This has left its mark on all spheres of society, politics, and the economy.

2. China is part of the "Third World." It is among the "developing" countries, which are poor and backward by comparison with the industrially developed countries.

3. Geographically, China is part of Asia. Numerous typically Asian attributes are therefore displayed in its history, its cultural heritage, its religious and philosophical traditions, and its people's way of life and relations with one another.

4. Whereas the previous three points concern similarities that China bears to three different groups of countries (other countries under the control of Communist parties, other developing countries, and other Asian countries), there are many things in which China is unique and cannot be compared with any other country. It differs in scale: its more than one billion inhabitants make it the most populous country in the world. It has a several-thousand-year-old culture, which was also the cradle of several other Asian cultures. The history of China, like the history of any country, is unique, individual, and markedly different from any other country's. The same applies to the history of the last decades. Mao Zedong was not the same as Stalin or Tito, and Deng Xiaoping is not the same as János Kádár or Mikhail Gorbachev. At every stage, the policy of China has differed appreciably from the policy pursued by any other country, socialist or otherwise.

There are schools of anthropologists and historians who emphasize this fourth point, in other words, the uniqueness of each country, society, and culture, and consider it futile to look for general regularities or the expression of general historical laws.

Others consider it fruitful to take a more general approach. They set out to study the features common to various groups of countries. For instance, many Sinologists place the emphasis on the second of the points in the list (China as a developing country), which in their eyes explains a considerable proportion of the phenomena they observe there. Others think the point most deserving of attention is the third: China's analogies and similarities with Japan, Korea, and India.

This book does not take the approach of rejecting generalization and "common regularities" of every kind, or agree that individual features alone exist in every country. It recognizes general influences that apply in similar ways in countries that differ greatly in other respects. On the other hand, the book eschews single-factor explanations of any kind, deeming it decidedly necessary to make a multicausal, multifactoral analysis of society. To build up a comprehensive picture of China today and attempt an explanation of the existing situation and the developments likely to emerge from it, one should consider all the factors listed above, plus a great many features and influences that have not been mentioned.

Although the indispensability of multifactoral analysis cannot be underlined too strongly, the book's attention will be confined nevertheless to a single group of factors: those covered by the first point in the list. The purpose is to study more closely the phenomena, causal relationships, and regularities that are similar in China, the Soviet Union, North Korea, Yugoslavia, and in general all countries where a Communist party was or still is in power. No one can argue (and this will be clear from what has been said so far) that this method yields explanations for all the aspects of China or the Soviet Union or Albania. But one can certainly say that identification of these similarities, kinships, and common regularities can serve as an important analytical instrument (alongside other, equally useful instruments) for studying these countries.

1.2 Socialist Countries

Table 1.1 lists all the countries where the Communist party was in power for a fairly long period (at least several years). The undivided power of the Communist party is the sole criterion for inclusion in the table. From now on those included will be referred to in this book as *socialist countries*.

At the time of writing, the Communist party is still in power in some of the countries in the table, while in others the political structure has changed [→16.3].[1] The term "socialist country" is used only during the period when the Communist party was ruling.

Figure 1.1 shows a map of the world. The shaded countries are those where the socialist system still pertained at the end of 1987. The socialist family of systems reached its greatest extent in the period 1980–87. Since then it has dwindled considerably.

At this point it is worth stating in advance one of the book's fundamental ideas, which runs as a leitmotif through all the chapters: that despite all the individual attributes that distinguish each of these socialist countries from all the others, they resemble one another and exhibit important attributes in common. Even though their actual systems differ in many details, they are all members of a broader, clearly identifiable class of social-political-economic systems that in this book will be called the *socialist system*. To draw a biological analogy, this system is a "species" of social systems. Just as the individual members of a biological species differ from one another while remaining members of it, so the various socialist countries differ while remaining members of the same species of systems. Clarifying the nature of this species of systems, describing and explaining theoretically the main characteristics of this class of systems, is the subject of this book. In the parlance of this book, these common phenomena and common properties are referred to as *system-specific*. The examination will be purposely one-sided, in that its aim is to identify among the plethora of phenomena those that are system-specific and distinguish them from those that are not. The book does not, therefore, set out to provide a comprehensive and detailed analysis of the situation in any particular socialist country. It aims to arrive at general statements applicable equally to any socialist country.

The first fourteen countries in the table are ones where the Communist party held power for at least three decades. That is long enough for the socialist system to *consolidate*. Of course, "consolidation" is a relative category; measuring in centuries, the rule of a system for a few decades is just a short, transitional period. But for a Czechoslovak or an East German citizen, say, who left university in 1948 or 1949—the year the Communists took power—and was a senior citizen by the time that power collapsed in 1989, the period amounts to his or her entire economically active life. The consolidation was robust enough for the attributes of the system to develop fully, so that they can be the subject of scientific observation, description, and analysis. The book is based on the general-

---

[1]Here, and in numerous other places in the book, the arrow in square brackets denotes a cross-reference to another chapter, section, or table of the book.

TABLE 1.1
The Socialist Countries, 1987

1 Serial Number	2 Country	3 Year Power Was Attained[a]	4 Population, 1986 (million)	5 Area, 1986 (1,000 sq. km)	6 Level of Economic Development, GNP or GDP per Capita, 1985 (USA = 100)	7 Share of People Employed in Agriculture, ca. 1985 (percent)
1.	Soviet Union	1917	281.1	22,402	50.0	19
2.	Mongolia	1921	2.0	1,565	—	53
3.	Albania	1944	3.0	29	—	50
4.	Yugoslavia	1945	23.3	256	40.4	30
5.	Bulgaria	1947	9.0	111	40.8	23
6.	Czechoslovakia	1948	15.5	128	59.2	12
7.	Hungary	1948	10.6	93	46.0	20
8.	Poland	1948	37.5	313	39.2	30
9.	Romania	1948	22.9	238	34.1	28
10.	North Korea[b]	1948	20.9	121	—	48
11.	China	1949	1,054.0	9,561	19.5	74
12.	East Germany[b]	1949	16.6	108		10
13.	Vietnam[b]	1954	63.3	330	—	70
14.	Cuba	1959	10.2	115	—	25
15.	Congo	1963	2.0	342	8.7	90

16.	Somalia	1969	5.5	638	3.1	82
17.	South Yemen[b]	1969	2.2	333	—	44
18.	Benin	1972	4.2	113	4.1	60
19.	Ethiopia	1974	43.5	1,222	2.4	86
20.	Angola	1975	9.0	1,247	4.5	60
21.	Kampuchea	1975	7.7[c]	181	—	90[d]
22.	Laos	1975	3.7	237	—	76
23.	Mozambique	1975	14.2	802	4.1	85
24.	Afghanistan	1978	18.6[c]	648	—	83[d]
25.	Nicaragua	1979	3.4	130	15.6	65
26.	Zimbabwe	1980	8.7	391	7.6	35
1–26.	All socialist countries[e]		1,692.6	41,654		
	Socialist countries as a percentage of world figures		34.4%	30.7%		

Source: Columns 4–5: *World Development Report* (1988, pp. 221–23) and Központi Statisztikai Hivatal (Central Statistical Office, Budapest) (1989, pp. 9, 14–15). Column 6: R. Summers and A. Heston (1988, Tables 3 and 4). Column 7: G. Baló and I. Lipovecz, eds. (1987).

[a]The year of attaining power in armed uprisings has been defined either by the year the uprising began (e.g., Soviet Union, 1917) or the year of its victory (e.g., Yugoslavia, 1945; North Vietnam, 1954). In the case of the Eastern European systems formed in a peaceful way it has been defined by the year of the fusion of Communist and Social Democratic parties.

[b]Here, as well as elsewhere in the book, countries are referred to by the names that reflect their geographical position, not by their official names. For instance, the country officially called the Democratic People's Republic of Korea is referred to as North Korea; the German Democratic Republic, as East Germany; and so on.

[c]Figure for 1987.

[d]Rural population.

[e]Certain countries (e.g., Burma, Cape Verde, Guinea Bissau, Guyana, Madagascar, São Tomé, and Seychelles) are borderline cases and are not included in the table. It is difficult to say whether or not they could have been counted as socialist countries in 1987 according to the criterion applied in this book.

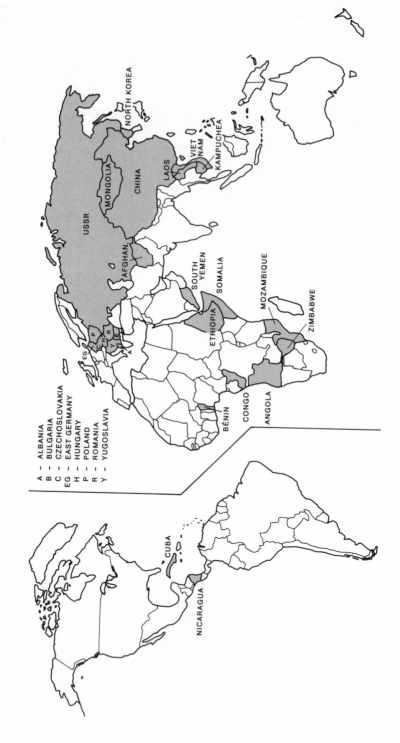

FIGURE 1.1 The Socialist Countries in 1987

A — ALBANIA
B — BULGARIA
C — CZECHOSLOVAKIA
EG — EAST GERMANY
H — HUNGARY
P — POLAND
R — ROMANIA
Y — YUGOSLAVIA

ization of the experiences of this group of consolidated socialist countries.[2]

From line 15 onward, the table shows countries where the power of the Communist party has a shorter history; in some it ceased while this book was being written, and in others it is likely to cease shortly. The socialist system in these countries did not consolidate, and it is doubtful, where it survives, whether it will consolidate at all under the rapidly changing external and internal conditions. For these reasons it would be arbitrary to draw general, theoretical conclusions from experiences of countries in the second group. The argument of the book includes the conjecture that the regularities observed in the consolidated socialist countries would develop sooner or later in the second group of countries as well, so long as consolidation occurs. This book does not attempt to check the truth of that conjecture.[3]

1.3 Interpretation of the Term "Socialism"

The association of ideas evoked by the expression socialism points in two directions: on the one hand conveying certain ideas, and on the other conjuring up certain formations in existing societies. As for the former, the range of ideas it conveys is wide and varied, and the book does not undertake a thorough discussion of them.

As for the actual historical formations, it was made clear in the previous section that this book deals exclusively with countries under the control of a Communist party. Many socialists, including numerous social democrats, Trotskyists, and adherents of the New Left, do not consider the system in the countries listed in table 1.1 "true" socialism at all. What is more, there have been cases in the last few decades of a country leadership within the group of twenty-six accusing another of abandoning socialism. Remember Stalin's condemnation of Tito or the mutual

[2]Most of the book's illustrative examples, data, and references to other works refer to a narrower subgroup within the group of consolidated countries. Following the order in table 1.1, these are the following nine countries: the Soviet Union, Yugoslavia, Bulgaria, Czechoslovakia, Hungary, Poland, Romania, China, and East Germany.

[3]Various written source materials are available on the countries in table 1.1 missing from the short list of nine countries, mentioned in note 2, including some synoptic, descriptive studies of economic conditions in a particular country. A few examples of factual country-studies: *Afghanistan:* B. Sen Gupta (1986); *Albania:* A. Schnytzer (1982); *Angola:* K. Somerville (1986); *Cuba:* C. Mesa-Lago (1981), M. Azicri (1988) and A. Zimbalist and C. Brundenius (1989); *Kampuchea:* M. Vickery (1986); *Laos:* M. Stuart-Fox (1986); *Mongolia:* A. J. K. Sanders (1987); *Mozambique:* H. D. Nelson, ed. (1985); *Nicaragua:* D. Close (1988); *North Korea:* F. M. Bunge (1985); *South Yemen:* T. Y. and J. S. Ismael (1986); *Vietnam:* M. Beresford (1988); *Zimbabwe:* C. Stoneman (1989).

condemnations by China and the Soviet Union. Albanian Communists considered the leaders of most of the other countries led by Communist parties to be traitors to socialism.

This book dissociates itself from such debates. The official leadership of every country featured in table 1.1 declared while it was in power that the system was socialist. Why seek a label for these countries other than the one they apply to themselves? Moreover, as will emerge later in the book, these countries' systems have attributes that at least some school of socialism or other would itself describe as socialist. This book, on the other hand, does not address the question of whether theirs is "true" socialism. It sets out to discover what their system is like, and not whether it merits the description "socialist" according to the criteria of some school of thought or other.

A term frequently used by politicians and by the press outside the socialist world is "communist system" or simply "communism." For the sake of easier perception by those who have not yet read the book, the subtitle refers to the political economy of communism. In the main title and throughout the book, however, I prefer to use the term "socialist system."[4]

There are other synonyms for "socialist system" in the literature on the subject as well, for example, "Soviet-type system," "centrally administered economy," "centrally planned economy," "command economy," and "state socialism."[5] Ultimately, the choice of the term is a matter of semantics, as long as the meaning is clearly defined, and therefore it deserves no further attention.

All of what has been said so far has advanced only half the argument: the reason why the term "socialist" has been used for the twenty-six

---

[4]My choice between the terms "socialist system" and "communism" is based on the following consideration. Marxism-Leninism, the official ideology of the Communist party, uses the expression "communist" in a quite different sense. It terms communist the unattained Utopian society of the future, in which all will share in social production according to their needs. The adherents of the Communist party in power never referred to their own system as communist. So it would be awkward to attach this name to it "from outside." The spirit of this book, which tries to interpret the system "from inside," is better served by adopting the term "socialist," which is how the system refers to itself.

[5]P. Wiles (1962) calls "socialist" an economy with considerable public ownership, and "communist" a country where the Communist party rules. Others, for instance, R. W. Campbell [1974] (1981) and J. Winiecki (1988), use the term "Soviet-type." From the German "zentrale Verwaltungswirtschaft" we get the term "centrally administered economy" used in W. Eucken's (1951) discussion of the Nazi economy and often applied to socialist economies. United Nations statistics refer to "centrally planned economies." The term "command economy" is often used to distinguish the system from a market economy (see, for instance, P. R. Gregory, 1990). More sociologically oriented writers, such as V. Nee and D. Stark, eds. (1988), often refer to "state socialism."

countries in table 1.1. The other half of the question is why the expression "socialist" has been applied exclusively to these countries. Could one not term socialist a Scandinavian welfare state where for decades there was a social democratic government and where a large degree of egalitarian redistribution has taken place? Or could one not so describe some African or Asian countries, which may not have a Marxist-Leninist party in power but consider themselves socialist and have certain features of a socialist kind?

This book provides no answers to these questions. As with the previous issue, it has no desire to take a position on whether systems like those just mentioned qualify as "true" socialism. All that needs pointing out for fear of misunderstanding is that the expression "socialist system" in this book exclusively signifies the system in the countries run by a Communist party. Other systems are mentioned only for the sake of comparison and otherwise fall outside the book's subject matter.

1.4 Political Economy

The subtitle of the book contains the expression "political economy" and not "economics." No distinction had yet been made between the two in the age of Adam Smith and Ricardo, but the two terms have gained appreciably different political and theoretical associations of ideas in recent decades, despite a good deal of overlap between them. Since no general agreement has been reached on these assessments and distinctions,[6] I must clarify what is meant in this book by the expression "political economy."[7]

Among the subjects the book will discuss are economic issues in the narrower sense: how decisions are made on production and consumption, investment and saving in a socialist economy, what decides the distribution of income, how efficient economic activity is, and so on. But

---

[6]For instance, advocates of the "public choice" theory, or traditional Marxism, or today's radical left-wing economists in the West all attribute a different meaning to it. For a comprehensive survey of intellectual history see the entry *"Political Economy" and "Economics"* written by P. Groenewegen in the *New Palgrave* (1987, 3:904–7).

[7]I am aware that the subtitle of the book may bring back unpleasant memories to many readers who were taught "the political economy of socialism" in the socialist countries. Several hundred million people were obliged to take this subject and read the official textbooks for it produced in the Soviet Union, China, East Germany, and so forth. The best known and most widespread of them was the official Soviet textbook of political economy, *Politicheskaia Ekonomiia Sotsializma* (1954), prepared under the intellectual control of Stalin. I do not deny a measure of irony in my choice of subtitle, which contrasts a new political economy of socialism with these distorted and compromised works.

a great many other problems will be examined as well. Here are a few examples:

- What connections are there between the political and the economic spheres? What influence do the system's framework of political institutions and its ideology exert on the workings of the economy?
- What social features mold the value system and choice criteria of the decision makers?
- To use the terminology of Marxian political economy, the book will not confine itself to studying the relations of "things." Its primary concern will be the social relations between people, and among the important themes analyzed will be the relations of superiors and subordinates, of those exercising and those obeying power. What molds these relations, and what influences do they have on economic activity?

Because of all these considerations, the reader can expect the book to exceed the bounds of "economics" in the stricter sense and to extend into the fields of political science, sociology, social psychology, political and moral philosophy, and history. This extension is what "political economy" is intended to convey.

Undoubtedly, there will be drawbacks to this extension of the subject examined, because it will encroach on the space available for detailed exposition of certain economic analyses. On the other hand, it will allow the internal relationships within the social-political-economic system to be examined more comprehensively.

1.5 Positive Analysis

The principal subject of the book is a positive analysis of the socialist system in reality, as it has emerged historically.

The official textbooks used for decades in the socialist countries themselves to teach the political economy of socialism have usually mixed reality with desires, the real attributes of the system that actually exists with the desirable attributes of a fancied socialist system that operates efficiently and fairly. This book will, of course, go out of its way to avoid so grave a distortion. It aims to depict what experience presents. It seeks to describe what is usual and characteristic in this system, and not what might happen if the system should operate as its apologists wish. The book tries over and over again to answer the question of what is normal, customary, and general in this system. It does not even pose the normative question of what would be optimal from the point of view of public welfare and the interests of society.

The task is to describe and explain the *regularities* that apply in numerous places for quite long periods. Social scientists do not establish universal, immutable laws. Regularity is a much more modest concept. Any regularity is generated by a recurrent constellation of circumstances that produces behavioral patterns, decision routines by economic agents, political and economic mechanisms, and trends in economic processes that are susceptible to explanation. A regularity does not remain valid forever, and it is bound to the particular system by which it was created. But one does find lasting regularities within a specific historical period and a specific system. The book sets out from the following general assumption: socialism has been in existence long enough for behavioral regularities to have developed and become set.[8]

The sole test of the validity of the positive descriptions and general conclusions in the book is to confront them with reality. The reader should be warned that this validation process is not and probably cannot be undertaken with perfect rigor at this time. So one can rightly consider many propositions as hypotheses awaiting strong validation. That does not mean, however, that the book fails to provide support for its statements. Most important of all, I am convinced that the statements cannot be confronted with an available scholarly examination capable of refuting them decisively.[9]

In many cases the conclusive "evidence" supporting a proposition is provided by those who live in a socialist country. Do they recognize the situation described in the book? Does what is written coincide with what they experience day after day as consumers or producers, managers or employees, buyers or sellers? I also see myself as a "witness" of this kind. Moreover, I have spoken over several decades with many other "witnesses" and read many case studies, accounts, minutes and written reports, interviews, and sociographical studies that can be taken as pieces of "evidence."[10] I put my propositions forward in the belief that this concurrence between the book's statements and everyday reality obtains.

---

[8]When talking about generally valid regularities the book uses present tense, while whenever a phenomenon or event in a specific country in a specific time is mentioned past tense is used.

[9]Wherever the correctness of a proposition is disputed in another professional work known to me, attention is drawn to this in the text or footnotes. In such cases, special emphasis is given to the fact that this is a disputed hypothesis.

[10]Many researchers airily dismiss such "evidence" as merely anecdotal and beneath the attention of men of science. In fact, this kind of evidence often leads much closer to an understanding of the truth than many more ambitious analyses on a higher plane that rest upon distorted official data.

I am prepared to rethink any statement against which essential "evidence" is laid.

Often there is no direct way of testing the truth of a more general, and thus more abstract, statement. What can be tested in such cases is the degree of accord between the general proposition and the special consequences and partial regularities, derivable from the general proposition, that are sufficiently proved in practice. The book attempts a consistency analysis of this kind in several places.

Some statements in the book are supported by statistical material, including eighty-six statistical tables, seven statistical figures, and a great deal of other data.[11] In addition, the footnotes refer to more detailed, empirical studies that support the book's statements, among them some econometric analyses.

To all this, however, I must add that the professional literature on this subject still falls short of empirically clarifying all the problems raised in the book. Many of the figures in the official statistics contain an intentional distortion and are expressly misleading. The gathering of data is obstructed by secretiveness. The continuity of the time series is broken by constant reorganizations. In many cases no regular observation and measurement of certain phenomena have been undertaken even if they were observable and measurable in principle. Such observation and measurement tend to be omitted particularly if the phenomenon is an embarrassing one for the system from the propaganda point of view.

In countries where the sole rule of the Communist party has ceased or been shaken, a great deal of previously secret information is coming to light, and earlier distorted reports are being reexamined and modified. This process seems likely to continue, although one cannot expect all the earlier statistical falsifications to come up for subsequent correction. The revision of some of the data, coupled with econometric analysis of the statistical reports available, may one day induce researchers into the socialist system to revise many of their earlier conclusions. Even so, the first draft of the theories cannot be postponed until all the required ob-

---

[11]Only a fraction of the statistical data used is based on my own research. Most of them come from publications by other scholars. The comprehensive nature of the book allowed me not to rely solely on primary, original sources in this respect. I am, consequently, contented with secondary sources provided they are well-founded, thorough, and suitable to illustrate the message of the book. In most cases the sources refer only to the works from which the data or tables were taken. These publications will provide the reader with detailed references to the primary sources, such as, for instance, national and international statistical source materials.

I take the opportunity to express my thanks to all the authors and to their publishers who have given me permission to use certain tables compiled and published by them. These adoptions are detailed at the appropriate places in this book.

servations and data have been gathered and subjected to statistical analysis in a conscientious and objective way. After all, it is often theoretical analysis itself that prompts the making of some observation, measurement, or empirical examination.

1.6 Models

The subject of the examination itself determines certain methodological principles that must be used in the analysis. The task is to generalize the experience of the socialist countries. This book, like so many other scientific works, employs models for the purpose of generalization.[12]

For instance, let us say we want to present the kind of relationship that emerges between the institution controlling investment resources and the institution requiring investment resources, not the relations in particular between a state-owned industrial firm and the industry ministry in the Soviet Union in 1951 or Czechoslovakia in 1985, but the relation in general in the socialist countries. In this case one cannot escape using a far-reaching abstraction. One must disregard the specific features differing from country to country and period to period, or in a particular country and period from sector to sector or region to region, and arrive at what is common to and typical of all these particular situations. Such a model cannot reflect accurately and in detail the precise situation in any country, period, or sector. Those who know the details well can always object that things are not quite the way the researcher claims. Despite these likely counterarguments, this examination will follow the procedure of abstraction, model-creation, and theoretical generalization.

It will not be explicitly and repeatedly underscored that the text is presenting "models" and not reality directly observed, but it will be worth the reader's while to remember throughout that simplified, abstract rep-

---

[12]The word "model" must be understood here in a wide sense. Economists of today are inclined to reserve this technical term of the philosophy of science exclusively for models expressed in the language of mathematics. While a mathematical formalization is one possible way of creating a model, it is certainly not the only one, and it has both advantages and drawbacks. There is a trade-off between accuracy and rigor, on the one hand, and the wealth of the description of reality, on the other.

The book employs "verbal" models ("ideal-types" or "prototypes"), which is at once a gain and a loss. The procedure certainly leads to looser, and at times almost vague, expression. On the other hand, it provides richer descriptions and analyses closer to real life, because it is able to build on the reader's association of ideas. It makes it simpler to make the frequent change between the various levels of abstraction and the various combinations of simplifying assumptions.

Readers interested in mathematical modeling will find references in the footnotes to the formalizations of various verbal models and conjectures.

resentations of reality are being advanced. The usage will also vary. In some places there will be references to a "typical situation," a "characteristic structure," or a "prototype," but all these expressions, where they occur, may be understood as synonymous with the term "theoretical model."

The book will present a large number of regularities. These exist not merely side by side and independently but in the closest of relationships with each other. There are some of a more profound nature and some others that explain more superficial regularities of lesser importance. I hope that this "hierarchy" of regularities will emerge clearly by the end of the book. In this respect the reader will encounter not merely loosely strung observations but a deductive train of thought that leads from a few main premises to an entire thought-network of conclusions. Many elements in the train of thought are found separately in other works. The special feature of this book is the deduction linking these and other, lesser known elements closely together [→15.1].

1.7 Evaluation

From what has been said so far, and from the emphasis placed on positive research and modeling assignments, it should not be assumed that a "value-free" analysis will be made. All social-political-economic systems can be judged by the extent to which they further a variety of ethical desiderata and how far they assist in implementing specific values.

The book is not intended to foist my own system of values on the reader. Although this system of values may appear unwittingly in the specific selection of the subjects, in the emphases placed, and in the way the facts are arranged, an attempt will be made to be as impartial as possible. Liberty, equality, social justice, welfare, and many other ultimate values will play a part equally in assessing the system's performance. One might say metaphorically that these values are the various "subjects of study." The book attempts to grade the socialist system in all subjects meriting serious consideration. As far as possible it assesses all the "subjects" customarily considered when comparing systems and projected by the system's own ideology.

To pursue the metaphor further, when school reports are made, all the persons concerned—parents, teachers, and students—weight each subject differently. For some, mathematics is the prime consideration; for others, physical education or history.

The book will have done what it set out to do if it proves capable of deciding, objectively and convincingly, what grade the system deserves in which subject, and how well it has promoted each specific value. This evaluation by "subjects of study" is a scientific task. People with the widest variety of world outlooks and party affiliations may well reach agreement on whether this book has performed its scientific task satisfactorily. If it has, it may help all these people with their various outlooks and political affiliations to clarify their thoughts.

Once that is done, the reader remains alone with his or her conscience and political and moral convictions. What goes beyond this, namely, the "weighting" attached to the various components of performance and contrasting of the system's overall performance with one's own set of values, is up to the reader, of course.

There are frequent references to a range of socialist ideas: Utopias, "blueprints" for the social set-up of the future, visions, and action programs. But all these are mentioned at most as secondary subject matter, for the purpose of examining the effect of the ideology in practice or contrasting some prior conception with reality. The book does not contain a methodical survey or evaluation of the history of socialist ideas.

Nor does the book go beyond positive analysis and assessment of the socialist system and erect a normative theory. It describes and explains the process of reform that takes place in the socialist system, but it does not make its own proposals for reform. For my conviction in any case is that ultimately, the countries living under the socialist system can only overcome the grave problems in their societies and economies if there is a change of system.

2

The Antecedents and Prototypes of the System

BEFORE starting the examination of the classical socialist system and the reforms, the main subject matters of the book, mention must be made of the antecedents. Although the intellectual history of socialism is not analyzed in detail, its outstanding importance justifies a sketch of the Marxian image of socialism. It is followed by a short analysis of the prerevolutionary system, and then by a brief description of the main prototypes of the socialist system. Finally, a quick glance is made at the era that connects presocialist society with institutionalized and consolidated classical socialism.

2.1 Marx's Image of Socialism

The bulk of Marx's scientific work[1] was concerned with capitalism; he wrote little about the future socialist society. However, one can compile from the scattered remarks he made a blueprint of what he had in mind, even if it is a sketchy one. Here I will take from that blueprint only what is relevant to the subject of this chapter, and I will return to Marx's ideas on socialism several times in other parts of the book.

Marx, as a revolutionary critic of capitalism, invariably spoke very highly of the ability of capitalism to develop the forces of production, eliminate medieval backwardness, promote technical progress, and bring to production better organization and greater concentration. Marx argued that this process takes place amid the exploitation of the proletariat. The accumulation of capital is accompanied by the increasing poverty of the exploited class. In the end the process leads inevitably to a revolution: the power of the capitalists is overthrown and "the expropriators expropriated."

Clearly, this train of thought includes the idea that socialism will "supersede" capitalism, to use a Marxian expression. It will arrive once the capitalist system has fully developed and become not just mature but overripe. The replacement will occur in places where the capitalist system of production has become an obstacle to the development of the forces

---

[1]The reader's attention is drawn to the following works summarizing Marx's ideas and Marxism: T. Bottomore, ed. (1983), L. Kolakowski (1978), G. Lichtheim (1961), and D. McLellan (1980).

of production but has also paved the way for a more highly developed system of production than itself by providing the material conditions for socialism. It will have made these preparations by causing the bulk of production to be undertaken on a large industrial scale, with modern technology and a high degree of organization within the company. This high degree of organization and concentration of production will leave only a handful of capitalist proprietors, who will be swept aside so that the proletariat can take over the running of production.[2]

According to this image of socialism, controlling production is a fairly simple matter. Production relations are easily surveyed once the view is unobstructed by the anarchy of the market and the complexities of the exchange of goods through the medium of money. In this clear-cut situation it will be possible to divide the work of the society into various tasks and ensure that it satisfies the needs of mankind directly.

There is a close logical connection in this line of thinking between the high standard of the production forces reached under capitalism and the smooth and simple way the socialist form of economic activity will operate. Marx considered it self-evident that the socialist order would take power first in the most highly developed of the capitalist countries.

2.2   System Prototypes

Three prototypes may be distinguished in the socialist system:
  1. *The revolutionary-transitional system* (the transition from capitalism to socialism).
  2. *The classical system* (or classical socialism).
  3. *The reform system* (or reform socialism).[3]

[2]"England alone can serve as the lever for a serious economic revolution," Marx wrote in 1870. "It is the only country where the *capitalist form,* that is to say combined labour on a large scale under capitalist masters, now embraces virtually the whole of production. It is the only country were the *great majority of the population consists of wage labourers.* It is the only country where the class struggle and the organization of the working class by the trade unions have acquired a certain degree of maturity. . . . If landlordism and capitalism are classical features in England, on the other hand, the material conditions for their destruction are the most mature here." K. Marx [1870] (1975b, p. 118).

Engels argued in a similar way that "countries which are only just turning over to capitalist production now" might arrive at socialism, but "the indispensable condition for that is the example and active assistance of the hitherto capitalist West." The more backward countries, he argued, could only set out on the road to socialism "if there has been an advance beyond the capitalist economic system in its own native land and in the countries where it has flourished." F. Engels [1894] (1963, p. 428).

[3]The classical system is discussed in chapters 3–15, and the reform system in chapters 16–24. Although an attempt has been made to consider this division in placing the statistical tables, it was not possible to apply it consistently in certain places, for instance, with inter-

These are three models. At no time in the history of any specific country has its system corresponded exactly to any of these three models. Even so, these models are not descriptions of ideal, Utopian socialism. They set out to provide abstract generalizations of historical realizations of socialism.

At first glance the three prototypes seem to refer to three consecutive *stages* in history. The revolution is followed by a transitional period, after which mature, classical socialism develops. Later, after quite a long period of history, it may give way to reform socialism.

After these stages of socialism comes a change of system; in this respect one can talk of a further prototype:

4. *The postsocialist system* (the transition from socialism to capitalism). Part 3 makes repeated references to this stage, but detailed discussion of it is not within the compass of this book.

Interpretation of the prototypes as consecutive historical periods can be accepted only as an initial and not entirely accurate approach. The actual course of history is far more complicated.

In some countries the order of appearance is different, or the stages alternate with one another. For instance, War Communism in the Soviet Union can be considered a revolutionary-transitional period that was succeeded first by a specific era of reform, the period of the NEP. Only after that was the classical system built up in full. In China the classical system had already emerged when there was a dramatic turn of events and the Cultural Revolution began, resembling in many respects what this book describes as the revolutionary-transitional system.

History has shown that the first type cannot survive indefinitely. It really is transitional and must give way sooner or later to the classical system. There is no evidence, however, of uniform, conclusive experience for saying that the classical system must necessarily give way to a reformed socialist system. There are countries where the classical system still survives at the time of writing (North Korea and Cuba). Elsewhere (for instance, in East Germany and Czechoslovakia), society avoided reform socialism altogether, making a jump straight from classical socialism to the postsocialist transition.

It may happen in a particular historical period and country that no single one of the types listed above prevails in its pure form. One type

---

national comparisons covering several countries over the same period. Chapters 3–15 contain a large number of tables in which data on the reform economies also appear.

This is clearly permissible if the table explores a phenomenon that applies equally to the classical and reform systems—in other words, if some constant feature of the socialist system can be illustrated with data from the reform economy as well.

In other cases the table itself shows that there was an appreciable difference between the situations under the classical and reform systems. The comprehensive nature of the table, however, requires that later data from the period of reform have to be referred to in advance, in chapters 3–15.

predominates, but attributes of another are woven into it, and the mixture may be accompanied by internal conflicts and the concurrent appearance of conflicting tendencies.

Even though it may be quite easy to date the duration of a particular prototype in a particular country to a specific period in history, no one could argue that the system remains unaltered throughout that period. The main attributes of the classical system were apparent in the social-political-economic system of the Soviet Union from the time when Stalin consolidated his power until his death (for the sake of argument, the twenty-five years from 1928 to 1953), but the system was different at the beginning, when these characteristics were developing and solidifying, and somewhat different again at the end. After the transitional experiments with reform under Khrushchev (1953–64), the classical system revived under Brezhnev (1964–82), yet there is no denying that the Brezhnev period considerably differed from the Stalin period. The prototype sets out to reflect an intertemporal average. To stay with our example, it picks out what the beginning, middle, and end of Stalin's rule and the whole period of Brezhnev's rule have in common. The attention is concentrated on the lasting, long-term states of society, and also on comparing these lasting states with each other (for instance, the systems of classical and reform socialism, or the socialist and the capitalist systems). The short-term vacillations and other changes within the duration of a particular prototype or socioeconomic system usually fall outside the scope of the examination.

Compiling the conceptual edifice of the prototypes serves the purpose of capturing several decades of history in a condensed form. They are not stills because they show the system dynamically, in motion, as will be seen, and they introduce the cast through their actions. It may be more appropriate to draw a literary analogy: it is as if a novel set over a long period of history had been condensed into four separate one-act plays. Clearly, a lot of the novel will have been lost, but the most important events, characters, and conflicts can still feature in the plays in a condensed form.

Neither in subsequent explanations of the events nor in actual prediction of the future can a comprehension of the prototypes be a substitute for concrete historical examination. Nevertheless, these models may prove to be useful conceptual tools in both descriptive and predictive research.

2.3 The System before the Socialist Revolution

Let us now look at the actual course of history, beginning with a description of the social system preceding the socialist revolution. The first question to ask is how similar the internal conditions in the various socialist countries were when each society embarked on building a socialist system. This being the question that needs answering, one should draw a strict distinction between the countries in which the socialist revolution was brought about by internal forces and those in which the socialist system was introduced by external forces, and examine the two groups one at a time. But only in the case of the Soviet Union, the first socialist country, is the verdict quite plain: Lenin's Bolshevik party was not assisted to power by any outside force. In the case of all the other socialist countries it is more ambiguous, because the forces preparing for the revolution received from the Soviet Union (and later from other socialist countries) at least moral support, and in many cases the support they might receive was of a far more tangible kind: political, organizational, financial, and military. Although it would be a gross exaggeration to state that socialism was simply "exported" to the other socialist countries, it is certainly true to say in the majority of cases that it resulted from combinations of internal forces and external support in varying proportions.[4]

For the purposes of this study there is no need to examine these proportions for each country in any detail. Instead, the following procedure will be applied:

Table 2.1 lists fourteen of the twenty-six countries featured in table 1.1 in whose cases scholars largely agree that the part played by external assistance was relatively smaller than the part played by internal forces; the Communist party largely came to power due to internal forces. It is not claimed that all such countries are given in table 2.1, but doubtful cases have been omitted. Nor is it claimed that the outside political, financial, and military assistance given to the Communist party coming to power was paltry, merely that internal forces in these countries played the main, or at least a particularly important, role in bringing the revolution about.

For the countries highlighted in the table, the following are a few of the main attributes shared by their social-political-economic systems, which served as antecedents to the socialist system.

1. The countries in the group were poor and economically undeveloped.[5] This is clearly demonstrated by the fact that their per capita pro-

---

[4]The question of the effect the specific initial state and historical development of the Soviet Union had on the shaping of the general features of the system, and the influence exerted by the Soviet pattern and the Soviet intervention on the other socialist countries, will be discussed later [→15.4].

[5]Mao Zedong (1977, p. 306) offered a revealing explanation of that fact. In 1956, he said: "Our two weaknesses are also strong points. As I have said elsewhere, we are first 'poor' and second 'blank.' By 'poor' I mean we do not have much industry and our agricul-

duction before the revolution was a fraction of the production of the most developed countries at the time.

2. The proportion of industry was low. They were basically agrarian countries in which the peasants and landless agricultural workers formed the bulk of the population.

3. The modern sector of industry consisting of large factories equipped with up-to-date technology and organized in an up-to-date way was relatively small.

4. Their social relations and property forms contained many precapitalist features.

5. There was striking inequality in the distribution of income, which was far less evenly spread than in the developed countries in the same period. The gulf between rich and poor was instrumental in revolutionizing the population.

6. In terms of their political systems, it is notable that not one of the countries listed in the table was a consolidated parliamentary democracy. All had systems that to a large extent suppressed political liberties, and more than a few were brutal dictatorships.

7. Quite a number, if not all the countries in the table, were partial or total dependencies of other states: colonies or semicolonies, countries under military occupation, or simply dependent economically and politically on one or another stronger, more highly developed country. Consequently, the attainment of national independence was on the agenda.

8. In most of these countries there were events in the years before the revolution that shook up the institutions of society: war against an outside enemy, civil war, guerrilla war, or repeated insurrections. Of these events, the warfare was tied up in some cases with the situation outlined under point 7.

The first four of these attributes clearly conflict with what Marx had expected: socialism does not emerge first in countries where capitalism is overripe and has done all it can to develop the forces of production. Socialism does not inherit developed, well-organized production concentrated into large units, if one discounts the relatively small modern sector. Moreover, it takes control of a society in the stage of upheaval.

The eight points constitute a summary of the main attributes common to the social-political-economic system before the socialist revolution. I shall return to the characteristics of the prerevolutionary situation and

---

ture is underdeveloped. By 'blank' I mean we are like a blank sheet of paper and our cultural and scientific level is not high. . . . This is not bad. The poor want revolution, whereas it is difficult for the rich to want revolution. Countries with a high scientific and technological level are overblown with arrogance. We are like a blank sheet of paper which is good for writing on.''

TABLE 2.1
Socialist Countries: Revolution Largely by Internal Forces

1 Serial Number	2 Country	3 Year Power Was Attained	4 Level of Economic Development, GDP per Capita[a] (USA = 100)	Before Communist Party Attained Power	
				5 Type of External Dependence	6 Type of Armed Combat
1.	Soviet Union	1917	21.8[b]	Independent state	World War I
2.	Albania	1944	—	Independent state, Italian occupation	World War II, war of liberation
3.	Yugoslavia	1945	14.0[c]	Independent state, German and Italian occupation	World War II, war of liberation
4.	China	1949	—	Independent state, Japanese occupation	World War II, revolutionary wars before and after the war of liberation
5.	Vietnam	1954	—	French colony, Japanese occupation	World War II, war of liberation, first against Japa- nese then against French
6.	Cuba	1959	—	Independent state	Guerrilla struggles inside the country

7.	Congo	1963	12.8	French colony until 1960	Colonial struggles for independence, military seizure of power
8.	Somalia	1969	5.4	Italian colony	Military seizure of power
9.	South Yemen	1969	6.0	British colony	Colonial struggles for independence
10.	Benin	1972	5.0	French colony until 1960	Military seizure of power
11.	Ethiopia	1974	4.5	Independent state	Military seizure of power
12.	Mozambique	1975	12.4	Portuguese colony	Colonial struggles for independence
13.	Nicaragua	1979	21.4	Independent state	Armed uprising
14.	Zimbabwe	1980	14.7	Former British colony, in practice independent	Seven-year guerrilla war

Source: Row 1: S. N. Prokopovich (1918, p. 66). Row 3: É. Ehrlich (1990, table 8). All other rows: I. B. Kravis, A. W. Heston, and R. Summers (1978, table 4).

[a]It would be more expressive to describe the level of economic development of each country by giving the corresponding data for the last year of peace before the revolution, but the scarcity of data made that plan hardly feasible. The unmarked data refer to 1970.

[b]The European territory of Russia in comparison to England on the basis of national income per capita in 1913.

[c]The datum refers to 1937.

the starting point for the emergence of the new system several times in the remainder of this chapter and in subsequent chapters. The inherited backwardness and the other characteristics of the initial state left a deep mark on the forms of socialism that struck root in the Soviet Union, China, and other countries that took the socialist road largely as a result of internal forces.

After that, it is worth looking at the countries where the socialist revolution was not brought about basically by internal forces. This group is very heterogeneous in terms of the eight criteria listed earlier. The characterization given for the countries in table 2.1 suits some of these countries, such as Mongolia and Afghanistan. But the majority of the Eastern European countries occupied by the Soviet Union after the Second World War had progressed beyond the low level of development that marked the countries in table 2.1 at the time of the revolution. In fact, two of them, Czechoslovakia and East Germany, belonged to the group of countries with the highest level of industrial development. These countries were, so to say, compelled by open and concealed Soviet intervention to adopt a system whose first historical realization had developed in a backward society.

The conclusion to be drawn here is that the initial attributes of this group of "externally revolutionized" countries are not the ones worth taking as a basis when attempting in the rest of the examination to clarify what caused the features of the socialist system to develop. The appropriate starting point is the initial state of the countries in table 2.1, above all the Soviet Union.

2.4   The Revolutionary Transition toward the Classical System

This section is concerned very briefly with describing the character of the period that leads from the presocialist system to the institutionalized classical system.

The transition took place in different ways in each country, but one can discern common features, mainly in the case of the countries that took the socialist road basically by their own efforts. The emphasis here is primarily on these common features. The summary that follows qualifies not as a specific historical description, but rather as a compound, model-like sketch of the transitional period in several countries.

It is not enough merely to review the most important actions taken. Also required is an idea of the public atmosphere and political climate of the period. The exponents of revolution are fired with enthusiasm. They feel a sense of triumph and of doing a great deed of historical justice. Having fought for the revolution and risked imprisonment, torture, and death, they are ready to sacrifice more to make their ideas come true. Working for the community is a self-evident obligation for them. The enthusiasm is not confined to a small group of active revolutionaries, for great masses of people are borne along by it. For this reason, this stage is often seen as the "heroic age" of socialism.[6]

"Expropriation of the expropriators" begins at once. Part of the factories, banks, and other institutions are taken into state or collective ownership. Work starts immediately on centralizing production and distribution.

The most important of the measures of redistribution is to confiscate the great estates of the landowners and divide them among the landless and the poor peasants.

What takes place is not simply a wave of nationalization and socialization—it is accompanied by a redistribution of property and income. The reader is reminded of the sharp inequalities of the prerevolutionary system; the new regime tries to eliminate them as fast as possible. The upper classes are deprived of their high incomes, and most of their property is confiscated. In several places poor families actually move into the homes of the rich. Palaces are taken over by schools and workers' vacation homes.

In most countries this initial revolutionary transformation takes place in time of civil war or war against an external enemy, when the economy is in a state of disruption. Therefore, among the most immediate tasks is to ensure that food is distributed fairly. Rationing is introduced, so that basic foodstuffs at accessible prices can be ensured also for the poor. Black marketeers who try to sidestep the rationing system are harassed and prosecuted.

However grave the economic problems are, a campaign of education covering the entire population begins, free basic health care for all is promised, and vacations for children are organized.

The impulse to dispense historical justice is not expressed exclusively in the redistribution of economic goods. The nobility, the wealthy, and the old regime's leading politicians and officials are also subjected to persecution. Many of them are imprisoned, sent to labor camp, or exe-

---

[6]This title was given by the Soviet economic historian L. N. Kritsman to his study on Soviet War Communism, *The Heroic Period of the Great Russian Revolution (1926)*. The period of War Communism is one historical realization of the prototype referred to in this book as the "revolutionary-transitional system." It agrees in many (but not all) of its attributes with the generalized model described in this section.

On the first years of the socialist regime, see, for the *Soviet Union*, M. H. Dobb [1948] (1960), A. Nove (1969, chap. 3), and L. Szamuely (1974); for *China*, H. Harding (1981) and M. Meisner (1986); for *Yugoslavia*, D. D. Milenkovitch (1971) and F. B. Singleton and B. Carter (1982); for *Hungary*, I. Pető and S. Szakács (1985).

cuted. Physical violence and merciless terror are common accompaniments of revolutionary periods.

The expropriation of material goods and the personal persecution of the old ruling stratum in society involve both spontaneous acts unsanctioned by the law and measures hastily introduced in new legislation. These occur concurrently and may even work against each other. There is no longer any law and order or legal security in society, which may well have been disrupted already by the civil and external warfare before the revolution. Symptoms of anarchy become widespread.

From the outset the country's population is divided. Alongside the revolution's supporters and those indifferent to it or simply intent on survival there also appear active resisters of the revolutionary changes. In some places the resistance manifests itself in small, localized actions, and in others it takes on an organized form that results in uprisings and civil war. This further increases the level of violence on both sides, with retaliation breeding still more ruthless retaliation.

The question often arises as to what would have happened if Marx's expectations had been fulfilled, if socialism had come to power in the most highly developed countries. What would the outcome have been if socialism had taken control, in time of peace, of modern forces of production developed on a vast scale by capitalism, so that it was able to supply the people amply with material goods right from the start?

The historical fact is that no socialist system has ever been installed in power by internal forces in any developed capitalist country. It is precisely the situation described in the previous section (backwardness of a largely precapitalist nature, poverty, striking inequality, brutal oppression, war, and then a deep crisis in society) that induces revolution and allows the Communist party to seize power. These conditions for a change of system are what elicit the characteristic events summarized above: enthusiasm and self-sacrifice on the winning side and resistance on the other, redistribution at dramatic speed, and disintegration of social order.

Numerous attributes of the revolutionary period are understandable in the light of prior events and easily explained by them. No less understandable is the fact that this period can be only transitional, since many of the factors that sustain this system are temporary.

In very few cases do revolutionary fervor and self-sacrifice last a lifetime. The average person, inspired by a great cause and a mass movement and confident of approaching victory, is capable of self-sacrifice for the community, but only for a short time. After that he wants to get back to normal daily life, and sense the connection between his work, the sacrifices he makes, and his own material welfare. It becomes vital for society to encourage people to perform well by dispensing material rewards and penalties.

Once all the wealthy have had everything possible confiscated from them, the scope for that kind of redistribution is exhausted. Production has been set back by the events preceding and following the revolution and the confusion of the transition.[7] It becomes clear that production, not confiscation, is the way to continue improving the population's material position. Production, of which the bulk is now in public, collective hands, requires organization and effective control.

The prerevolutionary system has left the country backward, and before they came to power the revolutionaries promised that once in power they would eliminate this backwardness. As society emerges from the bloody external and internal warfare and the chance comes for peaceful labor, those in power realize they must fulfill these promises by rapidly increasing the economy's forces of production. They would like to achieve swift and spectacular economic successes. Moreover, they feel the system is threatened militarily, and their desire to increase their military power rapidly trains their attention on fast economic growth.

Attainment of the goals outlined above is now hindered by the anarchy, the lack of law and order, and arbitrary local actions. No society of any kind can function without some sort of discipline. There is a growing demand for order to be restored.

All these altered circumstances prepare the ground for the country to step beyond the socialist revolutionary-transitional system. The spirit of revolutionary romanticism and heroism gradually fades and then dies, even in those who were enthusiastic about the revolution before; the new system becomes institutionalized and bureaucratic, and life normalizes. The classical socialist system emerges and consolidates.[8]

At this point it is worth making a short diversion to consider the specific historical development of Eastern Europe.[9] Yugoslavia and Albania basically took the socialist road by their own efforts, and accordingly, the validity of the model outlined above as a summary of the main fea-

[7]In the Soviet Union, for instance, industrial production in 1920 had fallen back to 21 percent of the 1917 level. See L. N. Kritsman (1926, p. 80).

[8]The process by which the revolutionary-transitional system is transformed into the classical system is dealt with in several historical works. (See references in note 6.)

[9]The painful dilemmas of postwar democracy in Eastern Europe are discussed by the outstanding Hungarian political scientist I. Bibó in his 1945 and 1946 papers, reprinted in his 1986 volume. Of the writings on the political history of the Eastern European countries between 1945 and 1949 and the role played in it by the Soviet Union, mention should be made of the seminal work by Z. Brzezinski [1961] (1967). See, furthermore, T. T. Hammond, ed. (1975) and C. Gati (1984).

tures of the socialist revolutionary transition can be extended to cover them. But as section 2.3 underlined, it was the Soviet Army that eliminated the German military occupation in Bulgaria, Czechoslovakia, Hungary, Poland, and Romania, and occupied East Germany after Germany's military defeat; the Soviet military and political presence in these countries represented an extremely strong support to the Communist party, which wanted to institute a socialist system. The Soviet Union imposed on these countries the socialist system, mainly by enforcing a domestic political situation in which the Communist party was able in the end to attain undivided power.

Multiparty parliamentary democracy operated in these countries in the years immediately after the war. They had coalition governments in which the Communist party's weight was greater than its share of the vote. The economy that emerged was a curiously mixed one, with a "regular" capitalist sector on the one hand and socialist elements on the other. A steady process of nationalization took place. Land reform was carried out on a large scale.

This period came to an end around 1948–49 with the amalgamation of the Communist and Social Democratic parties and the elimination of the multiparty system. From then on, construction of a socialist system began with full force, starting straight away with classical socialism.

The 1945–49 period in these countries had many of the attributes of the revolutionary-transitional system described above, but it also differed from it in many crucial respects. These differences are explained precisely by the fact that instead of an internally induced socialist revolution taking place in 1945, the pre-1945 system was demolished by an outside force, the Soviet Union.

Part Two

THE ANATOMY OF THE CLASSICAL SYSTEM

3

Power

THE KEY to an understanding of the socialist system is to examine the *structure of power,* which receives little or no attention in many comparative studies of economic systems. In my opinion, the characteristics of the power structure are precisely the source from which the chief regularities of the system can be deduced.[1]

This chapter, on power, and chapter 4, on ideology, are closely related. The present chapter deals with the institutions of power and the way they work, and chapter 4 deals with the objectives, value system, and ideas behind the political actions of those who possess that power. One might say that this chapter is about the body of power, and chapter 4 is about its soul.

The description and analysis will be brief, because they concentrate on the characteristics essential from the point of view of the book's subject: the economy of the socialist system. There is no discussion of several other attributes of the political structure that to a historian or a political scientist would be of equal interest.

3.1 The Party

The established practice in the social sciences is to make a distinction between a particular organization or institution's formal rules of operation, in the sense of its declared, internal rulebook and the official prescriptions of the law of the state, and the actual regularities governing how it works. How similar and how different are these two "rules of the game"? This distinction will be made in the following description of how the party, the state, and the so-called mass organizations operate.

---

[1]Let me propose the following procedure for the reader to consider:

Before beginning chapter 3, it might be worth reading chapter 15, which sums up the whole of part 2, dealing with the classical system. Although some of the concepts in chapter 15 may not be clear until chapters 3–14 have been read, the summary more or less projects the main conclusions, which makes the chapters that follow here easier to understand.

My proposal would be that the reader continue with chapters 3–14 after that; when chapter 15 is reached again, it would be worth rereading it in the light of the information gathered from studying part 2.

Of course, the train of thought can be followed clearly also without the advance reading of chapter 15.

The fundamental institution in the power structure is the Communist party.[2] (For brevity's sake it will be referred to hereafter generally as "the party," without qualification.) The socialist countries have a *one-party system* in which no other party can operate.[3] At the peak of its power, the party comprised a substantial proportion of the population (see table 3.1).

The chief organizing principle in the party's rules of organization is "democratic centralism." Entry into the party is voluntary; the admission of an applicant is decided upon by the party branch.[4] The branches are the basic cells of party, covering all party members in a specific territorial unit (e.g., a city or part of a city) or place of work (e.g., a factory). The leading body is elected at a meeting of the branch members for a specified term. The branch is headed by the party secretary.

The branches are under the direction of higher party organizations, usually arranged on territorial principles. For instance, a district party committee headed by a district party secretary has over it a county party committee and a county party secretary. At the top of the pyramid is the Central Committee (or in federal countries consisting of several states, such as the Soviet Union, China, or Yugoslavia, the federal Central Committee). The national (or federal) Central Committee elects a smaller, executive body of control from its own ranks; the customary term for this is the Political Committee. (The well-known Soviet term is "Politbureau.") The Central Committee also elects the party leader (general secretary) and his immediate colleagues, the national (or federal) secretaries.

---

[2]For a long time the *Short History of the Communist Party of the Soviet Union,* the Stalinist version of party history, was holy writ in the Soviet Union, underscoring the central role of the party. It later fulfilled similar functions in the Eastern European socialist countries.

For scholarly works on the history and functioning of Communist parties, see the following books. *Soviet Union:* J. F. Hough and M. Fainsod [1953] (1979) and J. F. Hough (1969); *China:* H. Harding (1981) and J. W. Lewis, ed. (1970); *Eastern Europe:* S. Fischer-Galati, ed. (1979).

[3]In several socialist countries, such as China and Poland, other parties existed formally even under the classical system, but they had no actual power or even independent influence over political matters.

[4]The specific terms used ("branch," "party leadership," "party secretary," etc.) may differ from country to country. In such cases the terminology in this book is an attempt to use terms unrestricted to a particular socialist country and applicable to all of them. With a few exceptions, the book also refrains from listing the specific terms used in each country.

The same procedure will be followed in the rest of the book for other unstandardized terms that differ slightly from country to country while having the same meaning nonetheless.

TABLE 3.1
Proportion of Party Members in Socialist Countries, 1986

Country	Party Members (thousand)	Party Members (percent of population)
Albania	147	4.9
Bulgaria	932	10.4
China	44,000	4.2
Cuba	524	5.1
Czechoslovakia	1,675	10.8
East Germany	2,304	13.8
Hungary	871	8.2
Mongolia	88	4.5
North Korea	2,500	12.2
Poland	2,126	5.7
Romania	3,557	15.6
Soviet Union	18,500	6.6
Vietnam	1,700	2.7
Yugoslavia	2,168	9.3

Source: R. F. Staar (1987, pp. 45–47).
Note: The data on membership are based on the declarations of the parties themselves. The share of party members is given as the percentage of the total population. A comparison to the adult population would result in even higher proportions.

Under the formal rules, all leading bodies and all party secretaries at every level are elected by the party membership, either directly or indirectly through delegates or acts of election by party leaders who themselves have been elected already. This electoral procedure, along with the rule that party resolutions can be passed only by elected bodies, constitutes the democratic side of the principle of democratic centralism. The other side is centralism: the decision of a higher party body is binding on a lower party body, and ultimately on every member of the party. A party matter is open to debate until it has been decided, after which it must be implemented without argument or protest.

In real life, centralism prevails very strongly. According to its formal rules, the organization is built up from below, but in practice it works to a far greater extent from above.

The central leadership has available a large staff of officials who concurrently constitute a bureaucratic hierarchy of department heads, deputy department heads, and employees. Under the formal rules, these appointed party officials have no power, since the right to decide belongs exclusively to the elected bodies. In fact, they exercise great influence on the management of affairs.

Formally, the general secretary is merely the one who executes the decisions of the central leadership, and between central leadership sessions those of the Political Committee. In practice, enormous power is concentrated in his hands. Here the prime example one thinks of is Stalin's role in the Soviet Union,[5] but the almost absolute power of the general secretary develops sooner or later, in an extreme or less extreme form, in every socialist country that arrives at the stage of classical socialism.

The post of secretary is a full-time job, at least in the larger branches. Alongside all middle-level party bodies and the larger, if not the smaller, branches, an organization of appointed party officials is established.

What ultimately emerges is a bureaucratic hierarchy that encompasses the whole of the party: instructions passed down from above must be carried out by the subordinates. Under such a system of superiority and subordination, the distinction between elected officers and appointed officials counts for little. Collectively, the elected (though full-time) party leaders and the appointed party officials are known in common parlance as the *party apparatus.*

Clearly, the nature of the selection process has been reversed. In practice, the elected body is not picking the members of the apparatus. Instead, the apparatus is choosing those who will join the elected body at the next election and whom they in turn will elect as secretary. Ultimately, the apparatus determines who gains admittance into the party, which party member becomes a member of the party apparatus (in other words, a party functionary), and which party functionary is promoted to a higher function. In a similar way, exclusion from the party or from elected party bodies is also in the hands of the apparatus. Formally, every detail of admission, promotion, entry into party bodies, demotion to a lower function, or exclusion is validated by electoral procedures or the decisions of elected bodies, but all this is largely an empty formality. The case has been decided before the election is held or the decision made.

3.2 The State

In its formal constitution, laws, and legal regulations, the state under the classical socialist system resembles any other modern state. It is di-

---

[5]There is a rich biographical literature on Stalin. See, for instance, I. Deutscher (1966), R. Tucker (1973, 1990), and A. Ulam (1973). Tucker in particular shows the interactions between the nature of the Bolshevik movement and the charismatic-terroristic leadership Stalin provided.

vided into three separate branches: a legislature, a state administration responsible for applying the laws, and a judiciary. The members of the legislature (which will be referred to hereafter as parliament) are elected by the general public. Parliament then nominates the government. Local legislatures (hereafter local councils) operate in each territorial unit (in federal countries in each state, and within states in each county, city, township, etc.). These local councils are independent within limits laid down by the law and have their own executive organizations.

In a number of socialist countries the constitution asserts that the leading force in the country is the Communist party, but the way this leading role applies in practice is not specified. As a first approach one might say that the activities of party and state are closely interwoven in a way that ensures that the party is the dominant force in their common activity.[6] Although the laws of the state do not define it, the party's jurisdiction in practice covers the following:

1. All major appointments, promotions, and dismissals are decided upon by the various bodies of the party. The regulations of the state are silent on the subject, but the rules of the party normally lay down precisely which party body's resolution is required before a specific post is filled, in other words, which personnel decisions are the prerogative of the Political Committee and which of the party leadership at the county, city, or branch level.[7] This prerogative of selection covers offices in the state administration and all major managerial positions in the economy. Party committees decide who will be president of the republic and who will stand for parliamentary and local government elections. Since in most of the cases there is only one candidate for each seat, the practical result is that the representatives are selected by the party. Similarly, party organizations decide on the appointment of judges and prosecutors.

The importance of the party apparatus's role in selecting the members of elected party organizations was pointed out in the previous section. It should be added here that the party apparatus also prepares the party committees' resolutions on other personnel matters, so that they are little more than confirmation of choices put forward by the party apparatus beforehand. One can conclude, therefore, that the party apparatus plays the key role in selecting the members of the legislature, the state administration, and the judiciary.

2. The party organizations reach decisions on every major affair of state before the state organization responsible has come to its own deci-

[6]In the 1950s I heard József Révai, the top ideologist in the Hungarian party, make the apt "dialectical" observation: "The party and the state are not one, but they are not two either."

[7]In Soviet professional jargon, this body of regulations is known as the *nomenklatura*. The term nomenklatura is also used in a figurative sense to denote the leading stratum.

sion. The major decisions of the government are preceded by resolutions of the party's central leadership or Political Committee, those of county councils by resolutions of county party committees, and so on.

3. The party apparatus is in direct touch with the apparatus of state. The effect is a curious kind of duplication in which a specific party functionary or group of functionaries within the party apparatus has responsibility for every important sphere of state activity. The central party apparatus contains departments responsible for industry, agriculture, education, culture, foreign affairs, military matters, and so on. The duplication, however, is not total.[8] One discrepancy is in scale: there are normally far fewer people in the party apparatus dealing with a particular area than there are in the parallel state organization. On the other hand, the small staff has great power. Its word is decisive, even though it may not formally issue instructions at all.

Additionally, and very importantly, the task of the party apparatus includes supervision of the state apparatus. It must report immediately on any irregularity it finds.

Under constitutional law there is no obligation on the state officials, members of parliament, and councils or judges to obey the instructions of the party. The majority of them are party members, however, and as such they are obliged to carry out the party's instructions. In practice, their obligation extends beyond the resolutions of elected party bodies to the individual behests of the appropriate party functionary, the blanket justification being that his or her instructions are designed to implement the party's resolutions.

Speaking of an interweaving of party and state, I have mentioned so far only the way the party (or rather its apparatus) holds sway over the state. Use of the term "interweaving" can be justified by the following circumstances:

Some members of the elected party bodies hold state office or leading positions in the state-owned sector, as ministers, deputy ministers, chief executives of state-owned firms, ambassadors, generals, police chiefs, and members of parliament. So to that extent the "state" has penetrated the party, not just the party the "state."

Interweaving also takes place in the careers of individuals. Someone who starts life as a lowly party functionary, of course, may advance exclusively within the party apparatus. The same applies to the apparatus of the state: an individual may enter it and remain in it throughout his or her career. But to switch from one to the other is far from exceptional:

---

[8]The party bodies at lower levels are organized on regional principles, but each regional party apparatus likewise contains bodies that correspond to a number of functional institutions of state (state administration of industry, agriculture, etc.).

a factory manager may be promoted to city party secretary and then return to the state administration as a deputy minister. Conversely, he or she may begin as a party secretary, continue as a chief executive of a large company or a chief of police, and later fill a high office in the party. For this reason it is customary in socialist countries to talk of "members of the apparatus," "functionaries," or "cadres" in a comprehensive sense, without necessarily stipulating where the function is performed (whether in the party or in the state). These are also the grounds on which some authors employ the term *party-state.*

A line of argument constantly put forward in debate is that despite the undoubted overlap between the party and the state, there is nonetheless a "natural division of labor" between them: the party performs political functions and the state administrative ones. But this distinction does not apply under this system. Politics influences all dimensions of life; there are no administrative affairs "free of politics." The Communist party considers itself responsible for everything and does not allow the organizations of state and those working in the state apparatus any autonomy at all. In fact, the existence of the "party-state" and the blending of the political and administrative functions is one of the main characteristics of the system.

3.3   The Mass Organizations

The various organizations and associations in society are termed collectively *mass organizations.*[9] With only a few exceptions, their main chareristic is for each to have an organizational monopoly in its own field. There is one labor-union movement, one youth league, and one women's organization. The Academy of Sciences alone has the right to represent science. It is worth mentioning particularly the various professional bodies: there is a single association of engineers, writers' union, musicians' union, motion picture union, and so forth.

This organizational monopoly makes it possible for the mass organizations to function concurrently as authorities. The labor unions of many socialist countries handle welfare funds provided out of the state budget and limit the benefits from them to their members. Membership in the appropriate arts organization doubles as a permit to engage in that artistic activity professionally; without that membership it cannot be pursued.

---

[9]Of the literature on mass organizations, the reader is referred to B. Ruble and A. Pravda, eds. (1986) and A. Kahan and B. Ruble, eds. (1979). Both books describe the role of the trade unions.

Legally and formally, each mass organization is autonomous and its officers are elected by its members, directly or indirectly, according to its statutes. In practice, the party decides who the candidates for election will be.[10] When all is said and done, a leading officer in a mass organization is as much a functionary as any member of the apparatus or any high state official. At this point one can extend all that was said in the previous section about state officials to cover officers in the mass organizations. They too are under the direction of the party, since the main resolutions they pass are preceded by decisions of the relevant party body. Members of the party apparatus actively intervene in the mass organizations' affairs; in practice, if not formally, they order them to take specific measures. The mass organizations' main function ultimately becomes one of conveying the ideas and intentions of the party to "target" sectors of society (the workers, youth, women) corresponding to the sphere of each organization. As Lenin put it, they are "transmission belts" between the party and the masses.

Also applicable to the mass organizations are the earlier remarks about interweaving. The leaders of the larger organizations (the unions, the youth league) are commonly members of the leading party bodies at various levels (national, regional, and branch). They represent their movements in the party leadership and the party in their movements. If they fail to do the latter, the party appoints others to their posts.

The observations on the careers of functionaries can be extended to the mass organizations in the same way. It is quite frequent for an officer in the labor or youth movement, say, to become a higher functionary in the party or state, or for a party or state functionary to move to a higher post in a mass organization.

3.4 Cohesive Forces

To refer to the organization consisting of functionaries of the party, the state, the mass organizations, and also the managers of the state-owned sector collectively, two terms will be used as synonyms in the remainder this book: *apparatus* and *bureaucracy*.[11] Where no specific reference

[10]In 1929 the Communist party of the Soviet Union (Bolshevik) dismissed Tomsky from his leading position in the labor unions. (Later he committed suicide.) Kaganovich, one of Stalin's closest associates, made this comment on the dismissal: "The greater part of the leadership . . . has been replaced. It could be said that this was a violation of proletarian democracy, but, Comrades, it has long been known that for us Bolsheviks democracy is no fetish." *Report on the Sixteenth Congress,* quoted by R. Conquest [1968] (1973, p. 41).

[11]"Bureaucracy" is used colloquially and in sociology in several different senses. Colloquially it has a pejorative ring, implying such things as roundabout handling of matters, unenthusiastic work, and delay in reaching decisions. By social scientists, particularly since

is made to a particular bureaucracy (the apparatus of the party or the state or a specific mass organization such as the labor-union movement), the terms apply to all the apparatuses collectively. So the party apparatus, in the terminology of this book, is part of the bureaucracy—not something external to it but an integral element of it—indeed, the most powerful part of it, dominating the other elements.

What forces bind the bureaucracy together?

1. *Ideology*. The bureaucracy, and particularly its leading force, the party, is held together by specific ideas, aims, and values. Many members of the apparatus are people guided by noble purposes who work long, hard hours in the firm belief that in doing so they serve the cause of their party and of the people, the common good and the interests of mankind. At this point I merely make reference to the cohesive force of a common ideology before turning to other forces. As mentioned before, the influence of ideology is so important that the whole of the next chapter will be devoted to it.

2. *Power*. The members of the bureaucracy, which includes the party, are bound together by their resolve to retain power. The bureaucracy constitutes the power elite of the classical system.[12] The power, of course, is shared unequally because of the multilevel, hierarchical way in which the bureaucracy is structured. The party apparatus plays a prominent part; it is "stronger" than the other provinces of the bureaucracy. Higher-level functionaries have greater power than lower-level ones. It must also be noted that everyone in the bureaucracy (apart from the paramount leader at the very top) is at once a master and a servant: one can order about those below one, but one must obey those above. Ultimately, however, this group in society rules collectively over the other citizens, deciding their destinies and disposing of the country's resources. As the possessor of power, the bureaucracy reproduces itself indefinitely, even though the people who make it up are constantly changing.[13]

Max Weber [1925] (1978, chaps. 3, 11), it has been used as a value-free technical term to denote a specific social formation irrespective of whether it operates in a good, speedy, and compassionate or a bad, tardy, and inhuman way. This book uses the term in the latter, value-free sense. (However, the bureaucracy under the socialist system differs in many features from the one with which Max Weber was concerned [→6.1].)

[12]On the concept of "elite," see the R. Michels [1911] (1962) and V. Pareto [1916] (1935).

[13]Some authors classify the bureaucracy of a classical socialist system as a ruling class. This idea arose first in the writings of L. Trotsky [1937] (1970) and M. Djilas (1957). Similar notions have been advanced by J. Kuron and K. Modzielewski (1968).

G. Konrád and I. Szelényi (1979) put their emphasis on the potential class-power of the intellectuals. In a self-critical follow-up, Szelényi (1986) revised some ideas of the earlier book concerning the willingness of the bureaucracy to share power and the chances of the rise of an entrepreneurial class. He discussed the latter point in more detail in Szelényi (1988).   Continued

3. *Prestige and privileges.* The members of the bureaucracy have prestige. This applies first and foremost within the bureaucracy, where a member in a higher position has prestige in the eyes of a member in a lower position. Under the system (save among a few exceptional professions such as scholars, scientists, artists, and sports figures, who have their own yardsticks of prestige), the level of the position attained in the bureaucracy is the sole measure of rank.[14] (This contrasts with the situation in societies based on a pluralist power structure and private ownership, where parallel measures of prestige exist, of which one of the most important consists of business success, income, and wealth.)

The ultimate instance of prestige attaching to high office is the phenomenon referred to in the socialist countries as the "the cult of personality." The highest leader of the country is literally revered as a person superhumanly talented, infallible, and omniscient. The prime examples to have emerged under the classical socialist system are Stalin and Mao Zedong, in the two largest socialist countries, the Soviet Union and China. Similar cults grew up around the party leaders in all the other countries during the Stalin period, and even after Stalin's death many features of the personality cult could be observed in countries where the classical system lived on.[15]

Similar symptoms, on a lesser scale than in the cult of personality surrounding the leader of a country, appear in the case of a regional or branch party secretary, who possesses a special aura, and whose every word is regarded as wise and unerringly true.

The prestige is accompanied by material privileges proportionate to rank [→13.5]. Actual pay is not particularly high, although the relative salary proportions between higher and lower positions are no less than those customary in the state bureaucracy of a capitalist country. By contrast, all the more importance attaches to the fringe material benefits in

---

The position in this debate depends, of course, on one's definition of the term "class." On alternative definitions of class and class conflict, and modern usage of this sphere of concepts, see R. Dahrendorf (1959).

In any case, definitional difficulties arise when one comes to analyze the power elite of a socialist society. For instance, I have just mentioned the enormous inequality apparent in the distribution of power. So this book will avoid using the expression "ruling class" for the bureaucracy in power under the classical socialist system.

[14]There exist not merely informal definitions of "equivalence" but ones for formal, protocol purposes, laying down, for instance, which state positions (minister, deputy minister, ministry department head, etc.) bestow the same rank as the various grades of party functionary, army officer, company executive, officer in a mass organization, and so on.

[15]For example, the cults of Nicolae Ceausescu in Romania, Fidel Castro in Cuba, and Kim Il Sung in North Korea.

addition to pay. They include benefits in kind, either free or at a very cheap price. Functionaries also have access to goods and services in short supply. The functionary can shop in special closed stores offering goods not available in ordinary stores; he or she has an institutionally owned apartment.[16] Functionaries receive medical treatment in hospitals that are better equipped and less crowded; they spend vacations in closed places better supplied than the usual company holiday center; and so on. These special services may even be provided in several grades: a higher-ranking functionary may be treated in an even better hospital, shop in an even better stocked store, use a chauffeur-driven, institutionally owned car, have a personal vacation home, and so on. Many of these material privileges are also available to the functionary's family.

Let there be no misunderstanding: in spite of these material privileges, a functionary's standard of living falls short of the level of the wealthy in a capitalist society. Nevertheless, the privileges are great enough for the withdrawal of them to come as a blow.

4. *Coercion.* I have mentioned that every party member is under an obligation to put party resolutions and instructions into practice. Clearly, it is also compulsory in the state bureaucracy to carry out measures decided on higher up. The final result is a party and state discipline whose observance is enforced.

There is a system of retributions within the party: various grades of censure, transfer to a lower function, and, as the ultimate punishment, expulsion from the party. Under the classical system, the last is a very serious penalty, since it brings a functionary's career in the apparatus to an abrupt end and is followed in many cases by prosecution by the state.

Infringement of state discipline can have the legal consequences customary under other systems as well, ranging from withdrawal of cash bonuses to demotion or dismissal. But the penalty can be much graver than this: a sentence in a labor camp or prison, or execution.

So far I have been referring to penalties for real infringements of party and state discipline, but the concept of discipline expands under the classical system. It is a functionary's duty not merely to obey precisely phrased instructions with blind obedience, but to follow faithfully a currently valid political line. Departure from this line (or in extreme cases a real or assumed intention to depart from it or grounded or groundless suspicions of such an intention) is enough to incur the discipline of the party or prosecution by the state. That leads to the next question: the conflicts *within* the bureaucracy.

---

[16]There is no complete translation of the term used in socialist countries (*sluzhebnaia kvartira* in Russian or *szolgálati lakás* in Hungarian). The apartment or the car is owned or rented by the employer (for example, by the company or government office) and allotted to the employee as a part of the package of fringe benefits.

3.5 Internal Conflicts

The bureaucracy and the party as the motive force behind it do not constitute a monolithic entity, since a variety of internal conflicts appear in them. During the periods of greatest repression, these conflicts are almost entirely submerged, but they reappear in various forms as soon as there is a slight relaxation.

The sharpest form of internal conflict is the operation of "wings" or factions within the party. In fact, they can amount to the germs of parties within the party, although they normally take a very loosely organized form. A faction is the concerted appearance of a group that represents a line of its own, differing decisively from the line other groups are taking, on issues of political import. For instance, a group with a separate political platform of this kind was formed in the Soviet party by the party leaders who opposed the plan for the forcible, swift collectivization of agriculture.

The operation of factions and separate political groupings is forbidden by the internal statutes of a Communist party. What usually happens sooner or later is that the political group in power at a particular time eliminates the groups that attack its political line.[17] For these reasons it can prove quite dangerous to start forming a political group within the party. Of course, when new and fundamental problems have to be decided upon, new factions, or at least new looser political groupings, often emerge all over again. But never, under the classical system, can any faction really strengthen itself to a point where it becomes a stable oppositional organization capable of surviving in the longer term.

Conflicts within the party can emerge also in a great many other dimensions, for instance, over the division of political influence among various ethnic groups or in the struggle for power between generations. The latter heightens particularly when the question of succession to paramount leadership arises.

Another type of conflict occurs when the functionaries of the state and the mass organizations chafe at the interference of the party apparatus, who for their part are discontented with the level of enthusiasm shown by the former in carrying out the party's instructions.

---

[17]Stalin used merciless terror to settle scores successively with all the political opposition groups. On this, see the classic work by R. Conquest [1968] (1973), and also the biography of Bukharin by S. F. Cohen [1973] (1980). In Eastern Europe, the real or assumed representatives of "national communism" were eliminated in a similar fashion. Another well-known example of a grouping opposed to the political line of the moment being eliminated was the trial in China, after Mao's death, of the "Gang of Four," Mao's immediate associates.

The classical socialist system is not immune to the social phenomenon known to Americans as the pressure group or lobby.[18] Representatives of the interests of the various branches or industrial sectors, professions, trades, and geographical regions attempt to pressure the central organizations (for instance, over resource allocation or appointments). Some groups of this kind extend right across the various sectors of the party, state, and mass-organization bureaucracy and have "their men" representing them in the widest variety of positions. The farming lobby, for instance, includes central leadership members of peasant origin, the leading party and state officials from agricultural counties, heads of the Ministry of Agriculture, members of parliament for farming constituencies, and professors of agricultural universities. There is a "mining lobby," a "cultural lobby," and so on. Each group strives to promote its ideas through its personal connections and by various means of exercising political pressure (sending delegations, speaking up at meetings, arranging for articles to be written for the newspapers, etc.).

Earlier in this chapter the cohesive forces binding together the various parts of the bureaucracy were underscored, but a full picture should also include the conflicts among them.

3.6 Repression and the Totalitarian Nature of Power

After describing the nature of the apparatus in the previous sections, it is time to make a few observations on the relations between the ruling elite and the rest of society.

The bureaucracy sets out to convince people to support their policy, using the whole arsenal of education and modern political propaganda for the purpose [→4]. Rallies and mass marches are political features of the classical system. But to augment the arsenal and give special emphasis to the words of enlightenment there is repression. Not only active political opposition and organization, but even half-stifled grumbling can have cruel consequences. In the most extreme periods of the classical system it becomes common for confessions to be extracted under torture, and for masses of people to be imprisoned, sent to labor camps, or executed.[19] The oppression extends beyond those who take up the struggle

---

[18]This idea was first worked out in application to the Soviet Union by H. G. Skilling (1966) and F. Griffiths and H. G. Skilling, eds. (1971). The wide-ranging debate around these issues can be followed through J. F. Hough (1972), W. Odom (1976), and S. Solomon, ed. (1983). A discussion for the case of Chinese politics is K. Lieberthal and M. Oksenberg (1988).

[19]The most important document to summarize this is A. I. Solzhenitsyn's famous book *The Gulag Archipelago* (1974–78).

in the political arena [→3.4] to many other groups in society on various grounds: well-to-do peasants, some religious denominations, certain groups in the urban intelligentsia, workers who demand higher pay, and so on. By the time the political structure of the classical system has been consolidated, the spirit of the vast majority of people has been broken to such an extent that they dare not even think of resistance. This mass repression is the basis on which enforcement of the regulations and instructions of the leadership rests. This is what ensures discipline in society.

In a number of senses the structure of power under the classical socialist system is totalitarian in nature.[20]

The influence of the bureaucracy extends to every sphere of life. Under any social system there are matters in which the state plays a part of some kind: it erects legal barriers, interferes by issuing state regulations, acts as a buyer or as the proprietor of a state-owned firm, and so on. Under other systems there also are "private" spheres in which the state cannot or will not intervene. This distinction between the state and "civil society," state affairs and private affairs, becomes entirely blurred under the classical socialist system. Of course, the bureaucracy is not capable of making decisions and rules on everything, but the limitation on what it does is solely practical. It is not prepared in principle to declare any matter outside its jurisdiction or say it does not wish to intervene in it [→6.7, 19.5, 19.6].

So the influence of the bureaucracy spreads to such traditionally private spheres as culture, religion, the life of the family, how many children people have, the relations of a household with its neighbors, how free-time is spent, the choice of career and employment, and much more. Nor have I even mentioned that every economic transaction qualifies as a matter of concern to the party and the state.[21]

---

[20]The classic references on totalitarianism are H. Arendt (1951), focusing on the psychology of totalitarianism, and Z. Brzezinski and C. Friedrich (1956), focusing on the analysis of general characteristics of the phenomenon.

[21]Some studies have likened the classical socialist system to "military dictatorship." The analogy is false for several reasons. For one thing, power in a military dictatorship is concentrated into the hands of the generals and the military staff. By contrast, the driving force behind the bureaucratic machinery under the classical socialist system is not the top military but the party, even though the army and the police organizations play, of course, an important part. In fact, in a totalitarian society, the military force is always under the control of the party. As Mao said, "Our principle is that the Party commands the gun, and the gun must never be allowed to command the Party." Mao Zedong [1938] (1967, p. 272).

For another, although military dictatorships (for instance, in Latin America, Africa, and Asia) impose brutal terror on the population, they are not "totalitarian" in character. There are numerous spheres of life that the leading groups of a typical military dictatorship make no effort to influence at all.

The power of the bureaucracy is also totalitarian in that it permeates the whole of society and influences every citizen. Account is kept of every resident and employee by the party branches, mass organizations, state apparatus, and police authorities of each locality and place of work. To take an example, every adult carries an identification document in which is stamped one's place of work, place of residence, and family status. A change in any of these is registered in one's ID, which one is obliged to present at the behest of any authority. To take another example, whatever function a citizen may perform, whether it is the lowliest post in the party, a mass organization, the state, or the economy, the item of information will be recorded by the personnel department concerned. From then on this file of information accompanies one for the rest of one's life. Wherever one goes to work there is, ultimately, a single and indivisible bureaucracy that passes one's file and all its information from hand to hand.

Finally, there is a third point of view from which power is totalitarian. The bureaucracy is not subordinate to any stable legal system. There is a constitution, but its wording is sufficiently general to leave the legislators a free hand. Formally the laws are passed by parliament, but in practice the party organization concerned, and so in effect the party apparatus, decides what the law should stipulate. Moreover, there are a vast number of state regulations that do not receive the rank of law even formally: they remain as government or ministerial orders, or, most common of all, simply the personal rulings of a particular member of the bureaucracy. For the bureaucracy itself decides the kind of legal shape it wishes to give to its various rulings.

Not infrequently the bureaucracy, particularly certain groups and branches within it, actually infringes on the laws that exist on paper. This creates an especially grave situation when the breach of legality is to the serious detriment of millions of individuals, when there is mass resettlement, exile, imprisonment, torture, and execution. But one should add that if those in power so wish, the "legal foundation" for mass repression can be laid at any time. Laws, government orders, and court sentences can be passed to give formal, legal sanction to the persecution of groups or individuals. This precisely supports the assertion made earlier that the bureaucracy is not subordinate to the legal system. The line of effect is in precisely the opposite direction: the formal system of law is subordinate to the current endeavors of the bureaucracy.

There are well-known theoretical models of bureaucracy that describe the relationship between the electorate, the legislature, and the bureaucratic organization ("bureau") and then try to deduce from it the behavioral regularities of the bureaucracy.[22] According to such a model, the

---

[22]See W. Niskanen (1971).

legislators, with an eye to the next election, have an interest in winning the confidence of the voters. Aware of that interest, they issue instructions to the bureaucracy accordingly, and monitor how the bureaucracy performs. In the realm of these models, the bureaucracy is subordinate to the legislature.

Such models do not apply to the classical socialist system because two of the models' main premises do not hold. (1) The legislature, in direct contradiction to the assumptions of the models, is not dependent on the voters; instead, its members are nominated by the bureaucracy itself, so that the legislature becomes a component of the bureaucratic apparatus. (2) For the same reason the legislature is not separate from the bureaucracy and does not regulate or control it; it is a part of it, and what is more, a subordinate part into the bargain.

As a consequence, the checks and balances that prevent the bureaucracy in a parliamentary democracy from acquiring and monopolizing power for itself permanently, or placing itself above the competing political forces, fail to operate. There are no independent courts that might check that the laws, ordinances, or activities of the state administration do not conflict with the constitution or earlier laws, that citizens might turn to for redress against the state, and that might protect the individual against the powers that be.

It was stated in the previous section that the power in the classical system is not monolithic, and that internal groupings and conflicts exist within it. Nonetheless, in the narrower sense now intended and according to the three criteria put forward here, the power structure under the classical socialist system is, after all, indivisible and totalitarian.[23]

[23]Western political scientists studying socialist systems have taken issue in their writings with the extreme interpretation of the theory of totalitarianism, and they have opposed to it the idea that there are groups in conflict with each other at work within the political structure. This book treats these as mutually compatible, complementary theories. It is true that the classical system is not "100 percent" totalitarian. Totalitarianism is a theoretical model that ignores some important phenomena, but it remains a sufficiently realistic approach to reality. So much so, in fact, that just as it was going out of style among Western academics, Eastern European dissident writers recognized its significance and began referring to it.

4

Ideology

IT IS not the intention of either this chapter or any other part of the book to provide a methodical analysis of intellectual history. Its purpose is a narrower one: to present those aspects of the ideology and of its ideas, beliefs, promises, values, and moral imperatives that actually contribute to the formation, stabilization, and maintenance of the classical socialist system.

4.1   The Official Ideology

I am concerned here with the official ideology as codified in the party's resolutions, party leaders' speeches and writings, textbooks on ideological subjects, leading articles in the press, and other official pronouncements.

Under full-fledged, stabilized classical socialism there is no open competition between alternative ideologies for the hearts and minds of the population. The bureaucracy enjoys an almost full ideological monopoly. There are tolerated alternative ideologies. For instance, it is not illegal to disseminate religious ideas, although churches run up in practice against a variety of administrative and economic obstacles, and they are subjected in certain countries and periods to merciless persecution. Ideologies diametrically opposed to the official one appear as well, but only temporarily, and by and large only semilegally or wholly illegally. Meanwhile, the official ideology is put forward by a vast apparatus of party, state, and mass organizations, served by the press, the other media, and educational, scientific, and cultural activity.

The official ideology is drawn from several sources and rooted deeply in the history of socialist ideas. It is laid down and solidifies in the way geological strata are formed.

The deepest stratum of all is the thinking of the early socialists and, later on, of Marx in particular. Also connected to these is the intellectual tradition of the European labor movement before the socialist revolutions.

The next stratum consists of the ideas, aspirations, and values of the revolutionary movements in the countries that later turned socialist [→1.2, 2.3].

Then comes the sphere of ideas that arose at the revolutionary-transitional stage out of the experiences of the Communist party once it had made the transition from a revolutionary party in opposition to a governing party with full responsibility, along with the pledges it made in that period to the people.

All these strata are overlaid with ideological elements that emerge as the classical socialist system is constructed. These tie in very closely with the system's development and stabilization-cum-rigidification, since they assist in these processes and justify what arises in practice.

In the Soviet Union's case this final stratum of official ideology is associated personally with Stalin, and termed Stalinism by many. Its influence is felt strongly beyond the Soviet borders in the official ideology of every socialist country.

A contribution to the shaping of this ideology is made by the leaders of the national parties themselves,[1] so that the official ideology of classical socialism varies from country to country. Other changes of various kinds take place with the passage of time.

The various strata are not irrespective of one another. The official ideology develops by selecting from the ideas in the earlier strata, some being forgotten and relegated to the system's "unconscious," and others gaining new emphases and contexts.

What this chapter ultimately attempts to do is to generalize from the several variants and identify in the official ideology of every country in which a classical socialist system is operative the traits that are common, characteristic, and permanent to the greatest degree.[2]

The forthcoming sections do not take issue with the official ideology, because it is merely its subject for description and analysis. The only fair demand to make of this description here is that it should portray its subject faithfully, without distortion. I shall refrain from pointing out repeatedly that what I am advancing is not my own point of view but an interpretation of the official ideology. Although there will be no debate on the official ideology of the classical system, it will be compared in later chapters with reality under that system.

4.2   The Socialist System's Sense of Superiority

The adherents of the official ideology are imbued with the Messianic belief that socialism is destined to save mankind. The conviction that the

---

[1]The part played by Mao Zedong should be specially noted, because he, after Stalin, was the leader who exerted the greatest influence outside his own country.

[2]Certain components of the official ideology will be discussed later in the book [→5.7, 7.1, 19.3, 21.1].

socialist system is superior to the capitalist is one of the most important ingredients in the ideology. The main assumption behind this is that socialist production relations offer more favorable conditions for developing the forces of production than capitalist production relations. Several factors point toward this:

Socialism can eliminate several attributes of capitalism that erode efficiency. Gross errors in the allocation of resources are caused by the anarchy of the market and the fluctuations in supply and demand. These problems can be overcome by planning, which does away with mass unemployment and the concomitant squandering of the most important production force of all, the human being. Planning allows one to avoid crises of overproduction and the incalculable losses they involve.[3] Competition based on private property leads to business secrecy, whereas under socialism innovations become common property. Competition leads to waste of other kinds, such as the proliferation of costly advertising and the eternal changing of models and types of product, which socialism can eliminate. Finally, it puts an end to the frittering away of resources on parasitical consumption by the exploiting classes.

Socialism has an additional advantage besides preventing the waste caused by private property, competition, and the market. Workers freed from exploitation work more enthusiastically and conscientiously than exploited proletarians. This enthusiasm increases performance and reduces the costs of supervision. Responsibility and enthusiasm for work will continue to grow until communism, the highest degree of social development, is reached, when they become a need in everyone's life, and it is possible to dispense entirely with the social costs of providing incentives to work, and thereby with those of selling goods for money and maintaining the remnants of the market.

Socialism's sense of superiority ties in with a conviction that capitalism has passed the stage at which it contributes to the progress of society and already exhibits many signs of decay.[4]

Marx and later Lenin emphasized that socialism's superiority is manifested in economic achievement and not (or not primarily) on an ethical

[3]The moment in history that most favored this sense of superiority was when the West was suffering from the grave effects of the 1929 Great Depression, when production fell back, and millions were thrown out of work, while in the Soviet Union the First Five-Year Plan was being briskly fulfilled.

[4]Albania's long-time socialist leader, Enver Hoxha, expressed it this way: "The so-called consumer society, so loudly advertised and praised to the skies by the bourgeoisie as the 'society of the future,' is nothing but a rotten, declining society, which is revealing more and more of the old permanent ulcers of capitalism which it tries to cover up. Such things will never occur with us." E. Hoxha (1975, p. 9).

plane.[5] The official ideology of classical socialism reflects a belief that this economic superiority follows from the system itself. Socialism achieves great accomplishments not because the population makes great sacrifices when required, nor because economic policy is better advised than in the capitalist countries, but because of the system's basic properties, which guarantee that sooner or later, once the initial disadvantage has been overcome, its superiority will plainly emerge.[6]

Among the main indicators of the end of the classical system is that this unqualified faith in the system's economic superiority is shaken; even socialism's advocates begin to doubt whether socialism necessarily or automatically favors economic performance more than capitalism and concede that capitalism has scored several good points in the contest between them. Once the idea that certain features of capitalism need somehow imitating or incorporating into socialism begins to pervade officialdom, the system is departing from its classical state.

Another important ingredient in socialism's sense of superiority is moral ascendancy, even though it does not count as a prime criterion in the competition between the systems. The official ideology states that socialism is a purer, nobler system that ensures social justice and equality. People themselves are transformed under this system, as they place themselves, voluntarily and increasingly, in the service of the common good, so conquering their own selfishness and individualism. This idea appears in Stalinist ideology, but it plays a particularly crucial role in Maoism. And this brings us back to the previous discussion: the profound change in human nature is an important factor for ensuring the economic superiority of socialism.

This book will return repeatedly to the problem of *values* [→1.7]. To use a philosophical term, the book will enumerate the social phenomena seen by one group or another in society to be of *intrinsic value,* and distinguish between those seen as *primary goods* and those seen merely as means or instruments for attaining some other intrinsic value or primary good. Official ideology suggests that the creation and maintenance of the socialist system is in itself a thing of value, a primary good. Even if it fails at a specific point to yield the performance of which its innate properties render it capable, it will yield it sooner or later. After all, any single factor of performance (e.g., material welfare, efficiency, or fair distribution) is only instrumental in nature and exists to further the real

[5]See, for example, Lenin's dictum: "Socialism calls for greater productivity of labor—compared with capitalism and on the basis achieved by capitalism." V. I. Lenin [1918] (1969b, p. 248).

[6]As Georg Lukács, the famous Hungarian Marxist philosopher, put it: "I have always thought that the worst form of socialism was better to live in than the best form of capitalism." G. Lukács (1971, p. 58).

purpose of creating and defending the socialist order. These factors will certainly appear as a by-product of the socialist system, even if there is a delay before they do so. Of greatest importance is the simple fact that socialism has been won.

4.3 The Basic Promises

One important ingredient in the official ideology consists of the basic promises made to the population by the party when it comes to power. What are the main achievements to be reckoned on, if not in the immediate future, at least later, after a decade or two?

Typically, the classical system emerges in a country that has been poor and backward before the revolution. In most cases the turbulence of the transitional period, coupled with warfare at home and abroad, has widened the gulf between the socialist country concerned and the industrial countries in the forefront of economic growth. The promise runs like this: soon the gap will be closed and the socialist country will catch up with the most highly developed capitalist countries. The potential for doing so lies in the superiority of the system, spoken of in the previous section. But it is only a potential that must be exploited. This can be done by concentrating resources on stimulating growth and making sacrifices on behalf of a high rate of growth [→9].

This promise to catch up with the capitalist economy is heard repeatedly.[7] Although the message takes different forms in different countries, according to their nature,[8] the germ of it remains the same: capitalism's level of economic development will be attained and surpassed within a historically foreseeable period. Several important features of the classical system's official ideology are exhibited here: self-confidence, a firm belief in the system's advantages; hope that the present problems are just temporary and a better life is within reach; and reassurance, mobilization for work and sacrifices in favor of a promising future.

Another group of promises concerns the citizens' way of life and the obligations the system undertakes. The socialist system, having inherited

---

[7]In East Germany, the slogan for a long time was "Überholen, ohne Einzuholen" (to overtake, without catching up), meaning that socialism was going to beat capitalism without reproducing any of its flaws.

[8]The idea was first framed by Stalin [→9.1] and then restored to the agenda by Khrushchev, who had this to say on the tasks of the Seven-Year Plan for 1960–67: By 1967 "or perhaps sooner the Soviet Union will emerge first in the world in both physical volume of production and *per capita* output. This will be a world historic victory for socialism in the peaceful competition with capitalism in the international arena." N. S. Khrushchev (1960, p. 56).

poverty and backwardness to start with, is still waging its initial struggle with external and internal enemies, and there is still misery and chaos, when the authorities take on a role similar to the one attempted by welfare states at a high level of economic development. Let every person do his or her task properly and the state will see to everything else. These ingredients of the ideology spring partly from the intellectual traditions of the labor movement and the European socialist parties, and partly from the platforms of revolutionary movements working under extremely unequal systems, whose unjust distribution of wealth they swore to eliminate should they come to power.

The first and perhaps most important factor to provide is jobs. There is to be full employment, if not at once, then in the foreseeable future. Everyone able to work has a constitutional right to work.

Several other provisions are due as civil rights as well. It is the state's obligation to provide the population with such basic needs as food, shelter, health care, education, vacations, and cultural goods and services. Typical first signs of a serious intention to fulfill the promise are the following. Basic foodstuffs are sold at very low prices subsidized by the state, in many cases through a rationing system that levels off the ability to buy. Urban apartment blocks are nationalized, rents subsidized heavily, and tenancies allocated by the authorities. A uniform system of state (or half-state and half-union) general social security is introduced, providing the population with health services free of charge.[9] Education is free also. The labor unions allocate free or extremely cheap vacation facilities. Books, phonograph records, and theater seats are subsidized heavily.

Although the initial, practical steps to fulfill the promise are taken right from the beginning through price and taxation policy, and by establishing a variety of institutions (e.g., a food distribution authority, housing offices, a social insurance center, networks of cultural and vacation centers run by firms), the complete fulfillment of the promise never occurs and never can occur [→13.7]. All through the period of classical socialism great tension builds up between the promises made in the official ideology and the system's actual economic performance. As time goes by, this failure to fulfill the initial promises becomes an oppressive burden [→18.3].

---

[9]In most socialist countries, health care is expanded to cover the whole population as a citizen's right at a comparatively late phase in the consolidation of the classical system. Initially, the right is acquired only by those employed in the state sector. Much the same applies to some other "basic needs" and their provision by the state.

4.4 The Self-Legitimation and Paternalistic Nature of Power

An important component of the official ideology is its views on the structure of power and the party's role in that structure.[10]

No attempt is made in the official ideology to disguise the fact that the system is dictatorial, since all political systems in existence are considered to be so. It is merely a question of who exercises dictatorship over whom. In a bourgeois society there is dictatorship of the bourgeoisie. Under a socialist system dictatorship over the bourgeoisie is exercised by the proletariat. The ideology states that the working peasants and other strata in society are allied with the proletariat, whose power they support, but they are not themselves in power. So pursuit of a class policy is openly admitted by those in power.

The working class does not exercise power directly; it is represented by the party. The party is the vanguard of the working class and so ultimately of the whole of society. As such it is destined to lead society.

Should the policy of those in power be opposed by certain political groups, this does not imply a problem with the policy; it means the groups concerned are obtuse, ill-willed, or plainly inimical—spokesmen of the internal and external class enemy. But the official ideology goes even further. Neither can broad mass opposition serve as evidence for the claim that a section of the people do not support those in power. The party knows better than the people itself what the people's interest demands: this is precisely what "vanguard" means.[11] The party is an organization that has proven its capacity to head the people by leading the revolution and defeating the revolution's enemies. The ideas and methods termed "scientific socialism" in the official ideology ensure intellectual superiority to those who know and employ them over the exponents of any other ideas and methods, since it supplies them with a reli-

[10]In considering the formative strata of the official ideology there is no reason at this point to delve into the deepest, prerevolutionary layers. Marx did not cover the subject, and what few short references to postrevolutionary power he made were very general. The dictatorship of the proletariat he envisaged implies some kind of collectivist self-management, not bureaucratic power at all.

The ideas presented here (the ingredients of the official ideology of the classical system having to do with power) were developed after the assumption of power in order to account and provide subsequent ideological justification for the situation that had emerged. The development of these views is associated mainly with the efforts of Lenin and Stalin.

[11]When in 1953 the people of East Berlin rose in revolt (as the first ones to do so in Eastern Europe) and were crushed by Soviet tanks the poet Bertolt Brecht, who lived in East Germany, wrote an ironic poem saying, "The people had gambled away the confidence of the government. . . . Would it then not be simpler if the government dissolved the people and elected a new one?" B. Brecht (1967, p. 1009).

able compass for comprehending any new situation and identifying the new tasks it poses. This is what allows the party to understand the people's interests better than the millions outside the party, making it superfluous for those in power to submit themselves to the control of an electoral process involving alternative parties. In fact, to do so would be a grave mistake and a crime against the people, since the majority of votes might go to a party that ill-served the true interests of the people. To quote Stalin, "The Party cannot be a real party if it limits itself to registering what the masses of the working class feel and think, if it drags at the tail of the spontaneous movement. . . . The Party must stand at the head of the working class; it must see farther than the working class. . . . "[12]

Stalin quotes Lenin on this: "It will be necessary under the dictatorship of the proletariat to reeducate 'millions of peasants and small proprietors, and hundreds and thousands of office employees, officials, and bourgeois intellectuals,' to subordinate 'all these to the proletarian state and to proletarian leadership . . . ' just as we must ' . . . in a protracted struggle waged on the basis of the dictatorship of the proletariat—reeducate the proletarians themselves, who do not abandon their petty-bourgeois prejudices at one stroke . . . but only in the course of a long and difficult mass struggle against petty-bourgeoisie influences.'"[13]

Thus power undergoes a curious process of self-legitimation. Whether the ruling group expresses the desires and interests of the majority, and whether the majority of the people supports them, are *not* measured by whether this support is manifested in some tangible form (for instance, a ballot). The possessors of power have appointed themselves as the manifest expression of the people's interests and the repository of a permanent public good. According to the elliptical thinking described, one can almost say they have legitimated their power "by definition."[14]

The classical system has a paternalistic nature self-evident from what has been said about self-legitimation: those possessed of power are convinced they know better what the interests of those whom they rule demand. The bureaucracy stands *in loco parentis*: all other strata, groups, or individuals in society are children, wards whose minds must be made up for them by their adult guardians.[15] This set-up ties in closely with

[12]See J. V. Stalin (1947, p. 82).

[13]See ibid., pp. 41–42.

[14]See the papers of F. Fehér, Á Heller, and T. H. Rigby, in T. H. Rigby and F. Fehér, eds. (1982).

[15]Condemnation of paternalistic government can already be found in Kant, as the following quotation shows: "Under such a *paternal government (imperium paternale)*, the subjects, as immature children who cannot distinguish what is truly useful or harmful to themselves, would be obliged to behave purely passively and to rely upon the judgement of the head of state as to how they *ought* to be happy, and upon his kindness at willing their happiness at all." I. Kant [1793] (1970, p. 74).

the caring role assumed by the bureaucracy and discussed in the previous section. So long as citizens do as they are told they will have not a care in the world, because the party and state will see to everything. The same stance can be seen plainly in the cult of personality that comes to surround the man at the pinnacle of power. As paramount leader he is not only the best of statesmen, generals, and scientists, he is above all the father of his people. The paternalistic role is one of the major ideological justifications for centralization and the bureaucratic organization of power.

4.5 Discipline, Willing Sacrifice, and Vigilance

An essential constituent of the official ideology is the code of moral imperatives. These are not codified formally, but they can be reconstituted from official statements, from the practice of rewarding and penalizing, and to an extent from literary and other works of art that have received the stamp of official approval.

As one would expect, a great many of the moral imperatives also apply under other systems and ideologies. The norms concerning family life, for example, are quite conservative and hardly distinguishable from the Victorian morals of Western civilization. Here it is worth being concerned exclusively with the moral norms specific to the system and relevant to the subject, political economy.

Discipline is expected of all citizens, particularly members of the party. Originality can easily be branded as affected eccentricity, independence as intractability and individualism (a pejorative word), and a critical outlook as disrespect for superiors, indiscipline, and destructiveness. None of these three attributes is prohibited, but they are all risky in practice. The characteristic certain to be appreciated is unconditional discipline. The prevailing political line must be followed, the decisions endorsed, and the commands of superiors obeyed without hesitation. This is the behavior valued and rewarded by the authorities and conducive to a successful career in the bureaucracy. The major criteria of selection are political reliability, loyalty, and fidelity to the party and its ideas (in other words, the official ideology). If these are apparent they can outweigh

---

I. Berlin, personifying the paternalistic dictator, phrases his line of thought like this: "easy for me to conceive myself as coercing others for their own sake, in their, not my interest. I am then claiming that I know what they truly need better than they know it themselves. . . . Once I take this view, I am in a position to ignore the actual wishes of men or societies, to bully, oppress, torture them in the name, and on behalf on their 'real' selves." I. Berlin (1969, p. 133).

deficiencies in ability or professional expertise.[16] The converse does not apply: not even the greatest talent or professional experience can make up for a lack of loyalty, reliability, or compliance.

When the antecedents of the classical system are examined one finds no such respect for loyalty or compliance either in Marx or in the prerevolutionary traditions of the European labor movement.[17] The earliest stratum in which the roots of such respect can be found is the revolutionary movement in the period before the establishment of the socialist system in countries where socialism triumphed through its own internal resources [→2.3]. These countries were repressive regimes where the revolutionaries, and in particular the members of the Communist party, were working amid persecution, and in many places and periods in a state of illegality. The movement could never have survived without discipline. Moreover, it was preparing for a revolution that would entail armed struggle, guerrilla warfare, revolutionary onslaught, and civil war, all of which required military discipline as well. After the victory of the revolution, civilian, peacetime power is taken over by persons who have grown accustomed to orders and obedience.

In the transitional period the party requires its members and the functionaries of the party and state to act in a disciplined fashion, because they are surrounded by chaos, because society has disintegrated and a new order must be established, and because a military struggle is in progress against inside and outside enemies. The nationalization of factories and other organizations has begun, and their management also requires discipline.

The most important layer of historical soil in which the attitude of considering discipline and loyalty as moral imperatives can grow is the process by which the classical socialist system is erected. Later in the book [→7.3, 21.10] there will be a detailed treatment of the bureaucratic regulation of society and the economy, for which this ethical stance is indispensable.

The virtues of discipline are closely linked with those of willing sacrifice. Individuals must be prepared to subordinate their own interests to higher interests, as defined in a specific situation by the bureaucracy. If need be they should take on extra work outside the officially prescribed working hours. If need be they should renounce the pleasures of improv-

---

[16]This criterion was formulated in an extreme form by S. Stasevski, a Warsaw secretary of the Polish Communist party at one time: "The party's personnel policy [is]: No one has to be competent in any post; he merely has to be loyal." Quoted by R. Toranska (1987, p. 187).

[17]Marx, an out-and-out member of the European Jewish intelligentsia, to whom these "military" qualities were totally alien, considered *de omnibus dubitandum* (one should be doubtful in all things) his favorite motto. See D. McLellan (1973, p. 457).

ing their material standard of living. If need be they should accept the subordination of family life to state interests, for most of the time of all adult family members is taken up with work and political activity. In this respect again, the official ideology embraces a kind of "military spirit"; all citizens should feel they have been mobilized. Metaphors taken from military life are common: "the labor front," "hero of socialist labor," "the battle for production," and so on. The building of socialism is likened to a long campaign in which all must do their duty. Those who do not (or are suspected of not doing so) are cowards, deserters, or traitors.

This "war consciousness" demands other virtues, such as vigilance against internal and external foes. Since there are no peaceful and civilized forms for expressing political agreement or opposition (e.g., voting between alternatives), one can never be quite sure whether anyone supports the system and agrees with the political line that happens to be in force at the time. What if they do not? One has to be on the watch for concealed enemies. That requirement in itself engenders an atmosphere of distrust, secrecy, and suspicion that requires the development, in fact the multiple development, of supervision.

The reason why distrust of the outside world and the capitalist environment arises is plain from the predicament of the socialist countries. Across the frontiers there are plenty of politicians and political movements opposed to the power of the Communist party and the creation of the socialist system and inclined to support (or actually supporting) activity aimed against that system. All this breeds a self-imposed isolation from the outside world. Insofar as possible, all influences emanating from the capitalist countries must be rejected, whether they are political, cultural, or simply expressive of their alien lifestyle. The greatest caution must be taken with any political or any economic, commercial, or financial relationship, because the outside enemy may abuse such relations and use them for blackmail or as means of applying political pressure. A symbol of this public atmosphere might be a defensive circle of wagons turned inward and prepared for an attack. Anyone consistently exhibiting this isolationist attitude counts as virtuous.

4.6 Power and Ideology

Once the party has seized power and become its sole possessor, it must never relinquish it under any circumstances. Stalin quotes Lenin's dictum that "the question of power is the fundamental question of the revolution" and then adds the following: "The seizure of power is only the beginning. . . . The whole point is to retain power, to consolidate it, and make it invincible."[18]

In the official ideology's system of values, power is no mere means of attaining other primary objectives; it becomes in its own right a primary good of intrinsic, ultimate value. This must be borne in mind when assessing how the socialist system performs. To return to an earlier analogy [→1.7], when grading the system the following can be considered as one of the subjects of study or assessment criteria: How firmly is power in the Communist party's hands? The official ideology would suggest that this subject has great weight in the school report. As mentioned in chapter 3, the classical system scores well in this subject, since it erects the institutional frame ensuring that power is retained.

As the introduction to the chapter emphasized, power and the official ideology are as inseparably linked as body and soul. It would seem futile to ask which came first, the institutions and organizations that created the classical system, or the ideas that motivated the members of those institutions and organizations. Throughout the process, before the revolution, in the transitional period, and during the evolution of the classical system, the word is made flesh in the deeds of living persons. Conversely, these deeds, and subsequently the emerging system's need to legitimate and justify itself, constantly adjust and modify these ideas until the official ideology of the classical system matures. Institutions, organizations, and movements, on the one hand, and programs, expectations, convictions, moral imperatives, and values, on the other, all combine to bring about and maintain the classical system.

In this respect there is some similarity between the role of the Communist party under the classical system and the role of the Catholic church in the Middle Ages. Both enjoy "secular" power bound up with state power, and both exert a vast ideological influence. Each in its period has an ideological monopoly guaranteed by power and persecutes all heresy and heterodoxy. Each has a strictly organized, centralized, hierarchical structure and maintains a tough discipline in its own apparatus.

Of course, one should not take the comparison too far. The role of the Communist party and official socialist ideology in the classical socialist system is something historically unique and incomparable with any other historical phenomenon.

Max Weber argued that Protestantism played an important part in creating and consolidating capitalism; that the diligence and thrift instilled by the Protestant ethic were an inducement and ideological support to capitalist accumulation, which relies upon expansion of private

---

[18]See J. V. Stalin (1947, p. 39).

wealth.[19] But neither Weber nor anyone else has claimed that the great or even monopoly influence of Protestantism was a vital prerequisite for the development of capitalism. Catholics, Jews, and Moslems too were among the pioneers of capitalism, which was able to flourish also where those religions predominated. By contrast, the classical system discussed in part 2 of this book develops and consolidates only where the official ideology of socialism just described enjoys a commanding influence.

[19]See M. Weber [1904] (1930).

5

Property

THE DISCUSSION begins with an explanation of the concepts involved in the problem. This is followed by a methodical examination of property rights under the classical socialist system.

5.1 Explanation of the Concepts

A simple distinction is often made: capitalism is associated with private ownership and socialism with public ownership. The statement is basically true, but a more accurate understanding of the situation requires a somewhat subtler system of concepts.

First of all one must distinguish *private goods* from *public goods*. An example of the former might be a garment, and of the latter the signal from a lighthouse at sea. If person A is wearing the garment, person B is precluded from wearing it at the same time. By contrast, the fact that skipper A is taking his bearings from the lighthouse signal does not preclude skipper B from taking his from the same signal. Three other examples of public goods are sunlight, the human language, and the knowledge of production processes that have entered the public domain.[1]

One must not confuse the concept "public good" with "public property." The mark of a public good is that one cannot establish at a particular moment whose property it is, whereas a private good can be owned. (The latter may be the property of an individual, a group, or the state, but the last case is still one of collective ownership of a private good.) This brings one to an important constituent of the property concept: its exclusivity. A nonowner may use an owner's property only by permission. For one to be able to speak of property at all, there has to be a social mechanism that enforces the assertion of the property rights, in

---

[1]There is no universally valid dividing line between private and public goods. The dividing line varies through history, depending on the state of technology and the social conditions. The high seas are public goods, but the maritime countries retain the prerogative of regulating fishing rights in coastal waters. This property right is enforced by international courts, by legal and economic sanctions, and as a final resort by naval force. To take another example, language is a public good, but in practice ordinary people are precluded from using it with the accent of well-to-do people: this language used by a particular social stratum serves as a private good for that stratum, whose property right is secured by the social mechanism of upbringing and education.

other words, excludes nonowners from making arbitrary use of the property without the owner's consent.

So property means, on the one hand, a relation between a person and a thing; for instance, a garment is the property of a single person. On the other hand, it means also a social relationship between persons:[2] the specific relationship between owners and nonowners supported by the social mechanism for the enforcement of property rights.

Property is a compound, comprehensive concept that is worth breaking down into its constituents. These will be examined by means of a number of different classification criteria.[3]

The first such criterion concerns what it is that the owner has in his or her possession. Here are some of the more important alternatives:

- An object (such as a garment or a machine).
- A resource (such as land or a natural asset).
- Information (such as a discovery or knowledge of a production process).
- Someone's personal faculty: physical and mental capabilities by virtue of which some service can be offered. (It is not self-evident that such a capability is owned by the person concerned. One only has to consider the case of slavery.)

It is common for one owner to possess several kinds of objects, resources, and information at once. For instance, the owner of a factory containing a variety of machines and buildings may own the patent for a production process as well. It is also worth noting, however, that a great many things "belonging" to the factory are not owned by the proprietor at all. For instance, one does not own the workforce, one only hires its physical and mental abilities. One may simply rent the site of the factory and some of the equipment in it. One may have received some of the capital for the factory as a loan, and so on.

In studying socioeconomic systems it is particularly important to clear up who owns the means of production with which further products and services can be made. Attention will be centered on this in the subsequent

---

[2]This aspect gets special attention in the Marxist approach to the problems of property.

[3]The seminal contribution to the development of the "property rights" school was the works of A. A. Alchian (1965) and A. A. Alchian and H. Demsetz (1972). The main ideas of this school originate in various earlier theories. To mention only the most important antecedents: F. Knight's theory on uncertainty and risk [1921] (1965) and R. H. Coase's classical work on the theory of the firm and transaction costs (1937, 1960).

E. G. Furubotn and S. Pejovich (1972) were the first to apply the property rights approach to the behavior of a socialist firm. See also F. L. Pryor (1973).

sections of the chapter. On the other hand, I will ignore the problems of property rights over objects for the owner's personal use.[4]

The second criterion for classification concerns who the owner is. Is it an actual person—an individual, family, or specific group of persons? Or is it a legal entity—a firm, a university, a pension fund or state organization, a central government or local authority?

The third criterion, which needs discussing in a little more detail, concerns what the owner is entitled to do. In the following, property rights are divided into three main groups, which are referred to in the ensuing analysis as property rights of type a, b, and c. It is necessary to emphasize even in advance that we are dealing in all three cases with a group consisting of a large number of concrete, specific property rights.

The individual may exercise the property rights all alone or share, under specified conditions, the ownership of one and the same property with other individuals. The latter applies in case of a joint stock company, for instance, where an individual's ownership of a property is defined by his or her share in it. In the first abstract discussion of the three main types of property rights in this section the above alternatives are not distinguished yet and the "owner" is talked about in the singular. I shall return to this problem later [→5.2].

a. *Rights to residual income.* The owner has the right to dispose of the income generated by the property. One generally arrives at a more accurate description by defining this right as one to the residual part of the income, meaning that having deducted all the costs associated with utilization of the property from the income obtained with the help of it, the remaining income belongs to the owner.[5] The owner is free to decide how much of the residual income to use for such specific purposes as individual and family consumption, investment, the acquisition of further property, and so on.[6]

The rights of disposal over the residual income are full if the owner can, if he or she so wishes, spend it all on personal consumption. (It will be seen later that in the case of a state-owned firm in a socialist society the rights of disposal are restricted in this respect.)

---

[4]This is termed personal property in the teaching of official political economy in the socialist countries.

[5]To clarify the concept of residual income it is worth considering the position of a tenant farmer who pays a fixed rent to the landowner for the use of the land. In this case the residual income is made up of the income from the produce of the land, less all costs, including the rent. To that extent, it is the tenant who has type a property rights over the produce and not the landowner.

[6]In the case of capitalist production, this right is described as follows in Marxian terminology: the owner of the capital has control over the surplus value. By analogy, this property right can be interpreted as existing under other social systems as well.

Full rights of disposal over residual income may be accompanied by an obligation on the part of the owner to assume financial responsibility for the debts incurred through use of the property, at least to the value of the property in question and possibly beyond this to the total value of the owner's private wealth.[7]

Full rights of disposal over residual income provide an extremely strong automatic, spontaneous incentive to the owner. If one makes successful use of the property there will be a positive residual income that one can use as one likes. If one fails one misses out on that income, and the property concerned, and under certain conditions even other personal wealth, may go toward making up the loss. All other individuals who collaborate in the utilization of some piece of property without enjoying full rights of disposal over the residual income must be given an artificial incentive before they have an interest in the success of the utilization. This is nothing other than the simple and well-known relationship whereby everything in the case of type a rights affects the owner's own pocket: the owner profits from a positive residual income and loses from a negative residual income. The statement can also be reversed: type a property rights are full if, and only if, the utilization of the property affects the owner's own pocket.[8]

b. *Rights of alienation* or transferability. Rights of this type are those that allow the owner to sell property for money, rent it out, present it as a gift, or bequeath it to heirs. Not all the four rights necessarily coincide. For instance, it may be permissible to rent out an object or resource, but not to sell it, or vice versa.

These rights combine with an automatic, spontaneous incentive as well. If the owner has obtained the property by purchase and disposes of it again by sale, he or she has an interest in ensuring that the net value of the property increases as much as possible between the two transactions. The same interest in increasing wealth applies, of course, if the property has been obtained by the owner as a gift or a legacy, or if it is disposed of as a gift or a legacy. The owner also has an interest in seeing that the property is rented out on the best possible terms, assuming the decision is to rent it out at all.

---

[7]The modern form of joint-stock company and other, similar legal institutions arose in order to limit this liability [→5.2, property form no. 3].

[8]An individual who can only dispose of the residual income provided he or she does not make use of it for his or her own direct profit and who is not liable to the extent of his or her own property for any loss incurred also belongs among those who need an "artificial" incentive in the sense used above. Even though he or she has partial type a rights, the way the property is used does not affect his or her own pocket, and in that sense he or she is not the owner.

c. *Rights of control.* Other important property rights are those that concern the utilization of property (management, decision making, and supervision). The simplest example of this is a small company in private hands, whose proprietor decides which employees to hire and fire, what to produce, what price to sell the products for, and so on.

As the example shows, there is not just a single "right of control," but a collection of numerous, specific rights of control. The owner can delegate to others, usually to paid employees, one or other, or even the majority, of these rights. The owner may delegate to different employees different functions of control. He or she may erect a stratified, hierarchical control organization. The owner may ensure that employees perform the functions of control satisfactorily by using a variety of incentive schemes.[9]

Although the spheres of rights grouped under a, b, and c can be closely linked to each other, they are detachable from one another to some extent. There is a particular significance in the fact that a high proportion of type c rights can become detached from type a and type b rights in many respects, that is, the rights of ownership can be separated from the rights of control.

There is a complementary relationship between the automatic, spontaneous incentive provided by full rights of ownership and the artificial incentive given to those with partial property rights but without that automatic incentive. Determining where and in the performance of which social functions to rely on automatic, spontaneous incentive and where on artificial incentive is one of the fundamental problems facing economic systems.

The fourth criterion for classification is to decide what constrains the owner in exercising property rights. In real life an unconditional property right is extremely rare. Many property rights are constrained by state and legal regulations, or at least by customary law, tradition, and accepted codes of morality. Even under the systems that allow the greatest freedom to enterprise and competition, the owner's hands are tied by a myriad of constraints.

---

[9]The *principal-agent* relationship is analyzed in a wide-ranging body of writing that covers an increasing number of problems. The pioneers of this research program are K. J. Arrow (1964), T. Groves (1973), S. A. Ross (1973), and J. A. Mirrlees (1974, 1976). Comprehensive summaries of the theoretical writings in this field are provided by O. Hart and B. R. Holmström (1987), the study by B. R. Holmström and J. Tirole (1989), and the entry by J. E. Stiglitz in *The New Palgrave* (1987, 3:966–72).

There is a noteworthy literature on hierarchies. The pioneer was O. E. Williamson (1967, 1975). The theoretical and mathematical analysis of hierarchies is dealt with in numerous works. See, for instance, G. A. Calvo and S. Wellisz (1978), T. C. Koopmans and J. M. Montias (1971), Y. Qian (1990), and S. Rosen (1982).

Finally, there is a fifth classification criterion: the distinction to be drawn between nominal property rights laid down in legally valid documents and real property rights.

5.2 Some Characteristic Property Forms before the Advent of the Socialist System

In terms of the classification criteria discussed in the previous section, a variety of *configurations* of property rights (or, to use a synonymous expression, a variety of *property relations*) can come into being. Each configuration can be described according to what object constitutes the property or what set of objects together makes up the object that constitutes the property, who the owner is and what property rights he or she possesses subject to what constraints, and finally, to what extent this "package" of property rights is nominal and to what extent it is real. In theory, the number of possible configurations is infinite,[10] but in fact, historical systems give rise to specific types of configuration. From now on these types of configuration will be called *property forms*. Each property form is actually a theoretical model in which one or other of the specific features in the previous classification is ignored and only a few general characteristics are emphasized.

Before turning to the actual subject of the chapter, the property forms that operate under the classical socialist system, it is worth considering briefly three property forms typical of contemporary capitalism.

1. *The family undertaking.* The main item in this category is the family farm, but, of course, family undertakings appear in industry, trade, and other service sectors as well.

Remaining with the example of the family farm, the family owns the land, all the main means of production for working it, and the livestock. The family owns its own house and farm buildings.

---

[10]This is one of the weightiest arguments against unqualified use of the Marxist interpretation of the category "class" [→3.4]. The customary Marxist definition of class is the set of those people whose property relations, primarily their relation to the means of production, is the same in the society concerned. But it is hard to decide, because of the large number of configurations of property rights, what degree of similarity to expect from the specific configurations in order to place various individuals in the same class. Are a complete pauper and one who has an interest-bearing bank account and a summer cottage rented out equally members of the "working class"? Can one consider equally as members of the "capitalist class" the person whose family owns an undertaking that employs a couple of hands with all the rights of type a, b, and c, and the opulent shareholder who by and large has type a rights to the extent of shares but does not intervene in the management of the company (type c rights)? Is a senior employee with a good salary who is also a significant shareholder at once a member of the working and capitalist classes?

There is no sharp division between the household and the production undertaking; part of the produce is consumed by the family itself and part is sold on the market. The family exclusively uses its own labor, not employing any outside manpower at all.[11]

At an advanced stage of economic development there can emerge family undertakings that are highly mechanized, highly capitalized, and very productive, to which it is debatable whether the expression "small-scale plant" applies. But in general this is not the case in the societies where a (self-induced) socialist revolution has taken place [→2.3]. In these societies, family undertakings are indisputably small-scale plants, and their possessor-families belong to the poorer strata in society.

In a family undertaking the owner possesses all the rights of types a, b, and c. There is no separation of ownership from control. The family (in a traditional society, usually the head of the family) is both the nominal and the actual owner, and at the same time the decision maker in all business and production matters. The family has the most direct interest possible in the success of the undertaking, and no outside incentives of any kind are needed for this interest to assert itself.[12]

All of what has been said about the family farm applies by analogy to family undertakings in the other sectors.

In the case of forms 2 and 3, described below, the owners of the basic means of production utilize their property with the help of hired labor.[13] These owners are *capitalists.* In this case this book adopts Marxist terminology, describing as "capitalist" those who in the above sense are proprietors of firms employing hired labor. The term "firm," by the way, will be reserved for organizations employing labor on a permanent basis. Forms 2 and 3 describe capitalist firms. Socialist firms will be covered in section 5.3.

2. *The owner-managed private firm with unlimited liability.* The decisive distinction between forms 1 and 2 is whether or not outside labor is employed. The difference is not conspicuous if the number employed is small, but it becomes so in the case of medium-sized or large firms.

---

[11]For simplicity's sake, casually employed outside labor is ignored. If a farm employs labor permanently, it is no longer a "pure" family undertaking.

The property form described in this book as a pure family undertaking coincides more or less with what is known as a "small-scale commodity production unit" in Marxist terminology.

[12]The problem is put lucidly in the title of an article by Lester Thurow (*Financial Times,* September 6, 1986): "Who Stays Up with the Sick Cow?" On a family farm the answer is clearly the family, or, more specifically, the member of it to whom the task has been given by the head of the family.

[13]By definition, the category "property rights" includes also the degree to which the individual is in command of his or her own labor or to which it is at the command of another: a slaveowner, a feudal lord, a capitalist firm providing employment, or the state.

The proprietor may be an individual or a family, but outsiders too can associate to bring common property into being. (Along with other differences, this last possibility distinguishes form 2 from form 1, an undertaking that remains strictly within the family framework.) The proprietors fully enjoy both the ownership rights (rights of types a and b) and the basic decision-making rights (type c rights). Production and marketing are directed by the owners themselves, who only concede lower managerial positions with a narrow sphere of authority to paid employees. So the proprietors work together with (and confront) their hired workers as living, visible persons.

The entire net profit belongs to the owners. If the firm should become insolvent, however, they are responsible for its debts to the extent of their private wealth, not just the wealth tied up in the firm. (As will be seen, this is the main way in which this form differs from the company form.) The private income and wealth of the proprietors are closely and unequivocally connected with the income and wealth of the firm.

3. *The joint-stock company in private ownership.* With this form a large number of proprietors own the firm collectively. Sometimes the bulk of the shares is concentrated into relatively few hands, in which case the main proprietors may become "visible," but frequently the shareholders are not personally to the fore, and in contrast to form 2, the property becomes "depersonalized."

The cases in which the majority of (or even all) the shares in a company are held by the state will be disregarded, and the discussion will be confined to companies in which the majority of the shares are the property of private persons, of legal entities not owned by the state, or of private institutions.[14]

The company's residual income belongs to the shareholder, who receives part of it in the form of dividends on shares, while the other part is reinvested (type a rights). The shareholder can dispose freely of shares, that is, the property consisting of the proportion of the company each share represents (type b rights).

Furthermore, the company form differs from form 2 in that liability is limited: the owner is liable for the company's debts only to the extent of his or her investment (i.e., the value of the owner's shares). A company is not the same as the sum of its individual proprietors, it is a separate legal entity. Should the firm become insolvent and the shares lose

---

[14]American and British terminology can easily mislead a reader not fully familiar with it. A company is called "public" if its shares are quoted on the stock exchange, having fullfilled the stock exchange's stipulations for quotation. The word public refers not to public ownership but to the accessibility of the shares to the public as items bought and sold on the stock market. Shares in such a public company may be exclusively in private hands, but they could also be owned by the state.

their value, the shareholders' private wealth is not affected. So the connection of private income and private wealth, on the one hand, and the firm's income and the firm's wealth, on the other, is not so total and symmetrical as it is in the case of form 2. Nonetheless, the connection remains quite strong: the shareholder has a prime interest in seeing that the company is profitable and has good business expectations.

The final word on the proportions in which the residual income is divided belongs to the general meeting of shareholders, but even in the preparations for the general meeting the leading executives play a decisive part. Nominally they are just employees of the owners, who may dismiss them at any time and appoint others in their place. The shareholders are often unorganized, however, and so the managers come to possess a high degree of independent authority. There is a separation of ownership from control not found in forms 1 and 2.[15]

So, in fact, one group of property rights, those of control (type c rights) pass largely—but not totally—into the hands of the leading managers. However great the independent authority possessed by the leading managers of a company, they still depend heavily on the shareholders. A variety of incentives emerge. If the company flourishes, grows, and enjoys good business prospects over an extended period, the leading executives will receive very high salaries and bonuses. Perhaps more important still are the negative incentives. Shareholders may vote with their feet: if the executives manage the company badly and the likely results are poor or negative, or if the company's position by comparison with its competitors worsens, the shareholders will try to get rid of their shares, whose price will fall. It can happen that an aggressive new group takes over the company, bringing the reign of the previous managerial group to an end. A manager's whole career can be affected by whether the company succeeds or fails and whether the proprietors earn a high or low profit.

All three forms belong to a broader class of configurations of property rights, that of *private property forms.* The class also contains other configurations that cannot be described here, but in any case, these three examples are enough to convey what should be understood as a property form.[16]

---

[15]On this see A. A. Berle and G. C. Means [1932] (1968) for an account of how the shareholders lose power to the management. Also see J. Burnham (1941), who coined the phrase managerial revolution, and A. D. Chandler's seminal work (1977).

[16]State-owned firms exist also under nonsocialist socioeconomic systems. Some are wholly owned by the state and some are mixed firms in which state ownership dominates (for instance, a company in which the state owns a majority shareholding). This property form will not be dealt with in any detail.

5.3   The State-Owned Firm

In line with the overall plan of the book, I shall not be discussing the historical process whereby the property forms characteristic of the classical socialist system came into being. Instead, I shall turn immediately to the "end-product," the mature, stabilized forms. At most, I shall mention briefly the course of development for a few forms along the way.

The first and most important property form is the bureaucratic state-owned firm.[17] (For brevity's sake the word "bureaucratic" will usually be dropped.) Table 5.1 shows the share of the state-owned sector in various socialist and capitalist countries.

The property form of the state-owned firm occupies the "commanding heights"[18] of the socialist economy, the positions that allow the other, nonstate sectors of the economy to be dominated: mining, energy production and manufacturing, transport, domestic wholesale trading, foreign trading, banking, and insurance. On the other hand, agriculture, retail trading, and other services to the general public do not qualify as "commanding heights," and although state-owned firms appear in them, other property forms occur alongside and may even predominate.

The nominal owner of a state-owned firm is the state represented by the national government. According to official ideology, the sector is the property of "the whole of the people" or "the whole of society." This distinguishes it from other, likewise nonprivate property forms, for instance, from a firm owned by a regional organization of the state, or from a cooperative, in which the owner, according to the official ideology, is only a part of the people (the population of the region concerned or the membership of the cooperative).

To look beyond the nominal ownership and analyze the real content of the property form, one must examine the various specific property rights more closely.

a. The first main group of property rights are those of disposal of the residual income from utilization of the property. Under classical socialism this residual income flows into the central budget of the state. No definitive distinction is made between what is described under capitalist systems as company "taxation" paid to the state and what qualifies as the profits of the firm. The sum of all payments to the state budget constitutes the centralized net income of the state sector.

---

[17]The state-owned firm in the classical socialist system shows a host of pronounced features that can be observed in state-owned firms in capitalist countries as well, although in a less extreme form. (See, for instance, discussion of the problems of depersonalizing of property in this section, the relationship between bureaucracy and the state-owned firm [→7.3–7.5], and the softening of financial discipline of the state-owned firm [→8.4].)

[18]The expression was coined by Lenin.

TABLE 5.1
The Share of the Public Sector: International Comparison

	Year	Share of Public Sector
Socialist countries		
Bulgaria	1970	99.7
Cuba[a]	1988	95.9
Czechoslovakia	1988	99.3
East Germany	1988	96.4
Hungary	1988	92.9
Poland	1988	81.2
Romania	1980	95.5
Vietnam	1987	71.4
Yugoslavia[b]	1987	86.5
Capitalist countries		
Austria	1978–79	14.5
France	1982	16.5
Greece	1979	6.1
Italy	1982	14.0
Spain	1979	4.1
United Kingdom	1978	11.1
United States	1983	1.3
West Germany	1982	10.7

Source: The data on socialist countries were compiled by P. Mihályi for this book, on the basis of, an official CMEA statistical yearbook (Finansy i Statistika) (1989b, p. 49) and Savezni Zavod za Statistiku (Federal Statistical Office, Belgrade) (1988, p. 93). The data on capitalist countries are taken from B. Milanovic (1989, p. 15).

Note: The figures refer to the percentage of national income in the case of socialist countries and to the percentage of GDP in the case of capitalist countries. The figures on socialist countries include not only state-owned firms and organizations, but also agricultural cooperatives and the net output of household farming, i.e., private plots used by the members of these cooperatives. The unrecorded contribution of the informal economy is disregarded. Because of the inclusion of the output of household farming and the exclusion of the informal sector, the figures do not reflect sufficiently the contribution of the private sector.

[a]Only state-owned sector.

[b]On the basis of Gross Material Product at 1972 prices.

In this context, it becomes a problem to say exactly what is meant by the expression "residual income." One and the same central bureaucracy is deciding on the state-owned firm's selling prices, the wages it pays its workers, the price of the means of production it uses, and the contributions it must pay into the state budget. The bureaucracy decides what proportion of the gross returns must be delivered by each state-owned firm under the heading of centralized net income (or what budgetary support the firm receives, i.e., how much its negative net income is). Of course, the same applies to the sum of all the state-owned firms as to each firm individually: the bureaucracy decides what proportion of the total budgetary income will derive from the centralized net income of the state sector, and the headings and other channels for the rest of the state income. Much the same applies on the expenditure side. The amount remitted from the central budget under any heading to any state-owned firm or to the sum of all state-owned firms does not depend on the amount received from the same firm or from the sum of all the state-owned firms.

To summarize: the residual income in the case of this property form is of an economic magnitude set arbitrarily by the bureaucracy. But once it has been set (in the technical terms of fiscal management) it flows into the central budget of the state, and in that sense the owner is the "state coffers." So one must rephrase the question to ask: Who has control over the state budget? And who sets all the economic parameters (prices, wages, taxes, etc.) that have just been established to be the factors determining the size of the residual income? The answer to both questions is the same: this right of disposal belongs to the bureaucracy. So behind the impersonal institution of the "state coffers" is the group in power, and the type a property rights are theirs.

These type a property rights are broader in one dimension and narrower in another than they are in the case of a private owner. In the private owner's case one is talking of residual income in the strict sense. Although the amount of residual income that remains in the private owner's hands depends on his or her own activity, it also depends on circumstances independent of the owner (such as market prices and state taxes), whereas the centralized net income from the state sector is determined, as has been seen, almost totally by the bureaucracy itself. On the other hand, this right of disposal is narrower, since no individual member of the bureaucracy has a total right of disposal over the residual income. The right of disposal is restricted by a web of regulations and prohibitions.

The type a property rights are concentrated most of all in the hands of those with the greatest influence on the setting of the plans, state income and expenditure, prices, and wages. But at these levels of decision-making rights, the personal income and wealth of the most influential individuals is unconnected with the income and wealth of the state-owned firms. None of the profit from the state-owned firm passes automatically into the pockets of these members of the bureaucracy, and, conversely, they need not contribute out of their own pockets to any of the state-owned firm's losses. Since the connection between the "personal pocket" and the residual income of the state-owned firm is entirely absent, those who otherwise have the deciding voice in how the residual income is used are not real owners at all from this point of view. The automatic, spontaneous incentive noted with private property does not apply. Society must rely wholly on artificial incentives.

It is customary under the classical socialist system to employ incentive schemes that could give the top executives of state-owned firms a measure of interest in raising profits, and the interest may even extend to the firm's whole workforce. But it is normally a loose and weak interest. The scale (usually small) and precise formula of the incentive are set arbitrarily by the higher authorities, so that it becomes a mere means of control, that is, an incentive of the kind described earlier as artificial, and not a type a property right under which the whole residual income belongs to the owner.

b. State-owned firms do not constitute objects for purchase or sale; they cannot be leased out, given away, or inherited. Under the classical socialist system the property rights of alienation cannot be exercised by anyone, not even the "state" as the nominal owner.

c. The property rights of control are exercised by the bureaucracy. The activities are controlled by a hierarchical bureaucracy within the state-owned firm, and this bureaucracy constitutes the lower levels of a hierarchy embracing the whole of society. There are still numerous levels above it, right up to the peak of the hierarchical pyramid of power, the top person in the system. Although the type c rights are exercised by the bureaucracy as a whole, they are unevenly distributed among it, according to the relative influence of individual bodies in the apparatus and individuals within those bodies. Bureaucratic control will be discussed in detail in the next chapter. Here it is only necessary to put forward a few notions closely connected with the subject of this chapter.

The bureaucratic apparatus exercising direct control (type c rights) over the state-owned firms is separated organizationally from the apparatus handling the state's financial affairs (and exercising type a rights). Only at the very top are these two branches of the bureaucracy under the common direction of the party general secretary, the Political Committee, and the government.

One can leave open the question of whether the bureaucracy is acting for the good of the whole people or in its own, narrower interest when it exercises its type a and type c rights, that is, disposal of the residual income and the rights of control, since it is irrelevant to a clarification of the nature of property. A private capitalist owner remains a private capitalist owner even if he or she constantly distributes all income for altruistic purposes and runs a factory in such a way that its production serves the needs of the people to the fullest possible extent. Likewise, even if the leading stratum of a bureaucratic socialist power should live an ascetic life, if it should consider its prime task to be the raising of the population's material standard of living, and if it should carry out this task effectively, the property relations of the state-owned firm remain bureaucratic in the sense described above.

It follows from the line of thinking pursued so far that the expression "property of the whole people" is merely ideological in nature. It does not express the real property relations that subsist in the state-owned firms of classical socialism.

Remember what was established in the previous section in the case of private property forms about the depersonalizing of property and about the separation of the rights of ownership from those of control as one moves from the family undertaking to the joint-stock company. Clearly, in the classical socialist firm both these tendencies are taken to their absolute limits.

The depersonalizing of property becomes extreme. Whatever state-owned firm one takes as an example, there is no individual, family, or small group of partners to whom one can point as owners. Since no one can pocket the profits and no one need pay out of his own pocket for the losses, property in this sense is not only depersonalized but eliminated. State property belongs to all and to none.

Within the impersonal, faceless bureaucracy there is a rigid division between the bureaucratic apparatus collecting the residual income and the one controlling production. But it must be added that by comparison with the division under modern capitalism, there is in a sense a degree of "reunion" taking place. After all, the bureaucracy under classical socialism is a centralized, uniform social formation that uses hierarchical division of responsibilities to exercise a specific set of property rights: some of the rights of ownership and all of those of control.

5.4 Other State Property Forms

Having discussed in some detail the property form of the firm owned by the national government, it is enough to mention briefly that other state property forms exist under this system too.

One widespread form is the firm owned by a regional organization of the state (in federal countries, a national or provincial government, or a county, city, or village council). All of what was said in section 5.3 applies also to this form, except that the nominal owner is the state organization of a smaller territorial unit. But in the last resort this regional state organization is itself part of the all-embracing bureaucratic power, and subordinate to higher levels of control.

The other, equally widespread form is the institution whose material wealth is owned by the state (either the central government or a regional state organization) and under state control, but which does not qualify as a "firm" under state law. The most common name applied to it is *budgetary institution*. This kind of organization is not obliged even nominally to make its income cover its expenditure. All income accruing passes to the state budget, which covers all expenditure incurred. (In this it differs from the state-owned firm, where it is merely the positive or negative balance between income and expenditure that flows between the firm and the state budget.) Examples of institutions in this category are the state-run universities, hospitals, and museums.

It is tempting to compare these institutions with the nonprofit institutions of capitalist countries, which themselves can be contrasted with capitalist firms intent on making a profit. But the comparison is not entirely apt. In fact, there is no real profit motive in the classical socialist state-owned firm either [→8.4], and the decision on whether the legal status of a particular organization should be a "firm" or a "budgetary institution" is fairly arbitrary.[19] In terms of the subject of this chapter, property relations, there is little real difference between them. All the property rights apply analogously in both. Each is a species of bureaucratic state property.

5.5 The Cooperative

The second basic property form under the classical socialist system is the cooperative.[20] Its importance is mainly in agriculture, and so this will be dealt with in more detail.

[19]In the official analysis of Marxist political economy a distinction is drawn between productive and nonproductive sectors, with education, cultural provision, and health care among the latter. Ordinarily, the organizations in the productive sectors are firms, while those in the nonproductive sectors operate in the legal frame of budgetary institutions.

[20]The state-controlled cooperatives about to be dealt with have to be distinguished from the small-scale cooperatives that emerge in the course of reforms. These resemble private partnerships [→19.2].

Different countries use different names, for instance, an agricultural cooperative in the Soviet Union is called a *kolkhoz*. In line with the overall plan of the book, the main emphasis will be on examining the features common to them all.[21]

In most countries the classic agricultural cooperative is exclusively a production and sales cooperative. Nominally, it is an organization based on voluntary association of its members, in which the means of production form the collective property of the cooperative, and the membership itself elects its leaders. In practice, it differs substantially from the foregoing description.

The process of mass collectivization took place in almost all socialist countries where the classical socialist system eventually stabilized.[22] Data about the collectivization in the Soviet Union are shown in table 5.2 and figure 5.1. Before this happened there existed agricultural cooperatives organized in a more or less voluntary way, but they accounted for only a small proportion of production. The dominant property form in agriculture was the small family undertaking that employed no outside labor on a regular basis. In addition, there were small private agricultural undertakings employing outside labor, but not in large numbers. According to the Marxist classification the former are small commodity producers and the latter capitalist farms. Other criteria besides regular employment of outside labor have been used to classify a farm as capitalist: ownership of more than a specific area of land or number of livestock, or of a threshing machine, or of some other large piece of equipment could suffice to classify a farm as capitalist. Small-scale capitalist peasants in the Soviet Union were known as *kulaks*, a name that spread to other socialist countries as well.

Aggressive persuasion, threats, and brutal sanctions against resisters were used during the mass collectivization to induce the owners of small peasant farms to abandon farming on their own account, join the cooperative, and hand over their land[23] and other means of production. The

[21]Economists inside and outside the socialist countries also use the expression *collective property*. This book refrains from using the expression because it could be misleading: the bureaucratic state property described in the previous section is also "collective," both nominally and in reality. This collective character becomes particularly apparent if one compares it to individual, private property.

[22]The history of Yugoslavia and Poland differs from this to some extent. Although there was forcible collectivization, the campaign was not carried through consistently, so that a significant proportion of agriculture remained as noncollectivized family undertakings. In this respect these two countries never arrived completely at the pure form of the classical system.

[23]In certain socialist countries the land was nationalized immediately after the revolution, so that it was nominally state property before the collectivization, although the property rights were actually exercised by the peasant farmers. (This was the case in the Soviet

TABLE 5.2
Collectivization of Soviet Agriculture

Year	Collective Farms (thousands)	Peasant Households Collectivized of Total Number of House-holds (percent)	Gross Agricultural Production (index)	Livestock Production (index)
1913	—	—	96	87
1918	1.6	0.1	—	—
1928	33.3	1.7	100	100
1929	57.0	3.9	93	87
1930	85.9	23.6	88	65
1931	211.1	52.7	84	57
1932	211.1	61.5	76	48
1933	—	—	82	51
1934	—	—	86	52
1935	245.4	83.2	99	74
1936	—	—	93	76
1937	—	—	116	83
1938	242.4	93.5	107	100

Source: P. R. Gregory and R. C. Stuart (1986, pp. 109, 111).

small capitalist (kulak) farms were confiscated. Their owners in the Soviet Union and several other socialist countries were subjected to terror
that extended to mass physical assault, deportation, imprisonment, and
execution. Often small-scale producer peasants were classified arbitrarily
as kulaks and subjected to the same treatment, which increased the anx-
iety of those around them and helped induce people to join the cooperative in mass.

The trauma of forcible collectivization[24] left permanent scars on cooperative agriculture. After the cooperative sector had become institutionalized and normalized, the brutal mass terror ceased. Since peasants under the classical socialist system have no alternatives, however, the

---

Union, for instance.) In other socialist countries (e.g., Yugoslavia) the peasants farming
individually possess the nominal rights to their land as well.

[24]For accounts of forcible collectivization in the Soviet Union, for instance, see R. W.
Davies (1980), M. Lewin [1968] (1974), and R. Conquest (1986).

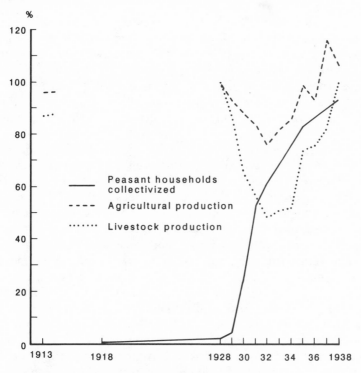

FIGURE 5.1 Collectivization of Soviet Agriculture
Source: P.R. Gregory and R.C. Stuart (1986, pp. 109, 111).

cooperatives cannot be described as truly voluntary associations even after institutionalization. They cannot choose freely whether (1) to leave the cooperative (or, if they have never been a member, to refrain from joining) and work in a family undertaking based on private property instead; (2) to employ permanent outside labor in their own agricultural undertaking if they can afford it; or (3) to join the cooperative on a voluntary basis (or, if they are already members, to remain voluntary members). Anyone wanting to work on the land must be a cooperative member (or possibly an employee of a state farm).

The leadership of the cooperative is only nominally elected by the members. In fact, they are appointed members of the bureaucracy, and in this respect they are in a position no different from elected officials of party or mass organizations or elected members of national or local legislatures [→3]. They too are totally dependent on the upper levels of the bureaucracy.

Nor can the leadership of the cooperative decide independently how to use the cooperative's income. The use is restricted by general regulations and by occasional, specific interventions from above. (Property rights of type a are absent.)

The leadership may not alienate the cooperative's means of production. Higher authorities decide on transfers of particular means of production and in cases where the cooperative merges with another. (There are no property rights of type b.)

The leadership does not have the freedom to decide how the means of production are used. The cooperative is as subject to the control of the centralized bureaucracy as any state-owned firm [→7]. (So property rights of type c are lacking also.)

It follows from what has been said that there is little real, tangible distinction under the classical system between the state-owned and the cooperative property forms. The latter is more or less a species of bureaucratic state property invested with a curious cooperative character. In reality, they operate as "nationalized" cooperatives and their property can be regarded as quasi–state property.

The only essential difference is that cooperative members in the Soviet Union and most Eastern European countries are entitled to till some private land known as a *household plot*. This is a tiny holding, and the peasant actually owns privately only a proportion of the means of production on it. The very small piece of land is assigned to an individual by the cooperative, which can take it back at any time and provide another little piece in its stead. Some of the equipment is rented from the cooperative or the state farm as well. Although the peasant family's property rights over the household farm are only partial, they do include the right to the residual income from it (rights of type a). That suffices to encourage intensive work on it: household farms account for a proportion of the total national production of animal products, vegetables, and fruit far in excess of the proportion of the agricultural land they occupy. Table 5.3 presents data on the household plots of Soviet kolkhoz members.[25]

What justifies bringing the cooperative sector of agriculture into being? There are two sides to the question. On the one hand, what provided the incentive to eliminate the private property forms? On the other, once that had happened, why was this not done openly, as nationalization?

While the collectivization is going on, great emphasis is put in official propaganda on momentarily relevant arguments. (For example, during the Soviet collectivization the main one was the grave difficulty in supplying the cities with grain.) But from the start the official propaganda

---

[25]The conditions in Bulgarian agriculture were comparable to the Soviet situation described in table 5.3. Here 37 percent of the chicken production, 46.5 percent of the meat production, and 53.1 percent of the egg production in 1985 came from family smallholdings, which accounted for only 12.8 percent of the cultivated land. R. J. McIntyre (1988, p. 105).

TABLE 5.3
Private Plots in Soviet Agriculture

| Year | Income from Private Plots of Kolkhoz Members (percent of total income) | Contribution of Private Sector to Total Output | |
		Meat (percent)	Eggs (percent)
1960	45		
1965		40	67
1970	35		
1975		31	39
1980	28		
1983		29	30
1985	26		

Source: Column 1: V. G. Treml (1987, table A3); columns 2 and 3: P. R. Gregory and R. C. Stuart (1986, p. 270).

about collectivization also lays great stress on longer-term economic considerations: the advantage of a large undertaking over a small, the principle of economies of scale. According to this argument, productivity is low in a small family undertaking and much is consumed by the household itself, so that the farm takes few goods to market. The claim is that in the large-scale undertaking productivity will be far higher. Even if self-consumption by the household does not fall, the proportion of produce sent to market will rise appreciably, according to the official ideology behind collectivization.[26]

In fact, this line of argument parallels the thinking found in Western economic theory.[27] It is worth combining small firms into large ones if the latter are more efficient, which will manifest itself in higher profits. Remaining with this line of thinking for a moment, the key question is clearly whether the efficiency of the large undertaking really is greater. To this question no general answer is valid and true for any sector of the economy or any process of consolidating small undertakings into large ones, irrespective of the social, political, and economic environment in

[26]Large-scale (state and collective) farming enhances labor productivity through cooperation: "Today . . . the peasants are able to combine their labor power with the labor of their neighbors, . . . and to produce much more than formerly." J. V. Stalin (1947, p. 312).

[27]See R. H. Coase (1937) as well as O. E. Williamson (1975) on the theories of transaction costs, and on the relationship between hierarchies and markets.

which the small or large undertakings are operating. Ultimately, large-scale cooperative farming under the classical socialist system has not proved more productive or efficient than small-scale farming.

The motives for collectivization, however, are not limited to economic considerations and efficiency. Just as big a part, or even bigger, is played by political intentions, the effort to bolster bureaucratic power.[28] Peasant farming based on private property is incompatible with the totalitarian power of the bureaucracy, because it could come to represent an independent social, political, and economic force, whereas large-scale cooperative management incorporated into the centralized bureaucracy fits integrally into the totalitarian power structure. The independence and self-determination of the private peasantry ceases and there is no longer any difference between the dependence of the rural population on the bureaucracy and the dependence of any other strata of the population.

Moreover, the very elimination of private property and creation of public property has intrinsic value in the eyes of those in power. This applies also to the small family undertaking, where it is thought that the peasant farming individually will be infected with "petty bourgeois" self-interest, with avoidance of service to the common good, and with avarice and backwardness. In addition, wherever small-scale production is widespread the process of accumulation will steadily bring capitalist property into being: the most successful or fortunate peasants farming on a small or medium scale will become kulaks [→19.3].

As for the other half of the question, utilization of the cooperative form (instead of open nationalization) and toleration of household farming is a compromise between the real, ultimate intention and momentary social realities. The real and feigned concessions markedly reduce resistance and make it somewhat easier for the mass of the peasantry to accept the loss of the chance to farm for themselves.

The extent to which this is merely a compromise is confirmed by the repeated official declarations that cooperative property is a lower form of social ownership than state property. So it can only be transitional, although the transition may take a long time. Ultimately, all production must be included in the framework of ownership by "the people as a whole."[29]

[28]On the relationship between the choice of organization form and the endeavors of political power, see S. Marglin (1976).

[29]This idea can already be found in Marx: "To save the industrious masses, cooperative labour ought to be developed to national dimension, and, consequently to be fostered by national means." K. Marx [1864] (1975a, p. 12). The last economic study Stalin wrote was a discussion of "what must be done to raise collective-farm property to the level of public property." J. V. Stalin (1952, p. 65).

In fact, state farms existed in the agriculture of the classical system from the very start. (In the Soviet Union the name used is *sovkhoz.*)[30] The long-term tendency toward relegation of the cooperative form is confirmed by the fact that the ratio of state-owned firms to cooperatives is rising steadily in several socialist countries.[31]

Compared with what has been said so far, the situation of the Chinese commune needs mentioning specially in one respect. Collectivization was taken even further than in the Soviet Union and many other socialist countries. Even such vestiges of private production as household farming on the Soviet kolkhoz were eliminated. Communes have not confined themselves to agricultural production; they pursue industrial, commercial, and other service activities as well. Collectivization of some of the consumption within the commune was introduced. The totalization of power was taken further, since the commune combined the functions of state administration with those of economic control. The commune became a bureaucratic authority, a firm (or rather a conglomerate pursuing a diversity of activities), and a consumption community above the individual households.

So far this section has considered agriculture. One finds cooperatives in other sectors of the classical socialist economy as well, but they do not differ in their basic features from the cooperative farms, and the relative weight of their production in their respective sectors is far less. I therefore refrain for brevity's sake from discussing them in detail.

5.6 Private Property and Production Activity of a Private Nature

Under the classical socialist system, private firms employing hired labor either do not exist or are restricted to a small segment of the economy. The almost total elimination of private capitalism is precisely what the official ideology considers a major, or even the main, criterion of socialism. Only state and cooperative ownership are recognized ideologically as socialist.

---

[30]Over a long period another kind of organization owned by the state operated in the Soviet Union alongside the sovkhoz providing agricultural produce. Known as the "machine tractor station," it rented out larger pieces of machinery (such as tractors and combine harvesters) to the cooperatives. For a long time the cooperatives did not even have the right to purchase larger machines, because ownership of them was monopolized by the state machine tractor stations. This further increased the cooperatives' dependence on the "openly" state-owned sector. Such stations were set up in several other socialist countries as well.

[31]In 1953 the sovkhozes (state farms) worked 9.6 percent of the sown area in the Soviet Union. By 1983 the proportion was 53.4 percent. P. R. Gregory and R. C. Stuart [1974] (1986, p. 269).

Even so, there survive a variety of private property forms (and partly related to them, production activities of a private nature), although they are dwarfed by the state and cooperative sectors. The following are the most typical of them.

1. *Small-scale private industry and commerce.* In some classical socialist countries, such as East Germany, Hungary, and Poland, small family undertakings can operate with an official permit,[32] but the sector accounts for a small proportion of industrial production and commercial services. For the sake of illustration, table 5.4 presents data on the pri-

TABLE 5.4
Elimination of the Private Sector in East Germany, Hungary, and Poland

| Year | Private Nonagricultural Employment in the Percentage of Total Nonagricultural Employment[a] | | |
	East Germany[b]	*Hungary[c]*	*Poland*
1949	—	20.3	11.6
1950	—	17.1	6.6
1952	34.0	4.5	4.7
1955	30.8	2.7	3.6
1960	21.6	—	4.8
1965	19.0	—	4.3
1970	16.5	3.8	4.4
1972	8.4	3.5[d]	4.0
1975	6.8	3.1	4.0
1980	5.9	2.9	4.9

Source: Columns 1 and 3: A. Åslund (1985, pp. 230–31, 247). Column 2, rows 1–4: Hungarian Central Statistical Office (1959, pp. 65–66); rows 7–10: Központi Statisztikai Hivatal (Central Statistical Office, Budapest) (1971, pp. 104–5; 1973, p. 109; 1975, p. 111; 1980a, pp. 128–29).

[a]The data start out in 1949, after the first wave of nationalization, when the "commanding heights" of the economy had already been nationalized.

[b]Figures include the semiprivate sector—private firms with state participation. In the 1960s their share amounted to 7 percent of the total nonagricultural employment. They were almost completely nationalized in 1971–72. A. Åslund (1985).

[c]Figures include only active employees. The water and forest economy is recorded as part of agriculture, so it is not included.

[d]January 1, 1973.

[32]Although by definition a small family undertaking cannot employ outside labor, in fact, a private artisan or trader with an official permit has been able to employ a limited number of workers, in practice usually not more than one person under classical socialism.

vate sector in East Germany, Hungary, and Poland.[33] In other countries the sector is not allowed to operate at all.

2. *Household farming.* This, in fact, is a hybrid form. As explained in the previous section, one part of a household farm's means of production is cooperative property and the other private property. The peasant family only receives the use of the land, the most important means of production. It may be repossessed at any time, and the family cannot alienate it. (In other words, they lack property rights of type b.) But the after-tax residual income from production on the household farm belongs to the peasant family (property right type a), which also decides the amount of labor put into it (property rights of type c).[34] So basically the form can be classed under private ownership and private economic activity.

3. *The informal private economy.*[35] This covers a wide variety of activity.[36]

a. Production or service activity performed by one individual for another for compensation in money or kind. Examples of nonmanual activity include medical treatment, legal advice, typing, translation, private language instruction, and babysitting. Some examples of manual activity are repair and installation work, house-building, cleaning, and personal and goods transportation.

---

[33]Table 5.4 shows that the process of eliminating the private sector took a much longer time in East Germany than in many other socialist economies.

[34]This property right too is restricted, because the peasant family must work certain hours or perform a certain quantity of labor for the cooperative. At most they can devote their remaining time to the household farm.

[35]In some economic writings the term "second economy" is applied to what this book calls the "informal economy." I join those who observe the following distinction: The *first economy* covers all that qualifies in the official ideology of the classical system as the "socialist sector," that is, the bureaucratic state and cooperative sector, while the *second economy* consists of the sum of the formal private sector composed of officially permitted, small family undertakings and the informal private sector.

[36]Out of the huge literature on the private sector, the second economy, and especially the informal activity in socialist countries, only a few comprehensive works will be mentioned. *General overviews:* S. Alessandrini and B. Dallago, eds. (1987), B. Dallago (1990), E. L. Feige, ed. (1989), I. R. Gábor (1979), G. Grossman (1985), M. Los, ed. (1990), and V. Tanzi, ed. (1982). *Soviet Union:* G. Grossman (1977a), T. I. Koriagina (1990a, 1990b), and the Berkeley-Duke Occasional Papers, which present theoretical studies on the second economy and summarize the findings of the interviews with Soviet émigrés. *China:* W. Zafanolli (1985). *Poland:* A. Korbonski (1981), S. Taigner (1987), and J. Rostowski (1989a). *Hungary:* P. Galasi and G. Sziráczki, eds. (1985). *Bulgaria:* D. C. Jones and M. Meurs (1991).

There have been many attempts to model the effect of the private sector on market equilibrium in a socialist economy in a general equilibrium framework with rationing. See, for example, R. Ericson (1983, 1984), D. O. Stahl and M. Alexeev (1985), S. Wellisz and R. Findley (1986), B. G. Katz and J. Owen (1984), and C. Davis (1988).

b. Production and marketing of foodstuffs (meat, fruit, and vegetables) by those whose full-time job is not agricultural.

c. Subletting of a privately owned or rented dwelling.

d. Trading activity outside the framework of state-owned, cooperative and officially permitted private commerce. Both black marketeering and the sale of goods imported legally or smuggled home after travel abroad belong here.

Some of the listed and similar activities exclusively require the labor of those pursuing them, while others require equipment as well. Some of those working in the informal economy use equipment owned by themselves (or possibly by the persons commissioning the work), and others use equipment in state or cooperative ownership. (An example of the latter is "black" transport of goods by a driver using a state-owned truck.)

Some informal activity is done by those employed in the state and cooperative sector outside their official working hours.[37] Other informal activity is done "on the firm's time" at the expense of official work.

It varies from country to country and from period to period which informal activities are permitted under the classical socialist system, which are prohibited by the legal regulations, and how strictly such bans are enforced. Related to this is the national and temporal variation in the scale of the informal economy and its relative weight in the economy as a whole. What is general is the existence of the informal economy; it never vanishes completely even when the strictest bans apply.[38]

A "shadow economy" exists under other systems as well, mainly as a way of evading tax. This is not the prime motive under the classical socialist system, where the bureaucracy seeks to confine all kinds of private property and private economic activity within very narrow limits, even when tax is being regularly paid. The informal economy represents an effort to overstep those narrow limits and operate without official permission, either by identifying opportunities not expressly banned by the letter of the law or by taking the risk of flouting the law. So this book uses the term "informal" as a comprehensive one that covers equally well nonillegal and tolerated activity, prohibited activity where the ban is lightly enforced, and activity that is strictly banned.[39]

[37]The graphic English expression for this is "moonlighting."

[38]As a crown witness Brezhnev is quoted by F. Burlatskiy in *Literaturnaya Gazeta,* September 18, 1988: "You don't know life. No one lives on wages alone. I remember in my youth we earned money by unloading railroad freight cars. So, what did we do? Three crates or bags unloaded and one for ourselves. That is how everybody lives in [our] country." Quoted by V. G. Treml (1990, p. 2).

[39]See A. Katsenelinboigen's (1977) article on "colored" markets and activities. They include white (legal), pink (informal activities involving state officials), gray (informal), and black (outrightly criminal) activities.

5.7   Capitalism, Socialism, and Property

So far this chapter has been concerned with property relations of the classical socialist system. Private property exists under it, but its scope is extremely restricted. The predominant property forms are the various kinds of bureaucratic public ownership: state and cooperative property in which the specific property rights are distributed in the configurations already described, which are typical of the classical system. In the official terminology of the classical system, the sum of the activities pursued within the frame of public ownership is known as the "socialist sector" of the economy.

In presocialist societies the various forms of private ownership, including capitalist ownership, develop and gain ground basically as a result of spontaneous economic processes. This transformation is paralleled in the legal system, which protects private ownership and enforces private contracts. Though the regulations of the state give a greater boost to capitalist ownership in certain periods, one certainly could not say that the state had organized capitalism's development and stabilization.

By contrast, the almost complete elimination of capitalist property relations and the creation and stabilization of the classical socialist system's property relations are not the results of spontaneous economic processes. This transformation is the consequence of revolutionary action by the party-state. It is immaterial whether the legal sanction of a particular state regulation has been penned at the moment the change is executed, or whether it is legalized retroactively. Whichever the case, the bureaucracy uses force to confiscate the overwhelming proportion of private property, nationalize the means of production, and coerce the peasants and other small producers who have hitherto worked their own holdings into the cooperative property form.

There is nothing surprising in this. The cardinal point in the program of Marxist-Leninist parties is "expropriation of the expropriators," in other words, the determination, as soon as politically practicable, to organize society on a basis of public instead of private ownership. This brings one back to the question of the system of values. To the followers of the Communist party, the value system is headed by three closely related values, each of which presumes the other and partly overlaps. Above all, socialism and its establishment and maintenance is not just an instrumental value of service to other, ultimate values, but an intrinsic ultimate value in itself. Socialism comes into existence only when and where the Communist party is in power; power is a fundamental, ultimate value. Socialism differs first and foremost from capitalism in having replaced private ownership with public ownership; so the elimination of private ownership and the establishment and stabilization of public ownership is an intrinsic value as well. Of course, instrumental values are expected as well from the creation of socialist ownership: it must ensure higher productivity than capitalist ownership provides. But it already has a vast intrinsic, internal value in that the capitalists are no longer exploiting the workers, the workers are no longer subordinate to the capitalists, and the capitalist class vanishes from the stage of history. Moreover, the two values have the closest possible relationship: the property acquired by the bureaucracy is a very important constituent of the bureaucracy's power.

The position and practical action taken on the question of property (for instance, on agricultural collectivization) is a clear example of what was said earlier about the vanguard nature of the party, about the self-legitimation of power, and about paternalism [→4.4]. Remaining with the example of collectivization, those in power are convinced that elimination of private property serves the people's interests, and that the peasants serve their own interests by giving up their independence and entering the cooperative. Their backwardness and shortsightedness prevent them, however, from recognizing their own interests, which is why they must be compelled, even if they resist the change. One purpose for which the power is needed is to force people against their will to adopt a way of life that eventually will be for their own good.

A system of values is being discussed that deeply influences the adherents of the Communist party, from the top leaders down to honest, enthusiastic party members who hold no function in the apparatus. This conviction spurs them to work, make sacrifices, and accept unpopular tasks, and to implement their program regardless of whatever mass resistance they meet. This is precisely where one finds cardinal differences between the Marxist-Leninist, communist value system and action program and those of other strands of socialism. The clearest difference is from those put forward by the social democrats. For example, in the social democratic interpretation of socialist ideas, the forms of public ownership of production and distribution have only an instrumental value. They must be introduced just to the extent that really furthers the values considered intrinsic: primarily welfare, social justice, and the assurance of liberty. Private ownership need not necessarily be abolished where it serves these intrinsic values better than nationalization or collectivization could do. One must certainly avoid making changes in the property forms by force or against the will of the majority of the population as expressed through the ballot box.

This book, in accordance with its plan, does not argue about values. It merely sets out to describe the extent to which the various features of the system promote each value and work against it. To say that the classical socialist system enforces the dominance of three values that the ideology of the Communist party considers most important is not a tautology but a statement that can be checked and either verified or refuted by experience. It applies the idea behind this movement: a society based on the undivided power of the Communist party, the (almost total) elimination of private ownership, and the general spread of public ownership indeed comes into being.

Having discussed the problem of values, I must mention a conceptual question that belongs here. Section 1.3 made clear the sense in which the phrase "socialist system" is used in this book. The corresponding problem is the interpretation put on the phrase "capitalist system."

When one considers societies in their entirety, each is in fact "mixed" from the point of view of property forms. History has not produced a society in which a single property form operates in sterile purity. At this point one school of social researchers inclines to stop and refuse to think in terms of families and species of systems at all, declaring they are all mingled, hybrid, and mixed in character, and the number of actual and conceivable mixtures and variants is infinite.

This book, however, does not follow that principle. Instead, it follows those willing to declare of whole systems that one is socialist and another capitalist.[40] At this point the way is open to expand and to express more fully the definitions to which only a first approach was made in section 1.2.

As stated earlier, the primary attribute of the socialist system is that a Marxist-Leninist party exercises undivided power. Now a further characteristic can be added: the party is committed to eliminating private property, and with its undivided power and interpenetration with the state, it manages sooner or later to put that program into practice, or at least come near to doing so.

On the basis of what was said just now about the difference in the way the presocialist and the socialist systems develop, the essential thing under the socialist system is what the ruling party wants to achieve and succeeds in achieving. With a nonsocialist system, on the other hand, one has to start from what has developed in society "of its own accord." The capitalist system is a society in which the capitalist forms of private

---

[40]The multitude of academic authors and politicians who subscribe to this terminological convention vary widely in their world views and theoretical and political outlooks. They include Marxists and anti-Marxists, those to whom "socialism" has a creditable ring and "capitalism" a pejorative one, and those for whom the two have the opposite association. The same applies to the authors and politicians who reject the socialism-capitalism pair of concepts. They are a thoroughly heterogeneous group as well.

The similar heterogeneity of both groups confirms indirectly that what is being discussed here is a value-free, semantic question.

When applying concepts, the main requirements are that they should be conceptually clear and unambiguous, and that their application as tools of analysis should prove workable.

property predominate.[41] To this must be added a negative criterion: there is no party in undivided possession of power that is committed to eliminating the predominance of capitalist private property.

In accordance with this line of argument, this book uses a broad definition of the concept of the capitalist system. It covers strongly individualistic systems like those of the United States and Switzerland, and more collectivist Scandinavian welfare states where a Social Democratic party has been in power for decades, and a number of regulations suggested by socialistic ideas have been introduced. The category covers countries with a measure of central planning (like India or France at certain times) and those with no sign of it; those with a fairly broad state sector (like Austria) and those with a very narrow one. No one would deny that the differences mentioned are very important and rightly the center of attention in numerous comparative analyses. But that does not preclude the viability of dividing twentieth-century social-political-economic formations into two great classes or species of systems: socialist and capitalist.[42]

[41]This is, of course, not an exhaustive comparison of all important differences between socialism and capitalism. Further attributes will be added, for example, the predominant role of bureaucratic coordination under socialism and that of the market under capitalism, as the analysis of socialism proceeds.

[42]Nor is it a deciding argument against the division into two classes that some specific systems found in twentieth-century history are difficult to squeeze into one box or the other. It is quite clear, for example, that an African or Asian society in which capitalist property forms have appeared only sporadically or weakly and precapitalist forms predominate instead, cannot be placed simply in the category "capitalist system."

A problem of classification is posed also by the social formation known as "African socialism" or "Islamic socialism" (of which Tanzania can serve as an example of the former and Algeria of the latter). Although there is a monopolistic force in power and it pursues an anti–private ownership, pro–public ownership policy, things do not go exactly according to the pattern described in this book. Not only the ideology but important features of the actual system that emerge are different.

Borderline cases, mixtures, and specific examples that are "not pure" occur with every classification introduced for the purposes of scientific analysis. Simple taxonomies divided into few classes are an aid to generalization on a large scale and also in creating models and theories.

6

Coordination Mechanisms

THE NATURE of political power, the prevailing ideology, and the property relations determine jointly the part (or at least the main feature of the role) that various coordination mechanisms can play in society. I shall state first in general what I mean by the concept of a coordination mechanism and then survey some of the main types, before returning to the central subject of the chapter: the place and function of the various coordination mechanisms under the classical socialist system and the relations they bear to one another.

6.1 Main Types

Each coordination mechanism is a subsystem of the social system. As the name suggests, a coordination mechanism coordinates the activity of the persons or organizations involved in it. Wherever a relation subsists between two or more persons or organizations, their activity requires coordination in some form.

The book discusses in some detail five main types of mechanisms: (1) bureaucratic coordination, (2) market coordination, (3) self-governing coordination, (4) ethical coordination, and (5) family coordination.

Each mechanism has its own range of characteristics: who the participants are, what relation there is between them, what communications flow between them to further the coordination, and what motivations encourage the participants to take part in the coordination process. Each mechanism has its typical procedures, and the relations between the participants have a specific "style," ethic, and written or unwritten code of rules.

Each main type embraces several varieties. The initial aim in the general definitions is to identify what is general and common to all bureaucratic coordination, all market coordination, and so on. In this sense I am discussing stylized, pure theoretical models whose structure at this level of abstraction disregards a variety of specific features.

1. *Bureaucratic coordination.*[1] Relations of superiority-subordination obtain between the individual or organization coordinating and the

---

[1]A distinction is made in the terminology of this book between the concepts of bureaucracy and bureaucratic coordination. The first refers to an organization and the second to a coordination mechanism. The bureaucracy primarily controls the processes in society

individuals or organizations being coordinated. Such relations are called *vertical linkages.* In many instances a hierarchy of superiority-subordination on several levels develops. An individual or organization acting as the superior of those on the level below it is concurrently subordinate to a superior on the level above. The vertical linkage is, however, asymmetrical. Though the superior depends on the subordinates to some extent, the subordinates depend on the superior far more. The superior is not chosen by the subordinates, but appointed over their heads.

The vertical flow of information consists of several kinds of communication, the most typical for this kind of coordination being the command, the order from the superior that the subordinate is required to obey.

Subordinates have several kinds of motivation for carrying out the superior's commands, the most characteristic being the effort to win the superior's approval, receive the reward offered, and avoid the penalty threatened for noncompliance. Subordinates know that the command is backed up by a legal compulsion, that failure to carry it out will incur legal sanctions.

2. *Market coordination.*[2] A buyer and a seller have lateral relations or a *horizontal linkage* in which the two parties rank equally in legal terms.

Under the transaction taking place between a buyer and a seller, the seller transfers something to the buyer. The transaction is accompanied by a flow of numerous communications of many different kinds, of which the most characteristic is the price.

The buyer and seller conclude a voluntary contract covering the conditions of the transaction. Both parties may have a variety of motivations for accepting the terms of the contract, of which the most characteristic is for both to be seeking a material gain from the transaction.

The mark of this type of coordination is that it is monetized: as the goods pass from seller to buyer, money passes in the opposite direction. (Of course, there may be a direct exchange of material goods instead.[3])

---

through the bureaucratic coordination mechanism, but it may also use other mechanisms to further its purposes, such as the market. The same applies in reverse: bureaucratic coordination may be used by individuals who are not themselves members of the bureaucracy. Shareholders, for instance, may use bureaucratic coordination in the management of the firms they own.

[2]As in the case of type 1, the book aims here at a description that is as general as possible. In other words, the definition of the market mechanism of coordination is not confined to one or another of the specific subtypes described in professional writings.

[3]In the socialist countries the terms "operation of the law of value" or "commodity and market relations," borrowed from the terminology of Marxian political economy, are employed in official economics teaching and professional parlance for what this book calls "market coordination." Using these key expressions, it is easy to make translations from one "language" to another. For instance, when teachers of political economy in socialist

3. *Self-governing coordination*. The participants in this type of coordination are laterally placed, equal members of a self-governing association. To this extent their linkage is horizontal.

The coordination is conducted according to a specific constitution or rulebook decided upon by the members. In many associations the entire membership is unable (or unwilling) to exercise directly the right of self-government in every respect, and the practical details are entrusted to a body of persons delegated by the members to perform the tasks of coordination. To that extent this mechanism does not consist exclusively of horizontal relations; there is a vertical element in the linkage between the members and the committee undertaking part of the government. Nonetheless, the mechanism must be distinguished strictly in theoretical discussion from the mechanism of type 1. Here the membership elects the governing body directly or indirectly and can dismiss it. That distinguishes the committee members clearly from the superior individuals or organizations of bureaucratic coordination, who are appointed over the subordinates' heads instead of being elected by them.

Again, in the case of self-government, numerous kinds of information flow among the members and between them and the governing body. The most typical are the votes of the membership and the collective decision.

Once more, the motivations are of various kinds, the most important being recognition of a community of interest, that is, the awareness that the interests of the individual members coincide with the collective interests of those participating in the self-governing coordination.

4. *Ethical coordination*. In this mechanism the participants are the donor individual or organization and the recipient of the benefit, who may be an individual, organization, or anonymous community. The recipient is not legally subordinate to the donor, and so a lateral, horizontal linkage connects the participants in the mechanism, as it does in the case of market coordination.[4]

The most typical of the many kinds of communication in this coordination are the application and the offer.

Once again, a great many kinds of motivation may be involved, but the dominant one cannot be fear of the recipient (in which case there would be a subordinate relation). Nor can expectation of material gain of the donor be dominant (because then there would be a buyer-seller relation). These two negative attributes are what distinguish this fourth

---

countries discuss, in connection with the reform of the socialist economy, "Is labor a commodity?" they are asking whether market coordination actually applies to the supply, demand, and employment of labor, and whether using this type of coordination is desirable.

[4]Individuals or organizations may perform these two functions by turns, or they may be simultaneously donors and recipients of each other's gifts. (To use Polányi's expression, a relation of reciprocity may obtain between them.)

type from the first two. The donor is moved by some altruistic motivation, which may be based on political or religious conviction; on an inner imperative to display noble conduct or generosity; on friendship, comradeship, solidarity, sense of community; or even on politeness or etiquette.

For a general definition it is immaterial whether the gift is in the form of money, physical goods, or an action, gesture, or communication. Ethical coordination, however, differs from the other horizontal linkage, the typically monetized market relation, in that monetization is frequently absent.

5. *Family coordination.* The participants in the mechanism are bound by family ties. (Although the definitions given so far have not stressed the fact, the participants in types 1–4 do not usually have family ties.[5])

Whether there are superior-subordinate or lateral relations, that is, vertical or horizontal linkages, among the members playing the various roles in the family depends on the specific structure of the family concerned.

One cannot single out any kind of communication as the most typical. The motivations are various, but certainly a major part is played by a sense of family love, complemented by an awareness of the family duty prescribed by morality, religion, and the law.

For each of the main types a few practical examples may be given displaying the theoretical models in a more or less pure form.

Bureaucratic mechanisms of coordination operate in the army and the police, in the internal administrative apparatus of a large modern firm, and in the regulation of rail traffic.

Market mechanisms of coordination occur in a city market place or market hall, in a bazaar, shop, or department store, or on a commodity or stock exchange.

Self-governing mechanisms of coordination apply in a choir, autonomous university, or professional association.

Ethical mechanisms of coordination obtain in a relief organization or when people voluntarily clear up litter others drop in a public place.

Family mechanisms of coordination govern the organization of communal consumption in a household.

Here the cases have been chosen purposely to exemplify the main features in the general definitions given earlier for each main type. The

---

[5]This need not be insisted upon strictly in the definitions. It may happen that family ties also bind subordinates and superiors in a particular bureaucracy, or that someone sells something to a family member for money. Members of one family may be members of the same self-governing association. To avoid overlap, it is worth stating about type 4 that it refers to the kind of altruistic relation in which the recipient is not a member of the donor's family.

names of the main types are used in this book in a literal, not a figurative, sense. One might play with words, for instance, by saying all human actions have a market nature and are based on some kind of exchange. Even religious martyrs, one might argue, give their lives in exchange for celestial bliss. Others might play with the words command and compulsion, saying the ultimate motive force behind every market transaction is economic necessity. Such play, however, can blur useful distinctions between social phenomena. The key words in the definitions above are used basically in the same way as they are understood by people not professionally involved in the social sciences.[6]

6.2 Some Observations on the Main Types

Several other, similar, or even synonymous concepts used in the literature can also help to shed some light on the notion of coordination mechanism. The term "control process" underlines the fact that the coordination mechanism controls the activity of those taking part in it. The term "adjustment mechanism" or "adjustment process" emphasizes that the participants in the coordination mechanism adjust to one another (and also to external circumstances). The term "integration mechanism" stresses that society is prevented from disintegrating into its constituent elements by various mechanisms binding it together.

Neoclassical economists frequently use the expression "allocation mechanism"; they consider analysis of the allocation of scarce resources as the purpose of economics. In the usage of this book coordination embraces allocation, but the emphasis is on the fact that it is living people who transfer inanimate objects, resources, and information from one place of availability to another and utilize them. It is living people who need coordination if the inanimate resources are to be allocated by their agency and direction. Each coordination mechanism denotes a collection of specific social relations.

---

[6]The typology presented in the section has achieved its purpose if the types are associated with the following images. (1) Bureaucratic coordination: commands, discipline, being at the mercy of superiors, rewards and penalties, strictness, legal stipulations. (2) Market coordination: price, money, gain, profit, business. (3) Self-governing coordination: membership, election, rulebook, constitution. (4) Ethical coordination: selflessness, unwritten commands, readiness to sacrifice, attention to others. (5) Family coordination: parent and child, brother and sister, family allegiance, common household.

The associations of images are "impressionistic" and not replacements for the definitions in the section. But they can still be useful as a way of conveying that the models in the typology depict characteristic relations drawn from life.

The typology introduced in the previous section cannot be said to offer an inclusive classification or the sole possible classification of all the conceivable types of coordination.[7] Numerous other types occurred in precapitalist societies. It might be useful, when describing the social systems of the present day, to add further types to the five introduced in the previous section. Many typologies related to this one but differing from it have been published.[8] In arriving at the present one, I have applied two main criteria. The first is the logical one that the main types should be independent in the sense that no single type can be described as a special case of another. The second is applicability to this particular book, which requires a typology capable of analyzing effectively the coordination mechanisms extant both in practice in the socialist countries and in the alternative visions, programs, and blueprints proposed for socialism.

The examples at the end of the last section were chosen for clarity's sake as ones approximating as far as possible the pure forms of the main types. But in real life many of the coordination mechanisms are combinations of several pure main types superimposed on one another. Both self-governing and bureaucratic elements are combined in the control processes inside a capitalist company. There is, for instance, a blend of ethical, self-governing, and bureaucratic coordination in the workings of a church congregation. Often the various mechanisms dovetail with one another. Internally, a large, privately owned firm under capitalism organizes itself bureaucratically, while a cooperative similar to an Israeli kibbutz uses self-governing coordination, and the production of a small-scale family undertaking is regulated by family mechanisms of coordination. Meanwhile, in all three cases, the unit takes part externally in mar-

---

[7]In an earlier piece of writing (1984) I employed a somewhat different system of classification and made the assumption that it was comprehensive. A revision of that earlier position is signified by the typology described in section 6.1 and the assessment of it above.

[8]K. Polányi (1944, 1957) distinguished three basic modes of transaction and integration: reciprocity, redistribution, and market exchange. In his 1944 book he mentions also "householding" as a separate principle of activities. The classification applied by C. E. Lindblom (1977) is this: authority, market, and preceptorial system. Both approaches stimulated the development of my own ideas, but I felt it necessary to depart from them. The similarities are clear, but it is worth singling out and justifying some of the differences. Bureaucratic coordination is a broader category than Polányi's redistribution; similarly, ethical coordination is a broader category than reciprocity. Lindblom's preceptorial system does not appear to be a distinct coordination mechanism, rather a method available to any of the five mechanisms appearing in this book. Neither Polányi nor Lindblom features the self-governing mechanism as a separate class, yet it is not a special case of any other mechanism.

ket coordination with the sellers supplying it and the buyers purchasing from it.[9]

Only family coordination has existed in some form since the dawn of human civilization, but the other four also have very long histories. It is hard to agree with the predictions of those who foresee a secure future exclusively for one or two types, and to anticipate or hope that the others will wither away.[10] All five types look very robust and set to remain so. But that does not mean they will continue indefinitely to live peacefully and equally side by side. It is highly typical of change in social systems that one type should lose ground in certain areas of life while another one comes to the fore; while entwined with other types it actually squeezes them out. It is possible for a movement, party, or association based on self-government to become bureaucratized or commercialized. Bureaucracies may have their functions taken over by business undertakings, or vice versa: the function of a business undertaking may be assigned to a state authority. Examples of all these changes or proportions and combinations can be found in presocialist societies.

6.3 Bureaucratic Coordination

Under the classical socialist system, bureaucratic coordination is the mechanism applied most widely and forcefully. The other main types exist, but they are repressed and to some extent atrophied, whereas bureaucratic coordination reproduces itself continually.

Of course, this type of coordination exists under the systems preceding socialism as well. In the case of modern capitalism, it is prominent within the state apparatus, the armed forces, large firms, and other large organizations, and such partial bureaucracies can wield great power. Classical socialism, however, is the first system in history to merge these partial bureaucracies into a single entity embracing the whole of society. That constitutes an essential difference from systems with partial, unmerged bureaucracies.

Separate chapters of this book have been devoted so far to power, property, and coordination, the intention being to explain in more detail and from various angles a related group of phenomena. This is the point

[9]On the problems of the hierarchy within the firm and the market that links firms, see the writings of O. E. Williamson (1967, 1975). Furthermore, see the references in section 5.1, note 9.

[10]For instance, for some, all roads lead to the market; the bureaucratic mechanism is an aberration that history will eradicate one day. For others, the future belongs to self-government; sooner or later both bureaucracy and the market will wither away.

at which to emphasize that the undivided, totalitarian structure of power, the state ownership of the bulk of social production, and the dominance of bureaucratic coordination over other mechanisms are three closely connected phenomena. The power elite, hierarchically structured and sharing power with no other group, has the exclusive right of disposal over the state-owned means of production. Within its own ranks it eradicates other coordination mechanisms to the degree it is able and relies as much as it can on bureaucratic coordination. Relations between state-owned firms are not coordinated by the market, nor does self-government apply within them. Instead, the relations between firms are bureaucratically coordinated, and within the firms this brings right down to the workbench the same vertical system of linkages that governs the company itself. At the apex of the pyramid is the top man in the party and state; at the base are citizens who hold no function in the apparatus: the working individuals and the members of their families. A continuous, vertical chain of relations stretches from top to bottom.

The concept of a perfect hierarchy, in which each member has one and only one immediate superior, at least for a specific activity, has been defined clearly in the theoretical writings on hierarchies. The hierarchy of classical socialism is not perfect in this sense. Under normal conditions, one and the same individual or organization, or, more precisely, each clearly defined activity of that individual or organization, will be regulated and controlled by several superior individuals or organizations. Mention has been made already of the overlaps in the activities of the party, state, and mass organizations [→3.2, 3.3].[11] The party organizations and the party apparatus within them manage and supervise the activities of all other organizations and institutions. Moreover, there are functional and regional vertical chains within the party apparatus, overlapping and controlling each other. Party leaders at all levels employ the political police to check on the reliability of candidate functionaries, prevent all kinds of political association, and remove those who are politically suspect. All these precautions extend even to the party apparatus itself, and in that sense the party as such is subject to a degree of supervision by the political police, which is managed and controlled in turn by the party leaders and organizations assigned to the task.[12] The same

[11]On parallel apparatuses, see T. Dunmore (1980). Dunmore also cites H. Simon's observation that every part of a hierarchy has its own objectives and motives, and its own background of information; this creates separatism and conflict with other parts of the hierarchy.

[12]In the most excessive periods of classical socialism (for instance, the time of Stalin's terror), this went as far as extreme intimidation of the members of the party apparatus. It is important to note, however, that this is no inevitable concomitant to the operation of bureaucratic coordination under classical socialism. What undoubtedly is a characteristic

duplication of functional and regional vertical chains, supervising and overlapping each other's activities, appears in the state administration. There the monitoring is done by special inspection institutions,[13] by the prosecution service, and by the political and economic police. There is a measure of control over the work of leading state and economic officials by the labor unions and other mass organizations, which can report any irregularity they find to a higher authority. Yet another network of control covers the general public on a residential basis. Every house or block has its appointee, who fulfills administrative functions (endorsing various permits, issuing or witnessing certificates) and observes what is happening on his beat.

At first sight this multiplicity of regulation and control seems dysfunctional, in that it can cause contradictory actions to be taken and conflicts to occur within the apparatus. In fact, it is quite understandable for bureaucratic coordination to be organized in this way. The cause is suspicion: no superior has full confidence in his subordinates. A well-known theory on how to build a reliable automaton out of unreliable components was put forward by John von Neumann:[14] the constituent parts must be multiplied. Redundancy within the system allows damage caused by any random unit malfunctioning to be prevented or rectified by another that chances to be functioning properly at that time.

The main direction of influence in the vertical chains is from top to bottom. A superior may issue a command to a subordinate, but not the reverse.[15] That certainly does not mean, however, that there is no influence at all exerted upward. To use the expression in Hirschman's theory,[16] there is "voice." The members of the apparatus at all levels, even the citizens at the very base of the pyramid who hold no functions, can make themselves heard by advancing proposals and criticisms. However, there are tight constraints on these. On no account may they concern the

---

feature of all classical socialist systems is the large part played by the political police in controlling and disciplining all branches of the bureaucracy.

[13]In the Soviet Union it was known for a long period as Worker-Peasant Inspection.

[14]J. v. Neumann (1956). Even the title of his paper points to the idea discussed above: "Probabilistic Logics and the Synthesis of Reliable Organisms from Unreliable Components."

[15]This is the main difference from self-government as a coordination mechanism. There the smaller decision-making body makes decisions binding on all the members (a downward influence). At the same time the member can mandate delegates to support a specific position in committee debate and make consistent representation of the member's position a condition for reelection next time (an upward influence).

[16]In his classic book (1970) A. O. Hirschman contrasts two kinds of feedback signal. If one wants to express the dislike one feels over the operation of the organization one belongs to, one can apply two feedback signals: the exit or the voice, that is, one exercises criticism, protests, and suggests changes.

basic principles of the system, the main political line of the party, or the overall economic policy expressed in economic plans. As for criticism of particular individuals, the danger of making it is proportionate to the height of the subject in the hierarchy and the depth of the subject's tolerance threshold. The situation varies by country and period, but one can say in general that criticism from below may be heard, although its voice is usually very feeble: the volume of discontent would have to exceed a critical lower limit to become audible or influential at all.

Staying with Hirschman's terminology for the moment, this ties in closely with the absence of "exit." An exit—opting out—is denied several times over to citizens under the classical socialist system. They cannot quit their jobs without leave from the firm or institution employing them [→10.4]. Should they receive permission to change jobs, they cannot in fact change employers, because with insignificant exceptions there is ultimately one employer: the state. It is extremely difficult to change one's place of residence, since this is impeded by administrative restrictions and the housing shortage. Party members cannot resign from membership; so demonstrative a step could easily jeopardize the peace of their existence, possibly their liberty, and in an extreme wave of terror their lives as well. But it is risky to resign even from the labor union, the youth movement, or any other mass or professional organization. The officials of the party, state, and mass organizations cannot resign to express disagreement.[17] Nor can the ultimate form of exit, emigration, be used: even an application would be dangerous. Of course, the preclusion, difficulty, or danger of every method of exit affects the voice, which is necessarily silenced or rendered far more timid. Thus the system denies itself the major factors of feedback from bottom to top.

6.4 Market Coordination

To show the place occupied by market coordination under the classical socialist system one needs to look at the entire flow of products and

---

[17]Max Weber [1925] (1978, chaps. 3, 11) described the kind of bureaucracy based on a parliamentary political structure and private enterprise. In that kind of bureaucracy the bureaucrats are personally free and only subordinate to a higher authority as far as their impersonal, official duty is concerned. Posts in the bureaucracy are filled under free contract, and the criterion for choosing the members is professional competence.

None of these features fits the bureaucracy under classical socialism. There is no free contract between the apparatus and its members that the official could terminate at any time of his or her own accord. If a post is assigned by the powers that be, it must be accepted. The main selection criteria are political reliability and loyalty to the superior, not professional competence. The control by higher institutions extends to every aspect of the lives of those on a lower rung.

TABLE 6.1

Input-Output Flow Between Units of the Social Sectors:
The Role of Bureaucratic and Market Coordination

Supplying Sector	*Consuming Sector*				
	1 State-owned Firms	*2 Cooperatives*	*3 Formal Private Sector*	*4 Informal Private Sector*	*5 Households as Buyers of Consumption Goods and Services*
1. State-owned firms	B	B	B + M	0	B + M
2. Cooperatives	B	B	B + M	0	B + M
3. Formal private sector	0	0	M (with intervention of B)	M	M (with intervention of B)
4. Informal private sector	0	0	M	M	M
5. Households as sellers of labor	B + M	B + M	0	M	—
6. Allocation of investment resources	B	B	0	0	—

Note: The meanings of the symbols are as follows: B = bureaucratic coordination, M = market coordination, 0 = no transaction in this entry.

resources. Table 6.1 is a schematic input-output table arranged according to social sectors. The rows represent the suppliers of goods and resources (in the case of market relations the sellers) and the columns the consumers of these goods (in the case of market relations the buyers). The table is concerned only with the division of labor between two kinds of mechanism, bureaucratic and market coordination, since that is the comparison from which the role of market coordination emerges clearly.[18] The table is designed to be comprehensive. It also mentions, at least briefly, the spheres of input-output flows dealt with in more detail later in the book.[19]

[18]Later sections of this chapter will return to the entries in table 6.1 in which other mechanisms play a part as well.

[19]There is one exception to this. Here there has not been any discussion yet of foreign trade [→14]. So the flow of goods between the country in question and other countries, namely, imports and exports, is not shown in table 6.1.

Entry 1.1 represents flows between state-owned firms.[20] This is ruled basically by the mechanism of bureaucratic coordination. The details will be discussed in the following chapter.[21]

Bureaucratic management of goods and materials is complemented by a few vestigial forms of market relations. If a firm is short of a means of production (material, semifinished product, component) it seeks to obtain, it will try bribing the representative of the supplier firm with favors, gifts, or even money. This effort replaces, in a distorted form, what would be in the case of market relations an offer of a higher price, except that the few officials involved in the transaction receive the extra, instead of the owner of the supplier firm. Factories often train a few staff expressly for dealings of this kind, who try to speed the flow of products toward the firm through aggressive intervention or corruption.[22]

The cooperatives differ little from the state-owned firms [→5.5]. In terms of the present subject the difference is immaterial. What has been said of entry 1.1 applies to entries 1.2, 2.1, and 2.2 as well, that is, to the flows between state-owned firms and cooperatives and among cooperatives themselves.

Where a formal private sector (craftsmen and retailers with a permit from the authorities and household farming) exists at all, those working in it are allowed to buy means of production from state-owned firms and cooperatives, within bureaucratic limits. Often they must pay a market price higher than the official price, or they are able to obtain the required inputs only through bribery. Accordingly, a combination of bureaucratic and market coordination applies in entries 1.3 and 2.3. With rare exceptions they are not allowed to sell their products to the state or cooperative sectors, as the zeros in entries 3.1 and 3.2 indicate.

Market coordination operates basically in entries 3.3, 3.4, and 3.5, that is, within the formal private sector, and in this sector's activities supplied to the informal private and household sectors. But except in entry 3.4, pure market coordination still does not apply, as official intervention is common, particularly in prices. This influence of bureaucratic coordination is referred to in the table in parentheses.

True market coordination applies within the informal private sector, and in sales by this sector to households and the formal private sector

---

[20]Sector 1 includes the state-owned firms under central government control and those controlled by regional bodies. For brevity's sake, no separate line or column has been given to the nonfirm, "budgetary institution" sector [→5.4]. What has been said about the state-owned firms applies to that sector as well.

[21]The exchange between state-owned firms is governed basically by bureaucratic coordination even when it takes place nominally as a purchase and sale accompanied by an account in money terms. This aspect will be dealt with in the next two chapters.

[22]These "expediters" are known as *tolkachi* in Russian economic slang.

(entries 4.3, 4.4, and 4.5). The informal private sector cannot supply the publicly owned sectors.

In entries 1.5 and 2.5 (where the seller is a state-owned firm or a cooperative and the buyer a household), a peculiar combination of bureaucratic and market coordination appears. For long periods in several countries, a part of the flows is governed by administrative allocation or a rationing system. The other part goes through conventional commercial channels, but, again, it is subject to a variety of bureaucratic influences, in the distribution of products among points of sale and in the setting of prices. Meanwhile households, as the buyers of consumption goods and services, behave like participants in a market transaction [→8.7, 12.6].

Entries 5.1 and 5.2 represent the sphere in which households are the sellers of labor and state-owned firms and cooperatives the buyers of labor. Once again, a peculiar combination of bureaucratic and market coordination applies [→10].

In general, the officially permitted, formal private sector is not allowed to employ outside labor. Where this is permitted, strict, very low upper limits are set. However, the table ignores this possibility (which is why entry 5.3 is marked zero).

It may be that a semilegal or illegal operator in the informal private sector will make use of outside labor (entry 5.4). Where this happens, market coordination applies.

Market coordination has at least a partial role in the allocation of labor, but investment resources ("capital") are allocated in the state and cooperative sectors through bureaucratic coordination (entries 6.1 and 6.2) [→9.2]. This sphere of allocation will also be considered in a later chapter. By and large, the formal and informal private sectors can make use only of capital accumulated out of personal savings. With insignificant exceptions, no private businessman can obtain either a loan or an outside source of finance, which is why there are zeros in entries 6.3 and 6.4.

From this survey it is clear that bureaucratic public property "attracts" bureaucratic coordination while private property and private activity "attracts" market coordination. This affinity between particular property forms and particular types of coordination is worth noting [→15.2, 19.4].

6.5 Self-Governing Coordination

Nominally, the mechanism of self-governing coordination exists in numerous spheres of the classical socialist system.

In politics the principle of "democratic centralism," laid down in the rules of the Communist party, covers the basic ideas of self-governing coordination [→3.1]. This principle provides the operating basis for all mass organizations, interest-representing and professional alliances, and social associations.

The power of the state is built upon self-governing principles. The members of all legislative bodies, from the lowliest district or communal council to the supreme parliament, are elected. The administration of state is subordinate at every level to the elected bodies. The major economic regulations, including the national plans, are invested by parliament with the force of law. So formally it seems as if the voters who have elected the members of parliament are governing themselves with these regulations.

Of the organizations of the economy, the cooperatives count nominally as institutions of a self-governing nature, whose running is performed by an elected leadership.

Earlier chapters have pointed out that the actual coordination in all these fields is provided by the bureaucratic mechanism [→3.1–3.3, 5.5]. The key question in this respect is the dependence of the elected bodies' members. Who, in fact, do they depend upon: those who voted them in, or those higher in the bureaucratic hierarchy who pick them out before the election, put pressure on the voters, and confirm them in their positions after the election? The answer can be provided by direct observation. The former is the case if there is generally a choice between more than one candidate; if candidates canvass for support; if the candidates of those in power can be voted out, others can be elected instead, and the voters make regular use of this opportunity; and if in practice the voters recall elected leaders from time to time out of dissatisfaction with their work. The latter is the case if it is exclusively the candidate of those in power who can be elected and the official candidate invariably is elected in practice; if opposing candidates are forbidden to canvass the voters' support; and if a higher body dismisses an elected leader when it is dissatisfied with him or her.

Experience leaves no shadow of doubt that in practice the latter is the case under the classical system. This was not yet true under the revolutionary-transitional system, when the self-governing mechanism applied in many areas, albeit not universally or unfailingly. The revolutionaries really did elect representatives to the bodies of the revolutionary political movements. In many places and for some time after the revolution had been won, the bodies of the new state power were chosen in real elections, often amid violent political struggles between various political movements and factions. This, however, proved to be temporary. A society has made the transition to the classical system once politics have become bureaucratized, elections have become nominal, and bureaucratic regulation has replaced genuine self-government. In this situation the "politician" and the "bureaucrat," as two separate roles, careers, and types of personality, become one. Those pursuing a professional political career are members of the bureaucracy; all bureaucratic activity is "politically activated."

Under the transitional system, voluntary cooperatives appeared, enjoying more or less real self-government. But these were transformed by forcible, mass collectivization and administrative establishment of rural and urban cooperatives into bureaucratically managed organizations very like state-owned firms.

Traces remain of the self-governing mechanism under the classical system. The role of "voice" and the emergence of proposals and criticisms from below [→6.3] adds up to the survival of some elements of the self-governing mechanism. But these elements are feeble, as stated earlier. The power structure of the classical system is fundamentally incompatible with the mechanism of self-government.

6.6 Ethical Coordination

This mechanism appears in a great many different forms. Our survey has been grouped according to the following principle: what motivates the donor?

The first group of motives is connected with political conviction: many are prepared to undertake deeds of selfless sacrifice for the party, the factory, and the country. Millions are ready to do unpaid voluntary work[23] in the factory or their part of town under the transitional system that follows the revolution. Townsfolk and students go to villages to help with the harvest. Doctors treat patients gratis, and actors perform before workers and peasants. These phenomena too are among the revolutionary-heroic features of the period.

This willingness later dies down [→2.4].[24] Where unpaid labor is done under the classical system, the cause is more often pressure than honest political enthusiasm.

What survives to a greater extent is sacrifice on behalf of a smaller community: voluntary work to provide a local kindergarten, school, or hospital, or to rehabilitate a playground.

---

[23]In the Soviet Union such voluntary, unpaid work was known as a "communist Saturday." Work of a similar kind was done with similar enthusiasm in China and other socialist countries.

[24]Times of war, when all peoples are prepared to make far greater sacrifices for their native land than they are in times of peace, constitute an exception to this general rule.

This leads to another group of motives: a high proportion of people are prepared to act selflessly or make financial sacrifices only because they are generous, concerned, and attentive to others. This kind of voluntary adaptation to others' needs, attentive gestures, and unselfish assistance often compensates for, or at least makes tolerable, the hardships caused by the frictions of rigid bureaucratic coordination. Its range of influence cannot be measured statistically, of course, but it plays nonetheless an extremely important part at work, in transport, when shopping, in the place of residence, and in all aspects of daily life. The significance of these spontaneous actions and gifts is all the more worth emphasizing because "charity" is looked down upon in the official ideology as something compromised under capitalism, since it sought to heal the wounds inflicted by exploitation with mere social remedies. Official moral teaching attaches no importance to petty, personal "good deeds." Instead, the emphasis is on respect for great sacrifices made for great causes.

It is worth mentioning at this point deeds based on mutual assistance and favors, even though they are not "pure" altruism. The manager of one firm will help the manager of another by supplying a component, for example, hoping that he can expect similar support next time. Friends will help build somebody's house, each one knowing he can count on similar assistance when he needs it. This reciprocity mechanism helps to fill the gap left by the frictions of bureaucratic coordination and the narrow scope left to the market mechanism.

6.7 Family Coordination

The family as a coordination mechanism proves to be the most robust of all. It survives the dramatic changes in the political and economic system to play a fundamental part in coordinating human lives and activities under socialism, just as it does under the presocialist systems.

There is ambivalence in the attitude of the official ideology and practical social, demographic, and economic policy toward the role of the family. On the one hand, its importance is emphasized. A great many opinions tending toward abolition of the traditional family forms became current in the revolutionary-transitional period. These are cast off under the classical system, where the dominant position is a conservative one that places many more moral and legal constraints on the family than one actually finds in the capitalist world of today. The household is organized largely on the basis of the family, to which the upbringing of children and organization of consumption are left to a great extent. (The latter is a very difficult task under the conditions of a shortage economy [→11, 12].)

On the other hand, strong tendencies toward constricting the role of the family and undermining its functional basis in certain important areas appear under the system. All the tendencies to be mentioned appear also under other, nonsocialist systems, in the developing countries following the capitalist road and in the industrially developed capitalist world. What distinguishes classical socialism here is the intensity, and in many respects the extreme force, of these tendencies.

1. A few exceptions notwithstanding, the socialist system appears in societies that have fallen behind in industrial development [→2.3]. So the family undertaking has played a large part before the revolution both in the villages and in the cities. The revolutionary-transitional system is accompanied by a land reform that raises the share of family undertakings in the economy even further. Later on, the establishment of the classical system involves an almost total elimination of the family undertaking.

From then on production is divorced from the family, apart from some vestigial forms (the narrow formal private sector and the broader but wholly or partly illegal informal private sector).

2. Forced growth [→9.5, 10.1] raises the demand for labor very rapidly, almost by leaps and bounds. Many men from rural areas who cannot find work in the villages are drawn by the rapid industrialization to industrial communities, and many are unable to bring their families with them. Most important of all, the employment of women increases extremely rapidly. Women are literally compelled by the family's financial circumstances to take employment. On the one hand, this change does help to give women more equal rights: the horizons and economic independence of women who go to work increase. On the other, it places very heavy burdens on women's shoulders: they still have to perform most or all of a housewife's and mother's traditional tasks, to which the work at her job is additional. As a result, new pressures are placed on family life, and the contribution of women to activities within the family inevitably falls.[25]

3. Another trend is closely connected with the previous one: a large number of the family's traditional activities are taken over by institutions (and to a lesser extent firms) under bureaucratic control. To a growing extent it is "large organizations" rather than the close family community that concern themselves with people from the cradle to the grave: the

---

[25]The breakdown of the existential bases of the traditional family (the elimination of family undertakings, the swift increase in the employment of women) contributes greatly to a rapid rise in the divorce rate.

day nursery, the kindergarten, the school summer camp, the hospital, and the old people's home.[26] A considerable proportion of the family's free time is spent not together but on organized activities tailored to age group and occupation, on outings and theater performances stipulated by the workplace, and on firm or office vacations. Some of the meals are transferred to the workplace canteen.[27] If the family standard of living rises, the next step is not to buy a private automobile as it would be in a household at a similar standard under the capitalist system; the purchase of private cars is restricted, and public transportation expands instead. Owner-occupied family houses at most remain customary in villages. In the towns people live in large state- or cooperatively owned apartment blocks. The vast majority of the new apartments are provided in housing developments made up of uniform tenement blocks. All these things together lead to a marked restriction of "private life," the sphere of activities coordinated by the family, and to an equally marked expansion of its opposite, the sphere of "collectivized," "institutionalized," "organized" activities coordinated bureaucratically.[28]

6.8   Spontaneous and Artificial Changes

Bureaucratic coordination already existed before the advent of the socialist system. During the course of history, partial bureaucracies, such as the armed forces, central management of the railroads, or protection against epidemics, were brought into being by state measures. Operation of the market at home and in foreign trade was assisted by central legislation; the legal compulsion to abide by private contracts was particularly important in this respect. There is central legislation on the legal aspects of the family community. It is central legislation again that provides legal guarantees for the activity of self-governing organizations. Finally and most important, the self-limitation of central state power is laid down in basic laws and constitutions.

But however great the role of the central power of the state, before the establishment of the socialist system it was *not* basically central de-

---

[26]In fact, the official ideology of the system promises a much greater degree and extent of state provision in this respect [→4.3] than it is capable of providing. These partly unkept promises—chronic shortages of day-nursery and kindergarten facilities, hospital beds, and places in old people's homes—cause a wide variety of tensions.

[27]The Chinese commune went even further in collectivizing consumption [→5.5].

[28]Several passages in the rest of the book deal with family property and the economic role of the family, including that of women. These analyses clearly imply an examination of family coordination as well, even when the term "coordination" does not appear explicitly in the text.

crees that decided what proportion of the coordination of society's activities would go to each main type; these proportions arose spontaneously during the course of history. They might be slowed down or speeded up by particular central measures of the state, but the measures did not decide the proportions.

It is unique in history for a central power to have intervened from above artificially by means of legal regulations in the development of society to decide that a particular main type, market coordination, should vanish, or at least be confined to insignificant positions, and replaced by centralized bureaucratic coordination. This was a fundamental change that did not occur spontaneously.[29] It was carried through by the central decisions of power, and by fire and the sword. It was then followed by numerous concomitants that arose spontaneously without any central decision expressly being taken: the atrophy of self-governing forms, the dwindling of enthusiasm for voluntary work for the community, and relegation of family and community life to a subordinate role. And there was another concomitant: a spontaneous self-generation, self-propagation, and excessive expansion of bureaucratic mechanisms that went beyond the expectations even of those who initiated and directed the epoch-making changes.[30]

[29]These two different paths of capitalist and socialist development are clear examples of the pair of opposites: "constructivist" and "evolutionary" development, in other words, the contrast between development of a man-made and a spontaneous order. These concepts were coined by F. A. Hayek. See F. A. Hayek (1960, 1973, chap. 1).

[30]Lenin [1917] (1969a, p. 473) wrote: "All citizens are transformed into hired employees of the state, which consists of the armed workers. All citizens become employees and workers of a single country-wide state 'syndicate.'"

Compare this to his exasperation in the circular letter of December 1921 to the heads of all central Soviet agencies: "It is necessary that an end should be put once and for all to the scandalous red tape . . . in your agency. My suggestion is that you pull yourself together at once. To confine yourself to formal replies and dispatches to other agencies also means breeding red tape and wasting paper." V. I. Lenin [1912] (1970, p. 423).

7

Planning and Direct Bureaucratic Control

THE LAST chapter concerned the division of labor under the classical socialist system between the main mechanisms of coordination. In chapters 7 and 8 the focus will be on the most important of these, bureaucratic coordination. Chapter 7 reviews this problem sphere comprehensively, while chapter 8 highlights the issues relating to prices and money.

7.1 The Precursors of Socialism on the Subject of Planning

The intellectual forerunners of the socialist system saw planning as one of socialism's great advantages. Marx put forward very emphatically the following line of argument:[1]

Capitalism produces a high degree of organization within the firm, but anarchy prevails in the market connecting the firms. This is inevitable as long as capitalist ownership remains. Socialism (by eliminating both private ownership of the means of production and the anarchy of the market) allows organization on a national economic scale. Marx reckoned that central allocation of social labor would be a very simple task. The fact that the social relations between people, and along with them the relation of people to products, would no longer be obscured by the market's "commodity fetishism" would make the task of allocation transparent and easy to survey. Nor did it seem particularly hard to determine people's needs and demands.

Neither the writings of Marx nor of his followers before 1917 make any mention of the likely difficulties of planning on a national economic scale or, for instance, of the matter of collecting and processing the information needed for planning. These thinkers deal frequently with the

---

[1]Marx, in *The Civil War in France* [1871] (1940), considers the nature of the future communist system to be that "united cooperative societies are to regulate national production upon a common plan; thus taking it under their own control, and putting an end to the constant anarchy and periodical convulsions which are the fatality of capitalist production" (p. 61). In *Anti-Dühring* [1878] (1975), Engels says that "with the taking over by society of the productive forces, the social character of the means of production and of the products will be utilized by the producers with a perfect understanding" (p. 266), and also, "In making itself the master of all the means of production to use them in accordance with a social plan, society puts an end to the former subjection of men to their own means of production" (p. 279).

question of what kind of incentive will be needed in general to make people prepared to work, but the problem of the planners and plan-implementing apparatus needing additional encouragement to do their special tasks is not raised.

I shall return to the subject of how experience under the classical system compares with the expectations of the precursors of socialism at the end of the chapter.

7.2   Initial Approach: Elaboration of the Plan

This section makes an initial approach to the subject of drawing up the plan, and section 7.3 to the question of how it is implemented. The two sections describe how these processes are conducted according to official regulations. The actual "rules of the game" together with the interests, motives, and conflicts of the participants are the subject of sections 7.4–7.6.[2]

It is expedient to begin the description with planning on a national economic scale. In most countries the plan is prepared by the most powerful bureaucratic agency, the national planning office, endorsed by the Central Committee on the party's behalf and the government on the state's, and then enacted by parliament.

In terms of the time-span of a plan, there are short-term, annual plans, and medium-term, usually five-year plans.[3] Of these the annual plan is the real operational tool for running the economy. The five-year plan tends more to be a statement of economic-policy intent, although the investment program it includes has a practical influence on how the investment process develops. In what follows, attention is centered on the annual plan, and where no qualification is stated, "plan" always means annual plan.

The national economic plan covers every aspect of activity in the economy.[4] Discussion will be confined to planning of the productive sphere. For reasons of space, planning of the so-called nonproductive sphere (i.e., the service branches) will not be covered.

[2]A concise description of how Soviet planning and management worked before Gorbachev can be found in E. A. Hewett (1988, chap. 4). H. Harding (1981) described the Chinese prereform planning and management.

[3]In certain countries and periods, the most important role has been played by quarterly plans. On certain occasions a few countries have also worked out long-term plans with a time-span of fifteen to twenty years. In most cases these have covered a part, not the whole, of the economy (e.g., the first Soviet electrification plan).

[4]The Soviet national economic plan used to have sixty thousand separate headings. A. G. Aganbegian (1989, p. 91).

The first chapter[5] of the plan deals with production. Aggregate indicators (e.g., figures for gross production value) prescribe a total production volume on a national economic scale and the distribution of this among the main sectors of the economy (industry, agriculture, transport, etc.). Apart from that, there are production figures for the most important so-called *priority products,* of which there may be hundreds or even thousands. Quantities for these products in the planning documents are given in physical units wherever possible. Only where this cannot be done are they prescribed in aggregate value terms.

The second chapter concerns the use to which products are put. The prescriptions primarily concern the distribution of materials and semifinished and finished products for the various spheres of use, which receive quotas for their various inputs. A quota is an upper limit. In this sense planning itself includes a "rationing" mechanism as well: it hands out "vouchers" or "coupons" without which a user (for instance, the sum of the firms under a particular ministry) will not gain access to an input even if it has the necessary purchasing power.

To allocate the priority products, *balances* (material, semiproduct, and product balances) are prepared.[6] One side of the balance consists of the sources (production, imports, reduction of stocks) and the other the uses (production use, exports, consumption by the population, increase of stocks). Enormous importance is attached in the planning methodology of the classical system to preparing the balances; their equilibration is considered one of the main criteria for judging whether the plan is consistent. The balances are agreed upon by a process of inching forward at repeated negotiations between the leading planners of the producers and the users, a procedure known as the "balance method" of planning.[7]

The third chapter covers labor: manpower quotas and wage funds are distributed among the various spheres; the main figures for any changes in nominal wages are laid down.

The fourth chapter is about investments. Aggregate investment quotas are broken down, and separate quotas are set for utilization of construction capacity and for imports of capital goods. This part of the plan

---

[5]The chapters are numbered merely to make the subject easier to survey. In fact, the way the actual plan documents are divided by subjects may vary from country to country and period to period.

[6]In the pre-Gorbachev period of Soviet planning two thousand balances were being prepared centrally at the State Planning Office (Gosplan), and several tens of thousands more at the State Material Supply Agency (Gosnab) and at the ministries. See E. A. Hewett (1988, pp. 125–26).

[7]Over the decades numerous experiments have been conducted in the Soviet Union and Eastern Europe, using mathematical models to help prepare the balances [→17.4].

additionally covers what are called high-priority investment projects, that is, the projects considered the most important.

The fifth chapter contains the targets for technical development: the new technologies for introduction, the fields in which to employ them, and the new products whose manufacture should be launched.

The sixth chapter, on foreign trade and international economic relations, sets the import quotas needed to equilibrate the balances and the export targets [→14.2].

The seventh and final chapter addresses financial affairs. It embraces the main entries in the state budget, the main targets for the banking system, and perhaps the decisions on pricing policy [→8.5].

If the plan were to decide every detail for every firm and institution in every field mentioned, several million target figures would be required. The physical impossibility of working out centrally such a number of planning figures is self-evident. So a practice of *plan disaggregation* evolves. Here an important practical principle is applied: the plan is disaggregated according to *addressees*. When the aggregate housing construction target is being broken down, for instance, it is stated how many dwellings should be built by the construction ministry, how many by the ministry of heavy industry, how many by the ministry of light industry, and so on. In this example the ministries are the "addressees." So each target figure is more than an "intangible" entry in the sectoral breakdown made by the statistical office. Each inanimate figure in the plan is matched by a live bureaucratic institution with a responsible (and accountable) head.

Disaggregation takes place on the same number of levels as exist in the hierarchy of national economic control. Taking the case of a hierarchy with four levels, first the planning office breaks down the national economic plan for the ministries. Then each ministry breaks it down for its own directorates (each directorate controlling several firms in the same sector or subsector), and finally, the directorate disaggregates its own plan for the firms belonging to it. The resulting compulsory annual plan for each larger firm contains several thousand figures.

Plan disaggregation is a basically downward flow of information. The plan a lower level receives from a higher is a *command,* not a recommendation.[8] The subordinate institution is obliged to fulfill the planning directive.

There is also a flow in the opposite direction: before the plan is finalized, the subordinate institution makes proposals and comments on the initial drafts. If necessary it can ask for the target to be amended during

---

[8]Stalin said of planning: "Our plans are not forecast-plans, not guess-work plans, but directive plans." J. V. Stalin [1927] (1954, p. 335).

the implementation of the plan. Finally, it must report on the implementation of the plan.

Apart from the vertical flow of information there is a horizontal one. Institutions on the same level coordinate matters with one another during the planning: for instance, discussion on the production and distribution of particular products will take place between representatives of the producer and user ministries, or, on a lower level, between those of the producer and user directorates. As a rule such discussion is held under the direction of the institution superior to the negotiating partners.

To sum up, one can state that elaboration of the plan is a monumental piece of bureaucratic coordination aimed at prior reconciliation of the processes of the economy. Thousands upon thousands of functionaries in the party apparatus, the state administration, the firm and cooperative managements, and the mass organizations negotiate, calculate, renegotiate, and recalculate before the millions of planning commands finally emerge at all levels.

7.3   Initial Approach: Plan Implementation and Management

The starting point for discussing implementation of the plan is the remark in the previous section: implementation is compulsory. This principle is so important that some authors have referred to it as the most characteristic feature of the system by attaching such names to the system as "directive planning," "imperative planning," or "command economy."

Elaboration of the plan devolves primarily on a specialized apparatus: the national planning office and the planning departments of ministries, directorates, firms, and institutions. But this apparatus is bound up with the organizations of management, particularly because the responsible leader at every level (the minister, head of the directorate, or director of the firm) is responsible personally for each phase in the work on the plan, from preliminary preparations through implementation to the report on its implementation. The specialized planning apparatus takes active part in formal and informal modification of the plan and in management in general.

The remainder of this chapter deals with the management of the public (state-owned and cooperative) sectors.[9] The decision-making problems that arise during implementation of the plan are surveyed briefly.

[9]The effects of bureaucratic control on the private sector will be covered later [→19.5]. For reasons of space it is not possible to include bureaucratic control of state institutions of a nonfirm nature (budgetary institutions), but its major features are analogous to those of the regulation of state-owned firms.

1. *Establishment of a firm*. In an economy based on private property the question of "entry" is decided within the framework of market competition. New firms are set up wherever entrepreneurs think it worthwhile. Under the classical socialist system the decision is the bureaucracy's.

2. *Liquidation of a firm*. The situation is similar. In a capitalist economy "exit" depends on competition; a firm that becomes permanently insolvent goes bust. The owners of firms decide whether to merge them or break them down, within the limits laid down by antitrust legislation. Under the classical socialist system it is the bureaucracy that decides whether to liquidate, break up, or merge firms.

Points 1 and 2 can be summed up in the following way: the "life or death" of a firm as a collective organization or organism is determined not by the "natural selection" of market competition but by the bureaucracy. There is a complete absence of what Schumpeter considered the most important driving force behind healthy economic development: the appearance of entrepreneurs who introduce new products or new technologies, establish new organizations, and conquer new markets, while obsolete production and ossified organizations are squeezed out. In other words, the system leaves no room for what Schumpeter called the revolutionary effect of "creative destruction."[10]

3. *Appointment, promotion, and dismissal of leaders*. The point has been made in chapter 3, but is worth repeating in the account of management for the sake of completeness: the selection of leaders is wholly in the hands of the bureaucracy.

The following spheres of decision making and control parallel the plan chapters discussed in the previous section. One might say management endeavors to ensure implementation of each chapter of the plan, and also to identify the tasks that even the highly punctilious plan cannot detail in advance.

4. *Management of production*. The constraints begin with the founder (normally the relevant ministry) defining the "profile" of the new firm, that is, its permitted (and compulsory) sphere of activities. The firm has no right to make products "alien" to its profile.

The most important constraint is the annual production plan, which lays down not just the overall output volume to be reached but annual production amounts for priority products (of which a firm with a wide range of products could have several hundred).

Moreover, the superior organization frequently intervenes directly in the production process, modifying the original program, prescribing new

---

[10]See J. A. Schumpeter [1912] (1968).

tasks and deleting others, pressing particularly for certain products to be made, and so on.

5. *Allocation of products and materials.* Mention was made in the discussion on planning of the allocation of priority materials and semi-finished and finished products, and in that connection of product balances. Disaggregation of these provides the overall frames for allocation of products and materials, but management goes into much finer detail. At this point it becomes especially plain that the bureaucracy takes the place of the market mechanism. For a great many products the bureaucracy assigns the user to a certain producer and lays down how much of a particular product the former is obliged to provide and the latter to receive. Certain producer (production or trading) firms are given a legal sphere of authority, with rights to decide which firm or budgetary institution gets "vouchers" for a certain product and who is left out.

Here again the higher authorities frequently intervene. They may alter the allocation prescribed in the plan or by lower-level organizations. If they consider a certain transaction particularly urgent, they can order deliveries to be diverted.

6. *Allocation of labor.* Once again, the overall constraints are provided by the plan, but management intervenes in the details and may even modify the plan itself. Workers can be transferred from one firm to another; firms can be compelled to increase or reduce their workforce. Wage rates are prescribed in minute detail trade by trade, according to levels of qualification. Strict limits are placed on the total wage bill.

7. *Regulation of the investment process.* This is mentioned here merely for the sake of completeness [→9.2].

8. *Technical development.* Normally, the tasks are merely outlined in the plan. A few priority areas of technical development are kept in the hands of the higher authorities: decisions on mechanization of certain processes, installation of new automated production facilities, and introduction of certain new products.

9. *Foreign trade and international economic relations.* These processes are retained in the hands of the higher authorities in a number of ways, among them import licensing and specific export directives, and tight control of the foreign exchange aspect of foreign trade [→14.2].

10. *Price setting* and 11. *Financial regulation.* These two are mentioned also only for the sake of completeness [→8].

The chief method used by the higher authority to control the lower in all the decision-making and management spheres listed is the command. Although coaxing, argument, and persuasion are used, and so are bonuses and penalties, their purpose is to compel subordinates to carry out the command. The chief executive's bonus depends on implementation of the plans and other operative commands of the higher authorities.

The penalties too, which range from a rebuke or dismissal to imprisonment or execution for "sabotage," are imposed for infringement of plan discipline and failure to implement other operative commands.[11] Thus bonuses and penalties are not directly linked with performance, but clearly intended to stiffen discipline and obedience to superiors.

The situation falls far short of the kind of partial autonomy in which the subordinate unit would receive a compulsory plan assignment from the superior unit and be left to implement it until it was time to report and receive the next plan. Apart from the plan, and if need be in contradiction to it, the superior unit intervenes daily in every detail of the subordinate's activities. Western writings often call the socialist economy the "centrally planned economy."[12] This term is one-sided, though the part played by central planning is great. The expression "centrally managed economy" is more apt because it better emphasizes the role of centralized bureaucratic coordination and control. Planning is only one of the means used in this form of coordination, although an extremely important one.

In this book the coordination mechanism described in sections 7.2 and 7.3 and typical of the classical socialist system is referred to as *direct bureaucratic control* of the economy.[13] This embraces the elaboration of plans with the force of commands and the administrative compulsion to implement them, the management based on the commands, and the practice of the superior organization intervening regularly in every detail of the production and allocation processes and day-to-day running of the subordinate organization.[14]

This mechanism of coordination is viable. The economy carries out its basic functions: it produces, allocates, and supplies the consumers. The plans are fulfilled by and large, if not precisely. The tasks those running the system consider of primary importance are particularly likely to be accomplished. This is a performance unmatched in the history of the

---

[11]I. T. Berend (1979) describes the 1959 decree introduced in Hungary to defend the planned economy under penal law. Berend writes that "a sentence of two years' imprisonment was prescribed for a substantial departure from a partial plan, if it was made 'without a compelling reason.' For a crime 'involving serious danger or damage to the national economic plan or any detailed plan,' a sentence of up to five years could be imposed" (p. 117).

[12]The term is recommended by E. Zaleski (1980).

[13]The expression belongs to the vocabulary of the Hungarian reform. The term "direct control" first appeared in Hungarian in writings of K. Szabó (1967), T. Nagy (1966), and L. Antal (1985), usually contrasted with the indirect control to be applied under the reformed mechanism.

[14]Among the pioneering studies on socialist planning and direct bureaucratic control, see J. Berliner (1957), D. Granick (1954), J. Kornai [1957] (1959), and J. M. Montias (1962).

world: in the field being examined (the sector in public ownership), the bureaucratic mechanism coordinates the activities and integrates the whole system while cutting the market mechanism out almost completely.

One must add, however, that direct bureaucratic control is inefficient in many respects. It is extremely rigid; there are long delays and serious losses before it adapts to changes in needs, technology, the domestic political situation, or the outside world. It provides no incentives for initiative, entrepreneurial spirit, or innovation.

7.4   The Motivation of Leaders in the Economic Bureaucracy

The mechanism of direct bureaucratic control would work well if perfect information on the past were available, if prediction of the future were precise, and if every command were faultless and carried out with impeccable accuracy. In real life the information is imperfect and imprecise, and there are a great many uncertainties about predicting the future. Moreover, both commanders and those who obey the commands are living, fallible people, not parts of a clockwork machine. The problems with the mechanism described in sections 7.2 and 7.3 mainly arise out of the motivations and conflicts of those taking part in it, and from the distortions in the process of collecting and utilizing information.

What motivations encourage an official in the bureaucracy to act? In what follows, attention will focus on the leaders, from the minister and the department head at the party center to the business director and party secretary in a factory, in other words, on those with staff directly subordinate to them.[15]

The motivations of the firm's management[16] and of other groups in the bureaucracy will not be treated separately. The object is to identify

[15]Space does not permit consideration of the staff member's motivation. It resembles the leader's in many respects but is not entirely the same.

[16]Under the capitalist system the unit possessed by the same owner (or group of owners) is clearly distinguished from the units possessed by other owners. If the word "firm" is reserved for this kind of unit (as it is in this book when capitalism is referred to), it is worth discussing separately the motivation of the top business executives whom the owners employ. Their motivation differs in important respects from the motivation of other leading officials operating under capitalism.

By contrast, a collection of production units is termed a "firm" according to arbitrary legal formulas under the classical socialist system. It is not distinguished from other "firms" by the above criterion (a specific group of owners). As the remainder of this chapter is intended to show, the behavior of leaders of firms resembles the behavior of the branch director superior to them; the relation of the firm's director to the branch director resembles the latter's relation to the minister, and so on.

the general inducements applying to all leaders in the economic bureaucracy.[17]

It is wise to avoid oversimplifying the account of the motivation or picking a single objective arbitrarily.[18] Instead, the sum total of the motives will be discussed.[19]

1. *Political and moral conviction.* Belief in the party's ideas, agreement with the official ideology, and enthusiasm for the plan's objectives are a major impulse.

2. *Identification with the job.* This acts as an inducement to anyone in a leading position under any system; one would like to do a decent job and is sensible of the "credit of the profession." If an executive of a firm, one at least wants production to run smoothly. If an engineer, one wants up-to-date technology employed and the technological regulations applied. If a chief accountant, one wants the books to be in order.

3. *Power.* Not everyone wants to have power; some have a positive dread of it. But such people do not accept leading positions. A person who becomes a leader is attracted by power. That person is pleased to have people obeying him or her. And once the person has power, he or she wants that power to remain, and indeed to grow.

4. *Prestige.* There is a close correlation in all societies between the rung attained on the ladder and the status attained in society. Other systems have several parallel ladders. This one in practice has only one: a career in the bureaucracy. A seeker of higher prestige must climb higher up this ladder.

5. *Material benefit.* All positive remuneration can be listed here: higher pay, bonuses, benefits in kind, and privileged access to goods and services.

6. *A quiet life.* Leaders want to avoid troubles, hindrances, and conflicts with their superiors, suppliers, and customers.

7. *Fear of punishment.* A mere rebuke from the boss is unpleasant, but punishment can be much graver, as mentioned earlier.

The relative weights these motives receive in society vary from country to country and period to period.[20] Of course, the relative strengths of the

---

[17]The case of the country's paramount leader will be ignored. All other leaders are known to have a superior (or superiors) and subordinates.

[18]Of course, this is no argument against a researcher picking out a specific motive for the purposes of a particular examination, within the frame of a model, to make a problem easier to discuss (assuming, of course, that neglect of the other motives does not jeopardize understanding of the very problem the researcher has undertaken to examine).

[19]A similar list is proposed by J. Berliner (1957). On managerial motivation in East Germany and Romania, see, furthermore, D. Granick (1975, parts 1 and 2).

[20]In China and Cuba, financial incentive played a far smaller part than in the Soviet Union or Eastern Europe during the period of the classical system.

various inducements to various individuals can be spread widely as well. The motives partly reinforce and partly conflict with each other. More will be said about this in the remainder of the chapter.

The official ideology suggests that every functionary should manage the activities entrusted to him or her "like a proprietor." In fact, it is impossible for a truly proprietorial motivation to develop at any level of the bureaucracy. Neither the director of a firm nor his or her superiors can pocket the residual income. They are neither able nor willing to bear full responsibility for their decisions, since they are instructed from above and there is constant interference in the way instructions once given are carried out. It is not worth taking any risk with the unit led— whether a firm, branch, or ministry—that might have negative results (for instance, introduction of a new technology or new product), because neither the unit nor its leader is likely to share in the gain or residual income from positive results. "Proprietorial" motivation cannot develop from persuasion if the actual social position of the official in the bureaucracy is not proprietorial in nature.

The internal incentives motivate leaders when they relate to their own environment. They deal with "partners" of three kinds: superiors (an upward vertical link), subordinates (a downward vertical link), and also their own suppliers and the receivers of their products, namely (in market parlance), with sellers and buyers (horizontal links "backward" and "forward"). None of these relations can be immaterial to leaders, not least because they are interrelated. For instance, either their subordinates or their customers are free to complain to the leaders' superiors if they are dissatisfied. Since they live in a shortage economy [→11, 12], they themselves are dependent on their suppliers. But the strongest of these four directions of dependence (upward, downward, forward, backward) is the first, their own dependence on their superiors.

All the motives listed earlier tie in closely with the fact that the subordinate depends on the superior; primarily the superior's are the eyes in which the subordinate wants to appear in a favorable light. Let me run through the motives again.

The superiors of the middle-level leader convey the "party line" to the leader on a daily basis, thereby influencing the mental process by which he translates his political conviction and enthusiasm into the language of his daily tasks. Those above assure him he is serving the party and socialism precisely by implementing the plan and the other commands. The superior explains in concrete terms the requirements for satisfactory accomplishment of the task and professional respect. His superiors will determine how he climbs the ladder, and thus what his power and prestige will be, what financial bonuses he gets, and what penalties he is given. Most of all it depends on the satisfaction of his superiors how peaceful or turbulent a life he has. The psychological process that translates the eight kinds of motives listed from innermost drives into practical deeds passes inescapably through the filter of his awareness of bureaucratic dependence.

All these circumstances affect directly the daily management of affairs, and perhaps even more important is the long-term effect on the character of each member of the bureaucracy.[21] It is unwise to criticize upward, come out with unusual ideas, or take initiatives. It does not pay to think for oneself or take risks on one's own. A subordinate wanting to do something should "cover himself" in advance by obtaining his superior's prior approval and spreading the risk over as many superior leaders as possible; then he will not come to grief. Since most people have at least some vanity, it is also worth flattering the superior.

These character traits develop not only after the individual has entered the bureaucracy. From the outset those with these attributes gain entry and above all advance quickly in their careers. The character-forming and training effect, and the selection criteria of bureaucratic control, reinforce each other: servility and a heads-down mentality prevail.

7.5 Bargaining and Inner Conflict

A leader is influenced in his actions by mutually contradictory motives; he labors under a conflict of values. A few examples follow.

Suppose a leader feels he has received an incorrect order. Should he carry it out or should he protest, out of party loyalty and professional pride? A leader finds the plan impossible to fulfill. If he accepts it without a word, he and his colleagues lose their bonuses, and could even be accused of sabotage. He wants a quiet life. Opposition could undermine that goal, but refraining from opposition could also cause complications.

Which course a leader chooses in a conflict situation of this kind depends also on one's personality. Much additionally hangs on the extent to which the specific embodiment of the classical system one lives in can tolerate opposition. Whatever the case, one finds typical attitudes and behavior patterns emerging as a frame for these conflicts and to some extent as a way of reducing them.

---

[21]The Soviet author A. Bek (1971, p. 76) wrote a novel called *New Appointment* about an industrial leader under the classical system. He described economic cadres like this: "Their era had left its imprint on them, and had instilled in them the highest soldierly virtue: to execute orders without questioning."

See also G. Kh. Popov (1987a) on this attitude at the root of what Soviet authors call the administrative command system.

One characteristic pattern is *vertical bargaining*. (The attribute "vertical" distinguishes this from the "horizontal" market bargaining that takes place between buyer and seller.)[22] The following example may be traced through. A branch directorate disaggregates for its firms the annual plan for production, materials allocation, and manpower. In this process the branch directorate plays the part of the allocator, and the management of the firm those of the submitter of the proposal and the claimant for the resources. To do so it needs information on the firms' production capacities and the relations between its inputs and outputs. Under ideal conditions the firms pass accurate information to their superiors, who objectively distribute the tasks so that every firm receives a realistic but mobilizing production assignment and saves materials and labor insofar as possible. In fact, this is not how preparation of the plan takes place. The head of the firm has an interest in receiving as easy a production assignment as possible and as plentiful a supply of materials and labor as possible to carry it out. That will result in the least conflict and minimize the risk of losing one's bonus or even incurring a punishment for falling short of the plan. These interests encourage one to distort the information by reporting a smaller capacity and a larger input requirement than one expects in the plan. On seeing the first draft of the plan, one does well to bargain: by complaining and perhaps requesting the party organizations and the higher authorities to intercede, one tries to obtain a looser plan, that is, a relatively smaller output assignment and a relatively larger input allowance. This coincides with the interests of one's immediate colleagues, who encourage the same behavior: a good boss is one who obtains a lighter plan assignment.

The directorate's experienced drafters of plans are aware of this tendency, however. In the initial phase of planning they prescribe a plan 10 or 20 percent tighter than they themselves consider realistic, calculating that the firm will want to beat them down. Another form of defense by the superior organization is to build into the assignment in advance the level the firm attained the previous year. For a firm that raised production from forty units to fifty last year, this year's task must be at least fifty. This is described in the planning jargon of the socialist countries

---

[22]In the classic work of R. A. Dahl and C. E. Lindblom (1953), bargaining is considered a separate basic form of coordination alongside other basic forms (the price mechanism, hierarchy, etc.). Categorizations of this kind (including the one used in this book) inevitably contain arbitrary elements. Nonetheless, it seems more consistent to consider bargaining one of the phenomena accompanying the various main types of coordination, not an independent main type. Vertical coordination involves bargaining between superior and subordinate, and horizontal bargaining between organizations on the same level.

as "planning in" the achieved base level.[23] Western literature[24] uses the expression "ratchet effect," comparing the constant raising of the plan assignment to a cogwheel that moves only forward, not back.

All tactical weapons elicit counterweapons. When a superior organization uses the weapon of "planning in," the countermeasure is to withhold performance. Even a firm capable of greatly overfulfilling its plan would be unwise to do so, because the following year that level would be compulsory. The optimum fulfillment is exactly 100 percent, or perhaps 101 or 102 percent. As a consequence, there is the self-fulfilling plan. The situation outlined here is one of the secrets of plan fulfillment to an accuracy of 1–2 percent.

The branch directorate's behavior in plan bargaining is ambiguous. It has two faces, like the god Janus. In the "downward" direction its interest lies in forcing more output and less input on the firm. Meanwhile, the directorate itself plays the subordinate in the bargaining process with its own superior, the ministry. Its "upward" role is just the same as the firm's in relation to the directorate: it is worth the directorate's while to hold capacity in reserve and conceal it from the higher body; it is worth "whining" for a lower output target and a higher input target. But if that is what it wants to do, its natural allies are its own firms, for theirs are the data and protestations it can cite. That being so, the directorate cannot put any real force into the combat with the bargaining behavior of its subordinate firms. The process leads ultimately to methodical distortion of the upward flow of information toward the underestimation of capability and the withholding of performance.

One can generalize from the example in several directions. It does not apply merely to relations among the three levels mentioned (the link between the branch directorate and the firm, and then the link between the directorate and the ministry). A similar bargaining process develops inevitably in any relation of superiority and subordination in the hierarchy. The example chosen concerned the annual production plan and the input quotas required to fulfill it. Similar bargaining can arise over any decision in which a superior body expects something of and/or grants something to a subordinate one.[25]

---

[23]I first described the process of plan bargaining in my [1957] 1959 book. Western researchers arrived concurrently and independently at similar conclusions. The work of J. Berliner (1957) deserves special emphasis.

[24]See J. Berliner (1957), J. R. Thornton (1978), M. L. Weitzman (1980), M. Keren, J. Miller, and J. R. Thornton (1983), and X. Freixas, R. Guesnerie, and J. Tirole (1985).

[25]For formal models of plan bargaining see J. Hlavácek (1986, 1990) and J. Hlavácek and D. Triska (1987). The authors introduce the term "Homo Se Assecurans" (self-securing) to characterize the producers' behavior under the conditions of a command economy and plan bargaining.

The actual outcome of the bargaining depends largely on the power relations between the superior and the subordinate. The stricter and more "military" the system, the riskier it becomes to bargain—although it is not impossible even then. The superior is likewise reliant on the subordinate,[26] which in addition has the information the superior requires. The subordinate gains a stronger bargaining position if it happens to have a monopoly in production or distribution, or if the supply of important and influential users depends on its activities.

Let us look again at the bargaining process from other points of view. In disaggregating the plan, the directorate makes an allocation decision: it allocates various resources to the producers under its control, who compete with each other for the resources, each striving to obtain for their assignment as much of the resources as possible. The producer's attitude toward these is not one of a buyer who has to pay but one of a recipient of a free grant. There is an absolute advantage in obtaining more, so long as the extra input is not used as grounds for a higher output commitment. They are like the farmers who strove to drive their own stock onto the common,[27] feeling it was not theirs and they had no reason to be frugal with it. This way, one cause of low efficiency in the management of resources and the emergence of excess demand for them has been identified [→11, 12].

This is precisely one of the essential differences between the bureaucracy within a large capitalist firm and the classical socialist system's totalitarian bureaucracy embracing the whole of society. However many levels the internal bureaucracy of the largest capitalist firm has, it is surmounted by an individual or collective owner, not a bureaucratic head. At this topmost level it can be clearly felt that the firm's general manager is responsible to the owners; what he does well or badly affects the owners' pocket, making them richer or poorer. But in a socialist bureaucracy each head has another head over him or her; and there is no real owner whose pocket is affected by good or bad performance. As for the paramount leader, his motivation is clearly political, not "proprietorial."

7.6 Planning, Management, and Politics

Under the capitalist system, the political sphere is distinct from the economic sphere, that is, from the world of business, despite some overlap-

---

[26]See R. W. Campbell (1978).

[27]The history of England's commons, which were everyone's prey, is well known. They were exploited without inhibition until they were destroyed. See G. Hardin (1968) and T. C. Schelling (1978, pp. 110ff).

ping between them. There is no such distinction under the classical socialist system, where politics pervades the economy.

As mentioned in section 7.2, the annual and five-year national economic plans are endorsed by the highest political bodies. But the apparatus of the party Central Committee plays a very active part in preparing the plan far earlier, from the time the very first outlines are drawn, and it has a decisive say in the development of the plan's main trends. The "plan law" itself is primarily a political document expressing the general and economic policy line of the party. Not infrequently the plan is preceded by a struggle between conflicting political forces, in which case it reflects the position of the winner (or a compromise between the two).[28]

Political events do not always coincide with the cycles of the plan. Not infrequently the plan has to be amended during the year because important political changes have occurred. This happens more frequently still during the period of a five-year plan, whose targets can be made obsolete by political changes.

Everything said about the plans applies, of course, to implementation of the plan, and in general to the management of the economy. That too is subordinate to politics.

I have already mentioned how the position of the leaders of the bureaucracy in a large capitalist firm differs from that of the officials of a socialist bureaucracy. At this point a further major difference is worth noting. Although the actions of capitalist managers may have political implications, they are fundamentally guided by business interests. They are faced with stable, lasting economic assignments: they must raise the present and future profit, wealth, and "net worth" of the firm; they must improve its market position and commercial prospects. By contrast, the economic tasks under the classical socialist system form only one factor in the policy of the Communist party; economic considerations are often subordinated to other domestic and foreign policy objectives. Nor are the relative weights attributed to the various political and economic tasks constant. This weighting system—the leadership's order

---

[28]Some theoretical models of planning assume that planners possess a well-defined, unambiguous preference ordering that stays unchanged for quite a long time, and that the planners optimize the plan accordingly when working out its details.

In fact, the planning decisions (and those made during the implementation of the plan) vary constantly according to the prevailing political power relations. What applies at most is the reverse of the statement. Ex post the political line is more or less reflected in the actual economic processes, that is, in some sense, revealed political preferences can be observed. But that is not entirely true either, because one often encounters phenomena that arise in spite of the policy makers' intentions.

of preferences, the "party line"—changes from time to time, and sometimes the changes can be very abrupt.

Let me return for a moment to the conflicts of interests mentioned in
the discussion of motivations. One of the major economic objectives under classical socialism is rapid growth [→9]. The top leadership devises
taut plans designed to force a rapid growth in production.[29] There is a
constant effort through official propaganda and in day-to-day management and control to attain volume targets.[30] The compulsion to pursue
this lopsided *quantity drive* comes not only from the instructions from
above but from the urging of users of the products. Meanwhile, the
quantity drive has numerous harmful effects, such as neglect of product
and insufficient care taken in expanding the product range.

This is a good example of a conflict of motives. One half of the leader's mind dwells on raising production volume, because he knows this is
his prime political task. But the other half thinks of other things. He has
an interest in withholding performance. (See the remarks on bargaining
and on "planning in.") He offends his own professional pride if he disregards quality or the chance to save inputs. Nor can he bank on his superiors invariably calling him to account on volume alone. One day it could
be a fall in quality or a rise in costs that gets him into trouble. These
circumstances give rise to an inner insecurity in leaders.[31]

Based on all this, one can state there is no justification under the classical socialist system for distinguishing the role in society of a "politician"
from those of a "bureaucrat," "technocrat," or "manager." These roles
become merged. The party secretary of a county or a firm spends hours
hurrying a shipment of raw materials or overseeing the start-up of a new
production unit.[32] Meanwhile, the leader of a firm or a ministry is ex-

[29]On the literature on taut planning, see H. Hunter (1961) and M. Keren (1972).

[30]Mátyás Rákosi, the "Hungarian Stalin," had the following to say in 1950: "A taut
plan is a good plan . . . a good plan is one which can only be reached on tiptoe." Quoted
by I. Birta (1970, p. 140).

[31]These conflicts of interest are among the factors that preclude the formulation of
satisfactory incentive schemes. The classical "principal-agent" models [→5.1, note 9] always assume the owner's objectives are clear and invariable. Where that is so, an incentive
scheme that encourages the agent to further the principal's purposes can usually be found.
The same assumption is not justified in the situation now being discussed, of a "superior-
subordinate" relation under the classical socialist system.

For early discussions of similar issues as related to socialist systems, see M. L. Weitzman
(1976), J. P. Bonin (1976), A. Bergson (1978b), B. R. Holmström (1982a), and D. Conn,
ed. (1979). For recent applications see, among others, P. Liu (1986) and K. Osband (1987).

[32]It is not clearly defined who the "top person" in the firm is: the party secretary or the
director. In most countries and periods under the classical system the party secretary has
not ranked formally over the director, but he has counted as top person in practice. In
China this was declared formally.

The extent of involvement of party secretaries, which turned them into *tolkachi* (expedi-

pected to inspire colleagues with political arguments as well. If one wants extra resources for one's own unit, one needs to support the application with political arguments, and if possible obtain the party organization's support. As a rule, purely economic or technical arguments will not suffice: it is worth supplementing them with political discourse, which may even substitute for the economic or technical calculations altogether. This "politicization" of the process of economic management often contributes to a distortion of information over and above the distortions described in an earlier section of this chapter.

7.7 The Problem of Information

There have been several references already to the problem of information, particularly the distorting influences on it. But disregarding distortion for the moment, the vast quantity of information required for bureaucratic coordination causes serious problems in itself. Assembly and processing of that huge mass of information, and coordination based on this information, is too enormous and difficult a task to be undertaken efficiently through centralized planning and management.

When the plan is prepared, the higher authorities are presented not with alternative, variant plans, but with a single plan proposal that its creators attempt to defend as the sole feasible and therefore "inevitable" plan.

As mentioned before, planning involves a process of reconciliation on several levels. It is as if the planners were trying to solve bit by bit a vast system of simultaneous equations. The only way it can be done, of course, is by repeated trial and error. Even a powerful computer is only able to solve iteratively large systems of equations (and nothing, in fact, as large as those involved in the problem of planning). Moreover, the time available for elaborating the plan is short; the collation process must be broken off arbitrarily before a fully reconciled plan has emerged. So the plan is full of concealed inconsistencies.

These reveal themselves one by one during the implementation. Then come improvised modifications for the remaining period of the plan, or not even those, for sometimes the plan is adjusted retrospectively to the actual performance. If one part of the plan or another is altered, corre-

tors) as well as politicians, can be surmised from the following comment by Boris Yeltsin (1990, p. 69), who became president of the Russian Federation in 1990 and then left the party: "When Gorbachev was first secretary of the Stavropol district committee, and I of the Sverdlovsk committee, . . . [we] often needed to help each other: from the Urals, with metal and wood, from Stavropol, with food products."

sponding alterations of the other parts should be made, since all the targets are interrelated. In fact, there is no time or energy to do so.

These technical difficulties with modifying the plan are one factor arousing opposition to the making of suitable adjustments by the bureaucracy to events unforeseen in the plan. This applies not just to unplanned-for problems but to favorable developments as well. It is hard to get any new invention applied or new product introduced if it did not feature in the original plan. The plan directs its implementers, but it also ties their hands, making it one of the sources of economic rigidity and lack of flexible adaptation.

If an assignment is bafflingly complicated, nothing could be more natural than for those undertaking it to try its simplification for themselves. One method applied widely is emphasis on the main tasks. Section 7.2 pointed out that the plan contains several tens of thousands of figures on a national level, and the number continues to grow as the plan aggregation proceeds downward. So a peculiar "order of importance" develops among the figures in the plan, the most important of all being those for volume of production in aggregate value terms and broken down for the products rated most important. (This system of priorities corresponds also to what was said in the previous section about the "quantity drive.") This is complemented, at least in certain countries, by forced export assignments. There is a strong insistence on priority investment projects being completed on time and on punctual deliveries of all the materials, parts, and machinery they require. Wage fund limits must be strictly observed. The incentives (bonuses, penalties) are tied to fulfillment of these priority tasks. But the concomitant is that the other planning directives become far easier to relegate, so that other tasks are neglected.

Nor would it help to change the "order of importance." Whatever is put to the fore, it would still be easier to fulfill the emphasized indices at the expense of the unemphasized. Only seemingly has it become simpler to ensure fulfillment of the plan and deal with the accompanying information problem. In fact, the procedure has solved nothing and led only to distorted one-sidedness.

Nor is it just a question of plan figures. The general principle of management practice under the classical system is to have "a grip on the decisive link."[33] A campaign is launched over the main link, the most pressing great task. Political mobilization is undertaken, and the many

[33]The expression comes from Lenin. Both Stalin and Mao Zedong emphasized the principle.

weapons of persuasion, reward, and compulsion are employed.[34] Meanwhile, the other tasks are relegated until such time as one or other of them joins the agenda in the form of a new campaign.

The methods of "emphasizing" tasks, declaring them main links and treating them through campaigns, leave a vacuum of control. That is followed by the appearance of spontaneous actions that the bureaucracy does not consider desirable. If the regulatory net is not dense enough, the holes have to be plugged with a succession of new regulations. The inevitable consequence is proliferation of the bureaucracy. The expanded reproduction of the bureaucracy continues. This can be measured by the increase in the number of employees and costs of the administrative apparatus, and by the increase in the number of legal regulations. The repeated resolutions calling for simpler planning and management are fruitless. The tendency to be complete, comprehensive, and watertight reappears constantly under the social conditions of bureaucratic coordination.

The great importance of the information problem was stressed by F. Hayek in the famous debate in the 1930s on planning and the market [→21.1]. The problem shared by all economic systems is utilization of the information (or, to use Hayek's expression, knowledge) possessed by society's members. If there is no barrier to free entry by private enterprise, and, in fact, this is facilitated by the capital market and the legal system, if there is adequate protection for private property and private contracts, and if the activities are coordinated mainly by the market, then the information is utilized in a decentralized way. Those using the information feel the benefits of it directly. Take the example of an entrepreneur well aware of the technical and market opportunities open to his factory. If he uses them effectively he makes a bigger profit. Not only an entrepreneur with a whole factory at his disposal but anyone with useful ideas or knowledge can apply it to his own direct advantage. The task of obtaining and processing information and the incentives to the actual utilization of information do not break apart but form an integral whole.

The situation is quite different if attempts are made to centralize crumbs of knowledge and information that have been scattered in all directions, and if the information in the subordinate's possession has to be "passed up the ladder." It may not be in his interest to transmit it, and he may fail to do so out of laziness. It may be fully in his interest to pass it up in a distorted form, of which examples have been given. Once the tasks are devised on the basis of the information transmitted,

---

[34]See A. Nove (1969) and K. A. Soós (1986).

a particular incentive has to be developed before use is made of the information. This incentive in turn may be one-sided or distorted: examples of that have been given also. Whatever the case, the processes of information and incentive have parted ways, which is one of the gravest problems inherent in bureaucratic coordination.

With that we are back at the starting-point of the chapter, with the ideas on planning held by the precursors of socialism. They expected planning to create order on a scale embracing the whole of society. But it emerged that direct bureaucratic control, which encompasses planning, is a curious combination of order and disorder, foresight and haste, service of great common interests and uninhibited assertion of partial interests.

Marx and his followers reckoned that planning would be a simple, easily soluble task. Experience has shown it to be an extremely complicated one. It can be solved somehow or other, but the practical solution is full of frictions, dysfunctional features, inefficiencies, and internal conflicts.

8

Money and Price

"MONEY circulation gradually dies away, supplanted by natural exchange, indeed, by the direct allocation of products. Foreseeing this, the People's Commissariat of Finance deliberately aims at the doing away of money." These lines appear in an article by N. Kovalevsky, one of the leaders of the Soviet planning office, published in 1926.[1] Having looked back with nostalgia on the revolutionary-transitional period of War Communism, the author concludes bitterly: "But this has not been our lot."

In terms of formal features, the classical socialist system is a monetized economy. But if one analyzes the actual processes behind the formal facade, following the procedure used in the book so far, it turns out there is merely an apparent monetization in many respects, since the role played by money in some of the relations is only weak or secondary. The desire to abolish money expressed in the quotation has been granted in part after all. Classical socialism is a *semimonetized system,* in fact. Moreover, the role of prices is far narrower and more restricted than it is under capitalism.

Sections 8.1, 8.2, and 8.3 survey the institutions of the financial system and the structure of the financial processes, while sections 8.4 and 8.5 examine the social relations expressed in those processes. The rest of the chapter is devoted to prices.

Later, chapters 11 and 12 will cover macroeconomic aspects of financial affairs and the price level, and, in connection with them, the question of inflation.

8.1 Banking

The entire banking system under classical socialism is state-owned. It consists seemingly of several organizations: the central bank and various specialized banks (an investment bank, a foreign trade bank, a savings bank for the general public). The specialized banks are nominally independent, but really they are regulated by instructions from the central

---

[1] The quotation and the information concerning it were taken from L. Szamuely (1974, p. 7).

bank; they are its "arms." These are grounds for speaking, as some do, of the existence of a *monobank*.[2]

Banks in a capitalist economy (apart from the central bank and perhaps some other exceptional institutions) are firms with an interest in increasing their profits and a market relation to their customers, whereas banks under classical socialism have not even a nominal interest in profits. They constitute collectively a rigidly centralized, hierarchical machine vested with rights of official authority. Banking amounts to a branch of the all-pervading bureaucracy, and the central bank, as the body running it, lacks even a nominal autonomy, since it is subordinate to the political-economic leadership (formally to the government), whose instructions it has to obey.

The central bank under classical socialism performs one of the customary main functions of a central bank under capitalism: the emission of money. It also has a function that is fulfilled in a capitalist economy by the commercial banks: to handle the entire short-term credit supply of the state sector (and in several countries of the cooperative sector, too). Each state-owned firm keeps an account at the central bank. Precise rules govern the amount of cash a firm may keep in its own till and what it may be used for. All other moneys must be placed in the firm's account at the central bank. Nor can the firm as "owner" of the money dispose freely of the money it has deposited in the bank, which is drawn upon almost automatically, according to a system of centrally set ordering, to cover the various kinds of expenditure.

The account is divided into various "subaccounts" between which there is no free flow of money. Money designed to cover the purchase of materials and semifinished products cannot be used to pay wages; money for wages cannot be used for materials, and so forth. The money is "earmarked."

The money earmarked for investment (accumulation of fixed assets) is segregated strictly from all the other funds, including, for instance, expenditure connected with material input for day-to-day production. In

---

[2]Lenin envisaged that "A single state bank, the biggest of the big, with branches in every rural district, in every factory, will constitute as much as nine-tenths of the socialist apparatus. This will be country-wide book-keeping, country-wide accounting of the production and distribution of goods." V. I. Lenin [1918] (1964, p. 106).

In 1986, before the moves toward a two-level banking system, the Soviet state banking system (Gosbank and the specialized banks) employed 406,300 people. N. V. Garetovskii (1989, p. 10).

For overviews of banking see the following studies: *USSR:* G. Garvy (1977) and H. Sigg (1981); *Eastern Europe:* G. Garvy (1966), Y. M. Laulan, ed. (1973), T. M. Podolski (1973), and A. Zwass (1978); *China:* G. C. Chow (1985); furthermore, G. Grossman, ed. (1968) for more general points.

certain countries and periods this segregation occurs at the central bank; elsewhere and at other times the financing of investment is undertaken by the investment bank (i.e., the arm of the central bank specializing in it).

In view of all this, one can say that money fails to perform the integration of all transactions; it is not actually a "universal means of exchange." The national currency is "not convertible" within the country: "investment money" cannot be converted into "materials money" or "wages money," or vice versa, even within the state-owned sector.[3] This "internal nonconvertibility" heightens the rigidity of economic activity and frequently prevents rational substitution taking place between the factors of production.

This applies even more to conversion between the national currency and foreign currencies. All kinds of financial relations with the outside world are strictly centralized into the hands of the central bank or its "arm," the foreign trade bank. Money is nonconvertible; all conversion is restricted by general regulations and detailed, case-by-case adjudication.

Returning to the firm's bank account, the banking sector has a full picture of all the firm's monetary transactions. Such full, centralized information on the movement of money has never been available under any previous social system. But, in fact, this huge mass of information is hardly used at all in the direct bureaucratic control of the economy. Instead, a million tiny direct interventions are made in the "physical" processes (prescription of production assignments, expediting of deliveries, etc.) [→7.3].

It is a convention of direct bureaucratic control to entrust the banking system with the monitoring of inventories. The information basis required derives from the provision of short-term credits, which also provides the means of intervening in a crude and slipshod way. If a firm is judged according to a variety of empirical norms to be overstocked, the bank limits the availability of working-capital credits. More important, it sends inspectors around and makes warning reports to the firm's superior bodies. This function might as well be performed by an "inventory-monitoring office." It is a piece of plain bureaucratic coordination that has nothing to do with a real bank's business activity, providing market coordination and induced by commercial motives.

One arm of the monobank deals with the transactions of the general public. There, and only there, may citizens keep their bank deposits. The supply of banking services to the general public is meager and backward.

---

[3]See W. Brus [1961] (1972), G. Grossman (1966), J. Kornai (1980), and M. Tardos (1981).

Apart from accumulating cash, the only legal way to invest money is in a savings deposit. Citizens may apply to this monopoly savings bank for credit to build their own home and, in certain countries and periods, to make installment purchases of certain durable consumer goods. The scale of the credit taken up by households is insignificant by comparison with a capitalist economy.

The banking system pays interest on deposits and charges interest on loans. All rates of interest are set centrally. The rates are usually very low, and in certain countries and periods the real interest rate is negative.

8.2 The State Budget

The discussion now turns to the state budget.[4] Table 8.1 compares the structure of the budget in certain capitalist and certain socialist countries. Table 8.2 shows some characteristics of the Soviet budget.

Both the revenue and expenditure sides of the state budget under the classical socialist system contain entries also found in the state budget under the capitalist system. The differences occur less in the formal features of the entries than in their relative sizes. The major items of expenditure will be considered in turn.

1. *Spending on administration*. This maintains the vast bureaucratic apparatus, and the items are relatively larger than in capitalist countries.

2. *Spending on the armed forces*.[5]

3. *State investment*. This entry covers the investment spending of state institutions of a nonfirm nature (budgetary institutions), just as it does under other systems. More system-specific is the financing of the state-owned firms' investment. The share of investment financed by bank credit or self-financed by firms is insignificant under the classical system. The entire outlay for almost every investment by a state-owned firm is provided by the state budget.[6]

---

[4]The description covers only the budget of the central government. The relative scale of revenue and expenditure in the budget for regional state authorities is tiny compared with those of the central budget, and both revenue and expenditure are closely controlled by the central management. The fiscal system is far more centralized also in this respect than in most capitalist economies.

For a more detailed discussion of the state budget in socialist countries, see F. D. Holzman (1955) on taxation, R. Hutchings (1983), and L. Muraközy (1985, 1989).

[5]The breakdown of expenditures may not reflect actual proportions, as some socialist countries tended to understate their military expenditures. Greater openness in this area only comes with reform, and the recognition of the necessity to reduce military expenditures [→23.3].

[6]In China, in the period of classical socialism, state investment as a percentage of total state expenditure has been as high as around 33–46 percent between 1968 and 1978. State Statistical Bureau, People's Republic of China (1985, p. 40).

TABLE 8.1

Size and Economic Expenditures of the State Budget: International Comparison, 1981

	Total Budgetary Expenditure (percent of GDP)	Economic Expenditure of the Budget (percent of GDP)	Economic Expenditure of the Budget (percent of total budgetary expenditure)
Socialist countries			
Bulgaria[a]	47.0	22.2	47.2
China	31.2	18.9	60.6
Czechoslovakia[a]	53.1	22.8	42.9
Hungary	63.2	26.9	42.6
Poland	53.2	32.5	61.1
Romania	43.5	22.2	51.0
Soviet Union	47.1	25.8	54.8
High-income capitalist countries			
Australia	33.6	2.8	8.3
Denmark	59.2	7.7	13.1
France	46.4	4.6	9.9
Switzerland	35.9	4.9	13.7
United States	34.8	3.5	10.1
West Germany	49.8	4.8	9.6

(*continued*)

The budget also covers a high proportion of investment in the cooperative sector (which is further evidence that cooperatives are "quasi-state-owned" firms).

Investment is made by a capitalist state as well, but the sum is a small proportion of total investment, whereas the central budget of a socialist state finances an overwhelming proportion of the total investment of the whole economy. This is one instrument of ensuring a high degree of centralization of the investment process.

4. *Subsidization of firms.* This embraces all kinds of grant, price support, or negative taxation whose beneficiaries are state-owned firms and cooperatives. The entry forms a very high proportion of expenditure.

TABLE 8.1
Continued

	Total Budgetary Expenditure (percent of GDP)	Economic Expenditure of the Budget (percent of GDP)	Economic Expenditure of the Budget (percent of total budgetary expenditure)
Medium- and low-income capitalist countries			
Argentina	32.5	4.0	12.4
Chile	29.5	3.4	11.5
Greece	41.5	6.9	16.7
India	21.3	6.8	32.2
Indonesia	27.0	8.2	30.5
Kenya	29.2	8.6	29.6
Panama	34.7	4.7	13.6
Tunisia	33.6	11.2	33.3

Source: Compiled by L. Muraközy for this book on the basis of the following sources. State budget: Europa Publications, various issues (1980–87); International Monetary Fund (1987). Output for capitalist countries: International Monetary Fund (1984, pp. 109–61). Output for socialist countries: estimates of P. Mihályi on the basis of United Nations, Common Data Bank.

Note: Based on the following classification of expenditures: (1) economic, (2) social and cultural, (3) defense, and (4) administrative expenditures. The second and third columns cover only expenditures of type 1. The data on the state budget are calculated according to IMF conception, except for Bulgaria, Czechoslovakia, Poland, and the Soviet Union, data for which are calculated according to the respective national statistical systems.

[a]1980.

5. *Subsidization of consumer prices.* Wherever the state's pricing policy is to set a consumer price lower than costs [→8.7], the difference is supplied by the budget. This may be considered a negative turnover tax.[7]

The items of expenditure numbered 3, 4, and 5 are components of the aggregate expenditure category that has been termed "economic expenditure" in table 8.1. The table shows that the weight of this by compari-

---

[7]In the period 1981–85, before Gorbachev's reforms were introduced, the total amount of subsidies (covering items 4 and 5 in the discussion above) in the Soviet Union accounted for 18 percent of budgetary expenditure. G. Ofer (1990, p. 39).

TABLE 8.2
The Structure of the Soviet State Budget

	1975	1984
	Revenues (percent of total)	
Turnover tax	30.4	27.2
Payments from profits	31.9	29.4
Taxes on population	8.4	7.6
Social insurance	5.2	6.6
Other revenues	24.1	29.2
	Expenditures (percent of total)	
Economic expenditures	51.6	57.8
Social and cultural expenditures, science	35.9	31.8
Defense	8.1	4.6
Administration	0.9	0.8
Other expenditures	3.5	5.0

Source: Finansy i Statistika (Finance and Statistics, Moscow) (1985, pp. 54–55).

son with other expenditures is conspicuously higher in socialist countries than in capitalist countries. This forms one of the safe measures of the extent of state centralization of the economic processes.

6. *Financing of free public services.* The entry covers spending on education, educational and cultural services, health, childcare, the pension system, and social insurance [→table 13.7].[8]

Although on paper certain items of expenditure should be covered by separate items of revenue (e.g., pension and social insurance contributions), in fact, the revenues and expenditures are completely divorced. Revenue and expenditure serving a certain purpose are not handled in the form of separate funds. For one thing, the pension and social insurance contributions are really separate taxes, whose rates citizens have no say in deciding. For another, when the bureaucracy decides the central budget it also decides how much it wishes to spend on these and other public services. They are spheres in which neither market nor self-governing

---

[8]In certain countries, certain public services (such as childcare or health care) are not entirely free. Those using them must pay a modest fee.

coordination apply;[9] bureaucratic coordination controls them almost entirely.

The main entries on the revenue side of the budget are these:

1. *The revenue generated by state-owned firms.* It includes both the profits and the taxes and levies paid by firms [→5.3]. The "grounds" and labels attached to the various payment forms are arbitrary and prone to frequent change, as are their proportions. The combination of the "negative" taxes on firms (number 4 on the expenditure side) with these positive taxes on firms constitutes an intricate network of redistribution composed of many "channels of income flow." The central budget takes money from the firms on a hundred different grounds and gives it to them on another hundred. This is precisely what makes it clear that the money accruing to a firm after the sale of its products and deduction of its costs is not the firm's; its disposal is directed centrally.

2. *Tax payments by cooperatives.* What has been said of state-owned firms applies self-evidently to cooperatives as well.

3. *Turnover taxes.* These are a major entry, providing a far higher proportion of budget revenue than in capitalist countries. The turnover tax is included in the price, so that the buyer of a good does not even know how much tax is paid at each purchase.[10]

4. *Taxes paid by the individual.* The general public pays taxes on various grounds (e.g., real estate and housing tax). Some strata, such as the self-employed, also pay income tax. But all in all the direct taxes paid by the general public are tiny compared with the other sources of budgetary revenue.

5. *Loans raised by the budget.* Two forms are worth mentioning. One is bonds issued to the general public, who are forced to buy them through aggressive political campaigns, not by advantageous financial terms. This is *forced saving* which is extorted administratively, and it must be distinguished from the forced saving induced by shortage [→11.1, 11.2, 12.6].

The other form is credit extended directly to the budget by the central bank. In economic terms this is tantamount to covering the budget deficit through an inflationary emission of money, whose size may be substantial in certain countries and periods.[11] The entry is usually concealed in published budgetary statements.

---

[9]There are scattered exceptions, of which the best known are the distorted and partly or wholly illegal elements of the market occurring in the health-care field, e.g., in the form of "gratuities" paid for special attention or immediate treatment.

[10]China's 1978 revenue from turnover taxes was 11.3 percent of the GDP, while in the capitalist countries at a similar level of economic development it was 4–5 percent. M. I. Blejer and G. Szapáry (1990, p. 457).

[11]In cases of long-standing budget deficit, the servicing of loans from the central bank is entered formally as expenditure, but the balance between the new credit raised and the

8.3 Survey of Money Flows

Table 8.3 is designed to make it easier to survey the circulation of money under the classical socialist system, and there will be several references to it in the rest of the chapter.[12]

The table distinguishes eight different money-holding sectors.[13] The rows represent the issuers of the money flow, that is, those from whom money passes to others: the recipients, who are shown in the columns. Some of the money flows within one sector, between units in the same sector. (These flows appear in the entries on the main diagonal.) The rest of the flows, shown in the other entries, are between sectors (or more precisely, between units in different sectors).

Only flows of money in the national currency, within the country itself, are covered in the table. Money flows to and from abroad and the conversion of them are ignored.[14]

The table covers all domestic money flows. However, there are flows of products (and services) unaccompanied by the flow of money, and so absent from table 8.3. For instance, nonfirm institutions, state-owned firms, and cooperatives provide individuals with free benefits in kind for which no service in return is exacted.[15] In the informal private sector, products and services change hands on a reciprocal basis, or one individual or organization makes a gift to another individual or organization with altruistic motivation. Although all these nonmonetary transactions play an important part,[16] their combined volume is very small compared with those that are nominally monetized.

---

servicing of the previous loans is positive, i.e., the indebtedness of the budget grows. This growth in net indebtedness covers the budget deficit.

[12]For money-flow models of socialist economies, see M. Augusztinovics (1965), P. H. Dembinski, and W. Piaszczynski (1988), and P. H. Dembinski (1988).

[13]Here "money holder" is taken to mean the nominal money holder. In terms of the survey's classification one can leave open what property rights the nominal money holder actually has.

[14]The survey is facilitated by some other minor simplifications. For example, money flows within the banking sector (entry 1.1) are not assessed; they are technical financial maneuvers whose analysis is irrelevant to the subject of this book. Money flows to do with interest payments are not shown. Nor are exceptional cases where certain nonfirm state institutions receive payment for some of their services, since the sum involved is insignificant.

[15]The state budget mainly finances social benefits to the public by maintaining through budgetary grants the budgetary institutions that then offer the public free services or cash payments. For instance, the budget finances public education, which provides its services to the public free of charge. Therefore, this flow appears in entry 2.3. The sum the state budget gives directly to households as a gratuitous payment is tiny, hence the zero in entry 2.8.

[16]The idea that classical socialism is only a semimonetized system, advanced in the introduction to this chapter, was not, or not primarily intended as, a reference to these money-

8.4 Soft and Hard Budget Constraint

Having surveyed the institutions of the financial system, the structure of money flows, and the formal principles and rules of operation, it is time to analyze the actual social relations that apply in the financial sphere. The situation becomes more comprehensible if acquaintance is made with the notions of the *hardness* and *softness of budget constraint.*[17] Let me begin the exposition by discussing state-owned firms.

The concept of "budget constraint" is familiar from the microeconomic theory of the household: the sum available to a decision maker places a constraint on the consumer's spending that he or she can choose to incur. This concept will be applied now to the case of a socialist firm. What happens under the classical socialist system if a state-owned firm's spending exceeds its budget constraint? And what happens if this is a regular, not an isolated, occurrence? The observation then is that the constraint will be adjusted to the repeated overspending. The firm receives regular external assistance, of which four main forms can be distinguished.

1. *Soft subsidy.* The adjective "soft" implies that this is not a case of a state subsidy at a level expressly laid down for a longer period. The amount of the subsidy is the subject of bargaining. Here and in several other places in the following discussion of soft budget constraint, one encounters repeatedly the phenomenon of vertical bargaining [→7.5]. A firm (or a branch directorate on behalf of several firms, or a ministry on behalf of several branches) bargains for more subsidy to cover its excess expenditure. Negotiations are made either in advance, before the amount of subsidy has been laid down, or during and after the period covered by the subsidy, to improve on the sum promised in advance.[18]

---

avoiding transactions. The next two sections will show that in some formally monetized transactions money does not play a primary part, and the advance comment on a "semi-monetized system" refers mainly to these areas.

[17]I introduced the concept in J. Kornai (1980) and restated it later (1986a). S. Gomulka (1985) distinguished between budget softness and budget flexibility. If firms can expect financial aid to be forthcoming, but not before a delay (budget flexibility is smaller than price flexibility), they will be more sensitive to changing relative prices; if they can trust that budgets will be adjusted immediately (budget flexibility is greater than price flexibility), they will not be. Other participants in the debate were K. A. Soós (1984), J. Szabó (1985), and J. Winiecki (1991).

Formal models related to the problem of the soft budget constraint include papers of M. Dewatripont and E. Maskin (1990), S. M. Goldfeld and R. E. Quandt (1988), J. Kornai and J. W. Weibull (1983), A. Lindbeck and J. W. Weibull (1987), J. Mitchell (1989), Y. Qian (1986), and M. E. Schaffer (1989).

[18]J. Szabó (1985) draws attention to the distinction between prior and continuous (concurrent or subsequent) softening of the budget constraint. The two phenomena are discussed in parallel in this brief description.

TABLE 8.3
Money Flow between Moneyholders

Issuer of Money Flow	Recipient of the Money Flow							
	1 Banking Sector	*2 State Budget*	*3 Budgetary Institutions*	*4 State-Owned Firms*	*5 Cooperatives*	*6 Formal Private Sector*	*7 Informal Private Sector*	*8 Households*
1. Banking sector		C	0	C, R	C, R	R	0	C, R
2. State budget	S		B	B	B	0	0	0
3. Budgetary institutions	0	0		P	P	0	0	W
4. State-owned firms	D, S	T, N	0	P	P	0	0	W
5. Cooperatives	D, S	T	0	P	P	0	0	W
6. Formal private sector	D	T	0	P	P	P	P	W
7. Informal private sector	0	0	0	0	0	P	P	W
8. Households	D, S	T	0	P	P	P	P	W

Note: The meanings of the symbols are as follows: B = benefit extended, C = credit extended, D = money deposited in a bank account, N = net income paid in, P = payment for goods and services, R = money withdrawn from a bank account, S = debt serviced, T = tax paid, W = wages paid, 0 = no flow of money in this entry.

2. *Soft taxation*. "Soft" does not imply that the amount of net income the firm is obliged to pay in (the "tax") is low. It means the amount is subject to prior and/or subsequent bargaining. The more possible it is to "beat down" the firm's taxation by pressure or pleading, the softer it is. Where taxation is soft, the obligations to pay net income into the budget are not set according to stable, uniform principles. They are assessed individually, case by case, almost as if the tax and profit rates were tailored to each firm or branch.

3. *Soft credit*. On the one hand, "soft" refers to the situation where the credit contract with the bank does not follow general, uniform principles, but a firm in trouble can "whine" for credit that actually includes a veiled grant. On the other hand, "softness" means that the bank does not insist on full adherence to the credit contract and its schedule. Contract fulfillment becomes the subject of bargaining.

4. *Soft administrative pricing*. Although price-setting is the subject of a later section of this chapter, I must mention here that a significant proportion of prices in a classical socialist economy are set administratively. These seem to be prices dictated bureaucratically to the firm, but, in fact, they can be "softened" by vertical bargaining with the price authorities. There is advance bargaining: the goal of the firm, branch directorate, or ministry is to make the pricing authority "acknowledge" the costs in the price, however low the efficiency of production. There is subsequent bargaining also. A price rise is sought if extra costs have been incurred. In some other cases a disguised price rise is made. The quality assumed when the price was set is lowered, or a good material is substituted by an inferior material, or certain finishing processes are omitted.

All four "softening" methods can be used separately or combined. One can maneuver among the various branches of the bureaucracy: the ministry responsible for direct control of the firm, the fiscal authorities, the banking sector, and the price authorities.[19]

A few supplementary explanations need to be added to the brief account given so far.

[19]This maneuvering involves a lot of legwork, searching for connections and supporters. Softness of the budget constraint produces what A. O. Krueger (1974) calls "rent-seeking behavior." Although this is costly and tiresome, it can be lucrative. It may be worth spending more time in the "corridors of power" than on the factory floor or in the office on sales negotiations. See, furthermore, C. Scott (1990).

S. M. Goldfeld and R. E. Quandt (1988) have confirmed with a mathematical model that a soft budget constraint induces firms to put much of their effort into bargaining and obtaining subsidies, and that this draws their energy away from improving production and sales.

Of course, any static interpretation would provide a highly simplified picture of the intricate social phenomenon termed here the softness of budget constraint. It depicts a static problem of choice, whereas this is clearly a case of a dynamic process in which an expenditure flow is opposed to an income flow.

When dealing with the softness of the budget constraint on firms, it is not permissible to take the case of a specific firm and put the question in the form: Is the constraint on it soft or not? The concept expresses the collective experience of a large group of firms, in this case the sum of the state-owned firms in the classical system. It asks what their expectations of the future are in terms of insistence on profitability.[20] In this sense one is dealing with a stochastic concept. The extending of external assistance is a random variable with a given probability distribution, of which the firm's decision maker (and his or her superiors) have a subjective "perception." The greater the subjective probability, that is, the safer the firm is in assuming it will receive external assistance, the softer the budget constraint.

Another interpretation is the following. The promise to enforce the observation of the budget constraint is a commitment of the bureaucracy that it will not tolerate persistent loss-making. Hardness versus softness refers to the credibility of this commitment.[21]

For simplicity's sake, the expression "soft" budget constraint has been used in the description so far. In fact, one would need a scale to register the degrees of softness and hardness from extremely soft via numerous transitional states to extremely hard.

"Hard budget constraint" is a concept akin to the principle of "profit maximization," but not exactly synonymous with it. Maximization of profits refers to the goal or internal motivation of a firm's decision maker: What does he wish to achieve? Softness or hardness of budget constraint, on the other hand, refers to a firm's external conditions: What will its environment tolerate? Although there is a clear relationship between internal motivation and external conditions, they are worth distinguishing on the abstract plane. Does the firm operate in a social environment that recognizes it will fail and exit from the economy in the case

---

[20]The collective experience of all state-owned firms was discussed here solely to simplify the account. In practice, this experience may not be uniform, but differentiated to some degree. For instance, firms in the branches with the highest central priority perceive a softer budget constraint than those in branches of the neglected sectors (C. Davis, 1989); there is a softer constraint on large firms than on small.

[21]The lack of *credible commitment* is the pivotal component in the game-theoretical modeling of the soft budget constraint syndrome. See the following studies: M. Dewatripont and E. Maskin (1990), A. Lindbeck and J. W. Weibull (1987), M. E. Schaffer (1989), and Y. Qian (1986, 1988).

of continuing losses and financial catastrophe?[22] Or will the environment be unable to accept this and bail it out? One manifestation of the softness of the constraint is a manifestation of the fact that a firm's survival and expansion do not depend on the market; it is decided in the frames of bureaucratic coordination and financial bargaining with the authorities.

To shed light on the complex phenomenon of the soft budget constraint let me make an analogy: the situation in the family. Five grades of *paternalism* are considered. I begin with the highest, grade 4: the parents provide for their child in kind, and the child accepts everything passively. That is the position of a newborn baby, who does not know yet what he or she needs and cannot express his or her wishes clearly. Under grade 3, there is still provision in kind by the parents, but the child is capable of expressing his desires. In the case of grade 2, the child is a student and receives money from the parents to spend freely, but remains wholly dependent on the parents, since she does not earn money herself. Under grade 1 the child is grown up and earns his own living. But the parents are still alive and help out if the child is in trouble. The child knows he can count on the parents in this way. Finally, there is grade 0; the parents are no longer alive, and the individual no longer a child; she knows she has only herself to rely on.

Turning from the analogy to the situation of a state-owned firm, elements of grades 4, 3, and 2, and to an extent grade 1, are combined under the classical socialist system. Grade 4 applies only in extreme cases, when the firm does not even dare to say anything. The phenomenon of bargaining (general under the system) points at least to grade 3, and even in part to grade 2 or grade 1. Although it is treated like an infant and the superior bodies look after everything for it, the firm makes itself heard and tries to exact better "provision in kind" and more "pocket money," that is, more resources and a softer budget constraint. This paternal control may be a burden and often an affront to its dignity, but the firm knows it also provides security. If the firm is in trouble the superior bodies will stand by it and not let it go bankrupt.

Paternalism, and soft budget constraint as one manifestation of it, is a typical social relation between superior and subordinate, higher authorities and management of the firm. The softness of the budget constraint does not simply arise because the higher organizations of control fail to keep tight financial discipline, or the tax authority, banking sector, or price office are overly tolerant. Its appearance is a strong regularity, deeply rooted in the basic traits of classical socialism.

---

[22]As P. Wiles (1962, p. 20) wrote about the capitalist firm: "It may not wish, as in Western economic textbooks, to maximize profit, but it will certainly be keen to avoid loss. For the basis of the market economy is that loss-makers cease to exist."

So far this section has dealt exclusively with the state-owned firm. Let me now turn to the other social sectors.

Everything said in the section about the softness of the budget constraint on state-owned firms applies accordingly to cooperatives as well. In other words, the budget constraint on them is also soft, though perhaps not as soft as on state-owned firms.

The budget constraint on the formal and informal private sectors, however, is thoroughly hard. The bureaucracy limits or even hinders their activity in a variety of ways, and it certainly does not give them paternalistic treatment or rush to assist an undertaking in financial trouble. In that respect, private business is quite on its own.

The budget constraint on households is basically hard as well. Their purchases are limited by various factors; for example, the goods sought may not be available [→11, 12]. But one cannot say of households what can be said of firms: that the main thing for them is the availability of the product desired, that the money for it will certainly be obtainable somehow [→12.5]. The presence or absence of the purchase money is a real hard constraint on households.

One can sum up by saying that the budget constraint is hard in the sectors not in bureaucratic public ownership.

8.5 Income and Price Responsiveness

Having discussed the hardness and softness of budget constraint, it is time to pose a broader question. How responsive are the various economic decision makers in the classical socialist system to their incomes and to prices?

Starting once again with state-owned firms, according to the official economic principles, such firms are required formally to cover their expenditure out of their income and to produce profit in addition.[23] That is what distinguishes them from budgetary institutions of a nonfirm nature, financed unilaterally from the budget. But in reality the principle does not apply.

A firm is wholly dependent on the bodies above it. In fact, the superior authorities convey in numerous ways which principles and instructions

[23]The principle is known as "independent economic accounting" (*khozraschet*) in Soviet economic parlance. In *Politicheskaia Ekonomiia Sotsializma* (1954, p. 465), the official Soviet textbook of classical socialism, *khozraschet* is defined as follows: "Economic accounting is the method of planned management of activity in socialist enterprises that requires the comparison of expenditures and results of production in money terms, the covering of the expenditures of the enterprise by its own revenue, and the guarantee of the profitability of production."

should be taken seriously and which are not really important. The quantitative targets are the most important of the plan's indicators [→7.7]. Attainment of them attracts financial bonuses, praise, and advancement. Failure to attain them brings rebukes from superiors, bonus denials, and punishment. In addition, there is strong insistence on meeting deadlines for certain investment assignments, observing wage discipline, and fulfilling export commitments [→9.2, 10.3, 14.2].

Reduction of prime costs and achievement of a specified level of profit feature among the assignments in the plan, but observance of them is not enforced. In fact, the methods used to soften the budget constraint make it always possible to plug the gap between a cost overrun and the "profitability principle," so as to disguise the loss. There is no particular danger in running a loss, and conversely, there is no particular advantage in making a profit. If a firm makes a large profit, it is taken away, and the higher profit is "planned in," that is, prescribed thereafter as a plan assignment, using the same procedure as for quantitative targets [→7.5]. Nonetheless, the leaders of the firm and their superiors are not absolutely indifferent to production costs and profit.[24] After all, reduction of costs and attainment of a certain profit feature in the general principles and the plan instructions. It is better to say that their interest in costs and profit and their *income responsiveness* are very weak and pale before other, stronger interests.

This has several consequences, of which just a few will be mentioned here. State-owned firms under the classical system have a weak *price responsiveness*. For instance, if one of two fully substitutive inputs became cheaper than the other, it is far from certain that the firm will heed this in selecting its input combination.

Let us consider a firm's demand curve for a certain input. Where there is hard budget constraint the demand curve slopes downward in the usual way. The softer the constraint, the steeper the slope, until it becomes quite vertical when the constraint is perfectly soft: demand ceases to react to price at all. Let there be no misunderstanding: it is not a case of the firm reacting less elastically to some particular price or other. The softness of the budget constraint blunts responsiveness to every price. The sure knowledge that external assistance is available acts like a tranquillizer, reducing the intensity of the reactions.

This weak price responsiveness is one of the main reasons for low efficiency. But it is not just in this indirect way that the soft budget constraint affects the efficiency of the firm. A hard budget constraint, a stronger profit motive (and, to add what is said in a later section of the

---

[24]If they were totally indifferent, it might not even be worth them acting to soften the budget constraint. Even so, the loss has to be covered in some form, from some source.

chapter, a rational price system), would compel a firm to use the most favorable technology from the point of view of costs. Without them the compulsion is relaxed.[25] The leadership of a firm feels capable of surviving even if its costs are higher than those of the other firms making similar products, the technology it uses is out of date, and it is bad at adapting to the needs of buyers. The important thing in the life and growth of the firm is not for the buyer to be content, but for the superior authorities to support it and help out in time of trouble.

The softness of the budget constraint plays a major part in causing a state-owned firm's demand for inputs to inflate and "run away" [→9.2, 11, 12].

A firm has to consider a great many things before procuring an input (for argument's sake, say, a particular raw material). Do the quotas in the annual plan allow the procurement? Has the material concerned been allocated to the firm by the management of material distribution? Do the suppliers have the material at all, and are they prepared to supply it, or will another firm receive priority? But there is scarcely any need to consider how much the material costs, whether there is money to pay for it, or how the future income will cover the present costs. Once the material is available it can be acquired—the money for it is always obtainable.

Everything declared about state-owned firms in this section and the last applies also to the cooperatives.[26]

The macroeconomic result of the micro behavior just described is that money plays a passive role in the sphere of firms in bureaucratic public ownership.[27] Instead of the actual processes being adjusted to the economic decision makers' financial means (the cash in hand, the credit, and all the money supply available to them), the opposite occurs: the cash in hand, credit supply, and all the available money supply of the firms are adjusted to the decision makers' actual actions. If there is any change in economic policy, for instance, this is done with the arsenal of methods of direct bureaucratic control [→7.3] (alterations to the production targets and to the input quotas, direct intervention in the firm's activities, etc.). If there is a resulting increase or decrease in a firm's or branch's credit requirement or profit, the consequence is one to which monetary and fiscal policy can be adjusted [→12.5].

---

[25]See the writings of S. Gomulka (1986), S. Gomulka and J. Rostowski (1988), and P. Desai (1986a, 1986b, 1987).

[26]Space does not permit consideration of the role of budgetary institutions. Their situation has singular features, but including them in the analysis would not alter the general conclusions.

[27]This expression first appeared in the works of W. Brus [1961] (1972) and G. Grossman (1966).

The arsenal of direct bureaucratic control also contains plan instructions, production assignments, and input quotas whose targets are expressed in value. If a physical unit of measurement cannot be interpreted (as it certainly cannot in the case of large aggregates), there is no choice but to calculate and add up in prices. So money is used in the direct bureaucratic control of the sphere of state-owned firms to that extent, but a clear distinction should be drawn between this role and the function of money in market coordination. Money, profit, and price are leading actors in market coordination but mere extras in bureaucratic coordination.[28]

It is now possible to summarize the justification for having termed classical socialism a semimonetized system in the introduction to this chapter. Money fails to operate as the general medium of exchange in entries 4.1, 4.2, 4.4, and 4.5 of table 8.3. Furthermore, in entries 5.1, 5.2, 5.4, or 5.5, that is, in the entries where the state-owned firms and cooperatives in bureaucratic public ownership conduct financial transactions with each other, the banking system, and the state budget, it merely plays a passive, supplementary, secondary role.

Turning to the other social sectors of the economy, it was established in the previous section that the budget constraint on the formal and informal private sector and on households is hard. Examining in turn all the aspects considered in connection with the sectors in public ownership, the results are found to bear the opposite sign:

■ Private undertakings and households are strongly responsive to price and income. Their purchases are radically influenced by their present and prospective income situation and by the relative price of the products and services they wish to buy. Thus, money plays an active role in this sphere.

■ The producers in the private sector are obliged to produce efficiently by the hard budget constraint and the strong incentive to increase profits.

■ The demand from private undertakings and households is under the hard constraint of the income and wealth available.

Simplifying slightly, one can divide the classical socialist system into two great spheres from the point of view of financial affairs: those with soft and hard budget constraint and with passive and active money.

[28]It has been argued that the function of money in the aggregate measurement of products is a crucial evidence of its activeness. This is, for example, one of the arguments used by K. A. Soós (1986).

Acceptance or rejection of this position depends on agreeing about terminology—what one includes within the "activeness-passiveness" of money: all possible money functions or only those that apply through the price-revenue-cost-profit mechanism of market coor-

8.6   Administrative Producer Prices

The next topic to consider is price determination. The prices used in various transactions will be taken in turn, grouped according to who is the seller and who the buyer.

Let me begin with interfirm prices in sectors in public ownership, in other words, the sphere in which seller and buyer both belong to this social sector (prices used in entries 4.4, 4.5, 5.4, and 5.5 of table 8.3). Known generally as *producer prices,*[29] these are *administrative prices* under the classical socialist system. They result from vertical bureaucratic coordination, not horizontal market coordination following from agreement between seller and buyer. The prices are set centrally while the economy remains undeveloped, but progressive differentiation of production makes this technically impossible to do. Pricing then becomes the province of a vast, multilevel, hierarchical apparatus.[30]

Economic theory has made it plain that demand, supply, output, quality, and prices have an inseparable bearing on one another. The quantities and prices are determined simultaneously by theoretical models.[31] In spite of that, the practice under the classical system is to separate the two completely; quantities and prices are handled by two quite distinct arms of the bureaucracy, which maintain substantial working relations in the field of consumer goods and services bought by households (considered in the next section) but pay little heed to each other on the matter of prices in the sphere of interfirm transactions.

Nominally, every single price is laid down officially for the producer firm, but in practice the pricing authorities are short of information on the vast number of products being made. So their decisions have to be based on calculations supplied by either the firm or a body superior to it (depending on the specific regulations). That often means in practice that the pricing authorities set *pseudo-administrative,* not truly administrative, prices, since they merely endorse prices set by the producer. This

---

dination? This book observes the latter convention. This does not entail a denial that aggregation performed in value terms has an influence on economic activity.

[29]Strictly speaking, the price of any means of production and services sold within the formal and informal private sectors is a "producer price" [→8.8].

[30]The actual form of organization varies between countries and periods. Normally, the topmost body (the central price office) is an authority with the rank of a ministry. At lower levels (within ministries and regional bodies) there are separate price departments under dual supervision (both by the ministry or regional body and by the central price authority).

[31]This is done in the so-called fix-point models (H. Scarf [1973], for instance) and the simplified versions of these made for practical calculation purposes, the "computable general equilibrium models." See, for example, K. Dervis, J. de Melo, and S. Robinson (1982).

price is not set through horizontal market bargaining either. It emerges from vertical bureaucratic bargaining.[32]

To set prices, the pricing authorities must apply principles prescribed officially. The following are those on which most emphasis is laid:[33]

A. Prices must reflect the socially necessary costs. The official expression of this principle is couched in the terminology of Marxian political economy.[34] Pragmatic application of it corresponds to what is known in Western business and economic circles as the cost-plus principle. To the actual cost is added the firm's profit considered normal and other net-income payments to the budget, and the price must cover the sum of these items.

The pricing bureaucracy comes up against a long list of grave problems when applying the first principle.

■ Prompted by the teachings of Marxist political economy, the price calculation is based on average costs. So a significant proportion of worse than average producers become lossmakers, even though their production is required to satisfy demand. (This alone is reason enough for softening the budget constraint.)

■ Under the same theoretical influence, the use of land and the employment of capital do not count as "costs," and neither land rent nor interest appears in the calculations.[35]

■ The level of nominal wages is unrealistically low compared with the price of other factors [→8.7].

■ The cost of import acquisition is not reflected adequately in the costs, because determination of the domestic price of imports is divorced from the actual cost of obtaining them, and the rate of exchange is arbitrary.

These distortions in themselves frustrate any consistent application of the first principle.

B. Prices should be the means by which the economic management encourages producers to perform specific tasks. For instance, the prices of certain more modern means of agricultural production (fertilizers,

---

[32]The producer makes a disguised price rise if all else fails [→8.4]. If the officially set price is considered to be too low, the quality is tampered with instead.

[33]G. Grossman (1977b) gives a similar list of criteria.

[34]The Marxian definition, in fact, implies that the price should only recognize the socially necessary cost. But in the absence of competition to enforce efficiency, there is no way of telling whether a producer has not invested socially unnecessary labor into a product. In practice, the Marxian principle is replaced by automatic recognition of the average cost.

[35]Even if interest is calculated on a pragmatic basis after all in certain countries and periods, the rate of it is absurdly low.

machinery) are kept low, the intention being to encourage the spread of modern technology.

Although there is reluctance to use expressions connected with the market mechanism in official corroboration of pricing policy, this is, after all, an attempt by the economic management to influence the supply and demand of producers in favor of its own preferences through price-setting. But the hope is illusory. As stated in the previous section, firms in public ownership are rather unresponsive to prices.

Since the automatic market mechanism that adjusts supply, demand, and prices to one another fails to work, the second principle necessarily comes into conflict with the first. The artificial lowering of a price makes long-term subsidization of production inevitable. Or, in the contrary case, the price is raised but the consequent extra net income is withdrawn by imposing a special tax or raising the proportion of profit the firm is obliged to pay in.

C. Prices ought to be stable. This is considered desirable for the sake of maintaining the purchasing power of personal incomes and helping in the technical process of planning. The economic management has inordinate fear of inflation.[36] To avoid inflation it is even prepared to accept the cataleptic rigidity caused by leaving prices unchanged for a long period (even decades in some areas).[37] Of course, this conflicts strongly with the first principle, because it prevents prices conforming to costs and renders necessary a complex system of subsidies and levies to bridge the gap between prices invariable in time and costs varying in time.

Concurrent application of the three principles has major consequences. One has been referred to repeatedly in passing: it is inevitably accompanied by the creation of a complex system of fiscal redistribution.[38] There develops an impenetrable web of subsidies granted on various grounds and extra levies, and taxes deducted on various grounds. This shows up on both the revenue and expenditure sides of the budget [→8.2]. Fiscal redistribution provides means (and also a reason) for softening the budget constraint.

The second consequence is this: since an attempt is made to use several mutually contradictory principles in economic management at the same time, none of them is really asserted. One function of price in market coordination is to convey information in a concise form on the relative scarcity of resources and products. No such information is conveyed by

---

[36]The leadership in several countries (the Soviet Union, China, Eastern Europe) has vivid memories of how the socialist system came to power when the economy was suffering from acute inflation and had great difficulty in restoring stability.

[37]For instance, many prices in East Germany were unchanged for thirty years.

[38]For detailed description and Hungarian data, see J. Kornai and Á. Matits (1987, 1990, pp. 54–98).

the prices here described. In fact, they impart almost no useful information at all, as it is almost all lost in the conflict between the disparate pricing principles. In other words, the relative prices emerging under the classical system are arbitrary and irrational.

The millions of prices in the price system are interdependent. Only a few fundamentally important prices need be arbitrary for a spillover distorting almost the whole price system: the arbitrariness of the output price affects the costs of the user, which affects the user's output price, and so on. Since there is far more involved than just the distortion of a few prices, the arbitrariness is enormously magnified through the mutual effects.

A vicious circle develops with the soft budget constraint and weak interest in profit on one side and the arbitrariness of the prices on the other. Since profitability is not a matter of life and death to a firm, it is worth neither the seller's nor the buyer's while to struggle forcefully for rational prices. If prices are generally known to be arbitrary, it is hardly worth reacting to them. But it seems to be justified to claim compensation for losses allegedly caused by the distortions of costs and sales prices.

One cannot base any kind of rational calculation on arbitrary prices. When a decision maker chooses between alternative input combinations (e.g., alternative production technologies, investments, or new products), it is far from certain that the more efficient will be identified by the calculation of costs and profit.

A further consequence is that the price system fails to contribute to creating equilibrium between production and consumption, supply and demand. These are not "market-clearing" prices; nor do the official pricing principles require them to be so.

In fact, the underlying causal connection is in the reverse direction: prices are arbitrary because market coordination, the mutual effect of supply and demand, seller and buyer, is forcibly excluded from the setting of them. Even if the bureaucratic coordination mechanism wanted to, it could arrive at nothing but arbitrary pricing.[39]

The real main function of prices in the sphere now examined is to create the weighting system needed for arriving at the aggregate volume indicators. From the angle of direct bureaucratic control, in fact, it would be desirable if all plan directives could be given in physical units of measurement. But that cannot be done; aggregation is inevitable in order to reduce the information task. So bureaucratic coordination is also confronted with one of the basic problems of the economy, that of

---

[39]The idea arose during the debate on socialism in the 1930s, primarily from O. Lange, that the pricing authority should set market-clearing, equilibrium prices [→21.1, 22.3].

measuring qualitatively unlike things. And if that must be done, there is no alternative to employing prices of some kind. In this case, that means the use of an arbitrary and irrational price system, which casts doubt on the economic meaning of each and every aggregate indicator of volume (output, capital stock, etc.) measured in value terms.

8.7 Administrative Consumer Prices

Let us now turn to the prices of products and services produced by the sectors in public ownership and purchased by households (those in entries 8.4 and 8.5 of table 8.3). These make up the bulk of consumer prices.[40] This sphere too has administrative pricing. The price setting is more strictly centralized than it is for most producer prices, since it rightly counts as far more of a political matter.

Apart from self-evident differences, the features described in the last section apply to this sphere. To the first three principles can be added two more principles valid expressly for consumer prices.

D. The consumer prices must be set so as to influence the demand of the population in the way those running the country consider desirable.

Unlike the second principle (influencing producers' decisions with prices), which the soft budget constraint on firms renders largely illusory, the fourth principle is realistic. There is a hard budget constraint on households, which are most responsive to relative prices. Therefore, consumer price policy does strongly influence households.

The ethical justification, if not the effectiveness, of the principle is debatable; whatever the case, it is certainly a vivid illustration of paternalism [→4.4]. The leaders of the economy believe they know what is really good for the consumers better than the consumers themselves; they are ready to defend them from their own faulty consumer decisions. All who set a high value on individual autonomy and consumer sovereignty object to this principle being applied. At most, the fourth principle can be endorsed only exceptionally under a system of values that respects the free choice of the individual.[41]

E. The determination of consumer prices should be used for the purpose of income redistribution. Accordingly, there should be special taxes to raise the price of luxury goods, for instance, while the price of basic,

---

[40]Of course, consumer prices also include the prices of products and services sold to households by the private sector. These are covered in the next section.

[41]For instance, it can be desirable to limit the consumer's freedom of choice in the case of narcotics and firearms. Even then the limitation of consumer sovereignty must be imposed by a competent democratic institution (e.g., a freely elected parliament).

staple articles and services should be lowered through subsidies. One manifestation of the principle is that the majority of basic public services (particularly health and education) are provided free. In certain cases, consumer price setting is used to further "class policy," for instance, by redistributing income from the villages to the towns.

One can say also of the fifth principle that it really works; use of it is accompanied by actual redeployments of income. Yet it poses grave problems. Above all, the goals of income redistribution are politically and ethically debatable, but even those prepared to go along with them may well doubt whether they should be applied through prices (rather than incomes). Redistribution through consumer prices cannot be "targeted" with sufficient accuracy: the subsidies are enjoyed also by those whom the income redistribution was not intended to support, and the high taxes place burdens on those it was not intended to include in the disadvantage [→13.6].

The remaining comments apply both to principles D and E. Consumer prices lowered artificially by subsidies (and as the extreme, the "zero prices" of free distribution) produce an inordinate growth in demand. That causes chronic shortage, since supply cannot keep pace. Among the promises in the official ideology of the classical system is a goal of satisfying people's basic needs [→4.3]. That is what consumer pricing policy (particularly principle E) should do. Instead, its effect is to highlight how the promise has not and cannot be kept at so low an economic development level. Often the very products and services it was intended to make "cheap" are those whose shortage is felt most acutely [→13.6].

The application of principles D and E exacerbates the conflicts between principles discussed in the previous section. Far from being insulated from producer prices, consumer prices react upon them in a number of ways. For one thing, firms too buy products and services bought primarily by households and so subject to consumer pricing policy. For another, consumer pricing policy affects the level of nominal wages. Since the wages set do not account for the true social costs of free or heavily subsidized consumption, labor appears relatively too "cheap" compared with other costs. The grave problem stated in the last section—prices are arbitrary and rational calculation is impossible—becomes graver still due to the backlash of consumer pricing policy.

There is no guarantee that consumer demand influenced by the state price will coincide with supply laid down in the state plan. If it does not, almost all the burden of adjustment falls on the consumers. Automatic market effects alerting producers via price and profit changes to any discrepancy between supply and demand, so obliging them to accommodate also, do not apply. Consumer preferences have no influence (or very little) on producers.

One can now explain why the entry of table 6.1 with the public sector as seller and households as buyer is marked "M (with intervention of B)." Formally, this is a horizontal market relation in which goods and money change hands. By one important criterion it is of a market nature: no one tells the buyer what to acquire; to that extent he enters into this relation voluntarily. But this market coordination is overlaid with bureaucratic coordination when the latter unilaterally and arbitrarily sets the administrative consumer prices.

Table 8.4 illustrates what has been said about consumer prices by comparing relative consumer prices in East Germany and West Germany. Most prices in the column on East Germany are administrative prices, but some market prices are also included. The arbitrariness of the socialist price system is conspicuous. There is no rational principle to account for the potato, for instance, being extraordinarily cheap, and butter and ladies' pantyhose being extraordinarily expensive.

8.8 Market Prices

Prices based on an unmistakably horizontal market relation, buyer-seller agreement, emerge only in the area where the seller is the informal private sector and the buyers are households or the formal and informal private sector (prices in entries 6.7, 7.7, and 8.7 of table 8.3).

With semilegal and illegal production, service, and trading activities, the market price must also cover the risk premium, as the seller may be punished. Punishment has no certainty, only a level of probability, and the risk premium is the likely value of the compensation expected for the loss incurred from punishment. The higher the probability of punishment, the higher the price.

Turning to the formal private sector, the price authorities try to lay down administratively the prices charged by private artisans and traders with official permits. But in practice it is hard to enforce these regulations[42] against prices sought by sellers and accepted by buyers, that is, based on agreement.

A special, intermediate category is the free market for agricultural produce. The main buyer on this market is the household sector, while the sellers belong to various social sectors: the cooperatives, with the part of their production they are entitled to sell on this market,[43] the household

[42]This is one means, but not the exclusive one, of bureaucratic restriction of the formal private sector. This is why entries 3.3 and 3.5 of table 6.1 are marked "M (with intervention of B)."

[43]The cooperatives in the Soviet Union and several Eastern European countries have to pay in their tax in kind (where such exists), or sell a specified proportion of their production

farms, and also people not employed in agriculture who sell produce (fruit, vegetables, meat) from their private gardens or dwarf holdings.[44] In this sphere buying and selling take place at true market prices. The prices on these free markets are universally far higher than administrative consumer prices, which indirectly indicates the insufficient supply from the public sector and the unrealistically low level of the administrative prices.[45]

I shall use the collective term *parallel markets* as a common term covering the legal free markets, and the various semilegal and illegal (grey and black) markets.

8.9 Nonprice Signals

In the chapter so far it has been discussed that all levels of the bureaucracy, including the leadership of firms in public ownership, react little to price signals. Moreover, prices other than the true market prices discussed in section 8.8 convey hardly any useful information, so that there would not be much point in heeding them in any case.

Yet all coordination mechanisms require information. At the risk of repeating in places what has been said earlier or anticipating material in later chapters, I shall look briefly, without attempting to be comprehensive, at the major nonprice signals prevalent under the system.[46]

1. *Planning communications.* The most important of these are plan instructions from above, which are complemented by planning proposals, criticisms, and reports from below [→7.2]. The bulk of these communications flow vertically, but horizontal flows appear too while the plan is being devised and amended: there are discussions between ministries, between branch authorities, and between companies.

2. *Other direct bureaucratic information.* To this category belongs communication within the framework of the management of the economy: moving downward there are improvised instructions, reminders,

---

to the state trading organization at artificially low official prices. Part of the produce is required by the cooperative itself for farming (sowing seed, etc.), and another part goes to the members for household consumption and perhaps for use on the household farm. If salable produce still remains after that (and very little or nothing does in many periods), the cooperative is entitled to sell it on the free market.

[44]In section 5.6, household farming was placed in the formal private sector and agricultural production by those not employed in agriculture in the informal private sector.

[45]For instance, the free-market price for milk in Romania in 1988 was 220–230 percent of the administrative price. The price ratios for some other foodstuffs were as follows: eggs, 330; potatoes, 320; cow's milk cheese, 180–220. P. Ronnas (1989, p. 554).

[46]On this see also R. P. Powell (1977).

TABLE 8.4
Relative Consumer Prices in East and West Germany, 1989

	Relative Consumer Prices (Numeraire 1 kg of wheat flour)	
	East Germany	West Germany
1 kg beef (for boiling)	4.39	8.04
1 kg beef (for roasting)	7.42	14.26
1 kg pork chop	6.06	9.02
1 kg potatoes	0.13	0.85
1 kg black bread	0.39	2.63
1 kg white bread	0.75	2.61
1 kg wheat flour	*1.00*	*1.00*
1 kg coffee	53.03	7.23
1 l milk	0.51	1.01
1 egg	0.26	0.20
1 kg butter	7.27	7.03
1 kg gouda cheese	5.45	10.02
1 kg sugar	1.17	1.54
1 kWh electricity	0.06	0.25
1 ton brown coal		
rationed	1.29	
free market	2.66	16.57
1 public transport ticket (within city)	0.15	1.69
1 ladies' pantyhose	10.60	4.23
1 washing machine	1,742.42	791.13
1 refrigerator	1,079.50	450.80
1 color TV	3,712.12	1,241.13
1 first-class domestic letter	0.15	0.80
1 square-meter rent in new public apartment	0.6–0.95	3.22–6.45
1 place in public kindergarten	11.36	72.58

Source: Compiled by C. Krüger for this book on the basis of the following sources: Statistisches Amt der Deutschen Demokratischen Republik (Berlin, East Germany) (1990, pp. 309, 311); Statistisches Bundesamt (Stuttgart, West Germany) (1990, p. 549); R. Götz-Coenenberg (1990, p. 15).

prohibitions, and callings to account, while proposals, requests, and protests move upward [→7.3].

3. *Operative horizontal information.* Although the vertical communications have a stronger influence, there is also a constant horizontal flow of information, of course. Authorities on the same level are in contact. Firms have direct contacts, too: orders and confirmation or rejection of them, disputes over delivery terms, expediting notices, claims, and so on.

4. *Signals of shortage and surplus.* This sphere of problems is treated in more detail in chapters 11 and 12. Here all that is noted in advance is that both shortage and surplus remain perceptible even when they are not reflected in the movement of prices. If the seller's stocks begin to decline or run out completely, or if the order book swells to more than its usual size, it probably indicates that demand has risen by comparison with supply. The same is implied if there are queues for products for which people did not line up before, or if previously existing queues for products have grown longer than normal. The opposites of all the symptoms listed presumably reflect that demand has fallen by comparison with supply.[47]

This form of information gains particular importance because it is, by its nature, decentralized: all firms and all factory units can observe their own stocks and order books, the queues they join, and those that form for their own products.

5. *Signals of catastrophe.* Normally, troubles accumulate steadily, but often they are noticed only when they have caused a catastrophe. A flood warns of neglect of flood precautions, an air crash of shortcomings in aircraft maintenance, and so on. Although this form of information takes a great toll, it is effective.

6. *"Voice."* Mention was made of Hirschman's apt expression for the important part played in coordination by proposals, criticisms, and protests from below [→6.3]. In fact, it appears as one ingredient in the information flows listed under types 1–5, although so far mainly in the form of feedback within the bureaucracy. But an additional role dependent on the system's level of political tolerance can be played by voice from the "very bottom": the complaints, low grumbles, or loud protests of the public.

Signals are mostly given when some economic variable has reached a critical value or, in other words, a threshold value. In certain fields these values are set by custom or routine (e.g., the critical value of input inven-

---

[47]It can be shown theoretically that given certain simplifying assumptions, sufficient information is provided by the stocks, order books, and observations of queuing to control an elementary, quantitative coordination of the system. See J. Kornai and B. Martos, eds. (1981), B. Martos (1990), A. Simonovits (1981).

tories) while in others by the tolerance limits of the economy's live actors (e.g., the size of fall in real wages leading to open protest).[48]

How system-specific is operation of the various types of information? Flows of nonprice information of types 3–6 are important under the capitalist system as well.[49] Type 2 is not unknown either, on the one hand within the various partial bureaucracies and on the other through the ubiquitous intervention of the state bureaucracy. But only in capitalist countries where national economic planning has been introduced in some form do some elements of type 1 appear, and even there sporadically.

As for the other side of the coin, the not inconsiderable part that price information plays even under the classical socialist system has been discussed in detail in the chapter so far.

In other words, the distinction is not that price signals alone operate under capitalism and nonprice signals alone under classical socialism, but rather that the systems differ in the relative weights they attach to them. In a capitalist economy, price signals carry the most important and effective messages, whereas under classical socialism that is done by nonprice signals.

In many respects, price and nonprice signals complement each other. But where they do not, and the latter replace the former, a wide variety of drawbacks occur. There is an automatic incentive attached to price signals in the case of private property and market coordination, whereas nonprice signals can be coupled to incentive schemes only by indirect means. Prices and costs are easily commensurable, but one cannot normally make a direct comparison between different nonprice signals with each other directly. Thus, the importance attached to each signal comes to depend on the decision maker's subjective judgment. To sum up: nonprice signals, too, are able to assure the viability of coordination. What they cannot do is fine-tune the system or ensure it operates efficiently.

[48]Remarkable research was done by I. Grosfeld (1989a) in the mathematical modeling of control according to tolerance limits. She used the model to analyze investment fluctuations.

[49]For a long time economic theorists neglected to study what functions nonprice signals perform under the capitalist system. But interest in the subject has grown more recently. For example, A. M. Spence (1974) studies the case where education is used as a signal in the job market. For a recent survey, see J.J. Laffont (1989).

9

Investment and Growth

CHAPTERS 7 and 8 dealt largely with short-term control of the economy, and medium and long-term control were mentioned at most in passing. The last of these is the subject of this chapter.

The first two sections describe the motives of the participants and the institutional framework of the investment process. The remaining sections examine the structure and dynamics of growth.[1] The literature has given a variety of names to the classical socialist system's specific type of growth: *forced growth, rush,* and *haste*.[2] The chapter tries to clarify what factors determine the rate of growth under the classical system, and what are the social costs of the growth process.

The main growth figures for a number of socialist countries are seen at the end of the chapter, in tables 9.10, 9.11, 9.12, and 9.13, followed by a summary appraisal of the growth performance [→9.7–9.9].

9.1 Expansion Drive and Investment Hunger

What are the motives behind forced growth, rush, or haste? The first part of the answer is an attempt to assess the system's supreme leaders in this respect.

By and large, the advocates of socialist revolution came to power in countries that had been poor and backward. In every backward country, whether a socialist system is in power or not, the signs can be observed of an impatience typical of the "late arriver," an oppressive awareness of having fallen seriously behind the more developed, wealthier countries.[3] This impatience, manifest in every developing country, is ampli-

---

[1]On the general theory of growth, see R. M. Solow [1970] (1988). On modern history of growth, see E. F. Denison (1962, 1967), A. Gerschenkron (1962, 1968), and S. Kuznets (1964, 1971). For applications to socialist countries, see A. Bergson and S. Kuznets, eds. (1963) and A. Bergson (1974, 1978a). See the subsequent sections of this chapter for more references to the experience of socialist countries.

[2]I coined the term "rush" (1971). For the epithet "haste," see M. Lewin [1968] (1974) and G. Grossman (1983). G. Ofer (1987) uses it as a synonym for "forced growth."

This chapter makes use of the excellent summarizing review by G. Ofer (1987). Although Ofer looks mainly at the literature on Soviet growth, it contains several general statements that go beyond it.

[3]The classical work discussing the consequences of backwardness and being a "late arriver" is A. Gerschenkron (1962).

fied in the case of socialist countries by a promise the socialist revolutionaries made before their victory: they would eliminate the backwardness
very quickly once they were in power. This is among the ideas that
brought broad strata in society over to their side. The promise is repeated
over and over again after the victory of the revolution. The revolutionaries themselves are impatient, but they also feel the pressure of the impatience among large masses of the public.

The original, oft-repeated promise rests on a belief that they can catch
up with the developed countries quite fast by virtue of the socialist system's superiority. This belief is a major constituent of the official ideology. The leaders insist on fast growth because it will provide further
evidence of that superiority.

Finally, the imperative to catch up faster with the more developed
countries is reinforced by military and defense considerations. Modern-
ization and economic strength are needed to create an army with striking
force.

It is worth quoting a speech of Stalin in 1931: "One feature of the
history of the old Russia was the continual beatings she suffered for
falling behind, for her backwardness. . . . We are fifty or one hundred
years behind the advanced countries. We must make good this distance
in ten years. Either we do it or they crush us."[4] Stalin's successors repeatedly returned to the same notion (Khrushchev made the memorable
threat that the socialist system will bury the Western world),[5] as did Mao
Zedong and other leaders of the socialist countries. The haste comes
across in the name Mao gave to one phase in China's economic history:
the "Great Leap Forward."[6]

The top leaders want to impose with an iron hand a policy of the
fastest possible growth. This is the leitmotif of the annual and five-year
plans. It is expressed in the production plans, which are intended to maximize growth in value and outrank all other instructions, in the quantity
drive apparent also in management, and in the highly ambitious plans
for investment.

It should be stressed, however, that a forced rate of growth is not a
policy the upper leadership need compel the middle- and lower-level lead-

[4]J. V. Stalin (1947, p. 356).

[5]Khrushchev said at a press conference during his visit to the United States:

"Q. It is frequently attributed to you, Mr. Khrushchev, that you told a diplomat at a
reception that you would bury us.

K. My life would be too short to bury every one of you if this were to happen to me.
. . . At the reception, I said that in the course of historical progress and in the historical
sense, capitalism would be buried and communism would come to replace capitalism."
N. S. Khrushchev (1959, pp. 76–77).

[6]One of the major slogans of the Great Leap Forward was "Surpassing Britain and
catching up to the United States (in the economy) within fifteen years."

ers to follow against their general will. On the contrary, these people already have a strong inner *expansion drive*. Let me return to the earlier analysis of the bureaucracy's motives in section 7.4.

The medium- and lower-level members of the bureaucracy are imbued by the same political conviction as the leaders. They sense the need for swift growth, which is conveyed to them also by the vast machinery for propagating the official ideology (motive 1).

Identification with their jobs also inclines them toward expansion. Anyone who considers really important the activity of the unit under his or her command wishes sincerely to see it extended. University presidents the world over wish their universities had more professors, more students, more lecture halls, and better equipment. Heads of hospitals aspire to more doctors and wards, and more and better facilities. The commander of an armed force demands additional and more modern arms (motive 2).

Leaders at all levels of the bureaucracy consider that their power and prestige grow in accordance with the expansion of the unit they lead, and so do their financial rewards in many cases (motives 3, 4, and 5).

Under the classical socialist system there is an additional major factor: middle- and lower-level leaders recognize the chronic shortage of the products or services their ministry, branch directorate, or firm provides. The pressure of unmet demand also pushes them to expand. In addition, the difficulties they encounter in obtaining their own inputs may prompt them to produce these within the firm or branch, which again requires investment.

Some of the impulses listed are system-specific, but others apply equally to bureaucratic leaders under capitalism, not just socialism. One might add that expansion drive is very strong not only among appointed, employed bureaucratic leaders but among capitalist entrepreneurs, who expect expansion to bring greater profits, and so greater power and prestige.

The main system-specific distinction lies not in the actual effort to expand but in the internally generated self-restraint that runs counter to it. In the eyes of capitalist firms' owners (or managers charged with running them on their behalf), expansion is an attraction, but also a big risk. They have to consider carefully whether the products of the enlarged company will be saleable, and if so, at what price and profitability. Any loss caused by a faulty investment decision hits them in the pocket. Though they expand in the hope of doing good business, the risk of doing bad business limits unbridled expansion.

This is the curb that the classical socialist system removes. Because of the chronic shortage, the extra production resulting from the expansion can probably be sold [→ 12.2]. Because of the soft budget constraint, the firm can reckon that liquidation will not follow from any faulty investment decisions, however high the costs and financial losses may be. A great many people at all levels of the hierarchy have a part in an investment decision, but no loss incurred will hit any of them in the pocket [→5.3].

Expansion drive is a fact of life for the bureaucracy.[7] And because this system has only bureaucrats and no real owners, there is an almost total lack of internal, self-imposed restraint that might resist this drive.[8] The *investment hunger* is ubiquitous.

Among the basic problems of the capitalism described by Keynesian macroeconomics is that entrepreneurs lack a strong enough desire to invest, precisely because of the self-restraint. The antidote is to stimulate entrepreneurs' "animal spirits," that is, expansion efforts.[9] This problem is entirely absent under classical socialism, where the investment hunger is insatiable. Of course, there remains a strong and effective curb, but it is not suggested from within to the firm or to lower- and medium-level decision makers in general because of fear of making a wrong decision. Instead, restraints from without are set by the process of bureaucratic allocation of investment, which fixes investment quotas and requires permits for investment projects.

9.2   Central Allocation and Investment Tension

The control of the investment process is far more strictly centralized than day-to-day production. The first things to examine are investment planning and decision making prior to an investment project.

On the one hand, the national economic plan distributes investment funds among the various ministries in the course of the planning and decision-making process. The disaggregation of the funds proceeds from the top downward in the customary way [→7.2]. The quotas are set in value terms and are usually broken down into a few main items of expenditure (e.g., a sum for construction and another for machinery and equipment, in the second case divided into machines acquired domestically and those acquired abroad). On the other hand, the central plan

[7]This feature of bureaucratic behavior is seized upon in the models in which the objective function of a bureaucrat is to maximize the budget at his disposal. See W. Niskanen (1971).

[8]It is worth mentioning two internal, self-imposed restraints. One is connected with motive 6: a leader wants a quiet life, whereas each new investment brings vexation and extra responsibility. The other self-restraint concerns maneuvers during the bargaining processes. A shrewd functionary will not give the impression of always demanding things but from time to time will exercise a measure of self-control.

[9]See J. M. Keynes (1936, p. 162).

decides case by case which, out of the set of all investment projects, will be the priority projects. It is determined centrally what the installation resulting from each priority investment project will produce, what technology it will use, where it will operate, when it should be ready, and how much it should cost to establish.

As noted in the last section, the investment hunger is insatiable, considering the totality of all firms and institutions in public ownership. Before the plan is finally endorsed, the subordinate units always demand more investment funds than the allocators on the higher levels are able to distribute.[10] There are always more priority investments proposed than the resources will stretch to. This specific form of excess demand is a manifestation of vertical shortage ("vertical" because it appears in the bargaining process between subordinates and superiors) [→11.3]. Pressure from above and below on those preparing the investment decisions is usually so strong that extremely ambitious and often unrealistic, overstretched plans result.

This is compounded by the fact that the devisers of a plan for an investment project frequently deliberately underestimate the expected investment costs and completion time so as to better the chances of acceptance. The desire of the lower- and medium-level managers above all is to have their proposal accepted and included in the plan. Once it has been, no one is going to halt the project, even if the costs turn out to be far greater than expected. The phenomenon is known in East European business parlance as "clambering into the plan."[11]

What basis does the superior allocator use to decide how to distribute the investment funds or endorse a priority project? There is no capital market where intended investors seriously consider the expected profitability of a project, the interest and repayment terms of the credit available, or the risk of the investment. No one makes a profit estimate, not least because no one regards a calculation from prevailing prices and prevailing interest and foreign exchange rates as competent to measure the efficiency of the project planned.

Although the guidance criteria customary under the capitalist system are lacking, the selection is not haphazard here either. Definite priorities apply in the allocation of investment [→9.4]. Other footholds are the balances worked out during planning, and the shortage signals the bureaucracy receives, from which it can deduce what new production facilities are needed to satisfy the probable demands. And, of course, alloca-

---

[10]Of course, not all sectors or all firms and institutions are equally aggressive in this scrimmage. Those who feel they may be set a big investment task but not ensured enough resources for it show particular caution.

[11]See T. Bauer (1981, p. 500).

tion, as mentioned earlier, is influenced also by the political pressure and lobbying from various quarters.

As for the execution of the investment plans, there is excess demand for investment goods and services called in economic parlance *investment tension*. Taken together, the investment projects that have been officially approved require more inputs than are physically available. This is a horizontal shortage that appears in the relation between the supplier and the utilizer of investment goods. The reaction takes place within the frame of direct bureaucratic control for the most part: the higher organizations intervene, making improvised decisions on who should receive the product or resource currently in short supply and who should be left out.

Normally, no project in progress is halted fully, not least because each has its powerful advocates in the bureaucracy. Instead, the holdups cause a number of different projects to slow down simultaneously. This practice leads to a dissipation of investment, severe lengthening of the approval and completion time,[12] and a large increase in the costs.

Before any investment decision comes a lengthy process of agreement and bargaining in which several branches and levels of the bureaucracy are involved. That precludes deciding quickly and flexibly on actions not previously planned. In any case, there are no free, uncommitted resources to use on a new project (say, quick application of a new invention or seizure of an export opportunity that suddenly arises). The rigidity mentioned earlier [→7.3] appears particularly strongly in the investment process.[13]

9.3 Investment and Consumption

The next thing to examine is the structure of the growth process. The first problem to study here is the breakdown of the expenditure of gross

---

[12]The process of obtaining permission takes so long that by the time the decision is made, the project is obsolete. In the Soviet Union in the 1980s, 25 percent of the projects had been devised ten to twenty years earlier. See R. Judy and R. Clough (1989). According to a representative survey, annual spending on between half and a third of the large projects begun in 1973 and 1974 was reduced from the second year onward, so protracting the investment period. See T. Bauer (1981, appendix, p. 172).

A comparison of investment projects in a number of industries shows that in the 1960s it took between twice and five times as long to complete a project in Hungary as it did in Japan. See Z. Pacsi (1979, p. 630).

[13]Y. Qian and C. Xu (1991) demonstrate in a formal model that because of the soft budget constraint, socialist economies rely heavily on bureaucratic procedures for pre-screening investment projects as their optimal organizational response to the problem of investment hunger. As a result of these bureaucratic procedures, projects are delayed and promising projects may be rejected.

domestic product and the proportion of it used for investment. The investment proportion in most periods is appreciably higher in most socialist countries than in most capitalist countries.[14] This is illustrated in table 9.1, which presents some comparative data.

The proportion of GDP spent under the classical socialist system on maintaining the bureaucratic apparatus and funding the armed forces is no smaller than in capitalist countries. More can go on investment only if less is spent on consumption, meaning direct, individual consumption

TABLE 9.1
Share of Investment in GDP: International Comparison

	Investment as Percentage of GDP	
	1980	*1988*
Socialist countries		
Bulgaria	28	27
China	24	32
Czechoslovakia	27	26
East Germany	24	27
Hungary	29	21
Poland	25	23
Soviet Union	30	30
Capitalist countries		
Brazil	23	22
France	23	21
West Germany	23	20
India	19	21
Italy	24	22
Netherlands	21	22
Spain	22	24
United States	17	17

Source: P. Marer et al. (1991).

[14]Since the discussion is of the general prototype of classical socialism, one must disregard the fact that the proportion of investment varied between socialist countries and also changed with time, sometimes rising and sometimes falling.

by households and collective consumption contributing to public well-being.[15]

Things happen this way mainly because the country's leaders, fully consciously, want them to happen so. Mention has been made of their impatience to achieve the fastest possible growth. Here one should add that they see as the main means of achieving it as large a scale of investment as possible. In the language of growth theory, they have dangling before them (even if they never heard of one) a Harrod-Domar model with just a single factor of production: capital. To their extremely simplified reasoning, the larger the proportion for investment, the faster the rate of growth.

Table 9.2 shows that investment in fixed assets grows appreciably faster in the socialist countries that feature here than it does in the capitalist countries with which they are compared. It is also worth noting that the gap between the growth rates of investment and GDP is far wider than in most of the capitalist countries. This confirms indirectly the observation made above regarding the forced expansion of investment. The table also records the low efficiency of investment: for output to rise over a long period by, say, 4–6 percent a year, investment has to grow by 8–11 percent a year. This is among the factors that impel the leaders of a socialist economy to enforce a high investment proportion.

The country's leadership not only wants a high investment proportion, it is fully able to impose its will. Never, under any previous system in history, has so small a group of people kept so tight a hold on the nation-wide investment-consumption ratio.

Economists argue about the ex ante causal relationship between investment and saving under the capitalist system. What one certainly can say is that both investment and saving are thoroughly decentralized processes in the hands of millions of decision makers. Also, in a high proportion of cases the two kinds of decision are separate, although voluntary saving influences investment and vice versa. This contrasts with the case under classical socialism. There investment decision making is extremely centralized and embraces decisions on saving as well. The saving, that is, nonconsumption, equals the amount the central authorities see fit to withdraw from consumption for investment purposes, whether the households, owners of the personal incomes, like it or not.[16]

[15]Here the analysis disregards whether particular socialist economies used foreign resources or not [→14.3, 14.6].

[16]Of course, an "investment equals saving" formula applies ex post under both capitalism and socialism. But this is a balance-sheet identity that has nothing to do with the ex ante causal problem, that is, with the degree to which the investment decision makers are influenced by past and expected future savings, and in reverse, how the decision makers on saving are influenced by the investment opportunities and the incentives connected with them.

TABLE 9.2
Growth of GDP and Capital Investment: International Comparison

	Average Annual Growth Rates, 1950–79	
	GDP	Gross Fixed Capital Investment
Socialist countries		
Bulgaria	5.43	10.89
Czechoslovakia	3.67	6.11
East Germany	3.77	8.52
Hungary	3.64	8.85
Poland	4.12	9.70
Romania	5.81	11.33
Soviet Union	4.95	8.02
Capitalist countries		
Australia	4.54	4.43
Canada	4.57	4.36
Finland	4.48	4.54
Greece	6.20	7.16
Italy	4.92	4.79
Netherlands	4.58	5.10
Norway	4.15	4.93
Sweden	3.69	4.18
West Germany	4.85	5.69

Source: F. L. Pryor (1985, p. 76).

Ultimately, what if anything limits the growth in the proportion of investment and the concomitant fall in the consumption proportion? As already shown, the classical socialist system lacks an automatic economic mechanism equivalent to the one operating under capitalism, namely, the interactions among individual savings and investment decisions, the capital market, and the commercial banking system. The country's leaders feel at most indirectly the limits to what the public can tolerate. These tolerance limits restrain the cutback in consumption.

There is no way of telling how concerned the supreme controllers of the classical socialist system really are with the public's material welfare.

Great emphasis is certainly laid on it in the published political programs. That obliges them to show some results of this kind, so as to legitimize the system and ensure it retains power. For this reason alone, consumption cannot be cut below the tolerance limits indefinitely.[17] It then depends on the political situation, primarily the degree of repression, where the limits actually lie: whether they allow stagnation or even reduction of per capita consumption for a longish period, or force some rise in consumption.

Ultimately, looking at the whole historical tendency of the classical system in the consolidated socialist countries, one sees a significant rise in consumption [→13.1]. But even in these countries, the consumption growth rate lags a good way behind GDP growth. In some, such as China, per capita consumption more or less stagnated for a long period.[18]

Although the bureaucracy would like to raise consumption, and the living-standard tolerance limits enforce a minimum level of consumption in any case, these circumstances are at most a curb on the top leadership's inner impulse to maximize the proportion of investment. It is not just the paramount leader or a narrow leading group at the top that prefers a high investment–consumption ratio. The vast subordinate bureaucracy inclines also toward fast growth of investment [→9.1, 9.2]. (Suffice it to repeat the key terms: expansion drive, soft budget constraint, investment hunger.) The micro motives of the bureaucracy and the macro policy of the central authorities coincide; the central leadership's decision in favor of a high investment proportion expresses the desire and purpose of the whole power elite.

The philosophy of historical "functionalism" would suggest that the institutional system of classical socialism and the motivation of the bureaucracy are as they are because that best helps a backward country to catch up. The political-economic-ideological mechanism indispensable to forcing fast growth emerges out of the impatient haste of a poor, undeveloped country.[19] Although this outlook has elements of truth in it, I

[17]In China in the period of the Great Leap Forward, the leadership's position was often characterized by quoting an old Chinese proverb: "Horses are required that gallop fast but don't need feeding."

[18]In China, the real wages of workers in state firms declined by 11.6 percent between 1957 and 1978. State Statistical Bureau (1985, p. 556).

[19]For a discussion of these issues, see A. Nove (1964, in particular chap. 1, "Was Stalin Really Necessary?"). In their monumental history of Soviet industrialization and collectivization, E. H. Carr and R. W. Davies [1969] (1974) implicitly adhere to the point of view that Stalin was the outgrowth of a particular growth strategy. For a discussion of the perceived need for coercion through the eyes of the Soviet economists of the 1920s, see A. Erlich (1960). A. Nove (1989) gives a survey of recent Soviet debates on this issue with many useful references.

see it as one-sided. This book's line of thinking suggests that a mutual influence is at work, with the power structure, ideology, and property relations on the one hand, and the type of economic growth on the other. The prime causal direction in this mutual influence is from the first to the second group of factors. Given the undivided power and official ideology of the Communist party, coupled with bureaucratic public ownership, the combined effect of all the factors is a forced rate of growth [→15.1].

Establishing the proportions of investment and consumption ties in closest with the problem sphere known in neoclassical economics as decision makers' time preference. The official ideology of classical socialism sought to proclaim the leadership's "future orientation," namely, request of a sacrifice from the present generation for a better life in the future. Mátyás Rákosi, Hungary's leader in the Stalin period, put it succinctly: "We won't kill today the hen that will lay golden eggs in the future."[20]

In characterizing the time-preference system in the age of forced growth, three phenomena can be distinguished. The first is the *sacrifice* the public makes in having to forgo part of its present consumption; more precisely, consumption of the kinds of products and services for which unmet demand does not accumulate and cannot be postponed to a later date. People consuming half the physiologically desirable quantity of milk for ten years will not be compensated by the assurance that they will be able to drink one-and-a-half times that amount for the next ten years. What the economy saves in the first period is saved once and for all.

The second phenomenon is *postponement*. Whereas sacrifice concerns a flow of consumption, postponement concerns the accumulation of stocks serving consumption: building of dwellings, retail stores, consumer goods factories, etc. Postponement is coupled with sacrifices, since it curbs current consumption. It is, however, no longer a case of "saving" consumption once and for all. Although, on the one hand, it frees resources for other investment tasks currently rated more important, on the other, the actions omitted must be performed later: the postponed tasks accumulate. It is like a loan raised on the next generation's account; every new postponement raises the burden of internal debt further.[21]

The third phenomenon is *neglect*. Pure cases of postponement do not do irremediable damage: unbuilt apartments, stores, or clothing factor-

---

[20]M. Rákosi [1950] (1955, p. 244).

[21]Postponement is not a system-specific phenomenon, since it occurs in a variety of forms in capitalist economies as well. An example is the neglect in numerous developed countries of infrastructural investment financed from budgetary sources.

ies can be built later. One can talk of neglect if there is irreversible damage. It occurs particularly in processes that demand *organic* development (fields such as higher education, health, or environmental protection). If in such cases specific tasks are neglected for decades, there is no way to compensate later by sudden resource reallocation or remedial campaigns of action.[22]

The marks of forced growth are extremely grave sacrifices by the public [→13.1] and conspicuous postponement and neglect in several development areas. The chapter's remaining sections return to them repeatedly. The policy is not notably far-sighted: maximizing the growth rate attainable in the next decade or two is preferred not only over present and future consumption but over laying the foundation in the present for production in the more distant future.

9.4 Priorities

The discussion of priorities applied in the allocation of investments begins by looking at the *sectoral structure*.

1. *Priority of investment goods.* The sectors developed are primarily those that directly cause an increase in fixed capital, that is, the production of investment goods. A concentric, self-repeating, self-inducing process occurs: the production of investment goods is raised so as to have more fixed capital, which must largely produce investment goods that contribute in turn to the growth of fixed capital, and so on. There is sense, therefore, in speaking of an internal spiral (or propeller), because the spiral motion advances, resulting in ever more investment, ever more fixed capital, and ultimately, ever more aggregate output.

The internal spiral, spinning at great speed, attracts to itself all the other sectors, although they grow far more slowly. Having adopted the idea outlined above, the allocators of investment will think it worthwhile developing the other sectors only as required to maintain the fast forward spin of the internal spiral. The general priority so arrived at is then translated into the language of several specific partial priorities, simple rules of thumb that apply when compiling the investment plans.

2. *Priority of domestic production over imports.* The development of the sectoral structure is stamped by the pursuit of autarky. This is mentioned here only for the sake of completeness [→14.1].

3. *Priority of the production sphere.* A distinction is made in Marxian political economy between "productive" and "nonproductive" activity

---

[22]The relationship among sacrifice, postponement, and neglect is discussed in more detail in my 1972 book.

[→5.4]. A practical meaning is attached to this in the planning and statistics of the socialist countries: manufacture of tangible material goods is viewed as the "productive sphere" and provision of most services as the "nonproductive sphere."[23] The priority: the productive sphere must have an investment advantage over the nonproductive, in other words, the production of material goods over services.[24]

There are several reasons why the nonproductive sphere is neglected. Part of the services under present-day capitalism are provided by private producers, and part by budgetary institutions and nonprofit organizations. In the former subsphere, the sovereignty of the consumer prevails through market coordination: private producers are prepared to offer as much housing, private education, private health care, and so on as there is demand. There are a great many profitable business opportunities here, which is why the subsphere develops rapidly. As far as the allocation of resources for public services is concerned, this is subject to the democratic political process, at least in a parliamentary democracy. The public service sphere cannot be neglected so long as the parties representing the majority of the public are willing to vote the sums for developing such services. By contrast, the allocators under the classical socialist system are not subject to any democratic control. Moreover, they have to make numerous allocational decisions that under capitalism are ultimately in the consumer's hands. These have passed under classical socialism into the hands of the bureaucracy, and in the eyes of those exercising bureaucratic control over the economy, there are always more important things to do than to develop services, which they feel can be postponed or neglected.

4. *Priority of class-one production.* Marxian political economy makes a further important distinction, between class-one and class-two production. The former makes means of production and the latter consumer goods.[25] The priority: class one must enjoy an investment advantage over class two.

---

[23]A clear exception to this is transportation, which according to Marx is productive, as an extension of production beyond the factory gates. The classification of commerce is ambiguous, since it combines both productive and nonproductive elements. For the statistical classification problem, see J. Árvay (1973).

[24]Another kind of classification appeared in the literature of the socialist countries: contrast of the productive-economy sector in a narrow sense with the "infrastructure." See É. Ehrlich (1985b). Space does not allow detailed clarification of how far the "infrastructure" agrees or disagrees with the definition of the "service sector" customary in Western literature. It is certain at least that the infrastructure is among the nonpriority, relegated spheres.

[25]The set of class-one products includes not only investment goods but materials and semifinished products for current production.

One problem of the classification (and also the priority) is that purely in terms of phys-

5. *Priority of industry.* Industry is considered to be the engine of growth. The strategy of forced growth primarily means fast industrialization. The priority: industry must have an investment preference over all other branches of the economy. The observation is illustrated in table 9.3.

6. *Priority of heavy industry.* According to the prevalent official view under the classical system, mechanization is the prime means of raising productivity and producing technical development. Large quantities of steel and other metals are used in both machinery and arms manufacturing. The priority: the industrialization preference must be given primarily to heavy industry, and within it to machinery and steelmaking.[26]

Rigid adherence to the priorities listed here leads to a disharmonious, deformed sectoral structure. In the early decades of forced growth, the extreme centralization of resources appears to succeed in speeding up the rotation of the internal spiral, as the priority sectors grow very fast. Meanwhile, other sectors fall behind, some of them very seriously. The farther they are from the internal spiral, the less they impede its rotation, at least for a time, and the more they are relegated. Sectors mainly producing consumer goods fall behind, and so do services, with housing construction, communal services, and trade affected particularly seriously. Agriculture and transportation fall behind as well.

Accompanying all this are the three phenomena noted in the previous section: grave sacrifices by the generation living in the period of forced growth; postponement of nonpriority, relegated tasks and accumulation of postponed tasks to the detriment of future generations; and finally, cases of neglect and irreparable damage.[27]

---

ical attributes, many items can serve equally as means of production or consumer goods. This is especially so if foreign trade is considered too: means of production can be imported in exchange for exported consumer goods; thus, class two also can generate means of production indirectly. (Or conversely, class one can supply consumer goods with foreign trade mediation.)

For all these reasons, the partial priority 4 fails to further expressly a consistent assertion of the basic priority 1.

[26]To illustrate this, first a Soviet figure: 84 percent of the industrial investment between 1917 and 1976 went to heavy industry. Statistika, Moscow (1977, p. 436).

The second illustration is Chinese: the number of heavy hydraulic presses equals the number of equivalent presses operating in all the EEC countries. Meanwhile, China's per capita GNP is only a twentieth of the EEC's. According to a Chinese economist, "The structure and scale of heavy industry exceed the dimensions the economy can bear." S. Zhou (1982, pp. 30–31).

Finally, a few Romanian data. More than half of the total investment between 1951 and 1981 went to industry. Of this, 77–80 percent went to develop heavy industry. M. Shafir (1985, p. 108).

[27]Cases of irreversible neglect have occurred in health care and higher education in several socialist countries. A grave situation developed lately in health care in the Soviet Union

7. *Priority of the arms industry.* The investment demands of the armed forces, including both the army and the police, receive unconditional priority over civilian development tasks.[28] For one thing, this ties in closely with priorities 3, 5, and 6, each of which serves not only to speed up the internal spiral mentioned under priority 1, but to develop the arms industry as well. For another, this priority appears of its own accord: the establishment of factories for purely military purposes receives particularly close attention when investment funds are allocated. This can only be gathered in part from the published plans, since a high proportion of the investments for military and police purposes are kept secret.

Having looked at the priorities to do with sectoral proportions, let us turn to the priorities that apply in the development of the microstructure, picking out three of them.

8. *Priority of new installations.* Those running the economy seek to set up as many new factories as possible while neglecting properly to maintain the old, existing ones. The motivation is mainly political.[29] Establishment of a brand new factory makes a far more spectacular example of overcoming backwardness and of achieving fast development than the drudgery of carefully maintaining an old factory's machinery and premises. Proud progress reports on the new facility can be made, and the festive inauguration can turn into a national event. The policy of forced growth needs this construction fervor, because the workers' enthusiasm is viewed as a production-boosting factor.

Although this priority is most conspicuous in the case of production investments, it also applies in other areas. More resources go into building new housing developments than into maintaining the housing inherited from the previous regime. The situation is similar with new schools, universities, railroads, and so forth.

---

and several Eastern European countries, contributing to unfavorable demographic trends: low life expectancy and high infant mortality. Between 1960 and 1984, the mortality rate went up from 7.1 to 10.8 percent per thousand of population, and average life expectancy went down from about 70 to 67.7, as compared to 74 to 78 in the West. Infant mortality was 25 per 1,000 in the USSR at that time compared with 6–10 per 1,000 in the Western developed countries. See A. G. Aganbegian (1989, pp. 228–29).

Even with a real turn in health care's favor in the distribution of resources (which has not happened yet), it would still take decades to reverse the damaging trends.

[28]It is worth mentioning here the sector's position in the coordination of current production. A sizable part of production for military purposes is organizationally distinct from civilian production, under the control of a separate ministry or sectoral directorate. But where there is an overlap, fulfillment of the military orders receives priority, even in cases of serious shortage. See C. Davis (1990).

[29]This phenomenon illustrates an earlier observation [→5.3]: a bureaucratic leader does not feel he is a real owner. No owner tolerates a constant decline in wealth if it can be helped.

TABLE 9.3
Industrial[a] Investment as a Percentage of Total Investment:
International Comparison

	Annual Averages at Constant Prices	
	1965–73	*1973–83*
Socialist countries		
Bulgaria	44.5	42.3
China[b]	51.5[c]	54.0[d]
Czechoslovakia	37.6	38.0
East Germany	50.2	—
Hungary	34.8	34.2
Poland	38.8	38.0
Romania	47.9	49.3
Soviet Union	35.0	35.3
	1965–73	*1973–80*
Capitalist countries		
Belgium	28.7	24.9
Denmark	16.1[e]	16.7
Finland	24.6	27.1
France	24.6	23.9
Ireland	25.9	29.0
United Kingdom	31.3	32.4
West Germany	25.6	24.4

Source: Compiled by P. Mihályi for this book on the basis of United Nations (1986c, tables 13 and 16), and Központi Statisztikai Hivatal (Central Statistical Office, Budapest) (1986, p. 28).

[a]In the socialist countries industry covers manufacturing, energy, and fuel-producing branches. In capitalist countries industry covers manufacturing, energy, and fuel-producing branches, and the electric, gas, and water utilities.

[b]State investment at current prices.

[c]1953–62.

[d]1971–80.

[e]1966–73.

This priority again has a postponing character. It temporarily releases part of the resources for maintenance and renovation for use in the short term on high-priority tasks. But sooner or later the postponement defeats its own purpose and becomes a brake on growth.

9. *Priority of big installations*. Those in charge of the economy are attracted to the big, and even more to the vast. Often a veritable "cult of scale" and gigantomania emerges.[30]

The phenomenon is not confined to material production. If at all practically possible, the various service institutions (whether universities, libraries, or hospitals) are established with as large a unit as possible.

Several factors push decision makers in the direction of this priority.[31] The first is the expectation of economies of scale from larger size and output volume.[32] But in practice, the greater volume is accompanied by extra costs as well as savings. The balance of the two determines the optimum size of a factory from the purely economic point of view.[33] The factory size most advantageous at a particular place and time depends on the nature of the sector, technology, ability of the managers, market structure, and many other factors. This explains why organizations of various sizes live side by side in market competition. By contrast, in the forced growth process often giant firms and institutions appear where several medium-sized or even small units would be more efficient. One can certainly say an indiscriminate preference for establishing larger units does not contribute to the fast rate of growth.

Considerations of power play a part equal to economic criteria or even greater. Superior leaders find it easier to control a smaller number of subordinates. As for the leaders of subordinate units, say a firm or a public institution, their power and prestige clearly increase if the unit they control becomes bigger.

10. *Priority products and investment projects*. There are several thousand priority products [→7.2]. Among these one can discern a smaller set consisting of "most important products of all." These receive special

[30]This preference applies not only to choosing the scale of a new installation but to development of the organizational forms of existing firms. In fact, the process began with nationalization and the collectivization of agriculture and small-scale industry, when large public firms and cooperatives were founded to replace small family undertakings and small capitalist firms. The process was complemented then and continued with successive waves of mergers among state-owned firms or cooperatives. As a consequence, there is a very strong concentration of production under the classical socialist system [→tables 17.2–17.6].

[31]A related but not identical question arose in the analysis of collectivization [→5.5].

[32]The economic concepts of Marx and Lenin, which lay great stress on the tendency to concentration and the large factory's advantage over the small, played a part in implanting this idea.

[33]See the references in section 5.5, note 27.

attention not only in the annual plans and the execution of them but in the allocation of investments and the implementation of investment decisions. The main thing in the steel industry is for the units that directly produce the steel and the most commonly used types of rolled steel to be ready as soon as possible. In farm machinery manufacturing, the most important task is to finish the units from which complete tractors and combine harvesters emerge. Far less care is taken to see that all the auxiliary plants contributing to the manufacture of the priority products, the component supplying firms, the transportation system, the repair shops, and the warehouses are operating on the right scale at the right time. The users (in these examples, the engineering industry processing the products of the steel industry and the farms employing the products of the agricultural engineering industry) not only need the priority products, but a thousand and one complementary products as well. Yet proportionate development of these lags behind the growth in the priority products.

This breeds a great many stoppages in production and is one cause of the chronic shortage [→12.1]. In spite of its manifest economic drawbacks, the tendency can be explained by the circumstances. Here again there arises the overall information problem [→7.7]: centralized bureaucratic decision making cannot give equal attention to a myriad tasks all at once. "Prioritization" is what makes the job manageable at all. Added to that there are considerations of mass mobilization, political campaigns, and propaganda. To be effective, these need focusing on a comparatively small number of actions.

The priority status of selected investment projects is a related phenomenon. In fact, the two partially overlap, since the bulk of priority investments will produce priority products when finished. Priority investment projects are the darlings of the power elite. The establishment of each new installation has a glamor about it; the media cover it in depth; all branches of the apparatus monitor its progress several times. Its requirements get the green light; supplies arrive even amid the direst shortages. Everything said in general terms in this chapter about the forcing of growth, about rush, and about impetuous haste can be experienced tangibly in the sequence of events surrounding a priority investment project.

From one point of view the one-sided attention to "priority products" and "priority investments" likewise belongs to the postponement sphere. If output of a priority product grows fast, the fact can be announced in plan reports. If a priority investment project is completed, it immediately supplies a graphic achievement. The relative lag in the production of the other, nonpriority products, the neglect of parallel construction of the ancillary production apparatus, and the halfhearted, less attentive handling of the nonpriority investment projects only make their braking effect felt after some time, although the effect comes in the end.

11. *Economic development at the expense of the environment.* Production growth takes place at the expense of ruining forests and other green areas, polluting water and air, and harming the natural animal kingdom. Further environmental damage is caused by other human activities (transportation, heating, urban civilization, etc.). The relationship of investment and environmental protection takes two forms.

First, is it ensured that investment projects for production or other purposes, and the installation created by those projects, do not harm the environment? Sparing the environment involves extra inputs. (For example, a more expensive method of disposing of effluent or filtering smoke may be required.) The answer is usually no. Amid forced growth, these extra inputs are forgotten. At a lower level of development, the view is particularly likely to be taken that there is still hardly any industry, urban transport, and so on, to cause air and water pollution; that is a problem only for the industrially advanced capitalist countries.

Second, do the plans (and particularly the priority investments) include any special investment projects whose purpose is expressly to protect the environment, perhaps to repair earlier damage? (Examples might be new sewage works or the establishment of factories to make environmental protection equipment.) Again, the answer is usually no. Such projects are far removed from the top priorities and the internal spiral of priority 1. By saving on special environmental protection investments, resources are freed for tasks with a higher priority.

Damaging the natural environment is not system-specific. All other social systems are susceptible as well; it is among the grave drawbacks of the capitalist system. Many thought environmental damage would be ended precisely by the abolition of the greed and selfishness of private property. But it did not happen. The bureaucracy of a classical socialist system in the midst of forced growth, rush, and importunate haste is even more shortsighted in this respect than the decision makers of other systems. This combines with a system-specific disadvantage: there is no way of organizing in society independent, strong environmental movements capable of confronting the economic decision makers if necessary. Table 9.4 compares the emission of sulfur dioxide, one of the substances behind the formation of acid rain, by the two groups of countries.

Failure to protect the environment is among the instances of postponement (and to a degree irreversible neglect). It cannot go on forever, for it sooner or later starts slowing production too, and its ill effect on the quality of life fuels public discontent.

One can conclude at the end of this survey of priorities that the list is certainly not complete but probably includes the most important of them. The official ideology emphatically states some of the priorities.

TABLE 9.4
Air Pollution: International Comparison, 1985

	Sulfur Oxides (kg per head of population)
Socialist countries	
Czechoslovakia	203[a]
East Germany	300
Hungary	132
Poland	116
Capitalist countries	
Austria	18[a]
Finland	73
France	31
Ireland	39
Portugal	32
Spain	75
United Kingdom	65
United States	90
West Germany	42

Source: Compiled by P. Mihályi for this book on the basis of United Nations (1987, p. I-30) and direct communication from the Secretariat of United Nations Economic Commission for Europe.

Note: Levels of industrial development and car density, on the one hand, and sulfur oxide pollution of the atmosphere, on the other, show a strong positive correlation. It is a sign of acute neglect of environmental protection that air pollution began to build up at a comparatively low level of economic development.

[a]Sulfur dioxide only.

Others are unstated, considered shameful, or even denied. But even the shame-inducing and denied priorities penetrate into practice.

For those who like to think in a framework of optimization models, the goal of forced growth can be defined as follows: The purpose is not maximization of social welfare in the broad sense. The time scale for the maximization task is not infinite, and not even truly "long-term" when measured on a historical scale. The goal is far more limited and short-sighted than that: to maximize the growth rate of aggregate output as recorded in the official statistics, and to do this on a historical scale only in the "medium term," in other words, for the next decade or two. This is the purpose served by the priorities outlined above, which are capable of promoting a faster growth rate only for a time.[34] As a consequence of priorities 1 to 11, the structure of the economy becomes disharmonious and sets in that disharmonious state.

9.5   Extensive and Intensive Methods

It is now time to examine the relations between the production factors and output in the growth process. There is a vast amount of general theoretical writing on this field. Several important attempts have been made to clarify the extent to which methods of analysis devised for the capitalist system, primarily aggregate production functions and the growth models based upon them, can be applied to the socialist system.[35] The greatest difficulty is caused by the lack of data, or the unreliability of them. The problems of measurement are returned to later [→9.7]. In any case, I cannot undertake to summarize the debate on the question or the numerical results obtained. The arguments here are solely intended to arrive at a classification of the main types of relationship between the production factors and output, and to shed light on the system-specific role of some relationships.

For simplicity's sake, I shall list the factor-output relationships under two main groups. The first group contains the effects caused by the growth of some factor. For instance, the stock of capital or the total labor expended on production grows, and that causes output to grow proportionally. The second group covers the effects caused by the growth

---

[34]Even this effect depends to a large extent on how the growth is measured. The result is only the semblance of growth in many respects. The problem is returned to later [→9.7].

[35]Of the statistical and econometric writings on the relationships between the production factors and output, the first mention should to go the work of Abram Bergson, who has greatly influenced other researchers as well. Of his more recent works, attention is drawn to his study of Soviet growth and technical development (1983). Outstanding contributions to the econometric analysis of Soviet growth have also been made by P. Desai (1976, 1986a, 1986b, 1987), V. Kontorovich (1986), and M. L. Weitzman (1970, 1983). An overall account of the factors behind Soviet growth is provided by E. A. Hewett in his book on reform (1988, chap. 2).

There are also several studies analyzing Chinese growth by econometric methods. The World Bank report (1985), and the study by K. Chen et al. (1988) can be singled out.

The literature on other socialist countries is scantier. T. P. Alton (1977) presents a summarizing account.

A comprehensive survey giving an account related in many respects to the classification used here can be found in F. L. Pryor's book (1985).

of the productivity of some factor. For instance, more efficient use is made of capital or labor, and that causes output to grow. This distinction and the accompanying terminology are quite widespread among Western writers, but writers in the socialist countries prefer to use another pair of expressions, distinguishing between *extensive* and *intensive* methods. The two pairs of expressions are synonymous: factor growth equals extensive methods, and factor-productivity growth corresponds to intensive methods. In what follows, the "Eastern" terminology is usually adopted.

Before going into details, another advance warning is needed. Strict dividing lines between various extensive or intensive methods can only be drawn in the framework of abstract analysis. In practice, they normally appear together. Even the most meticulous econometric examinations run up against a great difficulty when separation of the effects in numerical terms is attempted. No such attempt is made here, because there is no need to do so in order to accomplish the book's purpose of explaining the regularities of the system.

The dominance of extensive methods is explained primarily by the fact that the socialist system usually comes to power in backward, slow-growing countries that make poor use of their resources from the extensive point of view. Therefore, there are numerous opportunities for extending the utilization of them.

1. *Growth in the number of employed.* There is normally open unemployment at the time when power is taken, with hidden underemployment mainly in agriculture. The level of female employment is low. Considering only capital and labor, the two most important factors of production, an extremely high investment ratio can be squeezed out of the economy, and coupled at will with the ample quantity of labor available. The system takes advantage of this opportunity; the number of employed quickly grows [→10.1].

The two phenomena combined, namely, a high investment ratio plus a constant, fast growth of employment, are the two main factors explaining the high growth rate under the classical system, especially in the first one or two decades.

2. *More shifts and lengthening of working hours.* Although the volume of investment is huge, fixed capital is comparatively scarcer than manpower, which is abundantly available for a while. So those running the economy try to combine the fixed assets at their disposal with as much labor as possible, that is, they incorporate as many of the 24 hours of the day and 168 hours of the week as possible into the operating and working time of factories. By and large, in many of the factories and institutions of the classical socialist system, employees work more shifts than in many capitalist economies.

The lengthening of working hours can also be one of the factors that help to speed up the rate of growth.[36] In several countries the bureaucracy is reluctant to make concessions on the time worked even when the economy has reached a higher level of development and the workforce is demanding shorter hours. There are no independent trade unions to struggle for the workers' interests and win them their demands.

The extensive potentials discussed in points 1 and 2 are finite; after a time the reserve of labor runs out. When this happens, it becomes the most important factor behind the deceleration of growth.[37]

3. *Growth in the area farmed.* Hitherto uncultivated areas can be turned into farmland. This potential likewise runs out after a while.

4. *Wider exploitation of mineral wealth.* There can be extensive expansion in the use of mineral wealth, although in many places it can be done only at steadily increasing cost, or the potential eventually runs out.

One more summary comment can be added to what has been said about the extensive methods. The situation that results resembles wartime conditions under other systems. Even in peacetime, classical socialism has a *mobilization economy.*[38] I mentioned earlier the way a "war consciousness" is instilled constantly by the official ideology: building the economy is a battle against backwardness and enemies without and within, from which no one and nothing can withdraw [→4.5]. The struggle demands mobilization of all able-bodied men and all material resources.

I turn now to the discussion of various intensive methods, with the advance comment that they appear in combination with each other in the practice of forced growth.

1. *Intensity of labor.* The output attainable from given physical inputs depends to a great extent on the attention, care, and industry, in a word, on the intensity with which workers do their jobs. Socialists before and after the revolution believe that workers freed from the rule of capitalism will work far more willingly, industriously, and intensively than the hired wage-earners of capitalism. There are signs of this, at least, in the revolutionary-transitional period of socialist rule [→2.4, 6.6]. This conduct

---

[36]The trend in the various sectors of the economy is not uniform. A peasant or artisan working in a family undertaking drives himself and his family hard. The position changes after nationalization and collectivization. For agricultural cooperative members, the working hours on the agricultural cooperative are shorter than the total working hours of the whole family when they farmed their own land.

[37]The following formulation is widespread in the literature on the subject: when the reserve of labor is exhausted, the "period of extensive growth" ends and the "intensive period" begins. Although I used this division into periods in earlier works, I do not use it in this book because it is inaccurate.

[38]P. Hanson's (1971) apt characterization.

does not cease entirely under the classical system.[39] But in many people this initial enthusiasm gives way to apathy and an expectation that they will have to work only as much as they are paid for. At this point effective operation of the material and moral incentives designed to prompt the workers to more intensive work and discipline becomes the deciding factor. There are many serious problems with this [→10.4, 10.5]. The system does not find sufficiently effective incentive schemes.

2. *Technical progress*. Considerable technical progress takes place under the classical socialist system. Some of it ties in closely with the fervor of socialist construction: the first electric lamp in the village, the first tractor in the fields, the first automatic lines in the factories.

Thorough examinations have shown that although technical development really takes place, its contribution to growth is rather modest. What is more, even this moderate progress slows down in the later stages of the classical system.[40] Basically, this technical development is of a suit-following, imitative kind. New technologies and products introduced in the capitalist countries are taken over, usually after a long delay [→12.11].

3. *Development of manpower skills*. Although part of technical progress in a sense, manpower development is worth considering as a separate point. It is typical under forced growth that production, primarily industry, absorbs large masses of unskilled, inexperienced labor. Although ultimately, in the longer term, skill increases, the qualitative development of manpower lags much behind the fast-growing demand for it in production.

4. *Organizational improvement*. A distinction must be made between scheduled cessation of production (at night or on Sundays, for instance) and cases where production is interrupted, for example, because material has failed to arrive, a worker is not at his or her station, or a machine has broken down.[41] The more organized and disciplined the production and product flow to users are, the less time is lost in this way.[42]

---

[39]One expression of this in the Soviet Union was the Stakhanovite movement. Similar movements (so-called socialist work-competition, etc.) arose in other socialist countries. They combined truly productive efforts by extremely self-sacrificing, highly skilled people with manipulation and artificial setting of feigned records designed to spur others on. The ambiguity is presented graphically in the Polish director A. Wajda's film *The Man of Marble*.

[40]See remarkable data on Soviet technical progress in V. Kontorovich (1986). J. Klacek and A. Nesporová (1984) verify the low and declining contribution of technological progress for Czechoslovakia. For further references see section 12.11.

[41]The literature on employment of fixed capital distinguishes in this sense between extensive and intensive use. In this account the former is treated in point 2 of the discussion of extensive methods and the latter in point 3 of the intensive methods.

[42]The models in macroeconometric literature using production functions do not usually distinguish intensive methods 2 and 3. The so-called residual factor is intended to cover the combined effect of the two.

In this respect classical socialism comes out badly. The standard of management and the internal organization of production are backward. There is a concurrent appearance of circumstances symptomatic of all developing countries (e.g., a low level of adaptation to production among industrial labor freshly arrived from the village) and of system-specific effects (e.g., investment tension and other delays caused by chronic instances of shortage). So this is an intensive method that contributes little to production growth.

5. *Quantity at the expense of quality.* Here the word "quality" is meant in the everyday sense used of the quality of a machine or a material by an engineer and of the quality of the goods by the customer in a store. It covers many different attributes: modernity, appearance, perfect material and processing, durability, and so on. A producer trying to make as good a product as possible in terms of these and similar use characteristics normally requires more resources. And conversely, he saves resources if willing to sacrifice the quality of a given quantity of output.

The capitalist property forms and market coordination provide a strong incentive to improve quality. As Schumpeter's theory points out, entrepreneurs are in a winning position if they can capture the market with a new, better, and more modern product. The quality improvement is provided by internal incentives on a micro level, not by central measures. These inner motive forces are absent from the classical socialist system. Everything pushes an economic leader toward quantity in this quantity-quality trade-off. Mention was made earlier of the quantity drive [→7.6]. Both the plan and direct, bureaucratic control place the quantitative instructions at the fore: quantity is measured, where possible, in physical indices or aggregate, crudely weighted indices of volume with no capacity to reflect finer distinctions. Improvement of quality is customarily mentioned in official statements, but bureaucratic coordination is neither able nor very eager to enforce it.

Certainly, quantitative growth at quality's expense is among the intensive methods that contribute greatly to the high rate of growth that features in the official statistics.

6. *Overintensive use of service capacities.* This is mentioned as a separate point, although it can be interpreted as a special case of method 5. More residents are squeezed into a housing area, more patients into a hospital ward, and more students into a classroom than is desirable for a good standard of provision. The development of transportation and telecommunications is badly neglected, which means that the trains and roads are overcrowded, and there are too few telephone lines. As just one example to illustrate the overintensive use of capacity, table 9.5 shows the load on the railroad systems of certain socialist and certain capitalist countries. The difference is remarkable.

TABLE 9.5
Overloading of the Railroad Systems: International Comparison, 1979

	Freight Traffic Densities (millions of ton-kms per km)
Socialist countries	
Bulgaria	4.07
Czechoslovakia	5.56
Poland	5.55
Romania	6.84
Capitalist countries	
Finland	1.21
Greece	0.34
Ireland	0.32
Italy	1.14
Portugal	0.24
Spain	0.78
Turkey	0.71

Source: Compiled by G. Kwon for this book on the basis of United Nations (1981, tables 6, 8B).
Note: The index means the volume of freight carried per total length of railroad lines measured in km. The volume of freight is measured in units of 1 ton carried a distance of 1 km.

The overburdening of transportation and service capacities, coupled with the perpetuation or enhancement of congestion, allows the economic leadership to provide investments and other resources to the service sector as meagerly as possible and to allocate investment funds to sectors with a higher priority.[43] In this respect, the phenomenon noted here ties in closely with priority 3 [→9.4].[44]

[43]The symptoms of overburdening and overcrowding appear in a particularly acute form in the health sector under the classical socialist system. See, for instance, the study by C. Davis (1989) on the Soviet Union in this respect.

[44]In the language of Leontief's input-output analysis, the problem discussed here can be described as follows:

The coefficients of the sectors of the production sphere for both current utilization and capital are fairly rigid in a particular period. On the other hand, the coefficients for the utilizations of the service sphere both in production and in public consumption (the current input coefficients and especially the capital coefficients) are fairly malleable. The proportion of input to output can be cut at the user's expense for a long time and to a large degree.

One is justified in listing this phenomenon with the intensive methods because it yields more output for the same input of fixed capital (often coupled with the same input of labor). The only qualification to add, as in the case of intensive method 5, is that the output is measured by crude quantitative yardsticks (mainly crude physical indices: how many households housed, how many people treated in hospital or taught in school, and so on).

To sum up, under conditions of forced growth, extensive methods predominate, complemented by intensive methods 5 and 6, which have harmful effects. The contribution of intensive methods 1 to 4 is slight.

This general conclusion is supported by numerous econometric analyses. Although these run up against a variety of methodological difficulties, as mentioned at the beginning of the section, and although their numerical results conflict with each other in many cases, I have found no study that contradicts this qualitative conclusion. Table 9.6 gives extracts from some calculations as an illustration. From the last column on the right-hand side of the table it is apparent that total factor-productivity growth—that is, application of intensive methods—made a relatively modest contribution in the classical socialist countries to overall growth. The table shows clearly that this is a system-specific characteristic: the growth in factor productivity made a conspicuously bigger contribution to growth under the capitalist system in the same period.

9.6   Fluctuations in Growth; Cycles

I now turn to the consideration of certain dynamic characteristics in growth. Three kinds of fluctuation can be distinguished.

1. *"Calendar" pulsation.* This is connected most directly with the annual plans. Since there is a strong material and moral incentive to fulfill the quantitative targets of the annual plan, the pace of work speeds up toward the end of the year. Table 9.7 gives figures for the end-of-year spurt, when production is speeded up irrespective of cost, human exhaustion, and the decline of quality. At the start of the following year, performance suddenly dives again.[45]

The undulation caused by the five-year plan is less pronounced. A normal feature at the beginning of a planning period is for several new investment projects to start simultaneously.

2. *Endogenous investment fluctuation.* This is more pronounced in the smaller Eastern European countries, in China, and in Cuba in certain periods. First of all, one row each of Polish and Chinese data is given to

[45]See A. Bródy (1956), M. Laki (1980), J. Rimler (1986), J. Rostowski (1988), and J. Rostowski and P. Auerbach (1986).

TABLE 9.6

Share of Factor Productivity in the Growth of Output: International
Comparison

	Period	Average Annual Rate of Change		Share of Factor Productivity in Growth of Output
		Output	Factor Productivity	
Socialist countries				
Czechoslovakia	1960–75	3.0	1.0	0.33
	1976–80	2.2	0.7	0.29
	1981–88	1.4	0.1	0.07
Poland	1960–75	5.1	2.4	0.47
	1976–80	0.7	−0.6	—
	1981–88	0.8	0.2	0.40
Soviet Union	1960–75	4.6	1.2	0.26
	1976–80	2.3	0.5	0.22
	1981–88	1.9	0.5	0.13
Capitalist countries				
France	1960–73	5.8	3.9	0.67
	1973–79	2.8	1.7	0.65
	1979–88	1.9	1.5	0.75
Japan	1960–73	10.8	6.6	0.61
	1973–79	3.6	1.8	0.43
	1979–88	4.1	1.8	0.43
United Kingdom	1960–73	2.9	2.2	0.76
	1973–79	1.5	0.5	0.60
	1979–88	2.2	1.9	0.95

Source: Socialist countries: 1960–75: P. R. Gregory and R. C. Stuart (1980, pp. 378–79); 1976–80 and 1981–88, output: Soviet Union, 1976–80, A. Åslund (1989, p. 15), all other data are from P. Marer et al. (1991); factor productivity: M. Mejstrik (1991, p. 27). *Capitalist countries*: 1960–73: J. W. Kendrick (1981, p. 128); 1973–79 and 1979–88, output: OECD (1990, p. 48); factor productivity: M. Mejstrik (1991, table 2a).

Note: The measure of output is GNP, except for capitalist countries in the periods after 1973, where the measure of output is GDP.

illustrate this in figure 9.1 and table 9.8; they show a conspicuously high degree of fluctuation in investment. Table 9.9 offers an international comparison of variation coefficients that is used as a measure of fluctuation around the long-term average growth rate. The comparison does not lead to conclusive results. While some socialist economies grow relatively smoothly, others show wild fluctuations, even larger ones than many capitalist economies.

TABLE 9.7
End-of-Year Spurt: International Comparison

Country (Years of Observation)	December Production as a Proportion of Average Monthly Production[a] in Following Year (percent)
Socialist countries	
Czechoslovakia (1968–82)	102.4
Hungary (1968–82)	114.0
Poland (1971–81)	106.7
Capitalist countries	
Austria (1955–81)	99.9
Finland (1976–81)	94.5
Israel (1958–77)	93.4
Italy (1974–82)	92.8
Portugal (1968–81)	98.1

Source: J. Rostowski and P. Auerbach (1986, pp. 297, 301).
Note: The data refer to manufacturing.
[a]Average for months 1–11 of the following year.

Fluctuation appears primarily in investment starts, and also in total annual spending on investment. The variation in production is more muted, and employment fluctuates least of all.[46] Some of the undulations display no regular pattern. Some other fluctuations have specific, cyclical regularity of alternating "stop" and "go" phases, at least in certain socialist countries and certain periods. There are successive stages of sudden braking, slowdown and stagnation, cautious revival, and unbridled expansion, after which the braking and a similar succession of phases return. Then the cycle recommences, repeating itself constantly.

[46]This is notable indirect evidence that the system guarantees employment and job security [→10.1, 10.2, 13.3].

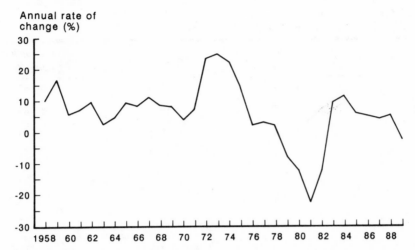

FIGURE 9.1 Fluctuation of Investment in Poland
Source: Period 1958–76, T. Bauer (1981, pp. 156, 176, 187); period 1977–89,
Glowny Urzad Statystyczny (1990, pp. xxxiv–xxxv).

Numerous researchers have set out to describe and explain this phenomenon. A range of alternative explanations has been put forward.[47]
The position presented here is subscribed to by several authors.[48]

At first sight, there are marked similarities between the cyclical fluctuations of the capitalist and socialist systems, but more careful examina-

---

[47]Of the early pioneers, the most remarkable are the studies by A. Bródy (1969b),
J. Gács and M. Lackó (1973), and J. Goldmann and K. Kouba (1969). T. Bauer's compre-
hensive work serves as a starting point for the subsequent researches and debates; it has
appeared in full only in Hungarian (1981). A few of Bauer's ideas have been published in
English (1978). Bauer's work is one of the main sources for the ideas on investment and
cycles in this book. Several writers have taken issue with his theory; see, for instance, K. A.
Soós (1975, 1986). Other notable contributions have come from P. Mihályi (1988) and
B. W. Ickes (1990). Some authors express doubts about the rightness of assuming a regularity at all in the fluctuation of investment and other economic variables.

Several authors have examined the fluctuation of investment in single countries on a
statistical basis or possibly with an econometric model. See, on *Hungary:* M. Lackó (1980,
1984), M. Marrese (1981); on *China:* B. Chavance (1987), M. Harrison (1985), and C. Hsin
(1984); on the *Soviet Union:* G. Roland (1987), M. Harrison (1985), and V. Kontorovich
(1990); on *Poland,* I. Grosfeld (1986); and on *Cuba:* C. Bettelheim (1987). A. Simonovits
(1991a, 1991b) devised theoretical mathematical models for the investment cycles. B. W.
Ickes (1986) is a summary appraisal of some aspects of the debate.

Incidentally, it is not surprising that economists examining the socialist economy should
have failed to agree on a generally acceptable theory. An army of researchers has been
dealing for a century with fluctuations of the business cycle in the capitalist economy, and
there is still no uniformity of position in their explanations. See V. Zarnovitz's review
(1985).

[48]The description mainly covers some of the ideas expressed by T. Bauer and M. Lackó,
and by myself in my earlier works.

TABLE 9.8

Fluctuation of Total Investment in Fixed Assets in China

Year	Annual Rate of Change (percent)	Year	Annual Rate of Change (percent)
1951	106.9	1969	62.9
1952	85.7	1970	49.1
1953	110.3	1971	13.4
1954	12.1	1972	−1.1
1955	2.5	1973	6.1
1956	52.8	1974	5.7
1957	−6.0	1975	17.6
1958	84.5	1976	−3.9
1959	31.9	1977	4.6
1960	13.2	1978	22.0
1961	−62.5	1979	4.6
1962	−44.1	1980	6.7
1963	33.7	1981	−10.5
1964	42.2	1982	26.6
1965	30.7	1983	12.6
1966	17.5	1984	24.5
1967	−26.3	1985	41.8
1968	−19.3	1986	12.2

Source: Calculated on the basis of the following sources: 1950–82: H. Chang (1984, p. 1287); 1983–86: State Statistical Bureau, People's Republic of China (1987, p. 60).

tion reveals profound differences. In capitalist economies the slowdown and contraction is usually connected with the inadequacy of demand. Production has expanded too fast for the present and the predicted future demand. Business prospects become uncertain. The economic decision makers, when they realize this, suddenly slow down. This braking is a decentralized process; no one "above" gives an order. The panic spreads horizontally, on the market.

In socialist economies, however, the process is centralized. The brake is applied by central control, and the instruction to decelerate passes ver-

TABLE 9.9

Fluctuation of Investment: International Comparison, 1960–89

	Coefficient of Variation of Annual Average Growth Rate of Investment (percent)
Socialist countries	
Czechoslovakia	131
East Germany	98
Hungary	171
Poland	187
Soviet Union	47
Yugoslavia	278
Capitalist countries	
Austria	127
Canada	94
France	106
Ireland	159
Japan	90
Spain	122
Sweden	130

Source: Calculation by P. Mihályi for this book, based on data from the United Nations Economic Commission for Europe, Common Data Bank.

Note: The coefficient of variation is the ratio of standard deviation and the mean. Western figures are based on data expressed at constant 1985 prices and U.S. dollar exchange rates. Eastern data are calculated at constant prices of various years.

tically down the levels of the hierarchy. Inadequate demand is not among the factors that provoke it. On the contrary, the leaders deciding to apply the brake sense an inadequacy of resources available to the accelerated process of growth. The entire cycle takes place amid conditions of rush, expansion drive, investment hunger, investment tension, and chronic shortage. These mark the conduct of decision makers at all levels in the bureaucracy. They would like to invest as much and as fast as possible; meanwhile, they meet constraints at the peak of the cycle that rule out further acceleration. One might put it like this: the top leaders receive signals notifying them of the obstacles to further acceleration. Three groups of signals can be identified.

First, imports and indebtedness cannot increase limitlessly [→14.3]. In many cases, particularly in the smaller countries of Eastern Europe, they have proved to be effective limits to further acceleration.

Second, the investment tension becomes intolerable. Economic and technical leaders feel that ever more common interruptions, delivery problems, and delays are unbearable.

Third, the expansion of investment cuts deeply into personal consumption, exceeding the public's tolerance limits. Discontent grows, becoming audible, and endangers the power of the ruling elite.

Sometimes just one of the three signals is enough to make those running the economy step on the brake. It can happen that two or even three constraints at once block the path of investment; then the panic is strongest and the braking most drastic. This coincidence appeared in its most extreme form in Poland, on more than one occasion, but it has happened in other countries, for instance, China and Hungary as well.

Every intervention in the investment sphere is transmitted onward through a web of delaying factors. That is why the downward and upward movements divide into several phases, and why the deceleration gives way only gradually to acceleration.

If the physical state of the economy and the foreign economic potentials allow it, acceleration is eventually renewed because permanent motivations begin to take effect. The expansion drive and the investment hunger have only been contained temporarily by the panic and the sober realization that the excessively taut plans are unrealistic. Sooner or later, these motivations revive. The leadership at all levels is reassured that tension has fallen, or even a measure of slack, an apparent underuse of resources, has appeared. So it is time to return to the customary, normal tension and expansion drive in production and investment. Everything starts over again.

3. *Changes in political line.* Classical socialism has certain basic features that apply constantly. (The whole of part 2 of this book is devoted to these.) But that does not preclude the occurrence of political struggles and faction-fighting in the bureaucracy [→3.5]. A change in the political power relations or the stance taken by the leader can lead to sudden, dramatic turns even during the same person's period in power. Examples include the transitions from War Communism to the NEP under Lenin, from slow development of cooperatives to swift and aggressive collectivization under Stalin, from the liberal policy of "letting a hundred flowers bloom" to the "Great Leap Forward" under Mao. In other cases the sharp change comes when an old leader dies and his successor takes a new policy course. Whatever the case, these sudden changes of line have far-reaching effects on the economy, producing great swings in a whole range of indices. For instance, Soviet collectivization was followed by a

dive in agricultural production; China's "Great Leap" suddenly raised investment, particularly development of heavy industry.

The idea has been put forward that these changes in course likewise have a regular pattern or rhythm, with comparatively "soft," restrained phases alternating with comparatively "hard," radical ones. The softer political line is more cautious, whereas the harder line brings tenser investment programs.[49]

The various kinds of fluctuation just described are not mutually exclusive.[50] The wave motions may be superimposed, and possibly reinforce each other's effects. For instance, an expansion phase at the end of an investment cycle coincides with the beginning of a new five-year plan, or a standstill within the endogenous economic cycle provides the reason for a change of political line, including changes of personnel. That happened, for example, in Poland in 1970.

One thing can certainly be said: socialist planning has belied the hope that it would produce smooth growth free of the fluctuations, standstills, and setbacks of capitalism. Although the fluctuations under socialism are induced by different mechanisms and have different consequences than those under capitalism, wave motions exist and cause damage of a great many kinds.

9.7   Measurement of Aggregate Output

Before concluding comments are made, a short detour is called for on the subject of measurement. In keeping with the general character of this book, I refrain from detailed discussion of statistical methodology, confining myself to the most necessary observations.

The official statistics of the socialist countries contain numerous distortions. These are not merely caused by inaccuracies of measurement; they are tendentious in seeking to present a more favorable result than the true one.[51] The concern here is primarily with the main factors dis-

---

[49]Á. Ungvárszky (1989) has identified a whole series of such changes in the history of the Hungarian economy. According to her findings, there is a close, observable correlation of movement among growth policy, foreign economic policy, and institutional changes within the rhythmically alternating political periods. See also D. M. Nuti (1986b) and E. Screpanti (1986).

[50]Other fluctuations also exist. J. C. Brada (1986), for instance, reports that the agricultural production of five Eastern European socialist countries fluctuates to a greater extent than it did when there was a capitalist system in those countries. The fluctuation is mainly connected with the frequent changes in production policy.

[51]There is a wide-ranging debate taking place on the distortions in the economic statistics of the socialist countries. See, for example, A. Bergson (1961, 1978a), A. Bródy (1964, 1979), Z. Dániel (1975), A. Eckstein (1980), M. Ellman (1982), P. Marer (1985), and A. Nove (1983).   Continued

TABLE 9.10

Official and Alternative Estimates of Growth: International Comparison

	1961–70	1971–80	1981–85	1986	1987	1988	1989
Bulgaria							
NMP (official)	7.7	7.0	3.7	5.3	4.7	2.4	−2.0
GDP (extended official)	—	6.8	3.4	4.2	6.0	2.6	−1.9
GNP (alternative)	5.8	2.8	0.8	4.9	−0.9	2.0	—
China							
NMP (official)	4.0	5.8	10.0	7.7	10.2	11.1	3.5
GDP (official)	—	5.5	10.1	8.3	11.0	10.9	3.6
GNP (alternative)	—	5.8	9.2	7.8	9.4	11.2	—
Czechoslovakia							
NMP (official)	4.4	4.7	1.8	1.8	2.7	2.6	1.2
GDP (extended official)	—	4.7	1.7	3.2	2.7	2.2	1.2
GNP (alternative)	2.9	2.8	1.2	2.1	1.0	1.4	—
East Germany							
NMP (official)	4.3	4.8	4.5	4.3	3.6	2.8	2.0
GDP (extended official)	—	4.8	4.3	3.9	3.3	3.1	2.3
GNP (alternative)	3.1	2.8	1.9	2.2	1.1	1.1	—
Hungary							
MNP (official)	5.4	4.6	1.2	0.9	4.1	−0.5	−1.6
GDP (official)	5.3	4.7	1.8	1.5	4.1	−0.1	0.2
GNP (alternative)	3.4	2.6	0.7	2.2	1.1	1.1	—

(continued)

torting the aggregate indices of output measured by value. The difficulties are surveyed in table 9.10, which gives the calculations for the total output of several socialist countries. Row 1 contains the official statistics, and the other rows alternative estimates. It is not this book's job to take a position in the debate. It is enough to point out one common characteristic: all the alternative estimates show a lower rate of growth

Great attention was aroused by an article by two Soviet authors, V. Seliunin and G. Khanin (1987), which revealed serious distortions in Soviet output statistics. Khanin had begun to reveal some of the distortions back in the 1960s, but there had been no opportunity earlier for him to publish his findings. Khanin later gave some further alternative estimates in another noteworthy article (1988). Surveys of the Soviet debate are A. Åslund (1990), B. P. Orlov (1988), and R. Ericson (1990).

The East German GDP has also been recalculated several times in the recent past, yielding progressively lower estimates. See *DIW-Wochenbericht*, February 14, 1991.

TABLE 9.10
Continued

	1961–70	1971–80	1981–85	1986	1987	1988	1989
Poland							
NMP (official)	8.4	5.4	−0.8	5.2	2.0	4.8	0.1
GDP (extended official)	—	5.3	0.1	4.2	2.0	4.1	−1.0
GNP (alternative)	4.2	3.6	0.6	2.7	−1.7	2.1	—
Romania							
NMP (official)	8.4	9.4	3.0[a]	3.0[a]	0.7[a]	−2.0[a]	−7.9[a]
GDP (extended official)	—	9.1	3.2	2.3	0.9	−0.5	−5.8
GNP (alternative)	5.2	5.3	−0.1	2.9	−0.9	−1.5	—
Soviet Union							
NMP (official)	6.9	5.0	3.2	2.3	1.6	4.4	2.4
GNP (official)	7.6[b]	5.5	3.7	3.3	2.9	5.5	3.0
GNP (alternative)	4.9	2.6	1.9	4.0	1.3	1.5	—

Source: Compiled by J. Árvay for this book, based on P. Marer et al. (1991).

Note: Official data originate from the statistical yearbooks of the given country or from reports submitted by national authorities to the World Bank. *Extended official* estimates were made by consultants to the World Bank, taking into account the level and growth rate of official NMP and the relation between NMP and GDP in periods where such data were available for a given country or the ratio in other countries. Therefore, any distortions embedded in official growth rates are included in the extended GDP growth rates, too. *Alternative* estimates are from Central Intelligence Agency (1989). These estimates in most cases use officially published physical quantity indicators that are then weighted by factor costs or adjusted factor costs of the products. The CIA volume is based on several sources, including the data of T. Alton and his associates in the Research Project on National Income in East Central Europe.

[a]In Romania the national accounts data for 1980–89 are the considerably revised figures published in 1990.

[b]1966–70.

than the official figures. The authors of these alternative estimates were primarily concerned to try to eliminate the statistical distortions described below.

1. Socialist countries use a different system of accounting than the rest of the world: the Material Product System (MPS) rather than the System of National Accounts (SNA).[52] To mention one of several larger or smaller discrepancies, the departure point of the MPS is a distinction between "productive" and "nonproductive" activity [→9.4, priority 3]. Consequently, gross output on the macro level ("social product") and net output ("national income," "net material product," NMP) refer ex-

[52]For details of how the two differ, see J. Árvay (1973) and United Nations (1977).

clusively to the production sphere and ignore the output of the service sphere. The underlying theoretical assumption is that the service sphere does not generate "value" (in the sense of Marxian political economy), and therefore the consumption of services means only a secondary distribution of national income. By contrast, the output measures under the SNA (gross national product, GNP, gross domestic product, GDP) include the services as well.[53] Under a system where the development of the service sector is overshadowed, this causes an upward distortion of the index for total output.[54]

2. A serious distortion is introduced into the accounts by the arbitrary features of the price system. For instance, an unrealistically low price is put on infrastructural services (which are neglected in any case) and housing provision, while many industrial products are overvalued.

3. The price system does not reflect properly the slow improvement, stagnation, or decline in quality. Simply adding the increased quantity produced at the expense of quality to the production volume [→9.5] distorts the index of aggregate output upward.

4. Under the classical system there is hidden inflation, which fails to appear in the official statistics [→11.7]. So the conversion indices (deflators) for eliminating the effects of the rise in the price level are too low, which means that stated growth is greater than real growth.

Although the existence of hidden distortions in the official statistics of the socialist countries, designed to give a brighter picture of performance than the real one, was known to experts before, the scale of the distortion has started coming to light only now, since a range of countries lifted the secrecy veiling their statistical work. Numerous quantitative examinations will have to be reexamined in light of the new, more accurate data.

---

[53]The central statistical offices of some countries and several researchers have calculated conversions of data originally in MPS into SNA and vice versa. By doing so (and making some other warranted adjustments) they made them comparable to data measured from the outset of SNA. See A. Bergson (1961).

For Czechoslovakia, V. Nachtigal (1989) has done a recalculation of NMP into GNP.

Hungary was the only socialist country that published production figures in both MPS and SNA terms since 1968.

[54]Take the following hypothetical example. In A, a capitalist country, the productive and nonproductive sectors both grow by 6 percent each, while in B, a socialist country, the productive sector grows by 6 percent, but the nonproductive sector by only 2 percent. If the MPS is applied to both countries, both will show an aggregate growth of 6 percent. If the SNA is used, however, the growth rate in A remains 6 percent, but the growth rate in B becomes a weighted average of 6 percent and 2 percent, which in all events will be substantially less than 6 percent.

Z. Dániel (1975) examined both this problem area and problem 2 below in a study on the "optics" of growth; calculating with the aid of an input-output model, the study also arrived at a numerical estimate of the extent of the distortions in Hungary's output statistics.

Until that happens, one must be content with the painstaking calculations made to try to correct the official socialist figures and bring them closer to Western methodology. Table 9.10 gave few estimates of this kind, and other tables attempt as far as possible to overcome the distortion factors listed above.[55]

9.8   The System-Specific Growth Type: Forced Growth

This chapter has attempted to present the main features of the growth process typical of the classical system. Some of these features appear in other systems, particularly developing countries pursuing a nonsocialist path. Even so, this configuration of features is system-specific. The sum of these main features defines the type described in the chapter introduction as forced growth. The word "forced" implies that the acceleration of the tempo, rather than arising from an integral, self-propeled movement in society, is compelled from above by the bureaucracy. The word "forced" also implies that the system tries to run faster than its legs can carry it.

This typical combination of main features may be summed up as follows:

1. Very high investment and low consumption proportions.

2. A specific set of priorities.

3. Accelerated utilization of the obvious potentials for extensive development; quantity drive at the expense of quality.

One is not justified in calling this combination of main features a definite "growth strategy." "Strategy" implies the kind of plan selected consciously by military commanders, whereas the elements of conscious choice in forced growth are diluted with spontaneous, concomitant phenomena, and even trends that develop in spite of the leadership's wishes. Priorities 1 to 6 are applied consciously, influenced by the ideas of Marx

---

[55]A very important undertaking is the United Nations International Comparison Project (ICP), conducted by I. B. Kravis and his colleagues. They try to eliminate the distorting effect of national price systems, expressing the figures for all countries in a fictional currency with a uniform purchasing power. There are numerous reports on their findings; see, for example, I. B. Kravis, A. W. Heston, and R. Summers (1978, 1982).

Also notable were the estimates of the Central Intelligence Agency (1989) and the Research Project on National Income in East Central Europe, headed by T. P. Alton. See, for example, T. P. Alton (1977, 1981).

The method of expressing the level of economic development of a country by the average of several indices measured in physical terms was initiated by F. Jánossy (1963), and used later primarily by É. Ehrlich (e.g., 1981).

An important contribution has been made by the statistical work under the auspices of the World Bank. See P. Marer (1985). This research is continuing; the data collection of the World Bank by P. Marer et al. (1991) is the source for several tables in this book.

and Lenin and other contributions to the official ideology. But no one adopts a conscious policy of neglecting quality, overstretching utilization of the service sphere, damaging the natural environment, in some periods reducing consumption, and so on. Yet the combination of main features forms an organic whole: the planned and spontaneous priorities, conscious and instinctive methods, and desired and undesired consequences go together. After all, these features were not chosen according to a particular planner's own preferences. This type of growth and the accompanying behavior and mutual relations of those taking part are formed largely by their social situation, which circumscribes their scope for decision making. A combination of prevalent power structure, ideology, property relations, and coordination mechanisms, together with the system's initial state characterized by poverty and backwardness, sets the process of growth on the system-specific path described in this chapter.

Space precludes a comprehensive examination of the features of forced growth in light of the diverse theoretical literature on growth. Discussion must be confined to a very short collation of them with three theoretical trends.

First, a sharp debate on growth policy took place in the Soviet Union in the 1920s,[56] when one of the foremost economists on the "left wing," Preobrazhenskii, put forward his notable theory of primitive socialist accumulation. Marx had well-known ideas about primitive capitalist accumulation, which was accompanied by brutal expulsion of the peasants from their land, enforcement of a high rate of saving, and thereby the first "big push" to speed up the growth of capitalism. According to Preobrazhenskii, something similar must inevitably occur under the socialist system. Investment must be concentrated on industry, particularly heavy industry, and retardation of light industry and agriculture consciously accepted. Resources needed for investment must be obtained by forced saving. Consumption must be kept on a tight rein, or even forced back. Produce must be bought cheaply from the peasants, whose purchasing power must be cut further by taxes and high industrial prices. There must be accelerated collectivization of agriculture, which among other things will free labor required for industrialization.

By a tragic irony of history, Preobrazhenskii and many exponents of his ideas fell victim to the terror of Stalin, who then went on to implement some components of his recommendation in a way even Preobrazhenskii probably did not envisage.

Second, one of the main ideas in Arthur Lewis's theory is expressed in the title of a classic article of his: "Economic Development with Un-

---

[56]P. R. Gregory and R. C. Stuart [1974] (1986) and A. Erlich (1960) provide a good survey of the debate.

limited Supplies of Labor" (1954).[57] Lewis analyzes the growth of capitalist developing countries, where a dual economy operates: a modern, fast-growing, capitalist sector coexists with a declining, backward, traditional sector. The former absorbs successfully the labor released by the latter. The wages of the labor flowing into the capitalist sector are decided by the social norms for living standards, not by endogenous market forces.

The description in this chapter makes clear the similarities and the differences between the situation Lewis describes and the forced growth of classical socialism. (Further contributions to the comparison are made in chapter 10.) In both Lewis's theory and the practice of forced growth, a key part is played by extensive method 1, the fast expansion of employment and practically unlimited supply of labor—until the scope is exhausted. Here only the major differences are mentioned. In our case, the modern sector is socialist, not capitalist. According to Lewis's analysis, the capitalist advance and the profit motive are capable of raising a stagnant developing country's saving proportion of 4–5 percent to 12–15 percent. The motivation described in this chapter, along with the historically unprecedented methods available to the socialist bureaucracy, can even force a saving proportion of 30–40 percent.[58]

Third, the theory of unbalanced growth is associated mainly with A.O. Hirschman and P. Streeten.[59] It is a normative theory; those subscribing to it recommend a growth strategy in which a few "driving" sectors pull ahead and their excess demand encourages the other sectors to catch up. It is not this book's task to decide whether that is really the preferable strategy for a developing country on the capitalist road. All one need mention here is that classical socialism follows this course in practice. This is brought about, among other things, by the combination of priorities described earlier. The pull of "backward linkages" recommended by the adherents of unbalanced growth and the chronic shortage of socialist systems [→11, 12] overlap as concepts in many respects.

9.9 Growth Performance

On reaching the end of the chapter, an attempt can be made to sum up the results of forced growth. Tables 9.11, 9.12, and 9.13 give the aggre-

---

[57]See, furthermore, A. W. Lewis (1955).

[58]There is an essential difference in wages as well [→10]. In the period of forced growth, the wage level is decided neither by "social norms" nor by market forces. Basically, it adjusts to what the bureaucracy decides should be the ratio of accumulation to consumption. This decision subsequently molds the social norms of consumption as well.

[59]See, for example, A. O. Hirschman (1958) and P. Streeten (1959).

TABLE 9.11
Growth of Aggregate Output: International Comparison

	Average Annual Growth Rate		
	1961–70	*1971–80*	*1981–88*
Socialist countries			
Bulgaria	5.8	2.8	1.2
Czechoslovakia	2.9	2.8	1.4
East Germany	3.1	2.8	1.8
Hungary	3.4	2.6	1.0
Poland	4.2	3.6	0.8
Romania	5.2	5.3	−0.1
Soviet Union	4.9	2.6	2.0
Capitalist countries			
Austria	4.7	3.6	1.7
France	5.6	3.2	1.9
Greece	7.6	4.7	1.5
Italy	5.7	3.8	2.2
Japan	10.5	4.6	4.0
Netherlands	5.1	2.9	1.3
Portugal	6.4	4.7	2.2
Spain	7.3	3.5	2.6
United States	3.8	2.7	3.2
West Germany	4.5	2.7	1.7

Source: Compiled by J. Árvay for this book. For the sources of data on socialist countries, see table 9.10, alternative estimates. The data on capitalist countries are based on OECD (1991).

Note: Socialist output data refer to GNP, but in the given period they almost coincide with GDP estimates. Capitalist output data refer to GDP. As discussed earlier, there are disagreements among experts concerning the validity of both the official and the alternative estimates for socialist growth. There is, however, a general consensus that the alternative estimates better reflect real growth. Therefore, these are used for comparison with the data on capitalist countries.

TABLE 9.12
Growth Rate of Aggregate Output in the Soviet Union and the United States

| | Average Annual GDP Growth Rates (percent) | |
Years	Soviet Union	United States
1900–13	3.5	4.0
1913–50	2.7	2.8
1950–73	5.0	3.7
1973–87	2.1	2.5

Source: W. D. Nordhaus (1990) based on A. Maddison (1989, p. 36).
Note: Maddison's estimates cannot be compared directly with the estimates of Soviet growth given in table 9.10 for several reasons. For example, the periodizations differ. Maddison's estimates are closer to the alternative estimates in table 9.10 than to the growth rates given in the official Soviet statistics.

TABLE 9.13
Growth Rate of Aggregate Output: China Compared to Capitalist Countries

| | Average Annual GDP Growth Rates (percent) | |
	1965–80	1980–87
China	6.4	10.4
Low- and medium-income capitalist countries		
Argentina	3.5	−0.3
Brazil	9.0	3.3
India	3.7	4.6
Indonesia	8.0	3.6
Mexico	6.5	0.5
Pakistan	5.1	6.6
South Korea	9.5	8.6
Thailand	7.2	5.6
Turkey	6.3	5.2

Source: J. Echeverri-Gent (1990, p. 105).

gate growth indices for several socialist countries and compare these with similar growth indices for capitalist countries.

For the time being the comment will be confined to the period of the classical system.[60] The growth performance is substantial, but not outstanding. Many countries on the capitalist road achieved faster growth than that. I must add, however, that particularly in the early decades, the countries under the classical socialist system managed to grow faster than a long list of capitalist countries. Classical socialism certainly took many countries from a state of severe backwardness at least to a medium level of development. If it emerges that the data must be revised even further downward, the recognition for this achievement must be moderated as well, or perhaps even be withdrawn.

Judgment in this respect must be suspended, but whatever the outcome of future auditing of the figures, certain observations can already be made.

Leaders of the socialist countries are inclined to attach high intrinsic value to the fast growth or even make a fetish out of the growth rate for aggregate output and go for its increase at any price. An impartial observer, however, cannot accept this shortsighted criterion of evaluation. Even if the rate should be high in some socialist country or other, at least for a period, the question remains: what sacrifice had to be made for that growth rate? And what kind of economic structure lies behind the aggregate index?

The price paid for forcing growth is very high. It involves a great deal of abnegation and causes contemporaries much suffering.[61] At the same time, this type of growth undermines its own economic performance. Even where a high growth rate is attained initially, it cannot be kept up; sooner or later, the growth rate starts to fall more and more conspicuously. Each generation leaves a baleful legacy for the next—of grave, postponed, and increasingly urgent tasks, and of an economy with a disharmonious structure.

[60]For several countries, the two tables also include the reform period. I shall return to these parts of the tables later [→16.1, 23.2].

[61]I shall return to this when I discuss shortage and consumption [→11, 12, 13].

10

Employment and Wages

ACCORDING to the Marxian system of ideas, a worker's labor power under capitalism is a commodity, an object of purchase and sale like the things that change hands for money on the market. One condition for liberation is that the commodity nature of labor power should cease.

The political economy taught officially in the socialist countries underlines that this has happened under socialism, and a person's capacity for labor is no longer a commodity.[1] Translating that terminology into the language of this book, this means the allocation of labor is not performed by the mechanism of market coordination.

This chapter surveys the allocation of labor under classical socialism.[2] At the end of this chapter the claim made in the official textbooks is examined again, to see how justified it is in light of the analysis presented in this book.

The chapter begins by presenting the characteristics of labor allocation in the long and then the short term. It goes on to study the behavior of those taking part in short-term labor allocation and their relations to each other.

Throughout this chapter only the employment problems of the sector in public ownership (i.e., state-owned firms, state institutions of a non-firm nature, and cooperatives) will be considered.[3] It has been shown already that the other social sectors play an inconsiderable part under the classical system, and so it is more expedient to consider their employment problems in a later part of the book, which covers the process of reform [→19.2, 22.2, 23.1].

---

[1]The following quotation is from the official political economy textbook of the Stalin period: "Wages under socialism are essentially and radically different from wages under capitalism. Given that under socialism, labor power has ceased being a commodity, the wage is not the price of labor power. It expresses not the relationship between exploiter and exploited, but the relationship between society as a whole represented by the socialist state and the individual worker who works for himself, for his society." (*Politicheskaia Ekonomiia Sotsializma*, 1954, p. 452.)

[2]For a general overview, see J. Adam (1982, 1984), A. Bergson (1944), J. G. Chapman (1963), M. Ellman (1985, chap. 9), and A. Kahan and B. Ruble, eds. (1979).

[3]Consequently, expressions in this chapter such as "employment" and "labor demand" refer exclusively to the employment, labor demand, and so forth of the sector in public ownership, even when the appropriate qualifying word is not stated.

10.1   The Road to Full Employment

The most important extensive method used in forced growth is to mobilize the *labor surplus* [→9.5].[4] The proportions within the surplus differ
from country to country, but the following survey lists all the sources of
labor supply that can be absorbed by the public sector.

1. *Open unemployment*. This covers all those (most of them city dwell-
ers) who had jobs but lost them for some reason. Some of the unemployed may have been inherited from the preceding capitalist system.
Open unemployment of this kind is recorded in many capitalist countries
officially, for instance, by labor exchanges.

2. *Latent (hidden) unemployment*. This appears mainly in poorly developed countries, and that, as mentioned earlier, is just what most socialist countries are when power is taken. The category is made up of
those who undertake casual wage labor, or perhaps receive income from
casual selling of a product or performance of a service, but hold no permanent job. Alternatively, they may work on a family farm, even though
the farm could easily dispense with their contribution. Such "underemployment" appears on a mass scale mainly in the villages but exists
in the cities as well. Some of the latent labor surplus in the villages
moves to the cities, hoping for better chances of work, but a high proportion of it remains unemployed there as well. Unlike those in group 1,
they are not recorded at labor exchanges even under the capitalist system,
but they can be several times as numerous. The poorer and more industrially backward and stagnant a country is, the higher the number in this
group.

3. *Workers in family undertakings*. Mass collectivization [→5.5] and
nationalization cause those who have been working on small family
farms or in small private industrial or commercial undertakings to become employees of the sector in public ownership.

As for the situation in agriculture, even before collectivization, some
had been working full-time as a main occupation, but they had worked
for themselves or their families, whereas they now work for a publicly
owned employer. Others really belong to group 2, but their labor power
was not well utilized and their status has not been apparent before, since
it has remained "within the family." Collectivization, however, makes
this underutilization of their labor tangible and visible. There is pressure

---

[4]The expression "surplus" is used as the opposing pair of "shortage." I have purposely
chosen a neutral word. "Reserve" has overtones of appreciation and approval, while "excess" has a pejorative, condemnatory ring. So a reserve of labor or an excess of labor will
only be mentioned where such approval or condemnation is intended.

A similar terminology problem arises in the broader context of surpluses of any product,
service, or resource [→11.4].

on them to seek work in the local cooperative or with another state-owned firm or cooperative, in their home village or the city. So collectivization of farming releases a vast labor surplus to the other sectors, notably industry.

4. *The "declassed."* The wealth of big capitalists, landowners, and other rich people is seized in the first wave of revolution, usually while the transitional system is still in force. Later, under the classical system in most cases, comes appropriation of the means of production owned by the middle classes who live off their property; even if their personal property is not confiscated, it is exhausted sooner or later. A major element in the campaign for mass collectivization is elimination of the class of rich peasants and full seizure of their property [→5.5].

Some members of these social groups emigrate, while others are executed, imprisoned, or sent to do forced labor. Those escaping such destinies or later released from prison or labor camp take jobs in the sector in public ownership.

5. *Women working in the household*. The group covered partly overlaps with groups 2, 3, and 4.

The mass entry of women into employment receives a strong inducement from the new norms of family living standards and the wage level that reflects them. As the growth process progresses, all families feel increasingly that they can only live at the standard dictated by the norms of society if both husband and wife are employed. A man's wages alone cannot give his wife and family members the customary, socially acceptable standard of living.

6. *Population growth*. This concerns the usual demographical increment in the manpower surplus. In most socialist countries there is an appreciable increase in the population as a whole and the population of working age under the classical system.

The leadership in certain countries and periods may become dissatisfied with the rate of population increase and resort to methods of bureaucratic coordination to speed it up. In other countries the purpose of the state's population policy is just the opposite: to try to prevent an increase in the population by brute force.[5] Whatever the end, the means

[5]An example of forcing population growth was Hungary in the 1950s and again in the 1970s. Typical tools for bureaucratic intervention are deliberately created shortage in the supply of contraceptive devices and a strict ban on abortion (not on health, moral, or religious grounds, but with open reference to the economic interests of society and the labor needs of production); financial rewards from the state for increasing the number of children.

The main example of the opposite type of intervention is China, which applied rude methods to prevent undesirable population growth.

is bureaucratic intervention in a sphere that is traditionally the closest preserve of family coordination.

Groups 1–6 together make up the external surplus of labor under the classical socialist system.[6] It is clear from the description that what is termed here a surplus far exceeds in number the group of open unemployed. Many classified here in the surplus have not been employed before, and to that extent are not "unemployed."

As the process of forced growth proceeds, it absorbs more and more labor from all six sources until, practically speaking, they run out, so that there is no more scope for using this extensive method.[7] Some data relating to this appear in tables 10.1 and 10.2.[8] The proportion of the total employable population actually employed, the so-called participation rate, has reached its limit of tolerance. Table 10.1 shows that the socialist countries reach a higher overall rate of participation than the capitalist countries primarily through greater involvement of women in production.[9] Here it is worth noting the phenomenon presented in figure 10.1. There is a loose positive relationship between the level of economic development and the participation rate. If one compares the participation rates of socialist and capitalist countries at the same level of economic development, it turns out that the socialist countries' participation rates are the highest on each level of economic development. This is clearly shown in figure 10.1.

The surplus of labor is a potential labor supply but does not become one under all circumstances. Certain specific inducements are required.

The first inducement is the actual opportunity. The underutilized labor force is vegetating in the village, until it turns out one day that a new factory is being set up nearby. The opportunity acts as a magnet; many who have not belonged to this category before actively seek employment.

---

[6]The attribute "external" is prompted by the following consideration: The system contains "unemployment within the factory gates," to be mentioned shortly. This constitutes the internal surplus of labor.

[7]One cannot speak of unconditional exhaustion in the case of source 6. Even if a country has absorbed its whole labor surplus at a particular moment, the growth of the population will continually produce a further source of labor supply.

[8]The Soviet participation rate (the proportion of employed among the whole population aged 15 to 64) was 86.6 percent in 1980, as opposed to 66.5 percent in the European OECD countries and 70.9 percent in the United States. The participation rate for women was 87 percent, compared with 48.5 percent and 59.7 percent respectively. G. Ofer (1987, p. 1793).

[9]Table 10.1 makes the high rate of participation by women particularly clear by picking out the 40–44 age-group. The women in this age-group are beyond the period of their own education, and even their children are normally in their teens, so that they require less parental control, while they themselves are still well under retiring age. As the table shows, participation is far more widespread in the socialist countries than it is in the capitalist countries.

TABLE 10.1
Activity Rate of Women in the Age Group 40–44: International Comparison

	1950	1960	1970	1980	1985
Socialist countries					
Bulgaria	78.6	83.4	88.5	92.5	93.3
Czechoslovakia	52.3	67.3	79.9	91.3	92.4
East Germany	61.9	72.7	79.1	83.6	86.1
Hungary	29.0	51.8	69.4	83.2	84.7
Poland	66.4	69.1	79.5	83.2	84.7
Romania	75.8	76.4	79.5	83.1	85.1
Soviet Union	66.8	77.9	93.2	96.9	96.8
North European countries	30.9	39.9	53.8	69.9	71.1
West European countries	34.5	39.5	46.4	55.1	55.6
South European countries	22.4	25.3	29.7	35.7	37.1

Source: Compiled by J. Köllő for this book on the basis of International Labor Office (1987).

Note: The covered countries are Austria, Belgium, France, West Germany, the Netherlands, Switzerland, Luxembourg, United Kingdom (Western Europe); Greece, Italy, Malta, Portugal, Spain (Southern Europe); Bulgaria, Czechoslovakia, East Germany, Hungary, Poland, Romania, Soviet Union (socialist countries); the Scandinavian countries (Northern Europe). Regional averages are unweighted. The classification of countries by regions in this table is different from the ILO's original.

They become part of the labor supply, and in that sense one can say that the demand for labor during the long-term process of growth creates its own supply.

The second, self-evident inducement is the financial interest in permanent employment. Those in group 1 hasten to find a job purely because they need a livelihood. Permanent, secure employment is a huge relief to the unemployed. The need for a livelihood sooner or later leads those in group 4, the formerly privileged classes, to seek employment as well. Mention has already been made of the specific financial motivation of group 5, women who remained hitherto in the household.

The third inducement is bureaucratic compulsion, which can take various forms. The socialist countries lay down by law not only the right but the duty to work, and that means in practice (with certain exceptions

TABLE 10.2
Growth of Workforce in the Soviet Union

Year	Workforce[a] (million)	Period	Average Annual Growth Rate of Workforce (percent)
1927	11.3	—	—
1932	22.8	1927–32	15.1
1937	27.0	1932–37	3.4
1950	40.4	1937–50	3.1
1955	50.3	1950–55	4.5
1960	62.0	1955–60	4.3
1965	76.9	1960–65	4.4
1970	90.2	1965–70	3.2
1975	102.2	1970–75	2.5
1980	112.5	1975–80	1.9
1985	117.8	1980–85	0.9
1986	118.5	—	—
1987	118.5	—	—
1988	117.2	—	—
1989	115.4	1985–89	−0.5

Source: Compiled by C. Krüger for this book on the basis of the following sources: 1927 and 1932: A. Nove (1969, p. 192); 1937: A. Nove (1969, p. 226); 1950 and 1955: A. Nove (1969, p. 342); 1960, 1970, 1980, and 1985: Finansy i Statistika (1987, p. 414); 1965 and 1975: Finansy i Statistika (1977, p. 463); 1986 and 1987: Finansy i Statistika (1988b, p. 38); 1988 and 1989: Finansy i Statistika (1989a, p. 48).

[a]Excluding *kolkhoz* members.

mentioned later) the duty to work for the sector in public ownership. Those who fail to are legally harassed as "parasites" and forced by the authorities to take work.

On the micro level a big part is played undoubtedly by the customary relationship of supply: raising wages increases the labor supply [→10.5]. But on the macro level being considered here, that relationship cannot be perceived. The reason why the supply of labor grows is not that the employers offer higher and higher wages. The total supply of labor still grows if the average nominal and real wages stagnate or even decline

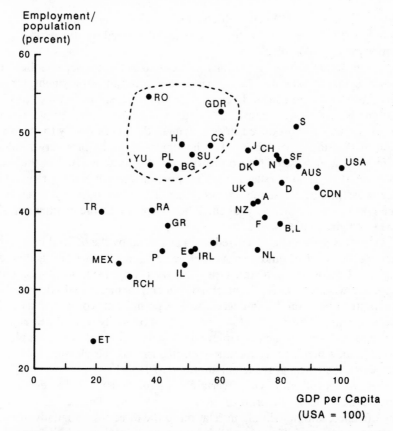

FIGURE 10.1   Participation Rates and the Level of Development, 1980
Source: The figure and the statistics on which it is based were compiled by
J. Köllő. The source for data on GDP is É. Ehrlich (1985, p. 100). The
figures on employment and population for the capitalist countries have been
taken from the *UN Demographic Yearbook* and for the socialist countries
from the *CMEA Statistical Yearbook*.
Note: For clarity's sake, the full names of the countries have not been
entered on the figure, and instead they are just listed here in order of GDP
per capita: Egypt, Turkey, Mexico, Chile, Romania, Yugoslavia, Argentina,
Portugal, Greece, Poland, Bulgaria, Hungary, Israel, Soviet Union, Spain,
Ireland, Czechoslovakia, Italy, East Germany, Japan, United Kingdom,
New Zealand, Denmark, Austria, Netherlands, France, Switzerland, Nor-
way, Belgium, Luxembourg, West Germany, Finland, Sweden, Australia,
Canada, and the United States. It should be noted particularly that all the
socialist countries feature in the ringed area above the capitalist countries at
a comparable level of development; in order of GDP, the socialist countries
included are Romania, Yugoslavia, Poland, Bulgaria, Hungary, Soviet
Union, Czechoslovakia, and East Germany.

over a long period.[10] Even with constant or declining nominal and real wages, the inducements for the groups just described to take permanent employment still apply.

The program of the Communist parties makes a promise, even before power is taken, to abolish joblessness and ensure full employment. Once the classical system consolidates, that promise is enshrined in the constitution. Nonetheless, it must be stated: it is no conscious employment policy designed to produce full employment that leads finally to absorption of the surplus of labor. The phenomenon is a by-product or side-effect of the process of forced growth. As discussed in detail in the last chapter, the system pursues the fastest possible growth at any price, and the most immediate scope for attaining this is provided by extensive method 1: speedy inclusion of the labor surplus into the production of the sector in public ownership.

Once this process has occurred and been rated by the official ideology among the system's fundamental achievements, it becomes an "acquired right" of the workers, a status quo that the classical system cannot and does not wish to reverse. Thenceforth full employment is laid down as a guaranteed right (and to a degree, so is a permanent workplace, as will be seen later). This is an actual, not just a nominally proclaimed right, ensured not only by the principles and practical conventions of employment policy but by the operating mechanism of the classical system, above all the chronic, recurrent shortage of labor.

Permanent full employment certainly is a fundamental achievement of the classical system, in terms of several ultimate moral values. It has vast significance, and not simply in relation to the direct financial advantage in steady earnings. It plays additionally a prominent part in inducing a sense of financial security, strengthening the workers' resolve and firmness toward their employers, and helping to bring about equal rights for women.

This achievement has its dark sides, however. First of all, one should consider again the path leading to it. Groups 1, 2, and 6, the previous victims of open and latent unemployment and the new generations seeking work, are clearly among the winners. But the way of life of group 3, the millions of peasants and other independent people, is overturned by collectivization. The majority are forced against their will, by an iron hand, to take employment in the public sector. Group 4, the formerly rich and privileged, suffer tragic losses. Nor is the position of group 5, the women leaving the household, devoid of ambiguity; they win in some ways and lose in others [→6.7]. These are some of the human costs of the transition: the victims along the road to full employment, and the

---

[10]In fact, as noted above, women might be driven into employment just because wages are low.

losses of those who are half winners. In addition, when full employment has been consolidated and become self-evident to subsequent generations, this state of labor allocation is accompanied by numerous economic drawbacks as well. Light will be shed on these in the later analysis.

One final observation is required on the connection between the growth process and full employment. Some of the socialist countries (the Soviet Union and the countries of Eastern Europe) reached full employment within the framework of the classical system. In others (such as China) this did not happen. The process of reform began when the surplus of labor was far from fully absorbed.

10.2 The Development of Chronic Labor Shortage

The socialist system has a large external labor surplus that it can mobilize until full employment is reached, but that does not preclude the appearance of partial *labor shortages* in the meantime. There are several reasons for this.

■ The majority of the surplus labor is unskilled, whereas the fast-growing economy, particularly industry, suffers from a shortage of labor with specific skills [→9.5, intensive method 3].[11] The shortage appears at all levels of qualification; there is a need for more skilled workers, more professionals with secondary and higher educational qualifications, and more experienced managers than are readily available.

■ Most of the surplus labor is in the villages, while the shortage is mainly in the cities. Before the surplus could move from the villages to the cities, urban housing and other services would have to develop quickly, but they are among the low-priority tasks constantly postponed.

■ Another cause of labor shortage is uneven regional development. Some regions develop fast, producing a big demand for labor, but the surplus often appears in other regions. The problem is especially acute if the development takes place in regions people find unattractive, for instance, if new industry is sited where the climatic conditions are harsh and the level of civilization comparatively low.[12]

[11]A shortage of unskilled labor may also emerge, largely in jobs requiring great physical effort or done under unpleasant conditions. This may tie in with the tradition that such jobs be done by men, while the prevalent surplus consists mainly of female labor. A frequent resort is for women to do heavy manual labor.

[12]An example from the Soviet Union is the development of Siberia.

All three phenomena are cases of *structural* labor shortage. This exists under any system, but the forms listed have system-specific features as well.

It would be mistaken to think an economy has either a surplus or a shortage of labor. The two are not mutually exclusive. Certainly, if one goes into the minutest detail, examining labor allocation at the submicro level, surplus and shortage are mutually exclusive. For instance, a factory at a particular time offers a specific number of jobs, which can be filled by people with specific qualifications. The area around the factory contains a specific number of inhabitants able and willing to fill those jobs. Comparison of the concrete, accurately specified supply and demand allows one to say whether there is a surplus or a shortage at that particular place and time. But if one takes a more aggregate look at the situation, adding up figures for several factories, trades, and regions, and for a longer period of time, there may be concurrent instances of excess supply and excess demand. The broader the sphere of aggregation, the more valid the statement becomes.

Figure 10.2 shows a so-called Beveridge curve.[13] It should be understood to refer to the total labor force of a socialist country, that is, as a survey on a macro level of the state of labor allocation at some particular time. The horizontal scale is one of the possible measures of labor surplus: the difference between the total number of people of working age and the total number in employment. The vertical scale is one of the possible measures of labor shortages: the number of vacant jobs. Each

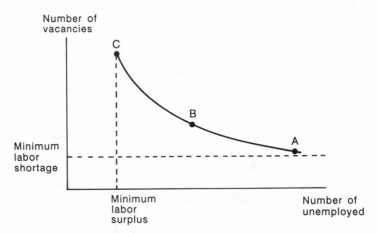

FIGURE 10.2   Beveridge Curve

[13]Named after the British labor economist W. Beveridge. The diagram is widely employed in labor economics. See the article by K. G. Abraham and J. L. Medoff (1982), for example.

point on the curve shows a particular combination of surplus and shortage.

Forced growth begins at point A: a large surplus, but some shortage already. As the process continues, the surplus steadily decreases and the shortage grows. Point B shows an intermediate state,[14] and point C the attainment of a situation where there is no more mobilizable surplus to draw into employment, and the labor shortage is very intense.

In what follows, the situation represented by point C is termed full employment, because it constitutes the upper limit of employment in a country's particular situation. There is a problem with the term, however. The figure also shows that even at this point employment is still not full in the sense of all people physically and mentally able to work having a job. The existence of groups capable of work who cannot be drawn into employment is explained by the following factors:

1. Some people choose voluntarily not to be employed, and the bureaucracy is prepared to exempt them from the general obligation to work if they fulfill certain criteria. For instance, it is accepted that mothers of large families need not take jobs in the sectors in public ownership. There is variation from country to country and period to period, on the one hand, in what individuals wish to do about employment, and, on the other, in the criteria applied by the bureaucracy when accepting or rejecting those individual desires.

2. There is temporary, frictional unemployment. To some extent this is inescapable under any system. An employee leaving a job, whether resigning voluntarily or dismissed, will not always find a new job straight away, even if there is a big shortage of labor. The phenomenon is linked closely with the structural disproportions between supply and demand for labor, discussed above, or, more precisely, with the adaptive features of the system: the degree of friction with which it operates and the speed with which it is able to adjust between supply and demand. In classical socialism's case, there are many restraints on the mobility of labor; some (such as the housing shortage) have been mentioned earlier, while others (the way employees are tied to their firms and other curbs on movement) are treated later [→10.5]. The reallocation of production and labor is impeded by the rigor of the bureaucratic coordination; the supply and demand of labor adapt sluggishly to each other. The Beveridge curve shown in figure 10.2 expresses the *friction* of adaptation, since there is still an appreciable surplus of labor at point C, which signifies full employment.[15]

---

[14]This point could represent the stage reached, for instance, by China when beginning its process of reform.

[15]There are people in many socialist countries, including the Soviet Union, who spend several months fruitlessly looking for a job even though there are a great many vacancies in the economy as a whole.

Continued

It becomes clear from what has been said why the attribute "mobilizable" has been added repeatedly to the word surplus even up to now: to arrive at the surplus, one must always deduct from all those capable of work but not employed those not in practice mobilizable for employment in the sectors in public ownership, for one of the reasons just given.[16]

Returning to figure 10.2, the vertical broken line represents the minimum surplus, that is, the number of those in the population capable of work but not mobilizable for employment: this barrier cannot be crossed during the labor-absorption process. The horizontal broken line marks the minimum shortage; the number of job vacancies can be no less than this, however great the labor surplus. The economy's employment situation lies within the inner area defined by the broken lines.

If the growth process ever takes the economy to point C, the state of the economy remains constant around that point. From then on, one can refer to a chronic shortage of labor. Point C in the figure shows the economy's normal state: the combination of the normal labor shortage and the normal labor surplus. No value judgment is attached to the concept of "normality" either by participants in the system or by the analyst of it. It may be that no one thinks state C truly desirable. "Normal" denotes solely that this is the accustomed state under the system, the one socially considered usual. Though the prevalent values of the shortage and surplus may vary, point C marks the intertemporal average of the data observed in reality.[17] (The concepts of normal shortage and normal surplus are returned to in more detail in the next chapter.)

The growing shortage of labor can be seen in a set of Polish figures shown in figure 10.3. This shows the proportion of vacancies to job seek-

---

Several authors rate this as open, not temporary, frictional unemployment, if the job-seeker fails to find employment within one month. Calculating on this basis, P. R. Gregory and I. L. Collier (1988, p. 617), in an article based on a survey of Soviet exiles using a questionnaire, arrive at an unemployment rate of 1.1 percent for the period 1974–79. I. Adirim (1989) reports a far higher proportion of unemployment, particularly in certain Asian regions.

[16]There is one more additional reason. Although the chapter does not deal with this generally, it must be noted that some people, with the agreement of the bureaucracy, work in the various parts of the private sector (self-employed members of the intelligentsia, private artisans, etc.). These individuals are not available for employment in the public sector.

[17]The following is important indirect evidence of chronic labor shortage: Cyclical fluctuation takes place in many socialist countries [→9.6]. It is worth noting that whereas the volume of investment fluctuates very strongly and production to a lesser extent, but still quite strongly, employment hardly varies at all. It falls very little even in periods of decline.

Table 9.10, which expressed the fluctuation in investment as a standard deviation around the average growth rate, is pertinent here. The data in the table show the standard deviation for investment in the six socialist countries of Eastern Europe combined to be 5 percent. By contrast, the standard deviation for employment (calculated in the same way) is only 0.4 percent. (For the data sources, see table 9.10.)

FIGURE 10.3 Vacancy/Job Seeker Ratio in Poland
Source: The graph was compiled by J. Köllő; the sources of the data are
Z. M. Fallenbuchl (1985, p. 33) and R. Holzmann (1990, p. 6).

ers. The index reaches the value of 1 when the shortage and the surplus
balance each other out as a whole, even if there is still a structural shortage and surplus. The Polish economy was already over this important
limit in the 1960s, and in two decades it came close to a value of 100. In
other words, there were one hundred vacancies for each job seeker.

It would be desirable to reach full employment without labor shortage
intervening. But a perfect eradication of surplus and shortage is possible
only in the realm of theoretical models, not in real economies operating
with many kinds of friction. Under classical socialism the main guarantee of really full employment is precisely this swing beyond "perfect
equilibrium" into chronic and intensive labor shortage; those who want
work can find jobs comparatively easily.

The labor shortage begins to spur those running the economy to
greater efforts to substitute capital for labor, in other words, to use relatively more capital-intensive technologies that release labor. It is not
profit calculations—not the fact that relatively scarcer labor has become
dearer by comparison with the price of using capital—that induces decision makers to do this. They pay little heed to price signals, even if they
reflect relative scarcities [→8]. (Moreover, price signals again fail here to
mirror scarcity changes [→10.5].)

Once again, decision makers are more influenced by nonprice signals
[→8.9]. Day after day they receive various signals of shortage. For

instance, there are no answers to advertisements for labor; employee-initiated termination of employment becomes more common, because employees know they can find other jobs easily. Time and again, the bureaucracy hits the upper limit of the availability of manpower, the most important resource of all. The decision makers feel almost tangibly that "this cannot go on"; adaptation to the chronic labor shortage is inescapable.

10.3 Direct Bureaucratic Control of Employment and Wages

For reasons of space, the subject in the remainder of the chapter must be narrowed down to the state of the classical system when it has reached, or at least approached, full employment. Until such time as the system reaches that state, the labor-allocation mechanism has features both similar to and different from those examined here, but description of them has to be omitted.

This section and the next deal mainly with vertical control, in two stages. Section 10.3 concentrates on the process within the bureaucracy, from central management through to the workshop head, while section 10.4 deals with the relationship between the bureaucracy and employees without bureaucratic functions.

Finally, section 10.5 examines the combined effect on wages of the bureaucratic and market mechanisms. Discussion of the economic and social problems of wages from other points of view is left to the final section as well.

Turning to the regulatory processes within the bureaucracy, it is worth recalling the description of annual planning and day-to-day management of the economy [→7]. Bureaucratic control of labor allocation integrally ties in with this, and so there is no need to repeat all the details. What need emphasizing are the features of economic management most typical of this part of it.

The process begins with education, when the young are "schooled" for the system. In other words, by severe restriction of the choice open to parents and the young people concerned, they are denied certain chances of further study and channeled toward others, or the path of further study may even be laid down by prohibitions and compulsory requirements. Once they have finished school, something similar takes place again: use is made of forms of intervention ranging from "channeling" toward a place of work to compulsory posting to one.

The ensuing account starts at the stage when employees have completed their studies and are at work. At this stage, the allocation of labor consists largely of control of employment and wages. Planning and management cannot devote equal attention to every plan indicator and to every aspect of economic activity [→7.7]. Instead, they give priority handling to some. Payrolls and wages are among the matters given highest priority. The strictest observance of the regulations on both is required.

Anyone thinking of a state-owned firm under capitalism might misconstrue the situation: here the object is not to stimulate the state-owned firm to employ the maximum number of people. On the contrary, the number employed is subject to an upper constraint.[18] One should not forget that there is now a state of chronic labor shortage in which the classical system tries to limit growth of the employment by bureaucratic means, prohibitions, and quotas. A vertical shortage occurs: the total workforce demand of the applicant firms is greater than the total quota the allocator can distribute.[19]

There are similar upper constraints on wages. These may take several different forms: an upper limit may be put on the sum payable in wages (known as the absolute wage-fund); average wages may be laid down (overall or by occupation); wages payable may be linked by some formula with the production accomplished; and so on. In fact, this is an instance of the "earmarking" of money [→8.1]. However much a firm saves on materials or another outlay, it has no right to use the saving on wage payments above the prescribed limits. The budget constraint on the firm's total expenditure is soft, but the constraint on one item of it, wage expenditure, is very hard.

The labor prescriptions in the plan are the subject of bargaining. The applicants hope for as slack a plan for workforce and wages as possible, because that will make it easier to fulfill the production plan (or, in the case of those realizing an investment project, to accomplish the investment task). The allocator displays the usual Janus face, trying to be strict with those below while bargaining for a slacker target with those above.

It is worth pondering the interests and behavior of leaders during vertical bargaining. While the bargaining lasts, it is worth them campaigning for more investment (inducement to expansion, investment hunger) and a bigger wage-fund to go with it (to make it easier to obtain labor and leave their employees more satisfied). One could also express this by say-

---

[18]Before the labor surplus finally runs out, the firms in many countries receive recruiting quotas prescribing how many new employees they must hire. The quotas are filled through aggressive recruiting campaigns. The economic leadership is prompted to use this procedure because certain firms are already up against a big shortage of labor, even though there is still plenty of surplus on the macro level. (See the comments on structural shortage in the previous section.)

[19]In a district with only a single sizable firm, the upper limit in the workforce bargaining is set less by the workforce quotas distributable on paper than by the actual constraint, perceptible in practice, on labor supply in the district.

ing they campaign concurrently for more investment and more consumption despite the plain macroeconomic contradiction between the two demands. Only the supreme central leadership ultimately counterposes the two conflicting demands when they divide the production between investment (along with other kinds of state utilization like the army) and consumption. They have the right to decide, but under the prevailing political and economic structure it is also a duty to decide, and whatever their decision is, they have no natural allies to support them of their own accord in curbing either investment or consumption and matching them up with the resources available. Everyone, even their own subordinates, presses them to raise both. So they have no choice but to create artificial allies through administrative instructions and bonus and penalty schemes that induce people to carry them out.

10.4 Employer-Employee Relations in the Factory

I shall now move from the corridors of power to the factories.[20] In many respects they present a similar picture to factories under any other system. At least at first sight, the similarity extends beyond the technological processes and organization of production (which are not considered here) to person-to-person relations. There are bosses, company managers, work managers, and foremen giving orders, and workers carrying them out. Although the bosses are actually also paid employees, like their colleagues in capitalist firms, they are the representatives of the employer, and in that capacity they are pitted against the employees in many respects.

The identity of their roles produces many similarities in their behavior. In line with the scheme of the book, attention is concentrated here on what is system-specific to a socialist firm.[21]

Both employees and employer are in a situation whose ambiguity is manifest in their behavior and their relations with each other. Taking employees first, I shall note the things that strengthen their position in relation to their employer, before turning to the factors that weaken their position.

In the period being considered, the labor shortage has already become acute. To borrow the terminology of the market mechanism, there is a

---

[20]The chapter refers throughout to firms and factories. Wherever there are more than two levels of division within the firm (e.g., the shops or independent shop units within the factory), the comments apply self-evidently to them as well.

Another possible expansion needs mentioning. The bulk of what is said about firms applies also to nonfirm state institutions.

[21]An excellent account of the conflict between bosses and workers can be found in M. Haraszti (1978).

"sellers' market," and in a true market environment the sellers (in this case the workers as sellers of labor) would be able to dictate their terms to the buyer (in this case the employing firm as buyer of labor). Although bureaucratic control plays a fundamental part, as explained in the previous section, the constant excess demand for labor still exerts a very strong market-style influence on the situation, and ultimately on the workers' behavior. If dissatisfied with working conditions and earnings, they are not usually restrained from leaving their jobs by any fear of not being able to obtain another.[22]Awareness that there is "exit" (to use Hirschman's expression again) gives the workers backbone, making them bolder about criticizing their superiors and opposing their orders. In this respect classical socialism is unique, as the only system in which full employment and chronic labor shortage persist so long.

The other main weapon workers have to protect their interests, besides or instead of quitting their jobs, concerns performance. Some "shirk" simply because they do not like hard work and can be sure of getting their wages without displaying any great effort. Others consciously hold back performance so as to be in a position to extract concessions from the bosses on wages and other conditions of work. They are induced to use this weapon by a sense of being indispensable and by the fact that the boss thinks twice before penalizing the workers.

An important element in the official ideology is its emphasis that the political system embodies the power of the working class. Whether a worker believes that, half-believes it, or disbelieves it entirely, he or she is encouraged by the declaration itself to act more openly against the bosses or resist them silently.

But there are factors that weaken the employees' position. No spontaneous defense of their own interests can compensate workers fully for their lack of independent trade unions. The official union movement openly adopts the role of a mass adjunct to the party in power, a transmission belt passing on the party's prevailing policy to its members. A good many union officials may feel contradictory attachments and therefore display ambivalent behavior, wanting to represent the membership, the workers in the firm, but also wanting to satisfy their superiors in the union bureaucracy and party organizations. The latter allegiance usually proves stronger under the classical system.

There are various strands of dependence of employees on their bosses of the company and their immediate place of work. Of course, the plain fact of this dependence is self-evident and common to all systems. Specific to the system is a special constellation of legal, economic, and politi-

---

[22]However, if the worker's occupational training and experience are such as can really be utilized only in his or her present job, that, of course, increases the risk to the worker of quitting that job voluntarily.

cal ties that applies in factories under classical socialism and is discussed in a moment, when the position and behavior of the employer are described. But let me say in advance what follows from it for the employees. Whereas the chronic shortage of labor and other factors noted already may encourage employees to oppose their bosses, perhaps holding back performance or quitting their jobs, they think twice before doing so after all, as the bosses too have effective weapons for imposing their will.

The resultant of the two opposing groups of forces is not always the same. Much depends on the country and the stage in its history, the strength of the repressive methods used by the bureaucracy, and the indispensability of the particular person at the workplace. Even individual character plays a part. Workers who put in excessive effort may appear side by side with shirkers, as may piece rates requiring a forced level of performance with payment schemes that reward good and bad work equally, and conscientious work side by side with slapdash. All may occur with varying frequency and in varying proportions.[23]

On the other side of the coin is the behavior of the employer, the bosses of the company and the factory. Each of them is subject to various types of pressure from various quarters. The description of the bureaucratic leader's motivation [→7.4] applies basically to these relations as well, allowing for certain additional, specific features. A boss most of all wants to be well in with his own superiors, since it is mainly they who determine his promotion, salary, and special bonuses and penalties. So everything said in the previous section about the compilation and execution of plans for manpower levels and wages applies to the lowest, intrafirm levels as much as to the suprafirm levels.

Bosses everywhere, however, depend on their employees. That applies equally in the relation between company and factory bosses and their workers. The more intense the labor shortage and the more demanding the workers concerned, the more a boss feels this dependence. His interest in smooth production and calm in the factory demands that he satisfy the workers' demands as far as possible. And if he embraces the official ideology with total conviction, he considers himself not an "employer" but a representative of his workforce, who should act in solidarity with the workers. All these factors prompt a boss to interpret the workers' complaints and demands to the organizations above him, making him the "voice" that utters their demands. In this respect he may assume the traditional role of the union shop steward to some extent.

Inevitably, his behavior is ambivalent. The same can be said of bosses as was said of employees: the relative weights of the two opposing groups of motives vary according to the country, period, and individual con-

---

[23]The question of work intensity has been discussed earlier [→6.6, 9.5].

cerned. But ultimately, it is typical of classical socialism for the bureaucratic interest of firm and factory managers to prevail.

The bosses of firms and factories possess numerous weapons. As mentioned already in the chapters on power and property, the economy or "business" sphere is not divorced from the sphere of politics and administration of the state. The leading group in the firm—the party secretary and the manager, with support from the union secretary—simultaneously perform the following functions:

■ Management of production. The production managers assign the workers their specific tasks, and at the same time set wages and bonuses within the general guidelines received from above [→10.3]. They have ways of favoring some people and discriminating against others. Since this is self-evident and not system-specific, no more need be said about it.

■ Supervision of a workplace to which workers have been assigned compulsorily. A major proportion of workers are assigned to a workplace rather than choosing one for themselves. The firm guarantees employment, but at the same time it binds its employees to itself legally. Under the stricter regimes of the classical system, even if the process of quitting the job can be initiated by the worker, it can only be done with management consent. "Arbitrary" resignation is precluded legally by the state. In some countries and periods, an employee may not even leave his or her place of residence (village or city) without workplace permission.[24]

■ Local representation of political power and ideology. The workplace is the scene of much of the political propaganda activity: the processes of convincing people and inspiring them, providing moral incentives, and refuting views considered incorrect.

■ Local representation of the all-embracing selection activity of the bureaucracy. The workshop can be the launching pad for a career leading as far as a seat in the legislature or a post as minister, but it can also land someone who behaves in an undesired way on a nationwide blacklist.

■ Local representation of the crime-prevention authorities. It is easy for the leaders of firms to arrange for the arrest or persecution in another form of "saboteurs" and "troublemakers," or those considered to be such by the local leaders.

■ Local representation of the administrative organizations of the state. Citizens need a consent or a special certificate from their firm for numerous kinds of official business, ranging from a change of

---

[24]This was the situation in the Soviet Union and China for a long time.

residence or acquisition of a passport or exit permit to applications for a telephone or a loan from the bank.

■ Local representation of the income-distribution authorities. Employees must report any separate income earned to their firm and obtain a workplace permit before taking on outside work.

■ The role of a local branch of paternalistic provision. Many firms provide institutionally owned apartments[25] and have their own doctor's office, holiday center, kindergarten, and day nursery. The bosses decide how these services are allocated. In many countries and periods, firms also deal with distribution of rationed foodstuffs and perhaps other scarce goods (such as color televisions or cars).

■ Family guidance. In certain countries and periods, the leaders of firms also intervene in family life: they can prevent a worker from initiating a divorce, persuade workers to have children or dissuade them from doing so, and help or hinder a worker's child applying for a place in a university.

All these functions[26] give the firm and the factory managers enormous power over their own employees. A firm becomes a cell of totalitarian power, not merely a scene of work.

Mention has been made of the dispersion of the alternative motives guiding the leaders of firms and of differences in their relative weights. Closely connected is the dispersion of the specific constellations of these functions and also the dispersion of the relative weights of the various methods used. The actual part played by any of the methods listed above in a particular firm or factory varies according to the country, period, and individual concerned. But whatever the case, all workers in a firm are largely at the mercy of their bosses. At the same time, they may share in the privileges that the bureaucracy extends via the firm to certain strata in society,[27] and in the special advantages that their bosses have managed to obtain for the workforce of that particular firm or factory.

[25]The allocation of institutionally owned apartments [→3.4] (or even the hope to get one) is one of the main bonds tying workers to their firms. Recalcitrance, such as voluntarily quitting a job, can lead to loss of the apartment, a heavy blow during a big housing shortage.

[26]Communes in China under Mao Zedong performed two other functions besides those listed: as plenipotentiary local organizations of state administration, and as institutions of collectivized consumption.

[27]For instance, in several countries preference over other strata in society is given to industrial workers, or to a narrower section of them, such as workers in large factories. Special advantages of this kind may apply, for example, in social security, health care, and housing provision. Similar preferential treatment may be furthered by allocation of consumer goods within the firm.

It would be a fine thing if industrious work became a need in the lives of all people.[28] It is no such thing for a high proportion of real people living under socialism. So, inevitably, there have to be bosses armed with incentive instruments to enforce labor discipline and wage discipline.

The property relations under capitalism cause both cooperation and class conflict between capitalist owners and wage laborers. Owners may feel how every extra dollar paid in wages comes out of their own pockets and how every minute a worker wastes loses them profit. They do not need to be ordered to maintain discipline. Capitalist owner-employers contracting wage labor are representatives of wage discipline and labor discipline in their own interest. By contrast, the bureaucracy under classical socialism is neither a real owner nor a real "employer." Its members receive no kind of automatic, direct advantage out of wage and labor discipline; its enforcement in fact sours their relationship with the workers. They are obliged by their integration into the bureaucracy to become enforcers of wage discipline and labor discipline. The bureaucracy fills a disciplinary vacuum left by the abolition of private property.

The described relationship between boss and employee, firm and worker, makes its influence felt in internal employment. Because it is hard to replace a worker who leaves, and also because there is the possibility of the superior organization being niggardly with future manpower plans, it is worth a firm accumulating an internal surplus. Just as goods shortages cause the hoarding of currently superfluous goods, so labor shortage breeds a tendency toward the hoarding of labor. Currently dispensable labor must be kept because it will be needed in the future. Then there is the additional fact that an appreciable proportion of the workers do not do their work really intensively, with full strength and attention. In fact, "shirking" is not unusual. The combined effect of these phenomena is to bring about *unemployment on the job*. In addition to what was said in section 10.2, therefore, chronic shortage of labor is compatible with and accompanied by not only a structural, frictional, external surplus of labor but an internal surplus of unemployment on the job.

Once such a situation has arisen, it is illusory to state the oft-repeated argument that there is no "real" shortage of labor because the shortage could easily be covered by mobilizing the internal surplus. The internal surplus does not result from personal error by particular economic leaders. It arises out of the essential attributes of the classical system and continues reproducing itself for as long as the classical system remains.

---

[28]Even Marx expected this only when the higher stage of communism was reached. See K. Marx [1875] (1966). It is doubtful whether it ever will happen, and one certainly can say that Marx did not hope for it in the foreseeable future, at the first stage on the road to a communist society, when the system had scarcely advanced beyond capitalism.

Sooner or later the classical system brings society to a point of full employment, but it cannot guarantee that all persons employed actually work to the best of their ability.

10.5 Bureaucratic and Market Influences on Wages

It follows from the two previous sections that bureaucratic and market coordination coexist and combine in the allocation of labor, and that the former predominates.[29] In examining how these two mechanisms affect wages, a distinction is made between relative prices on the macro and micro levels. An example of the former is the ratio between the prices of aggregate labor and aggregate capital, while the ratios between the wages for labor services differentiated according to profession, difficulty, danger, and other criteria are examples of the latter.

The bureaucracy basically determines the macro (average) level of wages in the economy as a whole. The intention is to set the planned annual average wage increase so as to harmonize with the macro plans for investment and consumption [→9.3]. When the central management decides the amount of investment, it seeks at the same time to stop runaway consumption from robbing investment of resources. Since the price level can be controlled quite effectively,[30] the planned level of wages plays a decisive part. The central management has very wide scope for taking sovereign decisions in this field: it is really capable of controlling whether nominal wages, the price level, and ultimately real wages rise, stagnate, or fall. No central management of the bureaucracy in any other society has such sovereignty in this vital area.

The macro relative prices of the basic factors of production (among them average wages) fail to reflect their relative scarcity and contribution to social production [→8.6]. When these relative prices are set, no attention is paid to each factor's abundance or scarcity. There is no capital market; a producer or investor either receives capital free or pays an interest rate that is arbitrary (and very low, despite the scarcity of capital). As mentioned before, the bureaucracy's wage policy adjusts the size of the average wage to the planned rate of real consumption (and the scale of customary, normal shortage of consumption goods on the market, as the next chapter explains).

In line with the program of this book, the problem is approached primarily through positive description. One can certainly say in this respect

---

[29]That is why the rubric "B + M" appeared in the cell for wage payments by the state-owned sector in table 6.1.

[30]Prices, however, are not regulated as strictly as wages. See, for instance, the account of disguised price increases [→8.6].

that the relative prices of the factors of production under classical socialism bear no relation to their relative marginal productivity.

Another question is how to assess the situation that develops in terms
of the efficiency of production. The arbitrary relative prices of the factors preclude rational calculation based on costs and prices when technology is chosen. That applies to the basing of decisions in both day-to-
day production and longer-term investment.[31]

One question closely related to wage setting is the proportion of individual to collective consumption [→13.3]. There is a strong tendency
under every classical socialist system to narrow down individual consumption of products and services bought directly by households for
money, and concurrently to increase the share of collective consumption
distributed in kind by the bureaucracy.[32]

Thereafter, of course, the take-home pay received by households is set
at a level where they would be incapable of paying for the products and
services they receive in kind. In the terminology of the official ideology,
the state "grants" housing, vacations, and medical care. But if all these
goods and services were sold for money at prices covering the costs and
the average level of profits and taxes, the workers, quite clearly, would
be unable to pay for them from wages set at the accustomed level. So
households have no option but to apply for all these products and services as a state donation.

This adds yet another distortion to the relative prices of the factors of
production. Wage costs are unrealistically low by comparison with what
the labor is actually costing society.

The next stage in the bureaucratic control of wages is the entire planning and management activity described in the last two sections. To
avoid repetition, I shall need only mention here, while emphasizing its
enormous significance, that it is precisely the sum of the millions of partial actions that ensures that the setting of wages remains by and large
in the hands of the bureaucracy.

The discussion now turns to the market elements that influence wages.

The analysis above began by examining how the average wage on the
macro level is set. What is the position with the dispersion about the
average on the micro level, the wage proportions between the various
trades and job areas, the wage differentials between different regions,
and the performance-related variations in wages, in a word, with relative
wages?

[31]In fact, this does not happen, because it is not in the interest either of the leaders of
state-owned firms, which have poor sensitivity to income and are under a soft budget
constraint, or of their superiors to make such a calculation.

[32]The book has dealt with this already in several connections [→6.7, 8.2, 10.4], shedding
light on the phenomenon from the angles of coordination mechanism, budget financing,
and paternalism within the firm.

Experience shows they are strongly influenced by the specific, prevailing supply and demand for labor. This is true to some extent even while the absorption of the labor surplus is still taking place, and it applies all the more at the stage of chronic labor shortage.

Workers taking short-term decisions weigh the attractions of various workplaces very carefully, looking at the work required, the working conditions, the physical difficulty and danger involved, and the pay. If they have a choice (and many do, as has been seen), they "vote with their feet," leaving a worse place of work for a better. They may only make threats, conveying their dissatisfaction with "voice" or by withholding performance. Bargaining between employed workers and their immediate superiors takes place on a massive scale. The more important and urgent the assignment and the more indispensable the employee, the stronger is his or her bargaining position.

Market forces also affect long-term individual decisions such as choice of career and place of residence. Certain trades are chosen by fewer and fewer people, while there are too many applicants for others; some regions become depopulated, and others overcrowded. These circumstances depend primarily on the likely earning prospects and other conditions.

The bureaucracy at all levels is obliged to react to these signals. It must do so within the firm, assessing the labor requirements in all the specific fields, along with their attractions or disincentives. The same must be done higher up, with the setting of wage proportions. Ultimately, one can say that relative wages are strongly influenced by the relations of labor supply and demand and the distribution of the relative excess demand. At the same time, the relative wages exercise a strong influence on the relative supply, namely, the occupational, workplace, and regional distribution of the total supply. (For reasons already discussed, they have far less effect on the demand.) In a word, market coordination has a strong influence here.

So far a distinction has been made on an abstract level between the problems of relative wages on the micro level, and of the macro, average wage level, relative to other factors of production. In fact, they are not wholly independent of each other.

In practice, the nominal wage under classical socialism is entirely rigid in a downward direction: open wage cuts are rare, although they have occurred at certain times (for instance, when the norm revision took place in the Stalin period).[33] So the kind of constant adjustment of relative wages described above usually involves the nominal wages of some

---

[33]This procedure is resorted to relatively rarely under the modern capitalist system as well, although it is not infrequent in times of depression for firms to reduce the nominal wages of some groups in absolute terms.

groups staying the same while those of other groups are increased. Adjustment of relative wages takes place through a series of partial wage raises. First the wages of group 1 are raised. But that means the earnings of group 2 are relatively behind, and sooner or later the problems of labor shortage there are exacerbated. So their wages have to be raised as well, at which point the problem of group 3 arises, and so on. Each in turn tries to press for higher wages, like a game of leapfrog.

What has been said here serves as another aid to understanding the vertical wage bargaining [→10.3]. The leapfrogging is accompanied by a spontaneous wage drift "from below." All economic leaders at all lower and intermediate levels work to obtain wage increases, pleading relative wage tensions. At the same time, there is strong resistance "from above." How the average wage level finally develops on the macro level depends on the prevailing power relations.

It may be that wage pressure breaks through to some extent, at least in terms of nominal wages. This can be interpreted as a market counter-effect to administrative setting of the nominal wage level, that is, the bureaucratic influence described above.

The central management normally seeks to counteract the wage pressure in order to spare the resources intended for other purposes (investment, defense spending) from the suction effect of consumer spending power in excess of the plan. The response tends to be to raise prices consciously (or accept the spontaneous price increases). All these relations play a major part in producing inflation, either open or hidden.

Examination of labor allocation and wages having been completed, it is possible to return to the question put at the beginning of the chapter: the assertion of the official textbooks of political economy that labor is not a "commodity" under socialism.

According to the observations presented in this chapter, the assertion in that strongly worded form is invalid. Market coordination has a substantial influence on the allocation of labor and on wages. However, the assertion is true insofar as the market influence is secondary; the influence of bureaucratic coordination is far stronger than that of the market.

What remains in doubt is how to assess that last phenomenon. When the early believers in Marxian ideas dreamed of a society in which labor would not be bought or sold like an inanimate object, they did not want to see employees ruled over with weapons of state power and economic constraints instead of market relations. In many respects the latter kind of oppression is graver than the kind of dependence produced by simple market relations.

11

Shortage and Inflation: The Phenomena

LITERATURE gives various labels to the group of phenomena discussed in the next two chapters: shortage, excess demand, disequilibrium, a sellers' market, suction, or repressed inflation, to list just the more common ones.[1] The terms do not coincide exactly and need more explanation later, but the list suffices to define the subject.

The intention is to explain shortage basically in terms of the system's inherent characteristics. As in the previous chapters, therefore, the effect of external relations is ignored for the time being [→14.3, 14.4].

The examination concentrates on the system's constant, lasting features. Factors influencing short-term fluctuations in the intensity and distribution of shortage phenomena are covered at most in passing. Attention is trained on parts of the phenomena that distinguish classical socialism lastingly from other systems, primarily capitalism.

---

[1] A substantial proportion of the ideas put forward in chapters 11 and 12 are based on my earlier works. Already my first book, *Overcentralization in Economic Administration* [1957] (1959), discussed the issue of shortage. Later that was one of the central themes in *Anti-Equilibrium* (1971) and *Economics of Shortage* (1980). A considerable part of the conceptual system and the analysis that follows has been taken over from those works of mine.

My ideas on the subject have altered several times during several decades of research, influenced partly by the works of other authors and partly by debates around what I wrote. In this book I have tried to include everything I can accept of the ideas of other authors. I aim to integrate all I am able to subscribe to into the account as a whole. I do not offer a more detailed breakdown of the remaining differences of opinion, apart from making comments of a dissociative kind in one or two places. In line with the general plan of this book, with only a few exceptions, I do not use its pages as a forum for debate. I would not wish to burden readers with a detailed account of how the position expressed in this book coincides with and differs from my earlier views.

The two sources of intellectual inspiration on the subject of shortage are Marx, who was an outstanding pioneer in analysis of lasting deviation from market equilibrium, primarily in his analysis of labor surplus (see chapters 23 and 24 in volume 1 and chapters 14 and 15 in volume 3 of *Capital* [1867–1894] 1978), and the work of Keynes (1936) on relations among unemployment, macro demand, and investment.

Recent literature on non-Walrasian equilibrium and disequilibrium has played an outstanding role in investigating the problem area. The pioneers of this school are R. W. Clower (1965) and A. Leijonhufvud (1968). See, furthermore, J.-P. Benassy (his comprehensive work of 1982), E. Malinvaud (1977), J. Muellbauer and R. Portes (1978), R. Portes and D. Winter (1980), and R. Portes et al. (1987). This group is called in many works the Disequilibrium School.

On the subject of chronic shortage under the socialist system, the following pioneer

The focus in the analysis of production is mainly on the sector in public ownership.[2] However, the formal and informal private sector, and, in conjunction with it, the gray and black markets, are mentioned among the sources of supply for households.

The subject is covered in two chapters: chapter 11 describes the phenomena of shortage and inflation, and chapter 12 discusses the causes of the two related phenomena.

11.1 Shortage Phenomena and the Shortage Economy

Using a somewhat simplified, stylized form, one can examine the choices facing the buyer of a product for personal consumption, for instance, a woman setting out to buy food. Assume she has a well-defined purchasing intention that accounts for prevailing prices, which she knows, and that beef features on her shopping list. Unless lucky, her shopping is not a single action but a process, a sequence of decisions whose stages and branchings appear in figure 11.1.

Event 0 is the most desirable: the product required is available in the first shop the customer enters, and she immediately buys it. For her this part of the shopping process is over.

In event 1, beef is available, but customers must queue for it. This is a familiar occurrence; under classical socialism customers very often have to queue. For some goods there is an actual, "physical" queue at the counter or outside the store. For others the expression can be used only figuratively. Customers receive numbers in order of application, and when their turn comes they are summoned to pick up the good. Returning to the customer, the good she seeks may not be available at all, either immediately or after queuing. In that case she must choose from a set of further alternatives.

---

works must be mentioned: L. N. Kritsman (1926), V. V. Novozhilov (1926), M. Kalecki (1970, 1972), F. D. Holzman (1960), and H. S. Levine (1966).

Attention is drawn particularly to the works that take issue with the ideas I expressed on the theme of shortage. The highly influential works of R. Portes and other members of the Disequilibrium School need underlining above all. Other important polemical works are K. A. Soós (1984) and S. Gomulka (1985).

Other references to major researches in the field of shortage can be found in the later footnotes to chapters 11 and 12. The volume edited by C. Davis and W. W. Charemza (1989) and the excellent summarizing article by J. M. van Brabant (1990) give a broad survey of the debate.

[2]The formal and informal private sector plays only a small part under the classical socialist system, gaining weight appreciably in the reform period. So analysis of the relations manifested between private production, on the one hand, and shortage and inflation, on the other, is postponed until later [→19.1, 19.5, 23.5].

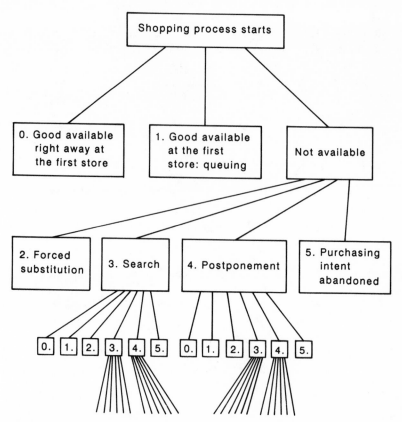

FIGURE 11.1   The Shopping Process

Event 2 is *forced substitution*. The customer abandons her original purchasing intention and instead buys something else that is more or less a substitute for it. It may be a close substitute, for instance, another kind of meat instead of beef, or a remoter substitute, some kind of deep frozen or canned meat, or it may be drawn from an even remoter sphere of substitutes: any kind of foodstuff at all. Forced substitution may involve the customer in a qualitative concession, buying a good less to her liking than the one she was looking for. Alternatively, she may be prepared to pay a higher price for a better product than the one she wanted to buy, or she may suffer a combination of the two kinds of loss.

Forced substitution plays a major part in understanding the shortage syndrome. It should be distinguished from voluntary substitution. If a customer has hitherto chosen the first of two products, A and B, which are close substitutes for each other and both readily available on the supply side, and then changes to the other (substitutes B for A) because her tastes or the two products' relative prices have altered, the substitu-

TABLE 11.1
Forced Substitution in the Car Market in Hungary, 1977

| Make Ordered | Make Preferred in the Case of Immediate Delivery | | | | | | |
	Trabant	Wartburg	Skoda	Zhiguli	Moskvich	Polski Fiat 126	Dacia
Trabant	47	21	1	19	0	5	1
Wartburg	16	7	7	53	0	1	6
Skoda	5	10	0	80	0	0	5
Zhiguli	5	30	7	30	1	3	2
Moskvich	25	25	0	25	0	0	0
Polski Fiat 126	25	11	11	39	0	0	0
Dacia	0	25	0	50	0	0	0

Source: Z. Kapitány, J. Kornai, and J. Szabó (1984, p. 239), based on Hungarian Market Research Institute (1978), Központi Statisztikai Hivatal (Central Statistical Office, Budapest) (1980b), Merkur Car Trading Co. (1980).

Note: The survey questioned 4,120 persons, and 1,406 sent evaluable answers. The proportion of forced substitution is expressed by the total of elements not in the main diagonal. Yet many totals stay under 100 since some of those questioned listed other makes outside the ones included in the list.

tion can be considered voluntary. But if she buys B because A is unavailable, the substitution is forced. Some deny these terms are appropriate, arguing that if product A becomes much dearer than B, the customer may be under an economic compulsion. There is no need to engage in a semantic argument on this; the main thing is for the distinguishing criterion to be clear. If both A and B remain available, there is a chance to choose between them, however expensive A becomes. (For instance, a customer who wants to stick to A at all costs may cut other expenses instead.) The position is quite different if A cannot be obtained. In that case the shortage unequivocally compels the customer to make another choice.

A case of forced substitution is illustrated in table 11.1. A representative sample of Hungarian automobile purchasers have been asked what model they would buy if all the imported Eastern European models familiar in Hungary were readily available without limits on supply or queuing. The main diagonal in the table represents those who would still buy the model for which they are queuing. They constitute only a small proportion of the buyers; the rest are making a forced substitution.[3]

[3]Z. Dániel and A. Semjén (1987) established on the basis of a questionnaire that more than two-thirds of the tenants in the rental housing sector of Budapest had carried out a forced substitution; they were living in dwellings of a different size and quality than those they would like to live in, given the prevailing rent structure.

Returning yet again to the food customer, she may not be prepared to make a forced substitution. Instead, her choice may be event 3, embarking on a *search* at other stores. If she is lucky, she finds some beef in the second store and the shopping process ends. But it may take three, four, or even more attempts before she finds any beef, the maximum number depending on how determined she is in her search.

Frequently she hears, perhaps at the first store or perhaps at a later one she visits, that the good is not obtainable at present but a further delivery is expected. Based on such information or past shopping experience, she may decide to wait on the purchase. Event 4 is *postponement*. It ties in with the fact that the consumer does not spend the money for the future purchase during the waiting period. Consequently, accompanying postponement (or a long period of search) there is *forced saving* as well.[4]

Finally, the customer can choose event 5: abandonment of purchasing intention.

Events 0, 1, 2, and 5 are alternative ends to the purchasing process. But with events 3 and 4, as the diagram shows, the process need not necessarily end at all. In the case of a search, the customer is faced constantly with all the alternatives, in store 2, 3, 4, and so on; the same situation arises when the shopping round is recommenced after a wait of a week, two weeks, and so on.

Events 1–5 are termed here collectively *shortage phenomena.* Although their specific contents and consequences differ, they are all brought about by a shortage of the good sought, and all cause unpleasantness, inconvenience, sacrifice, or some other loss to the customer.

The example above described the shortage phenomena arising when goods or services for personal consumption are purchased, so that the sufferer is a household. The item in short supply in the example was a material good, beef. Similar phenomena arise with so-called services of a nonmaterial nature: there can be a shortage of places in kindergartens, schools, or universities, in health or cultural facilities, and so on.

The same classification may be applied in full to the shortage phenomena that occur in the process of obtaining means of production, materials, semifinished products, machinery and equipment, and production services, when the sufferer is a firm. Event 1: the firm joins a queue at the input-supplying firm where orders have built up. Event 2: the firm is forced to alter the technology it originally planned, for instance, by using a poorer quality or more expensive input, because the input it

---

[4]A distinction is preserved between forced saving caused by shortage and forced saving compelled by administrative means, for instance, by forcing people to purchase state bonds [→8.3].

initially intended to process is not available. Event 3: the firm begins a search for the required input among various firms that manufacture or stock it, or may borrow from another user-firm that happens to have stocks of it. Event 4: the firm postpones its purchase because it has stocks left or, if it has none, because it has no option, and for this reason production may even cease. Finally, there is event 5: the firm abandons its intention of buying the input and prefers to try to change its production and materials-management plans.

One group of shortage phenomena in the production sector deserves a special mention: shortages of machines, equipment, and construction capacity for investment schemes, that is, the phenomena of investment tension [→9.2].

Largely similar shortage phenomena to those occurring during the acquisition of intermediate material products arise in the hiring and employment of labor [→10.2, 10.5].[5]

Shortage phenomena may arise in foreign trade, and in this connection in external financial relations [→14.3, 14.4].

Let me introduce the concept *shortage economy*. An economic system is a shortage economy if the following conditions coincide: shortage phenomena are (1) general, that is, found in all spheres of the economy (in trade in goods and services for consumers, in means of production, including investment goods, in labor, in exported and imported products, and in international means of payment); (2) frequent, and not only exceptional or sporadic; (3) intensive, making their influence felt very strongly on the behavior and environment of participants in the economy and the traits and results of the economic processes; and (4) chronic, applying constantly, not just occurring temporarily.

The expressions "shortage phenomenon" and "shortage economy" can be used to make an economic statement: the shortage phenomena under the classical socialist system are general, frequent, intensive, and chronic; the system is a shortage economy.

This statement can be supported primarily by experience. Illustrative data are given in tables 11.2–11.4 and in many other tables in this chapter and the next. Moreover, a copious and varied body of literature exists that support the statement empirically. Statistical proof of the state-

---

[5]Purely as an illustration, let us take the example of forced substitution and postponement. If a worker hired by a firm does not arrive for work on a day when his or her work is indispensable, the production manager is obliged to improvise by putting someone else in his or her place, perhaps a worker with less skill and experience. Ultimately, the manager does the work of the missing worker. Or the manager may alter the sequence of the production plan, bringing forward assignments for which the required workers are present and postponing the work for which the absent worker is needed. All such actions involve precipitation, holdups, and losses.

TABLE 11.2
Waiting for Housing: International Comparison

	Average Length of Time on a Waiting List in the 1980s (years)
Bulgaria	5–20
Czechoslovakia	6–8
East Germany	3–4
Hungary	4–6
Poland	15–30
Soviet Union	10–15

Source: Compiled for this book by G. Such and I. J. Tóth.

Note: Bulgaria: In larger cities, housing applicants were grouped in six categories: (1) families living under very poor housing conditions (e.g., in a kitchen, cellar, or attic); (2) those living as cotenants of a single divided dwelling; (3) subtenants, or those living under very crowded conditions (with less than 5 sq. m. of living space per capita); (4) those living under crowded conditions (5–12 sq. m. per capita); (5) those under less crowded conditions (12–20 sq. m. per capita); (6) those under the least crowded conditions (over 20 sq. m. per capita). In practice, state housing could be obtained only by those in categories 1–4. The average waiting periods for the categories were (1) 5–6 years; (2) 7–8 years; (3) 9–10 years; (4) 15–20 years. *Czechoslovakia*: Figure for larger cities in 1987. *East Germany*: National average for 1982. *Hungary*: Figure for Budapest in 1986. *Poland*: 1987 figure for purchase of a subsidized cooperative dwelling. No state housing was built in Poland in the latter years. *Soviet Union*: In practice, state-rented accommodation was allocated only to those with less than 5–7 sq. m. of living space per capita.

ment's truth is not needed, however, by those living in a socialist country. They experience the countless frustrations of thwarted purchasing intentions, queuing, forced substitution, searches for goods, and postponement of purchases in their daily lives as consumers and producers.

Shortage phenomena occur also in capitalist countries, quite frequently, intensively, and lastingly in some areas (e.g., the health or education sectors of numerous capitalist countries and the urban housing sector of many), and they may become quite general in exceptional circumstances such as a wartime economy. Nonetheless, if one considers the general, permanent state of the capitalist economy, one can say it is not a shortage economy.

11.2   The Process of Demand Adjustment

This section returns to buyer behavior in a shortage economy, and for the time being specifically to households as buyers of goods and services for personal consumption. The purpose at this point is to trace buying

TABLE 11.3
Waiting for Telephones: International Comparison

	Length of Waiting List as Proportion of Number of Telephone Subscribers (five-year averages, percent)		
	1971–75	*1976–80*	*1981–85*
Socialist countries			
Czechoslovakia[a]	25.1	30.2	11.3
East Germany[b]	23.3	36.7	—
Hungary[a]	36.6	47.2	55.5
Poland[b]	33.6[c]	45.7	57.1
Capitalist countries[d]			
Austria[b]	14.1	8.5	2.9
Belgium[b]	0.8	1.2	0.7
France[b]	13.1	7.9	0.9

Source: Column 1: Union Internationale des Télécommunications (1980, pp. 42, 52, 130, 154, 260) and (1982, p. 254); Columns 2 and 3: Union Internationale des Télécommunications (1986, pp. 56, 66, 150, 180, 280, 288, 348).

[a]Calculated on the basis of total demand for main lines. This includes new applications and applications for resetting. Resetting is a nominal demand for a main line in which a subscriber wishes to move a phone from one site to another.

[b]Calculated on the basis of the waiting list for main lines. This covers demand whose satisfaction has to be postponed because of a shortage of technical capacity (equipment, lines, and so on).

[c]1972–75.

[d]In many capitalist countries all telephone requirements can be satisfied practically straight away.

intentions, not actual actions (purchase, forced substitution, postponement, etc.). The shaping of these intentions is a dynamic process. To make the discussion clearer, practical problems of observation and measurement are ignored; it is assumed that one can discover a buying intention accurately at a particular time by questioning the buyer.

The first question to ask is what the buyer's buying intention would be, assuming prevailing prices, the buyer's prevailing income and wealth, and prevailing social and economic conditions, if there were not supply-side constraint on fulfilling one's buying intention. The buyer's answer to this question is the *notional demand.*[6]

To simplify the explanation, the question concerns the buying intention in the existing state. Indeed, one might ask what the buying inten-

[6]This term was introduced by the R. W. Clower (1965). For a more detailed discussion see J.-P. Benassy (1982).

TABLE 11.4
Waiting for Cars: International Comparison, 1989

| | Waiting Period in Years | | | | | |
| | Make of Car | | | | | |
	Lada	Skoda	Moskvich	Wartburg	Trabant	Dacia
Bulgaria[a]	10–12	5	2	2	1	1
Czechoslovakia	3–4	—	—	—	—	—
East Germany	17	16	—	14–16	14	15
Hungary	4–6	6	—	1	0	—
Poland	5–6	6–8	—	3–4	2–3	—
Romania[b]	—	—	—	—	—	4–6

Source: Compiled by Z. Kapitány for this book, partly based on Z. Kapitány and L. Kállay (1989).
Note: All cars are products of socialist countries.
[a]1988.
[b]For cars other than Dacia there are no data available or the makes were not available.

tion would be if the prices, income, wealth, and so forth were different from those that apply. In that case one would discover the notional demand function. The answer to the intentionally simplified question posed above merely reveals a single point on this function.

The discussion is also simplified by examining a partial problem as an initial approach. A stricter and fuller discussion would entail analyzing all the buying and selling intentions for all goods and services together.[7]

The second possible question is what the buyer intends to buy now that all supply constraints are known and the buying intention has been adjusted accordingly.[8] This answer can be called the category of *completely adjusted demand*.[9] The concept can be understood in terms of

[7]In fact, some further clarification is needed in the phrasing of the supposition of no constraint on the supply side. In practice, it implies goods and services that the buyer being questioned has actually encountered while shopping previously, but of which there might be a shortage momentarily, not goods and services known at most from hearsay.

[8]Thinking of a single buyer's single act of purchase, one ought in a determinist sense to possess accurate information about the supply. If one considers a multitude of buyers and/ or set of buying actions continually repeated in time, a stochastic analysis can be applied.

[9]This is not the same as the concept of "effective demand" of disequilibrium theory. The effective demand for product A is the buyer's answer to the hypothetical question of how much of A he would want to buy if he took account of the quantitative restrictions in connection with the purchase (and sale) of all the other products and services, B, C, and so on, ignoring only the quantitative restriction on A.

Forced adjustment of demand makes it very difficult (and according to some impossible) to separate demand from supply and establish demand and supply functions independent of each other.

Continued

expectation theory. This kind of buying intention is based on the expectation of the supply constraint at the time of purchase.[10]

Notional demand and completely adjusted demand can be seen as the theoretical extremes of the demand-shaping process. There are numerous intermediate grades, which may be given the collective term *partially adjusted demand*. They differ from notional demand in that the buyer has noted the supply constraints to some extent in arriving at his buying intention, but he has no accurate knowledge of them and/or still refuses to go far in compromising with the supply. For now he is unable or unwilling to divorce himself enough from his notional demand under the influence of supply constraint. In the following account, the term *adjusted demand,* without qualification, covers both completely and partially adjusted demand.

For the buyer, the road from notional demand via partially adjusted demand to completely adjusted demand is paved with a sequence of frustration, failures, dire rumors of impending shortages, and forced adjustment. Completely adjusted demand is the buying intention of a buyer resigned to chronic shortage.[11]

Of course, the shaping of demand is described here as a series of consecutive instances of recognition and adjustment in a time order only to simplify the account. In fact, the succession is far less "regular"; the adjustment of demand to the realities and expectations of supply occurs in real life against a background of possibly conflicting communications, hopes, and failures, and successful and unsuccessful acts of purchase. Often the buyer herself is unsure of her own intentions. She improvises, and she might be unable to answer a market researcher reliably even if she honestly tried.

This major problem of identification is akin, by the way, to the difficulty pointed out by R. E. Lucas (1985) of separating the behavior of the private sector from the state economic policy that affects it. J. P. Burkett drew my attention to the kinship between the two problems of identification.

[10]W. W. Charemza, in his study analyzing the scope for further development of the disequilibrium models (1989), stresses the importance of the relation between consumer adjustment and expectations on the market situation.

[11]Where there is no chronic shortage and the buyer's buying intention meets no demand constraints, the actual purchase can be assumed to reflect the notional buying intention faithfully. Under those conditions one is justified in taking the function attached to the real consumption figures as a demand function.

This assumption is unjustified in a shortage economy, since the actual purchase reflects the behavior of the buyer after making a series of forced adjustments. There is a debate taking place on this problem. Many argue that the demand functions in a shortage economy can only be estimated indirectly. For instance, Z. Dániel (1989) bases her estimates of the demand functions for rented housing in Hungary on direct questioning of the buyers. L. Podkaminer (1988) transfers the parameters of demand functions estimated in capitalist countries into functions describing the behavior of Polish households.

During the adjustment process, the buyer may abandon some buying intentions totally and irrevocably, so that they cease to feature later even as notional buying intentions. There is an analogy in this with the phenomenon described in Western literature on unemployment as "the discouraged worker."[12] Having sought a job vainly for a long time, many finally give up the struggle. Thereafter their names are not recorded at labor exchanges and so they are ignored in unemployment figures. Just as withdrawal by a seller of labor discouraged by lack of demand causes underrecording of the labor surplus, so withdrawal by a buyer discouraged by lack of supply reduces the observable shortage of goods.

Whereas a buyer's adjusted buying intentions for products in poor supply are lower than notional demand, his adjusted demand is higher than notional demand for goods that can be considered forced substitutes.[13] It is possible (but not certain) that the two contrary changes in adjusted demand will cancel each other out.

The adjustment of demand to supply is not entirely unreciprocated. To a lesser extent, a producer-seller also does adjust somewhat to likely demand.

Ultimately, it is possible (but not certain) that a curious state of equilibrium will arise. This can be called the *forced adjustment equilibrium.* The aggregate demand of all households for all products, adjusted to supply, can be satisfied from the entire supply available to households. Emergence of this forced adjustment equilibrium is compatible with a persisting sense of frustration in the buyer, since she is unable to satisfy her notional demand and obliged to spend her money on forced substitutes.[14]

What has been said so far is an aid to understanding what might be called the paradox of the shortage economy. On the one hand, consumers are highly dissatisfied and rightly complain about the items in short supply. On the other, "global equilibrium" (to use Eastern European professional jargon) can arise after all. The buyer's painful process of forced adjustment allows both sides of the paradox to apply.

---

[12]I have adopted this analogy from J. P. Burkett's article (1988).

[13]L. Podkaminer, in his study mentioned earlier (1988), gives an estimate of what the consistency of the notional demand would have been in Poland in the period 1965–78. He calculates that the notional demand for meat in Poland would have been substantially less than the actual demand had it not been for the spillover effect of the supply constraints and the distorted relative prices.

[14]The forced adjustment equilibrium discussed here, which basically arises through adjustment by the buyer, is compatible with a situation in which there are unsold stocks on the supply side. All the definition need stipulate is that a cumulative process does not occur, that is, there is no progressive increase of unsold stocks.

I declared just now that it is possible but not certain that a forced adjustment equilibrium will arise. A buyer may find no acceptable substitute and prefer to spend less than his total notional spending intention. In other words, a shortage-induced forced saving takes place. This may result from temporary postponement: the buyer sets aside the unspent money and makes his purchase when a supply to match his notional demand appears. In that case, the money accumulated through forced saving waits at the ready for the spending opportunity.[15] But there is a chance of this not happening. Perhaps the forced saving was not earmarked at all; the buyer just simply failed to spend it sensibly and no attractive spending opportunity arose later either. If this becomes a cumulative process in which more and more unspent and unspendable forced savings pile up in household hands, the household sphere moves further and further from a forced adjustment equilibrium, causing not only a notional but a genuine excess demand. A *monetary overhang* is generated, which expands over the sphere of consumer goods and services, creating tension in it.

Finally, yet another possibility needs to be considered. Households can spend part of their money in the formal and informal private sector, that is, on the legally permitted free market, or in the gray and black markets [→8.8]. Although some of the notional demand in relation to the sector of firms in public ownership remains unsatisfied and the buyer does not make a full forced adjustment in this direction, she is able to use all the money intended for spending after all. The parallel markets—the legal market at free prices, or the gray and black markets—may be able (wholly or partly) to prevent forced saving.[16] The consequent situation is considered likewise a kind of forced adjustment equilibrium; here the forced substitution in connection with the products of state-owned firms is complemented by purchases on the gray and black markets.[17]

So far trade in articles and services for consumer consumption has been considered. In other spheres of the economy, a forced adjustment equilibrium in the specific sense taken above may not arise at all, and

[15]M. Lackó (1975) proved this important relationship by econometric analysis. The population's real total consumption or saving depends closely on the state of the supply of cars and apartments. See also A. Simon (1977).

[16]G. Grossman (1977b) first put forward this idea.

[17]According to D. M. Nuti (1986a), the main explanation for the fact that several studies of the Disequilibrium School (see note 1) demonstrate a macro equilibrium on the consumer market is that the buyers are able to spend their money on the informal market.

In certain countries, the forced saving in the domestic currency can be spent on the black market for foreign hard currencies. W. W. Charemza and S. Ghatak (1990) demonstrated this phenomenon using Poland as an example.

a real, lasting excess demand prevails. One such sphere is certainly the transactions of investment goods.[18]

The question of which spheres typically have a forced adjustment equilibrium and which suffer from chronic excess demand will be left open for the time being. But I must add that even in the spheres where a forced adjustment equilibrium is finally attained, the unsatisfied notional buying intentions (and similarly, the partially adjusted buying intentions) are no mere notional quantities. They have a real momentum and a great influence on the behavior of both buyers and sellers. As mentioned before, buyers are embittered by the frustration of their original intentions. This bitterness is what "resigns" them and forces them to adjust. At the same time, the existence of the same notional excess demand fills sellers with confidence. They can bank on selling their products without much trouble.

Last of all, an observation on terminology is required. Some writers use the expressions "excess demand" and "shortage" as synonyms. This book and my earlier works follow the common parlance of the socialist countries in using "shortage phenomena" or simply "shortage" in a broader sense, as a collective term with a wide meaning. It covers not only excess demand, namely, unfulfilled buying intentions, but all forced adjustment forms, both forced change of intentions and actual adjustment actions (i.e., forced substitution, search, postponement, and forced saving).[19]

11.3 Horizontal and Vertical Shortage

The phenomena surveyed in sections 11.1 and 11.2 occur in the relationship between the seller and the buyer. In a legal sense, at least, they are horizontal relations. The seller is not the buyer's superior in an administrative sense, even though the seller has a power advantage. So this group of shortage phenomena will be termed horizontal shortage.

This is distinguishable from vertical shortage, which appears in the vertical relation between a superior and a subordinate [→9.2]. Take, for example, the setting of a firm's annual materials quota. The firm submits its requirements to its superior institution, the directorate, which fulfills

[18]M. Lackó's study (1989) shows how the trend in the investment credit demand of Hungarian firms adjusts itself closely to changes in the current credit supply. Yet the demand regularly and greatly exceeds the supply, that is, a full adjustment fails to take place.

[19]This has been an occasion of misunderstanding during the debates. "Excess demand" cannot be substituted for the word "shortage" either in my earlier works or in this book. The text contains the words "excess demand" solely where the reference is expressly to that, namely, to a specific constituent of the shortage syndrome as a whole.

the function of allocator in the relationship. The allocator has already received a quota from its own superior, the ministry, and that is the maximum it can distribute among its firms. As mentioned earlier, the firm has an interest in receiving as slack a plan as possible, in other words, minimum output commitments coupled with maximum input quotas. Under the circumstances, the sum of the requirements submitted exceeds the quota the allocator can distribute; this discrepancy is referred to here as vertical shortage.

The vertical shortage that arises during directorate–firm bargaining over rations of materials is a single example of a phenomenon common to all levels of the bureaucratic hierarchy (i.e., between directorate and ministry or ministry and planning office as well) and to allocation of all resources and products, whether semifinished products, components, machines, manpower, wage funds, investment quotas, or import allowances.

The situation certainly differs from the one in which the buyers' demand exceeds the sellers' supply. It amounts only to the antecedents within the bureaucracy of a real transaction that takes place later; a future buyer is obtaining a permit from its superior to make a later purchase with its own money. But the kinship between the two kinds of phenomenon, horizontal and vertical shortage, is apparent. It is the likely horizontal shortage that makes it so important to the firm to receive enough rations of materials to ensure a favorable position in the competition from buyers.

The two types of shortage are not independent of each other. During the bargaining process, the subordinate unit, expecting a horizontal shortage, submits an oversized application so exacerbating the vertical shortage.

A specific combination of horizontal and vertical shortage appears in the case of products and services distributed by the authorities to consumers through a bureaucratic rationing system.[20] In many countries coupon schemes are applied for a long period to staple foodstuffs, and in some cases to mass-produced consumer durables. A few examples are shown in table 11.5. In most socialist countries the following are rationed to the population throughout the classical period: state-owned housing tenancies, telephone lines, health services, places in educational institutions, and vacations in publicly owned vacation centers. Some of the

---

[20]The word "rationing" is given a broader, figurative meaning in what is known as disequilibrium theory; see J.-P. Benassy (1982), for instance. The existence of excess demand leaves no option but application of some procedure on the "short" side, that is, in the distribution of supply. The literature on disequilibrium terms all such procedures "rationing," even those that are not administrative forms of distribution. This book uses the word only in its literal, everyday sense.

TABLE 11.5
Rationing in Socialist Countries

Country	Rationed Products (monthly rations per head)
Cuba	Rice (2.3 kg), sugar (1.8 kg), fat (0.46 kg), edible oil (0.23 kg), beans (0.46 kg), meat (0.7–1.0 kg), chicken (0.46 kg), cigarettes (4 packs), cigars (1 cigar), tomato puree (2 cans), milk for children under 6 (30 liters), milk for 6-to-14-year-olds (3 cans), canned milk for people over 65 (6 cans) Soap (1 cake), soap for washing clothes (2 cakes), washing powder (0.23 kg), dish-cloth (1)
Poland	Coffee, butter (0.75 kg), meat (2.5–8.0 kg), fat (0.375 kg), flour (1 kg), rice (1 kg), sugar, chocolate (20 g), cigarettes, alcoholic drinks Gasoline[a] (24–36 liters); washing powder, soap, footwear
Romania	Bread (0.3 kg per day), eggs (10), dry pasta (0.5 kg), chicken (0.5 kg), pork or beef (1 kg), butter (0.1 kg), semolina (0.5 kg), rice (0.5 kg), wheat flour (0.5 kg), corn flour (1 kg), sugar Natural gas[b], (153–203 cn. m.), electric power (43 kWh)
Soviet Union[c]	Meat, flour, butter, eggs, sugar, cheese
Vietnam	Rice (9 kg), pasta (4 kg), meat (1 kg), sugar (0.7 kg)
Yugoslavia[d]	Coffee, edible oil, sugar Gasoline (40 liters), washing powder

Source: Compiled by G. Such and I. J. Tóth for this book on the basis of a large number of newspapers and journals.

Note: The table describes rationing in the 1980s. For brevity's sake, it does not include the exact dates on which rationing was introduced and abolished for each product in the various countries and regions of countries.

[a]The Polish gas ration varied according to the capacity of the engine, within the limits given.

[b]In Romania there were severe restrictions on energy consumption after 1984. In the towns, those exceeding the prescribed limits had to pay a fine, and their supply would be cut off until the end of the month.

[c]A variety of different coupon systems was introduced in several republics and cities in the Soviet Union. The table lists foodstuffs rationed in this way in many places.

[d]The coupon system in Yugoslavia was differentiated district by district. In Serbia in 1983, for instance, there was a coupon system in 80 out of 114 settlements.

rationing is done by state authorities, some by the monopoly firm or institution providing the relevant good or service, or perhaps by a mass organization (e.g., the trade unions), and some by workplaces [→10.4]. The proportions each undertake differ from country to country and period to period, but each is appreciable in every classical socialist economy.

There is a shortage in all spheres where a system of coupons or other form of rationing is employed. The allocating authority or institution feels the pressure of the vertical shortage; wherever applications can be made in advance (for instance, with housing or vacations) the sum of the requirements exceeds the quantity available for distribution. Intensive horizontal shortage appears at the same time. In all these spheres, the product or service concerned is made available to the user free or at a very low price. The question of whether it is shortage that makes bureaucratic coordination inevitable, or the reverse, is addressed later in the causal analysis [→12.3, 12.4].

11.4 Shortage and Surplus

The previous three sections dealt solely with the phenomena of shortage. It is now time to examine the opposite phenomenon, surplus.[21]

In the case of a single sale/purchase event, shortage and surplus are mutually exclusive. A buyer enters a store at a particular moment with a particular demand. The store, at that same moment, has a particular stock. If the buyer receives the good she is looking for and it is the last of that good in the store, there is neither a shortage nor a surplus after the transaction. But two other cases, strictly exclusive of each other, are possible: the buyer may not have received the good she was looking for (shortage), or stock of the good may remain in the store (surplus). So at that submicro level, there cannot be shortage and surplus at once.

The position is different if the situation is described in any kind of aggregate form, for instance, if several products, several buyers, several sellers, or a longer period of time are considered. In the case of a summation, there can be a coexistence of shortage (some demand from buyers remaining unsatisfied) and surplus (some sellers being left with unsold products).

---

[21]This raises again a terminological problem met with already in section 10.1. In my book *Economics of Shortage* (1980), I used the expression "slack" as the opposite of shortage, and I used the English word even in the Hungarian text. My aim was to avoid the approval implied by "reserve" and the pejorative flavor of "excess." "Slack" as the antonym of shortage has failed, however, to catch on sufficiently either in English or in Hungarian.

The usage of economists in English is not standard, but the most common antonym of shortage is "surplus." Although "slack" is perfectly comprehensible, it is rarer in English and tends to be used in another context. Taking all this into account, I prefer to use the word "surplus" here. I make reference to "reserve" and "excess" when approbation or disapprobation are implied.

The fact that the classical socialist system is a shortage economy does not preclude the appearance of surpluses. Indeed, there are several features of the system that directly encourage them to form.

The less certain the prospect of obtaining goods, the more intensively buyers have to hoard.[22] This hoarding tendency is apparent in firms, nonfirm institutions, and households. Buyers get used to shopping when goods are available (if their pockets allow), not when the time comes to use something. Large input inventories build up, and producers also try to create reserves of labor, which is in the shortest supply of all, and all kinds of capacity where a bottleneck may form.

Another inducement to a subordinate unit to build up reserves and then conceal them from its allocating superior is the phenomenon of plan bargaining [→7.5].

The producer-cum-seller is bad at adapting to demand (for several reasons considered in the next chapter). The frictions in the adaptation of production give rise to residual, unsalable stocks that cannot even be foisted on the buyers most embittered by shortage.

It is useful to observe and measure the two kinds of phenomena separately. Those suffering from a shortage of a particular product, service, or resource are not compensated by the knowledge that surpluses, unutilized capacities, and frozen stocks exist somewhere else in the economy. The inertia of the system, its many inflexibilities, and the strong frictions within it rule out any guarantee that one kind of surplus will be used in time to offset another kind of shortage.[23]

The frequency and intensity of the occurrences of shortage can be shown to bear a great many relations to the scale and consistency of the surplus. Some of these can be easily discerned in the figure resembling a Beveridge curve [→fig. 10.2]. Consider the following problem as an example. A buyer is looking for a specific good. The more varied the stock in each store, the fewer stores the buyer has to visit. Or take another example: the greater the variety of size, quality, and environment among the dwellings lying empty, the greater the chance someone

---

[22]A series of mathematical models analyzes the inducement for hoarding. See S. M. Goldfeld and R. E. Quandt (1990a, 1990b), J. Kornai and J. W. Weibull (1983), and R. E. Quandt (1986).

[23]Many economic analyses use the category of the macrolevel "net excess demand." In other words, the sum of the individual instances of excess supply is subtracted from the sum of the individual instances of excess demand. The difference is an indicator that can be used for a system whose adaptive features are favorable, in other words, where the individual instances of excess demand and excess supply soon cancel each other out. But this "netting out" calculation conceals the weaknesses of adaptation in systems with strong friction. For a further discussion of the problems of aggregate and disaggregate measurement of shortage and surplus see G. Roland (1990).

seeking accommodation has of finding something suitable quickly. There is a negative relation between the mobilizable surplus available to the buyer (or input-user) and the frequency and intensity of the shortage phenomena suffered.[24] It is common under all economic systems for greater or lesser phenomena of shortage to coincide with larger or smaller surpluses. These result from inevitable frictions in the adjustment between production and consumption and supply and demand. Only a perfectly adapted system could operate absolutely without friction, in other words, with no shortage or surplus of any kind. The system-specific feature of the socialist economy is that the friction is on a large scale; while the shortage is frequent and intense, the surplus is great as well, because a sizable proportion of it cannot be mobilized to supply the buyer or user better, and so lies unused.

11.5   Market Regimes: The Buyers' and the Sellers' Market

Those living in a shortage economy experience day by day that the buyer is at the mercy of the seller. The next topic is this unequal, asymmetrical relationship between the buyer and the seller.

A distinction can be made between two kinds of market regime: a *buyers' market* and a *sellers' market*. The word regime implies that the intention is to describe constant features of the buyer-seller relationship, not a momentary state. The main attributes of the two regimes can be seen in table 11.6. The purpose of the table and the comments appended to it is mainly to explain the two concepts. But one can add straight away an economic statement in accordance with the one made earlier [→11.1]. The classical socialist system is marked by a sellers' market, while the capitalist system, or, more precisely, the sphere of it operating in a framework of imperfect competition, is marked by a buyers' market.[25]

Accordingly, the sellers' market can be examined through examples from the classical socialist system, and the buyers' market through exam-

---

[24]For the mathematical modeling of this relationship, see J. W. Weibull (1983, 1984).

[25]There is total symmetry in the theoretical model of perfect competition: neither the seller nor the buyer has ascendancy. Spheres exist in capitalist economies where the actual operation approaches the theoretical model of perfect competition. Examples include the grain market, where large numbers of sellers and buyers confront each other on the grain exchange.

E. Domar (1989) and T. Scitovsky ([1951] 1971, 1985) have demonstrated that a buyers' market regime develops with full force in spheres of the capitalist system ruled by the various forms of *imperfect competition*. It is characteristic for these market forms to predominate in modern capitalism. I return to this subject in section 12.1, in connection with the causal analysis.

TABLE 11.6
Main Features of the Buyers' and the Sellers' Market

Main Feature	Buyers' Market		Sellers' Market	
	Buyers' Situation and Behavior	*Sellers' Situation and Behavior*	*Buyers' Situation and Behavior*	*Sellers' Situation and Behavior*
1. Information activity		Mainly by seller	Mainly by buyer	
2. Adjustment to other side		Mainly by seller	Mainly by buyer	
3. Effort to win over other side		Mainly by seller	Mainly by buyer	
4. Consequences of uncertainty		Mainly borne by seller	Mainly borne by buyer	
5. Relative power	Ascendency of buyer			Ascendency of seller

ples from the capitalist system and its sphere of imperfect competition. That entails repetition in some places of sections 11.1–11.4, to make as full a comparison of the two regimes as possible.

The lines of table 11.6 each consider separately spheres of phenomena that partly overlap. The divisions are a help, however, in picking out the individual conjunctions of problems.

1. *Information*. Information is required so that the seller and the buyer can meet up with one another. In a buyers' market this is mainly the concern of the seller, who advertises or sends a salesman around to the buyer. Of course, there are things for the buyer to do as well. It is not easy to find one's way around a wide range of choice; even in a buyers' market, price differences between close mutual substitutes are an incentive for search and discovery of the price-quality combination most favorable to the buyer.

In a sellers' market, information is mainly the concern of the buyer, who must obtain it. There is practically no advertising in a classical socialist economy. If not a household, a firm as a buyer sends a representative to the seller. The buyer often has to invest great effort in discovering where a desired product can be found.

2. *Adjustment*. In a buyers' market, the seller tries to identify as accurately as possible what the buyer needs, and adjust to it as much as he can. The goods he stocks are those for which he expects a demand. If he works to order, he tries to fulfill the orders as punctiliously as he can.

In a sellers' market, on the other hand, the buyer adapts to the seller. Forced substitution, search, postponement, accommodation of buying intentions to supply constraints, or complete abandonment of them are the various forms of forced adjustment caused by shortage. Of course, that does not mean the seller dictates totally to the buyer. The seller is obliged to some extent to consider the likely demand.

3. *The buyers' and sellers' efforts to win the other side over.* In a buyers' market, sellers compete with each other for the buyers' favor and confidence, and ultimately for their willingness to buy. So with justification it is also termed sellers' competition.

Under conditions of perfect competition, a generally applicable price level develops out of impersonal processes, and both sellers and buyers are pricetakers, that is, obliged to accept the market price. In practice, this kind of market operates only in the exchange of standard products, all of whose quality specifications are clearly known (as in the example of grain mentioned earlier). Since the price and quality are set, only one more decision remains for both seller and buyer: the quantity they wish respectively to sell and buy. (Naturally, one possible decision is to sell or buy none.)

The situation differs entirely under the conditions of imperfect competition that necessarily arise in the case of nonstandard, differentiated products. The seller of all differentiated products and services is a "monopolist" to some extent, whether it is the quality of the product or service or the place or particular time of sale that distinguish one seller from other sellers. The price is not set externally; the seller is the pricemaker.[26]

Sellers can win buyers from competitors with similar but not absolutely identical goods if they ask a lower price. In addition, they have a chance to engage in nonprice competition. They may win the buyers' custom (to repeat what was said under points 1 and 2) by advertising more convincingly, employing cleverer salesmen, and guessing better what the buyer needs. Other efforts can be added. Sellers will try to be as friendly and polite as they can to the buyers. They will perform many special services, if possible better than their competitors, offering a wide range, packing the good more attractively and carefully, perhaps providing delivery to the buyer, accepting a shorter deadline, or offering more favorable payment or credit facilities. Most important of all, they will woo the buyers with new products of better quality. The most important

---

[26]Tibor Scitovsky introduced the pricemaker-pricetaker distinction. The explanations of capitalism in this section rest to a large extent on the works of T. Scitovsky and E. Domar quoted already.

weapons of all in the competition for buyers are quality improvement and product innovation.[27]

All these efforts are mingled with harmful ones: attempts to manipulate buyers through misleading advertisements, cosmetic changes to the product, and pretense innovation. Corruption exists in all societies. In a buyers' market, the seller tries to corrupt the buyer.

The situation is the other way around in a sellers' market. Here there is buyers' competition for the seller's favor, or more precisely, willingness to sell. The buyer's efforts to obtain information and his or her forced adjustment have been mentioned. One can add to them the opposites of all the occurrences in the previous list. The seller is unfriendly and impolite with the buyer, while the buyer tries to flatter the seller and win his or her favor. The corruption points in the opposite direction: in retail trading, the buyer gives the "sweetener," an extra, under-the-counter payment to the sales clerk in order to obtain a good in the store at all. Firms employ "expediters" (*tolkachi* in Russian) [→6.4], who obtain the inputs their firms require through personal connections, by doing favors, and perhaps with bribes. The selection is narrow, the packing is ugly and flimsy, and the buyer has to transport his or her purchases as best he or she can. A producer or seller working to order quotes a long deadline and often fails to meet it. As a rule, there are no credit sales.[28] The gravest side-effect is that there is no competition spurring the producer or seller to improve product quality or to innovate.

4. *Uncertainty.* The economic processes take place amid uncertainty: no seller knows accurately the intentions and capabilities of the other sellers or the buyers, and conversely, no buyer knows accurately the intentions and capabilities of the other buyers or the sellers. The problem ties in with the acquiring of information, discussed under point 1, but other aspects need mentioning as well.

In an uncertain situation it is useful to have reserves. A buyers' and a sellers' market differ again according to who has to build up the reserves. In a buyers' market it is mainly the seller. The producer or seller in a trade whose technical nature dictates that sale from stock should be customary holds appreciable output stocks. In a trade whose technical nature dictates that production or delivery to order should be the custom, the seller holds appreciable reserve capacity. But even branches producing for stock normally keep some reserve capacity. The stocks of output

---

[27]The relationship between product quality and market regime is formalized in the article by myself and J. W. Weibull (1983). M. L. Weitzman (1987) models the seller's efforts to win the buyer in the two kinds of market state.

[28]The buyer gives credit to the seller in several socialist countries. One example is those on the waiting list for a car in Hungary, who, until 1989, paid half the price in advance.

and reserve capacity are needed so that the seller can adapt quickly to buyer requirements; if possible, no buyer should leave disappointed or unsatisfied, lest he or she become a competitor's customer instead.

But in a sellers' market, no appreciable output stocks can accumulate, as the buyers soon snatch up output, unless it is a frozen stock of some useless good. There is no real reserve capacity. The superior organizations try to tighten production to the limit of capacity. Even if the producer succeeds in concealing part of its capacity during plan bargaining it will not use that surplus for the buyer's sake, and so it does not count as mobilizable reserve capacity.

The shortage phenomena and the uncertainty of obtaining supplies induce the buyer to hoarding, that is, to build up large input stocks [→11.4]. Buyers make up for the absence of mobilizable producer reserve capacity by themselves producing the inputs they lack, if need be. This occurs even in the household in the form of handyman, do-it-yourself activity, and is thoroughly typical of the producer firms in classical socialism, whose high degree of vertical integration[29] is largely explained by the shortage syndrome. Wherever possible an engineering works makes its own components and has its own foundry, and even its own building department, because it does not believe any outside firm will deliver a part or a casting, or provide a construction service on time or in an orderly way.

This line of thought provides a basis for assessing table 11.7, which gives an international comparison of the composition of stocks. The figures show clearly that input stocks are relatively low in countries with a buyers' market, in line with the present hypothesis, and that the proportion of output stocks is relatively high. In countries where a sellers' market is assumed to operate, the proportions are reversed. This index number is quite stable; it varies little with the changes in the momentary state of the economy, which makes it highly suitable for distinguishing statistically the two kinds of regime, in other words, the lasting differences between a sellers' market and a buyers' market.

Some parties in the economy inevitably suffer losses from the uncertainty, even if they conduct extensive information activity and keep appreciable inventories. These losses are incurred mainly by the seller on a buyers' market. Some of the competing sellers have less skill or luck in assessing the likely situation, and so make smaller profits or even become insolvent. The buyer is less affected by the uncertainty.

---

[29]Here the word "vertical" is used not in the same sense defined in chapter 5 connected with subordination and superiority, but according to the definitions in the literature on industrial organization, namely, referring to the successive stages in the production process.

TABLE 11.7
Ratio of Input and Output Stocks: International Comparison

	Average Input Stock per Average Output Stock in Manufacturing, 1981–85
Socialist countries	
Bulgaria	5.07
Czechoslovakia	3.07
Hungary	6.10
Poland	4.49
Soviet Union	3.16
Capitalist countries	
Austria	1.06
Australia	1.36
Canada	0.92
Finland	1.92
West Germany	0.71
Japan	1.09
Norway	1.10
Portugal	1.66
Sweden	0.81
United Kingdom	1.02
United States	1.02

Source: Compiled by A. Chikán for this book.

By contrast, in a sellers' market almost all the consequences of uncertainty are borne by the buyers. If they weigh up the situation badly or have no luck (or connections), they do not receive the goods or have to make more forced adjustment. Sellers have nothing to worry about. They can assume that almost all output is salable, and if there should be any difficulties, paternalism and the concomitant soft budget constraint will see them through.

5. *Relative power.* The time has come to sum up the main attributes of the two regimes. Who is stronger? Who has power over the other? Who can force the other to do things he or she would not do of his or her own accord? The seller has ascendancy in a sellers' market and the

buyer in a buyers' market. Nor is this just a question of two possible discrete states. There is a scale of relative power.[30] Even if one cannot calibrate the scale accurately at this point, it is worth noting that it is possible for the seller to have, say, a small, medium, or very strong power advantage over the buyer, and vice versa. Remaining with the narrower subject of shortage, it depends on the frequency, prevalence, and intensity of the shortage phenomena whether the seller is stronger or weaker in relation to the buyer, and whether the buyer is at the seller's mercy to a greater or lesser extent.

In a particular country, the relative power can vary in time and between sectors of the economy. It may be that the seller's advantage over the buyer decreased in Czechoslovakia between 1978 and 1980 and increased in Hungary, and that in both countries the ascendancy was more pronounced in the state housing sector than in the clothing market. The present discussion, however, is not intended to deal with these short-term temporal changes and sectoral variations. What table 11.6 compares is the two regimes' lasting attributes, their natures.

The relationship between seller and buyer is among the most important social relationships. Marx turned to Greek drama for the metaphor of the masks worn by characters. There are tragic and comic, or heroic and villainous masks. The personal expression of the person concealed behind the mask is immaterial; the role that the actor plays in the drama is expressed by the mask. Social relationships develop character masks of this kind. No one can say that the sellers are benevolent in a buyers' market or malevolent in a sellers' market. It is the situation, one's own interest, and the role one plays under the prevailing conditions that induce the seller to be attentive and friendly to the buyer in the first case and inattentive and unfriendly in the second. The same person who is rude to the buyer when playing the part of seller is incensed by the indifference when she finds herself in the buyer's position. Ultimately, this is a social relationship in which power is divided between the seller and the buyer, to the advantage of one party and the detriment of the other.

Here a short terminological detour is needed. Though the detailed causal analysis comes later, it is already clear that there is a close relationship between the mass, chronic phenomena of shortage, on the one hand, and the dominant role of bureaucratic coordination mechanism, on the

[30]Many authors use the concept of *consumer sovereignty*. To interpret this expression with theoretical clarity, it in fact means one extreme on the scale, where all power is in the hands of the consumer. In reality, this never applies in such an extreme and clear way. Even where the buyer has a substantial ascendancy, it is still at most a case of division of power, and some power over the buyer remains with the seller. It is worth interpreting the expression "consumer sovereignty" more broadly, to mean a market regime in which the buyer has an overwhelming predomination over the seller.

other. This assumption is supported indirectly by the well-known fact that mass, lasting shortage does not arise in economies (or in certain spheres of those economies) where bureaucratic influences limit operation of the market mechanism of coordination to a small degree only. So, in fact, it is not a happy choice of words to describe as a "sellers' market" a form of coordination that hardly possesses or entirely lacks a market character. Nonetheless, I have been obliged to use the expression in this book, since it is the most prevalent one in other writings on the subject.[31]

11.6 Normal Shortage and Normal Surplus

Whatever system one sets out to describe, one of the most important characteristics is what market regime operates in it. One of the regularities of the classical socialist system is that a sellers' market prevails, in other words, that the system is a shortage economy.

Although all classical socialist systems without exception share this feature, countries, and within each country, spheres and periods in history, still vary in the intensity of the shortage and the scale of the seller's advantage over the buyer. In this respect appreciable variance can be observed.

Analysis becomes easier if the concepts of *normal shortage* and *normal surplus* are introduced.[32] These categories cannot be employed universally; they are applicable only when a degree of temporal stability can be observed in the shortage and surplus in a particular country over a fairly long period. One can say of country A, in terms of an intertemporal mean over quite a long period, that consumers typically wait an average of eight years for rented public housing and six years for a car.

---

[31]To add a personal note here, my book *Anti-Equilibrium* (1971) was the first to make a methodical comparison of these two situations and describe in detail the difference between what section 11.2 terms a "buyers' market" and a "sellers' market." The book tried to coin other terminology, calling a buyers' market "pressure" and a sellers' market "suction." The terms were based on a metaphor: products flow in a pipe system; in one case they are propeled to the buyers by the pressure of the sellers and in the other by the suction of the buyers.

The advantage of this pair of expressions is that they avoid the word "market," which is misleading in this context. I have to say, however, that the "pressure-suction" pair of terms has spread very little. There would be no sense in sticking quixotically to terms that have not become naturalized among economists, although (to my mind) they are clearer. That is why I use here the expressions "market regime," "sellers' market," and "buyers' market."

[32]A formal description of normal shortage was attempted by myself and J. W. Weibull (1978).

Though the quarterly observations vary around the averages of eight and six years, they do not depart from them greatly: there is always a waiting list, and the queue never lengthens much beyond the averages stated. Meanwhile, in country B, taking the average of a fairly long period, people typically wait only three years for housing and two for a car. Both countries in the example have shortage economies, and a sellers' market regime applies in the housing and automobile sectors of both. Yet the fact that the normal shortage is more intense in A than in B is an important distinction between them. Of course, the two queuing periods given are merely examples. One could conduct a similar analysis of the normal values of many other indices, ranging from ratios of forced substitution to the number of stores visited before a purchase is made, or to the ratio of rejected and accepted orders.

The numerical characteristics of normal shortage and normal surplus, comprehensively the *normal state* (or, in a dynamic setting, the *normal path*), are not valid in perpetuity. Even within the classical system, there can be changes in the external and internal political situation or the system of political and economic institutions in society, bringing about a new normal state. Such changes may result, for instance, from transitions from a peacetime to a wartime economy or the reverse, from replacement of a policy of fairly high growth with one of more moderate growth, and so on.

Classical socialism never changes from a sellers' market regime to a buyers' market regime; it never ceases to be a shortage economy. Even so, it is important to establish the scale of the normal shortage and normal surplus under various historical circumstances. Also worth following is the way the various indices of shortage and surplus fluctuate year by year and quarter by quarter around their normal values in a particular country over a certain historical period. For specific mechanisms are at work in the system, and although these allow short-term fluctuations, the shortage and surplus are drawn constantly back to values near the normal shortage and normal surplus. These mechanisms are discussed in more detail in the following chapter during the causal analysis.

There is no way of demonstrating what has been said with a comprehensive international comparison. It would have been most instructive to have regularly observed the phenomena of shortage and surplus, measure them, and publish the results, but unfortunately no socialist country did so. The situation is rather as if the capitalist countries would never publish figures for their system-specific problem, unemployment. The official statistical institutions cannot be excused by the admission that it would have been a highly difficult measurement task. These days there are plenty of known, usable indices for analyzing comprehensively the phenomena of shortage and surplus, the process of forced adjustment, and the behavior and mutual relations of the seller and buyer.[33] Some sporadic data on shortages are presented in this chapter and the next. Even these few examples confirm that it was feasible to observe and measure the phenomena of shortage.[34]

Shortage and surplus cause losses, which are discussed in section 12.11. But they belong to the accustomed, normal order of life under this system, which is what justifies referring to normal shortage and normal surplus. No one is surprised that commodities are in short supply or that one has to queue; housewives, buyers of inputs for firms, foremen, and workers have adapted their way of life and norms of behavior to the normal conditions of a shortage economy.[35]

Normal state is a concept related to equilibrium. The latter has several meanings, and so some conceptual clarification is required. In a wider sense equilibrium denotes the steady state of a dynamic system. That is how the concept is understood in the mathematical theory of dynamic systems and the natural sciences that make use of its apparatus. It is a value-free concept: no one argues that the state of equilibrium in a chemical system is "good." Many economists have taken over this meaning. Where that is the case, a system is in disequilibrium when it departs from its own state of equilibrium, the steady state typical of it. This is the sense in which Keynesian macroeconomics uses "unemployment equilibrium": there is a customary, steady rate of unemployment under the system, in which mechanisms operate to restore the customary unemployment if it is upset. In the same sense, one can talk of a *shortage equilibrium* as a synonym for normal shortage.[36]

Other economists use the concept of equilibrium in the narrower sense of a desirable state of equality between demand and supply. Theoretical writings use an adjective to distinguish this special type of equilibrium: Walrasian equilibrium. Of course, a shortage economy is not in equilib-

---

[33]No apt methodology has emerged for synthesizing the many partial indices that illuminate the various phases of shortage, surplus, and forced adjustment into suitable summary indices, although they are badly needed in theoretical analysis and economic management.

[34]In the case of measuring surplus, there is no justification for talking of special difficulties. The methodology for the measurement of unemployment and utilization of capacity has been devised in the statistical practice of the capitalist countries, and, with the requisite alterations, this can be taken over.

[35]In a work distributed illegally and later translated into English, Hungarian sociologist J. Kenedi (1981) gave a satirical account of a private building project: the trials of finding materials and skilled labor and the frequency with which resort had to be made to corruption. The book is a lifelike description of how citizens under a socialist economy must adapt to the shortage economy.

[36]E. Malinvaud (1977) speaks in this wider sense about Keynesian and classical unemployment equilibrium, and J. E. Stiglitz and A. Weiss (1981) about credit rationing equilibrium and excess demand equilibrium.

rium in that narrower sense. More precisely, there emerges in certain periods and certain spheres of the economy a specific kind of aggregate equilibrium, which was termed the forced adjustment equilibrium in section 11.2. It is accompanied, however, by a variety of discrepancies between demand and supply and numerous loss-inducing shortage phenomena covered in sections 11.1–11.5.[37]

11.7   Open, Declared, and Hidden Inflation

Study of the relationship between shortage and inflation is kept for the next chapter. The task here is to clarify a few concepts, and then arrive at some statements, still to do with the phenomenon of inflation.

Inflation is not system-specific; it can arise under any system. It always ties in with upward pressure on the prices of a great many (not just a few) products, and on the price level as a whole. This upward pressure can be traced directly from the pull of excess demand, the push of rising costs of products and services, or a combination of the two. The effects of demand and costs are usually closely connected.

A case where the market equilibrium adjusts once and for all to a single wave of price rises cannot be termed inflation, which is always a dynamic process: the original upward pressure on prices must constantly reproduce to cause an inflationary process.

If the price level steadily rises without administrative resistance, one speaks of *open inflation*. If the rise in price level (and the normally accompanying rise in nominal level of wages) is slowed or even halted by administrative price control (and usually administrative wage control), there is *repressed inflation*.[38]

Tables 11.8 and 11.9 contain official price statistics for a few countries, whose reliability will be examined in a moment. It emerges even

[37]The findings obtained by the Disequilibrium School with their econometric models can be reconciled with the above line of thinking in terms of substantive conclusions, if not of their terminology. (See the works referred to in note 1.) Using the apparatus peculiar to them, they describe how the short-term (annual) state of the socialist economy fluctuates around its own normal steady state, that is, around its shortage equilibrium. The studies referred to actually examine consumer markets where there might be forced adjustment equilibrium in the sense defined in section 11.2.

I uphold my objections in earlier works to the interpretation placed on the macroeconometric findings of the Disequilibrium School and to the terminology used. False associations of ideas can arise from interpreting short-term fluctuations as cases of the system tipping into either general "excess demand" or general "excess supply."

[38]For conceptual clarification in connection with inflation and the theory of repressed inflation, see B. Hansen (1951). D. M. Nuti (1986a) reviews the inflationary processes in the socialist countries and the terminological problems connected with them.

TABLE 11.8

Official Price Index in the Soviet Union: Long Time Series

Period	Average Annual Change of Official Retail Prices (percent)
1928–37	20.5
1938–40	5.9
1941–47	18.1
1948–57	−8.2
1958–76	0.0
1971–75	−0.1
1976–80	0.6
1981–85	1.0
1986–89	2.1

Source: For the period 1928–75: D. M. Nuti (1986a, pp. 42–44). From 1976: United Nations (1990a, p. 136).

from the column of official Soviet figures, however, that there was very strong open inflation for a long period. In spite of its strict central control of prices and wages, the classical socialist system fails to ensure a complete stability of prices.

Nonetheless, after the first wave of inflation following the Second World War, many socialist countries managed to stabilize the price level quite firmly, at least according to the official statistics. This is one of the achievements frequently cited in the official ideology, and it is eagerly contrasted with the far higher rate of inflation in many capitalist countries.

But how reliable are these official statistics? There are many methodological problems involved in measuring the price level in any country. Where there is political and scientific liberty, however, any bias in the state's figures can be challenged by independent experts, or by professional representatives of particular social strata, such as researchers working for the trade unions. This contrasts with the situation under the classical socialist system, where the central statistical offices have a total monopoly over the compilation of price statistics, and there is no opportunity for subjecting the calculations to open criticism. What is more, those running the economy have an interest in denying the scale of any inflation as far as possible. If price stability has been blazoned as a propaganda victory, an admission that the price level is rising will undermine

TABLE 11.9
Rate of Inflation: International Comparison

	Average Annual Change of Consumption Prices, 1960–80 (percent)
Socialist countries	
Bulgaria	4.05
Czechoslovakia	2.79
East Germany	1.21
Hungary	3.70
Poland	4.97
Soviet Union	2.30
Capitalist countries	
Austria	4.70
Finland	8.06
Greece	7.82
West Germany	3.95
Ireland	9.24
Italy	9.08
Spain	10.05

Source: F. L. Pryor (1985, p. 123).

the system's own arguments. Moreover, the high rate of growth is paraded as an achievement. The rate of output growth measured at prevailing prices would look far lower if a bigger deflator were used to calculate production volume at constant prices; in other words, conceding there was a rise in price level would weaken that argument for self-legitimation too. The official statistics are distorted methodically in various ways; there is a measure of *hidden inflation* that the price statistics cover up.

Hidden and repressed inflation should not be confused. Repression of inflation means prices do not rise despite the upward pressure, whereas prices do rise if there is hidden inflation, although the official statistics deny that the rise has occurred. In that sense, total open inflation consists of two components: the inflation declared in the official statistics, and the hidden inflation.[39]

[39]The statement that hidden inflation is one component in open inflation sounds a little paradoxical. Even so, this usage must be adopted as it is generally current.

The conceptual confusion is resolved if one does not associate the word "open" in this

Looking behind the scenes, one might find cases of conscious distortion of aggregate figures and the overall price index. But although the possibility cannot be excluded, there is no conclusive evidence either. The price index may become distorted, however, without any recourse to crude, central falsification. Four ways need mentioning.

1. The central price index relies on reports from below, from production and trading companies. As each report passes up through several levels in the hierarchy, those forwarding it realize that a price rise reflects badly on them; it is in their interest to gloss over any flagrant price increases.[40] So the center aggregates reports that have been distorted in advance.

2. Firms often impose disguised price increases [→8.4, 8.6]. Although profit is no matter of life and death to firms, as mentioned before, so that they are not in despair if they incur a loss, it remains more comfortable to avoid one by raising prices, rather than having to ask the superior organizations for help.

If a cost rises, in many cases it is not worth seeking official acknowledgment of it in a rise in the current administrative price. It is far easier to make some fairly simple modifications to the product, so that it becomes a "new manufacture" for which a new price can be calculated. The calculation then incorporates the increased cost in advance, which is acknowledged when the decision on the new administrative price is taken. In such cases the price authorities know what is happening too, but their motivation (a desire to demonstrate "price stability") coincides with the interest of the firm, and so they quietly acknowledge the procedure taken.

Let me add here that the firm is also interested in a disguised price increase because it can make the output plan, calculated at prevailing prices, easier to fulfill.

3. The statistical principle of comparability must be observed in the compilation of price indices. Note must be taken exclusively of products and services made in exactly the same quality last year as this when the price levels of the two years are compared. Generally speaking, that strict criterion is met by standardized products, whereas differentiated prod-

---

context with the idea of frank and honest statement of truth. The price determination process is open to inflationary pressure, and there are no administrative curbs on price rises.

[40]Hungarian researcher M. Petschnig (1985) recorded the following experience from detailed local observation at a time when the official inflation rate was less than 5 percent: The institution compiling the price statistics at the middle level accepted all reports of price rises under 5 percent without comment but demanded special explanations of all increases over 5 percent. Clearly, this put pressure on those reporting not to mention price increases above the critical value.

ucts do not usually satisfy the criteria of comparability because there are constant changes in their quality.

If there is no administrative control of prices and the market mechanism operates fully, a close correlation develops between the price movements of standardized and differentiated products. The prices of both groups settle freely, and there is no chance of the price level for standardized products lagging behind the level for differentiated products, because then it would not be worth making the former. So the calculation is not distorted by the components of the price index, on the long-term average, even if the whole of production is represented by the standardized products.

The situation differs under a system in which production and prices are coordinated bureaucratically. In the main, the price authority is able to set real administrative prices for standardized products, where price fixing can be enforced over a long period. For many differentiated products only pseudo-administrative prices can be set in real life. The price authority cannot control them fully, and disguised price increases are common. So there is a looser correlation between the price movements of standardized and differentiated products; in fact, the latter's price level may rise much faster than the former's.

If the standardized products are taken in this situation to represent the movement of the whole price level (pleading comparability), the price index is methodically biased downward.[41]

Technical advance and consumption growth necessarily raise the proportion of differentiated products in total production. The greater this ratio and the wider the sphere of pseudo-administrative pricing, the greater the bias in the price index.

4. There is an informal private sector even under classical socialism. The price changes within it are not covered by the official price index, whereas the big rise in gray- and black-market prices is the clearest reflection of the shortage of the state and cooperative sectors' goods and services. A truly comprehensive price index must be an average of the price levels in the formal and informal sectors weighted according to the sectors' real volumes. The bias can be sizable, depending on the informal sector's share of total output and the discrepancy in the two price levels.

Many Western economists have expended great effort on experiments in eliminating one or another of the distorting factors just mentioned and elaborating alternative estimates. Table 11.10 gives two examples of

---

[41]Even if a capitalist and a socialist country used exactly the same basket of products (fulfilling the comparability criterion and consisting mainly of standardized products) to compile their price indices, the former would be unbiased under the conditions just described and the latter certainly biased.

TABLE 11.10

Price Indices of Socialist Countries: Alternative Estimates

| | Average Annual Rate of Change of Prices (percent) | | |
	Official	Alton	Culbertson-Amacher
Bulgaria			
1963–70	1.1	—	3.4
1971–75	0.2	3.0	—
1976–78	0.5	3.2	—
Czechoslovakia			
1963–70	1.2	—	5.0
1971–75	0.1	2.2	—
1976–78	0.9	1.6	—
East Germany			
1963–70	0.0	—	3.4
1971–75	−0.3	0.7	—
1976–78	0.0	1.3	—
Hungary			
1963–70	0.9	—	4.1
1971–75	2.9	4.1	—
1976–78	4.3	4.4	—
Poland			
1963–70	1.2	—	5.5
1971–75	2.5	5.7	—
1976–78	5.9	8.0	—
Romania			
1963–70	0.4	—	6.3
1971–75	0.5	—	—
1976–78	0.7	—	—
Soviet Union			
1963–70	0.1	—	8.6

Source: D. M. Nuti (1986a, pp. 50, 52), who uses the following sources: 1963–70, columns 1 and 3: W. P. Culbertson and R. C. Amacher (1972); 1971–75 and 1976–78, columns 1 and 2: T. P. Alton et al. (1979).

Note: Although the periodizations of tables 11.9 and 11.10 differ, so that they cannot be compared directly, it is clear that the official indices given for several countries in table 11.10 are lower than those in table 11.9. The Western researchers from whom the figures were taken used differing official statistical sources.

this. The table shows that the distortion concealed in the official statistics is substantial. Of course, such experiments cannot provide a substitute for a conscientious internal audit of the statistics, since one could only obtain all of the figures required inside the country.

Without wholly reassuring figures to go on, it is hard to arrive at general statements, but the following can be put forward as a working hypothesis. The control mechanisms of the classical socialist system make it possible for the prices to resist the inflationary pressure. At least several countries over longer periods of time, if not every country all the time, managed to ensure price stability to quite a substantial degree.

12

Shortage and Inflation: The Causes

THE SHORTAGE and inflation found in the classical socialist economy form a group of phenomena whose appearance cannot be attributed to any single cause. Like most complex socioeconomic phenomena, it demands a multicausal examination.

There is wide-ranging debate among economists about the causes of the shortage and inflation that develop under socialist economic conditions. Most authors do not doubt that they result from the combined effect of several factors. The argument is concerned more with the relative importance of each explanatory factor and the degree to which they are causally connected. In other words, the question is whether there are primary causes from which secondary causes can be inferred: where are the causal chains?

This chapter is an attempt to synthesize the causal explanations advanced in the debate.[1] It does not confine itself merely to causes on the micro level, or merely to those on the macro level. Sections 12.1 to 12.4 deal with the former, while sections 12.5 to 12.9 cover the latter. Section 12.10 presents a brief summary.

Much of the literature starts out from an analysis of the consumer market and the shortage phenomena experienced by the household, and in some cases it confines the examination to them. The point of departure for the deliberations here is consideration of how the producer firm and bureaucracy running the production behave. The consumer market and the household are not drawn into the analysis until a later stage.

12.1 The Behavior of the Firm: Short-Term Decisions

It is worth continuing the comparison begun in section 11.5, opposing two pure cases or prototypes: a private firm under capitalism operating within a framework of imperfect competition,[2] and a state-owned firm

---

[1]All the reservations expressed in note 1 of the previous chapter about the attempt at integration apply to this chapter as well.

[2]The pioneers of the theory of imperfect competition were E. H. Chamberlin [1933] (1962) and J. Robinson (1933). Since then the theory has developed a great deal; H. R. Varian (1978), for example, gives a good summary of its present state.

The theory distinguishes various specific market forms of imperfect competition, monopolistic competition, the oligopolistic market (and the duopolistic market as a special case of it), and various special variants of all these. For a comparison with the classical

under classical socialism. For brevity's sake, the former will be called a competitive private firm and the latter a classical state-owned firm. The typical differences between them in terms of their interest and their behavior are summed up in table 12.1, on which a detailed, line-by-line commentary follows. The differences are explained primarily in terms of the difference between their property forms.

Considered first is short-term control of the firm's supply and the concomitant motivation and behavioral patterns. The end of the section turns to short-term control of the firm's demand, and the next section to its long-term investment decision making.

Line 1 of the table describes the interest motivating the two kinds of firm. The description is not intended to be complete; it is not stated that the decision makers in a competitive private firm are exclusively interested in profits, nor that the exclusive aim of the leadership of a state-owned firm under classical socialism is to gain the approval of its superior organizations, nor that the only way to gain this is to follow instructions accurately [→7.4]. Here the expression "maximizing" is better avoided; the present line of thought does not require a position to be taken on what formalism is most appropriate when modeling the motivation of a decision maker. It does seem certain, however, that the objectives mentioned exercise a decisive influence on the behavior of the firm.

Line 2 makes clear that a competitive private firm is surrounded by rivalry. There are numerous competitors making and selling close substitutes, and additionally, a new rival may appear at any time. This sense of threat from competition is absent from the life of a state-owned firm under classical socialism, where the bureaucracy alone decides what firms operate in each sector and what their "profiles" (lines of business) are.

As far as exit is concerned, it is worth looking at lines 2 and 3 of the table. In a competitive private firm's case, viability is determined by the market. The budget constraint is hard, and if the firm makes continuing losses, it is eliminated by the natural selection of the market. In the case of a classical state-owned firm, however, its death, like its birth, is in the hands of the bureaucracy. If the bureaucracy thinks fit, it can wind up a firm even though it is making a profit, and conversely, it can keep a firm going irrespective of any lasting financial failure. It possesses all the means of softening the budget constraint.

---

socialist state-owned firm, however, these fine distinctions are unnecessary, despite their importance in other connections.

The standard works on imperfect competition devote little attention to the sphere placed to the fore by T. Scitovsky and E. Domar, which plays a central part in the present line of argument: competition of a nonprice nature for the buyer. (For references, see chapter 11, note 25.)

TABLE 12.1

A System-to-System Comparison: The Short-Term Behavior of the Firm

Main Feature	Competitive Private Firm under Capitalism within Framework of Imperfect Competition	State-Owned Firm under Classical Socialism
1. Interest	Primarily increasing profits.	Primarily recognition from superior organizations. Chief criterion: performance of instructions.
2. Entry and exit	Determined by the market. Free entry. Business failure leads to exit.	Bureaucracy decides on all entries and all exits.
3. Budget constraint	Hard	Soft
4. Price responsiveness	Strong	Weak
5. Price determination	Firm sets selling price. Price higher than marginal cost.	Price authority sets selling price, but firm has influence on it. Relationship of price to marginal cost arbitrary.
6. Information on demand	Firm unsure of demand.	Firm sure of demand.
Producer-Seller's hypothesis	Does not expect notional excess demand. Quantity sold depends on own efforts.	Expects notional excess demand. Quantity sold does not depend on own efforts.
7. Notional excess supply	Would like to sell more at price set than buyer buys. There is notional excess supply and notional excess capacity.	Would not like to sell more at price set (approved) by price authority than amount it deems its production limit. There is no notional excess supply or notional excess capacity.
8. Demand for inputs	Constrained	Inclined to run away

From what has been said, it follows that a competitive private firm has very strong motives for winning the buyer over. These motives do not apply to a classical state-owned firm.

The difference is linked closely with the shortage phenomena. A competitive private firm (whether in existence or a potential entrant) has a strong interest in swift and flexible adaptation of its supply to the demand. If it notices that some demand is unsatisfied, it is worth its while to seize the opportunity. One should remember the information problem discussed earlier, quoting Hayek [→7.7]. A competitive private firm has a great interest in obtaining information about what shortages there are, using every scrap of knowledge it possesses and immediately expanding its supply to plug the gaps caused by the shortages.

A classical state-owned firm and its bureaucratic superiors lack all this motivation.[3] The firm has no interest in informing itself on its own account about what there is a shortage of or where there is unmet demand. It has no interest in adapting flexibly to the buyer by swiftly increasing or altering its supply; it is also constrained in adjustment because of mandatory output targets. It can expect the buyer to adapt to the seller instead.

Let me turn now to prices (lines 4 and 5). Both relative prices and the overall price level are covered in later sections. Only one aspect of the price problem is considered here: the relationship of the firm to prices. The main issue from this point of view is the degree to which a firm is responsive to prices, in this case to selling prices. A competitive private firm is strongly price responsive; after all, it "lives off the market." The price responsiveness of a classical state-owned firm is weak. Though not immaterial, the selling price is not vitally important to it. It really lives off the charity of the bureaucracy, not off the market.

The question of who determines the price and on what basis is secondary by comparison. Of course, if one compares the various market forms within the capitalist system, rather than the capitalist and socialist systems, the significance of price determination increases. On the one hand, a monopoly in the strict sense can dictate a price above the marginal cost without fear of losing customers, even if it makes no particular effort to recruit buyers.[4] At the other extreme, in the case of what is termed perfect competition, the selling price for the producer-seller is set. The producer then adjusts to the situation through the quantity of output. He

---

[3]This is the characteristic referred to primarily in the expression coined by K. A. Soós (1984): the "institutional inflexibility" of the socialist state-owned firm.

[4]This is true of monopoly in the strict sense. What laymen consider a monopoly is usually a firm operating under imperfect competition and facing competition from not too remote substitute products and services.

produces the amount needed to ensure that the price coincides with the marginal cost. There is no incentive in that case to make much improvement in quality, but nor can the firm afford to have the quality deteriorate. Either it abides by the written or unwritten standards of quality, delivery, and so forth, so that it is capable of selling its goods at the prevailing price, or it does not, in which case it is squeezed out of the market.[5] The phenomenon discussed in this section and section 11.5, namely, the effort of the producer-seller to gain the buyer from actual and potential rivals, applies in the case of imperfect competition, the middle ground of market forms between monopoly and perfect competition.

In the case of classical socialism, there is no clear statement one can make about how the firm's selling price relates to its marginal cost. The relationship is arbitrary. Nor does it appreciably affect the firm's behavior because of its weak responsiveness to prices.

Turning to line 6, a competitive private firm can guess the buyer demand roughly, but it has no accurate information. This uncertainty is what saves it from complacency. It cannot assume there is a latent notional excess demand among buyers prepared to purchase whatever it fancies producing. So it has to work very hard to convince buyers to prefer it over its rivals.

By contrast, a classical state-owned firm sees the demand as certain. In many cases it is tangibly manifested in queues for the product or orders covering production well in advance. The signs of shortage can take many other forms as well. The firm assumes the existence of latent notional excess demand. There would be buyers to match any increase in supply, and so there is no need to make any special effort to win buyers.

Although this section is mainly concerned with the firm and its micro behavior, the partial, microlevel elements in the expectations concerning demand (what demand the firm can expect for its own products) are combined with macrolevel elements of a general nature (how demand as a whole develops). That signifies in advance that the present causal analysis cannot be confined exclusively to examining the interest and behavior of the micro unit.

The phenomenon of notional excess demand has been treated in detail in section 11.2. An interpretation can be attached to a symmetrically equivalent category, *notional excess supply,* covered by line 7 of the table. The simplest approach, as in the case of notional excess demand, is

---

[5]The reference here is to a theoretically pure case of perfect competition. If a seller is able to distinguish himself from the other sellers by making special efforts (improving quality, offering better delivery terms, etc.), one has passed on into the realm of imperfect competition.

to shed light on the concept in question form. Sellers can be asked how much more of a product they would be willing (and would wish) to sell at the prevailing price than they do in fact sell, assuming there were no demand constraint on their doing so. The answer to the question is the notional excess supply. This quantity may take the form, partly or totally, of unsold stocks. But the producers may not have made it at all. It suffices for them to know that they are capable of producing it at relatively short notice. So notional excess supply is a category related to *notional excess capacity,* that is, the unemployed part of capacity that the producers would gladly employ, provided there were buyers to whom they could dispose of the products at the prevailing price.

In the competitive private firm's case there is such a notional excess supply or notional excess capacity. The line of argument that follows is well known from the theory of imperfect competition. A firm pricing a good sets its price above the marginal cost and sets the quantity of production accordingly, making the initial assumption that it can sell exactly that quantity at that price. That quantity is smaller, however, than the one at which the price would coincide with the marginal cost. The difference between the two is what is meant here by notional excess supply or notional excess capacity.[6] Many authors treat the existence of this excess capacity with a measure of disapproval, considering this to be the disadvantage of imperfect competition compared with perfect competition. But Scitovsky and Domar have shown it is far more an advantage than a drawback, because it is a major contributor to the impetus a competitive private firm receives to exert itself to win buyers.

This excess capacity is one explanation for the flexible adaptation in a market economy. If there turns out to be a buyer, there is always capacity to satisfy his or her demand. Moreover, this increases the buyer's self-confidence. The notional excess capacity's existence is a requirement before the buyer can threaten the seller with exit in Hirschman's sense. If buyers do not receive the right attention, they turn to a competitor, who is sure to have the free capacity to serve them.

With a classical state-owned firm there is neither notional excess supply nor notional excess capacity. Of course, the firm may have unused capacity. It conceals some of its capacity during the process of plan bargaining, but even so, it is unwilling to reveal it for the sake of a buyer. It may even withhold performance amid the direst shortage.[7] Alternatively, bottlenecks may result from the supply problems associated with shortage, causing other resources of the firm to remain unutilized. This is not,

[6]See H. R. Varian (1978, p. 95).

[7]K. A. Soós (1984) drew attention to the fact that this phenomenon plays a major part in erecting the supply constraint.

however, the kind of surplus that can be mobilized to satisfy demand. Although there are many factors that encourage a drive for quantity [→7.6], the withholding of performance and the physical constraints on inputs set an upper limit on the firm's production.

Ultimately, therefore, there is no notional excess supply or notional excess capacity to induce the firm to make efforts to win buyers. The lack of mobilizable excess capacities then makes adaptation even more cumbersome. All this is equally clear to the buyer, who even for this reason does not dare to employ the threat of exit.

As with line 6, warning is given of macro aspects of notional excess supply and notional excess capacity to be dealt with later.

Having considered the supply side, let us look at short-term control of the demand side (line 8 of the table). The motivation described in lines 1, 2, and 3 of the table and the price responsiveness signified in line 4 explain the interest a competitive private firm has in economizing on inputs. Since it need not reckon with shortage, it always obtains the quantity of inputs it requires, allowing for an expedient stockholding policy. The obvious conclusion from all this is that the demand for inputs is constrained.

A classical state-owned firm is in a different situation. To obtain the approval of its superior organizations and obey their instructions it should produce without interruption; the problems of obtaining supplies associated with shortage impede this. So the firm tries to stockpile inputs. In fact, only the supply constraint is effective; if a firm manages to gain access to the inputs, it can certainly finance the purchase of them, since its soft budget constraint presents no obstacle. It is not really responsive to prices, particularly not on the input side. So the firm's demand of the inputs for current production is not strictly constrained; instead, it is inclined to run away.[8] It is hardly worth asking how much the firm's voluntary constraint on demand would be, since even a smaller quantity than that would encounter the supply constraint (or the administrative constraint imposed by the authority rationing the inputs, which is discussed later). Mention is made later on of the macro aspects of the classical state-owned firm's input demand.

The phenomenon of "runaway demand" appears far more acutely in the allocation of investment goods, which is the subject of the next section.

12.2 The Behavior of the Firm: Long-Term Decisions

This section continues the comparison between the capitalist private firm and the state-owned firm under classical socialism. In the case of invest-

---

[8]I used the expression "almost infinite" demand for cases like this in my earlier works. This caused misunderstandings. I hope the expression used above ("inclined to run away") will be clearer.

ment there is no need to confine the discussion to the sphere of imperfect competition; a private firm can be chosen at will. To clarify the theoretical comparison, state intervention in private investment activity and investment by a capitalist country's state apparatus or state-owned firms is ignored.

The expansion drive and concomitant investment hunger are not system-specific phenomena, for the same endeavors affect capitalist private firms. The specific feature typical of one system or other is the kind of self-restraint shown by investment decision makers. What factors contribute to their ability and will to oppose the expansion drive, and to what extent are they able and willing to do so?

Reference has been made already to Keynes's remark that "animal spirits" are at work in the private entrepreneur, prompting him to develop his firm. But he cannot become dominated by them, because private owners bear the risk involved in an investment decision. That applies equally to a small firm in family ownership or a large joint-stock company. The residual income belongs to the proprietor [→5.2]. Even if the decision is taken directly by the managers, its success will make the owners rich and its failure hit their pockets. A serious crash swallows the family's wealth or the capital invested in the shares. So the investment decision is a matter of vital importance on which the careers of the managers who take it and implement it may depend.

The decision inescapably involves a risk. For that very reason, those taking it try to ascertain that the business prospects are good, that the future of the economy is promising, and that there really is a demand for the product of the investment or expansion, so that it can sell at a good price and yield a profit. This extensive, circumspect consideration encourages voluntary restraint on the efforts to expand.

Investment enthusiasm waxes and wanes as a function of the general business cycle of economic activity. Revival may bring a wave of optimism, with a proliferation of investment projects increasing demand, spawning further projects and ultimately causing an "overheating" of the economy. But at times like that, various factors able to impede the expansion even under such circumstances can intervene: increased demand for labor pushes up wages, growth in the demand for credit raises interest rates, and hitches may occur in supplies and delivery of materials (i.e., shortage phenomena appear, if only in a pale form).[9] These signals may be enough to produce a "cooling" of the economy, although that may not happen until there has been a severe depression. In all events, the worsening business prospects, increasing costs, and lower likely effi-

---

[9]For a description of the expansion phase in the capitalist business cycle, see, for instance, G. H. Moore (1983).

ciency of investment sooner or later encourage many entrepreneurs to restrain their investment intentions voluntarily.

The conclusion is obvious: demand for investment resources is constrained. Though it may rise steeply from time to time, there is no continuing runaway.

The situation is sharply different in the case of a classical socialist firm. The self-restraint just described fails to apply for numerous reasons [→9.1]. Since the budget constraint is soft, decision makers are not afraid investments may lead to financial failure. Any such fear is even less justified because responsibility is shared with the superior organizations, which have endorsed the investment project and may even have forced the firm to implement it. Whatever kind of financial rescue is chosen for an unsuccessful investment, the bill is ultimately picked up by the state, that is, by everybody—and nobody. There is no one like the owners of a private firm to be hit in the pocket when a loss is incurred. No one feels a true inner interest in ensuring caution in the handling of the money, which is the state's money—and that is the root cause behind the lack of voluntary restraint to counter the appetite for investment.

Sales prospects are no problem: whatever is produced, demand will adapt to supply. Chronic shortage ensures safe opportunities for sales.[10] The "overheating" produces no special signs of danger, on the one hand, because people have grown used to them (intensive investment tension is part of the normal state under the system); on the other, because wage rises can be blocked by administrative wage control and interest rates are set centrally (although they would not affect investment decisions in any case).

Again the conclusion is obvious. There is a constant runaway demand for investment resources from the state-owned sector under classical socialism. More investment proposals are submitted to the higher authorities for approval and financing than can be carried out. Demand for investment credit exceeds supply. The vertical application and horizontal demand for plant, construction, and installation is more than the allocating authority has at its disposal and more than the producers of them have physically available.

12.3 The Behavior of the Bureaucracy Managing Production

The last two sections contrasted one kind of firm with another, to make it easier to compare the two systems. In fact, one cannot examine a clas-

---

[10]Here (and at several other points in this line of thinking) one is up against a self-fulfilling expectation. The runaway demand for investment resources is one of the causes of the chronic shortage. At the same time, the chronic nature of shortage allows invest-

sical socialist firm in isolation. Earlier in the book it was explained how the leaders of firms form the lower levels of the bureaucracy on the production side. Although they exert a great influence over decision making through the various bargaining processes, a high proportion of the decisions, particularly the more important ones, are made at higher levels in the hierarchy.

What has been said already about the short- and long-term behavior of state-owned firms under classical socialism can be stated line by line about the middle and upper levels of the bureaucracy as well. To mention only one issue: the constant tendency for the bureaucracy's demand for inputs (especially investment resources) to run away. It is, however, worth making a few supplementary observations.

The allocator, during the planning process, tries to assign a taut plan to subordinate units, inducing them to extract as much output as possible from relatively little input [→7.5]. This intention in itself renders vertical shortage likely, since the meager allocations make it hard to cover the inputs for fulfillment of the output plan and for the quantity drive in general.

The higher the level at which a decision maker works, the more he or she is obliged to use aggregate indicators.[11] That brings us back to the information problem touched upon several times already. The head of a clothing factory, for example, is obliged to consider what styles, colors, and sizes of garments to include in the production plan. By comparison, the head of the clothing industry directorate thinks only in terms of broader aggregates: how many pieces of men's, women's, and children's clothing are produced. The minister of light industry deals with more aggregated indicators still, considering only the contribution of the whole clothing industry to total production value. The performance of a lower-level leader is judged on a report compiled on the basis of the aggregate criteria used at the next level up, and so it is not worthwhile to bother with detail or adapt closely to buyer demands. "The plan must be met" comes to mean that the targets for aggregate output must be reached, even at the cost of making far more green dresses and far fewer blue, far more baggy pants and far fewer tight ones than demanded. That is one reason why shortages and surpluses arise at the same time.

Like the setting of the output assignments, the bureaucratic allocation of inputs takes place on the basis of crude, aggregate quotas. To pursue the same simplified example, the clothing factory is allocated a set quantity of cotton or woolen fabric, classified, perhaps, into a few grades of

---

ments to be embarked on without fear of sales problems, which is among the factors contributing to the runaway investment demand.

[11]See A. Banerjee and M. Spagat (1987).

quality. But no exact breakdown of the fabric according to the 101 relevant quality specifications can be stipulated, not because the bureaucrats are negligent, but because the task is hopeless: there is no way of distributing administratively the modern production's myriad materials and semifinished and finished products. The coarse rationing system breeds a mass of allocational errors, shortages, and surpluses.[12]

The job of tackling the problems caused by shortage constantly faces the bureaucracy. That applies not only to every level of the state organizations controlling production but to the party apparatus. If there is a danger that a firm will fail to fulfill its production plan because a consignment of materials is late, it is seen as quite normal for the party secretary at the user firm to intercede with the party secretary of the supplier firm, the county party committee, or even the party center. Things done in a market economy by lowlier staff in the buying department become the common daily tasks of high political leaders. This is a burden to them of which they complain a great deal, but it is concurrently one of the manifestations of power. Functionaries manifest their power in their ability to speed up late assignments and obtain special treatment for the subordinate units that turn to them for help.

This is another phenomenon better described as a mutual effect than a one-way, causal relationship. Once there is shortage, it becomes essential for the bureaucracy to intervene constantly to overcome at least the gravest problems. But this very haste, the "fire-engine" approach, snarls up the input-output traffic, worsening the shortage at countless junctions in the economy.

[12]The charge was often made during the waves of terror under Stalin that the real cause of shortage was conscious sabotage by the enemy. It is worth quoting the records of the great trial of Bukharin and his associates. Vyshinsky, the chief prosecutor, stated, "It is now clear why there are interruptions of supplies here and there, why, with our riches and abundance of products, there is a shortage first of one thing, then of another. It is these traitors who are responsible for it." One of the accused, Grinko, said of another, "Zelensky, on the instructions of the bloc of Rights and Trotskyites, sent huge quantities of goods to the districts where there was a poor harvest and small quantities of goods to the districts where there were good harvests, and this caused goods to remain on the shelves in some districts and a shortage of goods in others." This means there is not enough money in the districts with poor harvests to buy the manufactures, while there are not enough goods in the districts with good harvests, where there would be enough purchasing power. The quotations are from R. Conquest [1968] (1973, pp. 563, 504).

In another trial, the manager of a food-trading firm confessed that the head of the counterrevolutionary group at the time of the adoption of the new Soviet constitution had set the participants "the task of intentionally discrediting the achievements summed up in the constitution. . . . We were to organize mass dissatisfaction among the population. . . . This could best be done by creating queues in front of the bread shops, organizing a holdup in the supply of bread." The confession was quoted in a speech by V. M. Molotov [1937] (1950, p. 24), one of Stalin's closest colleagues.

12.4 Relative Prices

Regarding the roles of prices, the analysis has been divided into two parts. They are examined first from the micro aspect, in terms of relative prices, and then from the macro aspect, with the general (average) price level along with the problem area of repressed inflation.

In line with the approach used so far in this book, the economy can be divided into two great spheres: (1) the interfirm sphere, where both the producer and the user are firms; and (2) the consumer sphere, where the producer is a firm and the user a household. (The former features in entries 4.4, 4.5, 5.4, and 5.5 of table 8.2, and the latter in entries 4.8 and 5.8.)

1. *The interfirm sphere.* Interfirm prices are certainly arbitrary and irrational, and they bear little information [→8.5, 8.6]. But that is not why there is shortage and surplus, as firms do not really pay attention to relative prices. Their budget constraint is soft and their responsiveness to prices low. Primarily their supply and demand both depend on the instructions and permits of their superior organizations and on other nonprice signals. The problem is not that the prices are "bad," but that they are ineffective. In other words, the market mechanism for mutually harmonizing demand, supply, and prices is eliminated, and production and consumption in the sphere are controlled by bureaucratic coordination instead.

2. *The consumer sphere.* Here the situation is quite different [→8.5, 8.7, 8.8]. The budget constraint on households is hard and their response to relative prices very sensitive. Administrative consumer pricing in many areas yields prices incapable of equating supply and demand; their rigidity makes adaptation harder still. The system of arbitrary and irrational relative prices is a major cause of shortage.

Apart from that general statement, the one aspect of consumer pricing policy needing rather more detailed treatment here is provision of some consumer articles and services to the public free of charge or compared to the costs at very low state-subsidized prices. These, in most countries under the classical system, include staple foods (bread, sugar, fats, etc.), public transportation, rental housing, and health, cultural, and educational services.

This pricing policy is not random, for it has deep roots in the official ideology of classical socialism, reaching down to the system's great "basic promises" [→4.3]. Society, it was promised, must at least satisfy the basic needs of all workers and their families. So these products and services must be available to all at accessible prices or free of charge.

Noble though the goals were, following them has numerous detrimental effects, of which the most conspicuous concerns the subject of this chapter: free provision or very low prices greatly swell demand, which the supply is unable to match. The result is a strong, if not uniformly intense, shortage of these products and services. This is an inevitable consequence of the pricing policy.

The function of allocating these products and services that satisfy basic needs passes from the market to the bureaucracy; they are distributed by administrative rationing. It is up to political scientists and social psychologists to say which is the prime force behind this and which the result. If the nobly meant principles of distribution and the pricing policy designed to apply them have produced shortage, is the bureaucracy forced to assume the task of allocation? Or is the real goal for the bureaucracy to take on the distribution of basic products and services as a major instrument of power, as it can do once it has removed the market mechanism from this sphere? The likely answer is that those two kinds of motivation are combined.

Several criteria can be applied in administrative rationing.

1. Need (size of family, state of health).

2. Recognition of economic or other social achievement (irrespective of political considerations).

3. Recognition of political merits. Political preference and discrimination, for instance, on grounds of social class.

4. Standing and prestige in the bureaucratic hierarchy.

5. Income and wealth situation.

6. Connections, bribery.

There may be either positive correlations or contradictions among these criteria. Some bureaucratic rationing schemes openly declare their criteria; others do not. Even when they do, there may be a discrepancy between declared and applied criteria [→13.6]. There may also be gray- or black-market allocation, alongside bureaucratic rationing or woven (semilegally or entirely illegally) into it.[13]

The artificially set relative consumer prices and administrative rationing system do more than allow redistribution among the various groups in society, that is, influence who partakes in the social product. In the same way the bureaucracy can influence greatly what citizens consume. This is among the major fields of paternalism [→4.4]. Although households retain some freedom of choice, the bureaucracy and the producers exercise dictatorship over the consumers.[14]

Here it is worth mentioning another ideological aspect of the pricing policy and rationing system for basic needs. Doctrinarian Marxists see

[13]A detailed evaluation of distribution comes in chapter 13.

[14]For the ethical, political, and social aspects of this see F. Fehér, Á. Heller, and G. Márkus (1983).

this distribution system as the first harbinger of a future period of history, *communism*. The well-known principle of communist distribution is this: "From each according to his abilities, to each according to his needs."[15] The argument runs that the principle can only be applied to a small area for now (for instance, to elementary education), but as the forces of production develop, it can spread ever more widely.

In reality, the principle is Utopian, with no realistic chance at all of application in either the near or distant future. Of course, single, precisely specified human needs can be fulfilled. Given today's telephone technology, for example, it is clearly possible to reach a stage when all have a telephone and use it as much as they like. The trouble is that the human need for telecommunications grows as technology develops. Once people can telephone as much as they like, they want to see the other person on a screen, have a phone in the car, transmit documents by phone, and link computers via the phone, just to mention a few possibilities known today. Experience shows without doubt that technical progress constantly creates new needs, so that the sum of all needs is infinite. The Utopia of the communist principle of distribution according to needs does not provide a rational justification for the experiments in distribution free of charge.

12.5 Repressed Inflation in Interfirm Relations

The causal analysis from the micro point of view in the previous sections is followed now by a discussion on the macro level. The subject of the previous section, examination of prices, continues, but instead of relative prices, the general price level is considered. The main purpose is to answer the following questions: What is the relationship between shortage and inflation? To what extent can the presence of repressed inflation explain the shortage?

The same distinction is made as in the previous section. Sections 12.5 and 12.6 respectively discuss first the interfirm sphere, in which both producer and user are state-owned firms or cooperatives, and second the consumer sphere, where the role of producer-seller is played by firms, but the user-buyer's by households.

Although the purpose is to reach conclusions on the macro level, one must start with microlevel statements, recalling and expanding on the observations made about line 8 of table 12.1. The effective curb on the firm's buying intention is on the supply side: it is applied either vertically (it does not receive as big an allocation from the allocating authority as

[15]See K. Marx [1875] (1966).

it would like) or horizontally (the firm producing or storing and distributing the input does not have as much of it available as the buyer firm would like). The demand conflicts with the supply particularly sharply in the case of investment goods, construction services, and imports of high-technology machinery.

The buyer-firm's own ability to pay is not an effective constraint on it. It has the right to obtain the physical inputs for all physical activities, whether current production or investment, prescribed or authorized by the plan, or at least interpretable as furthering fulfillment of the plan. If the input has not been allocated or cannot be obtained, the fact can be accepted. What cannot happen is frustration of the procurement by lack of money. This is a declared principle and applied practice of the planning and financial system under classical socialism. If the firm is able to pay out of its own cash reserves or a credit facility already supplied, there is no problem. But if these resources do not cover the bill, it can still raise the additional finance, using one of several techniques: an emergency loan,[16] postponement of debt-servicing or a payment to the budget, making free the firm's money reserves frozen by various ad hoc measures, and so on.

In macro terms the practice just described means this: the total money demand of the firms is decided basically by the financing needs of the real activity laid down in the plan. The total money supply to satisfy that money demand adapts to it passively. The monetary policy is permissive.[17]

One can add that interest plays no appreciable role whatsoever on the creditor's or the debtor's side. It does not influence the actions of the bank or the firm, nor does it affect either the supply of credit or the demand for it.

Financial policy, both fiscal and monetary, plays a subordinate, passive role.[18] Let us assume that the profit tax on firms, the interest rate, or the total money supply is reduced or increased. Under the capitalist system a change of that kind would certainly make itself felt in the business world, leading, for instance, to a contraction or expansion of the firms' real activity and a fall or rise in investment. Such fiscal or monetary moves have no effect under the classical socialist system. The real activity of the firms is affected only by measures like raising or lowering the production plan, sending a ministry commissioner out to the firm to

[16]For instance, see G. Tallós (1976).

[17]In Czechoslovakia, for instance, between 1971 and 1980, the total credit extended by the banking system grew about twice as fast as production. M. Hrncir (1989, p. 30).

[18]On the subject of the passivity of money see the references in chapter 8, note 3.

give extra instructions, or reaching a central decision to start an invest-ment.

From all this one can conclude that the firm sector is not "truly" monetized; it merely gives that impression. Although everything is ac-counted for also in money, the sector is only semimonetized [→8.5]. The semimonetized state of this sector (and the damage done by the passive-ness of fiscal and monetary policy, which comes to the same thing) is among the root causes of shortage. It allows demand to "run away" in several areas, as was mentioned earlier and is dealt with again in the remainder of the chapter. But even if one lists it among the fundamental causes, it is not an independent cause that could be changed in itself. The passivity of fiscal and monetary policy is nothing more than an ex-pression on the financial plane of the fact that the firm sector is con-trolled by bureaucratic coordination, in the main with the arsenal of di-rect control, and not by market coordination with the arsenal of prices and money.

That leads one to the problem of repressed inflation, but first we must return to the concept of monetary overhang [→11.2]. This denotes the buying power that "hangs over" the economy with the potential of de-veloping into buying intentions, and so effective demand. Normally, it can be understood as the accumulated, unspent stock of money in money owners' pockets (or bank accounts), which can appear on the market for goods as demand at any time. Now the classical socialist firm is not an autonomous owner of money. On the one hand, there are numerous ad-ministrative curbs on the way it spends its money, while part or all of its money stock may be frozen at any time. On the other, as mentioned above, it possesses a virtual "blank check." If it needs money for a "jus-tified" purpose, it can freely spend it, knowing that in some form or other the state stands behind to pick up the bill. In this sense the inter-firm sphere constantly has an overhang of money waiting to be spent and converted into effective buying intentions. Thus, in this sense there is repressed inflation in the interfirm sphere under classical socialism. It must be emphasized, however, that this is a very specific kind of re-pressed inflation that differs in several essential respects from the usual examples, such as the forms that arise in a capitalist war economy. The main difference is that a capitalist war economy contains privately owned, strongly profit-oriented firms. Sensing excess demand, they make forceful attempts to push prices upward, while the wartime govern-ment tries vigorously to force them back. "Forcing back" is an apt ex-pression here, because an intensive inflationary pressure must be forced back with might and main. The tension is increased because everyone feels that there is an unusual, extraordinary state of affairs that differs from the normal operation of the system. This all happens far less vehemently under the classical socialist system. For the reasons mentioned, firms are not so excited about prices; excess demand and administrative control of prices are an accustomed part of everyday life.

12.6 Repressed Inflation in the Consumer Sphere

The consumer sphere is truly monetized. The budget constraint on buyers is hard, and they are responsive to prices. That must be the point of departure for thinking over the problem of repressed inflation in this sphere.

To simplify the analysis, let us assume that the interfirm and consumer spheres are perfectly isolated from each other. The products and services offered by the firm sector to households cannot be bought by other firms. This assumption will be abandoned in the later part of the chapter.

Let me put forward in advance the statement that the section sets out to argue is true. It does not follow from the nature or basic attributes of the classical system that repressed inflation must appear in the consumer sphere, but its appearance and lasting presence are not incompatible with the system. Its appearance has no deep, system-specific roots; to a far greater extent it is the consequence of the economic policy pursued.

The argument takes place in two stages. First, the attributes of the system known so far are shown to be compatible with the absence of repressed inflation. Then the complementary statement is supported: the nature of the system does not exclude the possibility of repressed inflation.

1. Support comes from the observations in section 11.2 on the forced adjustment equilibrium, and in section 11.6 on normal shortage. On the demand side, all households have grown accustomed to normal shortage; they expect to queue for the customary period, make the customary proportion of forced substitutions, visit the customary number of stores before finding the good desired, and so on. They fully adjust their demand to the supply constraints. They make forced substitutions, but there is no forced saving.[19] The household's inclination to save is unchanged. On the supply side, the producer-seller firm treats the buyers' requirements with the customary indifference and need make no more than the customary adjustment to the buyers. In this way a forced adjustment equilibrium emerges in the consumer sphere.

---

[19]Or at most there is temporary forced saving absorbed by later supply that satisfies the postponed notional demand.

The central management of the economy makes no change in the prevailing consumer price level.[20] It has no wish to use price and wage policy to alter the customary intensity of the shortage, which it considers normal and a fact of life, as do the citizens who suffer by the shortage.

Unspent money does not accumulate in the consumer sphere of such an economy. There is no monetary overhang suspended above the market and ready to turn into purchasing power, nor any constant, actual excess household demand. So no repressed inflation appears.

2. The situation changes if shortage-induced forced saving arises, not just temporarily but repeatedly or even continually, in other words, if more and more unspent money piles up in household hands through a cumulative process. There may be several reasons for this.

a. The composition of supply departs so far from the composition of notional demand that the buyer is no longer prepared to make a full forced adjustment, preferring not to spend some of the money at all.

b. Those in charge of the economy allow nominal incomes to outstrip the price level, and so cause an increase in the intensity of the shortage on a scale that leads to forced saving.

This economy differs from the situation described in point 1 in that actual excess household demand arises and accumulates, perhaps to a steadily increasing extent. There is upward pressure on consumer prices. If the state pricing authority opposes that pressure, there is a case of "regular" repressed inflation.

The development of either situation is conceivable under the conditions of the power structure, property forms, and coordination mechanisms that prevail in the classical socialist system. Indeed, one finds historical examples of both.[21]

Where case 2b obtains, one can say that the creation of excess demand and the repressed inflation have been brought about by price and wage policy. It would be inept to attribute the emergence of the excess demand to monetary policy, since the monetary policy is passive and permissive (as mentioned in another context) and cannot be otherwise under the

---

[20]Reminder: the formal and informal private sectors are ignored at this point. I return to this issue at the end of the section.

[21]For a long time the consumer sphere in the Soviet Union, East Germany, and Czechoslovakia tended to create the impression of a forced adjustment equilibrium. J. Goldmann (1975) points this out in Czechoslovakia's case, for instance. But in other countries, such as Poland in the 1970s or the Soviet Union in the late 1970s and early 1980s (i.e., before either country had embarked on reforms), there were numerous signs of repressed inflation developing.

One can speak here only of "impressions." There is no firm, empirical evidence to back up the observations because of the distortions in the price indices and the unsolved state of the problem of measuring shortage.

system concerned. Those in political power decide their price and wage policy, whereas the financial authorities merely print enough money to carry it out.

I must return here to the role of the formal and informal private sector, and at the same time of the parallel markets (the legalized free market and the gray and black markets) [→11.2]. The public may spend all or some of the money intended for purchases that they are unable to make in the public sector in the private sector instead. This may contribute to the creation of case 2a, a forced adjustment equilibrium,[22] or it may alleviate the inflationary pressure in case 2b, where there is repressed inflation.

12.7   Excess Demand on the Macro Level

The discussion now turns to the economy as it really is, a connected whole. Bureaucratic coordination certainly prevents the whole economy from forming a single market by erecting various administrative restraints, applying quotas, and earmarking money in various ways, but there are still a number of spontaneous "leaks" and "siphons" between the vessels of the economic flows. More important, those running the economy have power to transfer products, resources, and labor from one sphere to another.

The first thing to do is to examine the components of demand on the macro level. No attempt is made at completeness, and attention is focused only on certain spheres of greater importance to the subject of this chapter. The main components of demand are not just listed; each is immediately classified in terms of the degree to which the demand of different sectors is liable to run away, and the force with which those creating each demand can intervene on their own behalf in the distribution of the products and services concerned.

1. Firms' demand for the inputs they need for current production. The meagerness of the input quotas for the taut output plans, the uncertainties of supply, and the expectation of vertical and horizontal shortage produce a hoarding tendency, inducing firms to buy all they can of what they may need in the future.

2. Firms' demand for investment goods; investment hunger induced by the expansion drive. Through this phenomenon, forced growth joins the list of factors explaining shortage [→9]. Normally, the almost insatia-

---

[22]As mentioned before, D. M. Nuti (1986a) considers this to be the main reason why many of the econometric surveys by the Disequilibrium School fail to demonstrate a lasting surplus demand.

ble investment hunger exercises the strongest effect of all on excess demand.

3. The foreign trade sector's demand for exportable products. This sector has a particularly strong demand for products salable for convertible currency. Although demand on foreign markets is limited, an appreciable proportion of domestic production is eventually salable abroad at suitably reduced prices (i.e., with the right measure of price subsidies). The demand from foreign trade, intent on forced exporting, is also liable to run away [→14.3, 14.4].

4. Demand from state institutions with a great influence on power for inputs they need for operation. There is a "weak" section of the bureaucratic apparatus that cannot make peremptory demands and must be content with the meager inputs assigned to it. (Examples are health care and education). But the "strong" institutions (such as the armed forces) are disinclined to exercise self-restraint; they make energetic efforts to secure for themselves products and services when they are being distributed.[23]

5. Demand from the consumer sphere. As pointed out in the previous section, actual excess demand may emerge here as well, but on the other hand it may not because a forced adjustment equilibrium has emerged.

The combined demand of these five spheres (and the other parts of the economy not mentioned here) confronts the combined supply. In terms of the macro totals, there is persistent excess demand under classical socialism.[24]

Spheres 1–4 have an almost insatiable appetite for the products, services, and resources they use. Their budget constraint is soft. Their demand is constantly liable to run away. To this sphere 5's demand, the excess demand of the consumer sphere, may be added, provided there is repressed inflation [→12.6, case 2]. But this is no precondition for the emergence of macro excess demand. Even if there is no repressed inflation in sphere 5 [→12.6, case 1], spheres 1–4 will generate enough excess demand to ensure it extends to the economy as a whole. Nor is it even

[23]This observation is well demonstrated in C. Davis (1989, 1990).

[24]There is debate about the degree to which excess demand on the macro level can be measured. Certain components in the demand of the interfirm sphere are difficult to pin down statistically. There are several economic and methodological problems in adding up the various items of excess demand. It is doubtful whether the statistics available can be used to arrive at an aggregate variable that can represent total demand covering the whole economy (or an acceptable approximation to that value).

So I have avoided using in my earlier works and in this book any means of expression in which the macrolevel demand (or excess demand) would be reflected by a single number. Instead, I prefer a metaphorical expression: certain components of demand (and thereby, in effect, the total demand) are liable to run away, leaving the supply far behind.

necessary for the demand from all four sectors to run away. In fact, the investment hunger arising out of the expansion drive is a sufficient condition in itself for excess demand in the economy as a whole, although it is usually coupled with runaway demand in spheres 1, 3, and 4 as well.

It is now possible to forsake the assumption made at the beginning of section 12.6, where the consumer sphere was isolated from the other parts of the economy to make the initial theoretical approach clearer. In fact, spheres 1–4 try to siphon off products and services from sphere 5, household consumption.[25] There are very few goods whose physical characteristics make them exclusively capable of serving the purposes of domestic households. If they are tradeable, then export of them can be reckoned with. Moreover, most consumer articles and services can find other domestic buyers than households. An office can move into an apartment, a taxi can be hired by a firm or institution, foodstuffs can be bought by the catering industry, furniture can be installed in offices, and so on.

In addition, finished products are not all that is liable to be siphoned off. Perhaps more important still is the possibility of redirecting the resources (materials, semifinished products, labor, premises, investment, foreign exchange available for imports) that can contribute to supplying the consumer sphere but also can serve the other parts of the economy. The threat is from all spheres with great political weight that they can use in plan bargaining over allocations [→7.5, 9.2].

So ultimately, the supply for the consumer sphere is confronted not only by households, with their own money limited by a hard budget constraint and their own buying intentions, but by the other sectors, with their soft budget constraint and their avid siphoning propensities.

The only reason why the whole supply is not siphoned away from households is that this is prevented administratively by those in control of the economy. They insist that a certain proportion of the supply should certainly reach households. They forbid firms to buy in stores where the general public makes its purchases and ban the use of housing for office premises. Even before that, they give plan quotas of inputs to the industries manufacturing consumer articles. Of course, all this is done by bureaucratic coordination with the weapons of direct bureaucratic control.

Whatever the case, the producer-sellers producing basically for the consumer market are aware of the existence of excess demand on the

---

[25]The phenomenon described here as "siphoning off" is related to the term "crowding out" in Anglo-Saxon business and economic parlance. By the latter is meant that in an allocation process (say, allocation of credits) the stronger group crowds out the weaker by bidding a higher price or with the help of state intervention.

macro level. Even if they experience no excess demand from the totality of households (i.e., a forced adjustment equilibrium has developed), they still receive no impetus to behave in the way a buyers' market regime would require of them. They feel that the sales problem is likely to be temporary; sooner or later, directly or indirectly, spheres 1–4 will appear as buyers. If there is macrolevel excess demand in the whole of the economy and the regime of a sellers' market dominates, their behavioral consequences spread everywhere; no islands of a buyers' market regime can remain for a long time.

Discussion of excess demand on the macro level impinges on the position with the allocation of labor, the problem sphere of chapter 10. There is a dichotomy during a longer period in the classical system: whereas shortage dominates over surplus in products, the contrary applies to labor. The dichotomy lasts until the absorption of the surplus labor has been completed. But ultimately forced growth may lead to a situation in which a labor shortage predominates and becomes chronic [→10.2].

The elimination of the initial dichotomy is inevitable and an integral part of the shortage syndrome. There is certainly rigidity in the adaptation of production and the development of technology, and a strict calculation based on prices and costs is not applied. Even so, planners and managers still sense the scope for substitution between labor and material inputs. They experience how there is often a shortage of one particular input or another—at one moment of workers and at another of materials or machines or other equipment. Under those circumstances they are often obliged to make improvised forced substitutions between inputs. That eventually leads to a situation in which there is no long-term surplus of any production factor to match the grave and lasting shortage in another, since shortage dominates in them all.

As stated before in another context, there is no chance in an interconnected economy of islands developing and surviving in which another market regime dominates than the one surrounding it. If the system as a whole is a shortage economy, sooner or later the allocation of labor will operate as a shortage economy as well.[26]

12.8 The Propensity to Inflation; the Relationship between Shortage and Inflation

It emerges from chapters 10 and 11 and from chapter 12 so far that the factors capable of producing and sustaining an inflationary process are

---

[26]The same applies to the opposite situation. Normative ideas arose that a sellers' market should be maintained in allocating labor to serve the workers' interests, while a buyers' market should be introduced in allocating products to serve the interests of consumers.

Continued

present under classical socialism. To mention only the major ones, (1) there is lasting excess demand on the macro level for products and services; (2) the producer-sellers have some interest in raising prices; (3) the labor shortage exerts an upward pressure on wages; (4) the permissive monetary policy may increase the money supply needed to such an extent that it generates excess demand.

These factors combine to create a propensity to inflation in the classical socialist economy. This term is intended to convey that the system, through its inherent attributes, contains within it the conditions for the process to arise, but that the process does not necessarily "break out," and if it does, it may be only in a mild form. Of the factors just listed, several are present, but do not exert great force. Only factor 1, excess demand, is very strong. Factor 2, upward pressure on prices, is not great. Under the soft budget constraint, profits are not a matter of life and death to firms; any loss arising can be compensated for in other ways than by raising prices, and in any case, the firm's interest points in a different direction. Factor 3, upward pressure on wages, is not strong. There are no independent trade unions or strikes, and administrative wage control is severe. Finally, as far as factor 4 is concerned, the monetary policy certainly is permissive. But it does not set about giving an expressly inflationary impetus to demand with an artificial injection of money supply to produce an expansion of business activity.[27] The incentive to expansion operates fully without special stimulus.

The chronic shortage and propensity to inflation under classical socialism derive from the same stock; they are created by the same or related factors. Are they merely concomitants of each other, or is there tradeoff between them? This idea has often arisen in economic literature. The question in this form is expressed in two general terms, and so it needs breaking down into two more specific ones:

1. Let us assume there is an inflationary process taking place in a classical socialist economy, but it is being partly or wholly repressed by the price and wage policy of the state. Meanwhile, shortage phenomena appear. Does the intensity of the shortage decrease if the repression of the inflation is partly or wholly lifted and the inflationary process does not cease, that is, if the repressed inflation turns partly or wholly into open inflation?

I agree with those who answer this question in the negative. This policy may overcome or ameliorate certain shortage phenomena temporarily, but the normal shortage returns later.

This dichotomy cannot be sustained in the long term precisely because of the potential for substitution (and the economic imperative to use it).

[27]Injections of this kind are made from time to time in capitalist economies, following Keynesian macro policy, to compensate for recessions and depressions.

This prediction follows from everything said in the previous sections. The interfirm sphere, with its soft budget constraint and low responsiveness to prices, would scarcely react to the price changes in the first place. The households, with their hard budget constraint and responsiveness to prices, would be obliged to react: their demand and their actual purchases would decrease. After the first wave of price rises, total household spending would fall. But if no other change took place in the system in the meantime, spheres 1, 2, 3, and 4 of section 12.7 would exert their strong siphoning effect on the products and services not bought by the households. The apartments vacated by households because of the high rent would be occupied by offices, which could easily pay the higher rate. The textile no longer required by households would be absorbed without any trouble by the army. The gasoline and heating oil that households did not buy would be purchased by state-owned industry or transportation.

Nor is it just a question of the unsold finished products and the services intended originally for households. More important still is the indirect effect via the direct bureaucratic control of allocation. A fall in household demand would allow inputs to be switched to areas where the planners thought the need was most urgent [→12.9], so decreasing the supply to the households.

In the end, the public would perhaps suffer the consequences of the price increases through a reduction in its real consumption, but the shortage would remain, or more precisely, shortage-cum-inflation would prevail.

2. Assume there is a process of open inflation whose rate has been steady so far. (For instance, the price level has been rising at a quite low rate of about 5 percent a year.) Alongside the inflation there have been shortage phenomena all the time. The question is, does the intensity of the shortage decrease if the inflation speeds up, for instance, from a rate of 5 percent to one of 10 percent a year?

Again, I concur with those whose answer is no. There is no need to give detailed arguments again, because they simply follow from the previous ones. Only a single line of thinking is picked out.

Let us start from the macro relationship [→12.7]. One assumes that there was excess demand in the system before inflation speeded up. Spheres 1, 2, 3, and 4 proved to have almost insatiable appetites. What would change if from now on all numbers measuring demand, supply, and actual sales and purchases had to be multiplied by 1.1, and by 1.1 again a year later, and so on? The significance here is in the proportion of supply and demand to each other, not in the kind of unit of measurement used (i.e., whether one unit of money has a larger or a smaller purchasing power).

To sum up, the attributes of the classical socialist system inevitably create a shortage economy. As far as inflation is concerned, they only produce a propensity. It then depends on the economic policy pursued how much that propensity is realized and in what form (how much the inflation is open and how much repressed, how much of the open inflation is declared and how much hidden).

12.9   The Self-Inducement and Reproduction of Shortage

Shortage breeds shortage. Of course, cross-effects of this kind are not among the prime explanatory factors. The genesis of the shortage must come first. But once it exists, awareness of it molds the behavior of the participants in the economy. The phenomena in question are commonly called *self-fulfilling expectations*. I shall list a few, all referred to before, so that a brief reminder will suffice.

Both sides on a sellers' market reckon on the likelihood of a shortage situation. That increases the seller's self-confidence and indifference to the buyer, and the buyer's humility and sense of defenselessness. Once the two sides have prepared themselves psychologically for the situation, the seller really need make no effort to win the buyer, and the buyer's forced adjustment really takes place.

Buyers are uncertain about future supplies and expect shortage, so they hoard. This hoarding tendency contributes to the development of excess demand.

All applicants during the plan bargaining for allocations anticipate a shortage of inputs. So they try to exaggerate their needs, which increases the vertical shortage.

Shortage can also be expected in the more distant future. Investors feel there will be no sales problem, which encourages them to apply no self-restraint in bargaining for investment resources. The result is that the consequently almost insatiable investment hunger becomes one of the most important factors producing excess demand.

These circular processes (and other like them) result in the self-inducement of shortage.

Note should be taken of the information and regulatory mechanisms acting in many fields to sustain and conserve the customary level of shortage, the normal shortage. Relative price movements under classical socialism fail to play the information role they have under market coordination, that is, they are signals of relative scarcity and draw the attention of the decentralized decision makers to shortages and surpluses. This price-signal system is replaced partly by signals of shortage and surplus, but in a fairly rough-and-ready way [→8.9].

Consider, for example, the experience of the Hungarian car market.[28] The country did not make cars. Instead, a monopoly car-dealing firm supplied buyers exclusively with cars imported from other socialist countries. People had grown used to waiting for a car for an average of two to three years. If the queue grew substantially longer, requisite measures (e.g., raising prices) were taken to make sure the waiting list returned to its normal length. Nor did a deviation in the opposite direction last for long. If the list became abnormally short, so that the shortage might have been eliminated, imports were curbed and the waiting list returned to normal. The intervention in either case is understandable from the angle of the firm and its superiors. A queue strikingly longer than usual might arouse discontent. A queue far shorter than usual might rob the seller of the advantage, making buyers too particular. Moreover, "too short" a queue is a sign that resources (e.g., import quotas) can be withdrawn from the area and transferred to places where the shortage is more intense than normal.

This line of thinking applies generally. Planners heed the signals of shortage and surplus. They try to expand the supply to areas from which more and louder complaints are being received of worse provisions than usual, longer waiting times, and more frequent forced substitutions. To make these transfers, of course, products and resources have to be withdrawn from somewhere. There is rarely a chance to do so from areas with a surplus in the literal sense. So, obviously, they have to rob areas where there are shortage phenomena, but they are less acute than usual.[29]

Taking a step upward, one can consider control of the entire consumer market. Macrolevel planning of household consumption [→7.2, 9.3, 12.7] needs to be returned to here. The controllers of the economy plan the consumer price level, the nominal income of the population, and the supply available for consumption. Usually they can also predict quite well how much of its income the general public will save, in other words, what the likely total expenditure will be. In the short term, those in

---

[28]The Hungarian car market was described in an article by Z. Kapitány, J. Kornai, and J. Szabó (1984), after which Z. Kapitány (1989a) continued observing its state and control mechanism. The exact details are contained in the articles; the workings of the market are described in a stylized and highly simplified form in this passage, which is merely intended to shed light on a general notion.

[29]The theoretical models of this allocation mechanism are contained in several studies in a volume edited by myself and B. Martos, whose title imparts the message of what is said above: *Non-Price Control* (1981). Several of the models described a feedback control mechanism that restores the normal state of the economy by reacting to departures from normal stock and order-book levels.

On the basis of the models, one can prove formally that such a mechanism is viable, that is, can coordinate the input-output processes, even though it does not ensure optimum allocation. For further references, see chapter 8, note 47.

charge of the economy are able to plan these macro measures, and also to ensure that the plans are implemented quite accurately.

With these tools available, in fact, they could also cut the frequency and intensity of the shortage phenomena in the consumer sphere dramatically with a single big decision. All they should do is to raise the supply channeled to the consumer sphere radically, leaving everything else unchanged.[30] But this is not what usually happens. It would entail suddenly withdrawing products and services from elsewhere, and there is likewise shortage and tension in the other spheres of the economy, production, investment activity, and foreign trade. Both the public and the economic leadership have grown used to the normal shortage in the consumer sphere. In the process of macro planning (at least in periods when the political and economic situation is sufficiently stable) they take special care to ensure that the shortage does not become more than usually acute.[31] No effort is made, however, to have supply grow faster than demand to make the shortage substantially milder than usual.

In effect, the system has fallen into the shortage-economy trap. Once it is in it, the shortage reproduces itself, not least through the force of habituation and inertia.

12.10 The System-Specific Nature of the Causes

The causal analysis is over; no further explanatory factors will be added to those given so far. The sequence of ideas that follows is intended to explain the "depth" of the causes: how random and superficial they are, or how deeply imbedded in the basic attributes of the system. Four types of explanation are distinguished, without claiming that the classification is either complete or universally valid. At certain points issue is taken with other views, usually found in public attitudes, political debates, and official statements about shortage, rather than in academic studies.

1. *The mistakes of participants in the process.* This is the most common explanatory formula in official propaganda and the media, and under their influence among the public, although not in academic writings. Some product or other is unobtainable because the commercial sector did not order it in time, the factory management failed to ensure its production, the ministry miscalculated the plan, the foreign trade firm was late in arranging to import it, and so on.

---

[30]In the sense of the line of thinking expressed in the previous section, the reduction in the shortage would only be temporary. This is ignored in the present argument.

[31]The econometric study by J. P. Burkett, R. Portes, and D. Winter (1981) shows that if excess demand appears on the consumer market, the controllers of the economy reduce the exports and increase the imports of consumer goods.

One can assume each such assertion is true in its own narrow context. All participants in all systems are frail humans, and errors slip into their work. But the purpose of scientific explanation is to discern why one kind of mistake, under specified circumstances, is more common than another—why the mistakes veer in some clearly apparent direction.

All systems, social as well as physical, exhibit frictions [→11.4]. The parts do not fit each other perfectly; the machinery squeaks. There is friction in the way both bureaucratic investment control and the stock market perform their allocating functions, but each kind of friction is system-specific. A scientific explanation must show why certain kinds of frictional phenomena apply in one system, and why they differ from those in another.

2. *Economic backwardness*. One often hears the shortage economy explained as something prevalent in poor and backward countries.[32] This widespread view confuses two conceptually quite distinct phenomena. One is a low level of economic development, with its concomitant low levels of production and consumption, while the other is shortage, the failure to satisfy buyers. East Germany was among the world's most highly developed countries in per capita production and consumption terms, yet it was still a shortage economy. East German citizens could not get the things they wanted to buy with their money. Meanwhile, many capitalist countries are economically backward without being shortage economies. The buyers' demand may be large or small depending on their income, but there are no supply constraints on their satisfying it.[33]

3. *Faulty economic policy*. In this case, the shortage is ascribed to a faulty line of political and economic control. The belief is widely held, particularly in the bureaucracy under the classical socialist system and among the early pioneers and advocates of reform. Several variants appear:

a. The production plan, or more commonly still the investment plan, is too taut. True, but the propensity to overtighten plans is inherent in the system.

[32]I reject the idea that poverty and backwardness could explain the shortage syndrome directly. This section makes clear my view that the system-specific causes of shortage are primary. But I concede that the birth of the system itself and the formation of its basic characteristics have a bearing on the economic backwardness of the countries involved. I dealt with this relationship earlier in the book [→2.2, 8.1].

[33]The concern here is to clarify concepts, not express value judgments. This line of argument does not endorse poverty or backwardness either politically or morally.

One more qualification is needed: reasons of space prevent this book from covering the way grave supply constraints can arise in some circumstances in developing countries taking the capitalist road.

b. The wage policy is wrong. The usual phrasing of the criticism is that the economic bureaucracy has not kept a tight enough hold on wages, which have grown too fast by comparison with productivity. In some cases the observation is valid. It was emphasized how such a wage policy can contribute to the formation of excess demand and repressed inflation on the consumer market [→12.6]. But this is just one factor behind the shortage-inflation syndrome applying in some instances, whereas several other factors apply continuously, irrespective of the economic policy selected [→12.7–8].

c. The pricing policy is faulty: the price of some group of products or services has been set too low. Section 12.4 dealt with the extent to which this is pertinent, and the whole chapter set out to show that this only explains part of the problem in any case.

4. *System-specific causes.* The line of argument in this chapter suggests that these are the most important factors behind the multicausal phenomenon. Their existence is a sufficient condition for the appearance of the shortage syndrome.

This chapter has treated the issue from both the macro and micro points of view. But one cannot ignore the fact that macro analysis is merely an analytical device of describing certain social events and processes in an aggregate form on a national scale.[34] There is no separate "macro explanation," since the processes described with the aid of aggregate indices are explicable also in terms of the way the participants in the economy behave.[35]

The various forms of macrolevel excess demand play an important role in generating both chronic shortage and the propensity to inflation [→12.5, 12.7]. But the various tendencies for demand to run away were retraced to the interests and behavior of the system's participants (the bureaucracy, and within it the managers of the state-owned firms), not to the administration's economic policy. Similarly, the attitude of the producer-seller toward the buyer on the micro level [→12.1] was seen also as a behavioral regularity. Earlier chapters showed how this interest

[34]It is worth noting a common terminological confusion: many people equate the term "macro variables" with the instrumental variables in the hands of central government. Take the example of prices. The central government can decide individual administrative prices and can also affect price development in other ways, but it does not decide the price index, average of all (state-set and spontaneous) price changes. The latter is a macro variable that is not an instrumental variable of the central government.

The government is one participant in the economic system. The macro variables are the combined attributes of the combined actions of all the participants—the government, bureaucratic apparatus, firms, nonfirm institutions, and households.

[35]This idea came to the fore in the debates on the macro theory of the capitalist economy and the micro foundations for that theory. See, for example, G. C. Harcourt, ed. (1977), R. E. Lucas and T. J. Sargent (1981), and E. S. Phelps et al. (1970).

and behavior link ultimately with the basic traits of the system: the structure of power, official ideology, bureaucratic public ownership, and dominance of bureaucratic coordination over other coordination forms.

There is no need to trace again the whole causal chain connecting chapters 3–6 with the discussion on the shortage syndrome. Just as a reminder, let me repeat that the ultimate system-specific causes are linked with the effect, the shortage syndrome, by certain intermediate, "medium-level" explanations. One such is, for instance, the interest of the firms' managers in gaining the recognition of their superiors. Others include the soft budget constraint and investment hunger. These three phenomena, with several others, form a major, direct cause of shortage, but equally they are also effects; they derived integrally from the system's deeper traits: the typical structure of power, ideology, ownership, and coordination [→15.1].

It is now time to return to the comparison of systems [→11.5–6]. The message is summed up in table 12.2, to which an explanation is added. This may also help readers find their way about the terminology used in the literature.

The two columns of the table compare the capitalist and the classical socialist systems. Each line picks out a typical dichotomy, a pair of opposing features. It needs saying beforehand that the two systems are compared with abstract clarity, so that a range of qualifications, exceptions, and atypical periods and sectors could be mentioned for both columns. In the first, for instance, one might allude to the sellers' market in a capitalist wartime economy, the widespread shortage of labor at peaks in the business cycle, or shortage phenomena in the socialized health sector. Similarly, in the second column one could point to the

TABLE 12.2
The Shortage Syndrome: A Comparison between Systems

Criterion for Comparison	Capitalism	Classical Socialism
1. Market regime	Buyers' market	Sellers' market
2. Dominant deviation from market equilibrium	Surplus	Shortage
3. State of labor allocation	Labor surplus	Labor shortage
4. Effective constraint	Demand-constrained system	Resource-constrained system (administrative quota, supply constraint, physical input constraint)

buyers' market in part of the formal and informal private sector. Rather than repeating the exceptions line by line, an attempt is made at a sharp contrast between the typical situations.

Line 1 needs no explanation, as it was discussed in detail in connection with table 11.1. A buyers' market is capitalism's typical market regime and a sellers' market classical socialism's.

According to line 2, the capitalist system is an "economy of surplus," as opposed to classical socialism's nature of a shortage economy. This comparison was made in Soviet economics as early as the 1920s. Kritsman, writing in 1925, states, "General surplus appears in a commodity-capitalist economy and general shortage in a proletarian-natural economy." In 1926, Novozhilov contrasted "general overproduction" with "general shortage."[36]

In the case of line 2 it should be noted that the two terms always denote the dominant one of the two deviations from Walrasian market equilibrium. Shortage and surplus are juxtaposed under every system [→11.1, 11.6], and the question is merely whether either of the two predominates.

Line 4 reveals which of the constraints on production and sales activity is really effective.[37] In a typical case, the capitalist system meets demand constraints on the output side and is therefore described as a demand-constrained system. The classical socialist system typically runs up against constraints on the input side. This can happen in several ways: allocation constraints through direct bureaucratic control, supply constraints on acquiring inputs, or the physical constraints of bottlenecks and input shortages in production. Bearing in mind all these constraints on the input side at once, one can employ this collective term: classical socialism is a resource-constrained system.

12.11 Economic Efficiency and Technical Progress

Having considered the phenomena and causes of shortage, it is time to look at the consequences shortage has for production and consumption.

---

[36]See L. N. Kritsman (1926) and V. V. Novozhilov (1926). T. Bauer and L. Szamuely drew my attention to these works.

Numerous economists in the Soviet Union in the 1920s concerned themselves with the theoretical analysis of shortage, but this body of writing was forgotten in the period of the Stalin terror. M. P. Afanas'ev (1990) reviews the debate.

[37]M. Kalecki drew attention to this (1970, 1972) when he made a distinction between supply-determined and demand-determined systems. Related ideas can be found in studies by R. J. Barro and H. I. Grossman (1971, 1974) and J. Goldmann and K. Kouba (1969).

These consequences, however, cannot be isolated from the effects of other phenomena discussed in earlier chapters, so a more comprehensive approach is called for. This section discusses in general terms the state of efficiency and technical development under the classical system, while the problems of consumer welfare are reserved for the following chapter.

Classical socialism, in spite of its promises, is not capable of achieving a high level of efficiency. A curious contradiction can be observed in production. On the one hand, the plans are taut, and those controlling production frequently complain that they are unable to produce the prescribed output from the input available to them. There are shortages of materials, parts, and labor. It seems as if there were a high degree of utilization of resources. On the other hand, all the international comparisons show that the utilization of resources and the proportion between input and output in production are worse under classical socialism than they are under capitalism.[38] This is demonstrated in tables 12.3, 12.4, and 12.5.[39] The productivity of labor and other factors in production

TABLE 12.3

Productivity in East and West Germany, 1983

	Productivity in Mining and Energy Production		
	East Germany	*West Germany*	*East Germany/ West Germany (percent)*
Brown coal produced per employee (tons)	2,699	5,905	0.46
Gas produced per employee (1,000 ccm)	904	2,251	0.40
Electric power produced in coal-fired paver plants per employee (MWh)	3,186	7,065	0.45

Source: Bundesministerium für Innerdeutsche Beziehungen (1987, tables 3.1–4).

[38]There is a wide range of literature concerned with intersystem comparisons of efficiency and productivity. The works by A. Bergson (1978a, 1987) and G. Ofer (1988) can be mentioned in particular.

[39]In tables 12.3, 12.4, and 12.5 the input and, in addition, in table 12.3 also the output have been measured in physical terms. That makes it possible to reduce the measurement difficulties involved in making the comparison.

Table 12.4 shows that a socialist economy uses more energy to produce the same quantity of output than a capitalist economy does. Econometric analysis in the study of J. R. Moreney (1990) supports this conclusion.

TABLE 12.4
Energy and Steel Intensity: International Comparison

	Energy Intensity in kg/Coal Equivalent Consumed per 1,000 U.S. Dollars[a] of Output[b], 1979	Steel Intensity in kg of Steel Consumed per 1,000 U.S. Dollars[a] of Output[b], 1980
Socialist countries		
East Germany	1,356	88
Poland	1,515	135
Six CMEA countries[c]	1,362	111
Capitalist countries		
France	502	42
Italy	655	79
United Kingdom	820	38
West Germany	565	52

Source: J. Winiecki (1986, p. 327).
[a]1979 U.S. dollars.
[b]The measure of output is GDP.
[c]The six CMEA countries are Bulgaria, Czechoslovakia, East Germany, Hungary, Poland, and the Soviet Union.

improves more slowly than it does under the other system [→table 9.7]. There is waste of material and energy.

What technical progress does take place under classical socialism consists almost exclusively of copying of innovations introduced in developed capitalist countries. But even this imitative technical development proceeds haphazardly.[40] Table 12.6 illustrates this general observation with an international comparison of the spread of an up-to-date metallurgical process.

The most important element in technical development is the discovery and industrial application of revolutionary new products that transform

[40]Of the vast literature on the subject, attention is drawn to the following: the comprehensive works by R. Amann, J. M. Cooper, and R. W. Davies, eds. (1977) and R. Amann and J. M. Cooper, eds. (1982, 1986), and J. S. Berliner (1976), S. Gomulka (1986), P. Hanson (1981), P. Hanson and K. Pavitt (1987), K. Z. Poznanski (1987, 1988), and A. C. Sutton (1968, 1971, 1973).

Y. Qian and C. Xu (1991) analyze the connection between innovation and a soft budget constraint with the aid of a mathematical model.

TABLE 12.5
Material Intensity: International Comparison

| | Intermediate Inputs per Unit of Gross Value Added for Years Around 1975 | | | |
	Economy[a]	Industry and Agriculture	Industry	Manufacturing
CMEA countries				
Czechoslovakia	1.43	1.65	1.67	1.73
Hungary	1.41	1.77	1.91	2.10
Poland	1.56	1.82	1.88	2.03
Yugoslavia	1.15	1.65	2.05	2.37
CMEA average	1.47	1.75	1.82	1.95
Capitalist countries				
Canada	1.07	1.21	1.32	1.70
Denmark	0.96	1.10	1.13	1.14
France	0.73	0.93	0.95	0.98
West Germany	1.12	1.45	1.46	1.51
Italy	0.93	1.24	1.40	1.40
Japan	1.12	1.60	1.77	1.85
Netherlands	1.23	1.68	1.79	1.83
Norway	1.15	1.44	1.54	1.80
Portugal	0.88	1.17	1.50	1.59
Spain	1.02	1.40	1.56	1.69
Sweden	0.98	1.20	1.28	1.37
United Kingdom	1.16	1.59	1.59	1.74
Capitalist average	1.03	1.33	1.44	1.55
CMEA average/ OECD average	1.43	1.31	1.26	1.26

Source: S. Gomulka and J. Rostowski (1988, p. 481).
[a]Defined as the material sphere of the economy.

TABLE 12.6
Continuous Casting in Steelmaking: International Comparison

	Continuous Casting per Total Production (percent)		
	1970	*1980*	*1987*
Socialist countries			
Bulgaria	0	0	10
Czechoslovakia	0	2	8
East Germany	0	14	38
Hungary	0	36	56
Poland	0	4	11
Romania	0	18	32[a]
Soviet Union	4	11	16
Capitalist countries			
France	1	41	93
Italy	4	50	90
Japan	6	59	93
Spain	12	49	67
United Kingdom	2	27	65
United States	4	20	58
West Germany	8	46	88

Source: Finansy i Statistika (Finance and Statistics, Moscow) (1988a, p. 109).
[a]1986.

production and people's way of life and consumption habits. Such innovations are for example the computer, the photocopier, synthetic fibers, and color television. Table 12.7 covers a large set of revolutionary new products that reshaped the picture of this century. There would be evidence for the superiority of the socialist system if at least a substantial proportion of these had been introduced in socialist countries first. With one or two exceptions, however, this was not the case.[41] This is one of

---

[41]Table 12.7 is concerned exclusively with innovations in civilian production. The question of whether the Soviet Union and the other socialist countries played a pioneering role in elaborating and introducing military innovations is not examined here.

Continued

the weightiest items on the negative side of the assessment of the system's performance.

There is no single explanation for the poor results with efficiency and technical progress. It is a multicausal phenomenon, among whose explanatory factors feature several connections already examined in this book. I shall briefly sum up the most important of them.

The system of rewards and penalties is weak. The owners and managers of a firm under capitalism that introduces an innovation are very likely to get vast financial gain. It is equally likely that low efficiency and technical backwardness will exact a high financial loss from them, and a very poor performance will lead to a fatal failure. These consequences are ensured not by intricate incentive schemes, but by the natural operation of the market mechanism and the market-clearing prices.

In a classical socialist economy, on the other hand, high efficiency and swift technical development does not produce a particular advantage, and a poor performance does not lead to failure. Any shortfall or waste is automatically excused in retrospect by the soft budget constraint.

Capitalism allows entrepreneurs to undertake the introduction of a new technology, a new form of organization, or a new product. They can try to carry this out through the existing organizations, but if they meet resistance, there remains the possibility of free entry; it is possible for new firms to be formed and get financing on the capital market. That is how a high proportion of the new products listed just now were introduced. The socioeconomic mechanism described by Schumpeter [1912] (1968) is an explanation of decisive importance for the dynamism of a capitalist economy.[42]

Under classical socialism, however, there is no place for new entries or enterprise driven by private interest. An initiative of any kind needs the endorsement and active support of the bureaucracy. In fact, the effect of bureaucratic coordination does not stop at making innovation next to impossible, for it also undermines the efficiency of routine, day-to-day production. Direct bureaucratic control is rigid. It is incapable of fine-tuning supply and demand, and of the millions of tiny measures that bring about an efficient combination of resources.

In any case, there is debate among experts about what the independent contribution of the socialist countries was to the development of military technology, and to what extent they relied on technical innovation of an imitative nature in this sector as well, for example, on utilizing inventions found through espionage.

[42]This idea is given strong emphasis in the analysis by P. Murrell (1990a, 1990b), which points to the lack of Schumpeterian entrepreneurs as the gravest shortcoming of both the prereform and the reformed socialist economy.

TABLE 12.7
Countries Where Major Technical Advances First Appeared:
International Survey

Product or Service	Pioneering Country	Data of Introduction
1. Information, Communication		
Components		
Transistor	USA	1947
Integrated circuit	USA	1958
LSI (large-scale integrated circuit)	USA	1968
Microprocessor	USA	1971
Optical fiber	USA	1973
Memory, storage		
MOS ROM (Read-only Memory)	USA	1967–68
Floppy disk	USA	1970
Programming languages		
FORTRAN	USA	1954
PROLOG	France	1975–79
Computers		
Electronic numerical integrator and computer (first generation)	USA	1945
Transistorized computer (second generation)	USA	1951
Integrated circuit computer (third generation)	USA	1960–70
Personal computer	USA	1975–81
Software		
Text editor	USA	1964
Computer network	USA	1981
Business, banking		
Credit card	USA	1950
Satellites		
Satellite	USSR	1957

(*continued*)

TABLE 12.7
Continued

Product or Service	Pioneering Country	Data of Introduction
Telecommunication satellite	USA	1960
Meteorological satellite	USA	1960
Geostationary satellite	USSR	1976
Television		
Videcon TV camera tube	USA	1945
Color TV	USA	1953
Video recording		
Black and white video recorder	USA	1951
Video disc	West Germany	1970
Laser video disc	Japan	1983
	The Netherlands	1983
Consumer electronics		
Quartz watch	Japan	1967
2. Energy (nuclear energy)		
Fission (nuclear) reactor to generate electricity	USA	1951
3. Materials		
Epoxy resin	USA	1947
Nonstick cooking utensil	France	1958
4. Machines and technology		
Steel and engineering		
CNC metalworking	USA	1965–69
Programmable robot	USA	1956
Assembling robot	USA	1980
Agriculture		
Plastic foil tent	Japan, France	1954
	USSR, Italy	1954
	Romania	1954
Green revolution hybrids	Mexico	ca. World War II

(*continued*)

TABLE 12.7
Continued

Product or Service	Pioneering Country	Data of Introduction
Deep freezing	USA	1950
Printing		
Computerized type-setting with laser projection	West Germany	1965
Land polaroid camera	USA	1959
Xerography	USA	1952
Laser	USSR, USA	1960
Laser printer technology	USA	1979
5. Aviation		
Supersonic aircraft	USA	1947
Passenger jet aircraft	GB	1949
6. Medicine		
Penicillin	USA	1945
Insulin (biologically produced)	USA	1982
Sabin vaccine	USA	1955
Oral contraceptive	USA	1957
Ultra-sound scanning machine	GB	1955
Use of laser for medical treatment	USA	1964
Computer tomography (CAT)	GB	1971
	USA	1974
Nuclear magnetic resonance (NMR)	USA	1981

Source: Compiled by P. Gerencsér and Á. Vészi for this book.

The situation is made even worse by the general, intensive, and chronic shortage. This causes constant hitches in production. Some input or other arrives late or runs out altogether, so reducing the efficiency with which the inputs available can be used and leading to frenzied haste and forced substitutions that are costly or detrimental to quality. Waste results from the hoarding tendency and the existence of unemployment inside the factory gates. The sellers' market eliminates the incentive of competition. It is not worth trying to cut prices, improve quality, or introduce new products in order to win buyers, because the sale is guaranteed in any case.[43]

To sum up, low efficiency and technical backwardness and conservatism can be attributed to the combined effect of a set of system-specific factors.

[43]The car industry in the capitalist countries is constantly striving to renew its assortment of products. By contrast, the Wartburg and Trabant models in East Germany and the Moskvich in the Soviet Union were manufactured for more than twenty years. But why should the East German or Soviet car factories have bothered with costly and risky innovation when customers were prepared to wait five, ten, or fifteen years even for these outdated models?

13

Consumption and Distribution

THIS chapter considers how the citizen lives under the classical socialist system. The first part of the chapter covers the average features of welfare, consumption, and economic security, while the second examines the distribution of these among the various groups in society.

13.1 The Growth of Consumption

Taking an average over a longer period, per capita real consumption tends in general to grow substantially. The result, however, is not particularly impressive compared with the consumption growth in countries developing under capitalism. Such a comparison is made more difficult because the various countries have different starting points in terms of their level of economic development. So an attempt will be made to establish how the ratio between the average real consumptions of individuals living under socialism and under capitalism changes in time.

The figures for the socialist countries given in table 13.1 have probably been distorted upward.[1] But even these figures show that over the long decades of classical socialism, the gap did not narrow but in fact increased in relation to the most rapidly developing capitalist countries.

Tables 13.2 and 13.3 provide an international comparison of living standards by showing that there are far fewer telephones, and private cars are much rarer in the Soviet Union and Eastern European countries than in European capitalist countries.

The most graphic comparison is between East and West Germany. The point of departure is roughly the same.[2] Table 13.4 contains several in-

---

[1] These figures have been affected by the same distorting factors mentioned in connection with measurement of output [→9.7]. Here, moreover, there is even more reason to suspect "cosmetic treatment" because the data on consumption have special propaganda importance.

G. E. Schroeder (1990a, 1990b) provides an account of the distortions in the official Soviet consumption time series and alternative estimates of them. In 1981–85, the final years before the Gorbachev period, one CIA estimate puts the annual average growth of real consumption at 0.7 percent; in other words, it was almost stagnating. See G. E. Schroeder (1990b, table 1).

[2] There were some initial disparities, but these do not explain the big discrepancy. The main reason is the difference between the two systems.

TABLE 13.1
Growth of Consumption: International Comparison, 1951–78

	Average Annual Rates of Growth in Real Consumption per Capita
Socialist countries	
Czechoslovakia	1.6
Hungary	2.6
Poland	2.9
Soviet Union	3.7
Capitalist countries	
France	3.9
Italy[a]	3.8
Japan[b]	6.5
United Kingdom[a]	2.1
United States	2.3

Source: G. E. Schroeder (1983, p. 315).
Note: The data refer to the growth rate of private consumption expenditure.
[a]1952–78.
[b]1953–78.

dices for comparing the material living conditions of the citizens living under the two economies. The comparison is all the more revealing because the classical system operated in East Germany right up to 1989.

The relative positions of the two systems are reflected clearly in table 13.5. For an article of consumption for which a West German citizen has worked one hour, an Eastern European has to work longer—twice, five times, or ten times as long in the case of some articles. The only exceptions are bread, and in some places tea and cigarettes.

The tables clearly display the way consumption by individuals under the classical socialist system lags behind consumption by those living under capitalism. The lag is greater in consumption growth than in production growth. That clearly results from the strategy of forced growth, in which investment is given priority over consumption. The population is compelled, without its consent being requested, to sacrifice some of its potential present consumption to investments designed to produce growth. It is quite another matter that the efficiency of investments is rather low, and in fact a faster rate of growth could be achieved even with a smaller sacrifice of consumption.

TABLE 13.2
Telephone Density: International Comparison, 1986

	Main Lines per 100 Inhabitants
Socialist countries	
Bulgaria[a]	15.1
Czechoslovakia	12.5
East Germany	9.8
Hungary	7.2
Poland	7.0
Romania[b]	6.7
Soviet Union[c]	9.0
Yugoslavia	11.6
Capitalist countries	
Cyprus	24.7
Greece	33.0
Ireland	21.2
Portugal	14.8
Spain	25.2
Turkey	5.3

Source: Compiled by P. Mihályi for this book, based on International Communications Union (1988, pp. 401–5).
[a]1983.
[b]1979.
[c]1982.

13.2 Other Factors in Material Welfare

The usual measures of material welfare—per capita real consumption, per capita consumption of various products, and so on—do not reflect adequately all the factors influencing the individual's material welfare.

The well-being of a consumer is reduced by the adjustment to supply of an original, notional buying intention, forced substitution, or abandonment of a buying intention. The sense of satisfaction if something is eventually obtained is weakened by the knowledge that the product is not what the buyer really wanted.[3] The delight of consumption is less-

---

[3]I. L. Collier (1986) made an interesting calculation of the effect of forced substitution. The question he put was what an East German citizen would pay for the right to satisfy notional demand at the prevailing prices. He measured the gap between the notional and

TABLE 13.3
Car Density: International Comparison

	Number of Cars per 1,000 Inhabitants	
	1980	*1987*
Socialist countries		
Bulgaria	56	127
Czechoslovakia	127	174
East Germany	151	209
Hungary	86	157
Poland	64	111
Romania	11	12
Soviet Union	26	44
Yugoslavia	108	129
Capitalist countries		
Austria	298	355
Denmark	271	309
Italy	302	392[a]
Japan	202	241
Norway	302	387
Netherlands	322	349
Switzerland	355	418
Spain	201	251
West Germany	388	462

Source: Z. Kapitány and L. Kállay (1980, p. 165); (1991, p. 90), and different national statistics for the capitalist countries.
   [a]1986.

ened similarly if the product or service can only be acquired after tiring queuing, a search, or even a long delay.

The loss shortage causes to consumers can sometimes be described as just a minor irritation. At other times the damage is worse, and shortage

---

real purchasing power of the East German mark as a percentage of the original consumer spending. He arrived at a discrepancy of 13 percent.

TABLE 13.4
Consumption in East and West Germany, 1970

	Consumption of East Relative to West (percent)
Endowment with consumer durables, per 100 households	
TV	93
Color TV (1973)	7
Refrigerator	66
Freezer (1973)	14
Washing machine	89
Automatic washing machine (1973)	3
Food and beverage consumption, per capita	
Meat	86
Milk	105
Cheese	46
Potato	149
Vegetables	134
Fruit	44
Tea	59
Coffee	51
Wine, champagne	29
Beer	68

Source: Consumer durables 1970: Statistisches Amt der Deutschen Demokratischen Republik (Berlin, East Germany) (1971, p. 345); Statistiches Bundesamt (Stuttgart, West Germany) (1970, p. 467). Other data: Bundesministerium für Innerdeutsche Beziehungen (1987, tables 4.3-1 and 4.3-2).

phenomena which gravely undermine the quality of life are not rare. Acute shortage of basic foodstuffs appears in certain countries and periods.[4] A shortage of telephones can wreck the lives of the elderly or sick, who cannot call for help when they need it. A housing shortage forces under one roof people who would like to live separately, damaging

[4]For instance, this occurred in Romania in the 1980s. According to the data of P. Ronnas (1990), in 1989 the per capita commercial sales in percentage of the 1980 per capita com-

their human relations and robbing them of the physical chance to lead an undisturbed private life.

Human contacts suffer damage that is statistically invisible but all the graver in human terms. Often the seller (or, in the case of a rationing system, the bureaucracy's official) is unfriendly and rude, while the buyers must grin and bear it, lest they get even worse treatment next time. The defenseless consumers frequently find themselves in demeaning situations.

With occasional exceptions, a buyers' market spares the consumer these losses. No one could say there was no price to pay for the better treatment. In setting a price on a buyers' market, the seller includes all the costs of attention to the buyer: advertising, sales teams, attractive store fittings, packaging, delivery to the door, the warehousing costs of offering a good range, back-up stocks and back-up capacity, extra staff to ensure prompt service, and so on. If not in all sectors or all geographical areas, there are many places where the buyer can choose between more expensive sales points with good service and cheaper outlets where service is less attentive. Experience reveals that a high proportion of buyers are prepared to pay the price of superiority in the buyer-seller relationship. One can only speculate on what the consumer would decide where this choice is unavailable.[5] My guess is that if there were voluntary choice, many would pay the extra costs of a buyers' market for the sake of the likely advantages.

When the purchase and consumption have taken place at last, the satisfaction is greatly reduced by the fact that there is frequently something wrong with the quality of the product or service: it does not do its job, it easily goes wrong, it soon wears out, it is out of date, its appearance is ugly, and so on. For instance, table 13.3 shows consumers under a classical socialist system receiving quantitatively less of each product or service than those living under a capitalist system. What the figures cannot express is the difference in quality. Just a few examples will be given. Far fewer individuals have telephones in the Soviet Union than in the United States or Western Europe. But those who have one have more trouble using it: it is harder to get a line, and they have to wait much longer before an international call is connected. The socialist countries are worse off than the capitalist countries not only because the housing

---

mercial sales were as follows: meat 46.6 percent, milk 74.6 percent, dairy products 47.6 percent, sugar 78.8 percent, and rice 43.6 percent (p. 15).

[5]F. L. Pryor (1977) worked out that a Soviet consumer in the 1960s spent about as many hours shopping (counting in searching and queuing) as the difference between the total hours worked by store staff in the United States and the Soviet Union. In other words, society spent the same time on consumer buying and selling in both cases. Under a seller's market regime, this time was sacrificed by the buyer, usually on top of a day's work, while in the other case it constituted the seller's paid working time.

TABLE 13.5
Work Time Required to Purchase Selected Consumer Goods: International Comparison, 1988

| Item | Unit | Hours of Work Required to Buy 1 Unit of Consumer Good (West Germany = 1) | | | | | |
		Bulgaria	Czechoslovakia	East Germany	Hungary	Poland	Soviet Union
Food							
Pork	kg	4.1	3.4	1.3	2.4	2.0	2.7
Beef	kg	5.9	3.7	1.0	2.6	1.7	3.0
Chicken	kg	5.4	4.7	2.8	3.5	2.8	5.5
Egg	piece	5.5	3.8	2.4	2.6	6.6	4.2
Milk	liter	2.7	2.0	0.5	1.8	0.7	2.9
Butter	kg	6.0	3.6	1.9	2.5	3.5	4.0
Bread (white)	kg	0.9	0.5	0.4	0.5	0.5	0.8
Sugar	kg	7.1	3.3	1.4	3.2	3.6	4.5
Potato	kg	3.7	1.1	0.3	3.2	—	1.6
Apple	kg	1.6	1.6	1.2	1.4	—	7.1

Wine	liter	2.9	5.8	0.5	2.8	10.6	13.4
Beer	liter	3.8	2.0	1.3	2.7	7.0	2.7
Coffee	kg	18.2	10.4	6.8	7.2	17.8	11.3
Tea	kg	—	3.2	1.0	0.7	0.7	2.4
Cigarettes	box	1.7	1.0	1.7	0.7	0.6	1.4
Nonfood							
Men's suit (winter)	piece	2.2	5.4	2.0	2.5	3.7	3.1
Men's shoes (leather)	pair	1.2	1.2	1.2	1.8	2.0	1.7
Motor car	piece	4.0	2.5	2.4	2.3	9.2	3.6
Color television	piece	5.3	6.6	5.6	4.0	13.4	4.6
Washing powder	kg	1.5	—	2.6	4.1	5.1	4.2
Gasoline	liter	8.1	7.0	2.6	5.7	5.0	4.0

Source: United Nations (1990a, p. 121).

area per household is smaller, but because the crowding is accompanied by further disadvantages: the standard of the buildings is much worse, and because maintenance is neglected, their condition continues to deteriorate; a high proportion of dwellings have no running water or modern sewage and heating systems. Automobiles made in the socialist countries are less reliable and less comfortable, consume more fuel, and look less attractive than cars of a similar size and performance produced in the capitalist countries.

The difference in quality can be explained by the discrepancy between the two systems. Without attempting to be exhaustive, here are some of the factors.

1. The command economy is only capable of issuing output instructions in terms of aggregate indicators; the fine distinctions of quality cannot be centrally prescribed. Thus, an adequate incentive to improve quality cannot be provided within a framework of vertical bureaucratic control.

2. Prices set under bureaucratic, central price control cannot reflect quality differences as accurately as prices determined on the market. Nor does the bureaucracy concerned with pricing try hard to make them do so. This criterion is relegated in all calculations in value terms based on the actual prices.

3. The strategy of forced growth results in priority for the quantitative growth of production even at the expense of quality.

4. In a sellers' market, the producer-seller can sell its output even though the quality of it is not faultless. In a buyers' market, quality improvement is among the methods used by producer-sellers to win buyers; this incentive-generating, coercive force is quite absent from a chronic shortage economy.

How does the population assess its own material situation? The answers depend on what chances there are for comparing their standard of living with the material conditions of the population in other countries. For a long period, the vast majority of people in the Soviet Union, China, or Mongolia were almost hermetically sealed off from the outside world: they could not travel abroad, and they could have no contacts with the few foreigners who visited their countries. They were not allowed to see a Western film or magazine that would have shown them the life of people there. Most people living under those closed systems did not become strongly dissatisfied with the level of consumption attained and its many unfavorable side-effects. They thought the hardships of their way of life were inescapable, and part of daily life in any society. They tended to feel that their position had improved since the more distant past. The acceptance of existing conditions and resignation of the prevailing material circumstances in those closed countries is one of the explanations for the robustness of the classical system.

The party-state was far less successful in isolating the peoples of Eastern Europe.[6] All comparisons with the West contributed toward the recognition that the system is incapable of ensuring the same standard of living that capitalism, the other system branded by it as inferior, provides for its citizens. So the dissatisfaction over material living conditions under the classical system was more intense in the small countries of Eastern Europe than in most parts of the Soviet Union or the Asian socialist countries. That played an important part in the fact that the reforms and revolutions started earlier in Eastern Europe.

13.3 Economic Security

Social security in the broader sense covers everything that guarantees a life without fear. That is out of the question under the classical system. Political repression prevails and breaks down all resistance, real and potential, and robs people of their basic political liberties [→3.6]. Nor is it only those who violate the prevailing laws and regulations or actually behave as enemies of the system who feel insecure, since the tyranny can strike at anyone. In that sense not even the system's own followers are safe. Particularly those who are politically active or fill an important function cannot dwell secure. The intelligentsia is pervaded by insecurity, since its very existence fills the bureaucracy with suspicion.

Let us turn now to economic security in the narrowest sense. This is the side of security that ties in closely with examination of the material standard of living. The discussion here will be concerned with those who keep well away from politics and show at least the minimal level of conformity that can save them with higher probability from political victimization. Once the classical system has been consolidated, the majority of the population falls into this category.

One major achievement of the system is to ensure basic economic security for the masses who conform to it. I shall list the basic factors in this security and at the same time note that the security is far from complete and has several shortcomings. The prototype of classical socialism considered in this description is mainly a generalization from the features of the Soviet Union and the Eastern European socialist countries, they being the societies where the system's internal tendencies developed most consistently. Far less in the way of economic security has been achieved

---

[6]This was true particularly in East Germany, where people could not be prevented from watching West German television. So all East German citizens were able to make regular comparisons of their way of life with that of their West German compatriots.

in China and other Asian and African countries at a lower level of economic development.

1. There is full employment, and what is more, a widespread shortage of labor, which applies permanently under the maturer conditions of the classical system. This is perhaps the most important factor. It frees people from the threat of unemployment, which has so oppressive an effect on workers under capitalism.

2. Public education is free. The health service is free to all in some countries and to certain classes in others.[7] Certainly, the quality of these services leaves much to be desired, but the fact that the state provides them free enhances its citizens' sense of security.

3. There is a centralized, comprehensive public pension system.[8] The level of pension is generally very low, but the fact that it is extensive, and in many countries covers the whole population, makes a further contribution to economic security.

4. According to the official ideology and the letter of the constitution, it is the state's task to provide housing.[9] In fact, housing is one of the low-priority, neglected sectors, and the housing shortage is acute [→table 11.2]. However, there are no homeless people overnight on the streets. There is a blanket duty to work, and with a place of work everyone can get shelter of some kind—if nowhere else, in a mass workers' hostel or some already crowded, multioccupied dwelling.

5. There is a welfare net to catch those incapable of fending for themselves: orphans, and the sick and old left helpless and alone. The care

[7]In the classical system free health care covers almost the whole population in the Soviet Union and the Eastern European countries. In China it only applies to employees in the state sector; the peasantry must contribute to the costs of their medical treatment, although in cases of serious illness, peasants and members of their families are entitled to numerous services free of charge.

As for the care being free, the habit of giving "gratitude money" to doctors and nurses is widespread, so that one cannot say people really have free access to the health service. But the tips are not compulsory. Those unable or unwilling to give them can still have treatment. So the statement that basic provision for the individual is guaranteed, at least on an elementary level, applies to health care as well.

[8]Here the situation resembles the one in health care. At the mature stage of socialism, all employees in the Soviet Union and Eastern Europe are entitled automatically to a pension. In China in the classical system, the centralized state pension scheme does not cover members of communes; the family and the commune have to care for the old.

[9]Under Article 44 of the Soviet constitution, "Citizens of the USSR shall have the right to housing. The right shall be ensured by the development and protection of state and social housing, the promotion of cooperative and individual housing construction, the just distribution, under social control, of housing space allocated in step with the implementation of the construction programme for comfortable dwellings, and also by low rents and low charges for communal services." Soviet constitution of 1977, quoted by B. Kotlove (1986, p. 17).

provided is not uniform, ranging from a wretched to an acceptable standard and varying between countries and periods, but on some level or other they are cared for by the state if there is no way of providing for them in a family context.

Among these basic security factors, the full employment, the overall duty to work, and the social safety net explain why there are practically no beggars under the classical socialist system. But that economic explanation must be qualified by saying there certainly would be people asking for alms from their fellow populace if begging were not prohibited by the law and the official public moral code. The ban is enforceable because the system really can ensure people the basic economic requirements of life.

But one must add that it really is only the basic material requirements that this safety net guarantees.[10] Recognition of its existence does not contradict the assertion that there is widespread poverty under the classical system: in fact, quite a few people are so disadvantaged as to be on the verge of inability to secure a basic livelihood.

6. Although crime exists, of course, public security is far tighter than in capitalist countries. This is partly connected with the factors of economic security mentioned earlier: there is less economic incentive to commit crimes. But partly this is the favorable effect of the otherwise highly depressing fact that the classical system is a totalitarian police state. Criminals have nowhere to hide. Everyone has to register with the police, even if they spend only two days in a strange place; should they fail to do so, the person providing the lodging must do it instead. Anyone discovering an offense must report it; failure to do so is punishable as well. Police spies permeate society; in addition, every apartment block or street has persons assigned by the apparatus to report all unusual events and the presence of any stranger for a longer period. Finally, sanctions are very tough on criminals caught and sentenced. Conditions in prisons and labor camps are extremely bad and in many cases unbearable.

The phenomena mentioned under points 2–5 are reflected as a whole by the distribution of total consumption between individual consumption the household pays for itself and collective consumption financed by the state budget. The problem is surveyed from various points of view in table 13.6. If one looks at the proportions of utilization of national production, there is no conspicuous difference between the systems; the European socialist countries do not prove be "welfare states" to a

---

[10]In line with the book's general approach, the developed prototype of the classical system is described. Situations different and far worse than this may arise in certain countries and periods. (Cf. the famines in the Soviet Union and China.)

TABLE 13.6

Collective Consumption: International Comparison

	Collective Consumption as a Proportion of GDP, 1976 (percent)				Divisible Public Consumption as a Proportion of Total Enlarged Consumption, 1969 (percent)[a]
	Education	Health	Welfare	Total	
Socialist countries					
Bulgaria	3.9	3.1	10.3	17.3	—
Czechoslovakia	3.9	3.8	16.3	24.0	—
East Germany	4.9	5.1	11.7	21.7	49.0
Hungary	3.4	5.3	11.6	20.3	40.0[b]
Poland	3.2	3.3	7.1	13.6	44.2
Romania	2.5	1.9	5.0	9.4	—
Soviet Union	3.7	2.6	9.3	15.6	48.9
Capitalist countries					
Austria	4.6	4.6	21.1	30.3	—
France	—	—	—	—	15.1
Italy	5.0	6.1	14.8	25.9	18.0
Switzerland	—	—	—	—	30.7
United States	5.0	2.9	11.3	19.2	—
West Germany	3.8	5.1	20.6	29.5	—

Source: Columns 1–4: F. L. Pryor (1985, p. 224). Column 5: V. Cao-Pinna and S. S. Shatalin (1979, p. 186).

[a]In the category of divisible public consumption belong all goods and services that could be distributed by market and nonmarket means as well, such as pharmaceuticals and hospital services. The total enlarged consumption is the sum of market and nonmarket consumption.

[b]Estimate for 1968.

greater extent than the capitalist countries they are compared with. But there is a very large difference in the last column. This covers the distribution of products and services that are distributable in terms of their physical characteristics, and in that respect could be allocated equally well by a bureaucratic or a market coordination mechanism. It follows clearly from the analysis so far that bureaucratic coordination is given far more emphasis under the socialist system.

That brings us to very knotty ethical problems. I pointed out earlier that the classical system scores a number of achievements in guaranteeing economic security. That is one reason why a substantial proportion of the population accepts the system and to some extent legitimizes it. But there is a concurrent dark side to all these achievements. One important component of the official ideology of classical socialism is paternalistic tutelage of the population by the party and state [→4.4]. This crops up in a number of forms, beginning with taxes and subsidies, which divert consumption away from the structure that would accord with the preferences of the public, continuing with the effect of bureaucratic rationing, and concluding with the phenomena connected with the demand for social security, which were just discussed. This kind of paternalistic state care is associated with constraints on the individual's freedom of choice, which are apparent in all of the six phenomena just mentioned.[11] The sense of security supplied by full employment and a chronic shortage of labor combines with bureaucratic constraints on the freedom to choose an occupation and a place of work; the right to work is coupled with the duty to work. Much of the paternalistic care is dispensed by the workplace, which strengthens the bonds tying the employee to his employer. Free education and health care are accompanied by compulsory assignment to a particular school, doctor, and hospital. If need be the state ensures shelter for all, but it decides who lives where and under what conditions. It cares for all the incapable, but everyone, capable and incapable alike, is caught in a state net embracing the whole of society. The solicitude follows the citizen from birth in a state hospital through a state day-nursery to a state old-people's home, and if need be, a state-supplied funeral, but this lifelong solicitude is paired with lifelong surveillance and ideological indoctrination. The police provide effective protection from criminals, but they keep an equally effective watch on innocent citizens too.

Welfare, solidarity with the weak, security within society, and individual liberty are requirements with a high intrinsic value according to the moral system of a large number of people. In many respects they are complementary—the assertion of one accords with the assertion of the others. But in several respects they come into conflict. Where that happens, it is up to everyone to decide according to his or her own scale of values which value should come first. To sum up, one can establish the following about the classical socialist system:

The system lags behind numerous capitalist countries in terms of narrowly defined material welfare, both in its pace of development and in the qualitative improvement of living conditions. The system's performance on solidarity and security is also ambivalent. Most important of all, the price of every achievement the system can claim in this respect is radical curtailment and grave, mass infringement of political, social, and economic liberties.

[11]For the ethical and political-philosophical aspects of the issue, see F. Fehér (1982).

13.4   First Approach: Distribution of Money Income

The next task is to analyze the distribution of welfare. There is a radical redistribution of wealth and income after the Communist party
takes power [→2.4]. Measured on a historical scale, the revolutionary-
transitional phase is the brief moment in which the socialist system comes
closest to applying egalitarian principles.[12]

The scope of this book does not cover the steady process of change of
the revolutionary-transitional system. Let us pass straight on to examining the mature classical socialist system.[13]

The first aspect examined is the distribution of money income among
the population. An international comparison is made in figure 13.1, using Lorenz Curves.[14] A number of indices are used to measure inequality.
Tables 13.7 and 13.8 present international comparisons of Gini Coefficients and other measures of inequality.[15] The figure and the tables show
that the distribution of money income in classical socialist economies is
more equal than it is in most capitalist countries.[16] But it must be added

---

[12]Since the confiscation of property acquired before the revolution and other redistributive regulations were mentioned earlier, here an observation is made only about the material
situation of those who come to power.

At this stage, when the revolutionaries who have advanced from illegality into the lime-
light assume power, the majority of the leading officials display puritanism. They refuse
to accept material privileges and claim only the degree of comfort absolutely necessary for
them to get on with their jobs. Lenin's very modestly furnished apartment can still be seen
in the Kremlin Museum. The new leaders' identification with the working people is even
expressed in their simplicity of dress. Mao Zedong stuck to his plain working clothes
throughout his life. In fact, the whole nation, during the years of Maoist rule, was compelled to wear clothes of the same kind.

[13]There is a wealth of writing on the subject, of which the following works can be singled
out: A. Bergson (1984), J. G. Chapman (1977, 1989), W. D. Connor (1979), and
A. McAuley (1979).

[14]The Lorenz Curve is to be understood as follows: The horizontal axis measures the
cumulative percentage of the population, and the vertical axis the percentage of total income. If the distribution of income is absolutely equal, the curve coincides with the diagonal between the two axes. The closer the curve approximates to the diagonal, the more
equal the distribution. The further it bulges downward, the greater the inequality.

[15]The Gini Coefficient is calculated as follows: the area between the Lorenz Curve and
the diagonal is divided by the total triangular area contained by the left bottom, right
bottom, and right top corners in figure 13.1. The value of the Gini Coefficient is 0 in the
case of absolute equality and 1 in the case of absolute inequality. The higher the value of
the coefficient, the greater the inequality.

The Gini Coefficients for the Lorenz Curves in figure 13.1 are found in table 13.8,
which also includes the coefficients for a few other countries.

[16]Distortion regularly occurs in calculations of the distribution of money income. On
the one hand, those with high incomes try to deny the existence of some of their income. On
the other, the statisticians never reach the very poorest, many of whom are uneducated
and cannot give a reliable account of their income. Both kinds of distortion can apply in

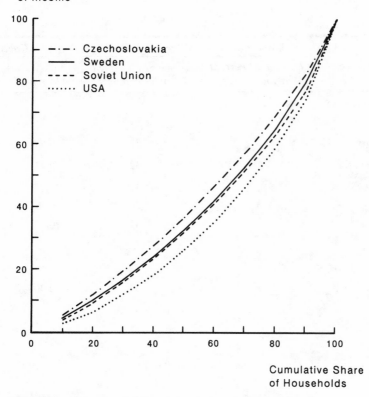

Cumulative Share of Income

- — · — · Czechoslovakia
- ——— Sweden
- — — — Soviet Union
- ········· USA

Cumulative Share of Households

FIGURE 13.1 Lorenz Curves: International Comparison
Source: C. Morrisson (1984, p. 133).
Note: The figure is based on the distribution of households, ranked according to household net income and classified in ten deciles. Income does not take into account nonmonetary income of the elite.

that the latter is not a uniform group. Taxation of a strongly redistributive nature has been applied in countries where social democratic parties governed for long periods and "welfare states" developed. That means money income after tax is far more equal there than in other capitalist countries.[17] For example, the distribution of after-tax money income in Sweden is more equal than in the Soviet Union.

---

the case of either system, although presumably more strongly under a capitalist system than under a socialist one. That presumption is based on the following line of thought:

As far as the topmost income group is concerned, their material privileges under socialist conditions tend to take forms other than money income. These are discussed in a moment. As far as the poorest are concerned, they are more tangible under the socialist system than under the capitalist one.

[17]For the capitalist countries, the basis taken is posttax income. Personal income tax is not levied in countries under classical socialism, so that this distinction plays no part in their case.

TABLE 13.7
Income Distribution: International Comparison

| | Proportion of Total Income Earned | | Gini Coefficient | |
	Poorest 40 Percent of Individuals	Richest 20 Percent of Individuals	Morrisson	Slama[a]
Socialist countries				
Bulgaria	—	—	—	0.21
Czechoslovakia (1973)	27	31	0.19	0.21
Hungary (1977)	26	32	0.21	0.25
Poland (1975)	23	37	0.27	0.22
Soviet Union (1973)	23	37	0.27	—
Yugoslavia	—	—	—	0.21
Capitalist countries				
Canada (1969)	20	37	0.30	0.39
Finland	—	—	—	0.47
France	—	—	—	0.52
Greece	—	—	—	0.38
Italy	—	—	—	0.40
Japan	—	—	—	0.42
Sweden (1970)	24	35	0.25	0.39
United Kingdom (1975)	24	35	0.25	0.34
United States (1970)	18	41	0.34	0.40
West Germany (1969)	—	—	0.32	0.39

Source: Columns 1, 2, and 3: C. Morrisson (1984, p. 133). Column 4: Sláma (1978, p. 315).
[a]The data in column 4 are for 1972–73.

13.5 The Distribution of Material Welfare: Other Manifestations

The distribution of material welfare is not fully expressed by money income. An attempt must be made to describe other manifestations of wel-

TABLE 13.8
Rural Income Inequality: China Compared to Low-Income Capitalist Countries

	Proportion of Total Income Earned		
	Poorest 40 Percent of Households	Richest 20 Percent of Households	Gini Coefficient
China (1979)	16	44	0.37
Asian capitalist countries			
Philippines (1971)	17	47	0.39
Indonesia (1976)	16	46	0.40
Thailand (1970)	14	51	0.45
Malaysia (1970)	13	52	0.48
India (1967)	13	53	0.48
Non-Asian capitalist countries			
Costa Rica (1971)	18	44	0.37
Mexico (1963)	13	55	0.48
Honduras (1967)	13	55	0.49

Source: M. Selden (1988, p. 147).
Note: The figures are the distribution of households in rural areas by total household income.

fare distribution as well.[18] Three phenomena are examined here, without any attempt at completeness.

1. *Turnover taxes and price subsidies.* Redistribution takes place not only by taxing incomes but through turnover taxes and price subsidies on the various items of consumption.

Take a simple example. The price of public transportation in the socialist countries is far lower than the real costs; the level of price subsidy is very high. Meanwhile, a high turnover tax is imposed on private cars. The thinking behind this procedure runs like this. Public transportation satisfies a basic need, whereas a car can be considered a luxury; the former is used by the poor and the latter by the rich. So this form of price subsidy and turnover tax is a redistribution in favor of the poor.

Not even in this comparatively simple example is it certain that the redistribution takes place only at the expense of the rich; at a higher level of economic development, the use of cars becomes widespread, and

[18]To avoid any misunderstanding of the line of thought, it is worth stressing that only the phenomena of welfare distribution are dealt with here. The explanation for the phenomena—the causal analysis—is discussed in section 13.6.

many people are almost obliged to use them for lack of public transport or because of the kind of job they do. And the redistributive effect of the majority of price subsidies and turnover taxes is far less clear-cut than it is in the case of cars. For instance, there are price subsidies to keep the prices of books, phonograph records, and theater, opera, and concert seats low, the idea being to make the arts accessible also to people with modest means. Yet experience shows that even when the prices are subsidized, the main customers for these services are the higher-income intelligentsia. Ultimately, the subsidies are a gift from the state to the higher-paid, rather than to the lower-paid.[19]

One flagrant example of a perverse redistributive effect is the subsidy that reduces the rent of public-sector housing.[20] The ostensible purpose of the subsidy is that everyone, including citizens on lower incomes, should be able to pay for their housing.[21] In fact, some of the housing stock is privately owned; that is the main property form in the villages and far from exceptional in the towns. These private owners have paid the full cost of building their home, and if they have sold it to someone else, the new owner has paid an unsubsidized price. In terms of income distribution, it is certainly not the case that all houseowners are rich and all state tenants poor; plenty of private owners are in low- or medium-income brackets, and the residents of state-owned housing are not confined to people on low incomes—many earn well and hold high positions. So redistribution takes place in favor of those who live in state housing and to the detriment of those in self-owned housing. Due to the income distribution of the groups given before, however, it also implies that money is effectively transferred from the pockets of relatively poor houseowners into those of relatively prosperous state tenants. Consequently, one cannot exclude the possibility that the net result of this complex redistribution is a more unequal, not a more equal, distribution of welfare. Figure 13.2 shows two Lorenz Curves referring to Hungary. One traces the distribution of money income and the other the distribution of housing. It can be seen that despite the state subsidies (or in part precisely because of them), housing is distributed less equally than money income.

The research done so far does not lead to unambiguous, general con-

---

[19]S. N. Zhuravlev (1990, p. 81) gives detailed calculations to show that although high-income households pay a greater amount of turnover tax on the items they buy than low-income households, they also receive more price subsidies, for instance, on their higher consumption of meat, fruit, and vegetables, and on the greater use they make of public transport and telecommunications.

[20]Z. Dániel's study (1985) served as a source for the analysis of the effect of housing subsidies. See also J. Ladányi (1975), I. Szelényi (1983), and M. Alexeev (1986, 1988a, 1988b).

[21]It is worth recalling the passage from the Soviet constitution quoted in note 9.

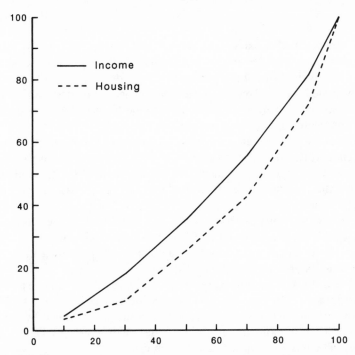

FIGURE 13.2 Distribution of Income and Housing in Hungary
Source: Z. Dániel (1985, p. 399).
Note: The income distribution data are based on the census, and the data
on the distribution of housing are based on the household statistics of the
Central Statistical Office. The unit of measurement for housing conditions of a household is the number of rooms of the dwelling, adjusted for
quality (for example, location, mode of heating, etc.).

clusions. However, fulfillment of the idea that the combination of turnover taxes and price subsidies can reduce the inequality in the distribution of material welfare certainly does not seem to be proved.

2. *Free goods and services.* In effect, this is the extreme case of price
subsidization: the state undertakes to bear the full cost of certain products and services, and dispenses them free. The problem is closely related
to the requirement of economic security [→13.3]. Providing educational
and health-care services free makes them accessible to all, at least to a
degree that satisfies basic needs, which enhances the security even of the
poorest people's lives. Supporters of this form of distribution hope also
that it will exercise an equalizing effect on the distribution of real consumption. In fact, this expectation is not consistently fulfilled. Various
inequalities intrude into the free provision of goods and services as well.

The quality of the schools and the health service is notably better in
the cities than in the villages. Employees of state-owned firms and institutions receive free vacations more frequently than members of agricultural cooperatives.

Members of the party and state apparatus are served by better-equipped, less-crowded health institutions denied to other citizens. In many places, high-ranking officials receive additional free benefits: they are provided with a free institutionally owned apartment, an official, chauffeur-driven car, and more comfortable holiday facilities than the vacation center of the average firm.[22]

Similar differences appear under all systems. What makes the phenomenon system-specific is the marked discrepancy between words and deeds. The egalitarian slogans of the socialist system's official ideology declare that everyone is entitled to the same free provision, but this is never attained.

3. *Access to goods in short supply.* In a chronic shortage economy, it makes a big difference whether everyone who is ready to pay for a good or service in short supply has an equal chance of obtaining it. In fact, such chances are very unequally dispersed.

Some of these inequalities are openly declared. There may be a rationing system, for instance, that favors specific classes in society [→12.4]. Various openly declared priorities apply in the allocation of housing or the selection of students for universities with more applicants than places. The next section deals with such cases.

The rest of the inequalities are concealed; these manifest themselves in various forms:

a. Here, in connection with shortage, the matter touched upon under point 2 above must be recalled: the network of restricted-access stores and service institutions that serve the members of the bureaucratic apparatus. These stores offer goods, such as high-quality imported industrial products, that are seldom or never available in stores open to the general public. The restricted-access restaurants and vacation facilities are more amply supplied, and guests are served foods unavailable in public restaurants, vacation centers, or food stores. Restricted-access hospitals have been mentioned already. In some countries and periods, the restricted-access network is vertically subdivided: higher-ranking officials in the bureaucracy can use stores offering a greater choice, more attractive holiday facilities, and hospitals with more modern equipment than officials of lower rank.

b. People obtain some items in short supply through their places of work, not through stores. The more severe the shortage of major food-

---

[22]Benefits of this type are given to high-ranking members of the state apparatus and firms under all systems, but the value of them under the capitalist system is insignificant by comparison with their money earnings. Under the classical socialist system, however, where money incomes are evened out to quite a large extent, these special benefits in kind become very beneficial in determining welfare differentiation.

stuffs and other articles of mass consumption becomes, the more this method of distribution is employed. The supplies to places of work are not uniform; various political and economic criteria are applied in favoring certain branches of the economy and regions of the country, and privileges are normally given to large factories.

c. Those with the right connections at the place of sale or with its superior authority can obtain items in short supply more easily.[23] This is not a question of the favored receiving the good desired more cheaply, but of him receiving it at all. For instance, it is set aside for him, or he is brought higher up the waiting list. Sometimes it is enough to be favored with information available only to a restricted group: he is told when the item in short supply will arrive in the store.[24] A great many things can help someone to obtain such special treatment: a high position, personal friendship with the salesperson, or bribery.

To sum up the conclusions from points 1–3: the real inequality that applies under classical socialism is greater than the inequality shown in figure 13.1 and tables 13.7 and 13.8.[25]

13.6   The Explanation for the Distribution

A combination of several factors explains the distribution of welfare. It would be desirable to present the phenomenon to be explained (the distribution of welfare), the explanatory factors, and the relationships among them in a precise numerical form. Unfortunately, there is no such research available. The relative weights of the explanatory factors cannot be presented in a numerical form, and one must be content with a great deal less: a list of the factors, and an attempt to assess the strength of their influence.

[23]In Eastern Europe the phenomenon is known as "socialist connections," in the Soviet Union as *blat*. In China people talk of service "by the back door."

[24]A Russian novel by the émigré writer V. Sorokin (1985), which appeared under the title *The Line,* begins with the assembly in a single square of all those who have learned through their personal connections that distribution of the serial numbers for a waiting list to buy a car will begin the next day. To repeat, they will begin to line up the next day not for cars, but for numbers on the waiting list for cars! This advance queue starts to form the previous night, and people wait in line for several days. It already counts as a privilege to have received the information as to when the distribution of waiting-list numbers will begin.

[25]C. Morrisson (1984), whose study is one source of table 13.8, gives an estimate of how the nonmoney benefits increase the inequality. For instance, the value of the Gini Coefficient calculated for the distribution of money incomes in the Soviet Union is 0.270, but when nonmoney incomes are included it is 0.309. The values of the same figures for Poland are 0.270 and 0.308.

The principal aim here is to present the real causal relationships, contrasting at certain points (if not for every factor) the distributive principles declared in the official ideology with the practice in real life. In addition, the principles will be contrasted with each other, because there are several cases where the declared values conflict with each other.[26]

1. *Work and performance.* The official ideology of classical socialism makes no promise of equality of incomes, and in fact takes issue with those who want it. Such a consistently egalitarian approach is more widespread among the New Left in the West. Under classical socialism the principle of socialist distribution stated in every textbook is, "To each according to his work."[27]

But the question remains of how performance can be measured and what the income proportionate with the performance should be. To an extent the principle of "distribution according to work" applies under capitalism as well, at least in the case of earned income. There performance is measured and rewards are set mainly (but not exclusively) by an anonymous, decentralized process: the labor market, on which the relative wages emerge.[28] Whereas in a classical socialist economy the question of what income is due for what quantity and type of work is decided arbitrarily by persons appointed to do so [→10.5]. Although those making the wage-control decisions pay some heed to the signals from the labor market when setting pay differentials, better earnings are a way of trying to attract labor to where there is a shortage.

Although the difference between the income of the top managers of firms and the average income of manual workers is sizable, it is far less than the difference in capitalist firms. Even in large firms under classical socialism the ratio is usually no greater than 5:1, whereas ratios as high as 20:1 occur in the United States.[29] This is partly explained by the different situation of the managerial labor market. Under capitalism, firms compete for the best managers; they are in short supply and can almost

---

[26]On the theory of distribution, see A. Sen (1973, 1981). On distributional principles in a socialist system, see Z. Dániel (1985).

[27]In phrasing this principle, reference is usually made to Marx's *Critique of the Gotha Program* [1875] (1966). The expression Marx actually uses is this: "The individual producer—after deductions—receives back from society precisely what he gave. What is given to him is his individual quantity of work. Unequal rights for unequal work."

Marx considers it necessary to apply this principle because the new socialist order has just been born from the womb of capitalism. Work has yet to become a basic need, as Marx predicts it will under communism. Under those conditions it is essential to have an incentive to perform, for which distribution according to work is required.

[28]The state intervenes in wage levels in several capitalist countries, for instance, by setting minimum wages. It is not this book's task to examine what mechanisms decide wages under capitalism.

[29]The Soviet ratio was around 4:1 in the 1970s. See A. Bergson (1984, pp. 1085–86).

dictate their own terms. The largest and most profitable firms outbid each other with offers of high pay. The zenith of a managerial career is to land one of the best-paying corporate positions.

The situation is quite different under classical socialism, where there is no need to entice talented managers from one post to another with high pay. Each manager belongs to the same centralized bureaucracy. Each is a soldier of the party, which decides on one's appointment, not confining itself to economic criteria in doing so. An appointment to head the very largest firm is far from the potential zenith of one's career. The road is still open to even higher posts: one may be made a minister or a county secretary of the party, or join the apparatus at party headquarters. These higher appointments are the real reward. So from the incentive point of view, there is no need for very high managerial salaries.

And there is an additional braking effect. Although the official ideology denies the principle of egalitarianism, an inclination toward leveling out of incomes can still be discerned.

2. *Political merits and positions of power.* Under the previous point, the discussion, tacitly, was of economic performance in the strict sense of the word. At least on a level of abstract analysis, another income-differentiating criterion can be distinguished from that: reward for political reliability and loyal service.

This mainly applies indirectly, through a linkage between career and politics. Those helped into high position by talent, and more importantly by unconditional service to the prevailing party policy, coupled with loyalty and discipline, enjoy continuing advantages in every dimension of material welfare, gaining the kind of privileges and connections discussed in the last section. In addition, there may be direct material recognition of political merits on different occasions, which can take a number of forms, ranging from money rewards attached to state honors and lucrative postings abroad to presentation with a plot of land or a holiday home.

This criterion is partly conceded and partly concealed in the official ideology. Its "meritocratic" aspect is acknowledged. Faithful political service to the system can be accommodated into the "work" concept contained in the principle of "distribution according to work" if the concept is stretched somewhat. The ideology prefers to hide the fact, however, that financial remuneration is being given for merits to which people should really be inspired solely for moral motives.

3. *Preferential treatment according to class, stratum, and region.* In many cases, the distribution of material welfare gives the cities an advantage over the villages, the capital over the other regions, and industrial workers over those on the land and in the services.

Particularly serious problems arise in large, multinational countries. In the Soviet Union, China, and Eastern Europe, appreciable regional differences in economic development and material welfare remain even after the system has been in power for a long time.

A part in determining the distribution of welfare in any society is played by the pressure that certain special-interest groups apply on politicians, the legislature, and the government.[30] This happens to a lesser extent under classical socialism than in parliamentary democracies, where there is more scope for organizing special-interest groups, but the phenomenon is not unknown [→3.5]. From time to time, groups championing particular occupations or regions manage to gain advantages for themselves by lobbying or political blackmail.

In many cases, this kind of discrimination conflicts with the principle described under point 1: distribution according to work. According to the practice under the classical system, individuals can receive different wages for the same work, depending on which sector or region they work in. In an efficient market economy, the mobility of capital and labor equalizes the pay for the same kind of work and the same performance to a greater extent than the classical system can, even though the latter prescribes this kind of equalization as a conscious ethical-political postulate, whereas the leveling tendency in the former results from the blind forces of the market.

4. *The need and the needy.* The classical system takes an ambivalent approach to the criterion of distribution according to need. This principle patently conflicts with the basic principle of distribution according to work sanctioned by Marx.[31] Marx postponed the application of the principle "from each according to his abilities, to each according to his needs" until the realization in the remote future of communism, the Utopian state of affairs in which people work without a material motive and the forces of production are so advanced that they can fully satisfy the needs of all [→12.4]. The pragmatically inclined official ideology tries discreetly to pass over this conspicuously Utopian concept. But there is no escaping from the tough question of the degree to which needs must be considered in the distribution of material goods, not least because certain of society's members or groups are clearly in need of assistance from the rest of society. Acknowledging that, the classical socialist system includes in its officially endorsed principles of distribution, alongside the main principle of distribution according to work, some other, auxiliary principles, based on the ethical values of solidarity and compassion for the weak.

---

[30]See M. Olson (1982) and A. Nagy (1990).

[31]In the work most often quoted in connection with distribution, *The Critique of the Gotha Program,* Marx states quite plainly that applying the principle of distribution according to work produces inequality in a certain sense, for instance, because a worker with several children personally receives less per person than a childless worker.

I turn now from description of the official ideology to analysis of the real situation. In many of their decisions about distribution, the authorities consider the size of the family, the number of a wage-earner's dependents, and decline in the ability to work. The assistance is given partly in money and partly as a benefit in kind; attention is paid to the disadvantaged in the allocation of housing, and so on. To that extent, the classical system too displays the redistributive, income-equalizing features of a welfare state, which can justly be marked down as an achievement by the system. But a number of qualifications that weaken this appreciative value judgment must be added.

One can excuse the fact that the absolute volume of all these welfare benefits is not great by pointing to the relative backwardness of the economy. But the fact that the relative proportion of public spending devoted to material support for the disadvantaged is lower than in some capitalist countries can be explained by the priorities of the growth pattern, not by the level of economic development.[32] Welfare expenditure tends to be residual in nature: it is given more emphasis in good times and pushed into the background in hard times. It was mentioned earlier in connection with economic security that poverty, and even utter destitution, continues to exist to an appreciable extent under socialism.

Throughout this book, the expression "socialist" system is used without any normative implications to denote the countries ruled by Communist parties [→1.6], but at this point it is worth suspending this definition for a moment. All over the world there are political currents that use the term "socialism" in a normative sense, attaching specific ethical principles to it. Although they interpret the value system of socialism in a number of different ways, most have a constituent in common: they see the combating of poverty and helping the needy, weak, and disadvantaged as one of the main objectives of socialism. By this definition, a socialist state has a duty to redistribute material welfare more fairly. Now measured by this yardstick, the classical socialist system just partly fulfills its mission. Some of its institutions help fulfill it, while others hinder; its policy in this respect is inconsistent and self-contradictory. For those who consider this criterion the hallmark of a socialist social system, the Scandinavian countries have made far more progress toward socialism than the socialist countries.

5. *Property and market success.* Individuals do obtain incomes under the classical socialist system through property instead of work, although the extent of them is comparatively small. Some of these are legal: here one can place the interest earned on bank deposits or from loans to the state (often forced loans). Others are tolerated by the authorities even

[32]See, for example, the data on welfare expenditures in table 13.6.

though they are not always legal: one might say this was the case with the rent from letting a privately owned house.

The private sector supplying products and services is very restricted, and part of it is illegal. The incomes earned from it depend also on several factors not covered under points 1–4 above.[33] To mention just a few: How intense is the shortage of the product or service the private enterprise supplies?[34] How clever is the owner in utilizing opportunities? To what extent are the authorities able and willing to intervene in the price the private enterprise charges the customer? All in all, one can say that the distribution of these incomes depends on market success.

The alien, hostile political and social environment in which the property and market operate pushes up the incomes of those who dare to enter the sphere after all. In an economy of chronic shortage, a peasant who takes produce not obtainable in the state-owned store to the free market obtains a higher price than would be the case if all produce were being sold on the free market. That applies even more to the black market, where the buyer must compensate the seller for the risk incurred by breaking the law. What was described just now as higher income induced by market success includes success in outwitting the authorities that restrict private transactions.

Here one of the distorted forms of high income obtained through the market mechanism needs mentioning: the private profit that often an employee in publicly owned commerce puts in his or her own pocket. Under healthy market conditions, excess demand pushes up the price and ensures the producer-seller a higher profit temporarily. The incentive of a higher profit causes the supply to grow, which then depresses the price, so that the extra earnings cease. The balancing mechanism fails to work under the conditions of a shortage economy and bureaucratic coordination. A seller bribed to supply an article in short supply to the briber does nothing, and can do nothing, to end the shortage. In fact, it would be against the seller's interest, since the shortage gives rise to the extra income. In an economic sense, this extra income can be considered a special kind of rent.

The sources of income just described are clearly alien to the socialistic principles of distribution. Even though their weight in the mass of all incomes is not great, they must be mentioned to make the survey complete. Certainly, the effect of these factors related to property and market success under classical socialism is dwarfed by the effect they have on the distribution of material welfare under the capitalist system.

[33]The word "also" is mainly justified because earnings depend also on factor 1, the work of those working in private enterprises.

[34]"Private enterprise" is used in its broadest sense. In this context it covers also a service smallholding, a private artisan working alone, and even a semilegal "moonlighter."

6. *Inheritance.* An individual's material welfare is dependent on what one has inherited from one's parents and what one's family background is. This consists partly of actual legacies and of tangible material assistance provided by the family. Fortunes of the size found under capitalism do not accumulate; in other words, the spread of legacies explains far less of the spread of current incomes, but their effect is not insignificant.

To give a single example: the distribution of housing. A young man starts out in life in a different way if he has grown up under comfortable housing conditions, his family helps him buy a privately owned apartment, or he inherits his parents' home,[35] and he does not have to wait for years for a state-owned apartment or buy or build a home of his own.

No less significant than the physical wealth inherited or received from the family is the intellectual inheritance. In terms of later life, it makes a huge difference also in the socialist countries whether a young person has grown up in a culturally backward environment or in a more educated family. The difference appears not only in the linguistic skill and intellectual training imbibed but in ambitions. Table 13.9 uses Hungarian data to demonstrate this relationship.

A person's life is also influenced by the parents' power position and place in the hierarchy. Everything described under point 2 applies to children as well as to heads of the family. "Cadres' children" stand a good chance of preference when applying for a school, university, or first job.

These circumstances and several other factors exercise an appreciable influence on social mobility. Table 13.10 compares internationally what proportion of children from working-class and peasant families become

TABLE 13.9
Aspiration to Higher Education in Hungary

Father's Level of Education	Children's Aspiration for Higher Education (at age 13, percent of sample)
University	51.5
Secondary school	40.1
Primary school	15.2
Less than the mandatory eight years of primary school	6.4

Source: M. Csákó et al. (1979, p. 124).

[35]In practice, the tenancies of state-owned apartments are inherited as well as the true property rights of privately owned housing.

TABLE 13.10
Social Mobility: International Comparison

	Manual, Nonagricultural Worker to Nonmanual Worker	Farmer to Nonmanual Worker
Socialist countries		
Bulgaria	22.6	10.1
Czechoslovakia	35.9	20.6
Hungary	27.5	10.7
Poland	27.6	10.3
Yugoslavia	26.1	17.1
Capitalist countries		
Australia	31.0	19.0
France	27.8	17.2
Italy	24.9	11.8
Norway	25.8	22.1
Sweden	29.7	17.7
West Germany	22.3	18.5

Source: W. D. Connor (1979) and sources cited therein.
Note: Studies on different countries were not conducted at the same time, but in various years.

white-collar workers. Although the socialist system declares itself to be a "workers' and peasants' state," the proportions are distributed in a not dissimilar way within the groups of socialist and capitalist countries. The upward mobility in more than one capitalist country is greater than in certain socialist countries.[36]

Clearly, this discrimination by birth and family background conflicts with the socialistic principles of distribution. Yet its marked effect on the distribution of material welfare is undeniable.

---

[36]R. Andorka (1988) describes an examination of social mobility in Hungary based on ample statistical observations, conducted in a way comparable with the numerical results of Western calculations. It was found that the establishment of the socialist system in Hungary initially made the chances of social mobility more even, but the process came to a halt at a later stage; society became more rigid, and in fact signs emerged of movement toward a closed, immobile society.

13.7   Tendencies toward Equalization and Differentiation

The factors affecting the distribution of material welfare have been listed under six main groups. Each factor has an effect that generates inequality; each contributes to the tendency toward differentiation that appears under classical socialism. So there can be no question of strict egalitarianism applying in this society.

On the other hand, there is a tendency toward equalization, whose effect is to even out incomes and compress the spread of living standards around the average. The main explanation for this tendency lies in the structure of the economy [→13.6, point 5]. Under capitalism, the dominant property form is private ownership; the main coordinator of the economic processes is the market. The range of incomes is expanded by the large incomes associated with property and market success. The material welfare of a high-ranking functionary under classical socialism may exceed by far the material welfare of a worker, but it looks tiny beside the vast wealth the most successful businessman can accumulate. The earnings of certain film directors, inventors, or sportsmen under the classical socialist system may seem large compared with the earnings of the average citizen, but they are nothing compared with the vast sums of money that similar "stars" receive in a market economy, where a high proportion of the great profits that their personal talents generate and the public will pay voluntarily goes into their own pockets.

What allows the equalizing tendency to preponderate is the almost complete liquidation of private property and the almost complete elimination of the market. In addition, ideological indoctrination clearly has an influence too. People are taught to consider an "excessively high income" immoral. Special condemnation is reserved for gains through "unearned income," "speculation," or "trafficking," and one can add here all gains in which private property and market success play a part. Influenced by official doctrine, people are inclined to lump income that would be considered in a market economy as honest profit together with income that would also be rated there as fraudulent, dishonest earnings. Suspicion and envy of higher earners, those at the upper end of the distribution scale, becomes deeply embedded in people's consciousness and emotional realm.[37]

---

[37]To some extent the officially proclaimed morality backfires, since the material privileges of the ruling elite can be condemned as well. Paltry though these are by comparison with the material advantages enjoyed by the upper stratum in a market economy based on private ownership, they fall foul of the puritanism of the official morality.

The indignation bursts forth from people when they learn, in the final phase of reforms or in the revolutions that lead to the replacement of the socialist system, of the luxury in

Of differentiation and equalization, the two mutually contradictory tendencies, the latter is the stronger. Ultimately, if one considers all dimensions of material welfare in the whole of society under the classical socialist system, the inequality is less than it is under the present capitalist system.

---

which, for example, the East German leader, Honecker, or the Romanian leader, Ceausescu, were living.

14

External Economic Relations

THE ANALYSIS of the classical socialist economy in chapters 3–13 has ignored external economic relations almost completely, apart from a few brief references. Once classical socialism has come into being (by internal effort and/or external influence) and stabilized, its basic attributes, like those of other systems, are determined by its internal features, not by its external environment. So the analysis of the various problems has rested on the simplifying assumption that a closed economy was being examined. Having reviewed the basic endogenous attributes, it is time to consider external economic relations, which may also contribute to a fuller understanding of the phenomena discussed so far.[1]

The external economic relations of all countries are greatly affected by their specific circumstances: size, level of economic development, geographical position, and natural resources. This chapter conforms to the book's approach so far in ignoring most of these differences and placing to the fore the characteristics common to all socialist countries' external economic relations. Most attention is paid to those that are specific to the system, consequent on its inner logic and so connected closely with the phenomena examined in the previous chapters. It will emerge that many important traits in external economic relations can be explained in terms of the main endogenous features discussed in chapters 3–13.

Some tables are given by way of introduction. Tables 14.1 and 14.2 show how the socialist countries' exports and imports divide up according to their main destinations and sources. Tables 14.3 and 14.4 shed light on international trade in a few major groups of products. Finally, table 14.5 uses an index of foreign-trade intensity to examine the structure of foreign trade, broken down by main groups of products and by destinations and sources. The greater the value of the intensity index above 1, the more some export or import flow exceeds the average, "normal" flow found in international trade, and vice versa.[2] Comments are made on these tables at several points later in the chapter.

---

[1] Analysis of the main features of foreign trade under the classical system is provided in E. A. Hewett (1980), F. D. Holzman (1976, 1989), A. Köves (1985, 1986), P. Murrell (1990a), P. J. D. Wiles (1968), and T. A. Wolf (1988).

Major help in writing this chapter was given by I. Szegvári and I. Salgó.

[2] Let us say that the exports of country A account for 5 percent of the world's imports. The exports of country A to country B equal the world average if country B obtains 5 percent of its imports from country A. The value of the intensity index is obtained by

TABLE 14.1

Export Structure of Socialist Countries by Main Markets

		Share by Importing Countries (percent)		
Exporting Countries		Socialist	Developed Capitalist	Developing Capitalist
Socialist countries	1938[a]	11.0	73.9	14.1
altogether	1958	69.8	19.5	9.2
	1970	59.4	24.5	16.1
	1980	47.6	33.9	18.5
from them:	1938[a]	12.7	75.0	11.0
European socialist	1958	70.6	20.8	6.9
countries[b]	1970	62.7	24.1	13.2
	1980	52.0	32.6	15.4
Asian socialist	1938[a]	3.1	69.0	28.6
countries[c]	1958	65.7	12.7	21.6
	1970	22.1	28.8	49.1
	1980	13.7	43.7	42.6
Soviet Union[d]	1958	71.8	17.5	10.7
	1970	57.8	21.2	21.0
	1980	45.3	36.1	18.6

Source: Compiled by I. Szegvári for this book, on the basis of the following sources: Központi Statisztikai Hivatal (Central Statistical Office, Budapest) (1965, pp. 172–73) and United Nations (1986b, 1:173).

[a]The data for 1938 contain the data of the countries that were socialist in 1958.

[b]Including Mongolia and excluding Yugoslavia for 1938 and 1958.

[c]For 1938 and 1958 non-CMEA member socialist countries.

[d]The Soviet Union is included in the total of European socialist countries, but its data are also shown separately.

comparing the actual proportion of the flow with the average proportion for the world. For instance, if country B obtains 15 percent of its imports from country A, instead of 5 percent, the intensity of this flow is 3.

Departures from the world average can be due to a variety of factors: the exporting country may be dumping its goods or applying political pressure on country B to buy them; alternatively, country B may be encouraging imports from A by applying a particularly favorable customs tariff. Geographical position, of course, plays an important role. In any case, if the intensity index is much greater than 1, there is "push" from the exporting country and/or "pull" from the importing country. Conversely, if the value of the intensity index is appreciably less than 1, one can assume there are barriers to the free flow of foreign trade in the exporting and/or importing country.

On the interpretation of indices of intensity and the highly informative results of examinations in which they are used, see A. Nagy (1979, 1985).

TABLE 14.2
Import Structure of Socialist Countries by Main Markets

Importing Countries		Share by Exporting Countries (percent)		
		Socialist	Developed Capitalist	Developing Capitalist
Socialist countries	1938[a]	15.6	73.6	10.8
altogether	1958	72.1	20.7	7.2
	1970	58.1	31.1	10.8
	1980	47.0	39.3	13.7
from them:	1938[a]	20.1	72.4	7.7
European socialist	1958	74.1	19.4	6.5
countries[b]	1970	62.6	27.7	9.7
	1980	51.3	35.2	13.5
Asian socialist	1938[a]	8.0	76.0	16.0
countries[c]	1958	61.6	27.0	11.0
	1970	24.4	56.5	19.1
	1980	18.6	66.2	15.2
Soviet Union[d]	1938[a]	12.5	78.6	7.5
	1958	77.4	14.9	7.7
	1970	58.6	26.2	15.2
	1980	44.7	39.4	15.9

Source: Compiled by I. Szegvári for this book on the basis of the following sources: Központi Statisztikai Hivatal (Central Statistical Office, Budapest) (1965, p.170); United Nations (1986b, 1:172).
[a]The data for 1938 contain the data of the countries that were socialist in 1958.
[b]Including Mongolia and excluding Yugoslavia for 1938 and 1958.
[c]For 1938 and 1958 non-CMEA member socialist countries.
[d]The Soviet Union is included in the total of European socialist countries, but its data are also shown separately.

14.1 The External Political Environment

One very important element in the ideology of the classical system is the notion that socialism is surrounded by enemies intent on destroying it [→4.5]. Adherents of socialism have a duty to guard against the hostile capitalist outside world and ward off its attacks. This view cannot be explained simply as a "persecution complex" from which Stalin or other leaders were suffering, since it is supported, at least in part, by actual historical experience. From the moment the Soviet Union was born, it was ringed by a hostile political environment. During the years of civil war, the forces inside the country intent on overthrowing the system received foreign backing in money, arms, and even military might. Similar

TABLE 14.3

Export Structure of Eastern European Socialist Countries by Destination and by Major Commodity Groups

		Destination: Share by Major Commodity Groups (percent)				
		Developed Capitalist Countries	Developing Capitalist Countries	Eastern European Socialist Countries	Soviet Union	Asian Socialist Countries
All food items	1970	17.8	9.0	8.7	10.7	10.7
	1980	6.0	9.0	5.5	10.1	7.7
	1987	7.9	6.7	3.8	8.1	1.8
Agricultural raw materials	1970	11.9	2.8	4.2	0.9	5.2
	1980	6.6	4.1	2.6	1.3	6.2
	1987	5.9	5.8	1.9	0.9	4.5
Ores and metals	1970	10.9	1.4	5.8	2.0	1.5
	1980	3.9	4.1	2.6	0.6	0.6
	1987	3.3	3.3	1.9	0.3	1.2
Fuels	1970	16.6	4.5	8.1	2.6	9.4
	1980	49.4	13.4	18.5	1.6	9.9
	1987	38.9	17.6	25.4	1.0	15.6
Manufactured goods	1970	36.3	57.8	67.5	82.9	69.4
	1980	26.3	51.7	62.0	83.6	67.1
	1987	34.6	45.4	58.1	87.7	57.3

Source: United Nations (1990b, p. 80).

Note: The table presents export data of all Eastern European socialist countries including the Soviet Union. In the breakdown by destination the figures in the fourth column include the import of the Soviet Union, but the Soviet import is also presented separately in the fifth column. The figures of each column do not add up to 100 percent, since there is a residual part of total export, not reported separately in the table.

TABLE 14.4
Import Structure of Eastern European Socialist Countries by Origin and by Major Commodity Groups

		Origin: Share by Major Commodity Groups (percent)				
		Developed Capitalist Countries	Developing Capitalist Countries	Eastern European Socialist Countries	Soviet Union	Asian Socialist Countries
All food items	1970	10.8	42.1	8.7	7.0	22.7
	1980	20.2	51.4	5.5	0.5	27.1
	1987	11.2	37.2	3.8	0.4	25.5
Agricultural raw materials	1970	7.0	20.6	4.2	9.1	11.8
	1980	3.9	8.7	2.6	4.4	9.5
	1987	4.2	7.1	1.9	3.0	6.6
Ores and metals	1970	3.7	9.5	5.8	12.0	8.0
	1980	3.6	6.9	2.6	4.4	11.7
	1987	2.0	5.7	1.9	2.9	10.8
Fuels	1970	1.3	2.4	8.1	15.0	0.0
	1980	1.5	22.3	18.5	40.8	0.0
	1987	1.7	15.4	25.4	52.6	2.8
Manufactured goods	1970	76.4	25.0	67.5	42.7	54.8
	1980	69.9	10.3	62.0	32.9	49.9
	1987	79.2	34.2	58.1	25.2	52.0

Source: United Nations (1990b, p. 100).

Note: The table presents import data of all Eastern European socialist countries including the Soviet Union. In the breakdown by origin the figures in the fourth column include the export of the Soviet Union, but the Soviet export is presented also separately in the fifth column. The figures of each column do not add up to 100 percent, since there is a residual part of total import, not reported separately in the table.

TABLE 14.5

Intensity of Foreign Trade According to Main Directions and Product Groups

	Primary Goods			Manufactured Goods		
	Socialist Countries	Developed Capitalist Countries	Developing Capitalist Countries	Socialist Countries	Developed Capitalist Countries	Developing Capitalist Countries
Socialist countries						
1955	7.43	0.33	0.32	8.60	0.19	0.24
1977	5.08	0.60	0.63	6.75	0.27	0.62
Developed capitalist countries						
1955	0.30	1.11	0.95	0.18	1.10	1.06
1977	0.66	1.07	0.93	0.44	1.09	1.02
Developing capitalist countries						
1955	0.26	1.04	1.24	0.25	0.81	1.53
1977	0.50	1.03	1.15	0.24	1.00	1.31

Source: A. Nagy and P. Pete (1980, p. 16).

events took place in the early history of several other socialist countries. Even after civil war and open intervention cease, there are still frequent unfriendly or hostile acts, ranging from support for internal anticommunist forces to obstruction or cessation of economic relations through blockades, embargoes, or various forms of trade discrimination.

It would be difficult even for a detailed historical analysis, country by country, to settle finally how far the fear of the capitalist outside world was induced by actual negative experience and how far such experience served simply as a pretext for use during internal political struggles.[3] All powers happily cite external perils if they are intent on curbing unrest and dissatisfaction with oppressive measures. This much seems certain: the state of affairs that came to be known as the Cold War in the years after the Second World War, but which had existed since the birth of the Soviet Union, arose from the mutual effects of political, military, and economic actions and hostile declarations by each side against the other.

To examine the situation, we can divide the outside world into groups of countries.

1. *Developed capitalist countries.* All forms of economic relations with these (exports and imports, credit transactions, use of foreign professionals, study trips, etc.) are subordinate primarily to political criteria. In the classical period, when the "siege mentality" outlined above predominates, the inevitable concomitant is isolation, which engenders a propensity to autarky. While the Soviet Union remained the only socialist country, this propensity applied exclusively to the Soviet Union itself. Later on, the Soviet Union and its allies together inclined toward isolation from the capitalist world; in other words, the propensity to autarky appeared at bloc level. This was accompanied by expansion of foreign trade within the bloc.[4]

The economic isolation is complemented by scientific and cultural isolation. Scientific, technical, and cultural relations with the West are crippled and sometimes prevented entirely by suspicion. The situation precludes a free flow not only of money, products, and capital but of experience and ideas. Only carefully selected persons may travel to the other side. This isolation is supported by the official ideology's condemnation of cosmopolitanism—"truckling" to the West—while at the same

---

[3]During the Stalin terror, the political rivals and enemies of those in power were falsely accused of being the agents of foreign secret services; they were alleged not merely to be spies but to pursue their domestic policy activities on the instructions and for the benefit of foreign powers.

[4]The proportion of exports to GDP in China during the classical period was 5 percent. When Mao's death was followed by an "opening up" (to use the Chinese reformers' term), the proportion rose rapidly to 10 percent, showing that there had been a propensity to autarky before.

time the political, economic, and cultural isolation makes life easier for
official propagandists, since it stops people comparing the actual situations, advantages, and drawbacks of socialism and capitalism at first
hand.

2. *Developing capitalist countries.* What has just been said applies
partly to relations in this sphere as well. It is worth adding that the governments of socialist countries (like those of developed capitalist countries) give strong consideration in these relations as well to their foreign
policy objectives. They are prepared to enter into economically disadvan-
tageous transactions with developing countries that they wish to support
for political or military purposes, and conversely, they are prepared to
forgo economic opportunities where political and military relations are
not being pursued.

3. *Allied socialist countries.* Here only a few observations are made
about the political background to the economic relations among the allied socialist countries. On the one hand, the official statements emphasize that they concern solidarity and mutual assistance. On the other
hand, representatives of each government try as far as possible to push
for what they consider their country's political and economic interest
demands. Other domestic and foreign policy considerations also exert a
strong influence on the allied countries' economic relations.

4. *Other socialist countries.* Conflicts among socialist countries arise
at various times, for instance, the split with Yugoslavia by the Soviet
Union and its Eastern European allies, and the later Sino-Soviet and
Sino-Vietnamese disputes. When relations are strained, each country's
government subordinates economic relations with the socialist country
with which it has a dispute to its domestic and foreign policy objectives.
If it feels it to be expedient, it scales down relations, applies an embargo,
recalls experts, or makes other reprisals.[5]

To sum up, the domestic and foreign policy of the state affect external
economic relations under any system. The system-specific feature in the
case of the socialist countries is the very great weight placed on political
considerations. They are the prime criterion for controlling the external
economic relations, and economic considerations in the narrower sense
are subordinated to them. The primacy of political considerations is well
reflected in table 14.1. This shows that the countries as a whole that
qualified as socialist in 1958 had been placing only 11 percent of their

---

[5]It is worth noting how modest the trade is between the two giant socialist countries,
the Soviet Union and China. China accounts for 1.5 percent of Soviet exports and 1.4
percent of Soviet imports, while 4 percent of China's exports and 3.3 percent of its imports
are with the Soviet Union. R. E. Feinberg, J. Echeverri-Gent, and F. Müller (1990, pp.
232–33).

exports on each other's markets in 1938, but the proportion had grown
to 69.8 percent two decades later. Clearly, the explanation for this radical
change is to be found not in their economic circumstances but in the
alteration in their domestic and foreign political situations.

14.2   The Institutional System of External Economic Relations

The description of the institutional framework for external economic relations in a socialist country begins with the institutions of foreign trade.
It is an officially declared principle of classical socialism that all kinds
of foreign trading activity are a state monopoly. Closer examination is
required to identify the organizational forms this monopoly takes.

A good starting point is to look at a state-owned production firm,
some of whose materials are imported and some of whose production is
destined for export, so that it has links with the outside world on both
the input and output sides. Under the classical system, such a firm is
strictly forbidden to have direct relations with its partners abroad. The
exclusive right to conduct import and export transactions and maintain
relations with foreign partners belongs to specialized organizations, in
most countries the foreign trade firms.[6] The choice of market for the
sale or purchase, the bargaining over prices, delivery terms, and deadlines, and in effect all the partial decisions involved in a foreign trading
transaction are the province of the foreign trade firm. The production
firm has no right to intervene in these matters, even though they will
ultimately affect its activity. This very division of rights opens a gulf
between home production and foreign markets.

Normally, each foreign trade firm has a clear profile. For instance, it
specializes in a specific product or group of products, or performs all
the foreign trading transactions for a specific production sector. Some
deal exclusively with either exports or imports. But however the operational spheres are defined, each has a monopoly in its own field. In the
legal sense, the foreign trade organizations function as firms, but as they
have full responsibility for the export and/or import of a specific group
of products, they possess many of the rights of an authority. It is far
more appropriate to consider the set of foreign trade firms as a branch
of the bureaucracy than as a group of genuine firms.

---

[6]The most widespread expression in academic writing is foreign trade organization. This
book draws a distinction under the classical system between a firm and a budgetary institution not operating under the legal category of a "firm" [→5.3, 5.4]. According to these
definitions, foreign trade organizations under classical socialism must be categorized as
firms, and that is why the expression is used for them in this book.

The division of decision-making spheres between the production and
the foreign trade firms is clearer still if one looks at prices. The price a
foreign trade firm pays a foreign seller for an import or receives from a
foreign buyer for an export is quite unrelated to the price the domestic
producer pays or receives from the foreign trade firm. Domestic prices
are normally frozen for long periods, and even if they alter from time to
time, most of the changes have nothing to do with changes in export or
import prices. Though the excuse given for a price rise in some product
on the domestic market may be a rise in the world-market price of the
imported product in question, the opposite may equally be the case: the
domestic price may be left unchanged despite a rise in the import price,
this being presented in official propaganda as one advantage of central
price control. It is a great achievement, runs the argument, that the stability of the domestic price system is unaffected by the whims of the
capitalist market.

The segregation of domestic prices from the import and export prices
paid and received on the foreign market relates closely to the absence of
a uniform rate of exchange between the domestic currency and each foreign currency. Nominally, an official exchange rate is set for each foreign
currency, which might give the impression that it is invariably applied.
But, in fact, this exchange rate is modified by various multipliers (greater
or lesser than 1). These multipliers vary from country to country and
period to period, but in all countries and periods there is a wide dispersal
of them according to the foreign market and product concerned.

A further influence on the effective conversion accompanying a foreign trade transaction comes from taxes and subsidies. A tangle of taxes,
tariffs, tax and tariff concessions, and temporary and permanent subsidies intervenes between the price paid or received on a foreign market
and the price at home.[7] Ultimately, there is no way of telling what a ruble
is worth in dollars. The domestic cost of earning a dollar by one export
transaction may be thirty kopeks and by another four rubles. It is a secondary matter of financial technicality what specifically caused the discrepancy between the two conversion rates in the example: different
exchange-rate multipliers, different positive or negative tax rates, or perhaps a combination of both. The essential feature is the almost complete
divorce of the domestic price of the product constituting an item of foreign trade from its price abroad.[8]

[7]The tariff system is not discussed separately, because it does not have an appreciable
separate role. It is one financial bridge built between the price of a product and its cost,
alongside the other bridges (taxation and subsidization).

[8]In any case, even if the link between external and domestic prices were closer, the state-
owned firm's price responsiveness would still be weak. In other words, it would not react
strongly to the price changes on foreign markets.

The divorce is both an effect of the tangle of taxes and subsidies and a cause of it. To continue the previous example, suppose that the import price of a material has risen and the price authority, on the initiative of the foreign trade firm, has raised the domestic price of the material. That raises the user firm's production costs. On such occasions the production firm feels it should be compensated for its losses, as it can claim they arose through no fault of its own. Some method of softening the budget constraint is used; the firm may be allowed to pass on the rise in cost by raising its selling price, for instance, or it may be rescued financially in some other way.

The situation just described explains the futility of any foreign exchange rate policy. In a capitalist market economy, the government seeks to affect the trade and current-account balances primarily by influencing the foreign exchange rates, or in certain countries by central control. The usual course taken if the debt is considered too high is to devalue the domestic currency, whose effect will sooner or later contribute to the reduction of imports and to the increase of exports. In a classical socialist economy this method fails to work because of weak cost- and price-responsiveness. Whichever way the exchange rate moves, the effect is absorbed by the web of taxes and subsidies and the softness of the budget constraint. Should the economic leadership under the classical system decide they want to reduce imports and raise exports on any market whatever, their only method available is direct bureaucratic control. They reduce the import quotas drastically and force exports by curtailing domestic demand for both consumer and intermediate goods more strongly than ever.[9] If the authorities manage to manipulate the trade and current account balances at all, it is only by bureaucratic means.

Mention has been made in connection with foreign exchange rates of financial relations with foreign countries. They now need examining more closely. Currency is not convertible under classical socialism, in other words, domestic currency cannot be converted freely into foreign currency. Foreign exchange transactions are strictly controlled; those possessing foreign currency are obliged to sell it to the "monobank."[10] Every conversion is made at a set exchange rate laid down by the central authorities.

The foreign exchange manager is the central bank. It may assign specific task-areas to some formally separate institution or other, for example, foreign trade financing to the state foreign trade bank, or tourist

---

[9]A clear example of this phenomenon is the Romanian foreign trade policy in the 1980s.

[10]Private individuals can only buy convertible currency within strict limits by special permission. The chance to do so is among the major privileges used to reward certain persons or groups.

foreign exchange transactions to the bank supplying credit to the general public. But these institutions are really arms of the monobank [→8.1]. In that sense, all kinds of financial relations with foreign countries are strictly centralized. The existence of the foreign trade firms and their monopoly over all foreign trading activities constitutes the first layer of insulation from foreign influence around domestic production. This layer is surrounded then by another insulator: not even the foreign trading apparatus has independent control over the financial relations of the foreign trade firms, as all financial transactions are conducted by the organizationally separate and very powerful monobank system, or the banking system's permission is needed for every transaction. This apparatus is known as a bank, but in fact it is the bureaucracy's foreign exchange authority, not a real bank performing business services at all.

What has been said so far demonstrates that the external economic activity of a classical socialist economy is controlled by bureaucratic, not market, coordination. The official idea is that the foreign trade and international finance sector should be in a similar position to the other sectors, operating according to the same principles of planning and bureaucratic management and using the same methods as the sector of production [→7]. The indicators for foreign trade and international financial relations make up one chapter of the plan and must be enforced through commands given to the foreign trade firms, to the other firms involved in exports and imports as producers and users, and to the banking system. But in real life a contradictory situation arises. Although the foreign trading sphere bears the mark of bureaucratic coordination and to that extent resembles the other spheres, it is out of line with them. It has been seen what a range of problems derive from elimination of the market and reliance on bureaucratic coordination even when the economy is assumed to be closed. The contradictions are compounded in this sphere, where the course of events depends to a large extent on the foreign partner. The foreign buyer, seller, and bank are under no obligation to take orders from the domestic planning office or ministry, and they cannot be prosecuted for flouting plan discipline. Understandably in the circumstances, there develops a system of institutions that artificially places several layers of insulation from the foreign market around domestic production. It does so for at least two reasons: because of the political considerations mentioned in the previous section, and because they shield the internal system of the command economy from the disturbances of the outside world.

In no part of the system is there a perfect hierarchy [→6.3]. All subordinates have more than one superior organization above them. This overlapping and often mutually contradictory intervention by the various branches of the bureaucracy is particularly conspicuous in the case of foreign trading. The responsibility falls primarily on the ministry of foreign trade, but the party apparatus, ministry of foreign affairs, the police and military organizations monitoring foreign relations, the foreign exchange authorities, the ministries controlling production, and the taxation, customs and price-control authorities all have a say as well. Clever managers of firms soon learn to maneuver among all these authorities, for instance, by winning the support of one when there are problems with another. Often a single decision is preceded by lengthy negotiations among the authorities concerned. More attention is paid to bargaining within the bureaucracy than with the foreign buyer, seller, or bank. The complication and lengthiness of the decision making exacerbates the inflexibility of foreign trading and credit activity. It is more important for the producer and foreign trade firm for a transaction to win the approval of the superior organizations than for it to leave a foreign customer satisfied, or for an export or import deal to make the maximum financial profit. The production sector is not obliged, let alone encouraged, to adjust flexibly and speedily to the situation on foreign markets. Foreign trade is a sphere that demands particularly subtle, speedy, and accurate adjustment even to shades of change. The only system capable of it is market coordination, which reacts sensitively to prices. The required fine tuning cannot be done with the sluggish, cumbersome range of methods available to direct bureaucratic coordination.

Despite the built-in fenders and layers of insulation, the unplanned changes taking place on foreign markets do have an influence on economic activities at home, and they often upset the plans and prevent them being applied. Ultimately, one cannot ignore the foreign partner's willingness or unwillingness to sell the products the country wants to buy, buy what it wants to sell, or extend credit. So some adaptation to external markets takes place, albeit after long delays and at the cost of many kinds of losses.

14.3 Capitalist Relations: Import Hunger, Export Aversion, and Propensity to Indebtedness

The two parallel sections that follow describe the participants' behavior and economic trends in foreign trade and financial relations, first with capitalist countries and then with other socialist countries. In the case of relations with capitalist countries, the discussion is narrowed down and some simplifications are made for reasons of space.

Attention is paid exclusively to transactions in convertible currencies (popularly known as hard currencies), which can be freely exchanged into other currencies. For simplicity's sake, "foreign trade for convertible (hard) currency" and "foreign trade with capitalist countries" are taken as synonyms in this section.[11]

In fact, there is no justification for treating trade with the capitalist countries as a single aggregate, since the political distinctions mentioned earlier, along with the capitalist partner-country's economic development and closely related technical level all have a part to play. Any importer knows the difference, for instance, between machines obtained from highly developed and more backward capitalist countries, just as an exporter feels a difference between a more highly developed country's demands on the product he offers and those of a less developed country. For space reasons, these differences are only mentioned occasionally.

1. *Imports.* One integral element of investment hunger [→9.1] and the hoarding tendency [→11.5, 12.7] is *import hunger,* particularly hunger for products from developed capitalist countries.[12]

Everyone hungry for investment, from the highest leaders down to factory foremen, long above all to obtain top-quality, up-to-date machines and equipment. Engineers who keep an eye on professional studies abroad and visit modern factories on study trips have good arguments to back their applications. The demand for up-to-date machines and equipment from developed capitalist countries is fueled by professional ambition, by endeavors to modernize, and by a desire for the smoother production that a reliable, trustworthy stock of machinery provides. This tendency is illustrated by table 14.6, which shows that the smaller European socialist countries import three times as many investment goods from the developed capitalist countries as they can export to them, and the Soviet Union imports twenty times as many.

Imports are also encouraged by chronic shortage. A customary, normal intensity of shortage develops in production inputs and consumer articles alike. If there is a bigger shortage than normal in some product or other, the handiest and quickest way of obtaining a substitute is to import it from a capitalist country.[13] Planners (or, in extremely urgent

[11]In fact, these are not accurately overlapping categories for several reasons. For instance, in trade between a socialist and a capitalist country barter deals occur, in which one consignment of goods compensates for another, so that payment in money is avoided; part of the trade between socialist countries is settled in convertible currency. However, the overlap is sufficiently large. The conceptual discrepancies do not interfere with the presentation of the tendencies discussed in this section.

[12]In the case of differentiated products, import hunger appears mainly in the demand for products from the developed countries, because they are likely to be of a high technical standard and a reliable quality. The distinction does not appear sharply in the case of foodstuffs, raw materials, and standardized products in general. In any case, the main suppliers of many agricultural commodities and raw materials are developing countries.

[13]The Soviet Union, for example, has imported huge amounts of grain and other foodstuffs, depending on the size of its own harvests.

TABLE 14.6
East–West Investment Goods Trade

	OECD Countries[a]: Export–Import Ratios with Socialist Countries			
	1971–75	*1976–80*	*1981–85*	*1986–87*
Bulgaria	9.5	7.3	13.2	17.8
Czechoslovakia	2.5	2.9	2.5	3.3
East Germany[b]	1.5	1.6	1.6	2.0
Hungary	5.4	4.5	3.7	3.9
Poland	6.1	3.7	2.3	2.8
Romania	7.8	5.1	1.5	1.4
Total Eastern Europe[c]	4.3	3.5	2.7	3.2
Soviet Union	13.4	20.3	28.5	20.2

Source: United Nations (1989, pp. 76–78).
[a]The Organization for Economic Co-operation and Development (OECD) was set up in 1960. At present twenty-four developed capitalist countries are members of OECD: nineteen European countries, Australia, Canada, Japan, New Zealand, and the United States.
[b]Excludes estimates of trade between East and West Germany.
[c]Regional aggregation calculated by the ECE secretariat, based on 1985 U.S. dollar weights.

cases, managers) do not consider whether the substitution of domestic production with imports will be profitable. The process takes place as a reaction to nonprice signals, not on the basis of price and cost signals.[14]

Of course, the top political and economic organizations, the party's Political Committee, the prime minister, and the head of the central bank are not indifferent to the total costs of imports, or ultimately to the balance of trade and the balance on the current account. In fact, they consider these one of their greatest concerns. But as in the cases of other problems of choice (see the decision on the proportions of consumption and accumulation [→9.3]), they cannot decentralize their problems by delegating them to lower levels of the hierarchy and ultimately to the producing firms. It is in the interest of everyone except those at the peak of the pyramid for capitalist imports to be as large as possible; there is

---

[14]Several socialist countries lay down that foreign trade efficiency calculations should be made to see whether it pays to substitute imports for domestic production or raise domestic production for export purposes. The calculations, however, have little effect on decision making. Often they are cooked so as to back up a decision taken already.

no internal inducement to limit the demand voluntarily. This situation makes direct control of import inevitable: the imposition of strict import quotas and the practice of requiring a special permit for each transaction. So there is a reciprocal effect: import hunger is one factor behind bureaucratic control, while bureaucratic control enhances import hunger, since each user tries to maximize his quota during the plan bargaining and build stocks of imports from the capitalist market.[15]

2. *Exports.* Here quite the opposite behavior is found. Whereas a hunger for capitalist imports appears spontaneously at every level in the hierarchy, no voluntary enthusiasm emerges for exporting to capitalist markets.[16] Why bother one's head with foreign buyers when one has at home a comfortable sellers' market in which queuing buyers are prepared to fit in with the seller? The more developed the country whose market is targeted, the more demanding the importer there will be about quality and delivery deadlines.[17] A private firm competing with its rivals in a capitalist economy is delighted to find a foreign market. Not so a state-owned firm under classical socialism, which is reluctant to export to a capitalist market and shows an *export aversion* that its superior organizations must combat with administrative compulsion. The practice of forcing export develops. Fulfillment of export assignments becomes one of the compulsory requirements of the plan, in fact, one of the top priorities on the list of planning instructions.

A foreign trade firm from a socialist country entering a capitalist market finds itself in a buyers' market. It is struck by the wealth and variety of the goods on offer, which enhances its appetite for imports. Meanwhile, it cannot compete on the market as an exporter with the domestic and foreign capitalist firms in terms of quality, modernity, or reliable delivery.[18] An economic system cannot have two completely different

[15]Import restriction is explained primarily by the statements above, rather than by a protectionist desire to defend a socialist country's domestic industry. Domestic producers are protected sufficiently by the sellers' market regime.

[16]Even in the most isolationist socialist country, Albania, the long-time leader, Enver Hoxha, had to admonish his people: "In the present situation, the tendency to expect everything from abroad must be sternly combatted. It is our duty to utilize all our possibilities and resources, relying on our own capacities and forces to produce as much equipment, spare parts and machinery as possible at home, and thus cut down imports of them. Besides this, we should take all-round measures to increase exports, to extend the range and to improve the quality of the goods we bring out. It should be clear to everyone that in order to import, it is necessary to export." E. Hoxha (1975, p. 10).

[17]M. Mejstrik (1984, p. 75) concludes from an examination of Czechoslovak product characteristics that only about 2 percent met the world technological standards in the late 1970s.

[18]The difficulties may be compounded by isolationism on the part of the capitalist country, for general protectionist purposes and/or as a manifestation of political discrimination.

faces, one pointing to the sellers' market at home and the other to the buyers' market abroad. If there is a sellers' market at home, it gets used to dictating to the buyer and does not care about quality requirements.[19] This kind of sluggishness and nonchalance necessarily makes itself felt in production for export as well. So long as the country's domestic economy lacks the stimuli that oblige firms to improve quality, develop technically, supply quickly and reliably, and adapt to buyers' requirements, it will always encounter grave difficulties with exporting for hard currency.

Under the circumstances, the only means for increasing the attraction of the products is price reduction, or in the last resort dumping. Many goods of poor quality can be sold for convertible currency if the price is lowered enough. This is often done, although it may not be apparent to the foreign buyer. A curious negative price-elasticity of export supply develops. Since the socialist country's purpose is to obtain a certain amount of foreign currency required to pay for its imports, the following relation applies when the export plan is set: a greater volume must be exported if the attainable export price is lower, but if it is higher, a smaller export volume will suffice.[20] In any case, the price-setting process is rendered impenetrable by the web of taxes, tariffs, and subsidies mentioned before. The public, and often the economic leadership, have no idea what domestic sacrifice is involved in obtaining a dollar or a pound. They do not know how much more cheaply a product is sold compared with the price offered by foreign competitors. Nor do they know how much domestic input went into making it.

The interest, social environment, and behavior of those handling import and export transactions largely explain the economic tendencies presented in tables 14.3 and 14.4.[21]

3. *The trade and current-account balance.* As shown earlier, the economic bureaucracy at every level, including the management of production firms, is interested in importing as much as possible from the capi-

---

[19]A counterexample often put forward is arms exports, which are successful on the capitalist market as well. It cannot, however, be considered a refutation of the argument just put forward. Both at home and abroad, arms sales do not take place on a sellers' market: the army, as buyer, has enough power to impose a buyers' market along with its accompanying quality conditions. See C. Davis (1990).

[20]On dumping and negative elasticity of supply, see F. D. Holzman (1976, 1983) and J. Winiecki (1984).

[21]I mention just a few remarkable tendencies. The proportion of machinery in the socialist countries' exports falls and the proportion of energy sources rises. It must be added that machinery exports are dominated by sales among the socialist countries. A comparatively small number of machines from socialist countries are bought by capitalist countries, particularly developed ones.

talist market. The opposite side has also been shown: the difficulties a socialist country encounters when it wants to export to a capitalist market.[22] The result is clear: a strong tendency for import expenditure to exceed export earnings.

Direct import of capital, that is, business investment by capitalist firms in the socialist country, is, with a few exceptions, forbidden. This follows logically from the politically motivated isolationism discussed at the beginning of the chapter. So the foreign trade deficit can only be covered by loans, extended by the exporting capitalist firms or by banks, covered in certain cases by government guarantees. An *inclination to indebtedness* thus emerges in relations with capitalist countries.

The economic leadership under classical socialism behaves ambivalently. On the one hand, it is hard for them to resist, as great pressure is on them to increase imports and it is tempting to solve easily some of the problems in the short term by using hard currency credit. On the other hand, the political considerations discussed in section 14.1 argue strongly against indebtedness, which arouses a perhaps exaggerated but not groundless sense of the peril of dependence. Which of the two influences is stronger, and by how much, varies by country and period.[23]

Even where the temptation to raise credit is opposed energetically, considerations relating to the balance on the current account play a very strong part in the management of the economy. An indebted country is forced to improve its current-account balance by the continual need to service its debt (its obligation to pay the interest and repayments that fall due) and its intentions of reducing its stock of debt. A country that has not got into debt would usually like to accumulate some hard-currency reserves.

On the basis of the line of argument here, it becomes comprehensible why the classical socialist system is always turning to import substitution as a means of improving the trade and current-account balance instead of successfully developing exports. Import substitution can be decreed by bureaucratic means. In the short term one simply has to ban certain import transactions and prescribe the use of certain domestic manufactures. In the long term, the same bureaucratic means must be used to prescribe the kind of domestic investments that will substitute for imports in the future. Moreover, this ties in well with the political objectives of isolation and the strategy of autarky. On the other hand, there is no

---

[22]Tourism is an appreciable supplement to earnings from exports of goods in many capitalist countries. This opportunity is severely curtailed under the classical socialist system by the policy of isolation. Nor can the neglected service sector make any appreciable contribution to exports.

[23]The data on foreign debt are presented in table 23.7.

way of ensuring the success of hard-currency exports by giving instructions. At most, direct bureaucratic control can press for them, and success is doubtful.

The subject of forced exporting leads, by the way, to one of the vicious circles that develop in a chronic shortage economy. Domestic shortage and tensions arouse import hunger. To compensate for the imports (and pay back the debts that mount up as a consequence of the imports), as much hard currency as possible must be obtained at all costs. As pointed out earlier, there are plenty of goods for which buyers can be found if the price is cut far enough. In that situation the foreign trading sector's demand for products salable on capitalist markets is almost insatiable. Since the sector appears on the domestic market as a buyer of these goods, it is practically insensitive to their domestic costs and prices. However high the domestic cost and price, the gap between the domestic and the foreign price can be bridged by some technique for softening the budget constraint. So, understandably, the almost insatiable demand for exports is among the forces that cause the chronic excess demand on the macro level [→12.7]. The forcing of exports for the capitalist market becomes one of the factors inducing the chronic shortage.

14.4   Socialist Relations: Tie-Ins, Export Preferences, and the Pursuit of a Zero Balance

Imports and exports. To begin with, a distinction is usually drawn between *hard* and *soft goods.* Such "hardness" or "softness" is not a constant, general feature of the good concerned. It is always an attribute applying only for a specific period in a specific relation between two countries. Whether the article forming the subject of negotiation is hard or soft depends on the prevailing circumstances in the two countries. In negotiating with the administration of the buyer country, the administration of the seller country considers a good it has produced to be hard if (1) it could be sold without much trouble on a capitalist market for hard currency, or (2) the buyer country's current domestic economic situation is such that the good concerned is badly needed, cannot be acquired from any other socialist country, and is only obtainable, if at all, on a capitalist market for hard currency at a cost of great difficulty and sacrifice. The two criteria often coincide, but not always. Say, for example, a seller country is negotiating a food export. Protectionist barriers may make it difficult to sell for hard currency, but if the buyer country is suffering from a grave food shortage and its leaders know they would have to pay hard currency on the capitalist market for the foodstuff they require to make up the shortage, the seller country's food export is "hardened" by the importing country's need.

A good is soft if there is a surplus of it in the seller country (which is therefore compelled to export it) and it would be impossible or very difficult to sell it on the capitalist market. A good is also soft if the potential socialist buyer-country can do without it comparatively easily.

The concepts having been clarified, the first question to address is the kind of behavior representatives of the government of a classical socialist system display when they negotiate an intergovernmental agreement prescribing the quantity and composition of exports and imports with a representative of another socialist country. (The subject here is the behavior of officials high in the economic or foreign trade hierarchy. The behavior of lower-level officials is covered later.)

Starting to negotiate, the government representatives look on their own country's hard export goods as their bargaining chips.[24] By offering them they want to achieve a number of things: (1) to obtain as much of their partner's hard goods as possible; (2) to sell as much of their own soft goods as possible; and (3) to accept as little of their partner's soft goods as possible.[25] When all is said and done, the negotiations are not primarily about the price at which the deal is made, although that plays a part as well. Much more prominent is the question of what the "basket" of goods exchanged between the two countries should contain. What proportion of hard and soft goods should there be in the basket? The more of their country's soft goods the representatives manage to pass off on their opposite numbers and the less of the other country's soft goods they are obliged to accept, the more successful they rate the negotiations. Ultimately, the process taking place at governmental level is the one known in commerce as tying in.

It is worth returning for a moment to what was said in the last two chapters about the concurrent appearance of shortage and surplus on the domestic market, since the above statements provide an additional explanation for this phenomenon. While there is a shortage of hard goods, there are unsold stocks of soft goods: the country has been unable to get rid of its own surplus at the foreign trade negotiations, and it may

[24]Some of the hard goods are sold by the producer country to the country in need of them for convertible currency.

[25]Of course, in this case as well, the duality of "hardness" and "softness" is used for the sake of clarification. In fact, the phenomenon can be also measured on a continuous scale. Although most of the machines qualify as soft goods, the machines from the industrially more developed countries, like East Germany and Czechoslovakia, in most cases are much harder goods than those from the less developed ones. Moreover, there can be differences in the quality of different products produced by the same sector within a given country.

even have been forced to accept some of its partner's soft goods as the only way of obtaining the partner's hard goods.

Let us now look at the behavior on the middle and lower levels of the hierarchy, beginning with the producer firm. The buyer country is short of hard goods, which means it cannot make tough demands about quantity, modernity, and delivery dates. It is therefore relatively easy for the producer to make goods which are considered hard by socialist trading partners. Similarly, it is relatively easy for the foreign trade firm in charge of exports to sell such goods on the socialist market. With soft goods the position is rather different, as it is not easy to squeeze acceptance of them into the intergovernmental agreement. But once the importing country has undertaken to accept them, neither the producer nor the foreign trade firm has any more problems here either. Apart from the lack of discrimination about quality, there is another advantage to the producer and the foreign trade firm: the long period that intergovernmental agreements cover, which increases their sense of security. Another advantage for the state-owned producer firm is the knowledge that it faces a sellers' market in the importing socialist economy.[26]

For all these reasons, behavior toward the socialist external market resembles, in part, behavior toward the capitalist external market and is partly the opposite of it. There is import hunger for the hard goods, but there is also import aversion to the soft goods. In general, there is no aversion on the export side; on the contrary, the lower levels of the production and foreign trading bureaucracy expressly prefer the comfort and security of socialist to capitalist markets.

There are presumably more hard products among the materials than among the manufactures. If this assumption is right, the effect of the tendency outlined above is reflected in table 14.5. The intensity of the flow of manufactures among socialist countries is very high. In addition, the intensity of trade in manufactures between the socialist countries is higher than the intensity of their exports of manufactures to capitalist countries. Among the other conclusions to be drawn from these differences in the intensity indices is that the socialist countries are able to

---

[26]The intensity of shortage is not the same in all of the socialist countries. The more intense the shortage is (and the graver the imbalance on the current account in convertible currency), the more the country needs imports from the other socialist countries. The governments of the exporting countries may feel reluctant to export to a country that is in a bad economic situation and hardly capable of supplying anything in exchange. However, for the producer firm—from the point of view of its own interest—it is a very reassuring feeling that for whatever it produces there will eventually be a buyer in need to purchase it. The effects of the domestic shortage economy are reinforced by the sellers' market on international scale.

impose their manufactures on each other, whereas their exports of them to capitalist markets remain far below the normal export proportions.

At this point let me diverge for a moment. Some writers on socialist foreign trade raise the question of which country exploits the other. Is there a concealed levy or subsidy in the foreign trading relations between them?[27] This book takes no position on this debate. Noteworthy though the question is, it is concerned in the last resort with a specific problem of redistribution over a set of socialist countries. Here the issue is who does comparatively well and who does less well out of a particular transaction. The trouble is that this is not a zero-sum game, one side winning as much as the other loses. Why is the efficiency of production and foreign trading low in both countries? Because the internal system of both operates at low efficiency.[28] Above all, by conducting the bulk of their foreign trade among themselves, the socialist countries rob themselves and each other of the incentive force and imperative to qualitative development of their economies which the high quality standards of the external market could provide.

Balance of trade and of the current account. In the absence of convertibility, a deficit in one bilateral relation cannot be set against a surplus in another bilateral relation.

If one disregards certain exceptions (which are mentioned in a moment), socialist countries do not invest in each other's economies. So the balance on the current account depends very largely on the balance of trade. And as a surplus cannot be converted on another market, no country likes its surplus to rise too much or its total lending to grow. The result is a specific tendency: the pursuit of a zero balance. A bilateral relation should produce neither a lasting surplus nor a lasting deficit.

Clearly, from what has been said, the socialist external market differs from its capitalist equivalent in that the behavior of the participants in it does not lead expressly to forced exporting in this relation. The superior authorities force an export only when the economy greatly needs a hard import likely to be the specific offset for the export in question, or where

[27]The study by M. Marrese and J. Vanous (1983) argued that the Soviet Union was a net exporter of hard goods at prices less than prevailing world market prices and a net importer of soft goods at prices greater than world market prices. It engaged in this kind of subsidization in order to maintain political dominance in the region. This proposition was criticized by J. C. Brada (1985), F. D. Holzman (1986a, 1986b), and A. Köves (1983).

[28]Soviet importers were justifiably disappointed that the Soviet Union was often obliged by its intergovernmental contracts to buy soft goods from Hungary, including many poor-quality products. At the same time, the Hungarian exporters bitterly complained, arguing they were forced by the same contracts to produce technically obsolete products. For instance, the underdeveloped telephone network in Soviet villages could use only substations compatible with the existing out-of-date equipment.

the government has undertaken under an international treaty an obligation it wants to fulfill at all costs, because of foreign pressure to do so or for some other political reason. Where one of these considerations applies, it adds to the forces inducing forced exporting.

Finally, there is a common conclusion to be drawn from sections 14.1 and 14.2. Let us return to tables 14.1 and 14.2. As mentioned earlier, the main explanation for the high proportion of the socialist countries' turnover among themselves is clearly not that trade with the former was manifestly more favorable in terms of macroeconomic or technical development. The decisive factors were the political considerations, namely, the desire for isolation from capitalism. Once the external economic relations with socialist partners have emerged and congealed, however, the continuance of these proportions is reinforced, at least on the export side, because in many ways the relations are comfortable and reassuring to the economic bureaucracy and the management of production firms.

14.5   An Attempt at Integration: The Council of Mutual Economic Assistance

All the phenomena introduced so far in this chapter leave their impression on the socialist countries' attempt at integration. A return must be made to the ideological antecedents before the practical experience is considered.

The classics of socialist thinking proclaim the idea of internationalism. Ever since the *Communist Manifesto* of Marx and Engels, "Workers of the world, unite!" has been one of the main slogans of the socialist movement. Before history produced a situation in which several socialist countries, segregated in national states, try to build economic relations with each other, many people hoped that the significance of national frontiers would decline and a supranational socialist economic community would emerge.

The hopes have remained unfulfilled in practice. Only one major, tangible step has been attempted up to now toward creating an economic integration of several socialist countries: the establishment and operation of the Council of Mutual Economic Assistance (CMEA, customarily known in the West as Comecon).[29] Examination of how the organization operated supplies the experience on which the above assertion rests.[30]

---

[29]The CMEA was set up in 1949 and dissolved in 1991. Its members in 1990 were the Soviet Union, Bulgaria, Czechoslovakia, East Germany, Hungary, Poland, Romania, Cuba, Mongolia, and Vietnam. Yugoslavia was a "limited participant."

[30]Of the extensive literature on the CMEA, the following are worth underlining: S. Ausch (1972), J. M. van Brabant (1980, 1989), L. Csaba (1990), and M. Kaser (1965).

The discrepancy between the idea of internationalism and the reality of the CMEA began with the extent of its membership. Neither China nor any other Third World socialist country apart from Cuba, Mongolia, and Vietnam had ever been a CMEA member. That is evidence in itself that no comprehensive internationalism arose; except in three cases, the relatively developed European countries did not enter into organized integrative relations with the countries that lagged well behind them in economic development.[31] One can assume there were antipathies on both sides. On the one hand, the governments of the more developed socialist countries feared they would have to transfer too many resources to the less developed countries at the expense of their own economies. This problem arose quite sharply in the relations between China and the other socialist countries. The idea of equalizing development levels, which would amount to a redistribution of resources among national states, may favor relatively undeveloped states and meet opposition from relatively developed ones.[32] On the other hand, the CMEA was not attractive enough to several African and Asian countries. Some were concerned that affiliation might jeopardize their economic relations with the capitalist world.

Conflicts with the other CMEA members led to the exit of Yugoslavia from the organization's activities in an earlier period and of Albania later on. These cases show that the application of day-to-day policy is stronger than either the moral idea of internationalism or economic considerations.

Another major question when examining the discrepancy between the idea of internationalism and the reality of the CMEA is the method of coordination between member countries. Market coordination played only a subordinate role within the member countries; the basic mechanism of control was bureaucratic coordination and, what is more, an extreme version of it: a strongly centralized command economy and direct bureaucratic control. The hypothetical logical extension would be a supranational centralized command economy. Above the hierarchy within each country there would be a further, supranational level. The central authorities for the socialist countries would devise the plan, disaggregate it into countries, prescribe compulsory output assignments and input quotas for each state, and set targets for the flow of products between countries, rather as the national planning offices have done with the plans for sectors or provinces.

This idea is not simply a hypothetical conclusion suggested by the logic of bureaucratic coordination. In fact, something of this kind was the

---

[31]Mozambique applied for admission to the CMEA but was refused.

[32]The problem of equalization occurred from time to time within the CMEA as well, but not openly and in a perhaps less intensive form.

ultimate purpose behind the power intentions of the strongest member country, the Soviet Union. Indeed, the notion tied in with the official ideology not only of the Soviet Union but of the Communist parties in the countries allied to it, where strong emphasis was laid on the leading role of the Soviet Union. Clearly, it follows from this recognition of Soviet supremacy that if a supranational planning center needed to be placed over the national planned economies, it could only be the top level of Soviet administration. That would be the place to prepare "socialist world plans" whose disaggregation would yield compulsory national plans binding on each country.

This idea was never realized, even though there were strong forces working to promote it. The strict centralization involved would be incompatible with the autonomy of the subordinate units, even though that autonomy is only partial in any case. Even in the periods when the power of the Stalin leadership predominated most strongly over the smaller countries of Eastern Europe and they were at their most accommodating, the foreign trade and financial agreements were still reached through a process of intergovernmental negotiations and bargaining. Bureaucratic coordination can only override the separate interests of a nation effectively if it can abolish totally its separate existence as a state and its state sovereignty of every kind. If that is not done, and it was not done in the case of the Eastern European countries, the disciplinary compulsion to fulfill the common plans is lacking.[33]

Foreign trade: quantities and prices. Tables 14.1 and 14.2 showed the distribution of foreign trade relations. The very high proportion of the trade with socialist partners, and within this trade, with CMEA partners, can be explained largely by the effects described in the previous sections. At the same time, however, a part in producing the situation was played by the activity of the CMEA as an organization perpetually striving to increase the trade among the socialist countries. Increasing the proportion of trade within the CMEA was considered one of the main yardsticks of success at every meeting and in every public assessment.[34]

Even so, the role of the CMEA in this respect should not be exaggerated. There was little real content behind the ceremonial forms at the

[33]This has taken place in the multiethnic socialist countries, notably the Soviet Union and China. The CMEA had never managed through simple planning instructions to reallocate resources from Poland or Hungary, say, to the Soviet Union or Vietnam. On the other hand, planning commands from Gosplan in Moscow sufficed under the classical socialist system to reallocate resources from Estonia to Siberia or from Georgia to Byelorussia.

[34]Official academic writings in the member countries classified all kinds of bilateral agreements as if they came within the competence of the CMEA and were reached by virtue of it. Authors were more able to do this because these bilateral agreements were sanctioned at joint CMEA meetings and interpolated into the multinational cooperation agreements.

official sessions; at most they lent a loose framework to the foreign trade relations, which were based mainly on bilateral negotiations.

One important element in foreign trade relations is the price applied to import-export transactions. The CMEA tried to develop uniform principles. The idea arose that the CMEA should devise "a price basis of its own" starting out from the average costs in the member countries. This never happened, because the export prices payable on the capitalist market, or the export prices attainable there, exercise too great an influence on the governments of certain member countries [→14.3 and 14.4]. So the CMEA accepted a compromise principle: although the foreign trade prices used within the CMEA had to be adjusted to the prices on the capitalist world market, member countries should be insulated from the market fluctuations in those prices.[35] This logically inconsistent idea led to a situation in which the production and foreign trade of the CMEA countries were unable to adapt flexibly to the outside world and were incapable of exploiting favorable changes or staving off detrimental ones.

Division of labor and investments. Despite repeated ritual promises, very little happened to promote a planned development of the international division of labor within the CMEA. In most areas the production structure that emerged in each country was taken for granted. Although there were agreements in a few industries to divide up the production range, the economic expediency of doing so proved doubtful in most cases. In a good many fields, different member countries set up parallel facilities with the same function, despite all the CMEA's declarations of principle prescribing a division of labor. Discounting a few joint projects, there was hardly any joint investment and no appreciable flow of capital between member countries.[36]

Financial affairs. The idea that the currencies of the member countries should be convertible at least with each other—that the Bulgarian leva, for instance, should be freely exchangeable into Polish zlotys or East

---

[35]This was the guiding idea behind the so-called Bucharest price principle agreed to in 1958. The principle was designed to adjust CMEA prices to capitalist world market prices every five years, at the beginning of each planning cycle. However, prices were to remain fixed within each five-year period.

The resolution was never applied with total consistency, and after the 1973 oil-price explosion it became unsustainable. Then "sliding" prices were introduced in 1975, adjusted annually on a moving-average principle, taking the five-year average as a basis. This kind of "sliding" price applied for a long time to oil trading within the CMEA. Meanwhile, the earlier, rigid method of setting prices continued to apply in many other fields, particularly in relations between the smaller member countries. Frequent price changes are difficult to incorporate into bureaucratic coordination of foreign trading activity.

[36]Meanwhile, the objection made by many of the member countries was that once completed, the few joint investments made turned out to be unfavorable to the countries involved in them.

German marks—was not even raised at official negotiations. Instead, a more modest goal was advanced: to institutionalize the *transferable ruble*. Transferability actually means that country A is free to spend the surplus accumulated in its bilateral relations with country B in member country C, D, and so on, for example, to pay off the deficits in the bilateral relations between countries A and C, or A and D. However, this kind of real transferability has never emerged either, for several reasons. Not even the institutional framework was established, not to mention the resistance to the idea from the economic leaderships of some member countries. (See the previous section.) To allow transferable rubles earned in trading between country A and country B to be spent freely in country C or country D would conflict with cardinal principles of bureaucratic coordination within the country. The transferable ruble could act at most as a uniform unit of settlement, not as a real tool for reallocating resources and products and transferring them across national frontiers.

After all, how could one expect a real application of convertibility or transferability of any kind when money is not truly convertible even within the member countries? In any case, the international agreements, in accordance with the processes of planning and control inside member countries, were expressed basically in physical units (or where that was impracticable in the value indicators used for aggregation purposes). It was not customary to measure foreign trade in terms of money and profit, in these "firm categories."

That brief survey is followed by some summarizing statements. The sluggishness and cumbrousness of the planning and operative control processes were treated in earlier chapters, and the earlier part of this chapter made the same observation about the management of foreign trade in each country. The CMEA's existence tended to increase rather than relieve that rigidity. Before any decision could be made, it was not enough for the two interested business partners or even the two governments above them to agree. They had to await the next session of the appropriate CMEA committee, whose consent was needed to validate the agreement.

It is worth comparing the situation with the integration endeavors of the Western European capitalist countries. Partial supranational integration can take place among these economies allowing a free market flow of goods, capital, labor, and money. In that case the market binds the associated countries together, which is what has happened with the aptly named European Common Market. A similar evolution was impossible in the CMEA, because each country functioned as a separate, bureaucratic command economy, and prices and money hardly played any part in the relations among its member countries.

The Coherence of the Classical System

THE DETAILED description of the classical system has been completed. The analysis provides a basis for drawing a few summarizing conclusions. This chapter sets out to identify the main connections among the regularities in the constituent elements of the classical system.

The word *theory* is variously defined by the various schools of philosophy of science and practicing scientists. I subscribe to the view that an edifice of ideas can be deemed a theory if it illuminates and explains the main relationships within an existing, observable, and constant group of phenomena. In that sense this chapter's task is to outline a few general statements within the subject-area of a positive theory of the classical socialist system.

To that definition of the task I must add right away that the exposition is not intended to yield a universal, comprehensive theory explaining simultaneously all the aspects of the classical system that call for illumination. It is quite compatible with other, complementary theoretical approaches that can play a likewise important part in explaining other aspects of this complex group of phenomena. But I trust that the edifice of ideas outlined in this chapter on the basis of the material of chapters 3–14 will prove to be of use in studying a few essential relationships.

15.1 The Main Line of Causality

The line of thought in what has been said about the classical system suggests that there is a clearly perceptible main line of causal connections, even though there are mutual influences in several directions between the various phenomena. The main line of causality is represented in diagram form in figure 15.1. The figure purposely ignores the reactions, that is, the reverse effects of all kinds that exist in real life, since it sets out expressly to highlight the main direction.

The key to explaining the classical socialist system is an understanding of the political structure. The starting point is the undivided political power of the ruling party, the interpenetration of the party and the state, and the suppression of all forces that depart from or oppose the party's policy. So the classical system, if one looks at its essential marks, is a one-party system (even if one or two socialist countries have other parties that exist nominally and play a formal part in a coalition).

Not all one-party systems lead to the formation of a classical socialist system. For that to happen it is essential for the party exercising power to be imbued with the official ideology of the socialist system. Common

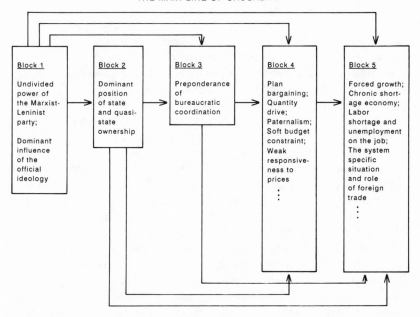

FIGURE 15.1 ˙ The Main Line of Causality

Note: The table shows the main line of causality from left to right. The arrows point out how each group of phenomena is influenced not only by the previous group of phenomena (i.e., merely the group one layer deeper), but by all the deeper factors, directly or indirectly. For instance, one of the groups of phenomena in the last block—the development and reproduction of chronic shortage— is not simply explained by such phenomena as the soft budget constraint or the weak responsiveness to prices; among the explanatory factors that act directly is the preponderance of state ownership and bureaucratic coordination.

The three points at the bottom of the blocks on the right hand side are intended to denote that the blocks contain only examples, not a full list. The book discusses numerous other phenomena which could be placed in the same block according to this scheme of logic.

parlance permits the term "Marxist-Leninist party," but the official ideology discussed in chapter 4 overlaps only in part with the ideas of Marx and Lenin. Much (but not all) has been taken over from them, and all kinds of additions have been made to their ideas.

The prime factor that brings the other system-specific phenomena about is the undivided power of the Communist party imbued with its specific ideology. It is worth recalling what was said at the end of chapter 4. The party's organizational existence and its ideology can only be distinguished on the plane of theoretical analysis: it forms an entity, like body and soul. So on the left-hand side of figure 15.1 they form block 1, the first link in the causal chain.

Under the classical system there is either a preponderance of state ownership (including quasi-state, cooperative ownership) or a situation in which at least the key positions, the commanding heights of the economy, are under state ownership. On the figure, this phenomenon is treated as the second factor in the causal chain (block 2).

Placing the role of property in second place has aroused debate. Some people rate it on a par with the political structure, and there is a view that the preponderance of state ownership is the chief criterion of a socialist economy.[1] The question is not wholly speculative, for it can be analyzed in the light of historical experience. If the Communist party gains undivided power in an economically backward country like China or Vietnam, it sooner or later begins a policy of nationalization and pursues it stubbornly. How fast the pursuit is and how often the process comes to a halt and starts again depend on the socioeconomic circumstances, the difficulties of organization, and the patience or impatience of the party. There are countries where even the barber shops and the village general stores are nationalized quite quickly, while elsewhere the system coexists for a while with the bourgeoisie. But all patience and coexistence of this kind is considered temporary by those in power, who can hardly wait for the nationalization to advance. Once banking, industry, and transportation have been nationalized, the authorities sooner or later set about eliminating private ownership in agriculture. The party openly proclaimed this objective even before it came to power. It is doing no more than putting its political program into practice.

It is not the property form—state ownership—that erects the political structure of classical socialism over itself. Quite the reverse: the given political structure brings about the property form it deems desirable. Although in this case the ideology plays a marked role in forming society, it is not the sole explanation for the direction of influence. The indivisibility of power and the concomitant totalitarianism are incompatible with the autonomy that private ownership entails. This kind of rule demands heavy curtailment of individual sovereignty. The further elimination of private ownership is taken, the more consistently can full subjection be imposed.

The three groups of phenomena discussed so far—the political structure and ideology typical of the classical socialist system, and the prop-

---

[1]There is a frequent tendency in the debates in this area to confuse a positive (descriptive, explanatory) approach with a normative one. Some of the schools of thought that call themselves socialist start from the following normative argument: the historical vocation of socialism is to eliminate private property and exploitation. Therefore, the dominance of state ownership is what primarily distinguishes the socialist system from other systems.

It is worth recalling here that this book concerns a specific group of countries [→table 1.1] described in the book's terminology as the "socialist countries." Assuming this definition, the question of which factors play a role that is primary, secondary, tertiary, and so on in producing these countries' main characteristics already belongs to the province of positive, causal analysis.

erty form—combine to account for the next cell on the figure, block 3, the system-specific constellation of coordination mechanisms. Here bureaucratic coordination takes the main part, and all other mechanisms play supporting roles at most or wither away. This is one of the corner-stones of the book's line of thought. The features of the system cannot be derived from the fact that it is not a market economy, or still less from the fact that the prices are irrational, and so on. Once the political structure, official ideology, and dominant role of state ownership are provided, they produce the dominance of the mechanism of bureaucratic control.

The actual forms of bureaucratic coordination vary from country to country and period to period. Fulfillment of one plan instruction is re-warded here and another there. Here ministries are merged and there they are split up. Meanwhile, officials in the apparatus and professional economists have lively debates on the advantages and drawbacks of one form or another. But certain essential factors remain unchanged: elimi-nation of free enterprise and autonomous actors on the market, and of the competition among them; centralization of decision making and in-formation; and the dominance of hierarchical dependence, vertical rela-tions over horizontal ones.

That brings us to the next cell, block 4 of the figure. To it belong the interest and motivation of the actors in the classical system, their consequent behavior, and the main features of the relations among them.[2] Some phenomena that may be placed here are listed in label form, without aiming at a complete list: plan bargaining, the quantity drive, the paternalistic behavior of superiors, the soft budget constraint, the weak responsiveness to prices, and so on. Whichever one is taken, it can be explained separately in terms of underlying factors, the nature of power, the official ideology, and the preponderance of state ownership and bureaucratic coordination.

The next cell, block 5, contains a list of a few typical lasting economic phenomena. The figure includes only the most important: forced growth, labor shortage, and unemployment on the job, the chronic shortage economy, and the system-specific role of foreign trade. The main features of these phenomena can be traced back to the explanatory factors qualified as deeper by the earlier logic. It is not because there is shortage that a huge and almighty bureaucracy develops; it is not because

---

[2]Some writers have described the approach that I customarily take in my works as "be-haviorist." However, this is not an accurate description. Though much can be explained by the participants' behavior, the behavior itself needs causal analysis. This is reflected in the structure of figure 15.1: the behavioral features can be found in the "middle zone" of the causal chain, midway between the underlying explanatory factors and the directly perceptible economic phenomena.

the aim is to force growth that the plans are made taut; it is not because import hunger appears that there is an import-permit system; and so on. Although reactions of this kind exist (and they are dealt with in detail in the next section), the main direction of causality is the contrary: the phenomena cited develop because a specific political structure and ideology have gained sway, as a result of which specific property forms have developed, which has led to the preponderance of bureaucratic coordination and the typical behavior patterns of the participants.

This line of argument contains elements that a researcher raised on Marxist political economy and philosophy can accept without much difficulty, while other elements in it differ radically from the ideas entrenched in the researcher's mind. He or she will be familiar with the approach reflected in the attempt to classify phenomena as "deeper" or "more superficial" and the desire to find the main directions of influence within the web of mutual effects.[3] It will be familiar and acceptable to attempt to explain a social group's behavior in terms of its self-interest and social situation, rather than contenting oneself with citing the preferences of individuals. Equally akin to Marxist tradition is the way the logical analysis (what is the main direction of causality?) combines with the historical approach (in what characteristic order in time did the main events occur?).

The same economist raised on Marxist political economy may be perplexed to find that the line of argument described here does not follow the usual pattern of discussing a relationship of "base and superstructure." Whatever meaning one attaches to the concept of "base," one cannot state that the base has determined its own superstructure. As noted in chapter 2, the historical point of departure, almost without exception, is a poor and backward country. It still has few large factories, and its production and the concentration of capital are low. It is certainly not the case that the forces of production are already being impeded in their development by the capitalist production relations, or that they can only develop once those relations have been destroyed. It is certainly not the case that one only has to drive the capitalists out for a well-organized, concentrated production system ripe for central planning to fall on the plate of the socialist planners. These countries are still in a state that Marx and Engels described in the *Communist Manifesto*, one in which they also say that capitalism is capable of giving enormous impetus to the development of the forces of production.

---

[3]This is one of the ways in which the Marxist researcher differs from the analytical economist living in a world of neoclassical models, who draws conclusions in his or her model from assumptions placed side by side, although there may be "deeper" and "more superficial" premises among the assumptions.

The historical development course of classical socialism is quite diffe
ent from the pattern presented in the handbooks on the Marxist philos
phy of history. The revolution shatters the old superstructure and artificially erects a new one, or, more precisely, it produces the seed of a new
superstructure which then pushes out almost of its own accord. The new
superstructure crushes the base that is alien to it and rearranges it entirely. It nationalizes and collectivizes; it steadily eliminates private property and squeezes the market into a smaller and smaller space. The bureaucratic apparatus of economic control springs up and spreads in all
directions. As this process goes on, as the property relations, coordination mechanism, and economic processes alter according to the new system, these changes react continually on the political forms and bring a
transformation of the ideology in their train.

15.2 The Affinity among Elements of the System

The discussion of the main line of causality in the last section contains
repeated references to the fact that the effect reacts on the cause: numerous interactions occur among the elements of the system. Previous chapters have cited plenty of examples of this, of which just a few are recalled
here as illustrations:

■ Once state ownership and the soft budget constraint have produced the investment hunger, the import hunger, the hoarding tendency, and wage-drift, it becomes necessary to use the administrative
tools of investment and import permits, material quotas, rationing and
allocation systems, and wage funds. Once such tools are being used,
it no longer suffices to encourage economic discipline with praise and
material rewards. It must be imposed with punishments, and firm
measures must be taken against "speculators" and "wage-swindlers."
This all has an effect on the political climate and the official ideology.
(Blocks 4 and 5 react on blocks 3 and 1.)

■ Bureaucratic control of state-sector wages, which combats the
upward pressure on wages even when there is a labor shortage, is incompatible with the higher incomes obtained outside the state sector,
on the free market. This and other factors tend to encourage as full
an elimination of the private sector as possible. (Blocks 3, 4, and 5
react on block 2.)

■ Once the economy has embarked on forced growth, the ideas to
explain the necessity and advantages of this type of growth need incorporating in the official ideology. (Block 5 reacts on block 1.)

■ If the managers of production fail to develop a strong intrinsic
interest in gaining foreign, hard-currency markets, due to the chronic

domestic sellers' market and several other factors, a mechanism and incentive system forcing them to produce for capitalist export purposes must be created. (Block 5 reacts on block 3.)

As the classical system consolidates, its elements develop a coherence. The various behavioral forms, conventions, and norms rub off on one another. To apply a chemical analogy, the phenomena exhibit affinity: they attract and require each other. The monolithic structure of power, petrified ideological doctrines, almost total domination of state ownership, direct bureaucratic control, forced growth, shortage, and distrustful withdrawal from most of the world (to mention just the main groups of phenomena) all belong together and strengthen each other. This is no loose set of separate parts; the sum of the parts make up an integral whole. In that sense as well there is justification in considering this formation as a *system*.

A curious "natural selection" comes to apply: new institutions, regulations, customs, and moral and legal norms that are easily reconciled with the nature of the system survive and take root; those alien to it are discarded.[4] Let us take a single example. No one planned in advance, before the first socialist system came into being, that personnel affairs— i.e., appointment, transfer, and dismissal—would be strictly centralized. There is no trace in a prior blueprint for socialism of the idea of establishing for the purpose a hierarchical apparatus in which the personnel decisions in every unit at every level would depend on the relevant party organization, on police institutions that keep track of people's political attitudes, on a superior personnel administrator, or on the official state, economic, or mass-movement leader in the field concerned. This very powerful institutional system with its precise forms of career control emerged step by step through trial and error, feeling its way with repeated reorganizations. It first became a permanent part of the system in the Soviet Union, and then developed in each socialist country in a more or less similar form. As a result, no other social system has such close control over individual careers as socialism, with its uniform, centrally controlled apparatus of personnel management. It illustrates that specific forms and institutions grow *organically* within the system.

Tendencies that have arisen and developed show a strong inclination to consummation. Direct bureaucratic control, for example, gains predominance, prescribing economic tasks in instructions [→7]. But once prescription of a firm's main assignments, in aggregate indices, has begun, there is no stopping there. Circumvention is too easy: the main

---

[4]The idea of natural selection among institutions appears in the works of J. A. Schumpeter and F. A. Hayek. For a more detailed explanation, see the article by A. A. Alchian (1950).

assignment is fulfilled, but the details and secondary tasks are neglected. Logically, the next step is to assign each task in more detail, and if that does not suffice, the subordinate's hands must be tied with an even minuter breakdown into even tinier parts. If the net of totalitarian power and its instrument, bureaucratic control, has too large a mesh, many actions can escape from it. The answer is a net with a smaller mesh that cannot be slipped through. The system's internal logic propels bureaucratic power toward "perfectionism."

The examples of positive selection, integration into the system, are followed by an illustration of the opposite process: rejection by the system. Private ownership and private enterprise are foreign to classical socialism, and in the long term it cannot tolerate them. The centralized, nationalized order of this society is disturbed not only by large-scale capital but by the existence of small-scale peasant ownership. Central power, sooner or later, depending on its tolerance threshold, sets about eliminating it. The Soviet Union waited more than a decade before launching mass collectivization. In Vietnam it was only a couple of years after the military victory, before much progress had been made on repairing the economic damage caused by the war, when the authorities embarked on eliminating the private farming and produce-trading sector and nationalizing and collectivizing its activities, with catastrophic economic results. The Ethiopian government launched in the midst of a devastating famine a socialist reorganization of agriculture that uprooted the rural population and resettled it on a collectivized basis. Going beyond examples, it should be stressed that property is not the only sphere of phenomena in which the classical system is unable to cohabit lastingly with institutions, customs, attitudes, and norms alien to it. The mature classical system cannot tolerate contrary political opinions, self-governing institutions, and organizations independent of the political institutions organized from above; cultures and world views other than the official ones; or free-market exchange between autonomous economic entities. All these phenomena, though they may recur time after time, are confined into an ever narrowing area. Individual behavior is deeply imbued with conformism: spontaneous use of the ideas and working abilities deriving from a spirit of enterprise is virtually ruled out, as are independent critical opinions and rebellion against the superior organizations.[5]

[5]The lines above emphasize a tendency against which countertendencies also apply. Even at a time of extreme totalitarian power, a measure of narrow individual autonomy survives in many spheres of life, though confined to a very constricted area. The spirit of enterprise remains latently present (and occasionally breaks out in a distorted form). Some people, if few of them, dare to oppose the repression. All these features suddenly strengthen when the social environment offers more favorable chances for them to develop.

To sum up the lesson common to these examples of integration and rejection: a natural selection of institutions and behavior patterns takes place, and ultimately enormously strengthens and greatly consolidates the inner coherence of the system.

Marx and Lenin expected the victorious socialist revolution to be followed by a transitional period in which the remnants of capitalism would still leave their impression on society. "What we have to deal with here is a communist society, not as it has *developed* on its own foundations, but, on the contrary, as it *emerges* from capitalist society; which is thus in every respect, economically, morally and intellectually, still stamped with the birthmarks of the old society from whose womb it emerges,"[6] Marx says of socialism. According to this view, later incorporated into the official ideology of classical socialism, the existence of the remnants of capitalism causes the difficulties in the transitional period, and once they have been done away with, all the communist system's beneficial features can develop unhindered. Experience, however, seems to deny that the tendencies and internal contradictions examined in the previous chapters have survived as a legacy of the capitalist system. On the contrary, the classical socialist system's characteristics *sui generis* have brought them into being.

15.3   The Prototype and the National Variations

It does not follow from what has been said that this book subscribes to the view that some kind of ultimate determinism or fatalism applies in history. There are two issues worth considering in this respect. The first is the departure along a specific historical path, and the second the broader or narrower determination of the path itself.

Beginning with the first issue, it depends on a conjunction of a great many circumstances whether or not a society sets out on the path toward classical socialism. As mentioned in the last section, the Communist party must gain undivided possession of political power for the process to get under way. This historical configuration bears the "genetic program" that transmits the main characteristics of the system to every cell within it.[7] This is the seed of the new society from which the whole organism grows.

---

[6]K. Marx [1875] (1966, p. 563).

[7]The analogy was inspired by the modern genetic theory of biology that inherited traits are transmitted by a particular substance, DNA, whose molecule has the special ability to control its own reproduction. It can transfer the inherited traits to further molecules formed under its control. The inherited genetic program is coded in the specific DNA chemical "language," and the code then reproduced in every single cell of the organism. Under the command of the program hidden in the DNA, all the biochemical, anatomical,

The approach outlined here contradicts the frequently expressed view that each elementary particle of the classical system is imposed artificially on the fabric of society, which resists it from first to last. According to this superficial notion, it is a case of nothing more than a merciless dictator and his slavish hirelings imposing their rule on the people by intimidation and violence. If that were so, this external layer would easily be shed by the body of society; but it is not a question of that at all. Throughout there is certainly resistance, sometimes weaker and sometimes stronger, which the possessors of power break by force, but the new structure proliferates with an elemental force, propagating itself and penetrating into every social relationship.[8] Once the start of the process is imposed upon the society, it goes on in a spontaneous manner, proceeding, to use Marx's phrase, "indigenously" (*naturwüchsig*). If another "genetic program" applies in some country at that particular historical turning point, the result will differ despite the similarity of the starting point. Consider North and South Korea, which were in the same economic position after the Second World War. The South resembled the North not only in its point of departure but even in certain features of its political and administrative structure applying in the postwar period: it was ruled by a relentless dictatorship that brooked no opposition; the bureaucracy of the state played a big part in running the economy, intervening in decisions on foreign trade, investment, and the extension of credit; and so on. Yet the difference is fundamentally significant: the official ideology in South Korea differed utterly from North Korea's; the possessors of undivided political power, far from intending to eliminate private property, cooperated with it and sought to assist its prosperity. Although a big part was played by bureaucratic coordination, there was no mention of abolishing the market, which operated with great vitality. As time went by, North Korea finally came to display all the classical system's essential features, while South Korea, after decades of suffering and sacrifices, developed a political and economic system that increasingly resembles Japan's path of development and differs ever more sharply from North Korea's. Similar statements could be based on com-

---

physiological, and to some extent behavioral characteristics of the biological organism are determined during its development. The consistency of the DNA in the living world is species-specific. See J. D. Watson's famous book (1968). For the short account above, I used a university biology textbook, N. A. Campbell (1987).

[8]The Hungarian poet Gyula Illyés describes this with moving force in his poem *A Word about Tyranny:* "You are a prisoner, and at once a warder . . . so that the slave himself makes and wears his chains. . . . Where there is tyranny, all are links in the chain; the stink and spew of its comes from you, for you too are tyranny." Illyés [1950] (1986, pp. 380–88), first publication in 1956.

paring Taiwan with mainland China or West Germany with East Germany.

Let us turn to the second issue raised at the beginning of the section: how widely or narrowly is the path determined? If in some country the power of the Communist party is consolidated and society departs on the path of historical development with its own "genetic program," according to the theory outlined in the book, certain main features are sure to develop. No one will be in any doubt later that such a country belongs to the family of socialist systems. At the beginning of the path it might have been uncertain what Czechoslovakia in the early years after 1945 or Cuba in the first years of Fidel Castro's rule might turn into, but by now it is indisputable that the systems that came into being are closely akin to the Soviet Union of Lenin and Stalin and to the China of Mao.

Whereas chapters 3–14 of the book have shed light on the main common features, it must be recalled here that this does not amount to perfect identity. Each socialist country has numerous individual characteristics. This too is suggested by the earlier biological-genetic analogy: not even the monozygotic twin offspring of the same parents are perfectly identical. To return to the subject, several factors affect the specific structure of a society and the economy within it: geographical and natural conditions, the economic and cultural legacy from the previous regime, the political line taken by the new possessors of power, the personal traits of the supreme leader, the behavior of foreign countries toward the country concerned, world political events, and so on. So it would be quite wrong to imagine that given the "genetic program," the accession of the Communist party to power, all has been determined and history will "take its course." The strength of application and the specific constellation of the tendencies described in this book will vary appreciably from country to country and from period to period. There is repression in every country at every stage in the classical system, but in one it applies on a mass scale in a particularly merciless way, while in another country or period it can be felt to be relatively mild. There is a command economy everywhere, but in one place it operates pedantically, with painstaking concern for the smallest detail, while in another it works sloppily and unreliably. Everywhere and always there is a shortage economy, but while the food shortage is unbearable in one country, the accustomed degree of shortage is quite tolerable in another.

The book describes the *inclinations* of the system. An inclination may prevail or it may be restrainable to some extent. A measure of choice affects the actual combination of mutually compensatory tendencies that arises. To take an example, the classical system is inclined toward forced growth. The more the leadership forces growth, the greater the problems in supplying the public and the graver the repression used to stifle the consequent discontent. If a more moderate leadership chooses to restrain the expansion drive and investment hunger (which happens in certain countries at certain times), it can afford to loosen the constraints on political and intellectual activity a little. So there is "play," some freedom to maneuver, although it is limited.

Here an emphatic reminder is needed of what was stated early on [→1.6, 2.2]: this book describes a theoretical model, a prototype of classical socialism, which does not act as a substitute for concrete historical analysis of individual countries. That task remains for other works. My aim here is merely to clarify where the constant constraints on choice in decision making lie or, more precisely, which constraints derive from the "genetic program," the basic, common features of this family of systems.

Some observers and critics of the socialist economy tend to ask why a better information and incentive system is not introduced under socialism. They think society can be perceived as the realization of a gigantic "principal-agent" model.[9] If the principal's purpose is known, an incentive scheme that best serves the objectives can be devised, and immediately the system will operate better. Willy-nilly, this line of argument implies that the principal has been rather stupid not to have lit before upon the information and incentive system that suits him best.

The approach in this book is not to start by deciding what the leadership's "objectives" are, not least because the objectives are difficult to observe. They are not necessarily reflected faithfully in public resolutions and political speeches, since these form parts of the official ideology. The only way of establishing the "true" purpose of the leaders is to observe their actual deeds, in which their intentions (and any forced modifications of their original intentions) are incarnated. Moreover, there is no community of purpose anyway, due to the multitude of conflicts within the sphere of the leadership.

All those controlling the classical socialist system, from the tip to the base of the bureaucratic pyramid, are not stupid at all. They are quite capable of asserting their interests and objectives. The system evolved in the way it did precisely because this is the structure that can perform the

[9]The author has encountered this approach mainly among Western theoretical economists without a close acquaintance with socialism but interested in its problems. A similar notion is not infrequently seen in the thinking of staff at the International Monetary Fund, World Bank, and other international agencies. Raised in the West, they suddenly engage in studying the problems of a socialist country, and even in preparing for practical decisions. For a long time a similar concept appeared among the mathematical economists in the Soviet Union: they sought to elaborate proposals for an "optimal economic system" for the official leadership of the day. For a description of this school, see, for instance, M. Ellman (1973) and P. Sutela (1984).

functions expected of it. It is naive to imagine that the main features of the system can be altered by applying a few ideas for reorganization.

The attention in another kind of critical approach is concentrated on the extreme examples. This course is taken by confirmed opponents of socialism who think they can present their message most effectively by drawing attention to the worst enormities, the unbridled mass terror, or the most conspicuous instances of waste. The same approach is taken by some confirmed adherents of socialism, who are glad to talk about the ultimate negative examples because they hope that the problems can be solved by curbing the "extremes" and "excesses." I try a different approach, focusing attention on what is general, typical, and normal in the system; in other words, on the average, the likely value of the random fluctuations. I do so in the hope that although this approach has less influence on the feelings of the reader, it may place the drawing of the conclusions on a sounder footing.

During the debates around the reforms and "de-Stalinization," one issue raised not infrequently is this: could the Stalin terror have been avoided? Was it worth paying the price signified by the victims of Stalin's rule that the socialist system might survive? Although the intellectual and moral content of these questions is fully understandable, it is not my intention to answer them here. The theoretical model being described is one that does not necessarily imply the extremisms of Stalin's rule, although it does not exclude them. The issue presented during the analysis of this prototype is as follows: Given the power structure, ideology, and property relations typical of classical socialism, what are the main features of the structure and operation of society that appear, at least as a tendency or inclination? Is the existence of this "genetic program," that is, the specific power structure and ideology, a sufficient and necessary condition for the inclinations and tendencies mentioned to arise? I consider this to be a stricter, not a more lenient, set of questions to put than the one at the beginning of the paragraph about the necessity or avoidability of the "extremists."

15.4 The Soviet Effect

What effect on the structure and main attributes of the classical system has been exercised by the historical accident that the Communist party first took power in former tsarist Russia? What kind of system would the socialist system have become if its development on a worldwide scale had started out from a different country?

Those posing these questions tend to point out how deeply the characteristics associated with Lenin's and Stalin's Soviet Union are rooted in

Russia's past. The KGB continues the practice of the tsarist secret police; the rigid and soulless apparatus is the heir to the bureaucracy of the old Russian governors and *chinovniks*; the bleakness of a *kolkhoz* village and the passiveness of a *kolkhoz* peasant recall the way of life of the *muzhiks* under the old regime. They customarily project the application of this line of argument beyond the Soviet borders as well. Socialism would have developed otherwise in other countries too if backwardness and a semi-Asian lack of civilization had not been branded upon it at the historical point of departure.

History cannot be reversed. There is no way of conducting an experiment in which the autocracy of the Communist country develops in some other country first and the new system in that other country exercises the global effect that the Soviet Union had in the actual course of history. To that extent one cannot give an answer with complete certainty to the question put at the beginning of the section. Nonetheless, the line of thinking in this book does suggest a few hypotheses.

1. One can certainly consider it an accident that the circumstances in which the Communist party could seize power should have arisen in Russia first. But the fact that *all* countries where the socialist revolution triumphed largely by internal efforts were backward and poor must be rated a recurrent regularity. The regime preceding socialism governed by brutal means; there were notably sharp inequalities in society [→2.3]. The specifically Russian antecedents may have played some part in developing the general features of the socialist system, but the antecedents equally characteristic of all the countries, listed in table 2.1, seem to be far more important. In not one of those countries had genuine parliamentary democracy developed; in not one of them had mature capitalism been attained; in not one of them had the market become the dominant coordination mechanism. All these countries were "late arrivers."[10] These common antecedents certainly had an effect on the political structure (total elimination of democratic institutions), the development of the pattern of forced growth for the sake of eliminating backwardness, the radicalism of the redistribution of income, and a good many other characteristics of the system. This is the type of society prone to accept the "genetic program" that creates the socialist system.[11]

---

[10] See A. Gerschenkron (1962).

[11] Another reason why this is worth underlining is that the crisis in the socialist world and the break made by many countries with the socialist system does not end that inclination once and for all. The leading Communists of Eastern Europe, the Soviet Union, and China are branded as traitors by Latin American guerrillas fighting to the death against the outrageous injustices of their own social systems. They trust they will gain power, and then they will be the ones who create true socialism.

2. The Soviet example played an important part in all countries in shaping specific elements of classical socialism (its official ideology, institutions, and norms of behavior).

In part the Soviet Union enforced this, by various methods. Great pressure was exerted on all the Eastern European countries under Soviet military occupation by the very presence of the Soviet troops. If the population tried to oppose the system, as happened, for instance, in 1953 in East Berlin, 1956 in Budapest, and 1968 in Prague, the resistance was crushed by the military might of the Soviety Army. Moreover, awareness of the threat of Soviet military intervention had the desired effect in the other countries as well.

Apart from direct intervention, another very influential factor was the tie that the Communist parties felt with the Soviet Union and its Communist party. The Moscow center imposed its will on the Communists of other countries with fire and sword in the early decades of the world Communist movement. Unconditional acceptance of every Soviet institution and action was the prime condition before a party could claim to be Communist. When the Communists took power in other countries, leaders who had returned from exile in the Soviet Union and continued to be controlled from the Moscow center played a big part in them; they unhesitatingly transplanted Soviet practice into their own countries. The presence of Soviet advisers exercised a great influence, and so did the fact that many politicians, army officers, and economic experts in the other socialist countries had completed their studies in the Soviet Union.

The compulsion was augmented and made more effective by voluntary zeal. The Communists who came to power after a long and often heroic struggle looked on the Soviet Union as the paragon of human progress. They were sincerely convinced that the more faithfully they copied the Soviet model, the sooner they would attain the socialism they ardently desired.

All this explains how the countries of classical socialism can be seen to have followed the Soviet example, not only in essential attributes but often in minor external details ranging from the design of the national crest and the uniforms of their soldiers to the managerial structure of their firms.

3. Strong though the Soviet effect was, an even stronger influence seems to have been exerted by the inherent logic of the classical system. Section 15.2 described the process of natural selection among institutions and operative mechanisms that ultimately welds the system into a coherent whole. Once the genetic program mentioned earlier starts to work (as the combined resultant of the Soviet effect and internal forces), the coherent features of the system develop and bring each other into being. It is not the following of the example of the Soviet shortage economy

that produces the East German or Mongolian shortage economy, but the inherent nature of the system. The counsel of Soviet security advisers is not the main factor behind the emergence in every country of the secret police, which builds up its network of informers and stamps out the least signs of resistance. This police apparatus arises out of the inherent needs of the system, which cannot survive without intimidation, repression, and limitations on civil liberties.

The following conclusion can be drawn. One of the explanatory factors behind the differences among the national variants of the system is the relative strength or weakness of the Soviet influence. But what shaped the prototype itself was not the Soviet impact but a combination of far more profound effects, namely, the causal chain outlined in section 15.1.

15.5 Verification

The previous sections contain a number of propositions:

1. The classical socialist system is distinguished from other system-families by several basic attributes; these are the system-specific features.

2. Specific causal relationships obtain between the groups of system-specific phenomena: there is a specific main direction of causality within the complex of mutual effects.

3. Certain conditions are necessary and sufficient for the system to emerge and consolidate. The seed of this "genetic program" is a particular political structure and related ideology: the undivided power of the Communist party and the prevalence of an official ideology whose cardinal precepts include the establishment of hegemony, and then dominance for public ownership.

4. This "genetic program" fashions society in its own image; it creates a coherent system whose various elements connect, and assume and reinforce each other.

On the one hand, this theory has a deductive character. The initial, basic assumptions and the intermediate conclusions act as the premises for the later analyses. So the internal consistency of the thought process can be checked: Does the analysis include no mutually contradictory assumptions? Have no logically faulty steps been made?

On the other hand, the theory has an empirical nature, resting ultimately on observation of the practice of classical socialism. So the relationship between the theory and historical reality deserves special attention.

It was stressed throughout the expositions that they outline a theoretical model compatible with the "dispersion" of actual historical realities around the theory. So the theory is not falsified if the situation in one particular country or other is not identical to the one defined in the model, or the events there differ somewhat from the course assumed in the model. But that poses a question: Is the book dealing with a theory at all, or just with the definition of a category, "classical socialism," which can neither be verified nor falsified?

In this respect I accept the criteria of the positivist theory of science,[12] in particular the criterion that a theory must be falsifiable. The wording of the definitions and the line of argument must not render the statements tautological, that is, exclude a priori the possibility of discovering the falsity of the statements in some way.

In the context of this book, the theory needs confronting with historical experience observed in many countries over a long period. It is not possible (or necessary) to prove or refute the theory with a mathematical-logical model. At most a few of the theory's partial conclusions can be tested econometrically, using a mathematical-statistical analysis of economic statistics.[13] The most important theses must undergo less subtle but weightier historical tests. For history (and those studying it) can or will be able to answer the following question:

1. Is there a previously consolidated socialist system in which the main features discussed in part 2 of this book cannot be demonstrated?

As mentioned before, this book draws mainly on the experiences of nine countries [→1.2]. It would be instructive to know also what the situation was in Albania, Mongolia, Vietnam, North Korea, and Cuba— other countries where the classical system consolidated itself over quite a long period. To what extent are the general propositions in chapters 3–15 confirmed by what happened in these countries? Little reliable information on these five countries has filtered out at the time of writing, but Albania has now ceased to be a socialist country, and reform movements are underway in Mongolia and Vietnam. So after the event, at least, more data and empirical information on them may become available.

---

[12]See K. Popper (1959).

[13]Should a statistical examination falsify one partial conclusion or another, one would have to examine the extent to which the phenomenon now known and described more accurately was compatible with the original premises of the thought process leading to the partial conclusions. If need be, those too must be altered. So in that sense statistical examination of a partial phenomenon is an important means of supporting or refuting the more general theoretical premises.

This procedure is well known in natural sciences. It is impossible to test the validity of certain fundamental theories directly by experiments. But then there are some less basic propositions, which are derived by logical reasoning from the fundamental theory, and which are empirically testable. If the test would prove the truth of the derived proposition, it would mean also a strong indirect empirical support of the fundamental theory.

It should be recalled here that in many contexts I have spoken only of tendencies and inclinations, not of a full application of those tendencies and inclinations. For instance, the failure of farming in Poland to undergo total collectivization does not falsify what was written in chapter 5, so long as efforts to collectivize appeared repeatedly and strongly in the Polish political leadership.

2. The most important testing ground is the process of reform taking place in socialism. Returning to figure 15.1, block 1 contains the "genetic program," the power structure and ideology. In many countries the reform proceeds as an attempt to alter blocks 2, 3, and 4 while keeping essential features of block 1 unchanged. The main characteristics of the power structure are retained, yet profound alterations in the system are awaited. Major indirect evidence of the theoretical statements just outlined is provided by the constraints, inconsistencies, and failures of the reform process and the tendencies to regress toward the classical system—the repeated restorations. If the whole system is capable, however, of developing new features in blocks 2, 3, and 4, sharply different from the classical ones, and if it is also capable of surviving and growing in this modified form without a fundamental change ensuing in block 1, the theory is weakened, or possibly falsified altogether.

The book suggests a revolutionary theory. The socialist system is not capable of a renewal that could free it of its dysfunctional features while retaining the sole rule of the Communist party and the dominance of the state sector. To use the terminology of figure 15.1, a profound, lasting, and from the economic point of view effective transformation of blocks 3, 4, and 5 requires a radical change in blocks 1 and 2—the political structure and property relations.

My belief in offering this book is that experience has yet to refute the propositions summed up in points 1–4. The remainder of the book examines the process by which several countries move away from the classical form of the socialist system and reforms and revolutions take place. These analyses support the theoretical propositions made above with further observations, although the ultimate verification or falsification of them can only be done by the future course of history and the scientific analysis that processes it.

15.6 The Viability of the Classical System

Can the classical system survive permanently? The answer depends on the time-scale applied, on how one defines the word "permanently."

The next chapter will give an overview of the duration of the classical system in several socialist counries. The period has ended, because the process of reform has started or a still more profound change of system has taken place. In any case, the country where the classical system lasted longest—more than six decades—was the Soviet Union.

There are only two countries where the classical system still prevails: North Korea and Cuba. All one can say about them is that so far, up to the time of writing, the classical system has operated in them for three or four decades. I have no desire to offer a guess as to what the future will bring for these countries when the general position in the world around them is that all the other socialist countries, including the two great powers, the Soviet Union and China, have gone beyond the classical system.

But even if one refrains from a direct prediction about those countries, one can certainly say that on the scale of centuries on which world history is measured, the classical system is transitory. It proves relatively short-lived compared with the socioeconomic formations that have managed to survive for centuries.

But alongside the scale of centuries for measuring world history there is a need to use other, shorter time-scales as well. The periods of decades from the emergence until the end of classical socialism cover the entire adult lives of generations. Taking a medium-term view, the classical system is viable. The analysis in chapters 3–15 has shown that it can perform the basic functions of controlling social activities vital for survival. It organizes production and supply to the public of the goods and services they need to survive. It ensures in its own way the discipline required for the coordination of activities and for human coexistence. It founds a legal and moral system in which people can find their bearings. What is more, the system enjoys the support of a certain part of society that feels such support is to its advantage. The system's elements cohere with each other. Under certain conditions it is capable not only of reproducing an existing standard but of expansion, growth, and qualitative development. It can gather a large military force, allowing armed defense in case of attack. Though the system is replete with contradiction and inner conflict, for a long time this does not threaten its existence as such.

The previous paragraph makes no value judgment. To return to the metaphor at the beginning of the book, a "school report" on a system can be compiled; in other words, one can rate its performance in relation to various intrinsic values [→1.7]. A succession of the most important general human values—material welfare, efficiency of production and ability to innovate, observance of individual liberties, equality, social solidarity—have cropped up during the analysis of the classical system. It has emerged that classical socialism fails to display superiority over the capitalist system in materializing some of them, for example equality and solidarity. What is more, for several other fundamental values, like welfare, efficiency, and liberty, the socialist system falls far short of the attainments of developed, modern capitalism operating under democratic political forms. This, however, is an assessment supplementary to the positive analysis, made from without. How the general public judges the system from within is quite another matter. Some members are biased in favor of the existing system because they share in power and benefit from it, and subscribe to the system's official ideology. Others are disaffected, but they cannot assess the performance of the system properly because they have no way of comparing it with other systems. Yet others hold strongly condemnatory opinions but have no chance of expressing them. If the discontent increases, those in power can ensure the survival of the system by stepping up the repression.

This leads back to the question discussed before. The classical system can survive while the discontent remains suppressed. Measuring its viability on a scale of decades, not centuries, the classical system looks tenacious and durable.

But one must add that the survival of the system is hard to ensure. Certain inherent contradictions are exacerbated. Not only is the socialist system behind in many areas in its competition with capitalism, but the lag increases. This all provides a motive behind the efforts to change the classical system, which brings us to the subject of part 3: the erosion and crisis of classical socialism, the reform, and the revolution.

Part Three

SHIFTING FROM THE CLASSICAL SYSTEM

16

The Dynamics of the Changes

IN THE coherence of the classical system lies its strength, but also its weakness. One might exaggerate slightly by saying it produces a fabric so closely woven that if one strand breaks, it all unravels sooner or later.

The world has been witnessing that disintegration in the 1980s and 1990s. Everywhere, with few exceptions, the end of classical socialism has come, and in many countries the change has gone further, for the socialist system as a whole has collapsed. Chapters 16–24 review and comment on the disintegration of the classical system. As a start, this chapter looks at the causes of the move away from the classical system and discusses the dynamics of the process.

16.1 The Inducements for Change

The change in all socialist countries that move away from the classical system in some direction is compelled by the accumulated tensions and contradictions.[1] Chapter 15 emphasized that the classical system constitutes a coherent entity and is capable of operating for an appreciable period. But that statement is compatible, logically and in terms of experience, with another: the classical system operates dysfunctionally, in a way replete with grave internal problems. Since each of these has been discussed in detail before, only a summary reminder of them is given. All the various negative phenomena can ultimately be placed in four main groups of inducements obliging the system to change. Although the various specific problems and contradictions appear to differing degrees in each country, in all countries operating under the classical system many of these problems are causing serious trouble.

The first group of symptoms is the accumulation of economic difficulties. The classical system is accompanied throughout by grave economic problems: the serious lag in technical development, shortage, backwardness in consumption, waste, and other losses. But concurrently the econ-

---

[1]For an overall analysis of the inner tensions leading to reforms and/or collapse of the system, see T. G. Ash (1990), Z. Brzezinski (1990), E. Hankiss (1990), and J. Staniszkis (1989, 1991), as well as the volumes published by the Joint Economic Committee, U.S. Congress (1989).

omy grows at an impressive rate, and the system's partisans may believe the difficulties are just the inevitable price of fast development. After a time, however, the growth rate slows down [→table 9.11].[2] Meanwhile, the earlier economic woes get worse. The strategy of forced growth cannot be pursued indefinitely. The postponed tasks mount up over a long period and accumulate into a less and less bearable debt: the worsening state of the seriously neglected sectors (housing, transportation and telecommunications, the health service, etc.) makes the functioning of the economy more and more difficult. The surplus that could be mobilized easily by extensive methods while there was fast growth is running out; in several countries the physical limit of labor supply has almost been reached [→table 10.2].

The grave problems in the economy, particularly the sluggishness of technical development and the inefficiency and blockages in production, become a threat to the military might of the socialist countries. The objective that the Soviet Union, along with its allies, should keep pace with the capitalist world in this respect demands ever greater, almost intolerable sacrifices. For the military power of the Warsaw Pact, which is on a far lower level in terms of volume of production, to maintain parity with the North Atlantic Alliance, it has to expend a far greater proportion of its production. Meanwhile, more and more economically very backward countries have become allies of the bloc in the last few decades; military and economic assistance to them is a heavy burden on the Soviet Union and its partner countries. All these circumstances increasingly encroach on the share of production intended for consumption, so preserving the low standard of living. The other countries operating under the classical system, those outside the Soviet bloc, come up against similar difficulties.

There is a partial connection between the economic situation and the second group of inducements to change: public dissatisfaction. There are frequent complaints from many sections of society—workers, peasants, officials, pensioners, students, teachers, health workers—about the low standard of living and the irritation, deprivation, and defenselessness caused by shortage. The low quality and narrow choice of products, the backwardness of the service sector, the shabbiness and bleakness of the manmade environment, and the destruction of the natural environment are all reasons why a sense of frustration develops and a dejected or even embittered mood of anger breaks out.

---

[2]For an examination of the slowdown in the Soviet Union, see A. Bergson (1978c), D. L. Bond and H. S. Levine (1983), P. Desai (1986a, 1986b), G. E. Schroeder (1985), and M. L. Weitzman (1983). For analysis of Czechoslovakia, see F. Levcik (1986), and of Poland, see L. Balcerowicz (1988) and B. Kaminski (1989).

But the dissatisfaction does not spring solely from the economic sphere in the narrow sense. Citizens are harassed by official insolence and bureaucratic arbitrariness. Everyone, particularly the intelligentsia, feels stifled by the very tight constraints on personal freedom, the lack of free expression, the prevarications or lies in the official propaganda, and the myriad forms of repression. However used to them people are, and however much they become the normal state of everyday life, it is beyond human nature to bear with them indefinitely.

Connected with the last two groups of phenomena there is a third group of inducements to change: loss of confidence by those in power. The classical system ensures the bureaucracy almost total power, but this can only be kept stable so long as at least the bureaucracy itself is still convinced of the legitimacy of its power, the superiority of the system it runs, the scientific basis and correctness of its ideas for transforming the society, its messianic mission, and the invincibility of its military force. Once this faith within the bureaucracy and among the sincere adherents of the Communist party starts to be shaken, change is on the agenda. And the deeper the crisis of confidence becomes, the nearer the whole system is to collapse.[3]

The recognition that as the economic difficulties in the socialist countries grew worse, the capitalist system was proving robust certainly contributed to the unease and lost confidence of those in power. There were spectacular achievements in economic growth, technical development, and exports by a whole range of countries like West Germany, Japan, and the so-called newly industrializing countries (NICs).[4]

Brutal repression is a vital disciplinary weapon under the classical system. However, it does not merely afflict the committed opponents of the regime; everyone, even the adherents of the system and the members of the ruling elite, is threatened by it. They too come to demand legal security and legality, at least for themselves. But by doing so they cast doubt on the legitimacy of using repressive measures unconditionally, even though that is one of the basic conditions for the classical system's stability.

---

[3]It is worth referring here to Lenin, the great expert on the theory and practice of revolution: "It is not sufficient for revolution that the exploited and oppressed masses understand the impossibility of living in the old way and demand changes; for revolution, it is necessary that the exploiters should not be able to live and rule in the old way." V. I. Lenin [1920] (1966, pp. 84–85).

[4]A. N. Yakovlev, one of Gorbachev's closest colleagues, said in a speech to the 1990 Congress of the Communist party of the Soviet Union, "We cannot repeal the fact that the volume of labor production in South Korea is ten times higher than in the North, and that people in West Germany live better than in the East," Quoted in *The New York Times*, July 8, 1990, p. 4.

The edifice of the classical system is bonded together with various kinds of cement: among others, with the faith of the elite wielding power, and the naked repression unconstrained by any laws or ethical norms. Both these bonding materials start to break down, and the edifice becomes unstable.

Finally, the fourth inducement to change is outside example. Each socialist country is influenced by the events in the other socialist countries. The political change in the Soviet Union and Eastern Europe had a mobilizing effect on the students demonstrating in Beijing in 1989. The East German and Czechoslovak movements in the dramatic times of 1989 were likewise a day-to-day influence on each other. Even in places like Romania and Albania, where the system had taken extreme totalitarian forms and long managed to insulate the population from news of the other socialist countries, the effort was fruitless in the end. Modern forms of communication know no frontiers and cannot be excluded with barbed wire and border guards: the fact that people listened to foreign radio stations and watched foreign television programs made a big contribution to the "domino effect" in the socialist countries. Apart from that, a decisive contribution was made by the alteration in Soviet foreign policy, which led to the relinquishment of its rule over Eastern Europe.[5]

16.2 The Depth and Radicalism of the Changes

The move away from the classical system is a complex process that takes place in several different spheres of social activity. There is change in the political structure, the ideology, the distribution of property rights, the relative weights of the various coordination mechanisms, the structure of economic growth, the relations of supply and demand, and so on. The behavior of many actors in the economy alters. To confine the analysis to some particular sphere could produce a one-sided picture.

In the case of each individual phenomenon one can observe, in a particular country at a particular time, how far the country has moved away from the classical system, or, more precisely, from the theoretical prototype of that system. Distance from the classical system is a multidimensional category. This book conducts the analysis in two dimensions, so as to make it simpler to survey.

The first dimension is the *depth* of change. "Depth" can be interpreted by referring back to figure 15.1. The closer a change is to the

---

[5]Although this change in Soviet foreign policy was an outside factor from the Eastern European countries' point of view, it was induced by a weakening of the system inside the Soviet Union.

beginning of the causal chain explaining the characteristics of the classical system, the deeper that change is, and the farther it is from the beginning of the chain, the more superficial it is. Accordingly, an alteration to the coordination mechanism (block 3) is deeper than a change that takes place merely in the growth priorities. But a transformation of property relations (block 2) is deeper still, and the deepest, really fundamental change is brought by altering the political structure (block 1). So the gradations of "depth" and "superficiality" refer to the sphere in which the system changes.

The second dimension is the *radicalism* of the change. Using the scheme of figure 15.1, one can say that a change in any block may be radical, partial, inconsiderable, or even spurious, a "surrogate" action. This mode of description is employed repeatedly in chapters 17–24; just a couple of examples are given here for the sake of vividness. When discussing the coordination mechanism (block 3), it is worth distinguishing between a full and a partial elimination of short-term planning instructions: the former is clearly a more radical change, and the latter a more moderate one. Or if one takes politics (block 1), there is a significant difference between an open proclamation of a multiparty system and implicit tolerance of opposition groups. The latter is an important alteration, but it is not a far-reaching one, whereas the former causes a fundamental change in the system.

There are several kinds of connection between the changes of varying depth and radicalism, and study of them raises a number of intriguing issues. How lasting can a more superficial change be if it is not based on deeper changes? Does a deeper change necessarily bring all the other, more superficial changes in its wake? What kind of delays occur? Can a radical change in one block (for instance, the coordination mechanism) be sustained permanently if there is only a partial, moderate change in a deeper block (for instance, property relations)? In all events, the analysis of the classical system, notably the summary of it in chapter 15, supplies tools for a combined, complex analysis of the depth and radicalism of the changes.

16.3 Reform and Revolution

There is no consensus in the literature dealing with the socialist system or in day-to-day political parlance on what should be termed "reform," "restructuring" (the Russian expression, *perestroika*, made famous by Gorbachev), "transformation," "transition," or "revolution." All one can do here is to clarify the sense in which these terms are used in this book.

Let me start clarifying the concepts with some negative statements. A change that fails to produce at least a moderately radical alteration in the basic attributes of blocks 1, 2, and 3 in figure 15.1 cannot be given the rank of a "reform." I do not deem to be a reform any change confined to blocks 4 and 5, that is, the last links in the causal chain, the superficial phenomena in economic activity, even if the change is an important one. Nor do I rate as a reform a change that affects the deeper spheres of the causal chain but produces only a modest alteration in them, or not even that, merely creating an illusion of change. Such pseudoreforms are dealt with in the next chapter.

Turning to the positive definition of the concept, I term a *reform* any change that permanently and essentially alters at least one basic attribute of at least one out of blocks 1, 2, and 3, but without taking the system out of the family of the socialist system. So the definition includes three elements:

1. It has to be deep: it must affect at least one out of the three spheres of political structure, property relations, and coordination mechanisms.

2. It has to be at least "moderately radical." A partial, moderate change is also termed a reform here, in line with common parlance.

3. At the same time, the term reform does not include a complete change of system, again in line with common parlance.[6]

When the most radical change possible occurs in the deepest link of the causal chain, the political structure—when the Communist party's monopoly of power is broken—the change "crosses the Rubicon." It is not a reform any more, but a *revolution*. In other words, reform covers essential, deep, and radical changes, but neither in depth nor in radicalism does it go so far as to abandon the basic distinguishing mark of the socialist system: the undivided power of the Communist party.

Once the Communist party's monopoly of power has ceased permanently, the country concerned is undergoing a revolution, which entails moving from one system's family into another. In this respect this interpretation employs the formula of Hegel and Marx: revolution implies a "qualitative" change, not just a "quantitative" one. The postrevolutionary system differs from the prerevolutionary one in its basic features.

This interpretation focuses attention on the end result of the change, not on any particular characteristic of the events leading up to that result. Historians and other social scientists, and also everyday speech, define the term "revolution" in several different ways. Three of these are: (a) Revolution takes place as a swift, sudden explosion, as opposed to evolution, which is a slow and steady process; (b) revolution is started "from

---

[6]The definition employed here is substantially broader than the one I used in an earlier study (1986b).

below" by pressure from the masses in the form of demonstrations, strikes, or even an uprising, while reform is initiated "from above" by enlightened members of the existing ruling group dissatisfied with the existing regime; (c) revolution is violent and accompanied by death, bloodshed, and possibly civil warfare, while reform is peaceful and nonviolent.

There is no denying that all three interpretations are widespread and no doubt that people are entitled to use them. All that needs emphasizing here is that the interpretation of the concept of revolution used in this book is not based on criteria a, b, and c; it exclusively considers the end result of the change, based on criteria 1, 2, and 3 explained above.

I must add that the changes taking place in the socialist countries are ambivalent in terms of the other definitions of revolution mentioned. (a) The big changes took place swiftly and sometimes explosively in some countries, but relatively slowly and steadily in others; (b) various combinations of changes initiated "from above" and forced "from below" appear; and (c) in most countries the change was nonviolent, but bloody, violent changes have also occurred (Hungary in 1956, Romania in 1989).

The radical turn of events in block 1—the end of the Communist party's monopoly of power—brings with it changes in the other blocks. This is the kind of transformation for which I reserve the expression *postsocialist transition* [→2.2]. Although society has inherited many features of the socialist system, it is in transition toward a capitalist market economy. A detailed analysis of this lies outside the scope of this book, and so it is only touched upon briefly in the final sections of each of the following chapters.[7] The discussion is confined to positive predictions describing the likely consequences of the legacy bequeathed by the previous regime. So in this book I say only as much about the postsocialist transition as follows directly from the analysis conducted.[8]

The distinction between reform and revolution employed here can be applied by the same logic to the capitalist system as well. In the sense that a reform is a complex of essential changes that may bring very radical restructuring but does not involve society stepping out of one family of

[7]The appendix to the list of references presents a selected bibliography of the literature in English on postsocialist transition. An attempt was made to cover the latest materials and include them in the book in the most updated form, at a time when the text had already been set. For this reason, no literary sources have been given for the short sections on certain aspects of the postsocialist transition at the end of the following chapters, and there are no references to the literature contained in the appendix.

[8]As mentioned in the preface, I summarized my normative position and economic policy proposals for the postsocialist transition in my book *The Road to a Free Economy* (1990). These proposals rely very largely on the positive analysis summed up in this book. Even so, the themes of the two works are clearly different: the subject of this book is a positive analysis of the socialist system, whereas the other is a normative proposal referring to the postsocialist system.

systems and into another, the renewal of capitalism by pursuing an active governmental economic policy on the lines advocated by Keynes and developing the welfare state was a reform, not a revolution. Neither Labour party Britain nor the Sweden of the Social Democratic party crossed over to the system family to which the Soviet Union, the Eastern European countries, and North Korea belong. On the other hand, it was a revolution that took place in Russia in 1917 and China in 1949, when the Communist party gained undivided power, so that the two countries entered the socialist system family. Consequently, I use the term "revolution" for the changes of system both in Russia in 1917 and in Eastern Europe in 1989; in both cases there was a qualitative leap from one family of systems to the other (even though the leaps bear opposite signs).

This book refrains from discussing whether some leap from one family of systems into another constitutes a revolution or a counterrevolution. In the official ideology of classical socialism, the approval implied by the word "revolution" is given to a leap taking the development of society "forward," that is, toward superior socialism, and the stigma of "counterrevolution" is attached to one pushing it "backward," namely, toward inferior capitalism. As said before, I reject this evaluation concerning superiority and inferiority. This leads to the rejection of this distinction between "revolution" and "counterrevolution" as well. A consistently radical change in the deepest fundamental attributes of some society—that and only that is what in this book qualifies as a revolution.[9]

Equipped with that system of concepts, let me return to movement away from the classical system. The revolution in some countries is preceded by a longer or shorter process of reform. That was the case in Hungary and Poland, for instance. But in other countries society passed directly into revolution and so into postsocialist transition, omitting the stage of reform. That is what happened, for instance, in East Germany.

The system of concepts outlined in this section introduces "pure" categories. Some actual historical formations can easily be described by one

---

[9]Many outstanding figures in the reform of socialism have termed the reform (i.e., the perestroika) a revolution. "Perestroika is a word with many meanings. But if we are to choose from its many possible synonyms the key one which expresses its essence most accurately, then we can say thus: perestroika is a revolution. Perestroika is a revolutionary process for it is a jump forward in the development of socialism, in the realization of its essential characteristics." M. S. Gorbachev (1987, pp. 50–51).

To avoid a confusion of ideas, it is worth underlining that in the usage of this book perestroika is an essential, deep, and radical move away from the classical system; in other words, a true reform. But it is not a revolution; at most it prepares the ground for a revolution or might grow into one step by step.

pure category or another. Others are less clear-cut. Here are a few examples.

Some republics in the Soviet Union and Yugoslavia were turned to a multiparty system; the first free elections were held, and the Communist party lost its power. To that extent a revolution occurred there. But in both regions the future of the union was unclear, and it was uncertain when and to what extent the constituent republics would realize their ambitions to become independent. Nor was it clear what forms the revolutionary change would take and what transitional stages would occur, or whether the process would move in the reverse direction.

The periods of reform socialism and postsocialist transition are quite clearly distinguishable in the chronology of historical events in Hungary and Poland, for instance, but the same cannot be said of the Soviet Union, where the two kinds of process became interwoven in various ways in the late 1980s and early 1990s, particularly in the political sphere. It is unclear whether the dramatic events in Romania, Bulgaria, and Albania in terms of their end result will conserve a hardly altered classical system, spark off a process of reform socialism, or come to constitute a true revolution that launches both countries on the path of a postsocialist transition.

The fact that these questions concerning these countries cannot be answered at the moment does not refute the workability of the conceptual framework. On the contrary, it is these pure, clearly defined categories that allow one to formulate precisely the questions about the state of transformation of the countries concerned. The manuscript of this book cannot be kept up to date on a daily basis. It may be that by the time the book appears in print, the situation in Romania or the Soviet Union will differ from the one when these lines were written. I hope, however, that the conceptual apparatus, the set of analytical tools, will remain workable, however the fate of the socialist countries may develop in the coming years. In fact, future developments will set the examination for the theoretical apparatus; they will confirm or deny its usefulness as a way of analyzing the latest information and events.

Even if the momentary state of some country or other cannot be placed in this conceptual framework with complete certainty, and even if an about-turn may occur any day in many countries, it certainly seems likely that all the consolidated socialist countries apart from the two bastions mentioned before (North Korea and Cuba) have moved away from the classical system. In 1977 about 32 percent of the world's population lived under the classical socialist system, whereas in the spring of 1991 the figure was 0.006 percent. So it seems justified to say that the classical system is a closed chapter of history. The overwhelming majority of the socialist world has gone beyond it, along the road of reform and revolution.

16.4 A Chronological Survey of Reforms and Revolutions

The last two sections introduced a system of concepts with the help of which the processes of moving away from the classical system can be surveyed and classified.[10]

Table 16.1 offers a bird's-eye view of one group of countries in the order in which the first move away from the classical system was made. The table sets out to show in which countries and when the change began with reform (column 1), the reform turned into a revolution (column 2), and the move began directly as a revolution, omitting the phase of reform (column 3).[11]

The table itself shows that the process is not unidirectional. There is no triumphant march forward from the classical system, advancing without a standstill until the system attains the desired degree of transformation. There is movement both forward and back, and in some place or other the cart may become stuck in a rut for quite some time, moving neither forward nor back. There were movements that were bloodily defeated or at least suppressed (suppression of the first Hungarian reform in 1954; military defeat of the Hungarian revolution in 1956; the halting of the first Soviet reform in 1958; the crushing of the Czechoslovak reform in 1968).

Table 16.1 demonstrates this dramatic movement forward and back only in terms of the three main alternatives (the classical system, reform, and revolution).

It is worth noticing particularly how each stage of reform or each revolution begins. The book describes several negative phenomena that develop under all socialist systems, although their intensity varies. These resemble the serious diseases of a living organism that take a long time to develop, lying dormant, perhaps for an extended period, without

---

[10]Summary surveys of the reform process in various countries have been elaborated. See, for *Yugoslavia,* D. A. Dyker (1990); for *Hungary,* I. T. Berend (1990), J. Kornai (1986b), and G. Révész (1990); for *China,* D. Perkins (1988), J. S. Prybyla (1990), and B. L. Reynolds, ed. (1988); for *Poland,* L. Balcerowicz (1988) and J. B. Kaminski (1989); and for the *Soviet Union,* J. Adam (1989), A. Åslund (1989), P. Desai (1989), E. A. Hewett (1988), and J. B. Tedstrom, ed. (1990). An outstanding overall analysis of the reform process is presented in W. Brus and K. Laski (1989).

[11]One important criterion for choosing the countries was the clarity of the information available at the time the book was being written. The choice has been confined to countries where there seemed to be no doubt involved in dividing their histories into periods.

TABLE 16.1
Reform and Revolution: A Chronological Review

| Country | Reform | Revolution and Postsocialist Transition | | Events Connected with the Dates |
		As a Continuation of Reform	Bypassing Reform	
Yugoslavia	1949–			1949: Yugoslavia breaks away from the Soviet bloc
Parts of country	1949–90	1990		1990: First multiparty elections in certain republics
Hungary	1953–54			1953: Prime Minister Imre Nagy announces government program of reform
				1954: Nagy ousted from power
			1956	October 23, 1956: Popular uprising
				November 4, 1956: Soviet military intervention
	1963–89	1989		1963: Political amnesty marks start of the easing of repression
				1989: Multiparty system declared
Soviet Union	1953–64			1953: Stalin dies
				1964: Khrushchev ousted, Brezhnev takes power
	1985–			1985: Gorbachev comes to power
Parts of country	1985–90	1990		1990: First multiparty elections in certain republics
Czechoslovakia	1968			January 1968: "Prague Spring" begins
				August 1968: Military intervention by Warsaw Pact
			1989	1989: "Velvet Revolution"
China	1978–			1978: Deng Xiaoping proclaims his reform policy: privatization of agriculture starts in 1979
Poland	1980–81			1980: Solidarity trade union forms
			1989	1989: "Round-Table Agreement" reached by Communist government and Solidarity
Vietnam	1987–			1987: Economic reform proclaimed
East Germany			1989	1989: Berlin Wall falls

Note: The table is not all-inclusive; it merely picks out a few of the countries that feature in table 1.1. An important criterion for choosing the countries was the clarity of the information, available at the time the book was written, for the periodization introduced in this chapter. The countries have been placed in order of the first occasion on which each made a move away from the classical system, whether in the form of a reform or a revolution. The right-hand column is intended exclusively as an interpretation of the dates in the table.

breaking out and consigning the patient to bed. The grave and long-term failures of the system must be distinguished from the ad hoc events that bring the problems out with dramatic force and provide the initial impetus for the subsequent changes. The gun has been cleaned and loaded, but a finger is needed to trigger off the process.

The sequence of events and the constellation of forces in various countries show no conspicuous regularity. In one country the process may be triggered by the death of a great leading figure in the classical system (Stalin in the Soviet Union or Mao in China), while in another the same leader who presided over the establishment of the classical system may head the reform process as well (e.g., Tito in Yugoslavia). In every case, both external and internal forces are involved, but their relative influences and the specific forms their effects take vary according to the country and the period. A big influence on the launch and advancement of the reform, and later on the preparations for revolution, is exerted by initiatives "from above," measures carried out by enlightened members of the ruling elite.[12] At the same time, there is a strong effect from pressure "from below," ranging from faint but perceptible murmuring to noisy protest, and from strikes to bloody uprisings. There is variation by country and period in the relative strengths and mutual effects of the impulses "from above" and "from below." The chapter began with an analogy: the classical system produces a fabric so closely woven that if one strand breaks it all unravels sooner or later. To develop the analogy, there is no regularity about the point where the strands start to break, or about the order in which the rest of the fabric unravels and how long it takes. All that seems certain is that if the strands begin to break at an essential point, the disintegration process takes place.

This book cannot undertake a specific historical analysis of the events, which is left to other works. The chapters that follow use a cross-section, not a temporal, longitudinal section, to examine the processes. The aim is to arrive at a generalization by taking a few *tendencies of changes* observable in all the societies abandoning the classical system, while refraining from giving an account of which countries each tendency appears in, what antecedents it has, and what conditions it develops under. In effect, each group of phenomena termed here a "tendency" is a model in itself. Each tendency is an abstraction distilled from the multiplicity

---

[12]In Hungary, the party invited an expert committee consisting of economic managers and economists to prepare a detailed blueprint for the economic reform of 1968.

The party leadership in the Soviet Union set up a similar committee in 1985 to devise the measures of reform. G. K. Popov (1987b) compares this process with the preparation of the "great reforms" under Tsar Alexander II, when there was likewise an accompaniment of bureaucratic bargaining.

of historical realizations to be found in the various countries at various periods in time.

To some extent the approach in part 3 differs from the one taken in part 2. Chapters 3–15 focused on the permanent characteristics of the classical system. This appeared to be feasible, because a mature system that had stabilized over a long time was being examined. A summary has been given of a period of history with a clearly defined beginning and end. The movement away from the classical system, on the other hand, presents less settled conditions; it is a historical restructuring that has yet to end. Even if one talks of a reform system, it is more in flux than its predecessor, since it is here that all the inner contradictions inherent in classical socialism break out. So it seems practical to place at the center of the examination the tendencies of the movement and the change, along with the countertendencies working against them.

17

The "Perfection" of Control

THE FIRST tendency is paradoxical. Although an impression of genuine change is conveyed by official declarations, regulations, and campaigns, the classical system in fact remains unaffected in any of its basic features.

17.1 General Description of the Tendency

The initiators of the events making up this tendency are influenced by the motives presented in section 16.1: they realize the classical system has encountered some serious inherent contradictions. They see that something has to be done to remedy the ills. Yet they remain convinced of the correctness of the classical system's basic principles and of its superiority. So they argue that all the difficulties are solely (or at least mainly) caused by a failure to apply the correct principles consistently enough. The system would operate substantially better if a few secondary principles, legal measures, and institutions were replaced by more effective ones and resolutions applied more consistently, while the primary principles were kept unchanged.

Many official resolutions and economic studies suggesting that line of argument contain calls like "let us perfect our system of planning," "let us perfect the organization of work," and so on. They convey the impression that the phenomenon they are discussing is very good as it is, and a few finishing touches will suffice to make it perfect.[1] Formulas like these have induced several authors to christen the whole trend the strat-

---

[1]E. Honecker, the last East German leader, for instance, in talking about the Kombinate movement [→17.3], called it "the most significant step in the 'perfecting' (*Vervollkomm-nung*) of the GDR economic mechanism." I. Jeffries and M. Melzer, eds. (1987, p. 57). The North Korean slogan ran: "Let us raise still higher the superiority of our country's socialism."

A similar formulation can be found in a writing of the Romanian dictator, N. Ceausescu (1978, pp. 41–42): "The fact that the working people are criticizing certain negative phenomena or mistakes committed in various sectors of society does not mean that they have doubts as to the socialist social system, but it is an expression of the desire of the working masses that such phenomena should be eliminated, and this is in keeping with the concerns of the Party for perfecting its forms and methods of conducting society."

egy of *"perfection" of the control,* using the quotation marks with an ironic intent.[2]

All the changes assignable to the perfection tendency leave unaffected the deeper basic features of the system, namely, the party's monopoly of power and the property relations. To use the terminology of figure 15.1, the alterations are mainly in block 3, but even there only very superficial changes occur. Bureaucratic coordination basically retains its dominant role; the main means of bureaucratic coordination continues to be direct control and planning instructions. All that the perfection campaigns tinker with are the methods and institutions of the command economy. The changes do not substantially modify the rules of behavior.[3]

Comparing the histories of the various countries, there is no clear relation in time between the attempts at perfection and the reforms. In some countries like Hungary and the Soviet Union, there was one period or more when officialdom tried first with perfection regulations and then embarked on the road of reform. There are countries like Cuba where repeated perfection programs have been proclaimed, but they have never gone further than that. There are yet other countries like East Germany that have leaped directly from the classical socialist system, or, more precisely, from a repeatedly perfected version of it, to the state of post-socialist transition, avoiding the stage of deeper and more radical reforms altogether.

In this account, the official and unofficial proposals for perfection programs are not segregated from promotion of them into party resolutions or state regulations, or from the subsequent implementation of such resolutions and regulations. Normally, the resolution or regulation is only faithful in part to the original proposal, and the implementation only applies in part the resolution or regulation. When one attempt proves fruitless, the next is started.[4] The perfection campaigns never at-

---

[2]T. Bauer (1987) provides a summary of this tendency. More detailed examination of the perfection tendency can be found for *Albania* in A. Schnytzer (1982, chap. 2); for *Bulgaria,* in R. J. McIntyre (1988, chap. 4) and M. L. Boyd (1990); for *East Germany* and *Romania,* in D. Granick (1975, parts 2 and 3).

[3]Observers may be misled by the fact that some economists and politicians advocating a strategy of perfecting the classical system use the term "reform" for their ideas. And why not? There is no patent on the use of the word reform; everyone defines it as they like.

It was mentioned in section 16.3 that this book uses the word reform in a restricted sense. But this conceptual clarification, which orients the reader within the terminology of this book, does not remove the difficulty of finding several other, often mutually contradictory definitions of reform in the flood of political statements and academic writings on this subject.

[4]G. E. Schroeder (1979) aptly named the repeated waves of Soviet perfection campaigns since 1953 "the treadmill of reforms." One stage in this series was the 1965 program often

tain the desired objective because the real roots of the problems lie much deeper, and the mending and patching is never intended to disturb them.

17.2 Reorganizations on the Upper Level

One recurrent concept goes like this: the response to the appearance of a harmful phenomenon must be to delegate the responsibility; in other words, to make an assigned state institution responsible for eliminating the problem. For example, the Soviet Union in 1986 set up a state organization with wide legal powers to monitor product quality. The activity of the organization Gospriemki led to frequent intervention and example making, and ultimately to a deceleration of the production process, but it solved none of the quality problems. The problems of the classical system, such as shortage and poor quality, have causes far too deep for the problems to be solved by a single state resolution or the appointment of a body responsible for overcoming them.

Repeated reorganization campaigns take place. These are particularly conspicuous examples of the fact that one is dealing with surrogate activities and spurious reforms that give the impression of change. The property relations are conserved, and along with them remains direct bureaucratic control as the basic coordinator of social production. The constant tinkering is done merely with the organizational forms. A line of argument often advanced in response to the rigidity and slowness of control runs like this: there are too many layers between the top leadership and the lowest executives in the hierarchy, and so authority and the firms must be brought closer to each other. Sometimes this is done by splitting up the organization of the ministries, on the grounds that this allows each ministry to run its firms more directly. Sometimes exactly the opposite is preferred: ministries must be merged to produce lower staffing in the apparatus, less direct intervention, and better coordination between sectors and firms controlled by the new larger ministry. The alternation of mergers and splitting of high authorities is illustrated in table 17.1.

Under bureaucratic coordination there necessarily must be some activities aligned to the performance of functions (control of finance,

---

referred to as the "Kosygin reform" after its presenter, the Soviet prime minister at the time. For a more detailed account of the Soviet perfection campaigns, including the Kosygin reform, see the work of G. E. Schroeder mentioned and M. Bornstein's study (1985). The perfection campaigns at the beginning of the Gorbachev period are returned to later [→17.4].

The literature on the perfection proposals and campaigns in East Germany is particularly extensive. See, for instance, M. Keren (1973) and G. Leptin and M. Melzer (1978).

TABLE 17.1
Number of Top Economic Authorities in the Soviet Union

Year	Number of Economic Ministries	Number of State Committees and Bureaus	Total Number of Top Economic Authorities
1939	21	—	21
1947	33	—	33
1958	13	11	24
1963	6	45	51
1966	41	12	53
1975	52	14	66
1979	55	20	75
1984	56	22	78
1986	51	27	78
1987	52	28	80
1989	48	30	78

Source: Compiled by C. Krüger for this book on the basis of the following publications: 1939 and 1947: A. Nove (1969, pp. 267, 295); all other data are from the serial publication *Directory of Soviet Officials: National Organizations* (Washington, D.C.: Government Printing Office, 1958, 1963, 1966, 1975, 1979, 1984, 1986, 1987, and 1989).

labor, technical development, and so forth) and others where territorial aspects come to the fore. One form of organizational juggling is to declare either the functional or the territorial principle to be dominant. Khrushchev, for instance, in 1957 suddenly reorganized the whole running of the Soviet economy on territorial lines; later, in the Brezhnev–Kosygin period, there was a new reorganization restoring priority to the functional principle. Reorganizations on territorial lines will be discussed later [→18.4].

17.3 Merger of Firms

Reorganizations are performed at lower as well as upper levels. The main trend is toward the merger of firms in both the state-owned and cooperative sectors. Some figures for international comparison are presented in tables 17.2, 17.3, and 17.4.

The tables show that the concentration of production is much higher in socialist economies than in capitalist ones. There are several reasons

TABLE 17.2
Size Distribution of Industrial Firms: International Comparison, 1970

	Socialist Countries[a]	Capitalist Countries[b]
Total manufacturing		
1. Average employment per firm	197	80
2. Percentage of those employed in large firms[c]	66	32
Textile industry		
1. Average employment per firm	355	81
2. Percentage of those employed in large firms	75	17
Ferrous metals		
1. Average employment per firm	2,542	350
2. Percentage of those employed in large firms	95	79
Machinery		
1. Average employment per firm	253	82
2. Percentage of those employed in large firms	61	28
Chemicals		
1. Average employment per firm	325	104
2. Percentage of those employed in large firms	79	35
Food processing		
1. Average employment per firm	103	65
2. Percentage of those employed in large firms	39	16

Source: É. Ehrlich (1985a, pp. 278–83).
[a]Sample, including Czechoslovakia, East Germany, Hungary, and Poland.
[b]Sample, including Austria, Belgium, France, Italy, Japan, and Sweden.
[c]Large firms are those where more than five hundred persons are employed.

for the difference. Although the phenomenon of economies of scale favors concentration in a capitalist economy too, there are forces at work in the opposite direction. For there are "diseconomies of scale" as well, and small and medium-sized units are able to survive permanently and

TABLE 17.3

Size Distribution of Construction Firms: International Comparison, around 1980

	Share of Firms in Total Employment within the Construction Sector (percent)		
	Less than 10 Employees	10–499 Employees	500 Employees or More
Socialist countries			
East Germany	—	21.0[a]	79.0
Hungary	14.6	15.4	70.0
Poland	8.7	15.1	76.2
Capitalist countries			
Austria	2.4	74.9	22.7
Denmark	41.8	51.5	6.7
Finland	13.3	66.7	20.0
France	48.3	47.1	4.6
Ireland	16.6	56.2	27.2
Netherlands	17.3	71.8	10.9
United Kingdom	28.1	45.2	26.7
West Germany	11.6	81.1	7.3

Source: Compiled by P. Mihályi for this book, based on United Nations (1986a, table IV.6) and direct communications with United Nations Secretariat.

[a]Firms with 1–499 employees.

successfully alongside large units in many industries. Free private enterprise allows continual entry by new small and medium-sized firms. The main regulator of the size distribution is the natural selection that occurs under the conditions of market competition. This can be somewhat affected by bureaucratic state intervention, which works in many cases against the trend toward concentration. Many countries have laws preventing the emergence of monopolies and cartels and the occurrence of certain kinds of mergers. In addition, some groups of small entrepreneurs, like farmers, self-employed craftsmen, and other people with small businesses, receive government support in the form of subsidies or tax or customs tariff reductions.

The classical socialist system creates a quite different situation, primarily by altering the property relations. The natural replacement for small and medium-sized units from new entries by private entrepreneurs

TABLE 17.4
Firm Size in East and West Germany, 1988

	Employees per Firm	
Sector	East Germany[a]	West Germany
Chemical industry	1,419	296
Construction material	712	71
Electrical engineering/ electronics	1,554	333
Food industries	480	125
Light industries	671	95
Mechanical engineering/ manufacture of vehicles	838	217
Metal industry	3,209	474
Textile industry	1,301	169
Total industry	893	190

Source: C. Schnabel (1991, table 3).
[a]Excluding apprentices.

ceases to occur. The newly created, publicly owned firms are large to start with. Later on they are subject to repeated mergers that result from bureaucratic intervention, not market forces [→7.3]. The bureaucracy has several motives for acting in this way [→5.5, 9.4],[5] of which just one may be emphasized here. The mergers make the business profiles of each firm more transparent: the fewer units there are to be controlled, the easier control and monitoring become. In fact, the easiest thing of all from the control point of view would be to eliminate all overlap between the production of firms and have perfect monopolies.[6] This line of argument conveys how well the effort to merge firms ties in with the classical system's "perfection" tendency.

Merging firms frequently serves as a substitute for deeper and more radical reforms. That was the case in East Germany, for instance. Table

[5]The supreme leaders are not the only ones with an interest in amalgamation, for the managers of large firms are glad enough to see a reinforcement of their economic and political positions. See E. Szalai (1982, 1989) on Hungary, and J. Winiecki (1989) on Poland.

[6]Monopolies developed in several branches in the Soviet Union. See R. I. McKinnon (1990a) and V. Tsapelik and A. Iakovlev (1990).

The amalgamation of firms and the creation of monopolies appeared in their ultimate form in East Germany, where the so-called combines covered all the units in whole subbranches, or all the units in a subbranch in a particular region. See P. J. Bryson and M. Melzer (1987), D. Cornelsen (1990), and W. Gössmann (1987).

TABLE 17.5
Firm Mergers in East Germany, 1950–70

Year	Number of Firms (percent)	Employment (percent)
1950	100	100
1960	68	135
1970	49	138
1980	19	150
1987	13	153

Source: H.-G. Bannasch (1990, table 2). Reprinted by permission of Kleuver Academic Publishers.
Note: The table covers manufacturing.

17.5 shows how the concentration proceeded without a break. The process strengthened particularly in Hungary when the opponents of change were attempting to use it as a way of postponing the reform. The effect of that campaign of amalgamation, which immediately preceded the major reform measures of 1968, appears in table 17.6. There were similar phenomena in other socialist countries.

17.4 The Development of Planning and Direct Control

Another major factor in the perfection tendency, apart from reorganizations, is transformation of the methods of planning and direct control. A few typical tendencies can be picked out of the multitude of proposals, experiments, and actual modifications.

TABLE 17.6
Firm Size Distribution in Hungary

	Size Distribution (percent)		
	1958	1964[a]	1968
Small firms (less than 100 employees)	27.9	13.6	11.2
Medium firms (101–1,000 employees)	62.1	57.0	54.2
Large firms (more than 1,000 employees)	10.0	29.4	34.6

Source: I. Schweitzer (1982, p. 35).
[a]The largest campaign of mergers was in the period 1962–64.

There is an initiative from researchers toward the use of mathematical methods and computers in the elaboration of plans.[7] This elicits an appreciable response, and some members of the planning apparatus join the academics in endeavoring to do this. In several socialist countries, separate sections specializing in the practical application of mathematical methods develop in the central planning offices. It is beyond the scope of this book either to describe this trend in full or to assess its intellectual and practical achievements and failures. Mathematical methods, theoretical and econometric models, and computer processes have their uses under any system in preparing for decisions at the upper, medium, and lower levels.[8] In this respect, brief mention is made only of experiments closely tied to the classical methods of planning and aimed at perfecting them.

The pioneers of mathematical planning hoped their methods would be welcomed. Their disillusion was all the greater when the planning bureaucracy, which often used rough guesswork, rejected their refined, lucid range of devices as an alien body. If one considers the actual sociology of the planning operation, not its declared principles, the resistance is understandable. The political leadership has no wish to state openly its real political goals in the form of "welfare functions" and "planner's preferences." All members of the planning apparatus strengthen their negotiating position in both vertical bargaining and horizontal reconciliation by keeping some items of information back and distorting others, upward or downward, according to their own interest. Complete candor would make their own lives harder. The aim of their calculations is not to serve any absolute "social interest" but to support their own viewpoint. That can only be hindered by careful outside checks and collation of their figures before they are fed into a computer; their manipulations are upset by the inexorable logic of a system of mathematical equations.

[7]For the pioneering works in the Soviet Union, see L. V. Kantorovich [1937] (1960, 1965), V. S. Nemchinov, ed. (1965), and N. P. Fedorenko, ed. (1975). For Hungary, see A. Bródy (1964, 1969a), J. Kornai and T. Lipták (1965), and J. Kornai (1965).

For a Western approach to the use of mathematical methods in planning, see W. Leontief (1953a, 1953b) and E. Malinvaud (1967).

For surveys and appraisals, see M. Ellman (1973), G. M. Heal (1973), P. Sutela (1984, 1991), and A. Zauberman (1975, 1976).

[8]The spread of mathematical methods of economic analysis in the socialist countries, including the writings on mathematical planning models, helped to break the intellectual monopoly of Marxist political economy and introduce economists to the international currents of modern economics. It trained its practitioners to respect strict logical relationships and facts and data instead of dead dogmas. To that extent it was useful in stirring up ideology, regardless of the part it played in conserving or transforming the old methodology of planning.

But assume for a moment that there were no resistance. Even the most up-to-date computer techniques would fail to solve a consistent calculation of the millions of variables in a national economy; the only "computer" capable of that is the market. Those hoping to replace the market with mathematics and computers were bound to be disappointed.[9]

Another trend in the perfection of planning is to try to transform the system of plan indicators.[10] The representatives of this tendency often stress the drawbacks of excessive centralization and the benefits of decentralization. Many proposals and subsequent rulings suggest employing other indicators than those used so far.[11] The compilers of them are not arguing for or against retaining the command nature of plan directives. Their concern is with exactly what needs prescribing. Here are some examples.[12]

1. The number of compulsory plan indicators needs cutting. There must be greater aggregation, but fulfillment of the smaller number of more aggregated indicators must be enforced without fail.

2. Greater scope must be given to indicators expressed in value terms and less to those measured in physical terms, as the latter tend to prompt more interference from above.

3. The system of plan indicators must not be based on indices of change from levels reached so far, as that encourages the withholding of performance and the production of false reports.

4. Under the classical system the plan indicator that is the "first among equals" is usually "total production value," that is, an indicator of gross output; tight prescription of this is the main way the authorities try to goad the producers into a quantity drive. But that can induce material-intensive production and a lopsided emphasis on products of high production value. So pride of place must go to other indicators like net production or the firm's profit.

---

[9]In fact, not many researchers in the mathematical planning camp placed hope on this. I myself played a leading part in devising and applying the first plan models in Hungary, but I never fostered the kind of illusions so aptly described by E. Neuberger (1966) as "computopia."

[10]The discussion earlier of the endeavors to introduce mathematical planning and now of the efforts to improve the system of plan indicators treated them as separate trends. Of course, they are not mutually exclusive; in several places they emerged in parallel, and possibly in conjunction with one another.

[11]Here mention must be made of the experiments in several socialist countries aimed at devising plans for the long term (periods of fifteen or twenty years). These operations left the methodology used for the annual and five-year plans or in the related regulatory mechanism unchanged. For this reason alone it is justifiable to rank them in the "perfection" category.

[12]For surveys of the discussion, see J. M. Kovács (1990, with a broad bibliographical coverage), and L. Szamuely (1982, 1984).

The proposals normally couple a new incentive scheme to the recommended alteration in the system of planning indicators.[13] In many cases this is accompanied by the proposal that the horizontal ties linking firms should be strengthened in the form of long-term contracts between them.

All these ideas just replace the old artificial formulas of information-gathering, processing, decision making, and execution with new, equally artificial formulas and "dodges." Firms can outwit any formula in fact, and if a new one is introduced experimentally, they will. When the superior organization focuses attention on one indicator, the firms improve this "chief indicator" of the day at the expense of indicators to which less heed is being paid. This is something that cannot happen in a real competitive market economy, where if one firm bungles something or misses a chance, another sooner or later grasps the opportunity in the hope of making a profit. Free entry and rivalry are hawk-eyed inspectors that no bureaucratic controllers can replace.

The last of the proposals mentioned, promotion of the firm's profit to the rank of "chief compulsory indicator," looks the most radical,[14] since it resembles the incentive formula of capitalism. In reality the fact that economic actors maximize their profits is not the most important attribute of a market mechanism based on private ownership. The major features are decentralization, free entry, and free competition.

Since the conditions for real decentralization are absent, the decentralizing proposals and amendments listed under points 1–4 do not really match the inner logic of bureaucratic coordination. If the mesh of the plan-indicator system and its complementary rules of direct bureaucratic control widens, it is easier for self-interest conflicting with the central design to intervene. Once experience begins to back that conclusion, the opposing perfection trend appears: proposals for increasing centralization instead of reducing it. The bureaucratic mesh must be narrowed, so that nothing slips through. If some designated aggregate indicator or other is evaded, more and more detailed indicators are required. If a regulation is too general and comprehensive, others that go into more

[13]The New Economic System introduced in East Germany in 1963 is a characteristic example of the "perfection" tendency: the transformation of the system of planning indices was combined with new incentive principles. See G. Leptin and M. Melzer (1978).

[14]Great attention was aroused worldwide by the proposals of E. G. Liberman [1962] (1972), which suggested that the incentives for firms should be linked to their profit. Some partial changes resulted from a few ambiguous measures taken in the Kosygin–Brezhnev period and inspired by the Liberman proposals. In terms of the classification used in this book, the Liberman concept can be placed on the border between a "perfection" tendency and a naive "market-socialist" tendency [→21], which is why it is mentioned in the discussion of both.

On the Liberman proposals, see M. Bornstein (1985), E. A. Hewett (1988), and G. E. Schroeder (1979).

detail are needed. If the existing apparatus cannot perform all its regulatory tasks, extra authorities need setting up.

The way bureaucratic coordination can perfect itself most is by completion, trying to regulate every detail. The obvious concomitant is more vigorous action to apply the decisions, tighter discipline. This was reemphasized in the Soviet Union not only under Andropov but in the early Gorbachev era, when attacks began on absenteeism and alcoholism eroding work discipline.

When one compares the histories of the various socialist countries, the effect of the perfection tendency is not uniform. Where the political structure of the classical system has become completely rigid and the stands taken in the official ideology are jealously guarded, as was the case in East Germany and Czechoslovakia in the 1970s, for instance, the spurious reforms of the perfection process help the conservative forces to maintain their positions. They mislead the disgruntled but gullible members of the apparatus, because it seems as if some change is taking place, even though only a semblance of change is being created. The situation is different in countries like Hungary in the 1960s or the Soviet Union at the beginning of the Gorbachev period, where some loosening of the rigidity of the political structure has begun, and concurrently some of the apparatus has begun to reassess the past. Even though the perfection campaigns there did not end the problems, their failure contributed to opening people's eyes. Every single setback worked to break down the self-congratulatory official ideology of the classical system.

The tendencies toward deeper and more radical change than the perfection of the classical system begin at the point where even the leading circles come to the realization that no reorganizations, no modifications to the system of instructions, and no vigorous measures designed to improve discipline will ever manage to master the constantly worsening problems.

17.5 Preview: The Organizational Structure under the Postsocialist System

The starting point of the postsocialist change of system is the state of affairs inherited from socialism, to which belongs the prevailing structure of institutions and organizations. Among the effects of the perfection tendency has been to make production far more concentrated than it is in economies where the distribution of factories of various sizes has been determined by the natural selection of the market. Sometimes a particular state-owned firm will have a total monopoly over vast areas of production or trade. Or even if the firm is not a true monopoly, the artificial mergers between firms will have given it a far bigger market share than it would attain under conditions of real market competition. These artificial formations oppose efforts to break them down into smaller units. That impedes the privatization process [→19.7] and the development of a real competitive situation.

A problem similar to some extent arises in the field of state administration. The perfection campaigns have brought numerous authorities and central organizations into being, and these fight doggedly for their survival, which hinders the fulfillment of one of the tasks of the postsocialist transformation: cutting the apparatus of the state.

On another plane the perfection tendency leaves a more favorable legacy. I noted earlier that the efforts to introduce mathematical methods of planning fail to yield any radical improvement in the way the system operates. But as mentioned before, they have at least a favorable educational effect. A new generation of economists grows up possessing up-to-date expertise in mathematics, statistics, econometrics, and computer technology, and at least some of them are familiar with the contemporary Western economic literature as well.[15] As a group they possess a more favorable intellectual grounding for the tasks set for economists under the postsocialist system.

---

[15] It is worth noting how important a role was played among the radical reformers in Hungary, Poland, and later the Soviet Union by economists who had immersed themselves in the study of mathematical economics at an earlier stage in their careers.

18

Political Liberalization

WHEREAS chapter 17 described a tendency toward pseudoreform, the following chapters present real reforming tendencies, beginning with the tendency toward political liberalization. What forms does the tendency take, and what are the forces whose influence causes it to appear? No less important, how are the counterforces intent on weakening or entirely eliminating the tendency asserted? The battle lines between these forces and counterforces differ from one country and period to another, and it is not among the aims of this book to chart them in detail. Attention is centered on the situations and conflicts one can consider most typical.

It is worth recalling the main conclusion of chapter 15: the primary role in developing and consolidating the classical system is played by a specific political structure; this forms the deepest layer in the causal chain explaining the system. It follows logically from this that the radicalism of the changes in political structure primarily decides how far the whole system can depart from its classical form.

In accordance with the parlance of academic writings on the socialist countries and political terminology, changes in the power structure and official ideology are called political reform, so long as they are appreciable and substantive but do not go more than halfway toward instituting real political democracy.[1] That conforms with the definition of reform given earlier [→16.3]. When changes of the most radical kind take place in the deepest layer, they are no longer a reform but a revolution. This is discussed briefly at the end of the chapter.

There are close relations between political and economic reforms. To some extent the political sphere must be extricated from this web of mutual effects so as to make the analysis clearer.

18.1 The Monopoly of Power

The one-party system remains so long as what takes place in the system is merely reform and no revolutionary political transformation occurs;

---

[1]For a discussion of the possibilities and limits of political reform in the Soviet Union, see A. Åslund (1989), S. Bialer (1980), W. D. Connor (1975), S. F. Cohen (1984, 1985), T. J. Colton (1986), M. I. Goldman (1987), and with focus on foriegn policy R. Pipes (1984a and b), and M. D. Shulman (1966).

the Communist party's monopoly of power continues. Without aiming
to be exhaustive, I shall examine a few important positions of power and
at the same time some manifestations of the undivided exercise of power.

1. *Appointments.* As before, under the classical system, the party decides in the reform phase who shall fill all the important posts. This
applies not only to party office but to more major state posts, more
important managerial jobs in the economic leadership, judicial appointments, and leading functions in the mass organizations.

The nomenklatura system typically remains [→3.2].[2] Although a self-
government mechanism operates formally for many selection procedures, so that the representatives of local state self-governing bodies
(soviets, councils, communes) are elected by the general public, heads
of the state administration by parliament, and leaders of local self-
governing bodies and mass organizations by their memberships, in fact,
the nomination of the candidates, or at least the endorsement of their
nomination, remains in the hands of the party organizations, with the
cooperation of the other branches of the bureaucracy.[3]

It is a problem to decide to what extent a new phenomenon, parliamentary elections with more than one candidate, fits this picture. In
some cases this is still mere pretense, since the same party organization
chooses the competing candidates, who support the same policy. But in
some parliamentary elections the official candidate faces a real opponent
with an alternative policy. Such opposing candidates either enter the election campaign of their own accord or gain nomination from some quasi-
organized or semilegal movement.[4] Parliament comes to include members who express their own independent political opinions on matters at
issue, not only criticizing the official policy but voting against party and
state proposals on some occasions. Certainly, the parliamentary majority
remains firmly in the hands of members who entered as officially selected
candidates; the government's decisions gain the required confirmation.
Yet one can still say that participation of independent candidates in the

---

[2]In Hungary this regulation was still in force over thirty years after the first wave of
reform began in 1953. The proportion of party members among local government officials
in 1985 was as follows: capital city and county councils, 99 percent; city councils, 96 percent; councils of large villages, 91 percent; village councils, 79 percent. See T. M. Horváth
(1988, p. 92).

A research project on Poland containing a survey of leading officials in the state apparatus and firms found that in 1986, 88 percent of the sample were Communist party members. See J. Wasilewski (1990, p. 750).

[3]It is worth noting that although the party still has the decisive word on appointments,
the proportion of non–party members in important positions increases. During the reform,
the Communist leadership wants to demonstrate that non–party members also have a
chance of a career in the hierarchy.

[4]This was the case, for instance, in the 1985 Hungarian and 1989 Soviet elections.

polls, followed by their election and activity in parliament, is a new kind of phenomenon which looks beyond the reform socialist system, almost "exceeds" it, and sketches the first pale outline of parliamentary democracy. When these representatives critical of those in power organize themselves into groups, the seeds of a multiparty system have appeared [→18.4].[5] This is among the elements of changes of a revolutionary nature.

2. *Government by decree.* An important mark of the monopoly of power is that separation of legislative, executive, and judicial powers fails to apply; the bureaucracy is not subordinate to the legislature, and citizens cannot appeal against the administration to the courts. In terms of essentials, the position in the reform phase has not changed since the classical system. Government is basically applied by decree even if measures may qualify formally as laws passed by parliament. So long as the ruling party's overwhelming parliamentary majority stays solid, its will almost automatically prevails.[6] Some decrees and internal regulations contradict the legislation passed by parliament. There are still numerous secret decrees and instructions.

Debates on the reform, particularly in the later phase of the process, often elicit a demand for the state to become a *state of law (Rechtsstaat* in German). The main criterion for this is that no person or institution be above the law. In that narrow sense not just the state of the classical system but the state of the reform phase, too, fail the test of a constitutional state. The party is above the law, and concurrently one can say that the whole bureaucratic apparatus is not subordinate to the law; on the contrary, the law is adjusted to the prevailing will of the administration.

3. *Disposal over the armed forces.* The organizations of the party-state dispose over the military, the police, the semicivilian, semimilitary party militia, and the penal authorities; this right of disposal is plain and indivisible. The party leadership decides on all essential personnel matters, dismissals, and promotions in the armed forces. The party leadership likewise decides the budgetary support and material resources available to the military forces. In this respect parliament's role remains formal; its members are denied even the most basic information.

The halfway advance of the reform on the road to political liberalization is clearly proved by the continued ability of those in power to use the armed forces for both outside intervention and suppression of unrest

---

[5]Such changes could be seen in the Soviet parliament in 1989–90.

[6]This automatic prevalence is precisely what the appearance of independent members of the legislature undermines.

at home.[7] Neither before nor after is there any need for endorsement of the decision to use the armed forces by the legislature (in the presence of other organized political forces or opposition movements and parties that might vote against it). So the party leadership has power over the armed forces. If one applies the Leninist theory of the state to its own system, the key issue of power is precisely disposal over the "organs of repression." In fact, from that point of view there is no appreciable difference between the systems of classical and reform socialism.[8]

18.2 The Easing of Repression

While the last section focused on the most important of the features of the political system that do not fundamentally change in the reform phase—survival of the monopoly of power—sections 18.2–18.5 deal with those in which appreciable changes occur.

The first change to mention is the easing of repression.[9] Under the classical system not just enemies but advocates of the system had lived in fear of arrest, imprisonment, torture, and death. Even functionaries who served the system devotedly often found themselves convicted on false charges. That is one of the phenomena that makes the classical system hard to sustain in its original form. In the reform period the situation changes; no loyal member of the bureaucracy need worry about being punished in spite of disciplined service. Yet this reassurance has mixed effects. While it reduces the tension within the bureaucracy, so helping to stabilize the reform, it leaves greater scope for criticism and opposing views within the bureaucracy, so weakening one of the classical system's basic cohesive forces: iron discipline extorted by fear.

[7]A couple of major historical events support this statement: The Hungarian leadership, in the midst of its internal reform process, was capable, for example, of committing armed forces to the intervention of the Warsaw Pact that strangled the Czechoslovak reform process in 1968. The Polish leadership in 1981 halted and reversed the reform process by mobilizing police and military forces and declaring a state of emergency. In addition, several times in China, the Soviet Union, and Yugoslavia, military and police forces have been used to crush minority movements, demonstrations for national autonomy, and protests against official policy, right in the middle of reform processes.

[8]There are plenty of signs that the influence of the army commanders within the party-state increased during the reform process in the Soviet Union and China, but even in those countries they did not become a separate political force.

[9]After Stalin's death, the repression eased also in most of the countries that in other respects did not embark on the road of reform and liberalization, but remained basically within the frames of the classical system.

Repression methods continue against those opposing the current political line, particularly if they seek to set up organizations separate from or opposed to the official political power.[10]

Some of the classical system's methods can still be used against individuals: a member can be disciplined by the party or excluded from it; any opponent is liable to loss of office or job, arrest, jail, internal exile, forced emigration, and so on. Meetings and demonstrations are broken up and associations and papers banned. All such weapons are used more rarely than under the classical system, and by and large less forcefully and mercilessly. More care is taken when applying the various repressive measures to observe legal formalities, which is a further inducement to moderation.

The changes in police, judicial, and penal practice are preceded or accompanied by condemnation of the previous extreme forms of repression. A milestone in exposing the crimes of the period of terror in the Soviet Union was Khrushchev's famous speech in 1956;[11] though heard at a closed party meeting, the news soon spread. A start had already been made on rehabilitating some of those condemned in the Stalin period and releasing some surviving prisoners. A second wave, exposing a far wider range of cruelty and terror, began when Gorbachev came to power.[12] Similar moves were made in Eastern Europe and China.

The effect of these events is not felt only by survivors of persecution or relatives of the innocent dead. They deeply disturb many sincere believers in the system who have not suffered repression personally. Chapters 3 and 4 on the structure and ideology of power stress how a high proportion of members of the party and officials in the bureaucracy act in total good faith with noble intentions. Many suffer profound mental shock, feeling they have been accomplices, if unwitting ones, in ghastly crimes. The moral crisis spreads beyond the intelligentsia to a great many functionaries, who feel duped and ashamed of letting themselves be mis-

[10]The bureaucracy still maintains tight control over the exercise of political liberties: a permit must be obtained for a demonstration, setting up an association or a newspaper, or even operating a photocopier.

[11]An English translation of Khrushchev's secret speech can be found in T. P. Whitney, ed. (1963).

[12]A growing number of documentary accounts of the consequences of Stalin's terror appeared in the Soviet Union in the 1980s, some as semilegal *samizdat* literature and others as legal publications. Particular mention must be made of R. A. Medvedev's monumental work, which later appeared in English as well (1989).

Official rehabilitation of the victims of the terror also took place. The breakthrough began with the 1988 party resolution that restored N. Bukharin and his associates to party membership. Bukharin, at one time general secretary of the Comintern and alongside Trotsky the main leading figure in the forces opposing Stalin, was vilified in 1938 in one of the notorious show trials, amid worldwide publicity, and then executed.

led. They want to turn over a new, clean leaf in the history of socialism. This group of "reform Communists" among the functionaries [→18.4] and the intelligentsia plays a highly important part in organizing the process of reform.

The easing of the repression is a change whose fundamental import, once grasped, provides one key to analyzing all other issues concerning the reform. The socialist system during the reform process is far from ensuring a life free of fear, but there is substantially less to fear than before.

18.3 The Constant and Variable Elements in the Official Ideology

It follows from its function that the official ideology should be always "up-to-date." Since the reform process's political line differs from the classical system's, revision of the earlier official ideology is inevitable. However, this is done tardily and reluctantly. The shapers and propagandists of the official ideology try to minimize the inconsistency between the ideas needed for ideological backing for the policy of the day and the traditionally proclaimed principles. Some principles are taken as axiomatic, and in their case the reform system's official ideology fully retains the doctrines inherited from the classical system. These need a brief review, at least in heading form, so as to understand the statements made in the period. As in chapter 4, they are just listed, without appraising their validity.

1. The Communist party is the competent leading force in society. Its monopoly of power is legitimate; preservation of it unchanged serves the people's interest. Tying in with this are the principles of the party's internal functioning: the ban on factions, the principle of democratic centralism, and the need for party discipline.

2. All essential precepts of Marxism-Leninism and its two classic exponents, Marx and Lenin, remain invariably valid.[13] Stalin, Mao Zedong,

---

[13]"Again, we are not turning away from socialism, from Marxism-Leninism, from everything that has been achieved and created by the people. But we decidedly renounce the dogmatic, bureaucratic, and voluntaristic heritage, as it does not have anything in common either with Marxism-Leninism or with real socialism." M. S. Gorbachev, *Pravda,* February 19, 1988.

The "Four Cardinal Principles," which were proposed by the designer of the Chinese reforms, Deng Xiaoping, were guidelines for the revision of the "New Constitution" in 1982. According to Peng Zhen, chairman of the Constitution Drafting Committee, "the drafting was done under the overall guidance of the Four Cardinal Principles, namely, adherence to the socialist road, to the people's democratic dictatorship, to leadership by the Communist party of China, and to Marxism-Leninism and Mao Zedong Thought." *Beijing Review,* December 13, 1982, p. 10.

and the leaders of other Communist parties in power under the classical system took wrong positions on many issues mainly because they strayed from the teachings of Marx and Lenin. The problems of the classical period arose not because the principles of Marxism-Leninism were realized in many respects, but, on the contrary, because of deviation from the precepts of Marx and Lenin.

3. Public ownership is superior to private ownership. Its predominance is an indispensable concomitant of socialism.

4. Other unimpugnable basic principles are appended to these in the socialist countries allied with the Soviet Union: unconditional fidelity to the Soviet Union and maintenance of the alliance with it, including the presence of Soviet armed forces in several Eastern European countries.

The list is not exhaustive, but it does convey the subject-areas in which the "taboo" ideas of the official ideology appear. So taboos continue to exist under the close protection of the state even in the reform period. There is no place for debate on these issues in lectures delivered under legal circumstances or in legally printed publications. The position has changed since the classical system only in that it is no longer compulsory to repeat a statement of allegiance to these principles in every lecture and piece of writing. These problems can be sidestepped, which makes work psychologically easier for those of the intelligentsia whose ideas on the taboo subjects conflict with the official ideology to a greater or lesser extent. But formal or informal censorship still prevents anyone putting a view different from the official one in these subject-areas.[14] Knowing that, a lecturer or writer usually exercises "self-censorship," omitting arguments generally known to be forbidden.[15]

These bans are ignored in *samizdat* materials published without legal permission and in lectures delivered at illegal "fly-by-night universities."[16] In addition, and often associated with the dissident literature at

---

[14]A state censorship authority exists in several reforming countries, such as the Soviet Union. In other reforming countries censorship is applied in an informal way: the appearance of undesired writings is prevented by editors appointed to head the newspapers, periodicals, and book publishers and by members of their staffs. Similarly, the principals of schools and universities are obliged to ensure that undesired lectures are not given, and so on.

[15]Independent-minded writers, journalists, and social scientists try to slip surreptitiously into their writings matter differing from the official line and critical of it. Men of letters learn to write between the lines and readers to read between them.

[16]The *samizdat* works written in the Soviet Union, Hungary, Poland, Czechoslovakia, and other socialist countries and the studies and books by political and intellectual émigrés amount to a library in themselves. This literature constitutes a source of fundamental importance to all research aimed at analyzing the socialist system. Unfortunately, much of this rich body of writing is still not available in public libraries, and few works have been translated into English.

The most influential work was A. I. Solzhenitsyn's *The Gulag Archipelago* (1974–78),

home, is the intellectual influence of the works written by the political exiles and smuggled into the socialist countries. The combined influence of these is wider or narrower according to the degree of repression and restriction in force. And that brings us to one of the main criteria for deciding when a reform process has passed over to a revolutionary change. The point is reached when the previously taboo subjects stop being taboo and start being questioned legally in the press, on radio and television, and at mass public meetings. The reform changes into a revolution when, without permission from the party authorities, in fact in spite of their protests, writings that would have circulated earlier only in *samizdat* form reach a wider and wider public.

While some ideas of the pre-reform official ideology are strictly conserved in the reform stage, other subject-areas undergo versatile revision. Graphic expression was given to the reform system's pragmatism by the leader of the Chinese reform, Deng Xiaoping: "As long as a cat can catch a mouse, it is a good cat regardless of whether it is white or black."[17] The major alterations occur in assessment of private property and the role of the market, but it is more practicable to return to these in the later chapters on the private sector and market socialism [→19.3, 21.1]. Instead, let us consider here how the official ideology of the classical system compares with its new version adjusted to the demands of the reform on certain other issues.

Earlier there was strong stress in the official ideology on the superiority of the socialist system over the capitalist [→4.2]. A curious arrogance arose: whatever happened under socialism was by definition better and of a higher order than what was happening or had happened under other systems. This sense of superiority is now shaken. It is hard to deny that the system's political institutions, far from shielding society from tyranny, have actually facilitated it, and that the institutions of modern parliamentary democracy ensure more effective protection against it. It is also hard to argue for socialism's economic superiority if the economic development gap between the advanced capitalist and the socialist countries has failed to narrow over a period of decades, and in fact has widened in the case of numerous countries. On many occasions even the

---

which circulated as a *samizdat* in several socialist countries. Some other examples of *samizdat* literature that had a great influence in the socialist countries and can be read in English are A. Amalrik (1970), V. Havel (1975, ed. 1985), E. Lipinski (1976), M. Lopinski, M. Moskit, and M. Wilk, eds. (1990), M. Meerson-Aksenov and B. Shragin, eds. (1978), A. Michnik (1985), J. Patocka (1977), A. D. Sakharov (1968, 1974, 1975, 1979), and A. Zinoviev (1984). From the Hungarian *samizdat* literature references have already been made to two works: M. Haraszti (1978) and J. Kenedi (1981). Excerpts can be read in G. Demszky, G. Gadó, and F. Kőszeg, eds. (1987). J. Kis (1989) is available in French.

[17]Deng Xiaoping [1962] (1989, p. 305).

official press and mass media point to the capitalist system's successes, for instance, when presenting the advantages of the market mechanism.

The classical system sought to develop a spirit of heroic sacrifice [→4.5]. The ideology of the reform system replaces the heroic ideas with more hedonistic ones. Less emphasis is placed on the idea of enforcing discipline; providing people with material incentives is promoted instead.

There is another change closely related to the previous ones: the official ideology of the classical system promised that the well-being of the masses would increase in the longer term. But there was no question of fulfilling this promise rapidly during forced industrialization. So the need to renounce the idea of a swift, steady rise in living standards features large in the ideology [→4.5, 9.3]. Today's rise in consumption has to be sacrificed for the morrow. The ideology of the reform system breaks with this, at least in periods of economic prosperity, and sets consumption growth to the fore. In this field the ideological traditions of the socialist movement are recalled. It is the sphere of ideas that Western journalists christened "goulash communism" during the first stage of the reform process in Hungary. During China's period of rising prosperity, emphasis began to be laid on the slogan "Get rich!" again. But the tendency lasts only as long as the swift rise in production and consumption. Once the problems of the economy worsen, calls for moderation, patience, and sacrifice are retrieved from the propaganda stockroom.

One important element in the official ideology was the paternalism assumed over and thrust upon citizens. The state undertakes institutional responsibilities to supply the public with cheap state-subsidized housing and free health care, education, and cultural provision, and provide infrastructural services and public transport out of the budget [→4.3, 4.4]. In the reform period these promises are withdrawn one by one. Amid the economic problems, it steadily transfers back to the individual, household, and family the costs of house building and housing maintenance, health care, the investment in setting up water supplies and telephone services, and the financial burdens of road transport [→19.6]. While shifting these burdens, it advances arguments for saying it is right to do so.

It is plain from what has been said that the official ideology of the reform period is a far less consistent mental edifice than the classical ideology was. It contains many more internal contradictions.[18] It is a

---

[18]To avoid any misunderstanding, the purpose here is not to investigate the degree of truth or falsity in what the official ideology under the classical system or during the reform process asserts, or to decide to what extent its promises can be fulfilled. The two ideological edifices are compared here solely in terms of the degree to which they contain precepts that concur or conflict with each other.

malleable alloy of old, set doctrines and new, more down-to-earth ideas enforced by real life.

As for the dynamics of the process, their most prominent characteristic is a steady disintegration. The original dogma loosens up, and the severity and relentlessness of doctrinaire thinking gradually gives way to a flabby permissiveness. Protests against "spiritual pollution" by ideas alien to the Communist party are fruitless;[19] the process is irreversible. Those who have abandoned an intellectual taboo previously considered unquestionable cannot reestablish that taboo in themselves. Those in whom the old view of the world has collapsed are no longer able to buckle down and restore their old beliefs and enthusiasm. Nor are the failures the only thing to have a disintegrating effect ideologically. If there should be successes at the expense of abandoning the classical dogmas (for instance, through reducing public ownership or planning), they too destroy the blind faith in the old dogmas of the official ideology. Ultimately, the disintegration of the official ideology undermines the system's foundations.

In discussing the official ideology, brief mention must also be made of the institutional framework. The bureaucracy retains its monopoly over the mass media and education, or rather over the parts of it organized formally. In fact, this can be added to the party's positions of power covered earlier [→18.1]. But the rule on the ideological front is not quite so totalitarian as it was under the classical system. There are alternative groupings with some (albeit largely informal) influence [→18.4]. The intellectual influence of the outside world also grows [→18.5].

It must be underscored separately that the power center controls the press, radio, and television less tightly than under the classical system. There is less uniformity in the mass media, and more independent opinions are heard, including criticisms, sometimes open and sometimes veiled. This is still a long way from what could be termed a free press, but it can perform far more of its indispensable calling: social control over those in power and expression of public opinion.

18.4 The Seeds of Pluralism

Not even the power structure of the classical system is perfectly monolithic; woven into it are strands, if faint ones, of political pluralism [→3.5]. These strands become notably stronger during the political reform. The centrifugal forces away from the center, opposing the centrip-

---

[19]For the Chinese campaign against "spiritual pollution," see Deng Xiaoping (1987).

etal forces pulling toward it, are stronger than under the classical system, but they do not become dominant. I present just a few of the changes: here attention is mainly given to those that affect the operation of the economy.

1. *Sectoral lobbies.* Even under the classical system there were groups or lobbies exerting pressure on the upper leadership on behalf of one particular sector or other. Their role increases during the reform process. This is a consequence of the weakening of centralization, but it also acts in the same direction, reducing the center's absolute sovereignty. The lobbies seek to influence decisions of many kinds, ranging from allocation of investment through wage increases to financial aid for loss-making firms.[20]

2. *Regional, national, and ethnic-minority pressure groups.* Under the classical system there were already regional lobbies trying to assert the real or imagined interests of some geographical or administrative unit, largely by winning more investment funding and financial subsidies for it. The strength of such regional lobbies grows substantially, the change being perceptible even in relatively small and ethnically uniform countries like Hungary and Poland. The problem is particularly strong in the multinational countries, such as the Soviet Union and Yugoslavia, where regional interests combine with those of particular national groups (in a minority compared with the country's majority national group).

The pressure from below may encounter efforts at decentralization in the central organizations. The latter are extorted by the information and administrative difficulties caused by centralization. Ultimately, there appears a strong tendency toward growth in the power position of the regional organizations (republican or provincial party committees and governments in states of a federal nature, and, taking the territorial breakdown lower, country and district party committees and state authorities).[21] This increase in the authority of regional organizations is accompanied by a broadening of the decision-making sphere in which some part is played by the self-governing coordination mechanism [→6.5]. (The qualification "some" is necessary because the democratic methods of election and control only apply within the regional organizations of state administration to a very limited extent.)

Although the central organizations themselves press to an extent for decentralization on a regional basis, they do not view the tendency favorably if it becomes "nationalist" (as the official ideology terms it). The

[20]See É. Voszka (1984, 1988) and E. Gaidar (1990).

[21]From the start this was among the main factors behind the reform in Yugoslavia. See A. Djilas (1991). Decentralization on regional lines was also prominent in Khrushchev's 1957 reforms. See E. A. Hewett (1988) and O. Hoeffding (1959).

more a tendency toward regional decentralization ties in with efforts by a historically evolved community seeking to conserve its traditions, culture, language, or religion to obtain national autonomy, the tougher the opposition at the center. In some cases explosions and bloody conflicts ensue. Nowhere, during the reform process, does it prove possible to fashion a truly federal state in which the rights and obligations of the member republics and the federation are harmoniously balanced. At the stage of reform socialism, no nation seeking independence has succeeded in seceding and founding a truly sovereign state.[22] Under these circumstances, national aspirations represent one of the strongest and most explosive forces within the socialist system on the road of reforms.

3. *Churches*. Under the classical system, a tendency with a force varying in time to abolish the churches or drastically limit their operations existed side by side with toleration of their activities. During the course of political reform, the former does not vanish but the latter becomes dominant. Meanwhile the churches' influence grows. In fact, it is hard to say how far this is an effect of the increased toleration shown by the bureaucracy or how far the reverse applies: the strengthening of the churches compels the bureaucracy to tolerate expansion of their activities. Whichever the case, the spread of religious beliefs is favored by the moral crisis in society and the widespread disenchantment with earlier socialist beliefs. Although the churches lack secular power, their spiritual influence independent of the prevailing power structure represents an appreciable force.[23]

4. *Unions and other bodies representing special interests*. The development of the Solidarity trade union in Poland and its acceptance of a role in public affairs is historically unique. It cannot be considered typical of the reforming countries as a whole. One can generalize to this extent, however: the tendency is for the bureaucratic nature of the trade unions to weaken. Union officials tend less to consider it their exclusive duty to act as a "transmitter" to the members of the commands and will of the party. It becomes more common for them to identify with their membership and begin to represent their interests more forcefully.

[22]In 1989–91, a succession of Soviet republics declared their sovereignty through their own legislatures. A similar process took place in several Yugoslav republics. But the actual status of these republics remains equivocal: although not subordinate to the federal government in many important respects, they still do not possess some basic features of sovereignty.

[23]One particularly big force was the Catholic church in Poland. The movement pressing for a change of system received a big boost from the fact that a Polish pope was chosen to head the Catholic church.

In some places the national aspirations of point 2 combine with religious distinctness. That is the case in Tibet, for instance. Also, to some extent Moslem-Christian antagonism lies behind the Azerbaijani-Armenian conflict in the Soviet Union.

One change worth remarking on is that the reform process in several countries legalizes strikes or at least tolerates them, something inconceivable under the classical system. If strikes occur, some take place under union auspices and others occur independently or perhaps with an unofficial union as the organizer.

A similar trend is apparent in other professional organizations that acted as integral parts of the classical system's bureaucratic apparatus. Examples of such bodies are the national academies of sciences; the associations of writers, movie staff, musicians, artists, and other branches of the arts; university student unions; societies of engineers; peasants' associations, organizations of artisans and private traders; and so on. These always had dual obligations, as transmitters "downward" between the upper leadership and the group belonging to the organization and as group representatives "upward." The latter role now strengthens appreciably, and self-governing coordination and organizational autonomy grow to some extent.

Here another feature of the political reform can be mentioned. New associations, clubs, and organizations appear in large numbers, with the widest variety of organizational criteria: members of the intelligentsia, pensioners, tenants in state housing, the disabled, and those engaged in charitable work form separate organizations. Environmental movements are organized. Some of the new associations also perform functions of group representation. Some engage in politics, while others seek to function in an expressly apolitical way. Whatever the case, their common feature is that their place is not assigned from above and they are not given instant monopoly rights. Instead, they are organized spontaneously through initiatives from below.[24] These early manifestations of a civil society independent of state power constitute a notable change from the classical system, whose totalitarian nature precluded any spontaneous self-organizing activity in society.

5. *Factions within the party.* The Communist party is not a monolithic entity even under the classical system [→3.5], but the slightest resistance to the dominant party line is ruthlessly hunted down. Again, the reform period brings a relaxation, and as disintegration of the system proceeds, organized factions start to develop. These group themselves in one country or another around some outstanding "reform Communist" personality. In effect, the seeds of a multiparty system appear within the ruling party at this point.

---

[24]Using the terminology introduced in chapter 6, the self-governing and ethical coordination mechanisms, which have withered away almost entirely under the classical socialist system, gain a greater role.

6. *Alternative political movements*. In the border area between legality and illegality under the reform system, one encounters political manifestations independent of those in power, or "alternative" movements whose political positions and program differ from the official line of the party. Political dissidence or opposition appears in a multitude of forms, among them in contributions to discussions in formal organizations or in meetings organized informally, in protest letters and the gathering of signatures to petitions, in the unlicensed publication and distribution of *samizdat* periodicals and books, and in street demonstrations, mass rallies, and political strikes.[25]

The legal status of all these activities is dubious. On the one hand, freedom of speech and association are codified in the constitution, but on the other, the penal code forbids "agitation against the state," "conspiracy to overthrow the state order," and "organizing activity against the state." Moreover, it does so without setting clear criteria for deciding when a deed falls into one of these categories. Under the circumstances it is up to the law-enforcement agencies and the judiciary, and ultimately the party-state organizations controlling them, to decide what kind of political activity counts as unlawful.

The change between the classical and the reform phases of the system appears in actual practice, not in the letter of the constitution and the penal code. There are still political trials, but far more rarely, and they are not usually preceded by physical torture of the accused. People are still jailed for political reasons, but in far smaller numbers, and their sentences are usually lighter. Those whose views are different from the positions of those in power run a risk, but the risk is smaller than during the terror under Stalin, Mao, or other leaders of that period.[26] In that sense one can conclude that the socialist system after the political reforms coexists with various independent, dissident manifestations, and although it puts constraints on them, it tolerates to some extent their existence.[27] The toleration is dictated by the political power relations.

[25]Sometimes the dividing line between the seeds of pluralism in groups 5 and 6 is blurred. B. Yeltsin, G. K. Popov, and others in the Soviet Union, for instance, began their struggle for reform as an opposition inside the Communist party, but they resigned from it to begin independent political organization. This represented a further shift toward a real multiparty system, and thereby toward a revolutionary change of system.

[26]This statement is not intended to underestimate the personal bravery or risks of those engaged in semilegal or illegal activity. The statements about the reduction in the risk are valid in a stochastic sense. No opposition activists can be sure that the persecution will not strike them and their fellows.

[27]Clearly, the police are aware of such movements. If participants in them remain at liberty, it is because those in power can only bring themselves to make limited use of police and judicial methods, not because of difficulties in detection or securing a conviction. Often attempts are made instead to make participants' daily lives harder: they are sacked from their jobs, not allowed to travel abroad, and so on.

Once the existence of groups opposed to official policy has been tolerated for some time, it becomes harder to clamp down on them, since it causes a stir and excites antipathy in the public and abroad.

The risk entailed in semilegal or illegal actions varies from period to period, along with the advancing or retreating tides of the reform process. When the bureaucracy takes fright at the growing influence and radicalism of the political opposition, it comes down on it harder, provided it still has the strength to do so.[28] The names of heroic resistance figures like Sakharov in the Soviet Union and Hável in Czechoslovakia, who suffered years of internal exile and imprisonment for their activity, are known all over the world. A long list could be given of people who may be less well known, but who made equal sacrifices and showed equal heroism in their struggles for democracy in Hungary, Poland, Czechoslovakia, East Germany, the Soviet Union, China, Vietnam, and many other socialist countries. These people and the movements they organized made an invaluable contribution to the disintegration of the old system and the processes of reform and revolution.

To sum up, public life under the socialist system as modified by the reforms cannot be described in terms of simplified dichotomies. It can be called neither a pluralistic nor a monolithic system. During the process of reform, as under the classical system, the bureaucracy and its official ideology is the dominant force, if for no other reason than because it has a monopoly of the administrative tools of power. But the presence of an informal alternative political sphere means it no longer has a monopoly over people's minds. A totalitarian monopoly over people's thinking would need either stronger faith or stronger fear; the political reforms have made both weaker than they were under the classical system.

18.5 Opening toward the Capitalist World

One of the major characteristics of the classical system is its hostile isolation from the capitalist world [→4.5, 14.1]. In this respect the reform brings a dramatic turn of events. The change is closely connected with the efforts in foreign policy at reduction of international tension, disarmament, and the defusing of local conflicts and explosive situations. Propaganda against the Western powers subsides, and greater weight is

---

[28]After Jaruzelski's military action in Poland in 1981, the active members of the Solidarity movement were arrested in large numbers. After the crushing of the mass student demonstration in Beijing in 1989, hundreds were arrested and later brought to trial and given stiff prison sentences.

attached to the principles of peaceful coexistence between different systems. Here the official ideology becomes more pragmatic: the idea of class war on an international scale recedes, as does the notion that the socialist countries, embodying the interests of the international working class, must defeat the capitalist countries, which embody the interests of the international bourgeoisie.

The expression *opening* in connection with the process of reform became current in China, but it can be used more generally to describe the change. Some degree of opening takes place in every sphere, although the opening is not full and remains subject to numerous administrative restrictions. The opening in external economic relations is examined later [→23.6]. Here a few remarks follow on the opening in the political and ideological sphere.

All forms of personal relations with the Western world become more widespread and intensive: correspondence, telephoning, and above all personal meetings between citizens of socialist countries and their friends and relations in capitalist countries, along with private tourism and official travel (business, scientific and scholarly, cultural, and so on) in both directions. It becomes more common for officials of the bureaucracy to travel to a capitalist country on official business or as a tourist. Several countries allow students, researchers, teachers, and artists to spend even years abroad; taking jobs abroad becomes more accepted.[29] These personal experiences have a deep influence on people.

People on a mass scale start listening to Western radio stations; Western literature, movies, and periodicals are allowed into the reforming countries in larger quantities with less political and ideological screening of them. It is not only high-standard, elite culture but "cultural goods" for mass consumption that reach citizens in larger quantities under reform socialism. Western dance music, clothing fashions, and consumer habits flood in. One sometimes has the impression that this flood, whether consciously or instinctively, has an ulterior motive: the public, particularly the young, are supposed to fall on the products of Western culture and civilization they have long yearned for, which distracts their attention from urgent public problems and active political involvement.

The behavior of the bureaucracy is not uniform. There is an alternation between more tolerant and more reserved periods. There have been campaigns in China on several occasions against Western spiritual influence, and similar tendencies emerge in the other reforming countries from time to time. Conservative party ideologists find allies in other schools of thought among the intelligentsia, influenced and made "anti-

---

[29]At the end of the 1980s, there were thirty-seven thousand Chinese students studying abroad, twenty-seven thousand of them in the United States.

Western" by rural romanticism, glorification of the past, chauvinism, or racism.

Although the opening is limited, its effect in the end is almost unstoppable. Fresh air enters a previously closed room, even if the door is left only ajar, not fully open. For decades it was possible to teach effectively that the citizens of the socialist countries were living in material prosperity while people in the capitalist countries were destitute. This myth and others like it become untenable once people have numerous chances to compare the two systems directly or indirectly. Not just scholars of "comparative economic systems" but growing numbers of people in the street perform "comparative studies" with increasing frequency. This may well be the most important result of the opening up, and one of the fundamental driving forces behind the process of reform.

18.6 Change in the Scale of Publicity and Candor

Gorbachev's reform program made the word *glasnost* familiar all over the world. It covers two closely connected requirements. One is to put a stop to secretiveness; the public must be informed of the decisions that affect them, and about the preparations for taking those decisions. The other is that the truth must always be told; the publication of false statements must cease.[30]

In the case of the first, the classical system never felt embarrassed about its secretiveness or treated it as a necessary evil. It made a virtue of it, considering it a fundamental requirement for vigilance [→4.5]. It was argued that all information could benefit the internal or external enemy. So every official was expected in general to divulge the minimum of information.

In the case of the second, telling the truth is, of course, a moral imperative generally accepted by subscribers to all world views. The opposite was never proclaimed in the ethics of the classical system; the commandment was merely broken in practice. It is important here to emphasize that cases where someone in possession of the full truth actually stood up and lied consciously were few and far between. Even then liars would usually reassure themselves by saying it was done in a good cause and the end justified the means. Most officials of the classical system were confused in their own minds about truth and falsehood. They believed

[30]These comments are not concerned with the question of whether the official assessment of some event on the government's part is correct or not, or whether it keeps its promises for the future. The distinction between "true" and "false" is examined exclusively in terms of whether the official statements on the events or data correspond with the facts.

their own statement because they believed in their own ideology, which had shaped their outlook; because they believed in their leaders, whose statements they repeated; because they were afraid to think in any other way; and because they were trained to be compliant, not doubtful and critical. These good intentions and this uncritical faith of theirs were imposed upon by those who made them believe so many lies: false allegations, for instance, used as a justification for oppressive sentences in show trials, or propagation of the myth that the leader was infallible.

It is not worth fostering illusions: secretiveness is prevalent to some extent in all political mechanisms, and so is governmental silence about awkward facts and misleading manipulation of public opinion. The question social science has to decide is the degree to which such behavior is impeded by the workings of society. The main question when analyzing glasnost is not whether the leaders of reforming countries are more inclined to insist on candor and openness than their predecessors under the classical system, but what mechanisms develop to prevent secretiveness and deceitful propaganda.

In this respect the reform has a radically different complexion. Secretiveness decreases, although it does not cease. A shift occurs between reliable and distorted information, in the former's favor.

Admittedly, the policy of openness meets a lot of resistance. Over the several decades it has become a conditioned reflex for the bureaucracy to try to hide any problem, difficulty, or crisis that arises, or release selective, distorted information about it. If that can no longer happen as it did under the classical system, thanks are mainly due to the changes reviewed in the previous sections. Take as an example a disaster at a nuclear power plant. Apparently, there was a very grave nuclear accident in the Soviet Union at the end of the 1950s. To this day it is not known exactly what happened, what lives were lost, or what health or environmental damage was done. Almost thirty years later came the nuclear catastrophe at Chernobyl. The initial reaction (the conditioned reflex just mentioned) was to be secretive and silent on the problem, and to release false information. But that could only be kept up for a few days. Correct information was extorted by the force of public opinion at home and abroad, and by the pressure of foreign governments and international organizations.

To return from the example to the overall subject, the main internal forces working against concealment, the glossing over of governmental negligence, and the release of misleading information are these: a press that dares to find out and to publish true information, officials who dare to defy their superiors when they try to force them to issue false reports, and independent organizations that write the true facts in their semilegal or illegal publications or spread them by word of mouth, even when official sources disguise them. Once a country has opened up to some extent to the outside world, news covered up at home can return in radio broadcasts and newspapers brought in from abroad. The freer the press and the stronger the alternative movements, the less people need fear oppression for contradicting official statements; and the more open the country to the outside world, the more certain it is that the truth intended for concealment will see the light. Thus, candor and openness become more habitual and natural.

This change, however, causes one of the fundamental internal contradictions of the political reform. The problems that breed popular discontent already existed under the classical system, or at least were rooted in it. But the repression then was so strong that people hardly dared to voice their discontent. The reform solves few of the problems, but the easing of the repression and the more candid, open atmosphere allow discontent to be expressed. Liberty is among the spiritual foods whose consumption whets the appetite for it. The freer the atmosphere, the greater the discontent turned angrily on the system. The phenomenon is well documented in history; it is demonstrated by the French Revolution, the Russian October Revolution, the Hungarian Revolution of 1956, the Iranian Revolution, and many other instances. In most cases, outbursts of popular rage, uprisings, and violent revolutions take place not when oppression is at its severest but when it is loosened and the system is liberalized.

This statement is backed up by the latest events in Hungary, Poland, China, and the Soviet Union. It appears to be contradicted, however, by what happened in 1989 in East Germany, Czechoslovakia, Bulgaria, and Romania. There the classical system remained until the very last minute, along with all its accompanying instances of repression, but there was, nonetheless, an outbreak of mass demonstrations that led to the fall of the old regime.

It would seem that outside influences played a big part in the course of events. To some extent the lack of the effect of an internal political liberalization was made up for by the external example, the revolutionizing influence of the changes in other socialist countries [→16.1].

There is a trade-off between repression and public satisfaction. The reform system works well amid a tolerable level of tension while the relative content coincides on the trade-off curve with relatively light repression. So long as the reform scores political and economic successes and satisfaction concurrently increases, the possessors of power can be more lenient on the subject of freedom of speech and association without putting their power in any fundamental danger. But once political and/or economic defeats ensue, the situation becomes strained and the leadership faces a dilemma: either to reimpose (or try to reimpose) the more repressive methods or to face the fact that its indivisible power may be imperiled.

18.7 The Limits to Political Reform

The specific historical course of political events varies from country to country. As mentioned previously, the liberalizing tendency of political reform is opposed by a very strong countertendency to conserve as much of the political structure of the classical system as possible. As many combinations of countervailing forces emerge as there are countries and periods.

The political situation in certain countries consolidates for a longer period of time, to produce a specific *equilibrium of political reform*. This happened, for instance, in Yugoslavia, beginning in the 1950s and continuing until the period before Tito's death. This was the case for fifteen to twenty years in Hungary under Kádár. The "reform equilibria" in these two countries were not the same; the specific combinations of liberalization and repression that accompanied the consolidated periods were different. But in both countries the combination that developed subsisted for a lengthy period. Neither the group of "fundamentalist" Communists intent on restoring the classical system nor the democratic opposition forces aiming to exceed the reforms of Tito or Kádár were strong enough in the period concerned to shift the system out of its ambivalent balance.

The equilibrium, however, was not a stable one even in those two countries;[31] after a while the tensions heightened, and in the end the balance of forces tipped decisively in favor of those pressing for liberalization. The political reform in other countries was unable to consolidate for a longer period even in that ambivalent, intermediate state. The political movement that surfaced in Poland in 1980 had such an impetus behind it that the Communist party felt its monopoly of power was in danger, and so used military force to disperse Solidarity in 1981.[32] Demonstrations by millions of people demanding democracy broke out in China in 1989, and there too the mass movement was crushed by mer-

[31]The meaning attached to these expressions is the one found in the mathematical theory of dynamic systems. There are two separate questions: whether the system is in a dynamic equilibrium and whether that equilibrium is stable. The former means that the overall resultant of all the forces affecting the system is zero, while the latter implies that there are internal mechanisms to restore the system to a path of equilibrium if it is perturbed out of equilibrium by a shock.

[32]Future historians will decide what part Soviet persuasion or pressure played, alongside the alarm of the Polish Communist party, in the decision to resort to military action.

ciless military intervention. But the brutal violence did not restore the political situation to its earlier intermediate, semiliberalized state. Further steps were taken back toward the political conditions and tougher repression of the old classical system.

Consider the problem from the point of view of the Communist party in power. It must face the possibility of losing its power, and it is determined to prevent that. There are several factors behind this determination, which is to be found at all levels in the party apparatus, not just among the supreme leadership. One should remember that power has a great intrinsic value for Communists. The official ideology has implanted deeply in the minds of the Marxist-Leninist party's functionaries that loss of power is irreversible and the worst conceivable tragedy [→4.6]. This fear may be accompanied by personal anxieties: a revolutionary change in the system may lose an official his or her position, personal power, and material privileges; he or she may even have reason to fear reprisals.

Assertion of the undivided power of the Communist party is the "genetic program" that pervades the whole organism of every socialist system [→15.3]. One expression of the unconditional determination to defend this power came in 1989 in the Chinese parliament from the party general secretary, Zhao Ziyang, well known to be a committed reformer: "The Communist party upholds the fundamental interests of the Chinese people. The Western type of multiparty system cannot be applied in China. There would be no basis or purpose in China for opposition parties to form. . . . The object of reforming the political institutions is certainly not to change the basic structure of the Communist party's leading role, it is to improve the operation of that structure. . . . The political institutions need reforming, but the position of the Communist party, namely the fact that it is the governing party, is inalterable. Only the specific methods of government can be altered."[33]

The quotation is from a Chinese Communist party statement, but similar ones have been made by the party leaders of the other reforming countries.[34] The bounds of the category of system termed the "socialist system" in these comments are transcended, or at least reached, by any country whose Communist party accepts even in principle the idea of party competition and parliamentary elections, since that entails accept-

[33]See *Renmin Ribao,* overseas ed., March 17, 1989. By a tragic irony of history, Zhao Ziyang was removed from the post of general secretary after the students' movement was crushed in June 1989, on the grounds that he had proved too indulgent toward the movement.

[34]"The solution of the tasks of *perestroika* which will determine the fate of the country and of socialism requires a strengthening of the leading role of the party, and new criteria for the evaluation of the fulfillment of its tasks." M. S. Gorbachev, *Izvestia,* July 5, 1988.

ing the possibility of losing its undivided power if the distribution of seats in parliament goes against it. A system remains within the socialist family of systems so long as its Communist party is determined to retain power by any means and is capable of effecting that intention.

Here the discussion of political reform can be concluded. A description has been given of the liberalizing tendency and the ambivalent state that develops in the political sphere. At times the tendency applies more strongly and at times it is beaten back. Sometimes the repression of it is by milder and sometimes by more brutal means. So long as the change can still be called reform at all and has not crossed over into revolution, it has clearly discernable political limits. In brief outline that is the political background behind the tendencies to economic reform described in the following chapters.

In 1989, the liberalizing tendency in Eastern Europe did not stop at the limits set by the Communist party. The demand for democracy was too strong and the resistance too weak for the limits to stand. One basic factor behind this was that the Soviet Union did not use military force to repulse the democratic revolution. That in itself is not enough, however, to explain what occurred; no less important was the internal disintegration of the system. It is the political side of the process of internal disintegration that this chapter is intended to convey; remaining chapters return several times to its other sides.

In this book I do not speculate on the future of countries in which the socialist system, in its classical or reformed form, survives at the time of writing. It depends on a number of factors, in combinations that vary from country to country, when and under what circumstances the change of system occurs, and how peacefully or violently it happens. All I can offer the reader are means of analysis: a presentation, one by one, of the forces tending to conserve or break down the system, and an examination of the relations among them.

18.8   Preview: The Political Structure of the Postsocialist System

The future political structure of the postsocialist system depends on a number of factors. Where the transition has actually begun, the first free elections have already been held. Taking part in them were several parties, and they were exclusively parties that had accepted the basic principles of a multiparty system and parliamentary democracy in their manifestoes. That applies also to the successor parties to the Communist party in power under the socialist system. To that extent the successor parties are not true Marxist-Leninist parties, but come closer to a Social-

Democratic party, since they have abandoned one of the basic pillars of the ideological edifice of Leninism: adherence to power at all costs.

The electors confirmed by a large majority their desire for the establishment and consolidation of parliamentary democracy. The majority of votes went to political parties and groups that declared that they wanted to introduce Western-style democracy.

These events are truly revolutionary in character, supplying the fundamental condition required for a change of system. But one must add that the subsequent course of postsocialist development depends on a number of internal and external factors.

For one thing, the point of departure is different in each country. There is a big difference, for instance, between Poland and Hungary, on the one hand, and Romania, on the other. The opposition movements in the first two countries have been organizing themselves a decade or two, and in many respects the liberalizing tendency described in this chapter had advanced a long way before the turning point arrived, whereas in the last, the classical system had survived in an extreme form; a merciless tyranny was in power until the very last day of Ceausescu's rule. The closer the situation of a postsocialist society was to the extreme Romanian case at the time the transition began, the closer it is to "starting from scratch" in developing the institutions and mentality of democracy.[35]

But the institutions of democracy are undeveloped even in places where the revolution was preceded by quite a long stretch of political reform. It takes time before newly legalized parties become conversant with parliamentary practice. It takes time before a judicial structure becomes truly independent, and a police force that was omnipotent under the totalitarian system gives way to one operating under legal control in the service of public security. It takes time to draft the laws and regulations needed for constitutionalism, the protection of property and private contracts, and the defense of civil liberties. It takes time before the media learn how to perform their indispensable task of criticizing the government of the day and investigating abuses.

The new system inherits a grave burden, not only in the weakness of the democratic institutions but in the ideological legacy still borne in people's minds. One finds a curious dichotomy of outlook over a wide area. Most people are prepared to accept the ideas and values of the

---

[35]The postsocialist transition of East Germany differs from that of any other country. East Germany was among the countries to leap from the classical system to postsocialism and skip the stage of reform, and to that extent there is a resemblance to the Czechoslovak and Romanian situations. What makes the circumstances unique is the unification of Germany. In a united Germany, the institutions of parliamentary democracy and the capitalist market economy await East German society almost ready-made.

Western world and, in fact, positively want to have democracy, guaranteed civil liberties, a market economy, competition, and security of private property. But concurrently they expect the new regime to redeem in the shortest possible time all the unfulfilled promises made by the old.

A particularly strong survival is the demand for paternalistic care from the state, for state action to shield the individual from all the buffets of transition and economic adaptation. Similarly strong is the survival of egalitarian ideas and emotions that cause people to greet with bitterness and antipathy the inequalities accompanying the market economy and expansion of the private sector.

The difficulties in the political and ideological sphere conceal inherent dangers that are compounded by the grave economic problems of the postsocialist transition. There may be a response in a still infant democracy to a populist, demagogue opposition; trends of extreme nationalism may appear. One can trust that the reins of power will remain in the hands of the democratic forces, but one cannot dismiss the chances of a swing against democracy. The more favorably the economic situation develops, the smaller this danger becomes and the more one can count on the consolidation of democracy.

19

The Rise of the Private Sector

THE RISE of the private sector is the most important tendency in the economic sphere during the process of reform. It brings a deep change, since it affects the property relations (block 2 in figure 15.1) and it does so in a radical way: private property appears alongside public property. But one must add straight away that this deep and radical change takes place only in a quite narrow band of the economy.

The private sector has been almost annihilated or diminished to a minor segment of the economy under the classical system. Private plants employing hired labor have been abolished in all their forms. Most socialist countries allowed a small number of private artisans and private traders to operate, and the dwarf household farms survived under collectivized agriculture. In addition, there was illegal private activity. This chapter reviews and analyzes the changes that take place by comparison with that starting position.[1]

One is confronted with an ambivalent phenomenon: a strong tendency to develop the private sector is matched by a countertendency, no less strong, to obstruct and restrict this development. An attempt will be made to present both sides of the process.

19.1 The Inducements behind the Development of the Private Sector

The private sector is not created "artificially" by the administration in the way the state and quasi-state cooperative sectors were established from above under the classical system. Large numbers of people voluntarily undertake economic activity on a private property basis. Not even constructive support is needed. It just means dismantling the bureaucratic barriers (or at least lowering them substantially). All the bureaucracy has to do is to annul at least some part of the measures the same bureaucracy had taken under the classical system to end the private sector's operation (or to decrease it to a very large extent).

---

[1]See references on the private sector and second economy in chapter 5, note 36.

Taking all the reforming countries together, one can say that tens of millions of people move spontaneously into the private sector, and the various forms of private enterprise sprout like mushrooms.[2] So there must be very strong inducements for people to enter the private sector, even though the environment is still unfriendly toward it. The first of these is a material incentive, the hope of a higher income. For many people, private enterprise opens the road to prosperity.[3] Some manage to grow rich in the literal sense. The chance of a break has a great mobilizing force, even if it does not occur on a mass scale. Earlier there was just a single career path to follow: rising steadily higher in the hierarchy. Now a second suddenly appears: getting steadily richer in the sphere of private enterprise.

Another very strong inducement to join the private sector is the desire for autonomy. Private ownership combines in the owner's hands the property rights of types a, b, and c.[4] Whether private entrepreneurs earn well or go bankrupt, they have unquestionable disposal over the residual income. Luck and bureaucratic intervention may greatly affect their income, but performance and income are linked far more plainly and clearly than they are in the public ownership sphere where impersonal and equalizing income distribution prevails. Private entrepreneurs find it gratifying to be their own masters. That applies not only to rich, highly capitalized proprietors but to the owners of the tiniest family workshops or peasant holdings.[5] Many people commit themselves to a private business even if the rewards are meager and uncertain, because they do not want a boss breathing down their necks, and independence has great intrinsic value for them.

The knowledge in itself that there is the chance of private enterprise and that an individual is able to leave the public sector and seek prosper-

---

[2]For a detailed analysis of the process of rural *embourgeoisement,* see I. Szelényi (1988).

[3]The irony is that a high proportion of those in the private sector earn a lot precisely because they operate not under capitalism but as a "foreign body" in the socialist environment of chronic shortage economy. Owner-cabdrivers or corner greengrocers who would belong to the lower middle class in the United States or Western Europe are among the "rich" in reform socialist countries.

The material inducements to the entrepreneurs are not the only ones contributing to the rapid growth of the private sector. The hired workers employed by production units in private hands also earn much more than those doing similar jobs in the state sector.

[4]In a larger private business, the owner may delegate some of his rights of control to employees, but he himself appoints them and can dismiss them [→5.2].

[5]Collectivization caused losses of many kinds, in human life, the grave initial setback to agricultural production, the subsequent sluggish rate of growth, and so on. But one of the worst scars, which never healed entirely, was left by the blow to people's sense of autonomy: a peasant was tied to his land and identified with it; once it was wrenched away, he ceased to be his own master and felt degraded by his subordination to the cooperative.

ity and a career elsewhere raises one's self-respect. The expansion of the private sector increases the opportunity for citizens to choose, and ultimately the liberty of individuals. Of course, not everyone desires autonomy, undertaking the responsibility, risk, and resulting stress of independence. Many are happy to be controlled from above as employees of an organization receiving wages and solicitude for their labor. The essential point here is that the reform system differs from the preceding classical system in providing those who want it with a chance of going into business independently.

Having identified the inducements for individuals to enter the private sector, the motives of the bureaucracy must be explained as well. The behavior of its members is ambivalent; one part of their split personality resists [→19.5] while the other assists in the development of this sector. They incline to the latter behavior primarily because they hope that private production will improve the supply to the general public and ease the shortage. In addition, it reduces some of the social tension, allowing a high proportion of the most active and enterprising people to occupy themselves with economic activity by going into business. That makes them more satisfied and, what is more, diverts their attention from political matters. The more clearly these relations are seen by the bureaucracy, the more consistent the regulations authorizing the private sector become.

19.2 A Survey of the Private Sector

In the production sphere, the most characteristic types of production unit and enterprise found in the private sector are as follows.

1. *The small-scale family agricultural holding.* The picture presented as a result of the reform is not uniform, so a few countries will be examined individually.[6]

The most dramatic change took place in China, where collectivization went furthest under the classical system [→5.5]. The reform did away with the commune system, and agricultural production passed to small-scale family holdings. This change was not reflected clearly in the legal forms, particularly to start with: the land nominally remained in social ownership while the family "took responsibility" only for tilling the soil

---

[6]The following studies can be selected from the wide range of literature: N. J. Cochrane (1988) as a summary on *Eastern Europe;* Y. Markish (1989), K. M. Brooks (1990), and S. Hedlund (1989) on the *Soviet Union;* K. Hartford (1990), N. R. Lardy (1986), M. Selden (1988), and T. Sicular (1985) on *China;* M. Marrese (1983) and N. Swain (1987) on *Hungary.*

and initially received only a short-term tenancy. Later the tenancy steadily lengthened, and the right of tenancy could be inherited or in some regions even sold. The land became de facto the private property of the small-scale family holding, and most of the farm livestock, machinery, equipment, and buildings joined this property form at the same time. (Some large-scale collective farming remained.)

The common name of the arrangement became the "responsibility system." This was a real privatization process: capital assets that had previously been in public ownership passed into private ownership. This mass, breakneck privatization of Chinese agriculture was not decided "from above." To start with, the administration merely loosened the strict commitment to making the commune the exclusive property form in agriculture and allowed a measure of experimentation. Initially, several new kinds of property form, variants of collective and individual farming, arose, but the "responsibility system," that is, private family holdings, soon obtained on a mass scale. The administration removed the bureaucratic barriers under the pressure "from below" of a spontaneous privatization movement, conceding in 1980 that the private sector could predominate in agriculture. The main explanation for the economic expansion in China during the first phase of the reform is the transformation in agriculture. The peasants set to work with an industry and energy they had never displayed under the commune system. The changes in property form and the rise in production are shown in table 19.1.[7]

TABLE 19.1
Property Forms and Output in Chinese Agriculture

	1978–87	*1978*	*1987*
1. Distribution of agricultural production by property forms (percent)			
state property	—	1.7	2.2
collective property	—	98.3	39.1
private property	—	0.0	57.7
2. Average annual rate of growth in agricultural production[a] (percent)	6.1	—	—

Source: Block 1: W. Ming (1990, p. 303); block 2: P. Marer et al. (1991, country tables).
[a]On the basis of agricultural GDP at constant producers' prices.

[7]The output of some agricultural products shows extremely high annual growth rates: cotton, 18.7 percent; oil-bearing crops, 14.6 percent; sugarcane, 11.1 percent; tobacco, 15.2 percent; and meat, 10.1 percent for the period 1978–84. *World Development Report* (1986, p. 105).

The period when the leadership in Yugoslavia sought to develop the classical system lasted the few short years from 1945 to 1949, without reaching the stage of fully collectivized agriculture. When they set about the reform (including the introduction of self-management), they did not disturb property relations in agriculture, which basically rests throughout the reform period on small-scale family holdings of a peasant nature.

Poland was the only Eastern European country in which a long reign of the classical system had the exceptional feature of not bringing about the collectivization of agriculture. Even before the process of reform began, one important constituent of it right from the start was a declaration that what had been private property in agriculture up to then would remain private property.

Mass collectivization was undertaken in Hungary in the early 1960s. The proportion of private, small-scale family farming remained minimal in the reform period, although its security increased. The substantial change took place in the role of the household farms of cooperative members and the auxiliary agricultural production.

The reform of agriculture got off to a very slow start in the Soviet Union, and it is still not decided whether it will take the more radical Chinese path in the future. The regulations introduced in 1988–89 open the way legally for it to happen. All along there has been far less spontaneous initiative from below toward private ownership and private activity and far more bureaucratic resistance to it than in China. To this day the Soviet peasantry has not been able to get over the ghastly trauma of collectivization.[8] Even though the people who experienced it personally are no longer alive, their children and grandchildren that feel there is no security for private property, and that the land may be taken away from them again. If they were to become prosperous farmers by farming individually, it could mean they would be branded as *kulaks* again, which could bring persecution, deportation, or death. Every gesture by the bureaucracy that seems inimical or even hesitant about restoring private peasant ownership reinforces the fear and uncertainty.

2. *Household farming and auxiliary agricultural production*. Both forms existed under the classical system [→5.5]. The reform introduces a new element insofar as it allows a strong growth of production under these two forms. It prompts the state authorities and the cooperative and state farms to support the household and auxiliary farms by making sowing seed, machines, transportation, and other means of production available to them.

---

[8]Therefore, the promotion of family leaseholds that was so successful in China did not quickly take root in those parts of the Soviet Union that were most hurt by collectivization, that is, in the Ukraine and Russia. In other parts, the process went faster: for example, the redevelopment of the old peasant farms in the Baltics.

TABLE 19.2
Growth of the Nonagricultural Private Sector in China

	1981 (thousands)	1988 (thousands)	1988/81 (percent)
Number of private firms[a]	1,829	14,527	794
Number of employees of private firms	2,274	23,049	1,014

Source: Column 1: *Beijing Review,* February 27–March 15, 1989; column 2: *People's Daily,* March 11, 1989.
[a]Individually and/or family-owned businesses.

3. *Small family undertakings in other branches.* Although the big breakthrough toward small family undertakings takes place in agriculture in most reform countries, the weight of small family businesses increases in other branches of the economy as well (see tables 19.2 and 19.3). The main spheres of activity found in this form are repair and maintenance, passenger and goods transportation, building construction, retail trading, catering, and other services.

4. *Complementary private activity in the nonagricultural branches.* This form existed under the classical system: an individual has a permanent place of work in the public sector but apart from doing that job takes on "extra work" for separate payment. This kind of private activity can be called complementary because the individual concerned complements his or her earnings at the main place of work with the income so obtained. In that it resembles form 2. Such activity can be clearly classified in the private sector if the buyer of the service is another individual or a household [→5.6].

TABLE 19.3
Growth of Private Small-Scale Industry and Private Retail Trading in Hungary

Year	Number of Self-employed Craftsmen (percent)	Number of Employees of Self-employed Craftsmen (percent)	Number of Private Retailers (percent)	Number of Employees of Private Retailers (percent)
1984	100	100	100	100
1985	104.8	108.1	113.7	121.5
1986	108.4	116.1	129.3	141.3
1987	110.8	183.1	142.1	169.6
1988	121.1	263.3	154.2	188.1
1989	125.8	346.3	176.9	208.8

Source: K. Balázs and M. Laki (1991, p. 504).

These activities become very frequent during the reform process, with a significant proportion of public-sector employees taking part in them. They turn into one of the basic sources of income.

The common feature of forms 1, 2, 3, and 4 is that the family basically makes use only of its own labor, hiring outside labor at most as occasional assistance. As mentioned in section 5.2, the customary Marxist classification for this kind of family enterprise is small-scale commodity production. This classification distinguishes it from the category of capitalist production, in which owners combine the capital they possess (or borrow) with outside hired labor (perhaps complementing this with the labor of themselves and their families). Remaining in the production sphere, regular employment of hired labor is the criterion for distinguishing these two social sectors according to the Marxist view of society, since permanent employment of hired labor amounts to exploitation of that labor by the possessor of capital. The form that follows falls into the category of capitalist production.

5. *The private firm employing hired labor.* Capitalist firms in this sense occur both in agriculture and other branches during the process of reform. Most are enterprises on the borderline between a small-scale family undertaking and a small capitalist firm. In some countries, such as China, Poland, Hungary, and Vietnam, medium-sized capitalist firms emerge as well, but very sporadically. Large capitalist firms develop too, but the number is small. Before the development of medium-sized and large capitalist firms can become more common, the country, on a political plane, has to reach the democratic revolution and enter the postsocialist phase, or at least arrive at a state where the elements of the reform process and of a revolutionary change of system are strongly mixed.

Tables 19.4 and 19.5 shed light on the development, during the reform, of the Soviet and Hungarian private sectors in the categories covered by points 1–5 in the survey above.[9]

Although they are not strictly part of the private sector, it is worth mentioning here two further forms that occupy the border zone between the public and private sectors and combine certain elements of both sectors.

6. *Leasing of state property.* The state remains the owner of the capital as far as type b rights are concerned, but rights of types a and c are invested in a private individual or group for the term of the lease in exchange for rent. In accordance with the type a rights, the residual income goes into the lessee's pocket, and if it is negative, he has to make

---

[9]The formally authorized, urban private sector was also growing fast in Poland. This category covered forms 3 and 5 in the list above. According to J. Rostowski's figures (1989a, p. 198), employment of hired labor by this sector was growing by 2–5 percent in the early 1970s, and the rate increased to 7–13 percent in the 1980s.

TABLE 19.4
Growth of the So-called Cooperative Sector
in the Soviet Union

Year	Cooperative Membership
January 1987	15,000
July 1987	39,100
January 1988	152,100
April 1988	245,700
July 1988	458,700
October 1988	777,000
January 1989	1,396,500
July 1989	1,660,000
October 1989	2,000,000
January 1990	2,573,800
July 1990	3,100,000

Source: The table was compiled by C. Krüger for this book, using data from *Pravda, Ekonomicheskaia Gazeta, Ekonomika i Zhizn'*, V. N. Beznosnikov (1990, p. 25), T. I. Koriagina (1990b, p. 145), and T. Kuznetsova (1989, p. 149).

Note: With the beginning of the reform, the term "cooperative" came into use as a cover name for part of the private sector. In some cases it meant a private partnership; in other cases it referred to a group of private owners who hired employees. In that sense the cooperative sector includes categories 2 and 5 listed in the text. The data exclude *sovmestitel-'stvo,* that is, the combination of state and nonstate jobs.

up the loss. As for type c rights, the lessee manages the enterprise and hires and fires the employees.[10]

In several reform countries the leasing form is widespread for a variety of units (e.g., stores, restaurants, and small firms).[11] It tends to gain ground where the assets can be easily valued at the beginning and end of

[10]The specific terms of the lease decide whether type c rights pass entirely to the tenant. The owner (the state authority or firm leasing it out) may retain some of the rights of control.

[11]The first country where lease arrangements occurred was Poland. As mentioned before, in legal terms the Chinese "responsibility system" started as a lease form, but in actual content it developed into a case of privatization. The agricultural resolutions adopted in the Soviet Union in April 1989 also allow a lease form (*arenda*).

TABLE 19.5
Relative Size of Social Sectors in Hungary

	First Economy (percent)	Second Economy (percent)
1. Distribution of total active time (excluding time spent on household work and transport) in 1984	67	33
2. Contribution of social sectors to residential construction (measured by the number of new dwellings) in 1984	44.5	55.5
3. Contribution of social sectors to repair and maintenance services in 1983	13	87

Source: Row 1: J. Timár (1985, p. 306); row 2: Központi Statisztikai Hivatal (Central Statistical Office, Budapest) (1985, p. 139), and P. Belyó and B. Drexler (1985, p. 60). Both studies rely on microsurveys (interviews and questionnaires).

Notes: The table covers both the officially recorded and unrecorded part of total activities. The figures concerning the latter are based on estimates elaborated by the researchers who compiled the data base of the table. The first economy figures include the traditional (kolkhoz-like) agricultural cooperatives [→5.5], and also the activities of so-called enterprise business work partnerships. The second economy figures include household farming and "auxiliary production of employees" (categories 1–5 in text). Figures in row 1 are aggregates of all branches of production, including residential construction. The latter is also surveyed separately in row 2. The second economy figures in row 3 are the sum of three parts: formal private sector, 14 percent; informal private sector, excluding "do-it-yourself" activities, 19 percent; and "do-it-yourself" activities within the household, 54 percent.

the lease, and where the tenant can be held responsible to the extent of any damage.[12]

7. *Firms in joint ownership.* In this case the ownership of a particular firm is shared by the state and individuals or privately owned firms.

[12]In the 1960s Tibor Liska, a Hungarian economist, proposed as the dominate property form under reform socialism a version of the leasing system that he had worked out in detail. His proposition was that the entire real fixed assets of the state, including all factories, should be leased to those who undertook to run them and bid the most favorable leasing terms in an auction. See T. Liska [1964] (1988), also J. Bársony (1982) and J. Szabó (1989).

Liska's ideas found a response not only in Hungary but abroad. The bureaucracy during the reform process cannot make up its mind to resign its types a and c property rights to the whole state sector. Under the prevailing power structure, it is hard to imagine a bureaucracy so "self-effacing" as to limit itself to the role of an "auctioneer" of leasing contracts. Nor is it certain that any large number of entrepreneurs would willingly take full

In a proportion of cases, the socialist state associates with foreign private capital. Such firms operate under privileged, artificial legal and organizational conditions, and their requirements receive special consideration.

In Poland, Hungary, China, and the Soviet Union there have also been experiments with joint ventures where the state associates with domestic private capital (or in some cases with both domestic and foreign private capital).[13]

Worth mentioning specially is a form that has appeared on a mass scale in Chinese villages, known as town-village firms. These are businesses pursuing nonagricultural activities, and with marked success; their production is growing very rapidly. The division of the property rights is not uniform or unambiguous; normally those of the village community and private persons are combined. A high proportion of them are clearly private enterprises.[14]

The survey has yielded a definition of the private sector in the production sphere: in a narrower sense it consists of the set of forms 1-5, and in a broader sense of the set of forms 1-7.

The private-sector income in all the forms discussed so far derives from production activity, from work. In most cases this work is coupled with privately owned capital. So the income generated is a combination in varying proportions of wages for labor, entrepreneurial profit for entrepreneurship, and rent for property. But alongside them there is an eighth form that contains no wage or entrepreneurial profit element, and simply yields rent received by virtue of ownership (or, more accurately, income in which the rent element is dominant and the wage and entrepreneurial profit elements are eclipsed).

8. *Income from property.* This takes several forms, of which the first four involve turning the money possessed by an individual to good account.

---

responsibility for a lease on a complete large firm without demanding type b property rights as well, that is, becoming private owners with full and irrevocable rights.

[13]In a few cases a joint venture arises in a formal sense when a state firm takes the legal form of a joint-stock company and assigns or distributes to the firm's employees as a bonus a small proportion of the shares.

[14]See W. A. Byrd and Q. Lin, eds. (1990). There are no reliable statistics that distinguished the privately owned, genuine collectively owned, and de facto state-owned firms in the official statistics of collectively owned firms. Casual observation shows, however, that the majority of rural collectively owned firms are de facto privately owned firms. This is particularly true of the rural firms established after 1984, which most of them were. Because government policy discriminates against private firms and favors collective firms, many private firms claim to be collective firms. To gain recognition from the government as collective firms, they have to pay fees to the government in the form of special taxes.

a. Interest on a deposit in the state bank. This form existed under the classical system. Several additional ways of investing money arise during the process of reform.

b. The yield from bonds issued by state organizations and state-owned firms. This has become widespread in several countries, including China, Hungary, and Poland.

c. Money loans to individuals on interest and repayment terms agreed mutually between the lender and the borrower.

d. Part-ownership of a private enterprise. The individual provides money of his own for the operation of a private firm and on that basis claims part of the firm's profits, irrespective of whether he works for the firm. This is roughly equivalent to owning some of the shares in a joint-stock company. But in these countries privately owned joint-stock companies are not legally permitted, so that part-ownership can only apply under legally unregulated conditions.[15]

e. The other main opportunity besides investing money is to let privately owned real estate: a plot of land, house, privately owned apartment, holiday home, garage, or commercial premises. (The letting may entail providing maintenance and other services to the tenant; to that extent the income is not just rent from property, since it contains elements of income from work and profit for entrepreneurship.)

The private sector's relative weight can be measured in various ways. One is to determine the proportion of output it accounts for, or the proportion of input it is using, in which case by definition only forms 1–7 can be counted in. Another possible calculation is to add up the income of all individuals, including all payments in money and kind.[16] To establish what proportion of that derives from the private sector, income from form 8 must be included alongside income from forms 1–7.[17]

There is one more point of view worth applying to a survey of the private sector. The two types of expansion of the private sector were mentioned in connection with Chinese agriculture, but they are worth stressing here in a more general form.

---

[15]The idea comes up in the debates on property relations that the state-owned firms should be converted into joint-stock companies and some of their shares sold to private individuals. This is only done, however, in exceptional cases during the reform phase. This kind of restructuring of property relations really comes into consideration in the postsocialist stage.

[16]For an empirical survey on Hungary, see K. Balázs and M. Laki (1991).

[17]Another diversion into the Marxist interpretation of the emerging situation is called for, because an understanding of it will be needed for evaluating the political environment around the private sector later on. In Marxist political economy, the incomes of a "coupon-clipping" possessor of money, a landlord pocketing house-rents, or a county landowner gathering rents for his fields are the fruits of exploitation. Someone receiving income on such grounds becomes, to the extent of that income, a member of the exploiting classes.

One path is for the private owner himself to establish the new private factory, buying capital goods with his own money, or credit or with the money of other investors, and so on. In this way the private factory comes into being alongside the state-owned factories, and the state-owned factories remain in state ownership.

The other path is for a factory in state (or cooperative) ownership to be sold to a private person or group of persons. In this case there is a "transfer" of property, so that private ownership comes instead of public ownership. This process is commonly termed *privatization*. The latter path may be combined with the former.

During the reform process, the first path is taken in most sectors, although there may be exceptions. The most important exception is the restructuring of Chinese agriculture, but privatization occurs in other sectors too (e.g., the sale in several countries of some state-owned apartments to their tenants). But one can say that mass, comprehensive privatization only takes place after the revolution, under the postsocialist system.

19.3   The Private Sector and the Official Ideology

Condemnation of private ownership and emphasis on the exclusive legitimacy of public ownership is a major element in the official ideology of the classical system [→5.7]. The official line under the classical system was that any form of private ownership is a vestige of capitalism tolerable at most in the short term.

That conception was rooted in the ideas of the Marxist classics. According to Marx, the future will bring an end to private ownership. Remember the oft-quoted lines from *Capital*: "The monopoly of capital becomes a fetter upon the mode of production, which has flourished alongside and under it. The centralization of the means of production and the socialization of labor reach a point at which they become incompatible with their capitalist integument. This integument is burst asunder. The knell of capitalist private property sounds. The expropriators are expropriated."[18] Engels put it this way: "Society will take all forces of production and means of commerce, as well as the exchange and distribution of products, out of the hands of private capitalists and will manage them in accordance with a plan based on the availability of resources and the needs of the whole society. . . . In fact, the abolition of private property is doubtless the shortest and most significant way to characterize the revolution in the whole social order which has been made neces-

---

[18]K. Marx [1867–94] (1978, chap. 32, p. 929).

sary by the development of industry, and for this reason it is rightly advanced by Communists as their main demand."[19]

This is one of the most agonizing and sensitive ideological dilemmas of the reform process. It is no small tactical detail, but as Engels rightly underlined, one of the main demands of the Communists and a cornerstone of the ideology.

Marxism raises a number of rational arguments against private ownership, of which some point to real disadvantages of this property form. At the same time, people in this case are influenced not only by rational arguments but by far deeper emotional layers of reasoning. Communists (and many non-Communist left-wingers) nurse an antipathy to private ownership or a downright hatred of it; they feel moral indignation against it, because the domination of private ownership is associated with privileges for the wealthy and an unjust distribution of income, because it produces unearned income, which they consider morally reprehensible, and because it lays the workers open to exploitation by their employers. They ascribe an intrinsic value to eliminating private ownership and establishing public ownership, even if they should be accompanied by disadvantages in terms of economic efficiency. Even a partial abandonment of this idea causes an upheaval as great as when a religious believer abandons faith in the immortality of the soul. One of the main explanations for the enormous strength of the resistance to expanding the private sector lies in the depths of ideological conviction.

Mikhail Gorbachev was in full accord with ideological tradition when he made this statement in 1988: "Thus *perestroika* in economic relations is called for in order to unearth the opportunities inherent in our system, in the various forms of socialist ownership. But private ownership, as is well known, is the basis of the exploitation of man by man, and our revolution was accomplished precisely in order to liquidate it, in order to hand over everything to ownership of the people. Trying to restore private ownership means to move backward, and is a deeply mistaken decision."[20] Zhao Ziyang, general secretary of the Chinese Communist party, made a similar declaration in 1989: "The ruling position of public ownership cannot be changed."[21]

The official ideology of the reform displays attempts to reach pragmatic compromises between the traditional opposition to private property and the reformist party line valid at the time, between partial toleration and encouragement of private property. Small-scale commodity

[19]F. Engels [1847] (1964, pp. 74, 78).

[20]Gorbachev's speech to the Presidium of the Supreme Soviet of the Soviet Union, *Pravda,* November 26, 1988.

[21]*Renmin Ribao,* March 17, 1989.

production is deemed to be compatible with the socialist system, and it is emphasized that it involves industrious workers, peasants, and ordinary townsfolk. There is indeed a tradition of political alliance with them in the Communist movement, although it applied only in prerevolutionary periods when the support of the peasantry and the urban petty bourgeoisie was necessary to the success of the revolution and the smashing of the tyrannical prerevolutionary order. Later, with the rural collectivization and the elimination of urban small-scale commodity production, this alliance broke up, but the idea now reappears as an auxiliary ideological prop.

The trouble is that there are strong ideological considerations weighing against this as well. Where does small-scale commodity production end and capitalism begin? Lenin gave a justified warning: "small production engenders capitalism and the bourgeoisie continuously, daily, hourly, spontaneously, and on a mass scale."[22] And, in fact, when the small-scale commodity producers appear on a mass scale under the reform socialist system, sooner or later the most talented and industrious stand out among them, along with the luckiest of them and those cleverest at bending the rules and deceiving the buyers. One way or another, they make bigger and more profitable investments than the others, extend their workshops, and ultimately grow up to be capitalists.

As mentioned above, the circle of problems is connected with the principles on the distribution of income. A believer in the socialist system of values cannot accept the idea of unearned income. The tradition goes back to Marx, who poured scorn on the idea that interest was the reward of frugality. This strikes a chord in the heart of many people whose lives of toil have brought them little, and they are outraged that others can be rich without working. This is fertile soil for ideological opposition to private ownership.

The antipathy is not confined to "unearned income." It extends also to people who undoubtedly work hard themselves, for instance, peasants or retail traders, but are felt to receive inordinately large incomes for doing so. A good many of the entrepreneurs grow rich rapidly. Most of those employed in the private sector earn better than their peers in the state sector. The anger, envy, and jealousy about greater wealth and higher earnings are closely related to the feelings of suspicion, antipathy, and hatred toward the private sector. The former provides fertile soil for the latter. In addition, the ideology of opposition to private property, drummed in for decades, has become deeply imbedded in the thinking of broad sections of the population, which further enhances the antipathy toward the private sector. Whenever some official measure or other is

---

[22]V. I. Lenin [1920] (1966, p. 24).

taken against "profiteers," "speculators," or "parasites," it regularly elicits approval from large masses of people.

For all these reasons, reform socialism is incapable of putting forward a consistent system of ideas on the subjects of private property, private economic activity, and income received on property. It is full of contradictions between the socialistic, anti-capitalist, anti–private ownership tradition, on the one hand, and the pragmatic requirements of the reform process, on the other; a deep-seated reflex reaction causes the former to dominate.

19.4 The Affinity of Private Ownership and Market Coordination

Let me return to an analogy used earlier [→6.4, 15.2]. *Affinity* is a term used in chemistry to mean chemical "kinship": certain chemicals are capable of combining with other chemicals. This expression can be used figuratively in political economy as well: certain property forms are capable of combining with certain coordination mechanisms. There is also a contrary phenomenon: some property forms cannot associate naturally, without force, with some coordination mechanism or other.

There is a close affinity between private ownership and the market mechanism.[23] The distinguishing marks of the market mechanism were described in section 6.1:

No private enterprise has administrative power over another. Their relations are of a horizontal nature.

A private enterprise is autonomous by definition: the property rights belong to a private individual or group of individuals. So self-evidently, these autonomous economic units enter into contracts with each other voluntarily, without orders from above. This ownership-based autonomy requires decentralized coordination.

The main incentive for an owner engaged in production is material gain. So no private proprietor can ignore the amount of income he gains by his activity and what his costs are, in other words, the price he gets for his output and the price he pays for his input. Thus he is at home with the information structure of the market, where the main role is played by prices and the advantages and drawbacks of each transaction are measured primarily in money.

---

[23]The close connection between the type of coordination mechanism and the property form is greatly emphasized in the positions taken in the debates on socialism by L. v. Mises [1920] (1935) and subsequently F. A. Hayek, ed. (1935). Attention was later drawn to the connection by the "property-rights school" [→21.1, 21.6]. (For references see chapter 21, note 43.)

The workings of the "invisible hand," the dynamics of the market, have been well understood since the time of Adam Smith. What needs noting particularly here is that the normal workings of the market require free entry for new entrepreneurs, rivalry between entrepreneurs, and failure of all entrepreneurs who come out worst in the competition.

All this needs to be repeated before turning to the actual subject of this section: the relations between the private sector and the market under the reform system. All economic relations arising among the private enterprises or between them and the general public are coordinated basically by the market mechanism. A natural advance by the market mechanism is inseparable from the expansion of the private sector.[24] Private enterprises need no central command before entering into market-mediated relations with each other and the households. It happens self-evidently and spontaneously; all that had to be done for the market to develop was to lift or at least ease the prohibitions.

The usual concomitants of true market coordination are conspicuous here. The buyer agrees freely on the prices and other terms of the transaction.[25] This sphere of the reform system's market operates with the usual dynamism: entrepreneurs pounce on opportunities that look profitable, so that rivalry develops among them (and possibly with the public sectors too). But if private entrepreneurs cannot make ends meet, they abandon the activity and may fail with grave losses. The budget constraint on a private enterprise is hard; no state under the socialist system rushes to aid an ailing private firm.[26] So the market performs the often merciless natural selection characteristic of it.

What comes about in this way is real flesh-and-blood market coordination. But two qualifications must be added. One is that this market is still under the shadow of the omnipresent bureaucratic coordination mechanism that dominates the whole of society. It can intervene in a hundred different ways even in the relations of private enterprises with each other and with households [→19.5]. Of course, even a capitalist

---

[24]The word natural is emphasized to contrast it with the artificial introduction of a market into relations between state-owned firms [→21.7]. This approach is inspired by the Austrian interpretation of market coordination, namely, by the works of Mises and Hayek, and by Schumpeter's theory of the entrepreneur's role. See also in this context P. Murrell (1990a, 1990b).

[25]This is still true if the administrative authorities want to dictate the private sector's prices. Except with a few, easily "identifiable" prices, the goal is quite illusory. There are plenty of ways around the administrative price.

[26]The bureaucracy does not obstruct exit, that is, it allows a private enterprise that cannot support itself to fail. It erects numerous obstacles to entry, however, which reduces rivalry [→19.5].

state that minimizes intervention erects prohibitions and limitations. It would serve no purpose here to go into the intricacies of the normative problem of what is the minimum intervention, limitation, and prohibition that all states must apply on the basis of the generally accepted ethical and legal norms. The instances of intervention, limitation, and prohibition found in the private-sphere market under the reform system reach far beyond that minimum scale. These are system-specific and mainly related to considerations of power and ideology.

The other qualification is that the market now being examined is primitive and backward. The market is an institution thousands of years old that appears even at quite low levels of civilization and technology. Whether one looks at the Western world in the Middle Ages or at the state of the third world fifty to a hundred years ago, one finds peasants bringing their own produce and livestock to the city and offering them for sale in an open marketplace or market hall; itinerant traders selling from the back of a cart; shopkeepers in cramped, ill-equipped stores; or travelers arriving from foreign lands with goods in their baggage that they have bought abroad and offer for sale at home. These market participants of yore have not vanished entirely even from the modern capitalist world, but they are no longer the leading actors. Their place has largely been taken by up-to-date forms of market operation. The fact that the market was almost entirely abolished for some decades under the classical system of socialism caused such primitive, medieval, "Balkan," "Asian" forms to enter the stage again when the market reappeared. What distinguishes the market linked under reform socialism with the private sector from the up-to-date market forms?

In the market mechanism of the developed capitalist countries the smaller economic units are connected by numerous decentralized organizations: wholesalers, commodity exchanges, warehousing and haulage companies, and advertising agencies. Estate agents are required for the operation of the market mechanism for real estate and housing. Stock exchanges, stock brokers, mutual funds, and investment firms are needed for the buying and selling of property rights. Smooth working of the market also involves a broad, decentralized financial sector of commercial banks, insurance companies, and other financial intermediaries.

In the reform socialist countries these organizations either are entirely absent or, if some exist, operate only in publicly owned, bureaucratic versions. Usually they serve only the public sectors and remain unavailable to the private sector or accessible to it only to a limited extent.

Up-to-date market coordination requires up-to-date technology: a widespread, efficient telephone service, quick and reliable mail deliveries, personal computers, photocopying machines, and so on.

Not even for the dominant state sector is there enough of this kind of technical equipment available, and the private sector is far more backward. Many private enterprises have no telephone at all. Even in the economically rather more developed countries of Eastern Europe, private enterprises conduct relations with each other at a primitive, backward technical level.

Even if market coordination in the private sphere were to be given free rein from the beginning of the reform, it would still take a long period of history to establish a modern market. And there is no question of a free rein. The backwardness just described can only be explained partly in terms of vestiges from the past and the antimarket legacy of the classical system. The rest of the explanation is the bureaucracy's continuing aversion not only to private ownership but to the concomitant market mechanism. That is why it obstructs the foundation of the network of private organizations needed for market coordination instead of encouraging it, and why the supply of technical equipment is meager.

19.5 The Private Sector and the Bureaucracy

It was mentioned earlier that the bureaucracy behaves ambivalently toward the private sector in the reform phase. Sometimes it reassures and assists it, and sometimes it undermines its confidence and hinders its operation. The ambivalence may take the form of support for the private sector in one branch of the bureaucracy coupled with obstruction of it in another, or of an alternation of periods favorable and unfavorable to the private sector.

Both kinds of behavior have their reasons. One side of the ambivalence, the bureaucracy's motives for allowing the private sector to operate, has been described. But although one of the bureaucracy's mental compartments is aware that it needs the private sector, another compartment of the same mind nurses a smoldering distaste and hatred for private ownership and individual activity. One explanation for the antipathy can be sought in the ideology [→19.3]. The other ties in with considerations of power. Leaderships of state-owned firms and quasi-state cooperatives are integral parts of the bureaucratic hierarchy; a manager or cooperative chairman is the bureaucracy's own person. One might say the bureaucracy governs the public sector from within, whereas it can limit the operation and income of the private sector only from without. It cannot appoint anyone to be an individual farmer or private artisan, and it cannot dismiss people from such positions. Even such a partial degree of autonomy is hard for a bureaucracy intent on totalitarian power to tolerate.

It was mentioned earlier in the chapter that private enterprise is not set up by taking conscious administrative steps; it arises spontaneously out of voluntary individual initiative. The same can be said of the bureaucratic resistance to it. The central administration in reforming countries does not usually direct its subordinate bodies to impede private-sector activity. The bureaucratic resistance likewise emerges spontaneously and automatically out of the power interests and ideology of the bureaucracy.

The points of contact between the bureaucracy and the private sector are as follows.

1. *Security of private property.* Based on their own or earlier generations' memories or the lessons of history, people recollect earlier acts of nationalization and how many people's house property and personal wealth were confiscated. They recall how the land was taken from the peasants. They do not feel that the private property they have now acquired is safe. Despite repeated reassurances, they still see no constitutional guarantees of security of private property.

2. *Legality; licenses to operate.* Free enterprise means the chance for anyone to start any kind of private enterprise without a special license from the authorities. There are exceptions to this principle even in capitalist countries based on free enterprise. Most countries insist on operating licenses for certain socially useful activities as well, if they have major external effects, like the establishment of a private hospital or school, a public transportation firm (operating airplanes, a railroad, or buses), and so on.

Even in the more permissive, reformed version of a socialist economy, the proportions are reversed. There are relatively few production activities that require no operating license. The reform phase differs from its predecessor in issuing licenses more liberally, not in abandoning its rights of authorization. This is another way in which it seeks to control the private sector.

Already in a classical socialist economy there was "black" economic activity: industrial or commercial services provided without a license [→5.6]. In this respect the reform brings two kinds of change. One is that certain previously banned activities are permitted, although pursuit of them is made conditional on a license from the authorities. For example, it used to be forbidden to use a privately owned car to provide a taxi service. Those who did so anyway ran the risk of prosecution. Now private taxis need a license to operate. In this instance, the color of the market for an activity has changed radically: a "black" market has turned "white." The other possible alteration is for a private activity to remain banned, but the ban is no longer enforced in practice. It is still forbidden, for instance, for one private person to do repair work on the side for another, without declaring it to the authorities or paying tax. The bureaucracy knows what is going on, but turns a blind eye. Here the change of market color is less radical: from "black" to "gray." The latter kind of change is very widespread in reforming countries. Masses of people perform semilegal, informal economic activity tolerated by the authorities.[27]

Work in the informal, semilegal sphere contributes greatly to improving supplies to the public and the incomes of those who do it. But it is a very chancy income; no one knows when the rigor of the law will fall on those working in the shadow economy. It is the part of the private sector that best escapes bureaucratic control, but it is highly dependent on the bureaucracy's leniency.

3. *Constraints on growth.* The bureaucracy consciously decides to place constraints on the growth of the private sector, not only on the macro level, to ensure that the sector as a whole does not exceed a set proportion of the economy, but on the micro level, to try to curb the size of each unit. This ties in closely with the principle just discussed of not letting small-scale commodity production become capitalist. The attempt is made partly with legal measures, for instance, an upper limit on the number of people a private enterprise may hire for wages.[28] But the constraint can also be applied by other methods, of course: appropriate tax levels, withdrawal of the operating license from a firm that grows "too big," or simply threats.

4. *Enforcement of private contracts.* The market coordination of the developed countries emerged spontaneously, but each step in its development was supported by legislation and legal practice. There are a great many refined legal regulations to protect decentralized private transactions, enforce the observance of contracts, ensure fair competition, remove the obstacles to free entry, provide orderly ways of "exit," and defend the rights of debtors and creditors. Of course, the law cannot give 100 percent security; it cannot prevent fraud. Nonetheless, coupled

---

[27]The term "second economy" is widespread in the academic writings of the socialist countries [→5.6], but as mentioned before, a terminological consensus has failed to emerge. Some works confine the term to the informal private sector and its "gray" or "black" activity. Others include the legal, "white" private sector in it as well.

This book uses the latter definition, defining the second economy as the entire formal and informal private sector.

[28]The number varies according to country and period. For a long time the employment limit for a private enterprise was seven in Hungary and eight in China.

In the Soviet Union, the first article of the law on "individual labor activity," passed in 1986, states: "Individual labor activity involving the use of hired labor with the purpose of extracting unearned income, or to the detriment of other socialist interests, is not permitted." *Pravda,* November 26, 1986. The wording, incidentally, demonstrates graphically the remarks about the official ideology in the previous section.

with correct practice by judges and lawyers and consistent enforcement of the legislation, it can provide a legal infrastructure for the smooth operation of a real market.[29] The market just starting to operate under reform socialism hardly possesses such a legal infrastructure at all.

Although steps in this direction are taken in the legal system and judicial practice of the reforming countries, they fall far short of performing these functions.

5. *Legal protection of private property and private firms from the authorities*. If the authorities act in a way damaging to the interests of a private owner or entrepreneur, there is very little chance of redress. It may be possible to lodge a complaint with the authority superior to the one in question or with another governmental body (the prosecutor's office or the so-called people's control commission), but no private person or firm can sue a state organization in the courts. This makes it easier for the authorities to become arbitrary.

6. *Taxation*. The ambivalence of the situation applies to the taxation of the private sector as well. On the one hand, the tax regulations constantly change, and they are frequently applied in an arbitrary way. There is often a tailor-made decision on how much tax someone will pay. In some countries and periods the taxes levied on private enterprises are so heavy that it becomes impossible to run them profitably.[30] On the other hand, arbitrary interpretation of the tax regulations, coupled with toleration of semilegal, "gray" activity over a wide sphere, makes tax evasion possible. The uncertainty of the situation precludes the development of a public moral climate in which people pay taxes honestly.

7. *Access to credit, foreign exchange, materials, and state orders*. The authorities allocating resources discriminate against the private sector in favor of the public sectors. This applies primarily to the banking system, which is a bureaucratic distributor of credit (and in foreign trade transactions of foreign exchange), rather than a real business partner. But cases also occur when a state authority allocates some material in short supply. State-owned firms also behave in a discriminatory way toward the private sector, either in obedience to legal regulations or arbitrarily.

One reason why the private sector is at a disadvantage in all the fields just listed is that there is no political party or movement to represent its

[29]The buying and selling processes of modern capitalism are coordinated by a complex mechanism in which market coordination predominates; this is supported and complemented by bureaucratic coordination through state guarantees and legal order, by the ethical mechanism through the principles of business integrity and keeping one's word, by the legislature, and by the self-governing mechanism through the activities of organizations representing special interests.

[30]Hungary's private artisans and traders handed back their operating licenses in droves when new tax rules were introduced in 1988.

interests forcefully. In a capitalist system power is frequently held by political parties or movements that represent the interests of private enterprise. But even if the party currently in power represents other interests, there are strong opposition parties to protect the fundamental interests of private enterprise and ensure the continuity of the laws that safeguard private property. By contrast, even under the reform version of the socialist system, the private sector has no chance of making itself heard in the political arena. It must resign itself to whatever the bureaucracy inflicts in the way of levies or constraints. Normally, it goes unchampioned even by opposition movements. Some dissident political tendencies are expressly anticapitalist.[31] Others may have liberal leanings, but they do not want to leave themselves open to any charge of trying to "restore capitalism."

Since the environment behaves ambivalently toward the private sector, the private sector behaves ambivalently too. On the one hand, the usual beneficial feature of private enterprises appear: diligence, intensive industry, cost economy, swift exploitation of business opportunities, flexibility, and so on. On the other hand, private entrepreneurs do not feel they can be content with slow, integral development, winning their customers' confidence and good will by degrees. Broad, productive accumulation and steady expansion of activity are not their purpose. Their timescale is foreshortened and their behavior marked by shortsighted maximization of profits. They go for the greatest possible profit in the least possible time, spend as much of it as possible,[32] and then, when the right moment comes, they go out of business. Most of the private sector has poor equipment and premises and neglects maintenance. Where chronic shortage persists, the private sector soon adopts the state sector's superiority and inattention to the buyer. Private entrepreneurs must often resort to bribery to combat the discrimination against them. Not infrequently they try to cheat both the buyer and the state. This all helps to make private entrepreneurs unpopular.

The ambivalence applies not only to the economic situation of the private sector but to the social position of those taking part in it. If success-

---

[31]In Poland the Solidarity trade union became the rallying point for the alternative political trends before the collapse of Communist rule, and one could not expect an organization representing employees to champion the interests of private employers. In Hungary and the Soviet Union in the 1980s there were influential alternative trends that placed a reawakening of the peasant past in the forefront and viewed with scorn and loathing American-style "business," speculation, and moneymaking, and the urban, petty-bourgeois way of life.

[32]Wasteful consumption is common among individuals engaged in the private sector and the members of their families. In addition, the following trend appears in investment: much of the profit is used for investments whose sole purpose is to preserve the value of savings (realty, precious metals, jewelry, fine art, etc.), not for development of the enterprise.

ful, they are envied, but also hated and despised. The members of their social environment have been instilled from the cradle with a strongly egalitarian outlook. High earnings command respect in the minds of a large proportion of capitalist society, because many people assume that they are probably the reward of outstanding performance. By contrast, to socialist society high earnings are suspect; people immediately assume they were obtained by foul means.[33] In any case, "petty bourgeois" is a pejorative term in the socialist world, and "bourgeois" even more so. Private entrepreneurs are quite aware of the climate of distrust and disdain surrounding them. So the person who becomes a private entrepreneur is not necessarily someone who best fits the business criteria for the position. It is someone who will take a political and social, not just an economic risk. The circumstances attract adventurers rather than sober, thrifty entrepreneurs.

So the position of the private sector under reform socialism enters a vicious circle. The ambivalent actions of the bureaucracy and the prejudice in society cause insecurity in private owners and entrepreneurs, who often show under these conditions the worst, not the best, side of capitalism. That heightens the antipathy toward them, which is a stimulus and argument for the bureaucracy to be even more hostile toward them, so that the negative features of their activities come to predominate even more. The system needs the private sector, and the private sector has to acknowledge the power of the bureaucracy, which is hostile toward it. But the result is a bitter coexistence, replete with mutual suspicion and conflict.

19.6   The Economic Role of the Family

As a diversion, it is worth dealing briefly with an important sphere in the life of society: the role of the family. The problems examined here impinge closely on the subject-area of the private sector, which has just been discussed, and partly overlap with them.

In the treatment of the classical system, family coordination was discussed as one of the coordination mechanisms. It was established that the sphere of activities coordinated by the family became much narrower than it had been traditionally before the socialist revolution [→6.7]. The

---

[33]The greater the disproportions in the economy and the discrepancy between the structure of supply and demand, the greater the profit a producer-seller can make under a true market mechanism by trying to contribute to satisfying excess demand. The very high earnings of these people is evidence, in fact, that they are performing a useful role. But it is to them, as "speculators," that public opinion under reform socialism is most hostile.

inner logic of the system tended to restrict the family's economic role still further. By comparison there are noticeable changes during the process of reform: activity coordinated by the family plays an appreciably greater part. It tends to be increased still more by the internal impetus of the reform process. Let us consider the most characteristic phenomena.

The most important change is the substantial role in the economy regained by the *family undertaking*, which the classical system wiped out almost entirely. It comes to the fore in the privatization of agriculture and in the other branches of the private sector. This form is capable of producing a sudden leap in labor intensity and in the increase of working hours; the family "drives" itself to do more work in a more disciplined way. Since the legal framework of private contracts, and within that the basis for individuals to extend credit and contribute capital, has yet to develop, particular importance attaches to the mutual trust ensured by family ties. It is reassuring that the wealth, capital, and money "stay in the family." This ties in with another motive behind the development of the private sector: the entrepreneur's desire to become independent of the state and prevent outsiders prying into what he does.

There are substantial changes in the *housing sector*. The classical system's housing ideal is an estate of rented tenements where people live in a large, easily supervised mass.[34] There is a change in the reform process in favor of owner-occupied family houses and apartments. Several countries (e.g., Hungary and China) start privatizing state-owned rented apartments.

The choice-dilemma of "a private house versus an apartment in a state-owned block" has several economic aspects in the narrow sense, ranging from the organization of construction and maintenance to the effect on both the family and the state budget, but here only the social effect is considered. Many people, if not all, take the English view that "their home is their castle." Most family life takes place within the walls of the home. For many people a family house is an embodiment of autonomy and one of the physical guarantees of the chance to retreat into private life.[35] It was mentioned in the discussion on the private production sector that one of the motivations behind a private entrepreneur is

[34]In Romania in the 1980s, it was described as merely a temporary compromise that the cooperative peasants should live in houses they owned themselves. A start was made on demolishing villages and forcing the peasantry into state-owned accommodation.

[35]One Soviet intellectual who is the owner-occupier of a modest house some distance from Moscow gave this ironic explanation in 1989: "In a Moscow apartment block they can turn off my water any time. Here I have a well in the yard; if necessary I can hold out for weeks."

a desire to be autonomous. The same desire leads many families to obtain a family house.[36]

The emphasis in *passenger transportation* under the classical system is on developing public transportation (except that the top functionaries in the bureaucracy would receive institutionally owned, chauffeur-driven cars [→13.5]). The reform brings a surge in the public's demand for private cars.[37] This demand is not based on a narrow calculation of economic efficiency, since it is more expensive for most households to run a car than to use subsidized public transportation. Moreover, a shortage economy means a long wait for an automobile, considerable inconvenience in maintaining and repairing it, and crowded roads. The main attraction of car ownership is a sense of autonomy and independence. To a lesser extent a car, like a house, is a "castle." The owner decides whom to let in and when to set off.

The reform changes the role of the family in *care of children, the sick, and the old*. The classical system, in its paternalism, promised that the state would steadily take this over. Appreciable steps were taken to do so, notably in providing childcare institutions (day nurseries, kindergartens, and after-school centers). Provision of free hospital care and old-age pensions for all (or large sections of society) tended in the same direction. But the classical system proved unable to keep its word, as it lacked the resources to pay for these enormous assignments. In any case, it had other priorities: many other tasks were rated more important [→9.4]. During the reform, the state admits or hints that it cannot fulfill these basic promises, and it begins to pass, or rather thrust, the tasks of caring for children, the sick, and the elderly back onto the family.

In a developed capitalist economy much of the *domestic work* is taken over by the commercial sphere, and this coincides with mechanization of the home. In terms of food, a network of restaurants and snack bars in various price ranges grows up; meanwhile, there is a growing supply of domestic appliances and machines to facilitate cookery, refrigeration, food storage, and so on. As for washing and ironing, laundry and dry-cleaning services become widespread; meanwhile, households are able to install washing and drying machines. The household gains a degree of choice about the domestic work it is able and willing to do, the labor-saving appliances it is able and willing to buy for the purpose, and the services it wants to buy outside the home.

[36]This is not the only motive. There may also be economic advantages, and in many areas of several countries plain necessity: citizens may be unable to obtain a home of their own in any other way.

[37]Khrushchev argued vehemently against private car ownership during the first Soviet wave of reform.

Classical socialism offers little in the way of commercial substitutes for domestic work. There is a shortage of restaurants and laundries operating commercially, and a shortage of refrigerators, washing machines, and up-to-date cooking stoves. Just one tendency can be seen: moves toward collectivization of consumption [→6.7], but even that does not go far. In any case, the reform halts and tends to reverse the trend. There is a surge of development in the branches providing services to the general public for money. State-owned firms in these branches also grow faster; this happens in the very fields (apart from agriculture) in which private enterprise appears soonest. Meanwhile, the public seizes the chance to acquire refrigerators, washing machines, television sets, and many other kinds of domestic consumer durables and appliances.[38]

Unfortunately, data on the distribution of ownership of the national wealth are not available. Observation of the direction of the changes suggests an appreciable alteration. Adding up the productive capital of the private sector and the value of buildings, cars, domestic equipment, and machines owned by households, along with other individually owned items of value, the proportion of material national wealth in private hands is appreciably higher than under the classical system. This shows society moving toward privatization of consumption and other life functions, not just of production.

Several explanations can be given for the increase in the family's economic role, and within it the privatization of wealth and life functions. It is worth shedding light parallel with the causal analysis on some of the conflicting phenomena that accompany the changes.

The increase is related to the growth in consumption by the public. Families can afford many purchases their income would not have stretched to before. More families can afford, temporarily or permanently, to forgo regular earnings by the wife and mother. Scrutiny of the budget in many families leads them to conclude that if the female spouse stays at home doing the housework and caring for the children, sick, and aged, there is a saving compared with trying to purchase these services for money. These financial motives are backed by ethical considerations: restored respect for the traditional role of a wife and mother; reinforcement of family independence; and alleviation of the defenselessness of the family in the face of the bureaucratic service institutions and the shortage economy.

These voluntary motives of the family come just at the right time for the bureaucracy. A serious budget deficit develops in all the reform economies [→23.3]; the financial authorities can hardly wait to be rid of the

---

[38]At the beginning of the Hungarian reform, the New Left critics of the changes scornfully termed the system "refrigerator socialism."

costs of subsidizing investment and operation of public transportation and consumer services. They want to pass the burden of these onto the public at a rate usually much faster than the households are willing or able to assume them.

In the last resort, households and families, particularly the women, are both winners and losers by the changes. Those who join the better paid in the regrouping of incomes that accompanies the reform process tend to feel the advantages. They are glad to be able to buy a family house, an apartment, an automobile, and domestic appliances. But those who fall behind are pressed on two sides. The formerly paternalistic state ceases to provide for them; the state budget cannot cover the subsidies, and housing and numerous public services begin to grow rapidly more expensive. Meanwhile their income is too low for them to buy themselves an apartment of their own, and the purchase of a car remains an unattainable luxury. Their wages were set in a period when state wage policy was based on an assumption that hardly any money need be spent on housing or utilities. Many women find themselves in a particularly difficult situation: those with only their own earnings to rely on, or those in households whose income is such that the separate income of the women cannot be forgone even though there is another earner, find it increasingly difficult (or expensive) to obtain places in institutions that will look after the children and the aged. The lower strata in society fall between the two stools of public ownership and paternalistic bureaucracy, on the one hand, and private ownership and the market, on the other. This is one of the main sources of the social conflicts that appear in the midst of the reform process.

But even if the burdens on the family grow, this is after all a tendency that results in a loosening of totalitarianism and greater autonomy for the smallest community in society: the family.

19.7   Preview: The Private Sector under the Postsocialist System

After the digression to the family, let us return to the main subject of the chapter, the private sector. The chapter can be ended with the idea with which it began: that the revival of the private sector is among the most important changes that take place in the socialist system during the process of reform. But the power structure of the system sets tight constraints on the sector's growth. While the Communist party retains undivided power, it is impossible for the private sector to become the dominant sector in the economy. This can happen when and only when the Communist party has lost its monopoly of power and the revolution takes place.

Under postsocialism, parties that support a capitalist system based on private ownership openly and legally become actors on the political state and emerge as electoral winners.[39] The privatization of state-owned firms comes onto the agenda; the legal institutions and executive agencies for this are created. There is debate on the most expedient way of transferring the wealth owned by the state to private hands. In the meantime, the process of privatization begins in practice, sometimes more rapidly and sometimes more sluggishly, and the expansion of the private sector in other forms speeds up as well.

In this respect the legacy of reform socialism has a positive side as well. The greater the extent to which both the formal and informal private sector has managed to develop within the framework of socialism, the faster the advance of the private sector will be after the change of system. In that sense the countries where there was a reform before the revolution start out under better conditions than those that jumped directly from classical socialism to postsocialist transition.

The course of history is not symmetrical. The private sector can be abolished by state command in a very short time. But the creation of the private sector cannot be performed by state command, only by the free will of the participants in it. Even if the government authorities do all they can to further a rapid growth, its development cannot take place from one day to the next. Inevitably, it will take many years before the private sector becomes the dominant sphere in the economy.

---

[39]Since this espousal sounds alien to ears used to socialist ideology, the terminology used tends to be indirect: politicians are more inclined to refer to "the market economy" or to "a Western-type economy" than to capitalism.

20

Self-Management

ANOTHER important tendency in the movement away from the classical system is the introduction of self-management into firms in public ownership. Unlike the tendency discussed in the previous chapter, which introduces an element alien to socialism—private property—the tendency to self-management is wholly socialistic: it promises a reinterpretation of public ownership. To that extent it brings a less radical change than the intrusion of the private sector, but the alteration remains significant enough to warrant classification as a true reform process.

Self-management is a specific configuration of property rights and at the same time of coordination. (In other words, its introduction modifies blocks 2 and 3 in the scheme of figure 15.1.) Its basic principle is that the heads of the firm, unlike those of a state-owned firm, are chosen by the firm's workers (type c property rights) rather than appointed from above [→5.1]. The workforce also disposes over the residual income after costs and taxes (type a property rights).

The alternative mechanisms of coordination were surveyed in chapter 6, and self-governing coordination was mentioned among them [→6.5]. To this day, the introduction of self-management into firms remains the experiment on the largest scale in using this mechanism in production. Its intellectual and political attraction for many is that it discards both bureaucratic coordination, which has been compromised by the classical system, and market coordination, which is tied up with capitalism, offering a special kind of third road that differs from them both.

20.1 Self-Management as an Intellectual and Political Trend

The intellectual forerunners of self-management are Robert Owen (1771–1858), Charles Fourier (1772–1837), and Pierre Joseph Proudhon (1809–1865), three thinkers whom Marx and Engels inclined to call "Utopian socialists." Proudhon was the man who coined the term anarchist. Ideas related to self-management crop up in the syndicalist, anarcho-syndicalist, and cooperative socialist movements.

Without offering a detailed description of the ideas of these great thinkers and intellectual currents,[1] it is worth picking out a few ideas

---

[1] A comprehensive account and analysis of the intellectual history of self-management can be found in B. Horvat (1982).

common to them. One leitmotif is strong condemnation of the role of the state and rejection of all kinds of "etatism." The ideal situation is a society with no state at all.[2] What is needed is economic democracy and workers' self-organization. The workers' production collective should govern itself. In the terminology of this book, the self-managing mechanism [→6.5] should replace the bureaucratic mechanism as the main coordinator of the economy.

Some elements of the ideas proclaimed by the intellectual current of self-management are realized in practice, at least in part. For instance, the historical formations like the Paris Commune in 1871, the soviets in the early days of the 1917 Russian Revolution,[3] or the short-lived workers' councils in the Hungarian revolution of 1956 bear some resemblance to the intellectual model of self-management.

Yugoslavia (in 1950) was the first country to introduce self-management generally,[4] and it remained the dominant property form in the public sector until very recently. Certain elements of self-management were also introduced by law in Poland in 1982 and in Hungary in 1985, if less consistently and generally than in Yugoslavia, and more recently in the Soviet Union.

The idea of self-management recurs repeatedly in the debates on reform in the other socialist countries as well. In addition, the realm of ideas embraced by self-management has been a major element in the radical and new-left movements of the United States and Western Europe over the last two or three decades.

Turning to the analysis of self-management in practical terms, important lessons can be drawn primarily from the economic history of Yugoslavia. In accordance with the plan of the book, this account does not

[2]It is a peculiar paradox of political philosophy that three completely different currents consider the demise of the state or at least a radical reduction in its role to be desirable:

"Left-wing" anarcho-syndicalism, which wants to replace the state with the self-organization of workers;

The official ideology of Marxism-Leninism, which approves the role of state force in the process of building socialism, but proclaims that the state will wither away at a higher degree of social development, with the coming of communism; and finally,

"Right-wing" libertarian philosophy, which seeks to reduce the role of the state to the ultraminimum in order to protect the liberties of the individual. See R. Nozick (1974).

[3]This can only be said of the soviets for as long as they actually remained the organs of power in the workers' revolution. Later, when the classical socialist system developed and ossified, the soviets became part of the bureaucracy.

[4]There were several motives behind the decision on self-management. One was to demonstrate that henceforward Yugoslavia was taking a different path than Stalin's Soviet Union and the other socialist countries following the Soviet pattern. Another motive was to consolidate popular support by reinforcing the notion that the factories were owned by the workers themselves.

For the political history of Yugoslavia, see D. Rusinow (1977).

provide a specific historical description of the Yugoslav economy.[5] The problem is studied on a more general level. Although references to Yugoslav experience are frequent, they are confined to cases where one can assume that use of the self-management form would yield similar phenomena in other socialist countries.[6]

In terms of the level of abstraction and nature of the premises, two types of analytical method otherwise permissible and indeed useful in theoretical analysis are avoided.[7]

No attempt is made at total generalization, that is, at devising a theoretical model descriptive of a self-managed firm's behavior irrespective of its political and social environment. Thus, the following assertions are not intended to be valid for an Israeli kibbutz, an Italian factory taken over from its capitalist owners by its workforce, or an American lawyers' partnership. Self-management is examined here only in the context of the socialist system controlled by a Communist party.

The account does not make assumptions about the self-managed firm's environment that one cannot expect a socialist system to fulfill. For example, it does not presuppose that the firm is linked to the other economic units by a freely competitive market, or that the state refrains from interfering in the operation of the market or the firm.[8] Like the rest of the book, the ensuing line of argument aims at realistic, positive observations and conclusions, not a normative theory of a desirable but imaginary system.

20.2   Political Relations

Let me begin by analyzing the introduction of the self-management form. The case in Yugoslavia was not that the workers in a few firms

---

[5]There is a rich body of writing on this: J. Prasnikar and J. Svejnar (1990) offer a summary appraisal. See also J. P. Burkett (1989), H. Lydall (1984), D. D. Milenkovitch (1984), S. R. Sacks (1989), and R. Stojanovic, ed. (1982).

[6]No reference is made here to phenomena connected with the peculiar circumstances of Yugoslavia (for instance, the problems in the relations among the seven Yugoslav republics).

[7]The problem-sphere of self-management presents an intellectual challenge to the economics profession. Numerous noteworthy works have appeared, including many studies that examine the behavior of the self-managed unit with the help of a formalized theoretical model. See the first pioneers of the theory of self-managed firms: B. M. Ward (1958) and J. Vanek (1970, 1972). For further elaboration see J. P. Bonin and L. Putterman (1987), J. H. Drèze (1976), S. Estrin (1983), and J. E. Meade (1972).

[8]This assumption is made, for instance, in the path-breaking studies by J. Vanek (1970, 1971), which summarize the normative theory of self-governing democracy and self-management.

voluntarily initiated the form's introduction and others joined until it became general. The idea of self-management arose in the supreme leadership, and when the party leader, Tito, accepted it, it became compulsory.[9] Yugoslavia did not undergo a process of natural selection between property forms and coordination mechanisms whereby the various forms existed side by side until those people rejected of their own accord and/or those proving economically unviable were eliminated.[10] Instead, it was the power of the state that turned the centralized state property into "nonstate" social property (the official Yugoslav term).

In Yugoslavia, self-management became an unassailable taboo, the exclusive form of nonprivate property. Until very recently (in practice, until the beginning of the revolution, bringing the appearance of a multiparty system), it was forbidden to argue for the rejection of self-management, just as it was forbidden to recommend the abolition of the dominant role of state ownership in the other socialist countries.

Self-management leads to a variety of macro- and microeconomic problems, which will be explored shortly. But the most important consideration seems to be the political and social aspect rather than the economic. Many supporters of self-management hope this property form will end the alienation of workers from their work, since leadership elections will allow them active exercise of the right of control, that is, type c property rights. Yet democratic self-government cannot apply freely inside the firm[11] if a monopoly of power by the Communist party prevails in the outside world. That is the basic inherent inconsistency in Yugoslavia's (and later Poland's, Hungary's, and the Soviet Union's) attempts at self-management.

Leadership elections are influenced by party and local government organizations in various ways. Potential candidates undergo screening and voters are manipulated, and if a leader disliked by the bureaucracy is still elected, sooner or later he or she is removed. In any case, the firm's

[9]M. Djilas recounts how the thought occurred to him, how Tito came to terms with the idea of self-management, and finally how the decision to introduce it generally was taken. The irony of the situation comes out in the fact that a hasty search was made in Marx's works for quotations to consecrate the idea, and Tito was actually reassured once the quotations had been found. See the interview by G. Urban in M. Djilas (1988).

[10]In this respect it is instructive to see how many people under the socialist system voluntarily choose some form of self-management, or the related form of a real cooperative based on voluntary entry. For instance, in 1928, before the beginning of forcible collectivization, the proportion of agricultural land in the Soviet Union farmed by cooperatives was only 1.2 percent. See A. Nove (1969, p. 150).

[11]The term "firm" is not used in Yugoslavia; other categories too were given names differing from both "Western" and "Eastern" terminology. Part of this terminology is presented later [→20.5]; in this analysis use is made of "Eastern" or "Western" synonyms instead, or, where none exists, of the closest generally understandable terms.

workers know it is to their benefit to elect a leader well connected in the party as well as in the central and regional state organizations, who can obtain favorable loans, tax treatment, investment funds, foreign exchange, and other advantages.[12]

One prerequisite for true self-management in any institution is that various groups should be able to put up alternative candidates. Candidates and the groups supporting them must be allowed to organize, run election campaigns, and criticize each other's programs, which in effect amounts to the basic rights to freedom of speech and association. Unless these are adequately guaranteed in all areas of society, they cannot apply consistently in self-management at the workplace either.

In a true parliamentary democracy, where political groups, organizations, and parties exist and compete with each other, in other words, where there are institutional guarantees against a monopoly of power and in favor of freedom of speech and association, the workers are more inclined to accept that they must give way to a superior in the firm or office. There too they demand the right of association to protect their interests and the chance of a say in production matters, but most of them do not insist upon having collective decision making and leadership elections within the firm.[13]

Under the socialist system there are wholehearted believers in self-management who are sincerely convinced that it is a fuller and more substantive form of democracy than "formal," "bourgeois" parliamentary democracy. But there also appear in the reform movements backers of self-management who see it more as an advantageous tactical move, a temporary "forced substitute" for real parliamentary democracy. They think that partial or total self-management is still better than full conservation of the undivided power of the party-state. It opens up a new political arena where opposition trends can begin the struggle for positions in firms, that is, a struggle also from below.

[12]On the Yugoslav experience in this respect, see the studies by J. Prasnikar and J. Svejnar (1988, 1990). For experience in Hungary with the election of the leaders of firms, see the study by K. Bossányi (1986). G. K. Popov (1988, p. 631) writes with concern about the likely effects of introducing the election of managers in the Soviet Union: "Attempts will be made to render the election of the manager meaningless; it will be necessary to elect persons acceptable to the ministry, upon which everything depends."

[13]Another demand raised on a wide scale under the conditions of a market economy based on private ownership and parliamentary democracy is the right of workers to participate in decision making. Of course, there are political battles and debates over the degree and specific form of participation there as well. See A. L. Thimm (1980) for a history of codetermination in Sweden and Germany, and a brief synopsis of the situation in other Western European countries. The debates in Germany are described in R. Judith, ed. (1986). An empirical comparison of the effect of codetermination in various countries, centering on West Germany, is B. Wilpert and J. Rayley (1983).

Nor can one exclude the possibility that self-management is promoted from above for expressly manipulative purposes as something capable of fulfilling the role of a forced substitute for the time being. Such people hope that the introduction of it will take the sting out of the movements aiming to break the party's monopoly of power. Self-management co-existed in Yugoslavia for decades with strict limitations on political liberties.

20.3 Economic Effects

Analysis of the economic effects of self-management bears closely on these political problems. Without attempting to be exhaustive, five questions are examined here.[14]

1. *Vertical dependence on superiors.* Under the pertaining power structure it is illusory to expect a self-managed economic unit to be truly independent of the bureaucracy. The influence on the choice of the head of the firm just mentioned is decisively important, but several other strands also bind the firm to its superior institutions;[15] they decide largely what financial subsidies it receives if it makes a loss, how its tax bill is drawn up, how much investment credit it gets, how much hard currency it has access to, and so on. It is also at the mercy of the nonprivate banking sector. A self-managed firm still has a soft budget constraint.[16] There is no private capital market or privately owned bank or other financial institution; the capital and credit market is a basically bureaucratic institution without a basis of commercial, profit-oriented activity.[17] The firm's horizontal dependence on the market is at least matched by vertical dependence on the party, the national and local organs of the state, and the nonprivate, nonmarket-oriented financial sector.

2. *The manager's dependence on his subordinates.* Clearly, the firm's workforce is not a truly sovereign community, but its position in relation to the head of the firm has strengthened. In that sense the manager's

---

[14]On a level of abstract analysis, this book discusses separately the tendency toward the use of self-management [→20] and the tendency to aim at the realization of market socialism [→21]. In fact, the former usually ties in with the introduction of market socialism. So here the discussion touches just briefly on a few questions that are explored in more detail in the next chapter. A measure of repetition and overlapping cannot be avoided, however.

[15]See J. P. Burkett (1989).

[16]On empirical evidence on the soft budget constraint in Yugoslavia, see P. R. Knight (1984), V. Konovalov (1989), J. Mitchell (1989), and L. D. Tyson (1977, 1983).

[17]Conspicuous evidence of this in Yugoslavia's case is the fact that the credit system has operated with strongly negative real rates of interest throughout the last few decades.

dependence on his subordinates is greater, so that he meets difficulties in ensuring that his instructions are obeyed, maintaining the discipline needed to coordinate the work, and preventing unjustified increases in wages and benefits in kind. How could he take strong measures against those on whom his reelection depends?[18]

This leads to the basic problems with the slogan "shop-floor democracy." There are communities whose members are capable of disciplining themselves: they restrain their financial demands voluntarily, and each member exacts intensive, careful work from himself or herself. The members also impose discipline on each other, by force of example, and if need be by peer judgment. One finds examples of such communities in Catholic religious orders or Israeli kibbutzim, or even in the work brigades of early socialism. This mode of operation usually works in small communities sharing a strong ideological conviction, whose members can easily keep an eye on each other and eject those who do not accept the common cause and discipline wholeheartedly.

Some left-wing schools of thought hold that this type of behavior can be made general. I am among those who doubt that, at least in the foreseeable future. Praiseworthy though efforts at selfless, voluntary discipline, and training designed to instill it, are, they provide an illusory basis for social production in the present day.[19]

3. *Short-term outlook*. The members of a self-managed unit lack type b property rights, the right of alienation,[20] an extremely important ownership criterion.[21] If workers have spent a long period devoting the best of their ability to the development of their firm and then have to leave it for some reason, they cannot take their "investment" with them. So

---

[18]M. L. Weitzman (1984, 1985) outlines a plan for a "share economy." Workers in such an economy have an interest in raising profits, that is, they receive part of the type a property rights, but they do not share in the type b and c property rights. These remain with the previous proprietors, at least in the capitalist environment about which Weitzman writes. (Or some of the type c rights of control may be exercised by managers designated by the proprietors).

The kind of behavior by firms induced by the Weitzman type of incentive system differs substantially from that which emerges under the self-management property form in a socialist country.

[19]A clear distinction must be drawn between self-management and the right of participation in the firm's decision making, or the right of consultation before a decision is made. The last two increase the chance for the workers in the firm to exercise an influence on the firm's activities, but they do not give them, even formally, either the right to or responsibility for control. So this more limited solution does not lead to the grave problems of imposing discipline discussed above.

[20]It is another matter whether or not the collective has the right of alienation. In other words, does the council elected by the workers have the right to sell the whole firm? The problem comes onto the agenda during the postsocialist transition [→20.6].

[21]On the free transferability of property, see A. A. Alchian and H. Demsetz (1972).

they differ from true proprietors in having no interest in the firm's long-term development. Faced with the fundamental economic dilemmas of "income today versus income tomorrow" and "consumption versus accumulation," their every interest prompts them to maximize income today and consumption.[22] They have no material interest in any expense or effort, for instance, a large-scale investment, research and development, or professional training, that yields an economic return only after a long delay. In such cases they ask themselves: What if I am not working for the firm any more when the sacrifice pays for itself? In this respect they are in an essentially different position than private shareholders, who have a stake in their company's "net worth," that is, the growth of its physical, financial, and intellectual capital.

4. *Inflationary pressure.* The inflationary process can strengthen under the reform system because of a number of factors. Self-management is not a necessary precondition for this. The same happened, for instance, in China, Vietnam, and the Soviet Union, where self-management was not introduced. One can add that self-management is not a sufficient precondition for the development of inflation. In Yugoslavia as well it came about through the combined effect of several factors [→23.5]. All one can say is that a self-managed firm tends toward the sort of behavior that fuels inflationary pressure.

Self-management reduces the resistance of the firm's leadership to raising nominal wages. Under the classical system, observance of the compulsory wage regulations is rigorously enforced [→7.3, 10.3]. Self-management abolishes this bureaucratic constraint, but it fails to replace it with the kind of proprietorial interest that could restrain wages. In a capitalist firm it is in the interest of the proprietor and the managers acting for the proprietor to oppose a wage rise, since it reduces profits. On the other hand, as has been seen, it is in the direct interest of the proprietors of a self-managed firm, its workforce, to secure as much income in the short term as possible. No manager who wants to remain popular with the workers will oppose this endeavor. If this inflationary wage pressure coincides with an indulgent financial policy, the mechanism of the wage-price spiral is in place.

5. *Unemployment.* The classical system tends to produce a swift rise in employment [→10.1, 10.2]. Mention was made of the expansion drive, which encourages a constant increase in production, while labor (at least until the supply is fully exhausted) is plentiful. There is no inducement whatever to be economical with labor.

The expansion drive remains under self-management introduced within a socialist system. But most of the expansion is not financed out

---

[22]See J. Prasnikar and J. Svejnar (1988, 1990).

of the firm's own savings. The firm divides up its resources like this: as much of the net income as possible is used for the nominal income providing the basis for the workers' current consumption, while it tries to milk as much as it can out of the state and the banking system to finance its investments. Bank loans bear a negative rate of real interest, so that in fact they also include a free subsidy.

It is worthwhile for a capitalist firm to increase its workforce so long as the increase still contributes to increasing its profits.[23] By contrast, the interest of a self-managed firm is not in profits but in raising the personal incomes of the workers it already employs. So it may shy away from the level of employment that maximizes profits if that level would entail reducing the income per existing worker below the maximum.

The circumstances described under points 4 and 5 may ultimately encourage the firm to carry out investments that are as capital-intensive as possible and require little extra labor, at the expense of the state budget, the credit system, and ultimately the inflation-bearing public. All this brings about the mechanism of effects that produces the simultaneous presence of inflation and unemployment.

To sum up, self-management introduced under the socialist system displays numerous negative features from the political and economic points of view. It is one of the dead ends of the reform process. Although a firm operating under the self-management property form differs substantially from a state-owned firm, they have a basic identity, or at least a marked similarity, in that they are both deeply embedded in the bureaucratic system.

20.4 Relations between Manager and Workers

Self-management produces a new relationship between the chief executive and the employees. It is worth noting that a similar change takes place even where self-management has not been introduced, but other tendencies to reform appear. The factors that work in this direction particularly are the measure of liberalization in the political structure and the erosion of the classical ideology [→18.4, 23.1]. The manager becomes far less inclined to enforce labor discipline among the workers and to resist pressure from them to raise nominal wages.

There are several reasons for the change. It ties in with some strengthening in the representative nature of the trade union, and with the fact that strikes become legal or at least tolerated. While the labor

[23]In other words, until the worker's marginal productivity coincides with the wages he is paid.

shortage persists, or may even worsen, the mobility of labor increases. The system is now less capable of taking administrative measures against those who change jobs of their own accord. So the management of the firm becomes more reliant on harmonious cooperation by the workers from the production point of view as well.

There is another change that has an even greater effect. The manager can reckon less on having the full support of a strong, tough bureaucratic hierarchy if he or she makes unpopular moves; nor can the manager rely so firmly on the unconditional support of the local party and union branches. In fact, he or she can count more on the chances that the employees, if they display noticeable antipathy or downright hatred toward the manager, will succeed in persuading the superior authorities to dismiss him or her. As the iron discipline of the bureaucracy loosens, the manager becomes more vulnerable, and under the circumstances more likely to become "populist" not only in personal behavior but in economic actions. That also means that one of the roles the manager assumes in negotiations with superiors is that of a "representative" of the employees' interests. Although such a role was not entirely alien to the manager under the classical system, such behavior is exhibited more strongly during the process of reform.

20.5 Ethical Coordination

The introduction to this chapter referred to the fact that the idea of self-management offers the glimmer of a third road to those who want to break with bureaucratic, centralized classical socialism but also reject capitalism. Similar intellectual and political considerations lend an attraction for some currents of socialism to ethical coordination [→6.6]. As in the case of self-management, which holds out the promise of establishing the self-governing mechanism, mention must be made here of the ideological traditions of socialism. Many people hoped that the production organizations and institutions of a socialist society would adjust to each other voluntarily and unselfishly, not as a result of state compulsion or the inducement of material gain.[24] The representatives of the collectives would agree upon the plans by negotiation.

No serious attempt to apply this concept was ever made in the Soviet Union or in most of the other countries under the classical system. Coor-

---

[24]The idea can be traced back to Proudhon, who wrote (1867–70, 2:414, 6:92–93) that a man whose self-awareness has been awakened does not need the external compulsion of discipline. The structure of the economy can be built upon mutuality (*mutuellisme*). Proudhon was strongly criticized by Marx.

dination was entrusted unhesitatingly to the bureaucratic mechanisms. In China the aspiration of voluntary mutual adjustment did become one of the pillars of the official ideology of Maoism.[25] In fact, however, very little of the idea was ever realized in the Chinese version of the classical system.

In the reform system's case, it was in the pioneering country, Yugoslavia, that the old socialist notion of voluntary mutual adjustment at all levels came to the fore in the early 1970s, along with self-management and in connection with it. The architects of the reform attributed great importance to establishing voluntary associations of economic units from the bottom up. The smallest cells are "basic organizations of associative labor," and the associations of these "work organizations of associative labor," out of which form "composite organizations of associative labor" at a higher level. The last are grouped into "industrial associations," which in turn are placed at a still higher level (usually one per republic) in "chambers of commerce."[26] However, the complete uniformity of the structure and even the names, along with the fact that production units can only combine into these organizations, in itself leads one to conclude that they did not arise spontaneously through initiatives from below, and that the structural blueprint was drawn up centrally. This all makes it obvious that in spite of the idea reflected in the terminology for the new institutions, this has nothing to do with real voluntary association.[27]

The idea of the reform was that the self-managing units and the various unions and associations of them would negotiate closely with each other at all levels and agree to the tasks on a basis of mutual consideration. The most comprehensive of the resulting agreements received a special name: "social compacts." All this was supposed to create a specific form of coordination. Since the agreement would come about neither by central command (in that sense not being of a bureaucratic nature) nor on a basis of prices and bargaining over conditions of purchase and sale (in that sense not being of a market nature), and since it was motivated by responsibility toward society and mutual willingness to assist, this comprehensive negotiating process at all levels could rightly be considered one version of ethical coordination.

In practice, very little applies of this artificial notion imposed on society by decree. Behind the "social compact," irrespective of it or in spite

[25]This was one of the attractions of Maoism to the New Left intelligentsia in the West. See J. Robinson (1969), for instance.

[26]See the studies of L. D. Tyson (1980) and J. P. Burkett (1989).

[27]An excellent account and appraisal of this sphere under the Yugoslav system is given in A. Ben-Ner and E. Neuberger (1990), whose expressive subtitle is "The Yugoslav Visible Hand and Negotiated Planning."

of it, great force is exerted on economic activity by the bureaucratic influences of superior organizations and market influences of buyers and sellers. The weakness of ethical coordination is apparent by comparison with the really strong mechanisms of bureaucratic and market coordination.

As a stark contrast, let us take a totally different form in which ethical coordination arises: the charity campaigns and associations that appeared in the reform socialist countries in the 1970s and 1980s. These are not allowed under classical socialism [→6.6] and are not organized under reform socialism by the state or by official mass organizations. They appear voluntarily as real initiatives from below, to perform specific, well-defined tasks. In Hungary, for instance, where the very existence of poverty had been denied for several decades, some groups among the intelligentsia woke up to the fact in the 1970s that an appreciable proportion of society lived in great poverty. So a semi-illegal charity organization, the Fund for Supporting the Poor, was set up and found plenty of people ready to help. Another development in Hungary was the charity movement to assist Hungarians fleeing from Romania. The first charity organizations are now appearing in the Soviet Union as well.[28]

Moreover, various groups arise to perform a number of other social tasks besides charity work: environmental protection, laying out parks, helping the aged, and so on. Every society contains latent forces of self-organization, people prepared to act for noble, ethical reasons; only the bureaucratic obstacles need to be removed. The mechanisms of ethical coordination are not capable of performing the basic control functions of society, including the economy, but they can play an auxiliary part that causes the economy to work more smoothly and people to live together in greater harmony.

20.6 Preview: Self-Management under the Postsocialist System

Countries that introduced self-management in the reform phase take a specific legacy into the period of postsocialist transition. The problems can be perceived clearly in Hungary and Poland, but the issue will be all the more pressing in Yugoslavia when the transition takes place there. There are advocates in these countries of the idea that the system of self-

---

[28]The so-called cooperatives, which, as was seen in chapter 19, are in fact private businesses, are the main organizers and contributors. Despite being in the start-up phase in 1989, cooperatives gave half a percent of their total revenue in charitable contributions. See *Moscow News,* April 1, 1990.

management should stay, and indeed become even more widespread.[29] If this were to happen, all the obstacles and dangers outlined in the previous sections would remain as well. In fact, they would be compounded by new difficulties. Two of these additional problems are covered here.

One is connected with the political situation. The development of a multiparty system in these countries has only just begun. There is certain to be strong rivalry among the parties for every elected position in every institution in society. If leadership of a firm becomes an elected position, it is inevitable that the firm itself will become an arena of party-political struggles. What would really be desirable after a long period in which the post of manager of a firm was one of the positions occupied by the political elite is the opposite tendency: the "depoliticization" of business and production, and the application of expertise and talent as the criteria for selecting managers.

The other problem ties in with the process of privatization. The elected leaders of a self-managed firm feel entitled to decide about the firm's future, including the sale of it. In this respect the legal stipulations are usually ambiguous; though they may not give the managers express powers to do this, they do not contain a sufficiently clear prohibition.

The main problem, however, is an ideological one. The propaganda of self-management tried to convey to the workers that the workers' collective was in charge of the firm.

This is an important legal and ideological argument in support of certain maneuvers in the course of privatization. The manager, with the knowledge and assistance of the elected council of the firm, agrees on the conditions for privatization with potential domestic or foreign owners. What the manager wants to achieve is that the conditions should give him or her and the firm's workforce an appreciable short-term advantage in terms of positions, pay, and employment, even if the transfer of ownership is detrimental in the long term.

Strange as it may sound, in the places where elements of self-management applied, the elimination of this property form and, in fact, some kind of initial nationalization of the public sector are placed on the agenda under the postsocialist system, because that opens the way for a privatization process conducted under reputable conditions.

---

[29]See, for example, the following proposition in K. A. Soós (1990, p. 68): "In the present period, full of political and economic uncertainties and radical changes, the practice of self-management, which, after all, has become accepted in our society, could be preserved as a valuable element of the status quo."

21

Market Socialism

THE FUNDAMENTAL idea behind the political and intellectual stream discussed in this chapter is for the market to become the basic coordinator of the socialist economy, or at least equal in rank with the bureaucratic mechanism, augmenting central planning, while public ownership remains the dominant property form.

Several currents of this broader stream are distinguishable from each other in many respects, one differentiating mark being the distance they want to go in establishing the market mechanism. But the notion they share is trust in the market, and so it is not unjustified to describe the whole stream as a movement in the direction of *market socialism*. The reformers at work in the socialist countries, particularly at the start of the process, tended to emphasize their desire to link planning and the market. So there is another justifiable term of the stream: the idea of a *plan-cum-market* economy.[1]

These ideas have a strong effect on the workings of the economy. The practical changes that point toward market socialism and plan-cum-market constitute one of the major tendencies in the move away from the classical system.

The subject of this chapter is the phenomenon of market socialism in the state sector. It does not cover what role the market plays in the other sectors of the economy. So to that extent it does not answer fully the question of what role the market plays in the economy of reform socialism. (Relations between the private sector and the market were discussed in chapter 19.)

21.1 Ideological Antecedents

The sphere of ideas embracing market socialism is profoundly alien to the thinking of the classics of Marxism. Marx appreciated the organiza-

---

[1] This book treats planning under socialism as one of the factors in bureaucratic coordination. So the "bureaucratic versus market coordination mechanism" features as a concept pair in the discussion on the reform process wherever I am expressing my own point of view.

But in presenting the intellectual trends that initiate and accompany the reform process, one must stick to the terminology used by the actual participants in the debate. That is the sense in which this chapter refers to advocates of "plan-cum-market."

tion prevailing inside the factory under capitalist ownership and contrasted it with the disorganization apparent outside the factory in the relations between firms: "the most complete anarchy reigns among . . . the capitalists themselves, who confront one another simply as owners of commodities," he writes in *Capital*.[2] Here is another quotation, also from *Capital*: "With collective production, money capital is completely dispensed with. The society distributes labour-power and means of production between the various branches of industry. There is no reason why the producers should not receive paper tokens permitting them to withdraw an amount corresponding to their labour time from the social consumption stocks. But these tokens are not money; they do not circulate."[3] Engels writes that communist society has no need of the "oblique and meaningless" form of expression represented by the value of goods. It takes account directly of the working time hidden in the products.[4] The Marxist classics repeatedly underline that the market is a poorly operating coordination mechanism that must be replaced by conscious planning. Karl Kautsky, the great exponent of Marxist ideas, summed things up like this: "The question is simply to transform this organization, which has hitherto been an unconscious one going on behind the shoulders of those engaged in it with friction, sorrow, and woe, bankruptcy and crisis, under the operation of the law of value, ever being adjusted into a conscious system in which a previous calculation of all modifying factors will take place of the retroactive corrections through the play of supply and demand."[5] One of the things Kautsky objects to here is precisely what Adam Smith saw as the market's chief virtue: that its hand works unseen behind the participants' backs.

The rational arguments and metarational feelings of those to whom Marxian political economy has become flesh and blood lead them to view with suspicion, antipathy, loathing, and contempt the market where crisis and anarchy, speculation, and dire competition reign, and all sound proportions emerge only after the event. One of the historical purposes of abolishing the system of private ownership is precisely to end this blind, hit-or-miss way of coordinating production and replace it by conscious planning. One of the axioms of Marxism must be abandoned by any who seek to combine what to Marx, Engels, and their truest followers were fire and water: socialism and the market.[6]

[2]K. Marx [1867–94] (1978, chap. 51, p. 1021).

[3]Ibid., chap. 18, p. 434.

[4]F. Engels [1878] (1975, pp. 294–95).

[5]K. Kautsky (1910, p. 151).

[6]*Neues Deutschland,* the East German Communist party's paper, wrote a few months before the collapse of Honecker's classical system, "And we should adopt these blessings of the market economy? Back to private ownership of means of production? Back to the

One of the most succinct intellectual precursors of the idea of market socialism is the classic work by Oscar Lange (1936–37). There was a debate on socialism in the West between the two world wars.[7] The great challenge came from a famous study by the Austrian economist Ludwig von Mises [1920] (1935), in which he stated that socialism, in the absence of private property and the market, is incapable of rational calculation. Lange took issue with this view, outlining an economy in which a firm in public ownership either maximizes its profits or follows a related formula for optimization. The central planning office tries to set market-clearing equilibrium prices, and does so, in fact, by simulating the market mechanism: when it sees excess demand it raises prices, and when it sees excess supply it reduces them. Lange's line of argument confirms that such a system is capable of balancing supply and demand.

It was argued during the debate that conscious central planning could not conceivably solve the vast system of equations involved in coordinating the supply and demand of millions of products. Lange countered by arguing that such gigantic calculations were quite unnecessary: socialism could adopt the operating principle of the market. The central planners adjust prices continually by reacting to the signals of excess supply or demand. In turn, buyers and sellers would respond to the price signals and ultimately their combined activities tend toward equilibrium. Lange's work offers no detailed practical proposals for reform, but the outline embraces many of the concepts basic to the intellectual current of market socialism: the autonomy of firms with an interest in increasing profits and reducing costs, the fundamental role of price signals, and the specific linkage between centralization and decentralization.

The sharpest repudiation of Lange's line of thought during the debate came from Friedrich von Hayek (1935). His main argument was as follows: the real big problem for socialism is not whether it can set equilibrium prices, but what incentives there are to obtain and speedily apply the necessarily dispersed information concealed in many different places. In this respect the market, competition, and free enterprise are indispensable. Looking back after fifty years one can conclude that Hayek was right on every point in the debate. Reformers who begin groping toward

---

exploitation of man by man? Back to free competition, to the free labor market? No, no way leads back to capitalism. The market economy, whichever attribute one may attach to it, cannot do justice to the essence of socialism, which is to do everything for the welfare of the people. That requires a unified economic and social policy and for that, there is only one basis—the socialist planned economy. The more effective and perfect we make it, the better for all.'' January 5, 1989, p. 5, editorial.

[7]Summary accounts of the Western debate on socialism in the 1930s were provided by A. Bergson's studies (1948, 1967). For present-day assessments, see A. de Jasay (1990), D. Lavoie (1985), and G. Temkin (1989).

market socialism along Lange's lines regularly learn by bitter experience in their own countries that the hope Lange held out was illusory.

Though disillusion usually follows in the end, the idea of market socialism must certainly have strong attractions if it captivates so many people. One secret of its influence lies in the intellectual sphere. To those who remain Marxists in political thinking but abandon Marxian economics in favor of the influence of the neoclassical school, the idea of market socialism provides an easy way out.[8]

Modern Western writing advanced long ago beyond the naive stage of idealizing the market: it is recognized that the market mechanism has its dark sides as well. Its automatic processes fail to reward the favorable external effects and punish the harmful ones, to ensure optimal supply of public goods, or to guarantee that the principle of social justice applies in the distribution of income. At the same time, enlightened critics of planning point to its many dark sides as well. Now the sphere of ideas embracing market socialism and plan-cum-market presents the prospect of a complementary application of the two mechanisms, in which each compensates for the other's shortcomings. Central planning and control will intervene when the market needs correcting on social welfare grounds. Conversely, the market relieves those in power of the daily chores of coordinating economic activity and has the added ability to issue signals when central planners make faulty decisions that damage the interests of the buyers and sellers. The tendency's adherents hoped that ultimately a system combining the advantages and minimizing the drawbacks of both mechanisms would emerge.[9]

The economic line of argument was augmented or reinforced by a line of political argument. Classical socialism had led to grave economic difficulties; it needed major changes. In the same period the capitalist system had scored numerous economic successes. Capitalism's "secret" is that its activities are coordinated by the market. This one aspect of it can and must be taken over, but everything about the classical socialist system of deeper significance must be retained. The power structure and dominant role of public ownership must be retained and combined with the market.[10] "Socialism" (for which read the one-party system, monop-

---

[8]Here a curious symmetry appears with the thinking of the early pioneers of mathematical planning. Both spheres of thinking link Marxist and Walrasian elements. In the theoretical realm of market socialism, centralization and public ownership coexist with a price-setting procedure that operates on Walrasian principles and with decentralized production. In the realm of mathematical planning, the structure of the programming model follows Walrasian principles. Walras's famous auctioneer is the price-control office; in the mathematical planning framework he is embodied in the model and the computer.

[9]I was also inclined to this view at an earlier stage (1965, 1971).

[10]The idea was expressed like this in one resolution of the Chinese Communist party: "Socialist economy is a commodity economy based upon public ownership." Resolution of

oly of power, and dominant role of public ownership) plus "market" (independence of firms, a contract system between firms, and the effect of price signals on producers and users): this is the combined form that is to resolve the problems of the socialist economy.[11] Acceptance of the idea does involve departing at a very essential juncture from the Marxist tradition, but it promises to remain compatible with the official ideology of the socialist countries in more profound, more fundamental areas.

The sphere of ideas bounded by market socialism and the "plan-cum-market" appears and exerts influence in every reforming country without exception. Some academic economists refer back to Lange, and others make a "rediscovery" independently of him. Many ideas that differ in important respects from Lange's also appear. Thinking in this sphere is shaped mainly by the intellectual motives mentioned above, although the experts devising the proposals may also be influenced by political considerations.[12] In adopting the market socialism sphere of ideas, the ruling circles of the reforming countries are guided, consciously or unconsciously, by the political line of thought briefly summarized above. All these motives merge and appear together. What can be said for certain is that the sphere of ideas of market socialism and plan-cum-market plays a central part in the official ideology of the reform socialist countries. The most conspicuous and cardinal difference between the official ideology of the classical system and the ideas of market socialism is

---

the Third Plenum of the Twelfth Congress, 1984, quoted in J. Wu and R. Zhao (1987, p. 312).

[11] "In short: the advantages of planning will be increasingly combined with the stimulating factors of the socialist market. But all of this will take place within the mainstream of socialist goals and principles of management," Gorbachev writes. M. S. Gorbachev (1987, p. 91). Or a later quotation: "The superiority of the market has been demonstrated on a world scale, and the question is now only whether, under the conditions of the market, one can ensure a high degree of social security. The answer is this: not only can one, but it is really the regulated market economy which allows to increase national wealth to a degree that allows the living standard of everyone to rise. And of course, state power is in our hands." M. S. Gorbachev, *Izvestia,* July 11, 1990.

[12] Here are a few of the pioneering studies, grouped by countries. *Yugoslavia:* B. Kidric (see his studies from the 1950s in the 1985 volume); *Hungary:* G. Péter (1954a, 1954b) and J. Kornai [1957] (1959); *Poland:* W. Brus [1961] (1972); *Czechoslovakia:* O. Sik (1966); *Soviet Union:* E. G. Liberman [1962] (1972); *China:* Sun Yefang [1958–61] (1982). See L. Szamuely (1982, 1984) for an excellent survey of the earlier debates. For an outstanding reflection on reform thought including criticism of its shortcomings, see J. M. Kovács (1988 and, in a shorter version, 1990), as well as I. Grosfeld (1989b), who establishes the link between reform thought and several branches of Western economic theories on market failures, comparative economic systems theory, principal agent and incentive theory, and the property rights school. For the Soviet Union, a first attempt to deal with the flood of reform thought unleashed by glasnost is A. Nove (1989). For a Czechoslovak perspective, see V. Klaus (1989, 1990).

that the former rejects and the latter respectfully recognizes the role of the market mechanism. One of the reasons why the revised official ideology of the Communist parties undertaking to accomplish market socialism is so full of internal inconsistencies is that it tries to reconcile incompatible elements: Marxian political economy and respect for the market.

21.2 Generalization from the Historical Applications

The ideas of market socialism and plan-cum-market did not remain simply in the realm of political and economic thinking. They had a tangible effect, persuading those in power in a range of socialist countries to make numerous practical changes. Without aiming to be exhaustive, it is worth picking out from the sequence of reform changes of a market socialist type a few countries where this type of control mechanism applied for a long time or continues to apply at the time of writing: Yugoslavia (1950–), Hungary (1968–89), China (1978–), Poland (1981–89), Vietnam (1987–), and the Soviet Union (1985–).

The discussion of the six countries is confined solely to control of the public sector. In Yugoslavia's case this includes self-managed units under "social ownership," and in the other countries, both state-owned firms and "quasi-state" cooperatives.

This book does not aim to provide a specific country-by-country history of the expansion, advances, and retreats of this tendency to change. Instead, the remainder of the chapter outlines a common general model of the "market-socialist period" in the six countries listed above. Something repeatedly stressed at similar places in the book must be said again: the description is strongly abstract; it ignores the many differences among the countries, and also the fact that the specific situation frequently changed within each country. It picks out solely the main features, inherent leanings, and specific tendencies that more or less applied in the six countries throughout the market-socialist period of reform.[13]

Yugoslavia, in certain respects, is a special, individual case, since the application of market socialism there was closely tied up from the outset with the introduction of self-management, which has been discussed in this book as a separate tendency toward change [→20]. Nonetheless, many phenomena similar to those discussed in more detail in this and the next chapter appear in Yugoslavia as well.

[13]Changes pointing in the direction of market socialism have been announced in several other countries as well.

The model that describes the operation of the public sector during the market-socialist period in the six countries mentioned is termed briefly the market-socialist economy in what follows.

Advocates of market socialism may take exception to this term on the grounds that the idea was only applied in the countries listed in a warped form. That is true, but is there any reason to say that the application departed from the visions and hopes of market socialism to any greater extent than classical socialism differed from the visions and hopes of the "fundamentalist" socialists? Just as the socialism of Stalin, Mao Zedong, and Rákosi is existing classical socialism, so the reform socialism of Tito, Kádár, Deng Xiaoping, Gorbachev, and Rakowski is existing market socialism. Following that line of argument, usage of the term seems to be justified.

21.3 Classification of Alternative Strategies for Deregulation

The distance traveled by the economic leadership along the road from some historical realization of the classical system toward the imaginary state of market socialism varies according to the country and period.[14] Overall one can say that a specific process of deregulation takes place. The discussion that follows uses the term "deregulation" exclusively for changes causing the removal of an economic phenomenon from the reach of direct, instruction-based bureaucratic control of a command-economy nature. According to this narrower definition, one cannot assume that a deregulated economic process is unaffected by the center or free from the influence of bureaucratic coordination. In this discussion the term simply means that its size is not set by a central, compulsory instruction.[15]

[14]Just a few comprehensive works are selected from the wealth of literature on the changes in the public sector: *Yugoslavia:* J. P. Burkett (1989); *Hungary: The Journal of Comparative Economics* (Fall 1983, special issue devoted to the Hungarian reform), J. Kornai (1986b), G. Révész (1990); *China:* B. Balassa (1987), W. A. Byrd (1990), H. Harding (1987), D. Perkins (1988), E. J. Perry and C. P. W. Wong, eds. (1985), C. Riskin (1989), M. Xue (1982); *Poland:* L. Balcerowicz (1988), Z. M. Fallenbuchl (1988), P. Marer and W. Siwinski, eds. (1988); *Soviet Union:* E. A. Hewett (1988), A. Åslund (1989), M. I. Goldman (1987); *Vietnam:* G. Porter (1990).

[15]To that extent that the interpretation of the concept is rather different from the one used when people speak these days of the deregulation of a Western capitalist economy. There it never occurred even in the period of so-called regulation that a state authority issued commands to a firm (which would usually be privately owned); at most, certain prices would be set and administrative constraints erected. However, although the specific contents of the deregulation process described in this book and the one going on in the Western world today do not coincide accurately, they both point in the same direction: toward a reduction in direct interference by the state. That is a further justification for using the expression here.

The alternative strategies for deregulation can be classified according to several criteria. The first question is how far the deregulation goes with certain especially important economic variables previously controlled by central command, that is, what the *degree* of deregulation is. I shall discuss this later [→21.4].

The second classification criterion for the alternative deregulation strategies is the *scope* of deregulation, the areas to which the process extends. The deregulation measures in Yugoslavia, and later Hungary, covered the whole sphere of state-owned firms right from the start. China and the Soviet Union first designated "experimental firms" to use the new control mechanisms, and for a long time segments of the sector operating under the principles of the old and new mechanisms functioned side by side. Later the number of firms under the new form of control was increased in several stages.[16]

That brings me to the third classification criterion, the *sequencing* of deregulation. The several changes in the ratios of the segments operating in parallel under different forms of control imply that the deregulation is performed in a sequence of stages, not as a single action. One important mark of the Yugoslav and Hungarian strategies was that the most conspicuous part of the deregulation—abolition of the command economy in short-term decision making—was performed with dramatic speed, at a stroke. (Even in those two countries, the other parts of the deregulation process were taken in several stages.) By contrast, even input-output deregulation moved only gradually in China and the Soviet Union, for instance.

The partial deregulatory measures have strong mutual effects. So both theoretical economists and committed reformers in the economic apparatus repeatedly argue that they are not worth applying singly, bit by bit, that they need gathering firmly into a package of measures that come into force at once. No one denies the packaging principle, but views differ on what a package should contain. Here the Hungarian reform process went furthest: the New Economic Mechanism introduced on January 1, 1968, embraced a very wide range of concurrent measures. Although the history of the reform contains such distinctive events, when single larger packages of measures were introduced at once, these, ultimately, also fall far short of covering all the processes of control.

---

[16]To some extent one can also list the case of China's special economic free zones here. Whereas in the experiments described above special conditions differing substantially from those in the rest of the economy were laid down for certain firms, in this case the special circumstances in respect of economic control are provided for particular regions.

The idea of setting up similar special zones has been voiced in other countries, for instance, the Soviet Union.

21.4   The Firm's Vertical Dependence

After pointing out that the degree, scope, and sequencing of deregulation differ by countries and periods, from now on these differences are ignored and the main features of a semideregulated state-owned firm are outlined in a general form. This abstraction is needed to prevent the main characteristics of the situation being obscured by the countless details.[17]

The firm is in *dual dependence*. On the one hand, it is vertically dependent on the state authorities, and on the other hand, it is horizontally dependent on the sellers and buyers.[18] To some extent the same can be said of any firm under any system: each is influenced by the state authorities, and each depends on the sellers of its inputs and on its buyers. What needs to be isolated in this dual dependence is the system-specific element in it.

In the account that follows, the many dimensions of a firm's activities are taken one by one, to see how far the vertical dependence survives the deregulation measures. The survey is intended to be as full as possible, and so some issues treated in more detail elsewhere in the book have to be touched upon again. The length of any point is no reflection of the weight attaching to the phenomenon it describes; some issues of the utmost importance are covered by a concise reference. More detailed discussion occurs only where the problem is not dealt with in another part of the book.

1. *Entry.* In general the bureaucracy still decides about setting up new, independent firms in public ownership. The bureaucracy also decides whether to permit import competition or the entry of private enterprise.

2. *Exit.* The bureaucracy decides whether to wind up a firm in public ownership. This relates closely to the phenomenon of soft budget constraint [→21.5].

3. *Mergers and splits.* The chance for firms to initiate a merger or a split has increased, but the bureaucracy still has the right to the last word.

4. *Appointment of leaders of firms.* The bureaucracy either decides directly or influences decisively the nomination, selection, and endorse-

---

[17]As the reader will see shortly, the conclusion is reached here that the role of bureaucratic coordination remains dominant. For that reason it is worthwhile, when summarizing the main features in the form of a model, to consider countries where the deregulation processes went further, rather than an "average" reform economy (e.g., Hungary and China rather than the Soviet Union). If the conclusion stands for a relatively more deregulated economy, it must be valid a fortiori for a less deregulated one.

[18]There is a third dependence as well: of the firm's leadership on its own employees, the firm's workers. This was discussed under the tendency toward self-management [→20.4].

ment of the selection. Table 21.1 surveys the phenomenon based on Chinese data.

Taken together, points 1–4 mean that the system did not move away from the situation characteristic of classical socialism, namely, that the principle of free enterprise fails to apply in the public sector. Rivalry between firms does not yield a natural selection between either enterprises or leading persons in the firms. The selection is artificial: the bureaucracy decides on the survival or demise of a firm and the promotion or dismissal of its top managers. There are ten more points to follow, but the first four must be said in advance to be the most important. So long as the conclusions above apply, there are enough grounds for concluding that of the vertical and horizontal dependencies, the vertical is dominant.

5. *Output* and 6. *Input*. Imposition of a command economy through short-term control of production in the sphere of state-owned firms ceased altogether in 1950 in Yugoslavia and 1968 in Hungary.

There was deregulation in China in 1984, but to a lesser extent than in Yugoslavia or Hungary. A so-called dual system was introduced: the state-owned firm receives a compulsory output assignment that in most cases does not tie down its whole capacity. Having fulfilled that compulsory output assignment, the firm has a right to produce more and sell this surplus freely. Input quotas for the compulsory output are rationed by the authorities in the way customary in the classical system, but the firm itself must acquire the inputs for the free output above the compul-

TABLE 21.1
Promotion of Managers in China, 1985

	Distribution of Different Channels of Managerial Promotion[a] (as percent of total)
Bureaucratic appointment	60.1
Bureaucratic appointment with consultation	30.7
Direct election	4.4
Direct hiring	1.8
Others	3.0

Source: Chinese Institute for Reform of the Economic System (1986, p. 173), quoted by Y. Huang (1988, p. 6). For an English publication of the data, see B. L. Reynolds, ed. (1988, table 5.10).

[a]Based on a survey of nine hundred firms. In this survey, 19.9 percent of the data are on collective firms.

sory plan; these are not supplied by the input-rationing authorities. The idea is that they should be obtained from other firms' free output above the compulsory plan.[19] The 1987 Soviet law on firms and the practice in applying it resembles the middle-of-the-road Chinese solution in content if not in technical detail. A sizable proportion of the firm's output is tied down by so-called state orders (*goszakaz*), which have de facto compulsory force, while the firm can decide freely about the rest of its output.[20] (See table 21.2.)

Even in Yugoslavia and Hungary, where output is not controlled by instructions, the superior organizations intervene in the determination of it in a number of other ways. The firm is under great pressure not only from buyers but from various party and state organizations to deliver certain consignments as soon as possible. If the wishes of the buyer and the authorities conflict, the latter prove stronger. In countries where the compulsory instructions have been only partially abolished, bureaucratic intervention in the decisions on output is all the greater.

Although central management of materials is less comprehensive than under the classical system, much procurement licensing and rationing remains. Moreover, intervention by the bureaucracy can be an effective

TABLE 21.2
Share of State Orders in the Soviet Union

	Share of State Orders in the Total Value of Production (Plan) (percent)	
Ministry	*1988*	*1989*
Machine building	86	25
Fuel energy	95	59
Metallurgy	86	42
Chemical and woodworking	87	34
Light industry	96	30
Construction materials	66	51

Source: E. Rudneva (1989, p. 27).

[19]Comprehensive data on the degree of deregulation are not known. The sporadic data present a picture in which the compulsory plan tied down 30–100 percent of firms' capacity on the output side at the end of the 1980s.

[20]For a more detailed discussion of the problems of state orders in the Soviet Union, see L. Voronin (1989), V. Sletsiura (1989), and E. Gaidar (1990).

help if there is trouble in obtaining an input. Such intervention in input procurement is often behind the informal interventions on the output side. Deregulation increases the role of voluntary contracts in buyer-seller relations. But when the interpretation or performance of a contract is in dispute, the referee turned to is some superior authority, not the courts.

7. *Exports and imports* and 8. *Foreign exchange*. There is a broad expansion in the role the producer firm plays in export and import trans-actions. But even if a firm gains the formal right to trade abroad without involving a specialized foreign trade firm, the superior organizations continue to intervene in numerous ways, setting export assignments, or putting strong pressure on the firm to fulfill certain orders, prefer certain markets and avoid others. For imports, quotas are set or each deal is tied to a licensing procedure. Linked with all this there is continued strict centralization of foreign exchange management.

9. *Choice of technology and product development*. Superior organiza-tions often intervene in the choice of technology for the firm and of new products to introduce. The firm's subsidy, credit facility, import license, and so on are often linked with the choice.

10. *Prices*. There is a partial deregulation of price-setting. A wide range of prices are still set by the authorities, however, which also inter-vene in the setting of prices that the seller and buyer are nominally free to set for themselves. Methods of calculation are laid down, profit mar-gins are fixed, and protests are made to the firm if prices are thought to be unjustifiably high [→22].

11. *Wages and employment*. Restrictions of several kinds prevent the employer firm and the employees from reaching free agreement on wages. There is frequent interference in employment through formal or informal setting of upper and lower employment limits.

12. *Taxes and subsidies*. Nominally, the tax system in force is more or less uniformly valid for all firms. In fact, taxes tailor-made for a particu-lar sector or firm are common, and so are tailor-made concessions on the amount of tax and the deadline for payment.

13. *Extension of credit and loan repayment*. Bureaucratic features continue to dominate the operation of the banking sector. The relation-ship between a bank and a firm is not a horizontal, commercial one in which the bank is concerned to make a profit for itself. It acts as a branch of the bureaucracy trying to keep the firm under control. The syndrome of soft budget constraint still applies in the spheres of points 10, 12, and 13 [→21.5]. Here again, the force of the firm's vertical de-pendence manifests itself.

14. *Investment*. Partial deregulation occurs in investment decision making. All reform socialist economies see a big rise in the proportion

of investments on which a firm can decide independently and whose main source of finance is the firm's own savings from retained profits. The proportion of investment covered by nonrepayable finance from the state budget falls, and the role of bank credit increases. (See tables 21.3 and 21.4.)

Although the proportion of a firm's investments financed from its own resources has substantially increased, as the tables show, the actual degree of decentralization is far more modest than that. Larger projects require extra finance on top of the firm's own resources, which leaves open the possibility of interference in the investment decision from the state financial organizations providing the contribution from the state budget or from the strongly centralized banking system. So the proportion of investments in which the central institutions are quite uninvolved in the decision is far smaller than the proportion shown in the tables.

These fourteen points cover all the main contacts between the bureaucracy and the firm. Only some of the interference by the superior organizations in the daily life of the firm can be traced through formal regulations that permit or even order them to do so. The legal provisions are augmented by millions of informal, "intangible" measures: leaders of

TABLE 21.3
Financial Sources of Investment in China

Year	Investment in Capital Construction (Rmb 100 millions)	Portion from State Budget (percent)
1976	376.44	83
1977	382.37	78
1978	500.99	78
1979	523.48	76
1980	558.89	54
1981	442.91	50
1982	555.53	42
1983	594.13	50
1984	743.15	48
1985	1,074.37	35
1986	1,176.11	35
1987	1,343.10	33

Source: State Statistical Bureau, People's Republic of China (1988, p. 498).

TABLE 21.4
Financial Sources of Investment in Hungary

	State-initiated Investments			Firm-initiated Investments		
	Percent financed by:			Percent financed by:		
	State	Firm	Credit	State	Firm	Credit
1980	83	14	3	10	68	22
1981	72	23	5	8	71	21
1982	69	27	4	8	73	19
1983	69	28	3	9	75	16
1984	81	19	0	10	73	17
1985	75	25	0	10	72	18
1986	61	39	0	11	76	13
1987	57	43	0	—	—	—

Source: Központi Statisztikai Hivatal (Central Statistical Office, Budapest) (1982, p. 78; 1984, p. 77; 1987, p. 75; 1988, p. 58).

firms are swayed by meetings, personal chats, phone calls, and letters, sometimes with honeyed words of bonuses, and sometimes with veiled or open threats.

Under the classical system, the structure of formal instructions and report-backs was clear, but under the semideregulated market-socialist system the flow of informal communications presents an amorphous picture. The relation between firms and superior organizations is full of vague, accidentally or intentionally ambiguous rules, improvisation, exceptional cases, and personal connections that evade the official "route." Various authorities all have a say in a single firm at once, often working at cross purposes. A smart manager learns to maneuver among many superiors, playing them off against each other. The repressive, military-like order of the classical system gives way to floppy, fluid ties and unclear relations of superiority and subordination.

Although there was constant bargaining between superiors and subordinates under the classical system, the superior decided the argument. Now the bargaining becomes more general; subordinates are in a stronger position to bargain, and use of misleading information in bargaining becomes more common.[21] Of course, the subject of the bargaining has also changed: firms used to push for a looser output assignment and more generous input quotas, whereas bargaining now is mostly

[21]See L. Balcerowicz (1988).

about officially permitted prices, wages, taxes, subsidies, credit terms, import licenses, and foreign exchange allowances.[22]

All the forms of intervention discussed can be viewed as indirect means of control. The ultimate difference between the two kinds of control can be summed up like this: the public sector in a classical socialist economy is subject to *direct* bureaucratic control and in a market-socialist economy to *indirect* bureaucratic control. A semideregulated economy develops.

The architects of the programs for market-socialist reform hoped that partial deregulation would also bring a change of role in national planning and central economic management. The idea ran as follows. National economic planning was to avoid being embroiled in detailed disaggregation of the short-term plan or in instructions to enforce it. That would leave more intellectual energy for economic analysis and compilation of short-term targets on the macro level and of long-term economic strategy. Here could be the link with central economic management, which would focus mainly on achieving the major fiscal and monetary targets and fixing the basic financial parameters (e.g., interest and exchange rates).

The idea fails to materialize. Instead of learning macro management, the central economic leadership continues intervening in the countless details of *micro regulation*. The reputation and influence of national economic planning are slowly but surely eroded. The planning routine developed under the classical command economy proves almost useless in the new situation. Meanwhile, staff in the central offices of reform socialist countries fail to learn the kind of analytical methods based on up-to-date professional expertise that economists in the economic management bodies of developed capitalist countries apply nowadays when preparing government decisions. The economic authorities are not conversant with issues of fiscal and monetary policy.[23] While the reform socialist coun-

---

[22]The term "regulators" is used in Hungarian economic literature for these financial, or at least value-term, parameters set by the superior organizations. The usual description of the change is that the plan bargaining customary under the classical system has given way to "regulator bargaining." See L. Antal (1979, 1985).

"Regulator bargaining" under Chinese conditions is treated in detail in G. Tidrick (1987), M. I. Blejer and G. Szapáry (1990), and P. Bowles and G. White (1989).

[23]Lack of the requisite understanding and experience in macro control is among the factors that divert the economic apparatus onto micro regulation. Its staff mainly have experience in hurrying consignments, speeding up an export assignment or investment action by setting bonuses, issuing special licenses or concessions, or imposing prohibitions. That is the area of tasks in which they feel at home.

The problem arose in a particularly acute form in the Soviet Union in the late 1980s, where there was a lack of basic macroeconomic knowledge in the central management of the economy. Errors in financial policy caused by misinterpretation of the situation were among the factors behind the development of the grave monetary and fiscal problems.

tries are still termed "centrally planned economies" in international statistics, they perform the ongoing management and restructuring of their
economies to no real plan, as a series of improvisations.

21.5 The Softness and Hardness of the Budget Constraint, and the Firm's Responsiveness to Prices

The need to give firms an interest in raising their profits is underlined in
the official documents of all reforming countries. That intention lies behind the system of payment and bonuses for managers; there is profit-
sharing among the workers; the size of the firm's welfare expenditure
depends on its profits. Savings from the profits retained by a firm become one of the financial sources for its investments. The reform programs conceived in terms of market socialism assume the firm will become price- and cost-responsive, so that price can become one of the
controlling tools of central management.

In spite of the stated principles and legal measures listed above, the
firm's profit incentive remains weak, even though it has been strengthened somewhat compared with the classical system's. Profitability fails
to become a matter of life and death or a central target of the firm because the budget constraint is still fairly soft.[24] Prices have a stronger
effect on the firm's reactions, but, again, there is no real breakthrough.

Use is still made in the market-socialist economy of all four methods
of softening the budget constraint:[25] (1) soft subsidization, (2) soft taxation,[26] (3) soft credit provision,[27] and (4) soft administrative pricing[28]
[→8.4].

---

[24]Hardness and softness are two extreme cases in a continuum; there are degrees of
hardness and softness [→8.4]. The hardness and softness of the budget constraint differ
according to country, period, branch, and type of firm. All groups of firms with a relatively
harder budget constraint also have a stronger price and cost responsiveness.

No great inaccuracy is committed if the finer distinctions are ignored in the analysis that
follows, and reference is made, for the sake of simplification without subtle qualifications,
to the softness of the budget constraint and to the weakness of the price responsiveness.

[25]There is a wide range of literature confirming by experience that the budget constraint
on a firm in the public sector of a reform economy really is soft. See, for example, the
following studies: *China:* M. I. Blejer and G. Szapáry (1990), P. Bowles and G. White
(1989), B. Naughton (1985), and C. P. W. Wong (1986); *Hungary:* J. Kornai and Á. Matits
(1987, 1990); *Poland:* L. Balcerowicz (1988) and M. E. Schaffer (1989a); *Yugoslavia:* S. J.
Gedeon (1985–86, 1987), P. T. Knight (1984), and L. D. Tyson (1977, 1983).

[26]This process is clearly demonstrated in the case of the Chinese economy in the study
by M. I. Blejer and G. Szapáry (1990).

[27]On this phenomenon, see É. Várhegyi (1987) in connection with Hungary and
P. Bowles and G. White (1989) in connection with China.

[28]"Enterprises do not have to watch costs or their various elements, . . . because any
changes in these parameters are automatically transformed, through the mechanism of

Some typical manifestations of this group of phenomena are as follows.

State money is used regularly to rescue consistently loss-making firms. This is demonstrated in tables 21.5. and 21.6. It is repeatedly promised in party and government resolutions and leadership statements that artificial resuscitation of loss-making firms will cease.[29] All reforming countries enact or prepare laws on bankruptcy proceedings, but these are almost never applied.

A high proportion of consistently loss-making firms are not merely kept alive with state subsidies or soft credits; their capacity is increased further. There is only a loose relation between the firm's past and future (expected) profitability and its investment, growth, and technical development.

A vertical bargaining process is going on. Firms can negotiate with the fiscal and foreign-trade authorities on subsidies, taxes, and customs duties, with the banks on loans, and with the price office on prices. There are plenty of "tailor-made" rules intended to cope with the specific financial woes of particular branches or firms. Where there are generally

TABLE 21.5
Bail-out of Loss-making Firms in China, 1988

	Number of Firms	Percent
Total number of firms investigated	403	100
Bailed-out firms	203	50.4
Deadline of paying the debt postponed	60	14.9
Debt being forgiven	3	0.7
New loan to pay the old loan	24	6.0
Loan repayment before tax[a]	98	24.3

Source: Direct communication of Dong Fureng (director, Institute of Economics, Chinese Academy of Social Sciences).

[a]Loans should be repaid after tax, out of profits. Repayment before tax, and accounted as cost, improves the firm's profit position.

'justified costs,' into the increases of the prices of the goods which they produce," the Polish Consultative Economic Council concluded. Quoted by Z. M. Fallenbuchl (1988, p. 125).

[29]According to Chinese economists, more than one-quarter of state-owned enterprises make a loss in China every year. *Renmin Ribao,* overseas ed., October 10, 1986. "China has expended more than 40 billion yuan, which is equivalent to one-half of the total profit of the [Chinese] industry, or two-thirds of total capital construction of the nation, to subsidize those state-owned enterprises." *Renmin Ribao,* overseas ed., August 18, 1988.

TABLE 21.6
Bail-out of Loss-making Firms in Yugoslavia, 1980–81

	Number of Economic Units[a]	*Number of Workers Involved (thousands)*
Total	13,667	4,848
1. Units with uncovered loss on 1980 annual financial report	1,303	277
2. Units where rehabilitation is in process	178	51
3. Units where bankruptcy procedure has been initiated	20	2

Source: P. T. Knight (1984, pp. 5, 78).

[a]Basic Organization of Associated Labor (BOAL) [→20.6]. A large firm can be composed of several BOALs.

valid rules, some allow case-by-case interpretation of the rule[30] or specify exceptions. And the rules are constantly changing; firms are quite uncertain what measures of the state's will affect their profits in the following year (let alone the more distant future).

A high proportion of firms' profits are deducted under myriad names through fiscal redistribution, and then handed out to the firms again under myriad other names. Each organization seeks to influence the firm in its own sphere of authority and enforce its objectives with bonuses and penalties, including subsidies and profit deductions. (It is another matter that in the end the myriad positive and negative incentives usually cancel each other out.)

Sometimes the money is taken out of one pocket and put into another pocket of the same firm. But there are usually winners and losers from the redistribution. A disproportionately large amount is deducted from firms that generate a big profit, and that is passed to the remainder. (See the examples of Hungarian and Polish firms in tables 21.7 and 21.8.) Egalitarianism is not alien to socialist distribution, but it is certainly a paradoxical distortion of the idea to apply it to the redistribution of

---

[30]A grotesque example of this was the profit tax on Chinese state-owned firms: the rate for each firm was set in an individual contract with the superior authority. See M. I. Blejer and G. Szapáry (1990).

TABLE 21.7
Leveling of Profits in Hungary

Transition from Original Profitability	To Final Profitability			
	Loss Maker	Low Profitability	Medium Profitability	High Profitability
Loss maker	0.233	0.500	0.122	0.145
Low profitability	0.038	0.853	0.103	0.006
Medium profitability	0.000	0.734	0.206	0.060
High profitability	0.008	0.394	0.515	0.083

Source: J. Kornai (1986b, p. 1697), based on the joint study with Á. Matits. See J. Kornai and Á. Matits (1987, 1990).

Note: The transition from "original" to "final" profitability means the transition from the pretax and presubsidy position to the posttax and postsubsidy position. Firms are classified in four categories: "loss making" means profitability less than −2 percent; "low profitability" is between −2 percent and +6 percent; "medium profitability" is between 6 percent and +20 percent; and "high profitability" is more than 20 percent. The figures refer to the proportion of firms in any given original profitability class that became members of a given final profitability class as a result of fiscal redistribution.

TABLE 21.8
Leveling of Profits in Poland

Transition from Original Profitability	To Final Profitability			
	Loss Maker	Low Profitability	Medium Profitability	High Profitability
Loss maker	0.000	0.161	0.625	0.214
Low profitability	0.000	0.706	0.279	0.015
Medium profitability	0.000	0.084	0.817	0.099
High profitability	0.000	0.011	0.413	0.576

Source: M. Schaffer (1990, p. 188).

Note: The table uses 1988 data. For the explanation of the term "transition" in this context see the note to table 21.7. Firms are classified in four categories: "loss making" means negative profitability; "low profitability" is between 0 percent and 6.8 percent, "medium profitability" is between 6.8 and 22.7 percent; and "high profitability" is more than 22.7 percent as far as the original profitability is concerned. For final profitability the categories are: "loss-maker" with negative profitability; "low profitability" is between 0 and 3.2 percent; "medium profitability" is between 3.2 and 10.5 percent; "high profitability" is more than 10.5 percent.

profits. Yet that is what happens: a clearly apparent tendency toward equalization runs through the redistribution of profits.[31]

All this experience becomes deeply embedded in the minds of the firm's leaders and molds their behavior. Their main conclusion is that it is not in production or on the market that a firm's profits are decided, but in the offices of the bureaucracy.

In fact, many people ask why the economic leadership does not impose tighter financial discipline. There are repeated resolutions and undertakings; why are they not carried out? On such occasions the radical reformers who champion the application of the ideas of market socialism reproach the party leadership and higher organizations of the government for their inconsistency. This analysis, however, sets out to decide why even the members of the ruling elite who take notions of decentralization, the market mechanism, profit incentives, and a hard budget constraint seriously are inconsistent in this respect.

The explanation is made up of several closely related factors.

1. *Political power.* The manager of a firm is a middle-level member of the ruling group, the bureaucracy, which holds power on every level. The upper level of the hierarchy cannot coldly view such a manager as an outsider, saying it is the manager's problem if the firm makes losses or faces financial collapse. The upper leadership chose and appointed the manager as head of the firm, the agent and main support of power.

A part is played by another major political consideration: liquidation of the firm may cause an outcry among the workers, so weakening the mass basis and the legitimacy of power, which are none too strong in any case.

2. *Ideology.* The bureaucracy undergoes a moral crisis. The ideological realm of reform socialism calls for efficiency, and sees the goal of maximizing profits as the expression of that. But such a goal can conflict with several of socialism's traditional values: the imperative of solidarity with the weaker side, the security to be guaranteed for the workers, the requirements of social equality, and the promotion of society's interests over those of individuals and groups within it. The bureaucracy, whose nucleus is the Communist party, is no profit-maximizing capitalist owner. With half his heart a reform Communist roots for the market, the independence of firms and the profit motive, but the other, stronger half binds him to traditional, socialistic values: he feels obliged to aid a firm in trouble; he certainly cannot throw workers out on the street; he has a responsibility to level off firms' earnings. Paternalism is his bounden duty. He does not believe an invisible hand can align the inter-

---

[31]A mathematical model for the analysis and theoretical interpretation of the tendency to equalize profits among state-owned enterprises has been devised by Y. Qian (1990).

ests of firms with those of society as a whole, and he feels that however important the profits of firms may be, they remain secondary. All this clearly encourages him to soften the budget constraint.[32]

3. *Property.* Under capitalism, there is a rather far-reaching separation of the roles in society of the state, the private owner, and the manager operating as an employee. The owner, an individual proprietor, or a shareholder in a corporation has a clearly perceived financial interest in raising profits. That is his own cause; he needs no state inducement or instruction to do so. If his capital does not produce the desired yield in some area, his own interest tells him to withdraw it. He pays the managers, and if they do not work to raise profits, he sacks them. Profits also motivate the commercial banks and other financial intermediaries. Financial discipline is imposed by the market in a blind and anarchic way (to use Marx's expression).

None of this can be awaited from public ownership under socialism.[33] It is useless for domestic and foreign advisers to call on the governments of market-socialist economies to be more forceful and impose financial discipline; the requirement cannot be met while public ownership remains dominant. The menaces of the center are not effective enough; firms are not even afraid they will be implemented.[34] The separation of functions does not apply here. Is the bureaucracy, which is the state, the owner, and the manager all at once, supposed to discipline itself? The budget constraint on firms can only become hard if the firm is really separate from the bureaucracy, that is, if it is self-evidently left to itself

---

[32]Let us quote from the statements of conspicuously high-ranking Chinese bank managers, as the phraseology they use well illustrates the syndrome: The task of the bank is "to praise the good and help the poor [firm]," according to one. "This is a public economy. We cannot shut enterprises; we have to help them live." The remarks are quoted by P. Bowles and G. White (1989, pp. 489, 492).

[33]Several researchers have drawn attention to the fact that symptoms of the soft budget-constraint syndrome appear also in the public sector of capitalist countries, where the weight of that sector is comparatively great. This was established, for instance, about the public sectors of Israel, India, Greece, Brazil, and Algeria.

[34]This phenomenon—the "credibility" of threats and acceptance of responsibility—is analyzed from many angles in the game-theoretical models concerning soft budget constraint. For references, see chapter 8, note 21.

Particular mention must be made of the study by M. Dewatripont and E. Maskin (1989), which examines the causes of the soft budget constraint syndrome. Using a game-theoretical model, the study confirms that if the extending of credit is centralized, a bank cannot fulfill its prior threat; instead, it must chase after its money and continue financing uneconomic investment projects as well. Where there is a real decentralization of the banking sector, on the other hand, the threat becomes credible, which hardens the budget constraint and scares off those proposing uneconomic projects.

in time of trouble. The only way of ensuring this separation automatically and spontaneously is by private ownership.[35]

The entrepreneurs who create dynamism in the economy can appear on the scene only after entry into production has ceased to be decided arbitrarily by the bureaucracy and comes to depend on the entrepreneurs' own initiatives and on their success in obtaining credit on the capital and credit markets based on private property. This is another way in which there is a strong relation between true market competition and free enterprise, on the one hand, and private property, on the other.[36]

4. *Coordination and control.* The practice in the market-socialist economy is for the superior organizations to exercise microregulation [→21.3], intervening in various details of the firm's activity. So they also share the responsibility. If failure ensues, the management of the firm can point out quite justifiably, with ample evidence to support them, that they discussed each important action they took with at least some higher party and state organizations or were specifically ordered to take that action. They can go on to plead that the losses were caused by faulty prices, the taxes or duties recently levied, the wage rises ordered by the state, and other measures taken by their superiors. Any firm on the verge of insolvency has dozens of high-ranking persons above it who possessed the same prior information as the firm's leaders, took part in taking the mistaken decisions, and so have a motive for disguising the responsibility. How, under the circumstances, can tough discipline be expected? The more bureaucratic control remains dominant, the less the budget constraint can be hardened.[37]

The following question often arises in the debates about the softness of the budget constraint: Is it possible to make the budget constraint on publicly owned firms hard under the prevalent market-socialist system? The four points above provide an unequivocal answer: No, it is not.[38]

[35]Exceptionally, the hardness of the budget constraint on publicly owned firms can be ensured artificially if there are not too many of them and they are surrounded by privately owned firms in a capitalist system. The behavioral norms of the narrow public sector then resemble the behavior of the dominant private sector of the economy.

[36]According to P. Murrell (1990a, 1990b), the gravest shortcoming of the experiments with reform conceived in terms of market socialism is precisely their failure to provide either the chance or the incentive needed for Schumpeter-style enterprise to develop.

[37]Micro regulation, as has been seen, is one of the causes of the softening of the budget constraint, because it precludes a total decentralization of responsibility and gives the superior organization a motive for glossing over the mistakes. But it is at the same time a consequence of the soft budget constraint, since the financial control is insufficient to provide the central organizations with an adequate means of transmission.

[38]My writings never suggested that the hardening of the firms' budget constraint would be feasible in a socialist system characterized by the dominance of state ownership. Later studies strengthened my doubts concerning this possibility. Along with colleagues of mine,

At this point it is worth stopping a moment to clarify the place taken by the theory of soft budget constraint in the critique of the market-socialist economy. This syndrome is not the deepest cause of the weaknesses and failures of the reform process. The ultimate causes lie in the power structure, and in the configuration of property relations and coordination mechanisms of the system reformed according to the ideas of market socialism. The combined effect of these deeper causes is crowned by a situation where the budget constraint, despite the promises, does not and cannot harden; the profit motive remains quite weak, and so prices fail to play their vital part in the operation of the market mechanism. In that sense the degree of softness of the budget constraint plays a pivotal role: numerous other, partial phenomena (runaway demand from firms, hunger for investment and imports, low level of efficiency) can be traced partly or wholly to this syndrome.[39]

Let us confront the visions of the reformers—the school of thought embracing market socialism and the plan-cum-market—with actual experience. The market differs from all other coordination mechanisms above all in making the actors in the economy react to prices. Even if the budget constraint is not inordinately weak—if it is only sufficiently weak to dampen substantially all demand and supply reactions—the market is incapable of fulfilling its role.

Even though the firm's responsiveness to prices is dulled, it is not wholly indifferent to costs and prices. It takes advantage of readily available chances to cut costs, but it does not bother to seize them all. It grasps every opportunity to raise prices, which tends to be more convenient than fiddling about with other methods of softening the budget constraint. Some firms react to certain conspicuous price changes either on the output or input side, provided other interests (e.g., fulfillment of some contrary desire of the bureaucracy's) do not argue against the reaction. But it all amounts to a rare, crude, distorted, and slow adjustment compared with the frequent, finely tuned, detailed, and swift accommodation produced by a true market mechanism forcing a sensitive reaction

---

I have since made some detailed empirical examinations—see, for example, J. Kornai and Á. Matits (1987, 1990)—and studied the material of several other surveys (see note 25). In addition, I have attempted a theoretical reappraisal of the connections. The theoretical line of thinking is outlined in this book. All these together have led me to the position summed up in the straightforward negative answer given above.

[39]This is worth underlining as misunderstandings have cropped up in the literature commenting on the theory of soft budget constraint. This phenomenon, as the present comments make clear, has an honored place in my line of thinking, but that is not inconsistent with a place within the explanatory theory of the system in the middle of the causal chain, not as its point of origin. In the conceptual framework introduced in figure 15.1, the soft budget constraint syndrome is a characteristic of block 4 [→15.1].

to prices, of the kind to which market economies owe their high level of efficiency.

One can add that the price signal itself may be faulty. For the low price-responsiveness and the soft budget constraint causing it have repercussions on that as well. If a firm can survive and even develop when its profit level is constantly low or negative, it is not even worth using every means available for adjusting prices. Such a price system as this leads to acquiescence in its own faults.[40]

Those preparing the plans for reform pointing in the direction of market socialism expected firms to react sensitively to prices. In that case the economy could be managed centrally by using so-called *financial regulators* instead of the old instructions in physical terms on inputs and outputs. Raise the interest rate and investment will fall. Devalue the national currency and exports will increase and imports diminish. Raise the price of product A relative to that of product B, and a firm will substitute A for B, and so on. These expectations were belied: it is fruitless for the center to try to exert influence through these regulators if the firm hardly pays any heed. It is like wanting to change the channel or volume on a television by remote control when no sensor has been built into the set. There is no option but to work it by hand.

It was established that the classical system is a semimonetized economy [→8]. The publicly owned sphere in the market-socialist economy that results from the reform process remains a semimonetized sector of the economy, even though the active role of money in it grows to some extent.

21.6 The Affinity between Public Ownership and Bureaucratic Coordination

The previous sections compared the sphere of ideas covered by market socialism and plan-cum-market with the real situation of the public sector during the process of reform. The question arises: Why do reality and the desired state differ to such an extent?

The planners of the reform hoped that the vacuum created by abolition or containment of the instruction system and the command economy would immediately "suck in" the mechanism of market coordination. This failed to happen. What the vacuum mainly sucked in was a modified form of bureaucratic coordination. Direct vertical control gives

---

[40]The situation on the labor market exercises a much stronger influence on relative wages because there is a hard budget constraint on the employee's household. So employees cannot acquiesce meekly if their wages fall short of the level they consider justified.

way primarily to indirect vertical control, and only secondarily is some space taken by the horizontal coordinating role of the market, in a feeble and often distorted form [→21.7].

Most observers recognize that the bureaucratic influence has remained very strong, but opinions divide on the description of the situation and on the causal analysis. Some people stress that although the firms want a reform that will introduce market socialism, the conservative bureaucrats oppose it. They usually go on to say that this conservative bureaucracy has its representatives, or even instigators (the "hard-liners"), in the leading bodies of the party. According to that analysis, the bureaucratic resistance is organized to some extent from above. Another version of the diagnosis visualizes the conservatives between two fires: more radical reform is demanded from above by the reform-minded supreme leadership and from below by the leaders at local and firm levels demanding independence, however, the obstinate, conservative bureaucrats dig in their toes.

I am among those who see some valid elements in these diagnoses but consider that they fail to describe satisfactorily the interests and behavior of the various social forces.

The bureaucracy as defined in this book is a hierarchically structured social group. It is not "outside" the society, it exists in every cell of it. On average every eighth or tenth family contains one or more members of the bureaucracy, whose daily lives, income, social status, and career are bound up in it. Every institution of the bureaucracy wants to survive and continue to function. There is no need to order or even encourage this behavior from above: it is natural that all responsible functionaries in it want bureaucratic coordination to continue, primarily because it gives them power. But that is not their only motive. They cling to their sphere of authority because they identify with their job and believe it is useful. The person in the price authority wants to set prices, the person in the wage authority wants to fix wages, the investment allocator wants to allocate investment, the personnel department staff want to allocate labor, and so on. If there is something amiss in these areas, each thinks: there must be a fuller intervention to restore order.[41] Each in his or her own field constantly reinforces the tendency described earlier as the completion of bureaucratic control, that is, preventing phenomena undesired by the bureaucracy from slipping through the net of rules, prescriptions, and bans.

---

[41]The constant reproduction of the bureaucracy and its repeated ability to return after retreating is confirmed by the fact that direct methods of control reappear immediately if any serious difficulty arises in the economy. Problems with the current-account balance, for example, cause the authorities to make even stricter use of the administrative methods of foreign exchange rationing and import licensing. See, for instance, J. Gács (1980).

The leaders of firms call for independence only halfheartedly. When all around them is in order, they would rather be left in peace and not have the profits, resources, and wage funds they have managed to obtain taken away through redistribution. But when a problem or obstacle arises, they expect or even demand intervention. The ministry or the county party secretary is asked to intercede if they have trouble obtaining inputs or the bank will not give them credit. Having spent a lifetime building up their connections, are they suddenly to lose this curious kind of accumulated "wealth" and be left without connections or patrons? If they suffer financial loss, must they face up to a hard budget constraint, insolvency, bankruptcy, and loss of their managerial positions? Lobbying for the right official decision, fixing things at the back door, and smart bargaining with superior organizations are the areas in which they feel at home. Competition and the ruthlessness of the market are unknown and alarming.

In a market, independent economic units enter into relations with each other. Official propaganda for the market-socialist reform stresses that it can reconcile central control and the firm's independence.[42] Yet they are a logically irreconcilable pair of opposites. There is no room to play with the meaning of words like "independent." A firm is only independent if neither it nor the other firms are subordinate to common superior organizations exercising real sovereignty. A firm is independent if and only if it is truly separate from the other firms, because each has different owners (or, in the case of corporations, nonidentical sets of shareholders).

All this explains how an affinity arises between public ownership and bureaucratic coordination too. The sundry methods of bureaucratic coordination constantly reproduce themselves spontaneously and naturally, without special compulsion. There is no need for a central command; on the contrary, bureaucratic coordination rises again even if some stern central resolution or other lays down that it must be curtailed.

---

[42]N. Ryzhkov, prime minister of the Soviet Union, in *Izvestiia,* February 2, 1985, puts it this way: "It is the goal of our work to elaborate effective methods of managing our gigantic economy and to give the enterprises and associations wide economic independence within the framework of the plan."

The highly important resolution from the Central Committee of the Hungarian Communist party that prepared the 1968 reform was expressed like this: "The combination of centrally planned control with the operation of the market mechanism makes possible and demands a significant increase in the socialist state firms' independence and sphere of decision-making, and concurrently in their initiative and responsibility." H. Vass, ed. (1968, p. 313).

According to a German report, at the Central Committee plenum of the Chinese Communist party in December 1990, the following simile was used: "The state enterprise is like a bird in a cage. It may move but it may not fly away."

Here I must return to the question of affinity between the elements of the system. The strands that started at two earlier places in the book [→15.2, 19.4] can now be tied together. Classical socialism is a coherent system, among other reasons because there is an affinity between public ownership and bureaucratic coordination; these elements in the system are organically connected and reinforce each other. Capitalism is likewise a coherent system, because there is an affinity between private property and market coordination, which are also organically connected and reinforce each other. The attempts to realize market socialism, on the other hand, produce an incoherent system, in which there are elements which repel each other: the dominance of public ownership and the operation of the market are not compatible.

This idea is not a new one. It was strongly emphasized by von Mises [→21.2] in the debate on socialism. The notion that a true market could function without private property was dubbed the "Grand Illusion" by G. W. Nutter (1968). The attention of economists dealing with the socialist system has been drawn to this idea repeatedly by A. A. Alchian, H. Demsetz, and other members of the "property-rights school."[43] This line of argument is greatly substantiated by the dismal consequences of the attempts to apply market socialism in practice.

21.7 Horizontal Relations of Firms in Public Ownership

How have the horizontal relations of firms in public ownership altered since the deregulation measures? Cases of bureaucratic intervention are still legion, but buyer and seller firms can now agree upon a great many things between themselves. They enter into purchase-and-sale contracts, alter them by mutual consent, agree upon prices, grant each other credit, and so on. Such ties existed under the classical system, but their role has grown substantially under the reform.

Yet the phenomenon needs cautious assessment. If one defines the term market strictly, these horizontal relations hardly deserve the label market coordination at all. A real market is impelled by the prices, the attainable profit in money, and the rivalry among competitors. These impulses are feeble in a semideregulated public sector. The official propaganda for the reform sets out to persuade managers to act as if the market were close to their hearts: they are urged in the press, on television, and in politicians' speeches to attend to buyers' requirements, pay

---

[43]See A. A. Alchian (1974) and A. A. Alchian and H. Demsetz (1972). For further discussion, see D. Lavoie (1985), G. E. Schroeder (1988), G. Temkin (1989), and J. Winiecki (1991).

heed to quality, and adapt to domestic and foreign demand. But such behavior is not susceptible to persuasion. In fact, it is not the market that controls the birth, growth, atrophy, or death of a firm. The firm comes to expect that its level of profit, the wages and profit share-out payable to its employees, its welfare spending, or its scale of investment will depend on what various superior authorities decide, not on the market.

Apart from trying to persuade firms to pay more heed to the market, the managers of the economy set out to simulate the market with cunning incentive schemes and contrived pricing arrangements [→22.3]. The trouble is that the most important factor in the operation of the market mechanism is whether living people have a personal interest in prices, supply and demand, and purchase and sale, not what formula governs the price movements. When a price rises, those with an interest act on that information: some are unable to fulfill their buying intentions and withdraw voluntarily from the ranks of the producers, while others seize the chance to join the producers of the product that has become more profitable. When a price falls, the opposite ensues. This direct relation between the information supplied by a price and the decisions affecting supply and demand is eclipsed in an artificially simulated market.

The last section pointed out the affinity between public ownership and bureaucratic coordination. One can now emphasize here again that there is no affinity between public ownership and market coordination. Market relations do not appear alongside public ownership in a spontaneous, natural way; there is merely an attempt to foist them artificially on the participants in the processes to be coordinated.

One vital requirement before the market can operate normally is that contracts between the buyer and the seller should be honored. In a market-socialist economy, these contracts are regularly broken with impunity. It is common for a publicly owned firm with payment problems to tide itself over simply by not paying another firm that supplies it. Such forced credit becomes one of the main forms in which the budget constraint is softened. The problem is then multiplied: the firm that has not been recompensed for its output fails to pay its own suppliers, who treat their suppliers the same way, and so on. The phenomenon is known in financial jargon as "queuing": forced creditors stand in line at debtor firms, hoping it will be their turn one day for their claims to be met. If queuing becomes widespread, the result is a real liquidity crisis.[44] Every

---

[44]For example, in Yugoslavia the annual growth rate of interfirm indebtedness was around 30–50 percent in the late 1970s and early 1980s. For a detailed analysis, see S. J. Gedeon (1985–86) and L. D. Tyson (1977). Similar phenomena occurring in Hungary are examined by É. Várhegyi (1989, 1990b).

firm can safely refuse to pay its bills, as it can be sure it will not be penalized and become bankrupt because of the financial crisis; in some way the state and the state banking system will rescue it.

This kind of forced credit and queuing cannot occur under the classical system because the central bank automatically debits the buyer firm's account and credits the seller firm's account with the claim. The market-socialist economy is "marketlike" in the sense that it permits commercial credit between firms. On the other hand, it contrasts sharply with the spirit and legal practice of a true market economy by tolerating mass infringement of payment obligations.

On the subject of horizontal relations, it is worth mentioning one important offshoot of the market-socialist sphere of ideas: the proposals to establish a state capital market within the frames of the socialist system.[45] The departure point for the proposals is a criticism of the way the market-socialist reform has worked so far. One of the main weaknesses of the original program is considered to be that it sought merely to create a market in goods, while what is needed is a united, comprehensive market that embraces a capital market as well.[46] The market-socialist reforms introduced so far have allowed only three methods of allocating the capital in public ownership: (1) allocation by the central state organizations of investment funded out of the budget, (2) extension by the state banking system of investment loans, and (3) "in-house," self-financed investment by the publicly owned firm from its own savings.

The idea is to allow a further method: (4) a firm in public ownership should be allowed to allocate capital to another publicly owned firm. For the capital market to develop, the legal position of the state-owned firm has to be changed, namely, by turning it into a joint-stock company. In this way it becomes possible for the firm to issue shares and for another firm to buy them. What arises is the phenomenon of *cross-ownership*: one state-owned firm becomes a part-owner of the other.

According to this scheme, not only is it possible for producer firms to buy each other's shares; state-owned banks can buy shares in a firm, and the other way around: firms can buy shares in banks, which likewise operate as joint-stock companies. The state-owned insurance companies and pension funds can invest their capital in the shares of firms as well.[47]

---

[45]This idea spread among reform economists mainly in Hungary, the pioneer being the Hungarian economist M. Tardos (1986, 1990). Similar ideas arose in other reforming countries, notably China and Poland. A more detailed exposition of the idea can be found in W. Brus and K. Laski (1989), which contributes many important ideas to the debate on market socialism.

[46]Those who put forward this idea usually add that a labor market is also required.

[47]It should be noted here that the whole pension system was run by a single monopoly state organization in a socialist economy in this period, even in the countries that went

This is complemented by the idea that state organizations of local government (such as city and village councils) and nonprofit state institutions (e.g., universities and hospitals) can buy shares too.[48]

The scheme assumes the shares are freely transferable within the sphere of owners mentioned. Trade in them is to be conducted through a stock exchange run by the state. Advocates of the proposal hope that a state capital market will produce a new form of public ownership more fluid than the old.

At the time of writing, this proposal has yet to be implemented anywhere. What is on the agenda in the Eastern European countries that have arrived at the postsocialist phase is the sale or the free transfer of the share in the firms transformed into joint-stock companies through a process of privatization, mainly to private domestic and foreign owners [→19.7]. One can expect a growth in the role of private property in the banking sector and sooner or later the establishment of private insurance companies, decentralized pension funds, and investment of part of their capital in shares by these institutions too. But all this is taking place in a socioeconomic environment different from the one assumed in the proposals just outlined: not in a market-socialist regime, but in a postsocialist one where the private sector will steadily gain a dominant role. To that extent the postsocialist experience in Eastern Europe is inconclusive to an assessment of what the actual effect of applying the proposals for a state capital market would have been.

There is no way to tell whether a state capital market will be established in the countries that still follow the path of market socialism, for example China. If it is, experience there will provide better grounds for a verdict. Without practical experience there is only guesswork to back any attempt to evaluate the proposal.

I cannot conceal my doubts. It has not proved possible to simulate a real market by artificial means even in transactions relating to goods. One fears that the state capital market would be an even paler simulation. It would involve nothing other than the transfer of state property from one state hand to the other state hand, regardless of whether the other hand is christened a "firm," a "bank," or an "insurance com-

---

furthest with reform. The insurance business is either handled by one state-owned monopoly company or at most concentrated into a few oligopolistic state companies.

[48]Most economists advocating the introduction of a state capital market leave open the question of whether shares can be sold to private persons. Although the proposals for shares remain unrealized even in the sphere of potential state-owned owners, the institution of bonds is introduced in practice.

One can consider the free purchase and sale of bonds in private ownership as the harbinger of a real capital market, even though it spreads only to a narrow band of the total capital.

pany." In fact, every new owner would be a firm with a soft budget
constraint, that is, a more or less bureaucratic formation. There cannot
be a real market in capital without capitalist private owners.

21.8   Proportions of the Two Kinds of Dependence

The conception of a semideregulated economy is based on the premise
that bureaucratic and market coordination can be combined in any proportion, let us say, in a ratio of fifty–fifty. Experience suggests this
premise is mistaken. Lively operation of the market is compatible with
a measure of state intervention, so long as it does not interpose too
often in the processes taking place when the parties to the market reach
free agreement. But bureaucratic intervention can attain a critical mass
that destroys the market's vitality. That critical mass is certainly exceeded by the million interventions in the public sector of the reform
economy.

The question raised at the beginning of section 21.4 must be returned
to. To some extent a firm has a dual dependence under any system, vertically on the state authorities and horizontally on the market. What system-specific features does this dual dependence show in the public sector
of a reform socialist system? The horizontal market dependence has
grown compared with the classical system, but it remains subordinate.
The arsenal of vertical dependence changes, with indirect bureaucratic
control replacing classical direct bureaucratic control, but vertical dependence stays predominant. The reform tendency born out of the notion
of market socialism brought large numbers of alterations in the actual
methods of coordination and control, but they did not lead to a radical
change.

Everything that has emerged about the dual dependence of the firm is
impressed on the position, motivation, and behavior of the manager,
which have changed appreciably since the classical system. The manager's dress, vocabulary, and demeanor begin to resemble those of his
or her Western counterpart. Managers no longer describe themselves as
soldiers of the party posted to the production front.

But, in fact, the change tends to be superficial. They certainly resemble
their fellow managers in the West in being paid employees, not entrepreneurs working at their own risk. They have been invested until further
notice with property rights of type c, namely, part of the right of control.
They do not possess the other property rights. But both the short- and
long-term interests of managers of capitalist firms accord with the owners' interest in profit and net worth. So they identify with the aim of
raising profits and feel their own destiny depends on the results achieved

on the market.[49] By contrast, the destiny of managers of socialist firms is tied, as has been seen, to those above them in the hierarchy. Alhough they have one eye on the market and the other on their superiors, the important thing, in fact, is for the eye cast upward to see clearly: their present bonus or penalty and their future promotion depend on their superiors. The proprietor, if any, is the sum total of the bureaucracy. But this is "intangible." What was established about the classical system remains true: public property belongs to all and to none [→5.3]. The hazy nature of property is the ultimate reason why the interest of the manager of a firm is hazy, ambiguous, and replete with contradiction.

Many people expect the reforms pointing in the direction of market socialism to produce a new "managerial class" whose members are independent of the party and the bureaucracy in general, and who will form a social group that may act as a counterbalance to the bureaucracy. At the same time, they will be independent of their workforces, and so personifications of the "employer" role against the "employees." Very little of these expectations is fulfilled.

The managers of state-owned firms remain members of the nomenklatura [→3.2, 18.1]. In fact, the behavior of managers of publicly owned firms in a market socialist economy reflects several roles: they are (1) bureaucrats at a middle level in the hierarchy, officials dependent on their superiors, and at the same time bosses themselves;[50] (2) co-owners who receive an ample share of the residual income;[51] (3) technocrats whose main concern independently, in terms of job identification, is with production and technical development; (4) elected self-management leaders who represent their employees' interests. In the market-socialist economy, the manager's identification with roles 2, 3, and 4 becomes stronger than under the classical system. What has remained unchanged is the dominance of role 1 in the manager's behavior.

21.9 The Relation between Publicly Owned Firms and the Private Sector

Many advocates of the market socialism and "plan-cum-market" ideas see the following as the desirable state:

[49]Several works deal with the relations between owner and manager and the divorce of ownership from control under the conditions of a capitalist joint-stock company. See A. D. Chandler (1977), E. S. Herman (1981), S. J. Grossman and O. D. Hart (1986), and E. F. Fama and M. C. Jensen (1983).

[50]On the other hand, the manager's position downward, in negotiations with employees, has weakened to some extent. There are several reasons for the change [→20.4, 23.1].

[51]If the manager is corrupt, the sum to be grabbed out of the residual income is larger. If scrupulous, the manager receives only the amount allowed under the rules of the pay and premiums of the leaders of a firm. In many countries this is quite a lot.

The public sector should retain its dominant position, but it should change over to market behavior. At the same time, there should be a private sector, but only with a complementary, secondary role. The two sectors should cooperate while concurrently engaging in market competition with each other. In this program the two tendencies discussed in this chapter and in chapter 19 are connected.

Some of these wishes may happen to be fulfilled. In Hungarian agriculture, for instance, certain large cooperatives effectively assisted the household farms of their members for extended periods by providing seed, transport, and other services. But the general picture of the reform economies as a whole over a longer period is less encouraging. Let us take the points of contact between the two sectors one by one.

Publicly owned firms are particularly disturbed by the fact that the private sector siphons off some of the labor force, often the best white-collar and manual labor. It is able to do so because numerous bureaucratic constraints prevent a publicly owned firm from deciding its own wages, and the private sector can pay much higher wages. That is just one manifestation of a more general phenomenon: the firm's managers, hampered by hundreds of different regulations, envy the private sector its autonomy.

Meanwhile, private entrepreneurs see the many privileges of publicly owned firms, particularly large state-owned firms, as unfair: their advantages in credit, imported materials, and foreign-exchange rationing, and the state subsidies and tax concessions for their investments. A publicly owned firm can rely on the support of the party and mass organizations and use the connections it has in every branch and at every level in the bureaucracy. Moreover, those employed full time in the private sector envy the privileges and job security of state-sector employees in many respects.

Having mentioned the competition for inputs, let us look at the output side. True "competition among sellers" arises in a few places like the food trade or the catering industry, but by and large the limits on entry conserve the monopoly, or at least the commanding position of the publicly owned firm. The chronic shortage remains over a wide area, and so the seller's advantage over the buyer is enjoyed by producer-sellers based on both public and private ownership. In this respect the two sectors live peacefully side by side.

Private entrepreneurs obtain some of their materials, semifinished products, and machines from other private entrepreneurs under real market conditions. But they can obtain the rest only from publicly owned firms, which places them in an exploited situation. Not infrequently, private entrepreneurs resort to bribing the officials of the selling firm to obtain the inputs they need.

There are cases of the opposite relationship, in which a publicly owned firm buys the products of a private firm, but these are limited by various administrative bans and restrictions. The vast and often highly profitable market that the public sector as a buyer represents to the private sector is largely denied to it and reserved for other publicly owned firms.

One can conclude ultimately that the conditions of "fair" competition have not been fulfilled. Each sector feels the conditions are detrimental to it and advantageous to the rival sector, and both are right with respect to different factors.

21.10   Interaction between the Mechanisms; Assessment of the Changes

A major element in the ideas surrounding market socialism and plan-cum-market is the hope that bureaucratic and market coordination will be complementary mechanisms that get along well and make up for each other's shortcomings [→21.1]. Very little of that expectation is fulfilled. I shall briefly size up the changes.

Partial deregulation of the public sector alleviates the extreme rigidity of classical direct bureaucratic control, which allows the managers of firms to adapt more flexibly to prevailing conditions. Various beneficial effects appear, even if the scale of improvement is not conspicuously great: in the case of many firms, the quality of the products improves and the range of them widens, new products are introduced more frequently, and more attention is given to buyers' requirements than used to be the case under the command economy; these changes alleviate the shortage in many areas.[52]

Perhaps more significant still than the achievements with economic performance are the sociopolitical effects. The economic atmosphere under a market-socialist type of reform is more human than it was under the classical system. Partial or total lifting of the command economy helps to dispel the barracks mentality of blunt orders and harsh reprisals against those who breach discipline.[53] Managers no longer live in fear

[52]The positive effects manage to assert themselves particularly if the partial deregulation occurs under comparatively favorable macroeconomic circumstances, as was the case in the early years of the Yugoslav and Hungarian reforms. Partial lifting of the command economy in itself contributes little to improving the situation if the macroeconomic situation is tense and other circumstances are unfavorable. I return to this question later [→23].

[53]One form of indirect control is this: the minister, instead of ordering the leader of the firm to do something, requests him to do it politely. Certainly, the head of the firm is dependent on the minister, and so he normally carries out the polite request just as if it were a command. Nevertheless, one cannot say the change is entirely irrelevant. "Le style c'est l'homme." The relations of superiority and subordination assume a more civilized

that the slightest mistake will be taken as sabotage and punished with imprisonment, forced labor, or execution. This contributes to a perceptible easing of the repression in other fields. Greater scope is available in economic relationships to living human contacts: fellowship, friendship, and unselfish readiness to help, in other words, the mechanisms summed up under the heading of ethical coordination.

But the favorable effects cannot obscure the general observation that basically the partial deregulation and the move toward market socialism fail to live up to expectations. In no reforming country does the public sector rid itself of the problems typical of it under the classical system. The initial achievements are not followed by a steady improvement in performance. Instead, there are setbacks and slowdowns. Once the slight increase in the firm's decision-making rights has absorbed the most obvious reserves, improvement in efficiency runs up against the constraints of the system. Numerous shortage phenomena persist. There is no sustained breakthrough in quality and technical development, and as a consequence, grave difficulties continue to arise with exports. Those are just the most striking problems. Moreover, the ambivalence of the market-socialist reforms creates new tensions as well: disequilibria that compound the old, classical macro tensions.[54] This will be discussed in more detail later [→23].

The result of the ambivalence in the reform of the public sector is that the shortcomings of the bureaucratic and market mechanisms, far from correcting each other, tend to reinforce each other. The sector falls between two stools. What takes place in the name of coordination is "neither plan nor market."[55]

There can be no coordination without discipline. Rigorous discipline was extorted by the classical system: it gave orders, rewarded obedience, and revenged itself on those who flouted discipline. No one could depart with impunity from the plan instructions, miss the publicly announced deadline for a priority investment action, or overstep the wage fund or the prescribed wage rates. That discipline is now lifted. Although instructions are given, there is no great risk involved in disobeying them (or more commonly in carrying them out sloppily and tardily). The center is unable to impose its will any more.

---

form, which reinforces the subordinate's sense of human dignity. Ultimately, that also makes it easier for him to say no to his boss.

[54]There are several indications that reform of a market-socialist type tends to undermine the efficiency of production rather than improve it, presumably because of the effects of the macro disequilibria. R. S. Whitesell's study (1989-90) uses an econometric analysis based on production functions to compare the efficiency of Hungarian and West German industry, concluding that Hungary's relative disadvantage increased further in the wake of the reform.

[55]This terse description was coined by T. Bauer (1983).

A market based on private ownership likewise imposes a discipline. The rivalry is merciless; a seller who goes under in a buyers' market is forced into exit. Sometimes the failure is tragic, and sometimes it is alleviated by several kinds of relief, but it remains a real failure. Banks insist that loans be repaid, and if need be sell the roof over the head of an insolvent debtor unable to service the mortgage on his house. Employers impose working discipline and wage discipline on employees. This rigor of the market based on private ownership is missing from a semideregulated public sector.

Here a brief digression must be made into public economic morality during the process of reform. For the market to work really well, there must be more than a material incentive and a legal compulsion for business partners to be persuaded to enter into fair contracts and abide by them. It requires business honesty as well, so that the forfeit of "good will," confidence, and reputation counts as a serious loss. There is a great need for the mechanism labeled earlier as ethical coordination to operate [→6.6]; otherwise, too much must be spent on lawyers, courts, and the collection of fines. In the reform economies, scrupulous business honesty fails to apply as a general norm; it is often breached by both the public and the private sectors.

The semideregulated public sector shows few signs of being influenced by respect for industry and thrift associated with private ownership, the market, and competition. What it does display is a spirit of cheap commercialism. This permeates the whole society: personal connections with officials in the bureaucracy are used by state-owned firms and private entrepreneurs in matters of production and by individuals in their own affairs, and bribery is often attempted.[56] Buyers suffering from shortage, whether firms, self-employed artisans, or consumers, try to do the same. The wealth of the state has no value in the public's eyes; people do not sense that it arose out of the taxes and sacrifices of taxpaying citizens, or that those handling the nation's wealth could be held responsible for it. Many of the public do not condemn defrauding or stealing from the state.

The phenomena described appear conspicuously in the Chinese economy, where the dual system based on plan instructions and freedom of firms to decide [→21.4] almost entices manipulation. During the customary bargaining under a system of control by plan instructions [→7.5], a firm would try to extract as small a compulsory output task and as large a quota of inputs as possible. This continues under the dual system, with the added feature that the firm, instead of using the material or ma-

[56]For a theoretical study of corruption under socialism, see P. Galasi and G. Kertesi (1987, 1989).

chinery allocated to it at the lower official price, may sell it at the market price to another state-owned firm or the private sector. Thousands of state-owned firms develop to deal almost exclusively with the acquisition of cheap state allocations through their connections and the resale of them at high prices.[57] Nominally, a firm of this kind is publicly owned, but, in fact, it becomes more or less the private property of its manager, who puts much of the profit in his or her own pocket.[58] It is the start of interpenetration by the bureaucracy and the private sector, not just in the form of legal joint ventures but through personal contacts. Private enterprises are set up by the dependents of high-ranking party and state officials or managers of firms, taking advantage of their familiarity with the "back door."[59] This would by no means be unusual in a capitalist society, but it sharply conflicts with the anticapitalist tradition of socialism and is hard to square with the official ideology of the reform socialist countries.

All this ties in with the appearance of high incomes. Some derive from real market success, but others draw on shadier sources: bribery, defrauding the state, or cheating customers. The man in the street does not make a stringent economic analysis or a police investigation. There is confusion in his mind. He is not even quite sure whether he is angry with the reform, the private sector, or the bureaucracy. He lumps higher earnings earned by real merit with those accruing from the privileges of power, and market profits with the ill-gotten gains of corruption. A surge of hatred for "speculators" and "corruption" breaks out.[60] That was one factor influencing the atmosphere of the 1989 student demonstrations in China. Stuck halfway, the reform process digs the ground from under its own feet, alienating a sizable section of the general public.

That completes the examination of how the reform programs derived from the ideas of market socialism and the plan-cum-market apply in practice. The narrower economic logic of these ideas is quite defensible: one can imagine a system in which autonomous, publicly owned firms and a perfectly objective and interest-free central bureau behaved as

---

[57]For a critique of the dual system, see the study by J. Wu and R. Zhao (1987).

[58]It is worth quoting from an article in the central daily of the Chinese Communist party: "These firms have both administrative and economic power. They combine the functions of government and economic life in one institution; they are sources of exploitation by the middleman, of resale for profit's sake; they make inordinate profits." *Renmin Ribao,* overseas ed., March 7, 1989.

[59]E. Hankiss (1989) termed this interpenetration the "grand coalition" under the reform system.

[60]Occasionally, a coalition forms among the Stalinist forces, the New Left who reject commercialism and the market, the populist people's romantics, and the conservative union officials who adhere to the notions of egalitarianism. These were the allies, for instance, during the first antireform wave in Hungary in 1972–73.

though they together constituted a market. The problem is that the tacit sociological and political assumptions behind the theory are unrealistic. Faced with the actual structure of the socialist system, the surviving traces of its earlier ideology, and its property relations, the attempts to implement the ideas of market socialism are doomed and cannot establish a robust socioeconomic system.

Nonetheless, these ideas and the attempts to apply them exert some beneficial influence, and not merely through the economic and political impacts mentioned at the start of this section. They have a leavening effect on society in general and particularly the part of the leading stratum of society with enlightened inclinations.[61] They shake the blind faith in the command economy, all-powerful centralization, and all-embracing planning as the highest form of control of economic processes. It awakens the desire to have autonomous economic units entering spontaneously and voluntarily into relations with each other. It starts to restore to the market and free enterprise the reputation that the previous doctrine has destroyed. Once people have accepted the idea that a market is needed in the public sector, they look with less prejudice and more sympathy on private enterprise. All these changes prepare the ideological ground for deeper and more radical movements in society.

21.11   Preview: The State Sector under the Postsocialist System

The starting point of the postsocialist transition is the dominant role of the sector in public ownership. Before the revolution, there were classical forms of control over this sector in Czechoslovakia or East Germany, for instance, and forms evolved according to market-socialist ideas in other countries like Hungary or Poland. What is to be done now?

One question is this: What proportion should the public sector occupy in the future? Clearly, this is the other, complementary side of the question touched upon in section 19.7: What should be the pace of privatization of public property and the development of the private sector in general? Market socialism has not lived up to the expectations of it. This is another inducement to the forces directing the transformation of society to speed up the privatization process as much as possible.

At a time when the process is commencing with the public sector's proportion at 70–95 percent, it is too early to examine where it will stop.

---

[61]According to the scheme of figure 15.1, market-socialist reforms mainly produce essential, although not consistently radical, changes in block 3 (coordination) and block 4 (behavior). At the same time they have a feedback effect on block 1, the structure of political power and the ideology.

Of course, it is worth discussing which spheres of a market economy based on private ownership are expediently left in public ownership, but examination of that exceeds the scope of this book.

Even if privatization proceeds at a quick pace, there will clearly be a period in which the proportion of the public sector remains considerable, and much greater than the proportion at which it will eventually stabilize at the end of the transition. And then another question arises: What forms of control over the operation of the state sector should the state use? When answering, it will be worth thinking over repeatedly the experiences with the forms of control born out of the ideas of market socialism.

A curious phenomenon has arisen recently in Eastern Europe—a kind of renaissance of market socialism. The first wave of it appeared among Communists intent on reforming the socialist system, but the present, second wave has influenced the ideas of some of Eastern Europe's non-Communist, indeed expressly anti-Communist politicians and economists. The idea that crops up among the economic policy makers and economists who were once in opposition and now exert influence in state functions and political parties or as advisers, and also among Western observers and advisers, is as follows: The old party-state was unable to induce real market behavior in state-owned firms. The new democratic system must show that it really can be done. This expectation will be confirmed or denied in practice. I cannot refrain from expressing doubts about the reality of it. My conviction is that the behavior of the managers of state-owned firms will remain ambivalent for as long as the state sector has great weight in the economy. Until that changes, they will still be half-businessmen and half-bureaucrats, and still use their connections with the bureaucracy to defend the protected and privileged positions of these firms (and the management of them). The managers of the remaining state-owned firms will behave more like genuine businessmen, as the private sector gradually evolves into a threatening competitor. Ultimately, market coordination will come to rule in the economy when and only when the private sector, the true social soil for the market mechanism, develops into the dominant social sector of the economy.

22

Price Reforms

ONE of the major tendencies in the move away from the classical system is modification of the price system. This relates closely to two tendencies discussed earlier—the revival of the private sector and reform of the control of the state sector in the direction of market socialism. So in that respect this chapter ties in closely with what has been said in chapters 19 and 21.[1]

Writers normally use the expression "price reform" to mean the compound set of changes. So the phenomenon to be examined needs to be broken down into its constituent elements. The following main factors can be distinguished:

1. *The method of determining prices.* To what extent does the bureaucracy retain control over prices, and to what extent does it cede the function of price setting to the market mechanism? There are two problems to distinguish in this area: the methods of determining product prices and factor prices [→22.1, 22.2].

2. *The principles of state price setting.* What economic principles are used in setting prices in the areas where state determination of prices remains? To what extent does the effect of these principles alter during the process of reform [→22.3]?

3. *Alteration of the system of taxation and subsidies.* How does this tie in with prices [→22.3]?

Once these factors in the price reforms have been examined individually, mention is made finally of some overall problems common to the partial processes [→22.4].

The price reforms analyzed in this chapter alter the coordination mechanisms (block 3 in figure 15.1) and the behavior of the participants in the economy (i.e., block 4). They do not cause a radical change, but they are sufficiently important to qualify as part of the reform process.

22.1 Determination of Product Prices

A distinction was made earlier among three types of prices, according to how the prices are determined: administrative, pseudoadministrative,

---

[1]Separate attention cannot be given here to the relation between the self-management discussed in chapter 20 and the price reforms. This partly overlaps in any case with the relation between market socialism and the price reforms, which is touched upon several times in the chapter.

and market prices [→8.6–8.8]. The reform process results in a substantial shift in the proportions of the areas in which each type applies to the determination of product prices.[2]

The sphere in which administrative prices apply narrows down. The sphere of pseudoadministrative prices broadens: the compulsion behind administrative prices is less vigorous, and the extent of the producer-seller's influence over the actual level of the price formally set by the authorities increases. One can also class as pseudoadministrative the prices for which calculation rules are set, but which the producers are allowed to calculate for themselves, since the rules can be bent without much trouble.[3] And a wider range of prices is openly declared to be free. Although these trends are general, there is a marked difference among countries (and periods) in how far they go and what factors explain the change.

One explanatory factor is the private sector's increased share of national production and turnover. The natural aspiration of private enterprise is to have its prices determined by voluntary contracts between the buyer and the seller. The greater the weight of the formal and informal private sector, the broader the area where market prices apply.

Another section of the changes ties in with the central economic leadership's efforts to deregulate. Yugoslavia went furthest in this: the bulk of the prices for products and services were freed in the very earliest phase of the reform process, and the area where administrative prices apply has remained very narrow.

There has also been a steady narrowing of the sphere of administrative prices in Hungary, but in 1989, the last year belonging to the period of reform socialism, a high proportion of the state sector's products and services were still subject to administrative pricing. This area of strict price control covered many basic raw materials, production and consumer services, and articles for mass consumption, so that administrative

---

[2]On price determination in *Hungary,* see B. Csikós-Nagy (1985) and W. Swaan (1990).

Of the wide-ranging debate in the *Soviet Union,* the following works can be mentioned: O. Bogomolov (1987), A. Komin (1988), V. Pavlov (1987), N. I. Petrakov (1987a, 1987b), and N. P. Shmelev (1988a, 1988b). The necessity of a price reform, the risk of inflation, and the social consequences of the changes all received emphasis in the debate. For Western analysis of the Soviet price problems, see M. Bornstein (1987) and E. A. Hewett (1988).

From the extensive debate in *China,* mention can be made of the writings of G. Liu (1986, 1989). For a survey of the debate in China, see J. S. Prybyla (1990, chaps. 11 and 12).

[3]In Hungary, several hundred thousand prices a year were being set. In 1985, for instance, investigations were made into 14,311 cases. In only 24 of these was a large fine imposed on the firm. L. Hübner, *Figyelő,* August 14, 1986, p. 5. One should add that imposition of the fine on the firm has little effect on the personal financial interests of the managers involved in the maneuvers.

price-setting had a wide spillover effect on the production costs of other goods and services, and on household budgets and so on wages.

In China, a dual system of regulating production was introduced [→21.4]. The complement to it in price determination is this: administrative prices are set for the compulsory output and rationed input, while the prices of free input and output turnover arise by free agreement between sellers and buyers, that is, according to market principles. That yields a dual price system for most products, with a lower administrative price and a higher market price. The producer firm may go on to find a way of operating as a curious kind of intermediary, not just a producer, selling cheap, rationed inputs at market prices to other producer firms, which may still find it worth their while to buy them for their own freely salable outputs. One finds a hybrid formation that crosses bureaucratic with market coordination: the rent concealed in the subsidized price of the rationed input is pocketed by the intermediary firm or possibly split with the buyer.[4]

The Yugoslav, Hungarian, and Chinese practices in price determination embody three typical states, various combinations of which are applied in the other reforming countries.

Particular note should be taken of the state price authorities' behavior over price trends in the private sector. They acquiesce in the deregulation of this sector's prices to an extent that varies according to the country and period. In some cases where they want to apply influence, they are content to prescribe methods of calculation or set a margin of "fair profit." In others, they try to set official, compulsory prices. Whether these turn out to be pseudoadministrative or true administrative prices depends on the consistency of compulsion by the state authorities. The harder the authorities aim for the latter, the more inspectors they need and the stiffer the penalties they impose for flouting the official price regulations. It can be done, of course, but the reaction is not confined to an increased likelihood of prescribed pricing being observed. Many private enterprises may have enough of the interference and return their licenses. They retreat into illegality, or cease their activity. Certainly, only a small proportion of private-sector turnover can be subjected lastingly and effectively to administrative price determination, since it is diametrically opposed to the nature of this property form.[5]

China's dual prices and the price authorities' interventions in the private sectors of all reform economies are cogent examples of a more gen-

[4]Some Chinese and foreign experts expected the free-price sphere under the dual system to promote the influence of the market mechanism on the regulated sphere. But according to the description above, this only happens in a gravely distorted form; in many respects the resulting dualism combines the drawbacks of bureaucracy and the market.

[5]Price determination is a good example in general of the ambiguity typical of the bureaucracy's behavior toward the private sector [→19.5]. It needs the private sector but still

eral sphere of problems: the parallel price systems applying in the reform economy.[6] There were signs of this under the classical system, but under the reform system it becomes really widespread.

Of course, there is nothing system-specific about a particular product not having a strictly standard price. A price can only be uniform if conditions of perfect competition pertain; under imperfect competition, the prices asked by the price-setting firms show a wide variance. But the phenomenon described here is not connected with that inevitable dispersion; it is a case of various mixtures of coexisting bureaucratic and market price control. There may, for instance, be a true "white-market" rent for an apartment of a particular size and quality, assuming the regulations allow the landlord and tenant to reach a free agreement without state intervention. Then there is another, clearly administrative but likewise "white" rent set arbitrarily by the authorities for housing rationed by the state. Typically that rent involves a big subsidy and is far lower than the market rent that would balance the demand with the supply. But there may additionally be a wide range of "gray-" and "black-market" rents depending on the degree of illegality lurking behind the tenancy agreement. For instance, someone moving into a state apartment pays "key money" to the person moving out for the transfer of the actual tenancy, which is then confirmed by the housing office through the appropriate rationing procedure. The housing official may need bribing too; if so, the amount of the bribe must be counted into the costs of the tenancy.

An important measure of the supplanting of the bureaucracy and the expansion of market coordination is establishing in which areas parallel price systems apply and the differences between the price levels. A few typical examples of this discrepancy can be found in tables 22.1 and 22.2.

There is frequent indignation against those who make a profit out of the higher prices of the parallel price system. The anger is understandable psychologically, but economically untenable. A market price cannot be judged on an ethical basis. A high white-, gray-, or black-market price signifies primarily that the supply falls short of the demand. Moreover, a contribution to the higher price is made by the risk premium, which depends on the degree of illegality and likelihood of punishment. The price will be driven down not by moral condemnation but by greater supply, and one requirement for that is legalization of free enterprise and free entry into production.

---

cannot bear to see private entrepreneurs setting their own prices on a free market and acquiring high incomes. It would rather prefer them to disappear, making their incomes "invisible" or withdrawing from production altogether.

[6]For mathematical models analyzing the operation and the effects of parallel markets, see M. Alexeev (1987, 1990), W. W. Charemza, M. Gronicki, and R. E. Quandt (1989), R. Ericson (1983), B. G. Katz and J. Owen (1984), and J. Kornai and J. W. Weibull (1978).

TABLE 22.1
Administrative and Market Prices of Foodstuffs in the Soviet Union

Item	Market Price as a Percentage of Administrative Price	
	1980	1987
Potatoes	360	345
Fruit	238	230
Meat	239	259
Dairy products	323	410

Source: Compiled by P. Mihályi for this book, on the basis of Soviet statistical reports.

22.2   Determination of the Prices of Production Factors

Changes take place also in the way the prices of the factors in production (factors for short) are determined. Factor prices include interest rates, the price of land and other natural resources, foreign exchange rates, and wages.

TABLE 22.2
Administrative and Market Prices of Cars in Poland

Year	Market Price as a Percentage of Administrative Price		
	Polski Fiat 126	Polski Fiat 125	Polanaise
1980	190	190	180
1981	210	190	170
1982	220	160	150
1983	230	200	180
1984	200	150	140
1985	190	140	140
1986	250	170	180
1987	300	210	280
1988	350	340	470

Source: Compiled by Z. Kapitány for this book on the basis of Z. Kapitány (1989b), interviews, and Polish statistical sources.
Note: In the period examined there was no free market for new cars in Poland. The price of cars sold outside the scope of central distribution was set through auctioning at the so-called automobile exchange.

The economic administration in all reforming countries tries to exempt factor prices from the trend toward deregulation and keep tight control over the setting of them. This effort succeeds to the extent that allocation of the factor concerned remains under the influence of bureaucratic coordination. Wherever there are parallel white, gray, or black markets, factor prices that evade central control inevitably appear as well.

1. *Interest.* The bulk of the credit supply is dispensed through the state-owned banking system, where centrally determined interest rates are imposed. The movements of real interest rates are illustrated in table 22.3, on the example of Poland. The real rate of interest, in spite of intense capital scarcity, is extremely low or even negative. This phenomenon is examined later [→23.4]. All that is worth noting here is that this is almost enough evidence alone for saying that market coordination has not become predominant in these economies. If the real interest rate is negative for a long period, it is unable to control the allocation of investments and gives false information to decision makers for all the decisions that compare present and future revenues and expenditures. The negativity of real interest has a spillover effect great enough in itself to cause serious distortion of the whole price system.

Credit transactions within the private sector are not infrequent, and the interest rate charged on a high proportion of them is substantially

TABLE 22.3
Change of the Real Interest Rate in Poland

Year	Rate of Inflation	Interest Rate	
		Nominal	Real
1982	104.5	29.2	−75.3
1983	21.4	8.2	−13.2
1984	14.8	8.4	−6.4
1985	15.0	7.8	−7.2
1986	17.5	8.2	−9.3
1987	25.3	8.7	−16.6
1988	61.0	22.5	−38.5
1989	244.1	160.0[a]	between −50.0 and −60.0[b]

Source: Data for 1982–88: G. W. Kolodko (1989, p. 16); data for 1989: personal communication by G. W. Kolodko.

[a]Data for December 1989.

[b]Estimate of annual average real interest rate.

different—much higher—than the official rates. But in the reform phase there is still no sign of a privately owned banking system. To the extent that there is a private credit market, its color is "gray" or "black"; private lending is against the law in most countries. The lender cannot rely on a legally enforceable contract. So again there is a parallel price system operating in this sphere, but the extent of the private credit market is insignificant by comparison with the volume of credit transactions conducted by the state-owned banking sector.

2. *Wages.* A parallel wage system develops.[7] There are opportunities for earning far more in the private sector than in the public sector. The income of those who work independently in the formal or even the informal private sector without the assistance of paid employees is not considered here. The analysis covers only paid employees. Their wages too are normally much greater than they would receive from a publicly owned firm for similar work. This is due to a number of contributing factors:

- Private employers try as far as they can to evade their obligations to pay tax, whereas a publicly owned firm would be unable to do so even if it wanted to, as it is strictly controlled. A proportion of the tax saved can be used to pay higher wages.

- The intensity of work is higher in a private operation: employees are more industrious and disciplined in their work, partly because they are earning more and partly because they are more strictly supervised. In addition, administrative costs and other overheads are far lower, so that even if the price were the same as the state price, it would cover not only the private entrepreneur's profit but the higher wages.

- In many cases the private sector is able to set a higher price than a publicly owned firm, which provides further cover for paying higher wages.

- Private entrepreneurs are not bounded by the wage limits imposed by the state, or if they do extend to them, they can easily evade the administrative restrictions. In general the influence of the labor-market mechanism applies in the setting of wages. Since there is a shortage of good, reliable labor, private employers are prepared to pay a wage that will attract the employee to them. The latter may either abandon a job in the public sector or may keep the job and work in the private sector after hours.[8]

---

[7]See R. I. Gábor and G. Kővári (1990).

[8]In the latter case workers are faced with the special problem of how to divide their energies. Frequently they will be sparing with their efforts at the publicly owned firm, reckoning that they will receive smaller payments there anyway. Far more effort is put into the extra work that can be classified under the private sector, because it pays more and because the earnings from it correlate more closely with the effort expended.

On the other hand, everything described earlier in connection with the classical system [→10.5] still applies on the labor market in the public sector:[9] bureaucratic and market coordination make their effects felt simultaneously.[10] The superior organizations set out to control wages in various ways, and they would like to obstruct the tendencies that push up wages. Yet they cannot entirely ward off market effects. The labor market's effect on wages has increased compared with the classical system, normally through the influence of two factors. One was mentioned already: where there is a tendency for the private sector to expand, its increasing labor demand pushes up the wages in state-owned firms and cooperatives too. The other factor is the tendency to deregulation in line with the objectives of market socialism, whereby attempts are made to dismantle one or two of the wage-management obligations of the classical system.

But although the effects of the market become stronger, particularly on the relative wages paid in different trades, jobs, and regions, the average wage level in the public sector remains basically subject to bureaucratic control. The stronger the influence of the bureaucratic mechanism, the greater the gulf that emerges between the wage levels of the private and public sectors.

The macroeconomic consequences of the phenomenon are returned to later [→23.1]. It is worth stopping for a moment here, however, and examining together the two factor prices discussed so far: the interest and wage expenditures in the public sector. According to normative microeconomics, the relative prices of capital and labor should express, more or less, the relative scarcity of the two resources. So if appropriate attention is paid to this price ratio when an investment decision is made, the combination of inputs will tend toward the socially desirable combination of capital and wages. What is the position with this in a reforming socialist economy?

A private artisan employing a handful of people, reaching agreement with employees on the basis of a free labor contract and borrowing privately to obtain labor-saving machinery, is forced to make such a calculation. But a state-owned firm or a cooperative is not obligated to make any such comparison of interest versus wages. For the budget constraint on investment funds is soft; if the calculation is faulty, the firm still survives. In fact, it is not worth heeding the ratio between the two factor prices at all, since it provides no kind of signal of the relative scarcity of capital and labor, any more than it did under the classical system. Both these factor prices of fundamental significance are arbitrary; the numerical proportion between them has no rational economic meaning.

[9]The analysis is concerned only with state-owned and quasi-state-owned firms; the special problems of self-managed firms are not discussed here [→20.3].

[10]On this subject see K. Fazekas and J. Köllő (1990).

3. *Land prices and rents.*[11] For publicly owned land, these are normally set by the local state authorities. For land used by a publicly owned firm or institution, the price or rent is more or less arbitrary.

A proportion of the land (differing according to country) is in private hands, its price or rent being determined by the market. One factor influencing the market price is that expectations of inflation in the reforming countries lead many to invest their savings in real estate as a way to preserve their value. They have good reason for this as there are few other value-retaining forms of investment.

Not infrequently a distorted hybrid of the two kinds of coordination mechanism develops: those who do best are those who obtain a state-rationed plot of land cheaply by personal influence and keep it as value-preserving private property.

4. *Exchange rates.* The central bank retains the right to set exchange rates along with its right to ration foreign exchange. Most reforming countries grossly overvalue their own currencies, which again causes a grave distortion permeating the whole price system.

The black market in foreign exchange, which existed even under the classical system, expands greatly in the reforming countries. The further a country goes with economic and political liberalization and the more open it becomes to the West, the more the parallel foreign exchange market used by the general public broadens. When that is compounded by accelerating inflation, people begin a veritable flight from domestic money. They not only try to invest their savings in convertible currency, but start reckoning the day-to-day transactions in it as well. Table 22.4 compares the official and black-market exchange rates in certain countries.

Of course, product prices and factor prices (including wages) are closely related. The authorities can exert a strong indirect influence on product prices through the factor prices as well. Those devising the reforms aimed at market socialism hoped these centrally determined factor prices would help them to control production indirectly. That hope was not fulfilled.

22.3 The Principles and Practice of State Price Determination and Fiscal Redistribution

This section is confined to examining administrative prices among state-owned firms.[12] Administrative price setting is connected closely with the

[11]This covers the price or rent of land for both agricultural production and other purposes (such as building construction).

[12]The price authorities also try to apply the price-setting principles described below to the sphere of pseudoadministrative prices. Incidentally, there the conflicts between the principles and the discrepancy between the principles and practices are even greater.

TABLE 22.4
Black-Market vs. Official Exchange Rates: International Comparison

	Black-Market Rate per Official Rate of U.S. Dollars (percent)				
Year	China	Hungary	Poland	Soviet Union	Yugoslavia
1985	109.4	137.0	401.0	723.6	111.2
1986	109.1	133.7	442.8	611.8	120.3
1987	120.4	134.8	412.0	915.6	110.9
1988	268.8	156.1	636.8	1,195.0	117.1

Source: International Currency Analysis, Inc. (1990, pp. 426, 620–21, 657–58, 699, 712).
Note: Ratio of black-market rate (national currency per U.S. dollar) and effective official rate at the end of the year, as quoted in source.

handling of the differences between prices and costs. If the difference is positive, in other words, the state-owned firm [→8.2] makes a profit, the treasury siphons off much of the surplus in various taxes. If the firm is in the red, the loss, or a good part of it, is normally made up. In the framework of fiscal redistribution, the income of a state-owned firm is drawn off into the state budget or augmented from it on hundreds of different grounds [→8.6, 21.5].[13] Its role is not reduced even in cases where a reform tendency aimed at attaining market socialism applies.

Under the classical system the authorities keep a range of principles in mind when determining prices, taxes, and subsidies. These need only be listed here, as they have been discussed earlier.[14]

A. Prices should reflect social costs.

B. Prices, taxes, and subsidies should be means by which the economic management encourages producers to perform specific tasks.

C. Prices, taxes, and subsidies should be stable.

D. Prices, taxes, and subsidies should influence the demand from the general public in the way the leadership considers desirable.

E. Prices, taxes, and subsidies should be used for the purpose of income redistribution.

All the principles listed are confirmed in the official documents of the reform; an attempt is made to apply each of them to a varying extent, but as they conflict with each other, none of them can, in fact, be applied consistently. These contradictions alone would ensure that the resulting systems of prices and fiscal redistribution remain arbitrary and ir-

[13]For references, see the notes to section 21.5.
[14]Principles A–E were discussed earlier only in relation to price setting [→8.6, 8.7]. This section extends the analysis to the principles of fiscal redistribution.

rational. But the conflicts among the existing principles can potentially be compounded by the addition of a new one.

F. Prices should assist in producing an equilibrium between supply and demand. According to Lange's model of market socialism, market clearing must become the prime (or even the sole) principle of pricing. But in the event no price office in any reforming country has ever set out to ensure the dominance of principle F, which rarely asserts itself in practice. There are frequent cases of persistent excess demand for some product or other (and much rarer ones of persistent excess supply); even if the price office is aware of such a case, it still does not alter the price.

It is worth referring back here to Oscar Lange's model of socialism, in which the state planning office should have simulated the market and raised or reduced prices according to the signals of excess demand or excess supply it received [→21.1]. No reforming country, not even Lange's Poland, has even conducted an experiment that approaches a realization of this theoretical model. It has not even been set as an objective, for at least two reasons. One is the pressing reason that it conflicts with the other principles of price determination, a high proportion of which follow closely from the official ideology and regulatory practice of the socialist system. The other reason is the technical difficulty of applying it. How could one observe the differences between supply and demand for millions of products? One of the reasons why the market is such an effective mechanism of coordination is that decentralized processes do this automatically.

It is instructive from this point of view to consider a short-lived experiment in Hungary. An attempt was made in the early 1980s to introduce a system of price control designed to adjust some of the domestic prices to world-market prices, using complicated formulas.[15] The experiment failed. On a real market, the export and import prices applying to real foreign trading transactions and the prices valid in trade between domestic producers and users develop in an extremely complex way. The individual interest of each participant is what governs his decision on his demand and supply and the demand and supply prices he offers, and ultimately the private contracts the participants conclude with each other. This lively teamwork cannot be replaced by inert schemes for calculation prescribed by decree.

Assertion of principle F would require prices that react as quickly as possible to the changes in demand and supply. This conflicts with principle C, the requirement of stability, which often, because of the impotence of bureaucratic control, cannot be applied in any other way than by setting rigid prices that remain unchanged for a long period.

---

[15]See B. Csikós-Nagy (1985), R. Hoch (1980), W. Swaan (1990), and L. Zelkó (1981).

The application of principle E (just redistribution of income) must be mentioned separately in connection with the fiscal redistribution affecting the profits of the firms. Those devising the incentive mechanisms for reform economies usually start from the following line of argument: a distinction must be made between the part of the profits that the firm has earned by its good work and the part it has gained without earning it, for instance, by inheriting good equipment from the period before the profit incentive was introduced, by having luck on the market, or by having a favorable price set for its products by the price authority. There is justice, so the argument goes, in siphoning off these unearned profits. In the opposite case, the firm may not be responsible for its losses: it may have inherited poor equipment, suffered bad luck on the market, or had an unfavorable price set for its output by the price authority. In cases like that, there is justice in compensating the firm for its losses. This kind of dispensation of justice through redistribution according to principle E may be called the *compensation principle*.

Now the compensation principle conflicts sharply with the nature of market coordination. The market is not "just"; it rewards good work and good luck in the same way, and it punishes bad work and bad luck alike. But in the long term it accustoms all participants in the market to adjust to the prevailing situation: to use the favorable opportunities to their own advantage and combat bad luck by their own efforts. The compensation principle, on the other hand, teaches a firm that in the long term it is not worth seizing a favorable opportunity, as the profit will only be creamed off. And if the firm has bad luck, the best course is to cry for help from the paternalistic bureaucracy [→tables 21.5, 21.6]. The compensation principle, E, and the equilibrium principle, F, conflict.

Here again one can sense the inseparable connection between the price system and the system of fiscal redistribution; they are almost mirror images of each other. If for some reason the price office sets the price well above the level of "costs plus normal profit," the tax office, in line with the compensation principle, has to draw off the excess income received by the firm. And once that has happened, the tax becomes established; even if the original reason for raising the price should cease to apply, the tax has become "built into" the price. (In the opposite case the subsidy is built into the price.) The link can come about from the opposite direction as well. For some reason or other the tax office levies tax on a product; the price office must take note of this and raise the administrative price accordingly. In the opposite case, if the price office takes advance note of a subsidy, it sets the price below the level of "cost plus normal profit" in the first place.

This brings the line of argument back to the issue of the soft budget constraint. Under the distorted, arbitrary, irrational price system that prevails, profitability fails to reflect the efficiency of a firm's activity. Each fault in the price system provides not only an excuse but a sound reason for fiscal compensation. The trouble is that the web of fiscal compensations makes it impossible to establish a rational price system. Three groups of phenomena—the arbitrary price system, arbitrary fiscal redistribution, and soft budget constraint—enter a vicious circle. They are each other's precursors, and once they have arisen, none can be changed without radically altering the others.

That brings me to the next subject: the scope and limits of comprehensive price reform.

22.4   The Scope and Limits of Price Reforms

Two tendencies are observable in the development of the price system during the processes of reform. One is an integral, spontaneous development toward a system of real market prices. The other is the obstinate survival of the arbitrary, irrational system of administrative and pseudo-administrative prices. The first connects with the extension of private ownership and market coordination, while the second ties in with the survival of public ownership and bureaucratic coordination in the key areas.

Both tendencies prevail, with neither managing to squeeze out the other permanently. There is also interaction between them. On the one hand, many of the bureaucratic hierarchy's institutions and a section of the general public are irritated by the market prices that manage to apply at all. Meanwhile, the arbitrariness of the administrative product and factor prices spills onto the prices of products and factors whose allocation and prices are controlled basically by the market mechanism. If the administrative interest rate, land price, foreign exchange rate, and general level of nominal wages in the public sector, along with the price of many energy sources, raw materials, public services, and so on, are arbitrary and irrational, the distortion is transmitted to the prices developing on the market, since the prices of the former affect the cost calculations of the latter. It is impossible to reach a satisfactory price system in some areas of the economy—those outside the sphere directly controlled by the state—while the basic characteristics of the old price system survive at the heart of the economy, in the state-controlled sphere.

In the sphere tightly controlled by state price determination and fiscal redistribution, the partial changes are made sluggishly, with occasional bursts of activity curbed again by fear of the consequences. There is no evidence at all of this series of partial changes converging on a rational price system that establishes an equilibrium between supply and demand.

Moreover, the effect of each partial price adjustment is cancelled out by inflation. If the price of product group A is raised by 50 percent by a conspicuous central measure, for the sake of more reasonable relative prices, the prices of product groups B, C, and so on rise after a while in response, less conspicuously but no less surely. Nor is the problem just that inflation cancels out the effect of the partial price adjustment. There is a contrary relation as well: under the conditions of widespread shortages, and open or repressed inflationary pressures [→23.5], the efforts to improve the relative prices have inflationary consequences. The effort to change the price relations is always made by raising the price of certain groups of products while the other prices remain proof against downward movement. Taken together, the series of partial price rises pushes up the average price level, that is, fuels inflation.

Nonetheless, it is not that inflationary effect of which the leadership of the reform economy is afraid.[16] They fear the trauma such a comprehensive price reform introduced all at once would cause. Although this might, in fact, release a wave of inflation, it does not necessarily fuel inflation persistently.

The path to comprehensive price reform is strewn with obstacles. Radical change is impeded at the first stage by the vicious circle mentioned already: the product prices, factor prices (including wages), taxes, and subsidies all need altering at once. It looks an impossible task to work all this out on paper in advance. Yet that would have to be done if the change is intended as a reform carried out while broad state determination of prices is retained, and not one accompanied by a general freeing of the market. To remain at a stage of partial and small changes in property relations and the mix of coordination mechanisms while conducting a radical and comprehensive price reform—the two objectives cannot be reconciled.

Radical price reform is also impeded at the second stage by its foreseeable effect on the mood of the general public. Even if the devisers of the price reform decided firmly that they did not want to cut per capita real consumption on average, redistribution on a large scale could not be avoided; there would be winners and losers. In that case the winners would keep quiet while the losers grumble or protest angrily. Those robbed even temporarily of their jobs by the hardening of the budget constraint would lose. So would consumers of certain goods and services subsidized before the reform.

---

[16]Some of the economists devising proposals for reform, far from being daunted by the risk of inflation, consider moderate inflation will be helpful by making the series of partial price adjustment easier to implement.

Here the analysis arrives at one of the basic internal dilemmas of the reform process. The more repressive the system, the more capable it is of making radical economic changes that entail a shock or great commotion. The more the repression eases, the more the elite in power has to reckon with the politically destabilizing effect of mass protest. But the popular discontent will not cease until the economic problems are resolved, and these cannot be resolved until the arbitrary price and fiscal redistribution systems have been abolished.

This is the point at which the process of price reform "seizes up." In every country, those in power choose a policy of small steps and gradual, partial modifications to the administrative prices, even though it leads them nowhere. Socialism on the road to reform proves incapable of bringing order into its price system. Unless that is done, the other changes cannot be wholly successful either. The private sector operates less efficiently than would be socially desirable, among other reasons because the price system emits distorted signals. And the public sector cannot take on a truly market character, because the interaction among price, demand, and supply cannot operate appropriately for several reasons, among them the distortions in the price system. The ultimate conclusion of this chapter needs to be added to the critical analysis provided on the practicability of the ideas of market socialism [→21.10]. Publicly owned firms fail to react responsively to prices and costs. But it is not really worth paying attention to prices in any case, because to a considerable extent they convey false information.

22.5   Preview: Prices under the Postsocialist System

The point of departure for the postsocialist transition is the distorted price system bequeathed by the previous regime. It inherits not only the prices but a dilemma: should it experiment with a comprehensive radical reform coupled with a general liberalization of the market, or should it try a gradual correction of the prices? Is it prepared for the great trauma that accompanies the first alternative? Or, if it decides in favor of the second alternative, will it not lead to a failure similar to the one suffered by the experiments with the reform of socialism: the price distortions are not eliminated, but the partial price reforms and the liberalization measures speed up inflation?

At the time of writing, a transformation corresponding to the first alternative has taken place, or is more or less taking place, in three countries.

The government of Poland undertook a radical economic reform starting on January 1, 1990; one element in it is the freeing of all product prices apart from a few exceptions, so conceding the determination of product prices to the market mechanism. The domestic price system is being induced to pay heed to world market prices through the introduction of internal convertibility and the liberalization of imports. At the same time as product prices are freed, an attempt is being made to apply tough regulations restricting the wages paid by the state sector. As far as the other factor prices are concerned, the interest and foreign exchange rates calculated by the state banking system are still prescribed administratively.

Radical change was taking place in Germany. On July 1, 1990, the West German mark became the legal tender in East Germany. The amalgamation of the two economies forced an adjustment of East German prices to the West German price system.

Czechoslovakia also instituted a comprehensive price liberalization covering the vast majority of products at the beginning of 1991, and this led immediately to a swift reorganization of the price system.

In other countries, such as Hungary, the policy of gradual liberalization of the price system and a step-by-step abolition of price subsidies was continued after the change of system.

Careful observation and comparative analyses of future experiences will reveal what advantages and drawbacks are attached to applying one or other of these alternative policies.

23

Macro Tensions

SEVERAL notable changes in the macro state of the economy can be observed in the socialist countries that undergo a process of reform. The discussion here is confined to just a few of the multitude of phenomena—the ones that tie in closely with the reform tendencies considered in the previous chapters. This is the question that needs answering:

What tensions result on a macroeconomic level when the private sector revives [→19], when the elements of self-management appear [→20], when the changes conceived in terms of market socialism are made to the coordination [→21], and when partial price reforms take place [→22]? The line of argument here does not assume that all four tendencies need to develop to the full before the tensions dealt with in this chapter appear. The decisive factor in this respect is whether or not the economy has shifted appreciably from classical socialism in the direction of market socialism. If it has, one can expect the appearance of the tensions due to be considered here. The other three causes also contribute, and analysis of them augments the explanation, but none of the three is either necessary or sufficient in itself to bring about the macro phenomena to be discussed now. The macro tensions relate closely to the changes that occur in the political field [→18].

These interactions of reform tendencies, resulting in insolvable contradictions, occurred most conspicuously in Poland in the 1980s, and from now on they will be termed the *Polish Syndrome*.[1] Whereas Poland in that period is the ultimate example, symptoms of the syndrome appear, perhaps with varying intensity, in Yugoslavia, Hungary, China, and other countries. The word ''Polish'' is only the term given to the syndrome; examples from other countries also appear in the account of it. At the time of writing, the syndrome is breaking out with exceptional force in the Soviet Union. There may be good reason in the future to rechristen it the Soviet Syndrome, on the grounds that the Soviet case has illustrated the relationships even more clearly than the Polish.[2]

---

[1]The term ''Polish Disease'' was introduced by P. Wiles (1982, p. 7). The combination of quasi-liberalization in the political sphere, the huge strike movement led by Solidarity, and the ambivalent steps toward a market-socialist economy resulted in a situation replete with internal inconsistencies, which already signaled the approach of catastrophe at the time Wiles was writing his article at the beginning of the 1980s.

[2]On the Polish Syndrome, see D. Lipton and J. Sachs (1990); also Z. M. Fallenbuchl (1989), R. Frydman, S. Wellisz, and G. W. Kolodko (1990), S. Gomulka and A. Polonsky,

Here the references are emphatically to tendencies, just as they are in all the previous chapters of part 3. Under certain circumstances, one tendency or another may exist only in a dormant form, but it breaks out when the circumstances change. In one place it may be effectively curbed, while in another there is no effort or even desire to combat it. Although this varies by country and period, this book does not go into the deviations.

I do not offer here a full, comprehensive macroeconomic analysis of the countries concerned. Nor do I undertake to provide a comprehensive assessment of all the macroeconomic consequences of the reform process, comparing all the achievements with all the problems. My sole purpose here is to describe and provide a causal explanation of the Polish Syndrome, in other words, of a typical combination of certain tensions.

23.1 Employment and Wages

Employment. The European reform socialist countries (including the Soviet Union) are marked by full employment and an intense shortage of labor. Open unemployment is negligible in scale.[3] However urgent the need for a radical transformation of the economic structure that would inevitably cause job losses, no such move is made. As a result of the soft budget constraint, the survival not only of the firm, but also of each job is largely guaranteed.

In the Chinese reform economy there is not full employment on a macro level; reserves of labor are still abundant.[4] Although there is no mass unemployment either, there is a substantial concealed surplus of labor in the villages. At the same time, there is a partial shortage of labor in certain branches and occupations, mainly in the cities. One might say the same of the state sector in China as of the European socialist countries: once someone has become the employee of a firm, his or her employment and even workplace is guaranteed.

---

eds. (1990), B. Kaminski (1989), G. W. Kolodko (1989, 1991), G. W. Kolodko, D. Gotz-Kozierkiewicz, and E. Skrzeszewska-Paczek (1990), D. M. Nuti (1990), and J. Rostowski (1989b).

On the Soviet Syndrome see A. Åslund (1989), K. Kagalovsky (1989), and R. I. McKinnon (1990b). There are also comprehensive surveys and appraisals elaborated by international organizations; see, for example, European Community (1990), and the joint study by the IMF, World Bank, OECD, and EBRD commissioned by the Group of Seven (G7) (1990).

[3]An exception was Yugoslavia, which had sizable unemployment [→20.3].

[4]During the process of reform, the hitherto concealed unemployment became more apparent in some Central Asian regions of the Soviet Union as well.

Under the classical system, strict employment plans were laid down. In the reform phase the compulsion behind these ceases or weakens. There is also a considerable loosening of the bureaucratic bonds tying the employee to his or her place of work. The labor shortage, combined with the loosening of these bonds, increases the frequency of cases where an employee leaves a job voluntarily. This threat has to be reckoned with by the leaders of a firm, and it improves the employee's bargaining position in wage disputes.

Wages. Under classical socialism, wage pressure does exist: employees try to push wages up [→10.5]. As the labor shortage grows, the wage pressure increases as well, but it runs up against decided bureaucratic resistance. The topmost leadership wants to keep consumption under control so as to fulfill the tight investment plans and prevent a more intense shortage on the consumer market causing greater dissatisfaction than normal. It firmly demands that all levels of the economic management maintain the wage discipline [→10.3].

Major changes by comparison result from the reform: wage pressure rises and bureaucratic resistance to it weakens. Employees become bolder about speaking out and making demands. Genuine organization begins and strikes take place. That would be impossible under the classical system, where the state would crush the first move, and knowledge of the consequences restrains employees from organizing.

The strongest such movement arose in Poland, where the formation of Solidarity amounted to the concurrent arrival on the political scene of an opposition political movement and an independent union movement representing workers' interests and pursuing their economic demands. Nowhere else did so comprehensive a mass movement emerge, although strikes became frequent in Yugoslavia, for instance, and even in the Soviet Union a sizable strike movement arose after several decades. The organization of the workers is a result and a proof of relaxation of the repression; at the same time it reacts upon it by breaking down the mechanisms of repression.[5]

Strikes and organization of a union nature are not the only measures of a stronger pressure from below by employees. The stance of employees and their representatives becomes more energetic at all discussions on wages, work-norms, and benefits, at shop-floor and firm level, individually or in groups. Merely the awareness of the threat that a strike could occur strengthens a worker's bargaining position and weakens that

---

[5]Under the prevailing relations of political power, the apparatus tries to suppress self-organization among the workers when it feels it has "gone too far." That happened in Poland in 1981 when the army took power and Solidarity was outlawed. But it only lasted a short while; in the end, Solidarity prevailed and formed a government.

of the production manager negotiating with the worker. The situation on the labor market only supplies the economic conditions for altering the bargaining strengths. No less influential on the behavior of the two sides is the change in the political climate.

Another contribution is made by the fact that the middle manager directly facing the employees has less feeling of being supported by higher organizations. This can be ascribed partly to the measures of decentralization. The greater the declared (and to a certain extent the actual) independence of the firm, the more dependent the leader of the firm becomes on the employees [→20.4]. This applies in an extreme form to the firm under self-management, where the employees elect the manager. But similar phenomena arise even where the self-management is only partial or not introduced at all. Popularity among employees becomes far more important to the chief executive of a firm. This again ties in closely with the general trend toward liberalization: the higher leadership is not keen to foist on the workers local bosses who are surrounded by the antipathy or hatred of their subordinates. Now the most immediate route to popularity is a wage increase; that is the simplest way of dispelling any tension.

The leader of a firm is all the more able to resort to it because the demand from above for wage discipline is far less strong. Wherever the command economy ceases wholly or in part, so do the strictly imposed wage plans. Demands for full managerial autonomy in setting wages become stronger.[6] Indirect methods of wage control prove insufficiently effective; firms can easily evade them. The bureaucratic directives on wages are not replaced by any forceful internal incentive. The profit motive fails to encourage a strict curb on costs, including economies on wage-related expenditure, because cover for losses from any increase in wage costs is easily found. (See the phenomenon of soft budget constraint [→21.5].)

Although firms have mainly been mentioned here, similar changes take place in the nonfirm sectors as well. The voices of workers in branches pushed into the background under the classical system become louder. Teachers and health workers come up with wage demands.

The situation where the tendency toward a *runaway of nominal wages* arises has now been outlined. This tendency strengthens as inflation accelerates and the wage-price spiral begins [→23.5]. The phenomenon shows up in the figures in table 23.1: in Poland and Hungary the increase of nominal wages exceeded the growth of productivity most of the time. Nominal wages do not run away because the planners have miscalculated the desirable level of nominal wages; the causes lie in the changed politi-

---

[6]See, for instance, E. Gaidar (1990) on the Soviet Union.

TABLE 23.1

Change of Nominal Wages and Output in Hungary and Poland

| | Average Annual Rate of Change | | | |
| | Hungary | | Poland | |
Year	Output per Capita	Nominal Wages	Output per Capita	Nominal Wages
1971	4.6	4.6	7.2	5.5
1972	1.6	4.6	6.1	6.4
1973	4.8	7.2	6.5	11.5
1974	2.4	6.7	4.9	13.8
1975	1.3	7.4	3.4	22.8
1976	−1.2	5.6	0.6	9.4
1977	5.9	8.1	0.7	7.3
1978	3.0	8.5	3.4	6.3
1979	0.7	6.1	−2.4	9.0
1980	0.1	6.0	−4.4	13.3
1981	0.1	6.3	−7.8	27.3
1982	3.4	6.4	−2.1	51.2
1983	−0.5	4.8	4.5	24.4
1984	1.4	12.2	1.1	16.3
1985	0.2	9.8	2.8	18.8
1986	2.4	7.2	2.2	20.4
1987	0.8	8.2	−2.8	21.1
1988	2.0	—	0.7	81.9
1989	−1.1	18.4	−2.2	286.1

Source: Nominal wages: United Nations (1990a, p. 389); 1971–85, GDP: calculation of P. Mihályi based on R. Summers and A. Heston (1984); 1986–89, GNP: P. Marer et al. (1991, country tables).

cal and social conditions. Bureaucratically imposed wage discipline has weakened, but wage discipline imposed by private ownership, market competition, and unemployment has failed to appear. The reform economy lacks any social force or mechanism to enforce wage discipline.

23.2 Growth and Investment

Growth policy. The policy position on growth under the classical system
is unambiguous: as fast a growth as possible has to be attained in the
medium term, regardless of cost or sacrifice. That expresses itself in the
priorities and methods applied in the strategy of forced growth [→9].

During the process of reform, this clear-cut line gives way to ambivalence and in many cases downright schizophrenia. The leadership half
wants to continue the forced growth, and half inclines to slow it in favor
of quicker results in improving the standard of living and rectifying the
previous disproportions.

Both these conflicting attitudes are backed up by the influence of a
range of factors. The leadership in several countries is distressed that
the growth rate is slowing down, and the sight strengthens further its
determination to combat the declining trend.[7] Among the reasons behind
the deceleration is that the potential for using the earlier extensive methods of attaining fast growth is being exhausted. This primarily relates in
the European socialist countries to the exhaustion of the surplus of labor.[8] The leadership repeatedly announces a policy switch to intensive
methods of growth, the strategy of "the new road of growth," but it
proves impossible to apply under the conditions of the existing economic
system. So at times of acceleration, it tries the most immediate method
of effecting growth centrally, which is to increase investment. That
brings us directly to one of the impulses behind a source of tension to
be treated later: overheating of investment activity.

In the discussion of the motives for moving on from the classical system [→16.1], the first to be mentioned was the slowing of growth, to
which the counterreaction was the "growth at any price" attitude just
outlined. But no less important a motive behind the reform is the dissatisfaction of the general public. Deciding how economic policy should
react to that poses a serious dilemma. On the one hand, the ratio of
accumulation to consumption must be altered in the latter's favor, so
that the growth in real consumption can speed up at last. But on the
other hand, people's living conditions and the quality of life are governed not merely by the flow of goods consumption, but by the capital
accumulated by the sectors directly serving consumption: their stock of

---

[7]The Soviet period of reform began, before the announcement of perestroika and glasnost, with Gorbachev proclaiming an acceleration of growth to be the watchword. Acceleration is identified in a similar way as a central task of the party and government in
Hungary, Poland, and China from time to time.

[8]Other factors forcing a deceleration of growth can contribute. In Hungary, for instance, the main justification given for the slowdown was the alarming growth of foreign
debt.

equipment and buildings. During the decades of forced growth the development of the housing sector, health care, domestic trade and catering, maintenance services, road transport, and other branches of passenger transportation has been neglected. Because of the constant postponement of the necessary development of them, a huge backlog has accumulated. If an attempt is made to start reducing this backlog quickly in the initial phase of the reform, vast investments are required. The housing and transportation sectors are particularly capital-intensive, but any accelerated development of a neglected branch requires investments. So the dilemma seems less and less soluble. A fast and if possible instant increase in consumption requires a fall in the share of investment, while a rise in investment is needed in the sectors directly affecting the quality of life. Within the general dilemma of investment versus consumption, there arises the specific dilemma of how to reallocate the investment among the sectors. The traditional beneficiary from the priorities of the classical system is industry, notably heavy industry. It now feels doubly threatened and applies more pressure to obtain its accustomed investment "allowances." If development of the previously neglected sectors actually begins, for instance, if the pace of housing construction increases, the high capital requirement of this activity draws investment resources from the "internal spiral" directly inducing growth [→9.4, priority 1] and causes the growth rate to slow. Whereupon the dilemma becomes even more acute: should the ratio of investment be reduced at all, and to what sectors should the resources be transferred?

There is no real solution to the problem. It resembles the position individuals get into if mutually contradictory demands are made of them: swings between extremes, heightening tension, and even crisis. There is alternate acceleration and deceleration of investment, and an oscillation can also be seen in the reallocation of investment in favor of the service sectors.[9] But if either of the constituents of this schizophrenic condition does come out on top, it tends to be the element of the ambiguous policy that inclines toward forced growth. This behavior has become a conditioned reflex for the bureaucracy. Implanted in the decision makers by the official ideology they have digested is the feeling that the faster production grows, the stronger the system becomes. The forcing of growth is a spontaneous inclination, whereas the other attitude of making concessions in favor of consumption and investment to serve consumption is suggested more by common sense, possibly backed up by fear at the sight of mass dissatisfaction. Unsurprisingly, the bureaucracy constantly

---

[9]M. Lackó (1984) on the example of Hungary demonstrates how the service sphere's ratio of total investment varies as a function of the favorable or unfavorable development of the overall economic situation.

relapses from the self-compelling, pro–living standards attitude into its natural, pro-growth behavior.

Decentralization of investment decision making. The reform conceived in the spirit of market socialism increases the jurisdiction of firms in public ownership over investment decisions. Although the actual regulations vary among countries and periods, there are two types of amendment fairly typical of the reform economies. One is a rise in the proportion of a firm's profits that it need not hand over to the state budget and can use to finance investment of its own. The other is a reduction within the entirety of the outside resources for investment in subsidies from the state budget that need not be repaid and an increase in bank credits that have to be repaid with interest.[10]

Those devising the reform hoped that the decentralization measures would provide profitability with a large role in investment decision-making. Firms would refrain from investments that threatened to show a loss. That does not happen, however, for several reasons.

In each of the reform economies, the real rate of interest is negative [→22.2].[11] So if for no other reason, excess demand for investment loans is inevitable because the loan always includes a gift element, a grant from the state. The obligation to pay interest does not play an appreciable part in the investment decision in any case. The firm's expansion drive and its investment hunger can still apply unhindered. Should the investment scheme ever lose money, the soft budget constraint will allow it to be covered.

There is a web of connections among the semi-decentralized banks, the superior authorities intervening in the running of the firms, and the leaders of the semi-autonomous firms themselves. The banks are unwilling to reject applications for credit, and if firms fail to meet their debt-servicing obligations, the banks tend to rush to their aid, not taking severe action against them [→23.4].

Understandably, under the circumstances, it is ultimately typical for a market-socialist firm not to be influenced by considerations of profitability when making an investment decision. Table 23.2 provides Hungarian data to show there is no appreciable correlation between investment activity, on the one hand, and profitability before and after the investment action of the investor firm, on the other.

[10]The state capital market and the phenomenon of cross-ownership have been dealt with earlier [→21.7]. In the later stage of reform in Hungary, these new forms gave firms a chance to obtain capital and investment resources.

[11]The long-term nominal interest rate was 0.82 percent in the Soviet Union in 1989. See E. Gaidar (1990, p. 24). This means that loans for investment could be obtained at a highly negative real interest rate.

TABLE 23.2

The Correlation between Profitability and Investment Activity in Hungary

	Average Level of Original Profitability in 1980–82	Average Level of Profitability after Fiscal Redistribution in 1980–82	Average Level of Investment Activity in 1980–82
Average level of original profitability in 1976–79	+0.83	+0.16	−0.06
Average level of profitability after fiscal redistribution in 1976–79	+0.17	+0.07	−0.07
Average level of investment activity in 1976–79	−0.01	−0.06	+0.18

Source: J. Kornai and Á. Matits (1987, p. 115).
Note: Based on data from all Hungarian state-owned firms.

To sum up, under the classical socialist system, the central planning decisions effectively used bureaucratic quotas to limit the amount that could be spent on investment. The reform process loosens the external bureaucratic constraints, but no self-restraint is built in by a profit motive or a fear of financial disaster. The overheating in the investment field typical of the classical system [→ 12.2] tends to increase rather than lessen in the reform economy. Just now I described the schizophrenia in growth policy, where a desire to force growth is coupled with a desire to eliminate the enforcement. The motivation and behavior in the investment sphere induce domination by the former of these two personalities, the tendency to force growth.[12]

23.3 The State Budget and Fiscal Policy

There is normally a substantial budget deficit in the reform economies; in several countries the deficit increases.[13] This can be explained partly by the governments of the countries concerned belatedly admitting to

[12]These phenomena appear sharply in Chinese growth policy. See G. Peebles (1990).

[13]For example, in the Soviet Union the budget deficit was about 2 percent in 1985, and increased to 11 percent by 1988. International Monetary Fund et al. (1990, p. 10).

a budget deficit that has existed before but been concealed from their parliaments and publics by various financial maneuvers.[14] The airing of the problem is one sign that political life is becoming more open.[15] But, of course, it is not solely a question of a secret coming out. The process of reform itself sets in motion or reinforces currents that tend to increase the budget deficit. Budget deficits also occur under other systems, sometimes in a very serious and stubborn form, as the case has been for a long time in the United States. Here again the task is to identify primarily the system-specific characteristics, or, more precisely, those brought about or exacerbated by the process of reforming the socialist system.

1. *Consumer subsidies.* According to the official ideology of classical socialism, the paternalistic state must look after the welfare of its citizens [→4.4]. The official ideology of the reform begins to abandon this notion, and economic policy incorporates an aspiration to pass on the costs of consumption increasingly to the individual, the family, and the household [→19.6]. The state would like to be freed from the promises it made earlier, which have proved impossible to fulfill;[16] it cannot, and no longer aspires so much to, create the impression of operating as a "welfare state." These radical ideological and social-policy changes are reflected also in the fiscal system and elsewhere.

Repeated resolutions are made to dismantle the subsidies on foodstuffs and other articles of mass consumption, and to reduce the budgetary support for the heavily loss-making state housing sector, transportation, and other public amenities. Sometimes these decisions are carried out, which leads to dissatisfaction, milder or sharper protests, strikes, and demonstrations among the masses; sometimes the authorities, seeing the great resistance, are deterred from acting on the resolutions at all. The sections of the population due to be robbed of their acquired rights by such a measure of "depaternalization" greet plans to withdraw existing subsidies with indignation, citing the welfare promises made by so-

---

[14]I. Birman (1980) was the first to draw emphatic attention to the problem of concealment of the Soviet budget deficit.

[15]K. Kagalovsky (1989, p. 450), who was among the first in the Soviet Union to address this issue, put it as follows: "At that time [1986] the greater part of the increase in the budget revenue was financed by a budget deficit, which, according to our estimates, now provides about 15–17 percent of its revenue. In the time of 'glasnost' there is no need to play hide-and-seek any more. It is not enough openly to acknowledge the existence of a budget deficit. It is high time to understand that this problem is of paramount importance. As the existence of a budget deficit was carefully hidden, there is no clear view about its influence on the economy in the Soviet literature."

[16]As mentioned before, the central budget in China encompassed lower welfare spending than in the Soviet Union and Eastern Europe, even under the classical system. Part of the housing, health, and pension expenditure was passed on to the firms in the first place, while the rest (notably in the villages) is still borne by the family.

cialism. Certain measures weigh to a tragic extent on the poorest and most disadvantaged in society—the very groups to whom the egalitarian measures of the classical system brought a modicum of relief at the time: subsidized food, articles of mass consumption, public amenities, housing, and medical care.[17] On some occasions the government tries to compensate for the reduction in price subsidies by granting money benefits. In that case, of course, the budget is relieved only in part of the burden of the subsidies that have been abolished.

Certainly, the amount of subsidy that remains is a heavy item on the expenditure side of the budget.

2. *Subsidies for loss-making firms in public ownership*. The running away of nominal wages and the higher prices for other inputs produces a rise in costs, while the pricing authorities try to block rises in output prices. This, along with many other kinds of distortion of the price system and several additional factors undermining efficiency, leads to a situation in which a high proportion of state-owned firms make regular losses [→tables 21.5, 21.6]. A growth of real output in the loss-making sphere concurrently increases the drain on the budget.

Ambivalence on the issue is found at all levels of the bureaucracy. Repeated pledges are made to wind up loss-making firms, yet in almost every case the threatened firm is reprieved with state subsidies after all.[18] One of the main explanations for the rising pressure on the budget is the softness of the budget constraint.

3. *Export subsidies*. The top leaders of the economy want to encourage exports, primarily those that produce a hard-currency income. Once the economy's trade and current-account balances deteriorate and foreign debt becomes a more serious problem [→23.6–7], the economic policy objective is to raise exports at any price. Subsidization of exports places an ever increasing burden on the budget.[19]

4. *State investment projects*. The overheating of the investment sphere has been discussed in the previous section; all that needs pointing out here are the budgetary consequences of it. Although the reform embraces

[17]The withdrawal of subsidies harms the middle and upper layers of society as well. In some respects the dividing line is not between "poor" and "rich" but between beneficiaries and nonbeneficiaries of specific allowances (e.g., between tenants of cheap, state-subsidized, state-owned housing and owners of apartments and houses built at great expense from their own scarce resources). So privileged groups too may oppose the abolition of certain subsidies.

[18]In Poland, for instance, subsidization of the state sector decreased very slowly: in 1982 it accounted for 47 percent of budget expenditure, and the proportion was still 38 percent in 1985. See Z. M. Fallenbuchl (1988, p. 126).

[19]Points 2 and 3 partly overlap. In some cases a firm starts to make a loss because it is forced to supply exports when the price is unfavorable.

a sharp reduction in the proportion of investment projects financed out of state budget, investment-hungry firms continue to try to squeeze as large a contribution out of the budget as possible.

The large share of subsidies and state-financed investment in governmental expenditures is demonstrated in table 23.3.

5. *Expenditure on the bureaucratic apparatus and the armed forces.* A succession of resolutions are made to reduce the apparatus of the party, the mass organizations, and the administration of the state, but little comes out of the decisions: each institution in the apparatus clings to its existence and its staffing level. If one organization should be dismantled after all, another grows instead. So no contribution to reducing budgetary spending comes from this source.

No satisfactory survey can be made of spending on the armed forces, since the published figures fail to show the size of the expenditure

TABLE 23.3

Budgetary Expenditure on Investment and Subsidies in a Few Socialist Countries

	Investment	Subsidy	Investment	Subsidy
	(percent of GDP)		*(percent of total budgetary expenditure)*	
Hungary				
1970	11.2	26.2	21.3	49.7
1980	9.6	27.9	16.3	47.1
1987	3.5	18.4	6.5	33.8
Poland				
1982	4.8	20.5	9.1	39.0
1988	5.5	15.1	11.2	31.1
Soviet Union				
1985	8.2	8.7	16.5	17.5
1989	8.9	9.3	17.1	17.9
Vietnam				
1984	5.9	7.5	23.1	29.5
1988	5.6	8.2	20.3	30.0

Source: Hungary: L. Muraközy (1989, pp. 105, 113, 115); *Poland:* D. M. Nuti (1990, p. 174); *Soviet Union:* International Monetary Fund et al. (1990, p. 10); *Vietnam:* D. Gotz-Kozierkiewicz and G. W. Kolodko (1990, p. 12).

clearly.[20] According to Western strategic experts, the military spending of the Soviet Union, China, and other reforming countries was stagnant or inclining to fall at the end of the 1980s. Even if this were so, the demand from the armed forces remains a constant source of tension on the budget.

6. *Servicing of foreign debt.* In the course of the reform, the inclination to become indebted to foreign creditors increases [→23.6]. Several countries are obliged to raise credit on steadily worsening terms. Debt servicing (repayments due and interest) comes to be a big, and in many countries increasing, burden on the budget.

The tendencies mentioned under points 1–6 are all connected with budget expenditure. Let us turn to the tendencies on the revenue side.

7. *Turnover tax.* This is the main source of tax revenue under the classical system. Collection is simple under the system's conditions, when almost all turnover is channeled through the state trading system, which can be easily checked. Under the reform system this form of taxation becomes far more problematic, because a sizable proportion of the turnover is transferred to the private sector, which is more difficult, or practically impossible, to control.[21]

8. *Tax revenues from firms and local authorities.* Decentralization raises the proportion of a firm's profit it can retain instead of passing it on to the budget. This is a major achievement from the point of view of increasing the firm's sphere of authority, but it concurrently reduces the revenue side of the state budget substantially. A similar change takes place with local authorities: they too can retain more of the taxes gathered in their areas. None of this would cause a problem if the decentralization of expenditure and revenue went hand in hand. But if the latter

---

[20]In May 1989, Gorbachev announced that military spending amounted to 77.3 billion rubles (*Pravda,* May 31, 1989), that is, 8.8 percent of GNP. That was twice as high as previously announced, although still lower than American estimates of 15 percent.

[21]Wage-related taxes exist under the classical system as well, but the public-sector employers deduct them automatically. Citizens do not notice they are paying tax, as both the turnover and wage-related taxes are gathered behind their backs. As part of the reform process, attempts are made to introduce income tax after the Western pattern. The first country to apply it in practice was Hungary.

The new Hungarian tax system caused a variety of tensions. Although one of its proclaimed purposes was to overcome injustices in the distribution of income, it failed to do so. It was not coupled with a negative income tax, and it did not help those in difficult financial circumstances, some of whom were worse off, in fact, than before. Yet it failed to cream off the incomes of high earners either. Many of those unable or unwilling to disguise their earnings preferred to accept less work, enter into fewer profitable undertakings, or abandon those they have pursued before. Thus, the tax acted as a brake on effort and performance, and so on supply. Others channeled previously open activity into the "gray" or "black" spheres, which the tax authorities could not control [→19.5].

progresses faster than the former, the process contributes to the budget deficit.

9. *The effect of inflation*. The problems of inflation are discussed later; only the effect the inflationary process has on the budget needs to be noted here.[22] When inflation begins to increase, a difference usually appears between the rates of increase in budgetary expenditure and revenue. The payment and collection of taxes takes time, so that revenue growth falls behind expenditure growth. This is exacerbated by the negative rate of real interest: even if interest is charged on late tax payments, it does not compensate for the loss of value caused by inflation.

Although the list cannot be claimed to be complete, nine factors that tend to maintain or increase the budget deficit have been mentioned. The economic authorities fail to respond to these difficulties with a carefully elaborated fiscal policy. A long time goes by before the leadership even grasps the magnitude of the problem. The classical system's bureaucracy has grown used to all the essential issues being decided by planning the physical volumes of input and output. The only other factor of any importance is the quantity of consumer goods absorbed at the fixed consumer prices by the money in the hands of the population. The financial processes are unimportant, and little attention needs to be paid to them. But under the reform system, the problems are suddenly joined by a phenomenon like the budget deficit. Having learned the art of physical planning and direct bureaucratic control—running a single, nationwide "factory"—the bureaucracy reacts in a bungling, dilettantish way to the fiscal problems (and, as will be seen, in a similar way to the monetary problems).

There are indications of haste: improvised measures are introduced;[23] often a regulation just announced is swiftly withdrawn again. When the government finally appreciates the dangers of the budget deficit, it exhibits a kind of "budgetary greed." Both firms and households get the impression that the administrators of public finance are seizing the smallest opportunities of raising extra revenue or ridding themselves of an item of spending regardless of the political and social consequences or the ability of those affected to bear the brunt.

Although one of the aims of the reform is to cut down the bureaucracy, the staff of the financial apparatus grows, more and more fiscal measures are taken, and the system of taxes and subsidies becomes ever

----

[22]The opposite effect is no less important: the role the budget deficit plays in generating inflation [→23.5–6].

[23]A characteristic example of this was the introduction of anti-alcohol measures not long after Gorbachev came to power. These did not help to combat alcoholism; they encouraged illegal home distilling on a mass scale and so caused a huge loss of income to the treasury.

more complex. The fiscal apparatus in the reforming countries becomes one of the bureaucracy's most influential branches.

What coordination mechanisms are at work in the institutions dealing with public finance? After the state budget has been drawn up and passed by the legislature, there is bureaucratic coordination of its implementation under any system; taxes are gathered and payments are made by administrative means. But budgetary decision making is another matter; the mechanism for that is system-specific.

Under a parliamentary political structure, all items of expenditure and revenue in the budget are decided upon ultimately through self-governing mechanism. The statement can also be reversed: true self-government can apply within a community only if the common expenditure and revenue are decided upon by the whole community or a freely elected body representing it.

The self-governing mechanism only applies ostensibly in a classical socialist economy. Under the given power structure, the decisions on the state budget are made ultimately by the same bureaucratic hierarchy (or, more precisely, the top level of it) that goes on to apply the decisions. By comparison, the element of self-government, including the role of parliament, increases somewhat under the reform system.[24] Nonetheless, all the basic guidelines of the budget are still decided at the top of the bureaucracy, and in this respect little has changed. The budget deficit therefore remains an issue dealt with at most by a few initiates and of scarcely any concern to the general public.

23.4   The Credit System and Monetary Policy

Institutions. What are the coordination mechanisms, or combination of them, that apply in the banking system of the reform economy?[25] This is a far harder question than the similar question put just now about the fiscal system. As for the banking system under modern capitalism, it is coordinated by a specific combination of bureaucracy and the market.

---

[24]There are clearly recognizable signs of when a parliament begins to take its responsibility for passing the budget seriously: when a real debate based on accurate figures is held on the expenditure on the armed forces, on budgetary support for the maintenance of the party and mass organizations, and on the official apparatus, and when views substantially different from those in the government's presentation are heard in the debate. This signifies that the system has reached the borderline of change in political structure at which revolutionary transformation begins.

[25]Detailed descriptions can be found in the following works: *Yugoslavia:* L. D. Tyson (1980), S. J. Gedeon (1985–86, 1987); *Hungary:* M. Tardos (1989) and I. Székely (1990); *China:* L. Wulf (1985), F. Levy et al. (1988), and X. Zhou and L. Zhu (1987).

The central bank is state owned, and the commercial banks and other financial institutions operating on commercial principles are governed by numerous state regulations. The banking system of a reform economy looks similar at first sight. The central influence of the state—the vertical link—is undeniably strong, but the impression, nonetheless, is that the managers and officials here are dealing with money; bank deposits come into being, loans are made, current accounts are run, checks and transfers are written, interest is calculated, bonds and shares are handled, and so on. All these indicate commercial transactions, horizontal relations, and "business," in other words, the presence of market coordination.

This impression is reinforced by the structural changes undergone by the banking system during the process of reform. Tendencies toward decentralization appear. Some of them are connected with the growth of regional autonomy;[26] separate banks are set up for each region. The rest are directed at replacing the earlier monobank with a *two-level banking system,* with the central bank operating as the upper tier and mutually independent commercial banks as the lower. So the impression is given that the decentralization has been accompanied by the appearance of competition among the commercial banks.[27]

But there appears to be a greater "marketization" than actually applies. To back that statement, one has to look more closely at the property relations of the banks in the reform economy, at the motivations of their leaders, and at their relations with the rest of the participants in the system.

If one examines the activity of a Yugoslav or Chinese regional bank or a Hungarian commercial bank, it emerges that no one in it has a direct, unqualified interest in profit. A publicly owned bank, like any other publicly owned firm in a socialist economy, belongs to everyone and no one. The managers are well paid, but their fortunes are not tied to the fortunes of the bank. They may be a little less indifferent to the bank's profit than bankers under the classical system, but one can say that basic control over their careers is in the hands of the bureaucracy, and they do not have to win and retain the confidence of real owners. So they frequently have to give way to bureaucratic pressure, to the wishes of the central and regional organizations of the state and the party, and of the heads of the most influential firms.

Although there are noteworthy differences, it is not possible here to discuss separately the situation in which the earlier classical monobank

---

[26]Yugoslavia and China made particularly important changes by building up a network of republican and provincial banks respectively.

[27]Hungary in 1988–89 was the first country to institute a two-level banking system completely. See M. Tardos (1989).

survives under the conditions of the reform economy and the situation in which partial decentralization has occurred.[28] In what follows, the expressions "bank" and "banking system" refer to the whole banking sector unless otherwise stated.

Interest, in a true credit system, is the price of credit. The lender extends a loan so as to profit by the transaction through the interest; the borrower makes a demand for credit dependent on whether the use of the loan will be worth as much as the interest to be paid. On a real credit market, a change of a fourth of a percentage point in the real rate of interest causes reactions in business.[29] The real rate of interest in the reform economies, on the other hand, is persistently and purposely negative [→23.2]. This is where it emerges that the banking system in a reform economy is fundamentally a bureau for allocating credit and collecting and storing money, not a network of institutions running on commercial, market principles.

Where the real interest rate is negative, anyone who takes up a loan from the bank can pocket a small donation from the state. Every practical argument speaks in favor of getting as deeply in debt as possible.[30] Credit demand from households, and particularly from the public sector, constantly exceeds the credit supply by a wide margin.[31] The interest rate fails to act as a balance in the allocation of credit.[32] The bank does not "sell" credit along commercial lines in the hope of making a profit through the interest; it allocates credit in accordance with noncommercial, bureaucratic criteria. Nor is it just a matter of clear, open criteria declared in advance; other factors—lobbying, vertical bargaining, personal connections, and corruption—are at work behind the scenes.

Clarification of the participants' behavior and the forces behind that behavior is an aid to understanding the monetary tensions that arise in

[28]When a partial decentralization has taken place, it becomes a more cumbersome process for the central bank to impose its ideas than it was when it simply had to order a branch of its own to perform some transaction. Under the conditions prevailing, this tends to increase the trend to be discussed below, namely, the running away of credit supply.

[29]The study by É. Várhegyi (1990a) demonstrates on the basis of an econometric analysis that the demand for credit from state-owned firms in the Hungarian reform economy is quite unresponsive to changes in the real rate of interest.

[30]This may also occur in a capitalist market economy in times of hyperinflation. There, in fact, it is a sign that the market coordination is disintegrating.

[31]The same phenomenon can be seen here as was discussed in connection with the market for goods [→11.2]: the demand adjusts to the expected supply. The firms have numerous informal links with the banks and do not submit credit applications with no chance of acceptance in the first place. So although the demand constantly and appreciably exceeds the supply, the sum of the excess applications for credit is always finite and not absurd in size. See the convincing study by M. Lackó (1989) on this.

[32]Without the balancing role of interest, it would be unjustified to use the term "credit market."

the reform economy. The constant excess of credit demand over credit supply is not the only thing the suppliers of credit have to contend with, since the power pressure and use of personal connections and influence tend to increase the credit supply.[33] Meanwhile, there is no proprietorial interest, real profit motive, or fear of business failure of any kind to restrict the credit supply. At most the central bank tries to stop, or at least curb, the unbridled increase in the credit supply by administrative means, but it has little success, because it is hard (if not impossible) to restrain the credit-allocating activities of the institutions dealing with commercial loans in the absence of an internal incentive for them to do so.

The capitalist credit system has had centuries of practical experience in which to evolve steadily a complex mechanism for coordinating the work of the central, state-owned bank with that of the largely privately owned commercial banks and other mediatory financial institutions, whose autonomy is not unlimited. The resulting development is a specific combination of strict legal stipulations (bureaucratic coordination), profit-based private contracts (market coordination), and impeccable business conduct (ethical coordination), which provides the central bank with effective means of influencing the running of the commercial banks.[34] There is no way this organically developed, finely tuned mechanism of control resting on a specific set of property relations and power structure can be "duplicated" and applied all of a sudden to the nationalized socialist banking system by central command.

So far the discussion has concerned credit transactions within the banking system. Extending credit outside the frames of the monobank system is strictly forbidden under the classical system; firms are not allowed to extend each other credit. This changes radically under the reform system, where the volume of commercial credit between firms steadily increases. Only a minority of this is based on voluntary credit agreements between two firms; the majority consists of forced credit: the buyer-firm simply does not pay the seller-firm's bill. Often the omission is because the former has not been paid by its own buyer. It may use a

---

[33]One high-ranking Yugoslav bank manager told me in a private conversation that more than once the prime minister of the republic (i.e., the region) or another member of the regional cabinet had intervened personally to get the credit application of some firm or other accepted. He had felt that it was impossible to deny so insistent a request.

[34]This mechanism, by the way, works with a lot of errors and frictions, and in more than one case it has proved unable to avert a grave financial catastrophe. The financial sector of a modern capitalist economy is the sphere where symptoms of the soft budget-constraint syndrome most commonly appear. The most recent alarming example of this in the United States has been the collapse of the savings and loan associations and the bail-outs carried out at the budget's expense, at dreadful cost to the taxpayers.

promissory note from a firm owing it money as a means of debt settlement. The postponement of payment and the chain of forced loans can bring a liquidity crisis upon a high proportion of the production sector. In the event, the banking system has to intervene from time to time, extending bank credit to make the insolvent chain of firms solvent again. But in the meantime, promissory notes flow around the firm sector as "quasi-money," preventing the banking system from keeping a real hold on the money supply.[35]

Monetary policy. The central bank cannot develop a monetary policy of its own in the reform socialist economy, any more than it could under the classical system. It too is subject to bureaucratic pressure; it is part of the central administration, not an independent body; its leadership is appointed by the highest leaders of the party and state. The bank has a duty to subordinate its activity to central control.

Here the problem of the budget deficit [→23.3] must be returned to. The deficit obviously has to be funded by credit. The desirable course from the economic point of view would be for firms, public bodies, and households to extend credit to the state voluntarily. The main form this takes in a capitalist economy is for these creditors to buy interest-bearing state bonds as an investment. This method is not used or hardly used at all in the reforming socialist countries. Instead, the central bank lends the money to the budget, a credit maneuver that is concealed from the public for a long time, for good reason. For it becomes clear at this point that the budget deficit is ultimately covered by the lenient central bank simply printing money, and that is one of the main forces behind the inflationary process.

The earlier remarks about the inexpert conduct of fiscal policy apply here as well. Formulation and implementation of monetary policy is a complex craft, and there has been no opportunity to learn it under the classical system. Grave mistakes are frequent.

Monetary policy during the process of reform vacillates between two forms of behavior: sometimes it is restrictive and tight, and sometimes it is permissive and slack. It sometimes resists and sometimes gives in to the pressures from above and below to extend as much credit as possible. But even when a general policy of monetary restriction is laid down, there are still plenty of gaps in it. If the political-bureaucratic pressure

---

[35]A graphic picture of this emerges from the writings of L. D. Tyson (1977), S. J. Gedeon (1987), and É. Várhegyi (1989, 1990b) [→21.7]. For example, in Hungary the total magnitude of forced interfirm credit was more than one-third of total outstanding short-term credit in 1989. Information communicated by É. Várhegyi.

The mass spread of forced loans between firms is linked, among other things, with what was said earlier: this is a kind of economy in which a respect for horizontal contracts and a firm economic, legal, and ethical basis behind contracts has failed to emerge.

is very strong, the banking system cannot resist it and permits credits even though they are incompatible with a consistent implementation of its restrictive policy.

Of these two opposing kinds of behavior, permissiveness usually prevails. Certainly, too much credit, and ultimately too much money, enters the economy during the permissive phases, creating too great a demand by comparison with the supply available.

23.5 Shortage and Inflation: Internal Economic Relations

An attempt must now be made to make a comprehensive review of the macro tensions in the reform economy and their combined effects. This is done in two stages. This section begins by ignoring the external economic relations and the effects of foreign trade and foreign credit on each country and focusing exclusively on the domestic relations. The following two sections draw the problems of foreign trade and foreign credit into the analysis.

The starting point is the subject matter of chapters 11 and 12: shortage and inflation under the classical socialist system. Most of the conclusions drawn there apply in the same way to an economy undergoing the process of reform and are not repeated in what follows. The main aim is to examine how much the picture drawn there changes as a result of the reforms.

The system moves away from its earlier normal state; the runaway of demand and build-up of macro excess demand increase. All the mechanisms working to stimulate demand were operating under the classical system, but bureaucratic brakes and barriers tended to constrain them. These constraints are weakened as a result of the reforms aimed at market socialism. The pressure for wage increases tends to break through, which fuels the demand from households. The firms' hunger for investment becomes greater, which raises demand from the firm sector. The inducements to increase excessively the money supply become more forceful. Here one must mention especially the budget deficit, which the central bank finances by issuing more money.

The macro excess demand under the classical system tends to elicit a price-raising tendency, but this is effectively opposed by the administrative setting of prices. In this connection the reform economy has the following alternatives:

1. It can retain the dominance of administrative pricing and resist the pressure for price rises. In that case forced saving begins, and the accumulation of unspent and unspendable money, that is, "monetary overhang," is formed. *Repressed inflation* develops. This was taking place in its most extreme form in the Soviet Union in 1990–91.

2. Some or all of the administrative shackles on price setting can be removed [→22.1, 22.4]. The price-raising forces are released and the overall price level starts to move. The repressed inflation is converted partly or wholly into *open inflation*. This took place with dramatic force in Poland, Yugoslavia, and Vietnam, and has occurred in Hungary to an appreciable, though far less drastic, extent. Data on the outbreak of open inflation can be found in table 23.4.

The profit motive of firms is not strong enough to become the main motive behind decisions, but it is not entirely ineffectual. A profit is an advantage to a firm; begging from door to door for subsidies, tax breaks, and soft loans is unpleasant. So the firm is strongly motivated to do all it can to raise its prices. The inducement to do so is much greater than it was under the classical system, when the profit plan played a very subordinate part in the list of targets and it was not worth trying to fulfill it.

Central price policy is intended to adjust the relative prices, in two ways. On the one hand, administrative prices are raised centrally in succession. On the other, the state-controlled price of first one and then another good or service is freed, giving rein to the pressure for a price increase. Whether either method or any combination of the two is used, the succession of partial price rises fails to attain its original objective of adjusting relative prices. At the same time, this course becomes one of the driving forces behind the general, continual rise in the price level.

3. Although an inflationary rise in price takes place, it is neither rapid nor widespread enough to restore the equilibrium between macro demand and macro supply. Any swift development of equilibrium prices for products is impeded by a variety of constraints and rigidities. In addition, a publicly owned firm is still not really responsive to prices, so that its demand for inputs is not checked by the rising prices of them. There comes about a situation in which open inflation and shortage exist side by side. The most extreme example of such a concurrent worsening of inflation and shortage was Poland, which is why the group of phenomena discussed in this chapter has been labeled the Polish Syndrome.

Alternatives 1 and 2 are never applied in their pure form; all one can say is that repressed inflation and shortage are dominant in some countries, and open inflation in others. Alternative 3, the coexistence of inflation and shortage, is perceptible in all reform economies, at least in traces, and on occasions in a form where certain sectors show signs of intense shortage while the economy as a whole is swamped by inflation.

The reform pays itself out for its own ambivalence. The inducements to a runaway of demand are not eliminated (notably the soft budget constraint); moreover, new ones are added, such as the stronger pressure

TABLE 23.4
Rate of Inflation in Reform Socialist Countries

Period	China	Hungary	Poland	Yugoslavia	Vietnam
1960–80	—	3.7	5.0	—	—
1965–80	0.0	2.6	—	15.3	—
1966–70	—	—	—	—	2.3
1971–75	—	—	—	—	0.7
1976–80	—	—	—	—	21.2
1980	6.0	9.1	9.1	—	—
1981	2.4	4.6	24.4	46	—
1982	1.9	6.9	101.5	30	—
1983	1.5	7.3	23.0	39	74[a]
1984	2.8	8.3	15.7	57	—
1985	8.8	7.0	14.4	76	—
1986	6.0	5.3	18.0	88	487
1987	7.3	8.6	25.3	118	316
1988	18.5	15.5	61.3	199	308
1989	17.8	17.0	244.1	1,256	96

Source: Row 1: F. L. Pryor (1985, p. 123); row 2: *World Development Report* (1988, pp. 222–23); *China:* 1980–89, T. Sicular (1990, table 1); *Hungary:* 1980–86, M. Bleaney (1988, p. 122), 1987–89, Központi Statisztikai Hivatal (Central Statistical Office, Budapest) (1990, p. 223); *Poland:* 1980–86, M. Bleaney (1988, p. 122), 1987–89, G. W. Kolodko, D. Kotz-Kozierkiewicz, and E. Skrzeszewska-Paczek (1990, p. 47); *Yugoslavia and Vietnam:* G. W. Kolodko, D. Kotz-Kozierkiewicz, and E. Skrzeszewska-Paczek (1990, pp. 23, 77, 79).
[a]Average of the period 1981–85.

on wages. Meanwhile, prices are more or less liberalized. So the price and wage stability of the classical system is destroyed without the chronic shortage coming to an end. In fact, if the reform measures are particularly ill-conceived (as in Poland or the Soviet Union), both the inflation and shortage get worse and worse.

The price rises induce employees to struggle more aggressively for higher wages.[36] The rise in input prices and wages increases costs, which

---

[36]Poland went furthest in this respect. Solidarity, before it came to power, managed to get wages indexed; price rises were followed automatically by wage rises, making it inevitable that inflation would speed up and take off as hyperinflation.

stimulates a further price increase. The well-known *inflationary spiral* has come about: price rises lead to rises in wages and other costs, which lead to price rises, and so on. In this case it is compounded by the self-reproducing mechanism of shortage. The sight of the symptoms of shortages causes stockpiling; both firms and households try to keep reserve stocks of articles in short supply.[37] The phenomenon is presented in table 23.5, which has a similar structure to table 11.7, and shows how the proportion of input inventories to output inventories grows as a result of shortage. This proportion is three to four times higher under the classical socialist system than it is in a capitalist economy, but in the Soviet Union, during the reform period, it reached almost six times the size of the proportion under capitalism.

The two kinds of spiral may intertwine. Although the partial price increases do not block off the shortage-reproducing mechanism, the instances of shortage provide a constant cause and excuse for raising prices, which helps to accelerate inflation. In reverse, the likelihood of price rises and the expectation of inflation induce stockpiling, which worsens the shortage. The intertwining of the two dynamic processes, each dangerous in itself, can push the economy into crisis.[38]

The new sources of tension produced by the move away from the classical system have been reviewed briefly along with their mutual effects. All that needs adding is that a new countertendency arises out of the move away from the classical system to combat the tendencies increasing the tension. As the private sector develops, it becomes capable of supplying a greater and greater part of the demand unsatisfied by the supply from the public sector, which enhances the adaptability of the whole economy. The revival of the private sector can also bring a demand-

---

The legitimacy and political credibility of the last reform-socialist government were so shaken that it could not withstand the demand for wage indexation. Everything stated in this book about the increase in the upward pressure on wages and the weakening of the administrative resistance to it took place in an extreme form.

The situation changed when Poland passed over into the postsocialist phase. Solidarity took over the government and the accompanying economic responsibility. Whereupon it performed a U-turn on the wage indexation it had previously fought for. Shortly afterward it initiated strict wage control by the state.

[37]Although alternative 1—open inflation—was dominant in Yugoslavia, instances of shortage occurred there as well. There was a notable piling of stocks, inspired partly by fear of a shortage of imported products and partly by inflationary expectations. See J. H. Gapinski, B. Skegro, and T. W. Zuehlke (1987) and J. P. Burkett (1989).

[38]The shortage of consumer goods became particularly acute in the Soviet Union. Taking a selection of almost a thousand kinds of foodstuffs and clothing and household articles, the finding was that only 11 percent were readily and regularly available. One institute found in a poll of consumers that over 70 percent of respondents would buy more meat, meat products, fruit, vegetables, and cheese if the supply were greater. See A. Voronov (1990, p. 27) and T. M. Boiko (1990, p. 85).

TABLE 23.5
Change of the Input and Output Stock Ratio in the Soviet Union

	Period	Input–Output Stock Ratio
Soviet Union	1980	4.8
	1981	4.9
	1982	4.6
	1983	4.6
	1984	4.7
	1985	4.7
	1986	5.2
	1987	5.6
	1988	5.8
	1989	6.2
Capitalist countries		
Australia	Average	1.4
Canada	for	0.9
United States	1981–85	1.0
West Germany		0.8

Source: A. Åslund (1991, p. 27) for the Soviet data and table 11.7 for the data on capitalist countries.

supply equilibrium closer on the macro level. The more extensive the private sector becomes and the fewer the administrative obstacles to it setting a market-clearing price, the bigger the role it can play in absorbing the excess demand.

23.6   Foreign Trade and Foreign Debt

A process of running into debt to the capitalist countries begins in all the reform economies; the size of the debt reaches serious proportions in several countries.[39] This becomes one of the most distressing macro tensions.

[39]A few examples from the wide range of literature on the indebtedness of the socialist countries are W. Malecki and G. W. Kolodko (1990), R. McKinnon (1990b), and I. Zloch-Christy (1987).

Any oversimplified, one-sided explanation for the causes of this must be avoided. A range of capitalist countries, including several Latin American economies, have become deeply indebted in the last decade and a half. Yet the same result—indebtedness—may have arisen from a different set of causes.

One cause common to all the processes of debt accumulation is the willingness of creditors in the 1970s and 1980s to distribute loans freely. It is not for this book to examine the reasons behind this willingness. But, certainly, when the great international credit-extending campaign began, it was thought that the socialist countries would prove good debtors. After all, they had always been punctual and reliable in the past, when the volume of credit extended to the socialist countries was still small (as the West was unwilling to lend and the socialist countries were unwilling to borrow).

So the sources of credit flowed abundantly, and that was a big temptation. But why was the temptation not resisted by the countries examined here? What needs to be decided is whether there is a connection between the indebtedness and the changes brought about by the reforms in the socialist economy. The propensity to indebtedness was already built into the classical system [→14.3], but by and large there was a will and an ability to resist it. That resistance has now weakened or broken down altogether.

One explanation for the change is an alteration in foreign policy. The classical system secludes itself from the capitalist outside world; it sees it as hostile and is afraid of it. It also fears the inciting influence that closer ties may have on its own citizens, through closer acquaintance with life in the developed capitalist countries and comparisons with the domestic conditions there. One major political element in the reform process is partial abandonment of this seclusion, or, to use the Chinese reform propagandists' term, an opening up to the West.

This opening up includes an intention of strengthening trading and financial ties with the capitalist countries. There is confidence that the following favorable reciprocal effects will be felt:

■ Among the expectations from Western imports and the other forms of economic cooperation are an acquaintance with the technology and organization and management methods of the developed capitalist countries and an extensive inflow of production know-how.

■ Western loans are seen as a means of expanding foreign trade and of supplementing domestic sources of finance. Foreign credit offers a flexible, easily handled outside source from which to finance straight away the import transactions desired so strongly.

■ The imports from the capitalist markets help to expand exports to the same markets, which means the imports can be paid for continuously. Long-term foreign loans are seen as useful for installing export capacity that will pay for itself rapidly, allowing both repayment of the loans and a further expansion of imports.

■ All these favorable reciprocal effects will be reinforced by the decentralizing reforms conducted in terms of market socialism. The greater autonomy of firms will include the authority to enter into direct relations with foreign sellers and buyers, bypassing the foreign trading firms, which have had monopoly rights in the past. In any case, their greater independence will allow them to adapt more flexibly to external markets, on the import and export sides.

Few of these expectations are fulfilled. At the same time, negative trends appear, and the interactions of them result in vicious circles that lead ultimately to the development and then the acceleration of a process of debt accumulation.

The failure manifests itself mainly in the fact that the reform economy does not manage to break through with its exports into the capitalist markets, while there is rising pressure from below for an increase in imports from those markets. Previous chapters have discussed the reason why the semibureaucratic, semimarket reform economy is insufficiently efficient and flexible. All that needs adding here to those features already identified is what expressly concerns foreign trade.

Even though the production firms partially receive independent foreign trading rights, there is still no strong incentive for them to export more effectively to the capitalist market or be thriftier with their imports from it. The foreign exchange rates are unrealistic; since they overvalue the local currency, they make imports cheaper and exports less profitable. That is precisely the opposite of the incentive that would be desirable—assuming that the exchange rates and foreign trade prices have any effect at all in the first place. In fact, what is true in general about the weakness of price responsiveness is doubly so when it comes to the effect of exchange rates and export and import prices. The armory of the soft budget constraint contains plenty of weapons for fending off foreign influence. If the price of an imported material rises or an export price falls, that is a good excuse for a foreign trade or production firm to request intervention to compensate for the loss.[40] This can be done through alteration of the customs tariffs, application of special multipli-

---

[40] All the socialist countries, whether classical or reform economies, adapted very poorly to the rise in energy prices. In the second half of the 1980s, for instance, the energy expended on one dollar's worth of production was over twice as high in the group of six smaller Eastern European socialist countries as it was in Western Europe. Almost half of Eastern Europe's steel was produced by energy-wasting "open-hearth furnace" technology, which has been all but abandoned in the West. See B. de Largentaye (1990).

ers to alter the foreign exchange rate, tax concessions, price subsidies, and so on. There is no great reward for the firm that adapts most cleverly, and no great penalty if it fails.

Removing the bureaucratic restraints and increasing the independence of firms, including the grant of independent rights to import, makes it easier for them to satisfy their appetite for imports. Meanwhile, there is still no strong profit motive, market competition, or hard budget constraint to make it a matter of life or death for a firm to find buyers for its goods. So the majority of firms fail to devote enough effort to exporting. And even the firms that do try to do well on the capitalist markets encounter a great number of difficulties, ranging from innumerable bureaucratic interventions and restrictions to shortage of inputs, including imported materials, semifinished products, and equipment. The result is that imports normally exceed exports, and the sum total of loans to cover the trade deficit constantly grows.

When that happens, a dangerous self-generation of the growth of debt sets in. The greater a country's indebtedness, the less favorable the terms on which it is obliged to raise new loans. If difficulties arise in debt servicing—paying the installments due and the interest—its credit rating deteriorates, which makes it harder still to raise further loans and the terms of them even less favorable. Although the debt began to mount originally because imports exceeded exports, the economy is now expected to yield a constant trade surplus to service the debt. Few of the reform economies manage that, and if they do, it is only for a short, temporary period. Not infrequently the process culminates in a grave payments crisis, and even if the country does not fall into insolvency, it only just manages to stop at the brink.

This line of thinking with its many constituents provides a basis for stating that the reform economy is more inclined to indebtedness than the classical system. This is permitted and at the same time encouraged by the changes encompassed by the reform in the political and the economic spheres.[41] The statement is also supported by observations. Tables 23.6 and 23.7 compare the debt burden in 1988 of two groups of European socialist countries: Hungary and Poland, which took the road of reform, and Czechoslovakia and Romania, which rigidly preserved the

---

[41]Romania had an enormous foreign debt of ten billion dollars in 1981, which it managed to repay in full by 1989. This was done through a particularly energetic forcing of exports and merciless limitations on imports, both of which were to the grave detriment of domestic consumption. Only an extremely repressive administration like Ceausescu's regime could do this. No quasi-tolerant, kid-gloved reform socialist economy would be capable of it. See A. Teodorescu (1990).

TABLE 23.6
Net Debt: International Comparison

	Ratio of Net Debt to Exports to the Market Economies (percent)				
	1984	1985	1986	1987	1988
Reform socialist countries					
Hungary	221	307	374	396	349
Poland	433	503	534	545	458
Classical socialist countries					
Czechoslovakia	42	50	53	66	62
Romania	93	97	100	70	33

Source: United Nations (1990a, p. 206).

classical system.[42] There is no doubt that the reforming countries got far deeper into debt.

The responsibility for a substantial proportion of the foreign debt in a capitalist country is borne by private firms. The government is only responsible for the loans raised by itself or the firms it owns, and for the loans to the private sector for which it has provided a government

TABLE 23.7
Net Interest Payments: International Comparison

	Ratio of Net Interest Payments to Exports to the Market Economies				
	1984	1985	1986	1987	1988
Reform socialist countries					
Hungary	17.5	19.0	21.0	20.2	18.8
Poland	43.1	43.7	43.2	42.4	36.8
Classical socialist countries					
Czechoslovakia	5.1	4.3	4.6	4.3	4.3
Romania	10.1	10.0	10.2	5.2	2.8

Source: United Nations (1990a, p. 206).

[42]East Germany is excluded from the comparison because its trading and financial ties with West Germany created special conditions. On West German help to East Germany, see J. Lisiecki (1990).

guarantee.[43] So both the grave problem of the debt and the activity of handling it are divided between the state and the private sector. By contrast, although some decentralization has taken place in a reform socialist economy, the issuing of permission to raise foreign credit and the servicing of foreign debt remain strictly centralized. That means all the problems in this connection fall upon the top leadership and the central bank apparatus directly assigned to the task. The firms in public ownership are not directly interested or involved in solving this grave national problem; not one of them goes bankrupt even if the whole country arrives at the brink of bankruptcy. The grave consequences are ultimately decentralized, however, as the public bears the costs of servicing the debt.

There is no role for the private sector in either the accumulation or the reduction of the foreign debt handled at governmental level. The reform economy does not legalize either private foreign trade or foreign currency transactions between private parties. But such activity still goes on. As a result of the political liberalization and the opening up to the West, more people travel abroad, it becomes easier to keep in touch with relatives and acquaintances living abroad, and more people study or work abroad. That makes it increasingly difficult to prevent the citizen of a socialist country from buying or selling hard currency either at home or abroad, from selling domestic goods abroad, and from selling goods obtained there at home. It is no longer a matter of an occasional transaction made casually on an official trip or a foreign vacation, for "shopping tourism," specifically for commercial purposes, takes on mass proportions. It is not rare for people to become semiprofessional dealers in foreign currency and foreign trade.

This area provides a clear instance of how inconsistent the official propaganda is in its reception of the market mechanism. Private foreign trading and currency transactions between private parties are branded as speculation, even though the dealings in most cases are socially useful. Ultimately, this activity raises the national income; it is among the factors behind the fact that the supply in these countries is better than the official trade and consumption statistics show. Even the country's foreign exchange reserves are in a better state than the official financial reports suggest, since the foreign currency kept illegally in homes, in fact, forms part of the national stock. In Hungary and Poland, where shopping tourism is most widespread, hundreds of thousands of people began in the late 1980s to spend at least some of their time on foreign

---

[43]Several Latin American countries have a very large state sector, and this primarily is what ran into debt. To that extent the origin of the process of debt accumulation there bears a resemblance to the process in the socialist countries.

trading, carefully calculating where and what it was worth buying cheaply for later sale at higher prices elsewhere.

The trouble is that this fundamentally useful private activity takes place amid great friction, in a way that squanders people's energies and time. Their path is obstructed by innumerable bureaucratic prohibitions, which they must expect to be applied in a quite capricious way; sometimes they are enforced and sometimes a blind eye is turned. This game of cat and mouse consumes an incredible amount of ingenuity and enterprise.

23.7 Shortage, Inflation, and Indebtedness

Section 23.5 examined the relation between the macro tensions discussed so far and their combined result: an interlocking of shortage and inflation. The examination at that point did not consider the foreign relations of the economy. Their effects can now be included in the analysis. The subject, therefore, is the triple relation among shortage, inflation, and indebtedness.

1. *Shortage leads to more imports.* The shortage economy tempts the managers of the economy to use imports from the capitalist market to fill specific gaps. This is the handiest and quickest course available, whether public dissatisfaction needs assuaging or blocks to production and investment removing. The leaders of a reform economy resort to this more easily than their counterparts under the classical system, because they are more alarmed by rumblings of discontent from the public or heads of firms, and less shy of raising the debt.

2. *Shortage leads to poorer export performance.* In a sellers' market, a producer is not reliant on finding a buyer on the capitalist market. Should he fail to, he can easily find a sales opportunity so long as the shortage remains in the home economy and the countries of his socialist trading partners. This enervating effect of a chronic shortage economy continues in all the sectors of the reform economy where the sellers' market persists.

3. *Debt leads to shortage.* Seeing the debts pile up, the managers of the economy are liable to place administrative curbs on imports and to force exports to capitalist countries by issuing state instructions or placing state orders, or perhaps even applying direct pressure. The problems with the current-account balance are among the main spurs to attempts to restore the prereform mechanism and retain the micro controls [→21.4]. The bureaucratic intervention is accompanied by the appearance of shortage, or a worse shortage of products imported in the past.

Alternatively, the shortage may become more intense because products are diverted for home consumption to exports.

4. *Debt leads to inflation.* Two kinds of causal relation apply here. One is that the leaders of the economy, if they react rationally to the trade and current-account deficits and the growing indebtedness, are obliged to devalue the country's currency. That makes imports dearer, which contributes to the cost–price inflation spiral.

The other causal relation is that servicing the debt demands a heavy expenditure by the budget and/or the central bank handling foreign exchange. That expenditure is normally covered by printing more money, that is, in an inflationary way.

This survey of the reciprocal effects is not full, but it suffices to show that the three economic problems of shortage, inflation, and indebtedness, grave in themselves, influence each other too. Once this reciprocal influence has made a whirlpool, the economy can reach a critical state. It happened in Poland in 1988–89, with inflation turning into hyperinflation,[44] shortage becoming prevalent and intense, and indebtedness fueling an approaching insolvency.

The Polish example, as the introduction to the chapter underlined, is an extreme one. But reciprocal reinforcement of the three perilous trends toward shortage, inflation, and indebtedness can be observed wherever they individually appear.

23.8   The Standard of Living

The effect of the reform processes and the accompanying macro tensions on the standard of living vary among countries and periods and among strata of the population in a particular country at a particular time. Again, the treatment must be confined to identifying a few fairly general phenomena.

The main winners are those who gain extra income by entering the private sector. In China that means several hundred million peasants, plus many tens of millions of citizens who engage in private activity outside agriculture, either full time or in addition to employment in the public sector. At the time of writing, there were already millions in the Soviet Union working in the "cooperative" (in fact, private) sector. Similar

---

[44]Polish hyperinflation assumed extreme proportions before the stabilization measures taken in 1990. Consumer prices increased by 636 percent between December 1988 and December 1989. D. Lipton and J. Sachs (1990, p. 105).

Also, the Soviet economy sunk into an inflationary whirlpool in 1989–90. On this, see the writings mentioned in note 2 and E. Gaidar (1990).

statements can be made about the other reform economies. The material living standard of these people improves appreciably.

In some of the reforming countries the supply situation improves, which is a gain for the whole population. This improvement comes from several sources. One is the resurrection and expansion of the private sector. For instance, the enormous boom in Chinese agriculture not only changed the lives of the peasantry for the better; it produced an almost instantaneous improvement in the food supply to the urban population. Anyone availing themselves of the services of the formal or informal private sector does so because their demand has not been satisfied by the public sector. Every ruble or forint of revenue that the private sector receives in exchange for consumer products or services means that the consumption of the general public has increased by a ruble or a forint.

Another improvement in the population's standard of living can be gained from the shift in the priorities of economic policy, so long as the shift is in favor of current consumption by the public or investment in the service sectors (housing, health) [→23.2]. The increase in imports of consumer goods can have a favorable effect. Another contribution to improving the quality of life comes from the fact that the measures of reform aimed at market socialism somewhat increase the independence of publicly owned firms, give slightly more scope to horizontal market relations, and so improve the quality and range of products to some extent.

The most successful country in this respect was Hungary. The living standards of quite large sections of the population improved substantially and continuously for about a decade and a half, due to the effects of the factors just outlined. Much the same can be said of Yugoslavia and China, and there was a far more modest, but detectable improvement, at least partially, in other reforming countries.

But sooner or later, even in the relatively most successful reforming countries, the trend of improvement is broken, and in the less successful ones it never really develops. No country escapes the macro tensions examined in this chapter. For a time the tensions remain latent, or the leadership consciously tries to conceal them, or even worse: it takes short-term measures that merely postpone the emergence of the difficulties while compounding the problem in the long term.

Consumption under the classical system is the residual variable of macro distribution. If there is trouble, the standard of living is forced down without hesitation, but investment and military expenditure are not interfered with, and no applications are made for foreign credit. The bureaucracy can act in this way because protest is ruled out by the totalitarian power over society and the tough repression.

Under reform socialism, the solution is no longer so self-evident. As a function of the degree of liberalization and glasnost, the general public is able to voice its dissatisfaction. Those running the country think discontent is worth avoiding. The reform began with a promise that the suffering caused by the classical system would end and life would improve. So the leadership does not resort automatically to the old methods of restricting consumption when the clouds start to gather over the economy. It may try something else instead.

Military spending is not usually cut.[45] That leaves two possibilities: curbing investment or raising foreign credits. These temporarily allow real consumption to continue rising, even if the pace is slower. If it cannot rise any more, at least it does not fall. Or if it falls, at least it does not nosedive. The programs concerning the standard of living promise less and less, but even then, the promise at any time is always greater than what eventually results.

That applies all the more because the two methods by which the leadership tries to prevent a shock fall in the standard of living thwart each other in the long run. Reducing investment undermines the bases for growth in the future and sooner or later causes production to stagnate or begin to fall. While the bureaucratic restriction of investment continues, the tension in the investment sphere heightens even more. Projects for investment constantly exceed the ever decreasing available funds. There is a mounting backlog of investment tasks; the bureaucracy of the branches and regions that do not receive an adequate share of the investment funds join the ranks of the discontented.

The dilemma of investment versus consumption can be avoided if the sum of the two, that is, aggregate expenditure, is raised by resorting to foreign resources. This was part of the basis, for instance, for Hungary's success in the 1970s in producing a seemingly durable increase in welfare, when the oft-mentioned "goulash communism" or "refrigerator socialism" was financed to a large extent with Western money. Foreign loans helped other reforming countries in a similar way to prevent their domestic macro tensions from manifesting themselves in a far greater fall in

[45]This also began to happen in the 1980s. The growing domestic economic difficulties forced the Soviet Union to display a greater willingness to reach agreement and withdraw from its earlier positions, among other reasons, because it needed the economic resources it was withdrawing from military use. So long as the Eastern European countries stayed closely dependent on the Soviet Union in military terms, they needed Soviet agreement before reducing their military spending as well. Roughly speaking, therefore, this reallocation was taking place in parallel in the Soviet Union and the other socialist countries allied to it militarily.

In fact, there is a long delay between cutting military spending and transferring the freed resources to civilian consumption.

the standard of living than actually occurred. But as mentioned before in this chapter, the problem is only exacerbated in the long term; a process of debt accumulation begins and then speeds up. In the end, the debt-servicing bill lands on the general public's doorstep just the same, and later, but to a far greater extent, they have to cut back their consumption.

There is another characteristic of the easing up of the macro tensions. When the limitation or reduction of real consumption takes place, the method is never to reduce nominal wages. The preferred method is to raise consumer prices in an open or hidden way, among other reasons because a rate of inflation that is relatively not too fast—still in single figures—is easier to handle politically than an open campaign to reduce nominal wages.

Inflation is compatible with the stagnation of average per capita real consumption, and possibly with a slight increase in it. At the same time, it inevitably produces a redistribution of real incomes: some sections of the population are able to defend their economic interests, while others (such as pensioners, and employees on fixed pay with a weak bargaining position) experience a steadily falling standard of living. The social tensions are heightened by the increasing inequality.[46]

The macro tensions covered in this chapter are the direct consequences of the attributes of the system, and to a large extent they follow from the reform itself. There is no magic potion capable within the prevailing system of eliminating the sources of these tensions. Each procedure used (reducing investment, raising credits, and so on) is only a postponement. The problem remains and asserts itself later with a force that is even more destructive.

Those running the country under the reform system do not recognize these interactive effects. The main problem is not a lack of the expertise to recognize them,[47] but the existence of an ideological block. The more firmly an individual believes in the socialist system, the less capable he or she is of seeing that the ever worsening problems derive from the system itself. One must not assume a cynical desire to deceive the people in the Communist leaders who promise an improvement in life at the start of the reform process and then, on seeing the difficulties, repeatedly extend the deadline for fulfilling the original promises. They really be-

[46]For an analysis of social tensions and inequality under reform socialism, see T. Zaslavskaya (1990), esp. pp. 86–153, and Z. Ferge (1988).

[47]In certain periods and countries there is trouble with this as well; an economic leadership reared on the official doctrines fails to understand the financial processes and macro interrelations that take place in the economy, largely as a result of their own actions.

lieve (if perhaps with steadily weaker conviction) that the problem will be a temporary one.[48]

The deterioration in public feeling is not merely caused by the fact that the state of the economy is manifestly bad. It is soured further by disillusionment over the leadership's promises. Each unfulfilled promise contributes to the undermining of confidence. The heightening of the macro tensions, the stagnation or decline of the standard of living, and the leadership's loss of credibility prepare the ground for revolutionary changes.

The revolution becomes inescapable when those in power finally lose confidence themselves in their ability to overcome the mounting problems. Alternatively, it may occur when the masses become discontented and turn their backs on the system to such an extent that they can break through in spite of the leadership's resistance.

23.9 Preview: Macro Tensions in the Postsocialist System

The postsocialist system, once it has replaced the socialist system modified by the process of reform, inherits the macro tensions described in this chapter. Upward pressure on wages occurs in the state sector of the economy. The situation in the investment sphere is tense. The state budget is in deficit. The demand for credit exceeds the supply; there is great pressure for an excessive increase in the money supply. Inflation continues and, in fact, may be speeding up. The shortage is intense in several spheres. The balance of trade with the capitalist countries is in a poor state. The debt is large and growing.

The general public experiences the joys of a political turn for the better in the months when the system is changing, but its economic situation does not alter in such a short space of time. It has been tired by the earlier periods and finds it hard to believe in new promises, even if they are made under an utterly different political system.

The new democracy inherits the macro tensions from the previous system, and right from the start it is faced with the very dilemmas that system was unable to resolve. Should there be a series of partial changes extending over a long period, or should a single package of measures, a comprehensive and coherent macro stabilization, be implemented with a

[48]A quotation from Gorbachev's New Year Address (*Pravda,* January 1, 1989): "And all the same, the economic reform has not worked at full speed. The results that have been achieved cannot satisfy us. There are still manifestations of shortages that have not been overcome and other difficulties in daily life. . . . We have to do a lot next year, in order to change the situation in the economy decisively for the better. And these changes will come."

firm hand, so as to restore order in wage control, eliminate the budget deficit, restrict the supply of credit, liberalize prices, and introduce convertibility simultaneously?

Some of the tensions discussed in this chapter are absent and some present in a less intense form at the starting point for the change of system if the revolution has not been preceded by a process of reform and the classical socialist system has survived to the last minute. As has been seen, the classical system, with its repression and bureaucratic constraints, is better able to resist a high proportion of these tendencies than the half-relaxed, half-regressive reform system. One must reckon with the possibility that macro tensions that the previous governments of Ceausescu, Zhivkov, and Husák used tough methods to repress may begin to develop in these countries after the revolution.[49] Precisely because the administration of the state will be in the hands of democratic governments in the future, there is a danger that they will be unable to resist forcefully enough the negative tendencies produced by an economy that is still dominated by a state-owned sector. There is a chance that wage pressure will grow, inflation accelerate, and foreign debt rise in these countries as well.

One can also expect the development of considerable unemployment, for which society is unprepared. Employees under the socialist system took full or almost full employment for granted; the very arrival of the problem is a shock to them, both financially and psychologically. Apart from that, society still lacks the institutions for treating unemployment, for instance, for registering the unemployed, paying them benefits, retraining them, or channeling them toward new jobs.

The intention here is only to draw attention to the likely problems and dangers, and of these only the ones that appear in the macro economy of the postsocialist system as a legacy from the previous regime. An examination of how the new system might overcome these tensions falls outside the scope of this book.

---

[49]No mention is made here of East Germany. Although the antecedents are similar (a jump from classical socialism to postsocialism), the circumstances of the transition, within the frames of the unified Germany, are unique.

24

Concluding Remarks

WHILE the previous chapters have dealt one by one with the most typical tendencies in the move away from the classical system, a few remarks are now made on the relations between those tendencies. A summary and appraisal of the reform process is provided from several points of view. Finally, to conclude this book on the socialist system, there is a further look forward at the transformation that supersedes the system.

24.1 The Depth and Radicalism of the Changes, and the Main Line of Causality

For an explanation of what follows, readers should recall figure 15.1, which shows the main line of causality among the main features of the classical system, and also section 16.2, where two criteria for analyzing movements away from the classical system were introduced: how deep and how radical the changes are. With the help of this analytical apparatus, the main tendencies discussed in the previous chapters are examined in table 24.1.

The phenomenon at the top of the table, numbered tendency 0, has been labeled "perfection" of control. In terms of depth, this is directed at the middle of the causal chain, at modifying the coordination and control, but even in that sphere it does not alter the essential features found in the earlier period of the classical system. Even though the tendency rates as a reform in the official propaganda, its effect is to conserve the existing classical system.

After the reference to pseudoreforms, the table continues with the real processes of reform, which are numbered 1–6. They are placed in order of the depth of the reform.

Tendency 1, political liberalization, affects the deepest layer of causality: the structure of power and the official ideology of the classical system are substantially altered. Nor is this merely important in itself. It is also an essential condition for any appreciable change in all the other spheres. So long as the Communist party is in power, the system can only move away from the classical system if the party makes the alteration itself, or at least tolerates it. It then either co-opts the change into the system's official ideology, or makes an ideological concession and ignores the phenomena that conflict with its ideas.

TABLE 24.1
The Depth and Radicalism of the Changes

Tendency	Depth (Placing in Figure 15.1)	Degree of Radicalism
0. "Perfection" of control	Block 3: coordination	No appreciable change
1. Political liberalization	Block 1: power and ideology	Moderate or middling
2. Revival of private sector	Block 2: property	Radical, but only in a narrow segment
3. Self-management	Blocks 3 and 4: coordination and behavior	Middling
4. Market socialism	Blocks 3 and 4: coordination and behavior	Moderate or middling
5. Price reforms	Blocks 3 and 4: coordination and behavior	Moderate
6. Macro tensions	Blocks 4 and 5: behavior and lasting economic phenomena	Middling

The process of reform does not take the change in the political structure very far: the liberalization is not consistent and does not develop fully. Nor can there be a comprehensive and consistently radical transformation in the other spheres while the key feature of the old classical structure, the Communist party's power, remains. Although the monopoly of power is shaken and the official ideology begins to break down, they remain strong enough to obstruct any consistent, full change in the system's other elements.

Tendency 2, revival of the private sector, causes a radical upheaval in the second deepest layer: property relations (block 2), although only in a narrow segment. This is the most important of all the many phenomena associated with economic reform; it brings a genuine, not a spurious, feigned change.

In the band where private activity is pursued on a basis of private property, an element alien to the socialist system appears. It is unable to fuse completely with the other parts of the system. Though the political system is more liberal than its classical predecessor, it is unable and un-willing to tolerate a free development of the private sector, and it places tight constraints on its operation and expansion.

Tendency 3, self-management, also brings a change in property rela-tions (block 2), but it is far less radical than the one caused by the revival of the private sector. In block 3, the introduction of self-management entails an appreciable change in the forms of coordination and partial abandonment of the centralization of control.

Both its origin (imposition by central bureaucratic command) and its day-to-day operation link it with the power structure, which differs only in part from the classical version.

Tendency 4, the reforms deriving from the ideas of market socialism, causes substantial changes in block 3 and 4, the coordination mechanism. In fact, the "blueprint" does not question either the key feature in block 1, the Communist party's monopoly of power, or the key feature in block 2, the dominance of public ownership. The essence of the idea is to link public ownership with market coordination within the prevailing political structure. The command economy is wholly or partially elimi-nated, increasing the autonomy of publicly owned firms.

Insofar as the blueprint for market socialism is realized at all, it can thank for its existence the fact that an important classical doctrine is reluctantly dropped from the official ideology: that planning, bureau-cratic coordination, is superior to market coordination and can replace it. It can also thank the fact that the bureaucracy is obliged to abandon its most appropriate weapon, the command, and the higher level of the hierarchy relinquishes certain areas of decision making to functionaries at a lower level.

But some complementary propositions must be added to the fore-going. The official ideology proves incapable of absorbing consistently the idea that socialism should be based on a market economy. More im-portant still, the higher officials in the bureaucracy are neither able nor willing to abdicate their rule over the public sector. Under the prevailing political structure, there is no escape from bureaucratic micro control, constant intervention in firms' affairs, and predominance of vertical sub-ordination over horizontal dependence to the market. So long as the characteristics of blocks 1 and 2 remain basically unchanged, there can be no radical change in blocks 3 and 4 either. The blueprint of market socialism cannot be followed consistently; there is an inevitable ambiva-lence about the way it is applied.

Tendency 5, the series of partial price reforms, brings changes in blocks 3 and 4. The introduction of the price reforms is propelled by the combined effect of tendencies 1-4. Without aiming at a full list, I shall mention some typical causal relations. The ideological changes induce the abolition of some paternalistic subsidies, which affects prices. The revival of the private sector is accompanied by the appearance of market prices in certain segments of the economy. The changes inspired by the idea of market socialism give firms a greater role in price setting; they reinforce the demand for the development of market-clearing prices.

Here, as with tendency 4, some complementary statements can be made. Numerous elements of the official ideology remain the same, which means that a great many old, nonmarket principles of pricing and taxation are conserved. The bureaucracy does not want to relinquish the power derived from the fact that a central pricing policy applies over wide areas and a high proportion of prices are set by the state. Vertical bargaining between the price authority and the firm over prices becomes a daily occurrence in the public sector, while operation of the private sector, whose natural form of price is the market price, is still confined to a narrow field.

Political liberalization, even if it is partial, tends to enable mass dissatisfaction to be expressed. The political climate is such that the leadership cannot bring itself either to introduce a comprehensive liberalization of prices or, if a large degree of administrative price-setting was maintained, at least to undertake a comprehensive price reform. These are sufficient explanation why this tendency is confined to a series of partial price measures that are inflationary without converging toward a rational, market-clearing system of prices.

Tendency 6, the joint appearance of macro tensions characteristic of the reform process, occurs in blocks 4 and 5—the behavior of the participants in the economy and the long-term economic phenomena. Some of the tensions (inflation, indebtedness) appear under other systems as well. What needs emphasizing here is that the process of reform, through specific lines of transmission, heightens certain tensions: wage pressure, runaway investment, budget deficit, inflation, chronic shortage, and indebtedness. To translate that into the terms of figure 15.1, it has been shown how the main features of blocks 4 and 5 during the reform process can to a large extent be explained by the changes that occurred in blocks 1, 2, and 3.

The brief survey of the seven tendencies reinforces the general theoretical inference [→15.5] that the main line of causality runs from block 1 toward block 5, that is, from power and ideology toward lasting economic phenomena. Ultimately, the sphere of politics, power, and ideology is the decisive one. This supplied the "genetic program" for bringing the socialist system into being [→15.3], under whose influence the classical system developed. There can be strong, or even desperately aggressive, resistance against radical change in block 1, for the sake of maintaining as much as possible its original classical properties. When and only when this genetic program is modified does a deep, radical, and persistent change take place in the whole organism. An understanding of the state of block 1 provides the most important analytical tool for understanding all the other blocks and revealing the progress and limitations of the reform process. The foregoing survey also reinforces the highly important (even though secondary) role played by property relations in explaining the process.

At the end of the examination of the classical system it was asked how the truth of causal explanation presented in chapter 15 could be confirmed. The main test proposed was whether the change of the system complies with the prediction made by the theory. Even though the reform process and the postsocialist transformation, when one considers the set of all socialist countries as a whole, is far from over, one can state from the observations so far that experience up to now confirms the theoretical statements made about the main line of causality.

While the main line of causality proceeds from block 1 toward block 5, that is, from deeper causes to more superficial ones, a number of feedbacks, reactions, and interactions apply. Just three important relations have been chosen as examples.

One interaction is that the reforming tendencies increase the autonomy of individuals, groups, and organizations in several respects. This applies to independent political movements, associations in society, private businesses, self-governing local authorities, self-managed firms, state-owned firms that become more independent in accordance with the ideas of market socialism, and so on. Various combinations of autonomy and subordination appear, but within them the weight of autonomy grows as a result of the reform, and as it increases, so the totalitarian power of the central leadership decreases. In the multinational countries, national independence movements evolve and gather momentum. Once some degree of growth of autonomy has taken place, it becomes a self-generating process; the reins with which the bureaucracy could drive every organization and individual at will slip from its grasp.

Another example of a reaction is the impetus the macro tensions give to the growth of the private sector. Private entrepreneurs are encouraged to enter by the big profits they can make alleviating shortage in the areas where the public sector cannot satisfy the demand and the private sector is permitted to operate (or at least is not persecuted).

Finally, there is a third, particularly important reaction: inflation, shortage, and stagnation or decline of the standard of living increase public discontent. The economic tensions generate political tensions; they can lead to an explosive outbreak of strikes and demonstrations. Ultimately, the economic crisis can spark off a political crisis and set into motion radical, revolutionary change.

But all in all, important though these relations are, they do not constitute the main line of causality and can only be described as reactions to or interactions with the main causal effects. A few other countereffects are mentioned in the next section.

It should be noted that the order in which tendencies 1–6 are placed, which is expressed in the arrangement of the chapters and the summarizing table 24.1, ties in with the logical structure of the relations. Quite distinct from that is the question of the actual historical order in which the events of the reform took place. As emphasized earlier [→16.4], there is little regularity to be seen in this respect when one studies the course of history in the reforming countries. In China, for instance, a property reform affecting several hundred million peasants takes place right at the start of the move away from the classical system, but there was still little change in the political sphere in that period, whereas in the Soviet Union, dramatic changes were going on in politics for some years, but for many years there have been only timid moves to transform the property relations.

There is one regularity to be seen, and it also follows deductively from the line of thought above. A considerable change must take place in the thinking of the Communist party leadership before it can bring itself to make an appreciable departure from the classical system, or at least resign itself to such a departure taking place. To that extent the point of departure everywhere is to be found in block 1, in the combined effect of measures from above and spontaneous initiative or pressure from below. If the Communist party stubbornly resists all changes, either it succeeds in suppressing all efforts at change (as one can say, for instance, of Cuba or North Korea in 1990) or the revolution literally breaks out, jumping the stage of gradual reform altogether (Czechoslovakia, East Germany, and Romania in 1989).[1]

24.2 The Incoherence of the Tendencies to Reform

The classical system forms a coherent whole [→15.2]. An affinity applies between the elements of it, so that they mutually complement and attract each other. At least as a pure theoretical prototype, it resembles a building in which all the blocks tie in with each other. The building may be a

---

[1]In the case of Czechoslovakia and East Germany, the stubborn resistance to change of the group in power was ultimately broken by an unambiguous message from the Soviet leadership. Gorbachev informed them that they could not now count on the help of Soviet tanks in putting down any uprising; the earlier military interventions in Eastern Europe would not be repeated.

prison, but the bars really divide it from the outside world, the locks are secure, the guards can look in through the peepholes in the cell doors, and the prisoners and informers go about their business in a disciplined way.

The reform destroys the coherence of the classical system and proves incapable of establishing a new order in its place.[2] The old regularities apply only partially, and new permanent regularities fail to coalesce. Everything is fluid, or rather gelatinous. Society is full of elements that have no affinity; they repel rather than attract each other. A great many of these internal inconsistencies have been presented in the preceding chapters. Some will be repeated now, as examples are given of the inconsistencies and incoherences to be found in the phase of reform. Let us examine some pairs of phenomena and inquire to what extent the two members of each pair tally, whether they have an affinity, or what conflicts arise between them. The first members of the pairs of phenomena are taken in the order dictated by their logical place in figure 15.1.

The Communist party, amid the processes of reform, wants to retain its monopoly of power, but in the meantime, it releases political forces that immediately demand the abandonment of this monopoly. The party proclaims "glasnost," but instead of showing gratitude, people dig up all the tragedy and injury they have undergone, for which they hold the party and the system responsible. The Communists declare their willingness to renounce all the merciless methods of intimidating the people, but as there becomes less to be afraid of, an elemental demand breaks forth from the people for full abolition of arbitrary rule and institutional guarantees of democracy. This places the power of the Communist party in danger, and in a strained situation in mortal danger.

As control over events weakens, so does control over ideas. During the first waves of reform of the ossified dogmas, justifiable reference can still be made to Marx and Lenin, who were not rigidly doctrinaire themselves; they were averse to others attaching a mythical significance to their ideas. But it is hard to order a halt to the process of disillusionment. A functionary who has honestly believed in the system in the past and been, to use party jargon, a "trained Marxist-Leninist" starts by wondering whether Stalin could have erred in one or two of his writings

---

[2] Yuri F. Orlov, the prominent Soviet dissident who emigrated in 1986 and returned for a visit to the Soviet Union in 1991, characterized the situation this way: "Gorbachev understood nothing when he began. . . . All he knew was that socialism must be improved. His idea was simple, and close to Western thinking: if you take socialism and add democracy and free speech, all will be well. But what he discovered was that the system designed by Lenin was such that once you pulled out one brick, the whole thing fell apart. Now he's trying to push the brick back in. This is the farce and the tragedy." *New York Times,* February 10, 1991, p. 4.

or propositions; then he begins to regard Stalin as someone who applied the correct teachings of Lenin in an erroneous and perhaps criminally wrong way. One wave of disillusionment later, the same man is doubting the foundations of Leninism, and from there he is only a step away from rejecting Marxism.

One manifestation of the tendency to liberalization is that the people, notably the intelligentsia and the research scientists, are encouraged to think for themselves and honestly analyze reality. But where does that lead? They begin to wonder what the cause of all the detrimental phenomena can be. The process of recognition is a long one, the first stage being to seek the fault in individuals. At this point, Stalin and all the national petty Stalins are branded as evildoers who bear the main blame for all the problems. The next stage is to ascribe the problems not simply to individuals but to a faulty political line taken in a certain period. Later on, not even this provides an adequate explanation. Socialism is a good system, but the particular version (special "model") of it applied so far is faulty. It is not socialism that should be abandoned, but "étatism" (the official Yugoslav viewpoint in the 1950s), the old "command mechanism" (the official Hungarian stance in the latter half of the 1960s), or the "command-administrative system" (the official Soviet view at the end of the 1980s). A "change of model," not a change of system, is required. Later, when the next wave of disillusionment breaks, people realize that the trouble is in the system, not some specific version of it.

The ideology of the classical system was taut and logically closed. It rested on axioms against which there was no appeal and which needed, as axioms, no proof. One axiom, for instance, was the superiority of the system. Whatever negative phenomenon appeared was a legacy of capitalism, or the fault of a specific individual, or the result of sabotage by the class enemy, but not, under any circumstances, a consequence of the system. Another such axiom was the leading role of the party (i.e., the party's monopoly of power). Whatever change may take place in the party line, there is no cause to doubt the truth of the axiom. Quite the opposite, in fact: willingness to correct itself is a sign of the party's wisdom. Questioning the axioms becomes permissible under the reform, but all at once that causes the carefully assembled logical structure to collapse.

None of the old principles and none of the old moral postulates can be retained unaltered. How, without ideological confusion, could one square a faith in public ownership with toleration and even encouragement of the private sector, extolment of planning with ever more complete abandonment of it, or the traditional disparagement of the market with the new publicity on its behalf? Previously people were urged to make sacrifices and observe discipline, whereas during the reform process materialism, the practice of "not moving a muscle without pay," hedonism, and adoption of the values of the "consumer society" have become more common behavior. Puritanism and the asceticism of the professed revolutionary count as a grotesque anachronism.

Two other incoherent pairs of phenomena have been discussed in detail in earlier chapters: the symbiosis between the bureaucracy and the private sector [→19.5], and the linking of the party-state's political power and state ownership with the market mechanism of coordination under market socialism [→21.6].[3] It is enough at this point to give a reminder of these two relations and the exceptionally important part they play in creating the internal inconsistency of the processes of reform.

Study of the history of the reforming countries yields no signs of a steady clarification or a gradual resolution of the internal inconsistencies. On the contrary, each inconsistency breeds new conflicts. The history of every reforming country is replete with cases of improvisation and hastiness. Experiments are made in creating something new, but time and again there is a retreat in some area or other toward reviving the old classical system, even though it can no longer be restored in its original form. As the problems grow, the leadership tries to solve them by denying they are there or, if nothing else works, by stepping up the repression.

To sum up, so long as the classical system can be sustained at all, it has a degree of stability and robustness, whereas the system undergoing the contortions of reform is inherently unstable. There are places where it can only subsist for a short time, and others where special circumstances allow it to continue for longer, but nowhere has it been able to survive lastingly (and the prediction from the line of thought put forward in this book is that it will be unable to do so in the future).

While on the subject of the instability of the reformed socialist system, it is worth digressing briefly into the discussion of the third road. The following notion is widespread among the initiators of the reform: we must reject the classical form of socialism because of its grave sins and shortcomings, but we must still not revert to the capitalist system. A third road must be found instead. This idea was expressed by Gorbachev in one of his speeches: "What alternatives are before us? . . . One is maintain the command-administrative system, the strict planning, and the commands in culture as well as the economy. The other, based on the conviction that the road we have trodden in the past has wholly com-

---

[3]Widespread political repression broke out in China after the defeat of the student demonstrations in Beijing in 1989. That obstructed and, in fact, reversed the process of economic reform as well, although the new leadership emphatically declared that it did not oppose the economic reform. Taking the expression "market socialism" as a pattern, the British China specialist C. Lin described the Chinese system in 1989–90 as "market Stalinism."

promised the choice of the October Revolution, suggests reverting to capitalism. Can we take either of these roads? No, we reject them. . . . We see another road that leads to social progress. . . . The new image of socialism has a human face. That accords with the thinking of Marx, to whom the society of the future amounted to a real humanism attainable in practice. And to the extent that perestroika rests on his work, we can say quite justifiably that we are building a humanist socialism."[4]

Mankind has experimented with a great many third-road solutions. The reform of the socialist system, directly affecting the lives of almost 1.4 billion people, is the biggest third-road undertaking so far. At the end of this book, based on the analysis in the nine chapters devoted to the reform, one can risk putting forward the following statement: this gigantic experiment has failed up to now. One can go on to add that if the prediction that follows from the line of thinking in this book proves correct, it will never succeed in the future either.

As stated before, the incoherence, internal contradictions, and lack of stability in the reform socialist system suggest that it is not lastingly viable. The process of reform yields a heteromorphic formation that contains the seeds of its own destruction: inner tensions that build up until it bursts. One alternative by which these can be relieved is for the possessors of power to combat the discontent of the people with violence and lead society back to the second road. The other alternative is that the reform process transforms into a process of revolutionary political changes. That offers the opportunity of free political choice, in which case the majority of the public choose the first road.

In my view, historians will view Gorbachev and all the others who initiated and supported the process of reforming the socialist system as people who earned undying merit. But that merit was not earned by leading mankind along a third road to redemption. They deserve posterity's gratitude for quite other reasons. There is benefit in the short term in every strand of the reform that eases the lives of the contemporaneous generation even a little: many people's living standards improve, at least to some extent; people's liberty and autonomy are enhanced; humiliation is less frequent; fear is lessened. And in the long term the reform causes an erosion of the foundations of the classical socialist system, decomposing its power structure and its control over ideas and morals. By doing so it clears the way for a real change of system.

---

[4]See *Pravda,* November 26, 1989. These sentences of Gorbachev's echo an oft-quoted idea put forward in 1968 by Alexander Dubček, general secretary of the Czechoslovak Communist party and leading figure in the Prague Spring: one has to create "socialism with a human face."

24.3 Reforms and Public Sentiment

With some social changes, it is quite simple to establish which groups in society support them and which oppose them. In the case of the process of reform in the socialist system, this cannot be done. It seems to be impossible to arrive at a general and unequivocal statement about who its adherents and its enemies are.

The following stereotype has gained currency: actually the entire people supports the reform, including the enlightened functionaries in the apparatus, but there is resistance from the conservative members of the party, and possibly the leadership of the secret police and armed forces. In fact, the situation is far more complex.

One long-standing cohesive force in Yugoslavia was national feeling, which approved the break with the Soviet Union, including the rejection of the Soviet social model. In Hungary's case, the shock of the bloody defeat of the 1956 revolution created a broad social consensus: the demand on a mass scale for peace and quiet, an "apolitical" life, and a tangible improvement in the standard of living, and the willingness for a long time to be content with small political concessions and official tolerance of the earnings to be made in the second economy. But even in these two countries, where the reform equilibrium lasted relatively longest, the attitude of the population toward the changes was, in fact, ambivalent [→18.7]. That applies all the more to the other reforming countries. The stratum that all along remains obstinately opposed to all change is relatively restricted. The rest are simultaneously glad and sad, confident and anxious.

As a result of the reform, the pressure of totalitarianism is substantially reduced. Merciless, unpredictable mass terror gives way to pressure in its milder forms, applied only against active resisters. The scope for criticism and protest is widened. But anyone who appreciates the true taste of political liberty cannot be satisfied by these limited tidbits of freedom. This is the point at which the demand for full freedom of speech and association really begins to break out with elemental force from a rising number of people, notably members of the intelligentsia.

Most people are glad that their independence is growing and the authorities are less wont to interfere in their lives. But they also fear losing the protection provided by paternalism at the same time. Heads of firms have reason to be afraid of real market competition and the regime of a buyers' market, and so have employees to fear the end of guaranteed jobs and the security of full employment.

The price system, and along with it the system of fiscal redistribution, is confused; anyone understanding it on the basis of an economic analysis can see that order between prices must be restored. But people have grown accustomed to this confused system of prices and taxes. Masses of people are the beneficiaries of the subsidies on foodstuffs, other goods for mass consumption, and state-owned housing. If those subsidies cease, the same masses will feel they are losers.

Wherever a partial measure of decentralization is taken, it pleases those whose sphere of authority has increased. But it means the power of those above them has decreased, which the losers do not usually welcome.

The growth of the private sector favors those active in it, but even they, once they have begun the activity, start to complain of the various bureaucratic constraints, tax burdens, and other drawbacks. Those buying in the private sector are pleased that the supply has improved, but they grumble meanwhile about the high prices.

Without continuing the list of ambivalent reactions, one can say that the masses fail to line up behind the ideas of the process of reform, because of the inherent inconsistency in those ideas. A mass movement may break out in a certain country at a certain time in favor of a specific idea for reform. The most conspicuous example was the Chinese students' protest of 1989, whose guiding notion was a demand for democracy, but even in that case, one cannot say the students and the citizens of Beijing who joined them had the purpose of supporting a comprehensive program of reform. In other countries (Poland, Yugoslavia, and the Soviet Union), strikes have broken out to protest against the food shortage or the price rises. Although these were not antireform demonstrations, one cannot say they were plainly designed to support the reform or some tangible partial program within it. What really mobilized people was disillusionment with the earlier promises and indignation at the deterioration in the economic situation.

The strikes express in an emphatic form something apparent over a wide sphere in a less demonstrative way: as time goes by, the initial enthusiasm of many people for the reform wanes. Although the reform wins new supporters among previously conservative functionaries who now wake up to the untenability of the old conditions, more and more people are coming in the meantime to feel disillusioned or even cheated. That was the case in the ultimate phase at the end of the 1980s, when in Poland and Hungary the reform came to a point where it switched over to revolution. Something similar could be seen in the Soviet Union, where bitterness and disillusion were spreading more and more widely, and political tension was increasing in 1989–90. However many favorable changes the reform may bring in everyday life, people give little credit to them. They feel far more intensively the widening of the yawning gulf that divides the promises of the reform and their own rising expectations from fulfillment of them. Measured against a historical scale, reform socialism is incapable of stabilizing in the long term.

24.4 Preview: The Socialist System's Legacy and Postsocialism

The subject of this book is a positive analysis of the socialist system, and it does not take a normative approach to dealing with the postsocialist system; it does not put forward practical proposals for the countries where that transition is on the agenda.[5] All that can be risked are a few predictive conjectures that follow immediately from the arguments in the book so far.

A revolutionary transformation takes place in society. In some countries important political events are condensed into quite a short period and occur almost like an explosion: there are turbulent mass demonstrations over a period of a few days or weeks, the Communist government then resigns, and a new government including the opposition takes its place. That is what happened in Czechoslovakia and East Germany, for instance, in 1989. But a change of government is not a change of system, merely one of the political preconditions for it. The change of system is a historical process that seems likely to require a long period of time. Its point of departure is the legacy received by the new system from the old. Chapters 17–23 each ended with a section that presented a particular component in that legacy. Without aiming to be exhaustive, it is now time to sum up by reviewing that legacy.

The new system receives a *national wealth* in poor condition. All the distortions that the classical system has caused and the reform system has failed or made no attempt to improve have left their impression on the national wealth, which is marked by technical backwardness and a seriously worn and ill-maintained stock of machinery and buildings. The deterioration is notably great in the commercial network, transportation, housing, and health institutions. The task of catching up with the arrears has been postponed constantly over a long period; now everyone sees that further postponement threatens an ever more serious catastrophe. Production and the daily life of the population have settled into ways that constantly damage the natural environment; environmental protection is also among the tasks to have been perilously neglected.

The poor state of the material wealth is coupled with weaknesses in the *human capital* inherited from the previous system. By comparison with the developed industrial countries, the professional skills of the

---

[5]For the literature on policy recommendations see the appendix.

workforce are backward in many areas, and labor discipline is lax. Managers and white-collar workers are unfamiliar with the workings of a modern market economy. Nor is the skill of the rising generation to replace them very promising, as there have been serious shortcomings for decades in education as well. Great efforts would be required to carry out the tasks postponed and neglected even if the whole economy were growing at a fair pace. In fact, the new regime usually comes to power in a critical situation of stagnation or recession, so that establishing harmonious proportions in the economy can take a fair time.

The new system inherits grave *macro tensions*, particularly in the financial sphere: inflation and shortage, excess demand and a stock of money that cannot be spent. In several countries there is the serious added burden of foreign debt. Some of the tensions are system-specific—bequeathed by the socialist political structure and property relations—and these may be heightened by the tendencies emerging out of reform socialism. It is likely that the inherited macro tensions will persist for a while. Of course, much depends on the new regime's willingness and ability to undertake a radical program of macro stabilization.

The new system inherits the old network of *institutions*: the specific structure and multiple-level hierarchy of the state apparatus, the set of legal regulations, and so on. All these have developed by a decades-long process of evolution in which the old system selected from the possible forms according to its needs. The new regime does not want to employ the Leninist formula of starting to build the new by ruthless destruction of the old; it aims at a peaceful and smooth transition. For that very reason, the old institutions may hamper the development of the new system for a long time. It takes a good while for the new institutions to evolve.

Also bequeathed are the old *property relations*: a dominant public sector, certain elements of self-management, and a weak semi-open, semi-covert private sector. There are a great many plans for privatizing the economy; some proposals appear to offer an accelerated solution. But whichever is applied, the new stratum of owners and entrepreneurs to provide a broad social base for capitalism will not emerge in a matter of days or weeks.

The new system takes over the old system's *staff of experts*. Since the subject of the book is political economy, the remarks here will be confined to the members of the bureaucracy and business leaders. The political turnabout certainly has personal consequences for many people. There are worse chances in the redistribution of functions for those more closely tied up with the previous regime, and better chances for those whose relations with the new political trend in power at present are stronger. However, we can speak only about probabilities. There have been no witch hunts so far in any of the countries where the postsocialist transition has begun. Those with a position before either retain it or transfer to other areas (e.g., a public official may become a far better paid manager in a private firm).[6] The opening of the frontiers encourages many to emigrate or take jobs abroad, which then increases the demand for the expert staff who stay at home. The distribution of positions among the experts changes somewhat, but a more or less identical staff remains in service. That enhances the continuity between the old regime and the new, and also the survival of the ingrained habits and norms instilled under the old regime.

Under these circumstances, there continues for a long time to be a curious *dual system* in postsocialist society.[7] It is a "mixed" system in which many elements of the socialist and capitalist societies exist side by side and interwoven with each other.[8] If the actual process of development follows the programs announced by the parties and movements taking power, the capitalist element will prevail. There are great chances of this happening, but even if it does, the inheritance of the socialist order will remain for a long time in all dimensions of socioeconomic activity. This duality will be the source of many kinds of conflict,[9] of which just one problem-sphere will be mentioned here—the likely transformation of the *moral values* accepted and respected by citizens—but even discussion of that will be confined to putting just a few questions.

It is no exaggeration to say that the vast majority of the population in the countries taking the road of postsocialist transition have become deeply disillusioned with the socialist system; they look back on it with ill feelings, and many of them positively loathe it. But that statement is compatible with the observation that great masses of people continue to adhere to moral values—attributes of a notion of a "good society"— that their upbringing taught them to rate as socialistic values.[10] Mean-

---

[6]There are frequent protests that the old possessors of power, including those with sins to their names, are "salvaging" themselves by obtaining prestigious, highly paid jobs under the new conditions. The protests have forestalled the salvage operation in a few specific cases, but the phenomenon remains quite common.

[7]This situation is predicted in my book (1990) mentioned above. A similar prediction is made independently, based on a markedly different line of thought, by P. Murrell (1990a, 1990b); even the expression used is the same in the two writings.

[8]Almost a prelude to this is the coexistence of socialism and the private sector under the system of reform socialism [→19.5], but in that case the private sector was in a subordinate, tolerated position. One can expect the power relations to change under the postsocialist system. The private sector will become, sooner or later, the dominant branch of the economy, recruiting the support of the state power behind it as well.

[9]In the earlier chapters, the final sections dealing with postsocialism have pointed in several places to the likely sources of conflict.

[10]One cannot claim that these values appear exclusively within the ideological realm of socialism. Many of them integrate into the moral concept of the Christian religion, or into

while, they are confused; they are also drawn toward moral values that contrast starkly with these values instilled over a long period. Let us take a few examples.

To what do citizens of a postsocialist country aspire? To be left in peace at last by the state, undisturbed by a million regulations, and unrestricted by a hundred obligations? Or do they demand an active state that takes wise measures, cares for the unfortunate, protects the environment, and regulates the uninhibited rise in prices? Do they accept or even welcome the fact that all may earn as much as they can, or are they outraged by high incomes and demand that they be heavily taxed?

If the political scene develops calmly, without excesses, both the politicians and the officials of the state apparatus will learn how to intervene with moderation and finely tuned methods in the workings of society and the economy, without tangling them and robbing them of their inherent forces of incentive. But until that happens, the attitude of people remains ambivalent: they want to see the state intervening cleverly, but they remain suspicious of it. That suspicion is going to take a long time to dispel.

One can expect many citizens to remain faithful to the ideas of solidarity, fairness, compassion for the weak, and rationality at a societal level, that is, to values that attracted so many honest people to socialistic ideas. But there is also the possibility that many will relapse from time to time into the discredited ideology of bureaucratic rule, etatism, paternalism, and egalitarianism. There is no telling how rapidly or consistently the change and clarification of the system of values will take place. And beyond the development of public sentiment, there is no predicting how long the profound transformation of all other properties of society will take. The transition will certainly be made easier if those involved in it, particularly those in responsible positions, realize as fully as possible where it started and what the nature of the old order was that has left such deep marks on the new. This thought was my primary inducement to write a book analyzing the socialist system, and this knowledge may reassure the reader that it was worth reading the work all through.

---

the ethics of the intellectual strands of Western freethinking. But the generations now transferring to the new regime as adults, perhaps in the middle or toward the end of their lives, have grown up and learned to respect these values under the socialist system.

References

Abraham, Katharine G., and James L. Medoff. 1982. "Unemployment, Unsatisfied Demand for Labor, and Compensation Growth, 1956-80," in *Workers, Jobs and Inflation,* edited by Martin Neil Baily. Washington, D.C.: Brookings Institution, pp. 49-88.

Adam, Jan. 1984. *Employment and Wage Policies in Poland, Czechoslovakia and Hungary since 1950.* London: Macmillan.

———. 1989. *Economic Reforms in the Soviet Union and Eastern Europe since the 1960s.* London: Macmillan.

———, ed. 1982. *Employment Policies in the Soviet Union and Eastern Europe.* London: Macmillan.

Adirim, Itzchak. 1989. "A Note on the Current Level, Pattern and Trends of Unemployment in the USSR," *Soviet Studies,* July, *41* (3), pp. 449-61.

Afanas'ev, M. P. 1990. "János Kornai: argumenty defitsita" (János Kornai: The arguments of the "Economics of shortage"). Moscow: Institute of Economics, Academy of Sciences of USSR. Manuscript.

Aganbegian, Abel G. 1989. *Inside Perestroika.* New York: Harper and Row.

Alchian, Armen A. 1950. "Uncertainty, Evolution, and Economic Theory," *Journal of Political Economy, 58* (3), pp. 211-21.

———. 1965. "Some Economics of Property Rights," *Il Politico, 30* (4), pp. 816-29.

———. 1974. "Foreword," in *The Economics of Property Rights,* edited by Erik G. Furubotn and Svetozar Pejovich. Cambridge, Mass.: Ballinger, pp. xiii-xv.

Alchian, Armen A., and Harold Demsetz. 1972. "Production, Information, Costs, and Economic Organization," *American Economic Review,* December, *62* (5), pp. 777-95.

Alessandrini, Sergio, and Bruno Dallago, eds. 1987. *The Unofficial Economy. Consequences and Perspectives in Different Economic Systems.* Aldershot, England: Dartmouth, and Brookfield, Vt.: Gower.

Alexeev, Michael. 1986. "Factors Influencing Distribution of Housing in the USSR," *Berkeley-Duke Occasional Papers on the Second Economy in the USSR,* December, no. 8.

———. 1987. "Microeconomic Modeling of Parallel Markets: The Case of Agricultural Goods in the USSR," *Journal of Comparative Economics,* December, *11* (4), pp. 543-57.

———. 1988a. "Markets vs. Rationing: The Case of Soviet Housing," *Review of Economics and Statistics, 70* (3), pp. 414-20.

———. 1988b. "The Effect of Housing Allocation on Social Inequality: A Soviet Perspective," *Journal of Comparative Economics,* June, *12* (2), pp. 228-34.

———. 1990. "Retail Price Reform in a Soviet-Type Economy: Are Soviet Reform Economists on a Right Track?" *Berkeley-Duke Occasional Papers on the Second Economy in the USSR,* February, no. 19.

Alton, Thad P. 1977. "Comparative Structure and Growth of Economic Activity in Eastern Europe," in *East European Economies Post Helsinki*. Joint Economic Committee, Congress of the United States. Washington, D.C.: Government Printing Office, pp. 199-266.

———. 1981. "Production and Resource Allocation in Eastern Europe: Performance, Problems and Prospects," in *East European Assessment, Part 2*. Joint Economic Committee, Congress of the United States. Washington, D.C.: Government Printing Office, pp. 348-408.

Alton, Thad P., et al. 1979. "Official and Alternative Consumer Price Indexes in Eastern Europe, Selected Years, 1960-78," *Working Papers*, L. W. International Financial Research, Inc., New York, September.

———. 1984. "Money Income of the Population and Standard of Living in Eastern Europe, 1970-1983," *Occasional Paper*, no. 83, Research Project on National Income in East Central Europe, New York: L. W. International Financial Research.

Amalrik, Andrei. 1970. *Will the Soviet Union Survive until 1984?* New York: Harper and Row.

Amann, Ronald, Julian M. Cooper, and Robert W. Davies, eds. 1977. *The Technological Level of Soviet Industry*. New Haven: Yale University Press.

Amann, Ronald, and Julian M. Cooper, eds. 1982. *Industrial Innovation in the Soviet Union*. New Haven: Yale University Press.

———. 1986. *Technical Progress and Soviet Economic Development*. New York: Basil Blackwell.

Andorka, Rudolf. 1988. "A magyarországi társadalmi mobilitás nemzetközi öszszehasonlítása: A férfiak nemzedékek közötti társadalmi mobilitása" (Hungarian social mobility in international comparison: Male intergenerational social mobility), *Szociológia* (3), pp. 221-40.

Antal, László. 1979. "Development—with Some Digression. The Hungarian Economic Mechanism in the Seventies," *Acta Oeconomica, 23* (3-4), pp. 257-73.

———. 1985. *Gazdaságirányítási és pénzügyi rendszerünk a reform útján* (The Hungarian system of economic control and finance on the way of reform). Budapest: Közgazdasági és Jogi Könyvkiadó.

Arendt, Hannah. 1951. *The Origins of Totalitarianism*. New York: Harcourt Brace Jovanovich.

Arrow, Kenneth J. 1964. "Control in Large Organizations," *Management Science*, April, *10* (3), pp. 397-408.

Árvay, János. 1973. *Nemzeti termelés, nemzeti jövedelem, nemzeti vagyon* (National production, national income, and national wealth). Budapest: Közgazdasági és Jogi Könyvkiadó.

Ash, Timothy G. 1990. *The Magic Lantern: The Revolution of 1989 Witnessed in Warsaw, Budapest, Berlin and Prague*. New York: Random House.

Åslund, Anders. 1985. *Private Enterprise in Eastern Europe. The Non-Agricultural Private Sector in Poland and the GDR, 1945-83*. Oxford: Macmillan, in association with St. Antony's College.

———. 1989. *Gorbachev's Struggle for Economic Reform. The Soviet Reform Process, 1985-88*. Ithaca: Cornell University Press.

―――. 1990. "How Small Is Soviet National Income?" in *The Impoverished Superpower: Perestroika and the Soviet Military Burden,* edited by Henry S. Rowen and Charles Wolf. San Francisco: ICS Press, pp. 13-62.

―――. 1991. "The Soviet Economic Crisis: Causes and Dimensions," *Working Paper,* no. 16. Stockholm: Stockholm Institute of Soviet and East European Economics.

Augusztinovics, Mária. 1965. "A Model of Money Circulation," *Economics of Planning, 5* (3), pp. 44-57.

Ausch, Sándor. 1972. *Theory and Practice of CMEA Cooperation.* Budapest: Akadémiai Kiadó.

Azicri, Max. 1988. *Cuba: Politics, Economics and Society.* Boulder: Lynne Rienner Publishers.

Balassa, Béla. 1987. "China's Economic Reforms in a Comparative Perspective," *Journal of Comparative Economics,* September, *11* (3), pp. 410-26.

Balázs, Katalin, and Mihály Laki. 1991. "A pénzben mért magángazdaság súlya a magyar háztartások bevételeiben és kiadásaiban" (The share of private economy in monetary terms in Hungarian household income and expenditure), *Közgazdasági Szemle,* May, *38* (5), pp. 500-22.

Balcerowicz, Leszek. 1988. "Polish Economic Reform, 1981-1988: An Overview," in *Economic Reforms in the European Centrally Planned Economies.* New York: United Nations, Economic Commission for Europe, pp. 42-51.

Baló, Görgy, and Iván Lipovecz, eds. 1987. *Tények könyve, 1988. Magyar és nemzetközi almanach* (The book of facts, 1988. Hungarian and international almanac). Budapest: Computerworld Informatika Kft and Móra Ferenc Ifjúsági Könyvkiadó.

Banerjee, Abhijit, and Michael Spagat. 1987. "Productivity Paralysis and the Complexity Problem: Why Do Centrally Planned Economies Become Prematurely Gray?" in M. Spagat, "Supply Disruption in Centrally Planned Economies," Ph.D. dissertation. Harvard University, pp. 2-20.

Bannasch, Hans-Gerd. 1990. "The Role of Small Firms in East Germany," *Small Business Economics,* December, *2* (4), pp. 307-11.

Barone, Enrico. [1908] 1935. "The Ministry of Production in the Collectivist State," in *Collectivist Economic Planning,* edited by Friedrich A. Hayek. London: Routledge and Kegan Paul, pp. 245-90.

Barro, Robert J., and Herschel I. Grossman. 1971. "A General Disequilibrium Model of Income and Employment," *American Economic Review,* March *61* (1), pp. 82-93.

―――. 1974. "Suppressed Inflation and the Supply Multiplier," *Review of Economic Studies,* January, *41* (1), pp. 87-104.

Bársony, Jenő. 1982. "Tibor Liska's Concept of Socialist Entrepreneurship," *Acta Oeconomica, 28* (3-4), pp. 422-55.

Bauer, Tamás. 1978, "Investment Cycles in Planned Economies," *Acta Oeconomica, 21* (3), pp. 243-60.

―――. 1981. *Tervgazdaság, beruházás, ciklusok* (Planned economy, investment, cycles). Budapest: Közgazdasági és Jogi Könyvkiadó.

———. 1983. "The Hungarian Alternative to Soviet-Type Planning," *Journal of Comparative Economics*, September, *7* (3), pp. 304–16.

———. 1987. "Reforming or Perfectioning the Economic Mechanism," *European Economic Review*, February/March, *31* (1–2), pp. 132–38.

Bek, Aleksandr. 1971. *Novoe naznachenie* (New appointment). Frankfurt am Main: Possev.

Belyó, Pál, and Béla Drexler. 1985. "A nem szervezett (elsősorban illegális) keretek között végzett szolgáltatások" (Services supplied within nonorganized, mainly illegal, framework). Budapest: University of Economics. Manuscript.

Benassy, Jean-Pascal. 1982. *The Economics of Market Disequilibrium*. New York: Academic Press.

Ben-Ner, Egon Neuberger. 1990. "The Feasibility of Planned Market Systems: The Yugoslav Visible Hand and Negotiated Planning," *Journal of Comparative Economics*, December, *14* (4), pp. 768–90.

Berend, Iván T. 1979. *A szocialista gazdaság fejlődése Magyarországon, 1945–1975*. (Development of the socialist economy in Hungary, 1945–1975). Budapest: Kossuth.

———. 1990. *The Hungarian Economic Reform*. Cambridge: Cambridge University Press.

Beresford, Melanie. 1988. *Vietnam: Politics, Economics and Society*. Boulder: Lynne Rienner Publishers.

Bergson, Abram. 1944. *The Structure of Soviet Wages*. Cambridge: Harvard University Press.

———. 1948. "Socialist Economics," in *A Survey of Contemporary Economics*, edited by Howard S. Ellis. Homewood, Ill.: Irwin, pp. 1412–48.

———. 1961. *The Real National Income of Soviet Russia since 1928*. Cambridge: Harvard University Press.

———. 1967. "Market Socialism Revisited," *Journal of Political Economy*, October, *75* (5), pp. 655–72.

———. 1974. *Soviet Post-War Economic Development*. Stockholm: Almquist and Wicksell.

———. 1978a. *Productivity and the Social System: The USSR and the West*. Cambridge: Harvard University Press.

———. 1978b. "Managerial Risks and Rewards in Public Enterprises," *Journal of Comparative Economics*, September, *2* (3), pp. 211–25.

———. 1978c. "The Soviet Economic Slowdown," *Challenge*, January/February, *20* (6), pp. 22–27.

———. 1979. "Notes on the Production Function in Soviet Postwar Growth," *Journal of Comparative Economics*, June, *3* (2), pp. 116–26.

———1983. "Technological Progress," in *The Soviet Economy: Toward the Year 2000*, edited by Abram Bergson and Herbert S. Levine. London: Allen and Unwin, pp. 34–78.

———. 1984. "Income Inequality under Soviet Socialism," *Journal of Economic Literature*, September, *22* (3), pp. 1052–99.

———. 1987. "Comparative Productivity: The USSR, Eastern Europe, and the West," *American Economic Review*, June, *77* (3), pp. 342–57.

Bergson, Abram, and Simon Kuznets, eds. 1963. *Economic Trends in the Soviet Union*. Cambridge: Harvard University Press.

Berle, Adolf A., and Gardiner C. Means. [1932] 1968. *The Modern Corporation and Private Property*. New York: Harcourt Brace and World.

Berlin, Isaiah. 1969. "Two Concepts of Liberty," in I. Berlin, *Four Essays on Liberty*. Oxford: Oxford University Press, pp. 118–72.

Berliner, Joseph S. 1957. *Factory and Manager in the USSR*. Cambridge: Harvard University Press.

———. 1976. *The Innovation Decision in Soviet Industry*. Cambridge: MIT Press.

Bettelheim, Charles. 1987. "Les grands cycles de l'économie cubaine, 1959–1985," in *Régulation, cycles et crises dans les économies socialistes,* edited by Bernard Chavance. Paris: Éditions de l'EHESS, pp. 241–62.

Beznosnikov, V. N. 1990. Participant in a conversation in *Individual'no-kooperativnyi sektor* (The individual cooperative sector), edited by Abel G. Aganbegian et al. Moscow: Ekonomika, p. 25.

Bialer, Seweryn. 1980. *Stalin's Successors*. New York: Cambridge University Press.

Bibó, István. [1945] 1986a. "A magyar demokrácia válsága" (The crisis of Hungarian democracy), in I. Bibó, *Válogatott tanulmányok. Második kötet, 1945–1949* (Selected studies. Second volume, 1945–1949). Budapest: Magvető, pp. 13–79.

———. [1946] 1986b. "A magyar demokrácia mérlege" (An evaluation of Hungarian democracy), in I. Bibó *Válogatott tanulmányok. Második kötet, 1945–1949* (Selected studies. Second volume, 1945–1949). Budapest: Magvető, pp. 119–83.

Birman, Igor. 1980. "The Financial Crisis in the USSR," *Soviet Studies,* January, *32* (1), pp. 84–105.

Birta, István. 1970. "A szocialista iparosítási politika néhány kérdése az első ötéves terv időszakában" (Selected issues of the socialist industrialization policy in the period of the first five-year plan), *Párttörténeti Közlemények, 16* (4), pp. 113–50.

Bleaney, Michael. 1988. *Do Socialist Economies Work? The Socialist and East European Experience*. Oxford and New York: Basil Blackwell.

Blejer, Mario I., and György Szapáry. 1990. "The Evolving Role of Tax Policy in China," *Journal of Comparative Economics*, September, *14* (3), pp. 452–72.

Bogomolov, Oleg. 1987. "Skol'ko stoiat den'gi" (How much does money cost), *Literaturnaia Gazeta*, September 16 (38), p. 12.

Boiko, Tatiana M. 1990. "Nash potrebitel'skii rynok" (Our consumer market), *EKO*, April (4), pp. 84–86.

Bond, Daniel L., and Herbert S. Levine. 1983. "An Overview," in *The Soviet Economy: Toward the Year 2000,* edited by Abram Bergson and Herbert S. Levine. London: Allen and Unwin, pp. 1–33.

Bonin, John P. 1976. "On the Design of Managerial Incentive Schemes in a Decentralized Planning Environment," *American Economic Review,* September, *66* (4), pp. 682–87.

Bonin, John P., and Louis Putterman. 1987. *Economics of Cooperation and the Labor-Managed Economy.* New York: Harwood Academic Publishers.

Bornstein, Morris. 1985. "Improving the Soviet Economic Mechanism," *Soviet Studies,* January, *37* (1), pp. 1–30.

———. 1987. "Soviet Price Policies," *Soviet Economy,* April/June, *3* (2), pp. 96–134.

Bossányi, Katalin. 1986. "Economy on the Way of Democratization," *Acta Oeconomica, 37* (3–4), pp. 285–304.

Bottomore, Tom, ed. 1983. *A Dictionary of Marxist Thought.* Cambridge: Harvard University Press.

Bowles, Paul, and Gordon White. 1989. "Contradictions in China's Financial Reforms: The Relationship between Banks and Enterprises," *Cambridge Journal of Economics,* December, *13* (4), pp. 481–95.

Boyd, Michael L. 1990. "Organizational Reform and Agricultural Performance: The Case of Bulgarian Agriculture, 1960–1985," *Journal of Comparative Economics,* March, *14* (1), pp. 70–87.

Brabant, Jozef M. van. 1980. *Socialist Economic Integration. Aspects of Contemporary Economic Problems in Eastern Europe.* Cambridge: Cambridge University Press.

———. 1989. *Economic Integration in Eastern Europe. A Handbook.* New York: Harvester Wheatsheaf.

———. 1990. "Socialist Economics: The Disequilibrium School and the Shortage Economy," *Journal of Economic Perspectives,* Spring, *4* (2), pp. 157–75.

Brada, Josef C. 1985. "Soviet Subsidization of Eastern Europe: The Primacy of Economics over Politics?" *Journal of Comparative Economics,* March, *9* (4), pp. 21–39.

———. 1986. "The Variability of Crop Production in Private and Socialized Agriculture: Evidence from Eastern Europe," *Journal of Political Economy, 94* (3), pp. 545–63.

Brecht, Bertolt. 1967. *Gesammelte Werke* (Collected works). Vol. 10. Frankfurt am Main: Suhrkamp.

Bródy, András. 1956. "A hóvégi hajrá és gazdasági mechanizmusunk" (Rush at the end of the month and our economic mechanism), *Közgazdasági Szemle,* July/August, *3* (7–8), pp. 870–83.

———. 1964. *Az ágazati kapcsolatok modellje. A felhasznált absztrakciók, azok korlátai és a számítások pontossága* (Input-output tables: The abstractions used, their limitations, and the accuracy of the calculations). Budapest: Akadémiai Kiadó.

———. 1969a. *Érték és ujratermelés. Kísérlet a marxi értékelmélet és újratermelési elmélet matematikai modelljének megfogalmazására.* (Value and reproduction. An attempt at formulating the mathematical model of Marxian theory of value and reproduction). Budapest: Közgazdasági és Jogi Könyvkiadó.

———. 1969b. "The Rate of Economic Growth in Hungary, 1924–65," in *Is the Business Cycle Obsolete?,* edited by Martin Bronfenbrenner. New York: John Wiley, pp. 312–27.

———. 1979. *Prices, Production and Planning.* Amsterdam: North-Holland.

Brooks, Karen M. 1990. "Soviet Agriculture's Halting Reform," *Problems of Communism,* March/April, *39* (2), pp. 29–41.

Brus, Wlodzimierz. [1961] 1972. *The Market in a Socialist Economy.* London: Routledge and Kegan Paul.

Brus, Wlodzimierz, and Kazimierz Laski. 1989. *From Marx to the Market. Socialism in Search of an Economic System.* Oxford: Clarendon Press.

Bryson, Phillip J., and Manfred Melzer. 1987. "The *Kombinat* in GDR Economic Organization," in *The East German Economy,* edited by Ian Jeffries and Manfred Melzer. London: Croom Helm, pp. 51–68.

Brzezinski, Zbigniew. [1961] 1967. *The Soviet Bloc: Unity and Conflict.* Cambridge: Harvard University Press.

———. 1990. *The Grand Failure. The Birth and Death of Communism in the Twentieth Century.* New York: Macmillan.

Brzezinski, Zbigniew, and Carl Friedrich. 1956. *Totalitarian Dictatorship and Autocracy.* Cambridge: Harvard University Press.

Bundesministerium für Innerdeutsche Beziehungen. 1987. *Materialien zum Bericht zur Lage der Nation im geteilten Deutschland 1987.* Bonn.

Bunge, Frederica M. 1985. *North Korea: A Country Study.* Washington, D.C.: Foreign Area Studies, The American University, Government Printing Office.

Burkett, John P. 1988. "Slack, Shortage and the Discouraged Consumers in Eastern Europe: Estimates Based on Smoothing by Aggregation," *Review of Economic Studies*, July, *55* (3), pp. 493–505.

———. 1989. "The Yugoslav Economy and Market Socialism," in *Comparative Economic Systems: Models and Cases,* edited by Morris Bornstein. Homewood, Ill.: Irwin, pp. 234–58.

Burkett, John P., Richard Portes, and David Winter. "Macroeconomic Adjustment and Foreign Trade of Centrally Planned Economies," *Working Paper,* no. 736. Cambridge, Mass.: National Bureau of Economic Research.

Burnham, James. 1941. *The Managerial Revolution.* New York: John Day.

Byrd, William A. 1990. *The Market Mechanism and Economic Reforms in Chinese Industry.* Armonk, N.Y.: M. E. Sharpe.

Byrd, William A., and Qingsong Lin, eds. 1990. *China's Rural Industry. Structure, Development and Reform.* Oxford: Oxford University Press, published for the World Bank.

Calvo, Guillermo A., and Stanislaw Wellisz. 1978. "Supervision, Loss of Control, and the Optimum Size of the Firm," *Journal of Political Economy*, October, *86* (5), pp. 943–52.

Campbell, Neil A. 1987. *Biology.* Menlo Park: Benjamin-Cummings.

Campbell, Robert W. 1978. "Economic Reform and Adaptation of the CPSU," in *Soviet Society and the Communist Party,* edited by Karl Ryavec. Amherst: University of Massachusetts Press, pp. 26–48.

———. [1974] 1981. *The Soviet-Type Economies: Performance and Evolution.* Boston: Houghton Mifflin.

Cao-Pinna, Vera, and Stanislaw S. Shatalin. 1979. *Consumption Patterns in Eastern and Western Europe. An Economic Comparative Approach. A Collective Study.* Oxford: Pergamon Press.

Carr, Edward H., and Robert W. Davies. [1969] 1974. *Foundations of a Planned Economy*. New York: Macmillan.

Ceausescu, Nicolae. 1978. *Speeches and Writings*. London: Spokesmen.

Central Intelligence Agency. 1989. *Handbook of Economic Statistics, 1989*. Washington, D.C.: CIA.

Chamberlin, Edward H. [1933] 1962. *The Theory of Monopolistic Competition*. Cambridge: Harvard University Press.

Chandler, Alfred D. 1977. *The Visible Hand: The Managerial Revolution in American Business*. Cambridge: Harvard University Press.

Chang, Hsin. 1984. "The 1982–83 Overinvestment Crisis in China," *Asian Survey*, December, *24* (12), pp. 1275–1301.

Chapman, Janet G. 1963. *Real Wages in Soviet Russia Since 1928*. Cambridge: Harvard University Press.

———. 1977. "Soviet Wages Under Socialism," in *The Socialist Price Mechanism*, edited by Alan Abouchar. Durham, N.C.: Duke University Press, pp. 246–81.

———. 1989. "Income Distribution and Social Justice in the Soviet Union," *Comparative Economic Studies*, Spring, *31* (1), pp. 14–45.

Charemza, Wojciech W. 1989. "Disequilibrium Modelling of Consumption in the Centrally Planned Economy," in *Models of Disequilibrium and Shortage in Centrally Planned Economies*, edited by Christopher Davis and Wojciech W. Charemza. New York: Chapman and Hall, pp. 283–315.

Charemza, Wojciech W., and Subrata Ghatak. 1990 "Demand for Money in a Dual-Currency, Quantity-Constrained Economy: Hungary and Poland, 1956–1985," *The Economic Journal*, December, *100* (403), pp. 1159–72.

Charemza, Wojciech W., Miroslaw Gronicki, and Richard E. Quandt. 1989. "Modelling Parallel Markets in Centrally Planned Economies: The Case of the Automobile Market in Poland," in *Models of Disequilibrium and Shortage in Centrally Planned Economies*, edited by Christopher Davis and Wojciech W. Charemza. New York: Chapman and Hall, pp. 405–25.

Chavance, Bernard. 1987. "Fluctuations et cycles économiques en Chine," in *Régulation, cycles et crises dans les économies socialistes*, edited by Bernard Chavance. Paris: Éditions de l'EHESS, pp. 263–83.

Chen, Kuan, et al. 1988. "Productivity Change in Chinese Industry: 1953–1985," *Journal of Comparative Economics*, December, *12* (4), pp. 570–91.

Chinese Institute for Reform of the Economic System. 1986. *Gaige: women mianling de tiaozhan yu xuanze* (Reforms: Our challenges and options). Beijing: Chinese Economic Press.

Chow, Gregory C. 1985. *The Chinese Economy*. New York: Harper and Row.

Close, David. 1988. *Nicaragua: Politics, Economics and Society*. Boulder: Lynne Rienner Publishers.

Clower, Robert W. 1965. "The Keynesian Counterrevolution: A Theoretical Appraisal," in *The Theory of Interest Rates*, edited by F. H. Hahn and F. P. R. Brechling. London: Macmillan, pp. 103–25.

Coase, Ronald H. 1937. "The Nature of the Firm," *Economica*, November, *4* (16), pp. 386–405.

——. 1960. "The Problem of Social Costs," *Journal of Law and Economics,* October, *3,* pp. 1–44.

Cochrane, Nancy J. 1988. "The Private Sector in East European Agriculture," *Problems of Communism,* March/April, *37* (2), pp. 47–53.

Cohen, Stephen F. [1973] 1980. *Bukharin and the Bolshevik Revolution: A Political Biography, 1888–1938.* New York: W. W. Norton.

——. 1984. "The Friends and Foes of Change: Reformism and Conservatism in the Soviet Union," in *The Soviet Polity in the Modern Era,* edited by Eric P. Hoffman and Robbin F. Laird. New York: Aldine, pp. 85–103.

——. 1985. *Rethinking the Soviet Experience.* New York: Oxford University Press.

Collier, Irwin L. 1986. "Effective Purchasing Power in a Quantity Constrained Economy: An Estimate for the German Democratic Republic," *Review of Economics and Statistics,* February, *68* (1), pp. 24–32.

Colton, Timothy J. 1986. *The Dilemma of Reform in the Soviet Union.* New York: Council on Foreign Relations.

Conn, David, ed. 1979. "The Theory of Incentives," special issue of *Journal of Comparative Economics,* September, *3* (3).

Connor, Walter D. 1975. "Generations and Politics in the USSR," *Problems of Communism,* September/October, *24* (5), pp. 20–35.

——. 1979. *Socialism, Politics and Equality. Hierarchy and Change in Eastern Europe and the USSR.* New York: Columbia University Press.

Conquest, Robert. [1968] 1973. *The Great Terror. Stalin's Purge of the Thirties.* New York: Macmillan.

——. 1986. *The Harvest of Sorrow.* New York: Oxford University Press.

Cornelsen, Doris. 1990. "Die Wirtschaft der DDR in der Honecker-Ära," *Vierteljahreshefte zur Wirtschaftsforschung,* DIW, no. 1.

Csaba, László. 1990. *Eastern Europe in the World Economy.* Cambridge: Cambridge University Press.

Csákó, Mihály, et al. 1979. "Közoktatási rendszer és társadalmi struktura" (Public education system and social structure), in *Rétegződés, mobilitás és egyenlőtlenség* (Stratification, mobility, and inequality), edited by K. P. Kálmán. Budapest: MSZMP KB Társadalomtudományi Intézet, pp. 85–164.

Csikós-Nagy, Béla. 1985. *Árpolitikánk időszerű kérdései (1985–1988)* (Timely issues in our price policy, 1985–1988). Budapest: Közgazdasági és Jogi Könyvkiadó.

Culbertson, William P., and R. C. Amacher. 1972. "Inflation in the Planned Economies: Some Estimates for Eastern Europe," *Southern Economic Journal,* *45* (2), pp. 380–93.

Dahl, Robert A., and Charles E. Lindblom. 1953. *Politics, Economics and Welfare.* New York: Harper and Bros.

Dahrendorf, Ralf. 1959. *Class and Class Conflict.* London: Routledge and Kegan Paul.

Dallago, Bruno. 1990. *The Irregular Economy: The Underground Economy and the Black Labor Market.* Aldershot, England: Dartmouth, and Brookfield, Vt.: Gower.

Dániel, Zsuzsa. 1975. "The 'Reflection' of Economic Growth: Experimental Computations to Revise Synthetic Value Indicators of Output," *Acta Oeconomica, 15* (2), pp. 135–55.

———. 1985. "The Effect of Housing Allocation on Social Inequality in Hungary," *Journal of Comparative Economics*, December, *9* (4), pp. 391–409.

———. 1989. "Housing Demand in a Shortage Economy: Results of a Hungarian Survey," *Acta Oeconomica, 41* (1–2), pp. 157–80.

Dániel, Zsuzsa, and András Semjén. 1987. "Housing Shortage and Rents: The Hungarian Experience," *Economics of Planning, 21* (1), pp. 13–29.

Davies, Robert W. 1980. *The Socialist Offensive: The Collectivization of Soviet Agriculture, 1929–30*. Cambridge: Harvard University Press.

Davis, Christopher. 1988. "The Second Economy in Disequilibrium and Shortage Models of Centrally Planned Economies," *Berkeley-Duke Occasional Papers on the Second Economy in the USSR*, July, no. 12.

———. 1989. "Priority and the Shortage Model: The Medical System in the Socialist Economy," in *Models of Disequilibrium and Shortage in Centrally Planned Economies*, edited by Christopher Davis and Wojciech W. Charemza. New York: Chapman and Hall, pp. 427–59.

———. 1990. "The High Priority Military Sector in a Shortage Economy," in *The Impoverished Superpower: Perestroika and the Soviet Military Burden*, edited by Henry S. Rowen and Charles Wolf. San Francisco: ICS Press, pp. 155–84.

Davis, Christopher, and Wojciech W. Charemza, eds. 1989. *Models of Disequilibrium and Shortage in Centrally Planned Economies*. London: Chapman and Hall.

Dembinski, Pawel H. 1988. "Quantity versus Allocation of Money: Monetary Problems of the Centrally Planned Economies Reconsidered," *Kyklos, 41* (2), pp. 281–300.

Dembinski, Pawel H., and Waclaw Piaszczynski. 1988. *The FOF Matrix Methodology*. Geneva: Cahiers du Département d'Économie Politique, University of Geneva.

Demszky, Gábor; György Gadó, and Ferenc Kőszeg, eds. 1987. *Roundtable: Digest of the Independent Hungarian Press*. 2 vols. Budapest: Beszélő, A Hirmondó, and Demokrata.

Deng, Xiaoping. 1987. "The Party's Urgent Tasks on the Organizational and Ideological Fronts," in Deng Xiaoping, *Fundamental Issues in Present-Day China*. Beijing: Foreign Languages Press, pp. 24–40.

———. [1962] 1989. "How Can Agricultural Production be Recovered," in *Deng Xiaoping wenxuan* (Selected works of Deng Xiaoping, 1938–65). Beijing: People's Press, p. 305.

Denison, Edward F. 1962. *The Sources of Economic Growth in the United States and the Alternatives Before Us*. New York: Committee for Economic Development.

———. 1967. *Why Do Growth Rates Differ? Post-War Experience in Nine Western Countries*. Washington, D.C.: Brookings Institution.

Dervis, Kemal; Jaime de Melo, and Sherman Robinson. 1982. *General Equilibrium Models for Development Policy*. Cambridge: Cambridge University Press.

Desai, Padma. 1976. "The Production Function and Technical Change in Postwar Soviet Industry: A Reexamination," *American Economic Review*, June, *66* (3), pp. 372–81.

———. 1986a. "Soviet Growth Retardation," *American Economic Review*, May, *76* (2), pp. 175–80.

———. 1986b. *The Soviet Economy: Efficiency, Technical Change and Growth Retardation*. Oxford: Basil Blackwell.

———. 1987. *The Soviet Economy: Problems and Prospects*. Oxford: Basil Blackwell.

———. 1989. *Perestroika in Perspective. The Design and Dilemmas of Soviet Reform*. Princeton: Princeton University Press.

Deutscher, Isaac. 1966. *Stalin: A Political Biography*. New York: Oxford University Press.

Dewatripont, Michel, and Eric Maskin. 1990. "Credit and Efficiency in Centralized and Decentralized Economies," *Discussion Paper*, no. 1512. Cambridge: Harvard Institute of Economic Research, Harvard University.

Djilas, Aleksa. 1991. *The Contested Country. Yugoslav Unity and Communist Revolution, 1919–1953*. Cambridge: Harvard University Press.

Djilas, Milovan. 1957. *The New Class. An Analysis of the Communist System*. New York: Praeger.

———. 1988. "Between Revolution and Counter-Revolution. Djilas on Gorbachev. Milovan Djilas and George Urban in Conversation," *Encounter*, September/October, *71* (3), pp. 3–19.

Dobb, Maurice H. [1948] 1960. *Soviet Economic Development since 1917*. London: Routledge and Kegan.

Domar, Evsey. 1989. "The Blind Men and the Elephant: An Essay on Isms," in E. Domar, *Capitalism, Socialism, and Serfdom*. Cambridge: Cambridge University Press, pp. 29–46.

Drejtoria E Statistikes (Directorate of Statistics). 1989. *Vjetari Statistikor I R.P.S. Të Shgipërisë*. (Statistical yearbook of Albania). Tirana.

Drèze, Jacques H. 1976. "Some Theory of Labor Management and Participation," *Econometrica*, November, *44* (6), pp. 1125–39.

Dunmore, Timothy. 1980. *The Stalinist Command Economy: The Soviet State Apparatus and Economic Policy, 1945–53*. London: Macmillan.

Dyker, David A. 1990. *Yugoslavia: Socialism, Development, and Debt*. New York: Routledge.

Echeverri-Gent, John. 1990. "Economic Reform in India: A Long and Winding Road," in *Economic Reform in Three Giants*, by Richard E. Feinberg, John Echeverri-Gent, and Friedemann Müller, New Brunswick: Transaction Books, pp. 103–33.

Eckstein, Alexander. 1980. *Quantitative Measures of China's Economic Output*. Ann Arbor: University of Michigan Press.

Ehrlich, Éva. 1981. "Comparison of Development Levels: Inequalities in the Physical Structures of National Economies," in *Disparities in Economic Development since the Industrial Revolution,* edited by P. Bairoch and M. Lévy-Leboyer. London: Macmillan, pp. 395–410.

———. 1985a. "The Size Structure of Manufacturing Establishments and Enterprises: An International Comparison," *Journal of Comparative Economics,* September, *9* (3), pp. 267–95.

———. 1985b. "Infrastructure," in *The Economic History of Eastern Europe 1919–1975,* vol. 1, edited by M. C. Kaser and E. A. Radice. Oxford: Clarendon Press, pp. 323–78.

———. 1985c. "Economic Development Levels, Proportions and Structures." Budapest: MTA Világgazdasági Kutatóintézet. Manuscript.

———. 1990. "Országok versenye" (Competition among countries), *Közgazdasági Szemle,* January, *37* (1), pp. 19–43.

Ellman, Michael. 1971. *Soviet Planning Today. Proposals for an Optimally Functioning Economic System.* Cambridge: Cambridge University Press.

———. 1973. *Planning Problems in the USSR: The Contribution of Mathematical Economics to Their Solution, 1960–1971.* Cambridge: Cambridge University Press.

———. 1982. "Did Soviet Economic Growth End in 1978?" in *Crisis in the East European Economy: The Spread of the Polish Disease,* edited by J. Drewnowski. London, Croom Helm, and New York: St. Martin's Press, pp. 131–42.

———. 1985. *Capitalism, Socialism and Convergence.* London: Academic Press.

Engels, Friedrich. [1894] 1963. "Nachwort (1894) [zu 'Soziales aus Russland'],'' in *Karl Marx, Friedrich Engels Werke.* Vol. 22, Berlin: Dietz Verlag, pp. 421–35.

———. [1847] 1964. "Principles of Communism," in K. Marx and F. Engels, *The Communist Manifesto and the Principles of Communism.* New York: Monthly Review Press, pp. 67–83.

———. [1878] 1975. "Anti-Dühring," in K. Marx and F. Engels, *Collected Works.* Vol. 25. New York: International Publishers, pp. 5–309.

Ericson, Richard. 1983. "On an Allocative Role of the Soviet Second Economy," in *Marxism, Central Planning, and the Soviet Economy: Economic Essays in Honor of Alexander Erlich,* edited by Padma Desai. Cambridge: MIT Press, pp. 110–32.

———. 1984. "The 'Second Economy' and Resource Allocation under Central Planning," *Journal of Comparative Economics,* March, *8* (1), pp. 1–24.

———. 1990. "The Soviet Statistical Debate: Khanin vs. TsSU," in *The Impoverished Superpower: Perestroika and the Soviet Military Burden,* edited by Henry S. Rowen and Charles Wolf. San Francisco: ICS Press, pp. 63–92.

Erlich, Alexander. 1960. *The Soviet Industrialization Debate, 1924–28.* Cambridge: Harvard University Press.

Estrin, Saul. 1983. *Self-Management. Economic Theory and Yugoslav Practice.* Cambridge: Cambridge University Press.

Eucken, Walter. 1951. *The Foundations of Economics: History and Theory in the Analysis of Economic Reality.* Chicago: University of Chicago Press.

Europa Publications. 1980–87. *The Europa Yearbook*. London.

European Community. 1990. *Stabilization, Liberalization and Decentralization*. Brussels.

Fallenbuchl, Zbigniew M. 1982. "Employment Policies in Poland," in *Employment Policies in the Soviet Union and Eastern Europe*, edited by Jan Adam. London: Macmillan, pp. 26–48.

———. 1988. "Present State of the Economic Reform," in *Creditworthiness and Reform in Poland. Western and Polish Perspectives*, edited by Paul Marer and Wlodzimierz Siwinski. Bloomington: Indiana University Press, pp. 115–30.

———. 1989. "Poland: The Anatomy of Stagnation," in *Pressures for Reform in the East European Economies*. Vol. 2. Joint Economic Committee, Congress of the United States. Washington, D.C.: Government Printing Office, pp. 102–36.

Fama, Eugene F., and Michael C. Jensen. 1983. "Separation of Ownership and Control," *Journal of Law and Economics*, June, *26* (2), pp. 301–25.

Fazekas, Károly, and János Köllő. 1990. *Munkaerőpiac tőkepiac nélkül* (Labor market without capital market). Budapest: Közgazdasági és Jogi Könyvkiadó.

Fedorenko, Nikolai P., ed. 1975. *Sistema modelei optimal'nogo planirovanii* (The system of optimal planning models). Moscow: Nauka.

Fehér, Ferenc. 1982. "Paternalism as a Mode of Legitimation in Soviet-Type Societies," in *Political Legitimation in Communist States*, edited by Thomas H. Rigby and Ferenc Fehér. Oxford: Macmillan, pp. 64–81.

Fehér, Ferenc, Ágnes Heller, and György Márkus. 1983. *Dictatorship over Needs*. Oxford: Basil Blackwell, and New York: St. Martin's Press.

Feige, Edgar L., ed. 1989. *The Underground Economies*. Cambridge: Cambridge University Press.

Feinberg, Richard E., John Echeverri-Gent, and Friedemann Müller. 1990. *Economic Reform in Three Giants*. New Brunswick: Transaction Books.

Ferge, Zsuzsa. 1988. "Gazdasági érdekek és politikák" (Economic interests and policies), *Gazdaság, 12* (1), pp. 47–64.

Finansy i Statistika (Finance and Statistics). 1977. *Narodnoe khoziaistvo SSSR v 1977* (The national economy of the Soviet Union in 1977). Moscow.

———. 1985. *SSSR v tsifrakh v 1984 godu* (The USSR in figures in 1984). Moscow.

———. 1987. *Narodnoe khoziaistvo SSSR za 70 let* (The national economy of USSR for seventy years). Moscow.

———. 1988a. *SSSR i zarubezhnye strany 1987* (The USSR and foreign countries, 1987). Moscow.

———. 1988b. *Narodnoe Khoziaistvo SSSR v 1988*. (The national economy of the Soviet Union in 1988). Moscow.

———. 1989a. *Narodnoe Khoziaistvo SSSR v 1989*. (The national economy of the Soviet Union in 1989). Moscow.

———. 1989b. *Statisticheskii ezhegodnik stran-chlenov Soveta Ekonomicheskoi Vzaimopomoshchi* (CMEA statistical yearbook). Moscow.

Fischer-Galati, Stephen, ed. 1979. *The Communist Parties of Eastern Europe*. New York: Columbia University Press.

Freixas, Xavier, Roger Guesnerie, and Jean Tirole. 1985. "Planning under Incomplete Information and the Ratchet Effect," *Review of Economic Studies*, April, *52* (2), pp. 173–91.

Frydman, Roman, Stanislaw Wellisz, and Grzegorz W. Kolodko. 1990. "Stabilization in Poland: A Progress Report." Revised version of a paper prepared for the conference on Exchange Rate Policies of Less Developed Market and Socialist Economies, Berlin, May 10–12. Manuscript.

Furubotn, Eirik G., and Svetozar Pejovich. 1972. "Property Rights and Economic Theory: A Survey of Recent Literature," *Journal of Economic Literature*, December, *10* (4), pp. 1137–62.

Gábor, István R. 1979. "The Second (Secondary) Economy. Earning Activity and Regrouping of Income Outside the Socially Organized Production and Distribution," *Acta Oeconomica*, *22* (3–4), pp. 291–311.

Gábor, István R., and György Kővári. 1990. *Beválthatók-e a bérreform ígéretei?* (Can the promises of the wage reform be fulfilled?). Budapest: Közgazdasági és Jogi Könyvkiadó.

Gács, János. 1980. "Importszabályozás és vállalati viselkedés" (Import regulation and the behavior of the firm). Budapest: Konjunktura és Piackutató Intézet. Manuscript.

Gács, János, and Mária Lackó. 1973. "A Study of Planning Behaviour on the National-Economic Level," *Economics of Planning, 13* (1–2), pp. 91–119.

Gaidar, Egor. 1990. "Trudnyi vybor" (Tough choice), *Kommunist*, January, (2), pp. 23–34.

Galasi, Péter, and Gábor Kertesi. 1987. "The Spread of Bribery in a Centrally Planned Economy," *Acta Oeconomica, 38* (3–4), pp. 371–89.

———. 1989. "Rat Race and Equilibria in Markets with Side Payments under Socialism," *Acta Oeoconomica, 41* (3–4), pp. 267–92.

Galasi, Péter, and György Sziráczki, eds. 1985. *Labour Market and Second Economy in Hungary.* Frankfurt: Campus Verlag.

Gapinski, James H., Borislav Skegro, and Thomas W. Zuehlke. 1987. "Modeling, Forecasting, and Improving Yugoslav Economic Performance." Tallahassee, Fla.: Florida State University, and Zagreb: Economics Institute Zagreb, October. Manuscript.

Garetovskii, N. V. 1989. "Voprosy sovershenstvovaniia bankovskoi sistemy" (Issues in perfecting the banking system), *Deng'i i Kredit,* (11), pp. 8–16.

Garvy, George. 1966. *Money, Banking and Credit in Eastern Europe.* New York: Federal Reserve Bank.

———. 1977. *Money, Financial Flows and Credit in the Soviet Union.* Cambridge, Mass.: Ballinger.

Gati, Charles. 1984. "The Democratic Interlude in Post-War Hungary," *Survey,* Summer, *28* (2), pp. 99–134.

Gedeon, Shirley J. 1985–86. "The Post Keynesian Theory of Money: A Summary and an Eastern European Example," *Journal of Post Keynesian Economics,* Winter, *8* (2), pp. 208–21.

———. 1987. "Monetary Disequilibrium and Bank Reform Proposals in Yugoslavia: Paternalism and the Economy," *Soviet Studies,* April, *39* (2), pp. 281–91.

Gerschenkron, Alexander. 1962. *Economic Backwardness in Historical Perspective. A Book of Essays.* New York: Praeger.

———. 1968 *Continuity in History and Other Essays.* Cambridge, Mass.: Belknap Press.

Glowny Urzad Statystyczny. (Central Statistical Office). 1990. *Rocznik Statystyczny 1990* (Statistical yearbook, 1990). Warsaw.

Goldfeld, Stephen M., and Richard E. Quandt. 1988. "Budget Constraints, Bailouts, and the Firm under Central Planning," *Journal of Comparative Economics,* December, *12* (4), pp. 502–20.

———. 1990a. "Rationing, Defective Inputs and Bayesian Updates under Central Planning," *Economics of Planning, 23* (3), pp. 161–73.

———. 1990b. "Output Targets, Input Rationing and Inventories," in *Optimal Decisions in Market and Planned Economies,* edited by Richard E. Quandt and Dusan Triska. Boulder: Westview Press, pp. 67–81.

Goldman, Marshall I. 1987. *Gorbachev's Challenge. Economic Reform in the Age of High Technology.* New York: W. W. Norton.

Goldmann, Josef. 1975. *Makroekonomická Analyza—a Prognóza* (Macroeconomic analysis—a prognosis). Prague: Academia.

Goldmann, Josef, and Karel Kouba. 1969. *Economic Growth in Czechoslovakia.* White Plains, N.Y.: International Arts and Sciences Press.

Gomulka, Stanislaw. 1985. "Kornai's Soft Budget Constraint and the Shortage Phenomenon: A Criticism and Restatement," *Economics of Planning, 19* (1), pp. 1–11.

———. 1986. *Growth, Innovation and Reform in Eastern Europe.* Brighton: Wheatsheaf.

Gomulka, Stanislaw, and Anthony Polonsky, eds. 1990. *Polish Paradoxes.* London: Routledge.

Gomulka, Stanislaw, and Jacek Rostowski. 1988. "An International Comparison of Material Intensity," *Journal of Comparative Economics,* December, *12* (4), pp. 475–501.

Gorbachev, Mikhail S. 1987. *Perestroika.* New York: Harper and Row.

Gössmann, Wolfgang. 1987. *Die Kombinate in der DDR.* Berlin: Arno Spitz.

Götz-Coenenberg, Roland. 1990. "Währungsintegration in Deutschland: Alternativen und Konsequenzen," *Berichte des Bundesinstituts für ostwissenschaftliche und internationale Studien,* no. 20. Cologne.

Gotz-Kozierkiewicz, Danuta, and Grzegorz W. Kolodko. 1990. "Stabilization in Viet Nam," *Working Papers,* no. 11. Warsaw: Institute of Finance.

Granick, David. 1954. *The Red Executive.* New York: Columbia University Press.

———. 1975. *Enterprise Guidance in Eastern Europe. A Comparison of Four Socialist Economies.* Princeton: Princeton University Press.

Gregory, Paul R. 1990. "The Stalinist Command Economy," *Annals of the AAPS,* January, *507,* pp. 18–26.

Gregory, Paul R., and Irwin L. Collier. 1988. "Unemployment in the Soviet Union: Evidence from the Soviet Interview Project," *American Economic Review,* September, *78* (4), pp. 613–32.

Gregory, Paul R., and Robert C. Stuart. 1980. *Comparative Economic Systems.* Boston: Houghton Mifflin.

———. [1974] 1986. *Soviet Economic Structure and Performance.* New York: Harper and Row.

Griffiths, Franklyn, and Gordon H. Skilling, eds. 1971. *Interest Groups in Soviet Politics.* Princeton: Princeton University Press.

Groenewegen, Peter. 1987. " 'Political Economy' and 'Economics'," in *The New Palgrave. A Dictionary of Economics,* edited by John Eatwell, Murray Milgate, and Peter Newman. London: Macmillan, and New York: The Stockton Press. Vol. 3, pp. 904–7.

Grosfeld, Irena. 1986. "Endogenous Planners and the Investment Cycle in the Centrally Planned Economies," *Comparative Economic Studies,* Spring, *28* (1), pp. 42–53.

———. 1989a. "Disequilibrium Models of Investment," in *Models of Disequilibrium and Shortage in Centrally Planned Economies,* edited by Christopher Davis and Wojciech W. Charemza. New York: Chapman and Hall, pp. 361–74.

———. 1989b. "Reform Economics and Western Economic Theory: Unexploited Opportunities," *Economics of Planning,* 22 (1), pp. 1–19.

Grossman, Gregory. 1966. "Gold and the Sword: Money in the Soviet Command Economy," in *Industrialization in Two Systems,* edited by Henry Rosovsky. New York: John Wiley, pp. 204–36.

———. 1977a. "The 'Second Economy' of the USSR," *Problems of Communism,* September/October, *26* (5), pp. 25–40.

———. 1977b. "Price Control, Incentives, and Innovation in the Soviet Economy," in *The Socialist Price Mechanism,* edited by Alan Abouchar. Durham, N.C.: Duke University Press, pp. 129–69.

———. 1983. "Economics of Virtuous Haste: A View of Soviet Industrialization and Institutions," in *Marxism, Central Planning, and the Soviet Economy. Economic Essays in Honor of Alexander Erlich,* edited by Padma Desai. Cambridge: MIT Press, pp. 198–206.

———. 1985. "The Second Economy in the USSR and Eastern Europe. A Bibliography," *Berkeley-Duke Occasional Papers on the Second Economy in the USSR,* September, no. 1.

———, ed. 1968. *Money and Plan.* Berkeley: University of California Press.

Grossman, Sanford J., and Oliver D. Hart. 1986. "The Costs and Benefits of Ownership: A Theory of Vertical and Lateral Integration," *Journal of Political Economy,* August, *94* (4), pp. 691–719.

Groves, Theodore. 1973. "Incentives in Teams," *Econometrica,* July, *41* (4), pp. 617–31.

Hammond, Thomas T., ed. 1975. *The Anatomy of Communist Takeovers.* New Haven: Yale University Press.

Hankiss, Elemér. 1989. "A 'Nagy Koalíció' avagy a hatalom konvertálása" (The 'great coalition' or the conversion of power), *Valóság,* February, *32* (2), pp. 15–31.

———. 1990. *East European Alternatives: Are There Any?* Oxford: Oxford University Press.

Hansen, Bent. 1951. *A Study in the Theory of Inflation*. London: Allen and Unwin.

Hanson, Philip. 1971. "East-West Comparisons and Comparative Economic Systems," *Soviet Studies,* January, *22* (3), pp. 327–43.

——. 1981. *Trade and Technology in Soviet-Western Relations*. London: Macmillan, and New York: Columbia Univeristy Press.

Hanson, Philip, and Keith Pavitt. 1987. *The Comparative Economics of Research Development and Innovation in East and West. A Survey*. New York: Harwood Academic Publishers.

Haraszti, Miklós. 1978. *A Worker in a Worker's State*. New York: Universe Books.

Harcourt, Geoffrey C., ed. 1977. *The Microeconomic Foundations of Macroeconomics*. Boulder: Westview Press.

Hardin, Garett. 1968. "The Tragedy of the Commons," *Science*, December 13, *162* (3859), pp. 1242–48.

Harding, Harry. 1981. *Organizing China: The Problem of Bureaucracy (1949–1976)*. Stanford: Stanford University Press.

——. 1987. *China's Second Revolution: Reform after Mao*. Washington, D.C.: The Brookings Institution.

Harrison, Mark. 1985. "Investment Mobilization and Capacity Completion in the Chinese and Soviet Economies," *Economics of Planning, 19* (2), pp. 56–75.

Hart, Oliver, and Bengt R. Holmström. 1987. "Theory of Contracts," in *Advances in Economic Theory. Fifth World Congress,* edited by T. Bewley. Cambridge: Cambridge University Press, pp. 71–155.

Hartford, Kathleen. 1990. "From Agricultural Development to Food Policy." Manuscript.

Havel, Václav. 1975. "Letter to Dr. Gustav Husak, General Secretary of the Czechoslovak Communist Party," *Survey, 21* (3), pp. 167–90.

——, ed. 1985. *The Power of the Powerless*. London: Hutchinson.

Hayek, Friedrich A. 1960. *The Constitution of Liberty*. London: Routledge, and Chicago: Chicago University Press.

——. 1973. *Law, Legislation and Liberty*. Chicago: University of Chicago Press.

——, ed. 1935. *Collectivist Economic Planning*. London: Routledge and Kegan Paul.

Heal, Geoffrey M. 1973. *The Theory of Economic Planning*. Amsterdam: North-Holland.

Hedlund, Stefan. 1989. *Private Agriculture in the Soviet Union*. London: Routledge.

Herman, Edward S. 1981. *Corporate Control, Corporate Power*. Cambridge: Cambridge University Press.

Hewett, Ed A. 1980. "Foreign Trade Outcomes in Eastern and Western Economies," in *East European Integration and East-West Trade,* edited Paul Marer and John M. Montias. Bloomington: Indiana University Press, pp. 41–69.

——. 1988. *Reforming the Soviet Economy. Equality versus Efficiency*. Washington, D.C.: The Brookings Institution.

Hinton, Harold C., ed. 1980. *The People's Republic of China, 1949-1979: A Documentary Survey.* 5 vols. Wilmington, Del.: Scholarly Resources.

Hirschman, Albert O. 1958. *The Strategy of Economic Development.* New Haven: Yale University Press.

———. 1970. *Exit, Voice and Loyalty.* Cambridge: Harvard University Press.

Hlavácek, Jirí. 1986. "Homo se assecurans," *Politická ekonomie, 34* (6), pp. 633-39.

———. 1990. "Producers' Criteria in a Centrally Planned Economy," in *Optimal Decisions in Markets and Planned Economies,* edited by Richard E. Quandt and Dusan Triska. Boulder: Westview Press, pp. 41-52.

Hlavácek, Jirí, and Dusan Triska. 1987. "Planning Authority and Its Marginal Rate of Substitution: Theorem Homo Se Assecurans," *Ekonomicko-Matematicky Obzor, 23* (1), pp. 38-53.

Hoch, Róbert. 1980. "A világpiaci árak és az árcentrum" (World market prices and the price center), *Közgazdasági Szemle,* October, *27* (10), pp. 1153-58.

Hoeffding, Oleg. 1959. "The Soviet Industrial Reorganization of 1957," *American Economic Review,* May, *49* (2), pp. 65-77.

Holmström, Bengt R. 1979. "Moral Hazard and Observability," *Bell Journal of Economics,* Spring, *10* (1), pp. 74-91.

———. 1982a. "Design of Incentive Schemes and the New Soviet Incentive Model," *European Economic Review,* February, *17* (2), pp. 128-48.

———. 1982b. "Moral Hazard in Teams," *Bell Journal of Economics,* Autumn, *13* (3), pp. 324-40.

Holmström, Bengt R., and Jean Tirole. 1989. "Theory of the Firm," in *Handbook of Industrial Organization,* edited by Richard Schmalensee and Robert Willig. New York: Elsevier, pp. 61-133.

Holzman, Franklyn D. 1955. *Soviet Taxation.* Cambridge: Harvard University Press.

———. 1960. "Soviet Inflationary Pressures, 1928-1957: Causes and Cures," *Quarterly Journal of Economics,* May, *74* (2), pp. 167-88.

———. 1976. *International Trade under Communism. Politics and Economics.* New York: Basic Books.

———. 1983. "Dumping by Centrally Planned Economies: The Polish Golf Cart Case," in *Marxism, Central Planning, and the Soviet Economy: Economic Essays in Honor of Alexander Erlich,* edited by Padma Desai. Cambridge: MIT Press, pp. 133-48.

———. 1986a. "The Significance of Soviet Subsidies to Eastern Europe," *Comparative Economic Studies,* Spring, *28* (1), pp. 54-65.

———. 1986b. "Further Thoughts on the Significance of Soviet Subsidies to Eastern Europe," *Comparative Economic Studies,* Fall, *28* (3), pp. 59-63.

———. 1989. "A Comparative View of Foreign Trade Behavior: Market versus Centrally Planned Economies," in *Comparative Economic Systems: Models and Cases,* edited by Morris Bornstein. Homewood, Ill.: Irwin, pp. 463-84.

Holzmann, Robert. 1990. "Unemployment Benefits During Economic Transition: Background, Concept and Implementation." OECD conference paper. Vienna: Ludwig Boltzmann Institute für Ökonomische Analysen.

Horvat, Branko. 1982. *The Political Economy of Socialism: A Marxist Social Theory.* Armonk, N.Y.: M.E. Sharpe.

Horváth, M. Tamás. 1988. "Kisvárosok politikai viszonyai" (Political relations in small towns), *Valóság,* July, *31* (7), pp. 89-98.

Hough, Jerry F. 1969. *The Soviet Prefects: The Local Party Organs in Industrial Decision-making.* Cambridge: Harvard University Press.

———. 1972. "The Soviet System: Petrification or Pluralism," in *The Soviet Union and Social Science Theory,* edited by Jerry F. Hough. Cambridge: Harvard University Press.

Hough, Jerry F., and Merle Fainsod. [1953] 1979. *How the Soviet Union Is Governed.* Cambridge: Harvard University Press.

Hoxha, Enver. 1975. *Our Policy Is an Open Policy, the Policy of Proletarian Principles.* Tirana: "8 Nëntori" Publishing House.

Hrncir, Miroslav. 1989. "From Traditional to Reformed Planned Economy: The Case of Czechoslovakia," *Czechoslovak Economic Papers, 27,* pp. 25-45.

Hsin, Chang. 1984. "The 1982-83 Overinvestment Crisis in China," *Asian Survey,* December, *24* (12), pp. 1275-1301.

Huang, Yasheng. 1988. "'Web' of Interests and Patterns of Behavior of Chinese Local Economic Bureaucracies and Enterprises During Reforms," lecture at the conference on Social Implications of Reforms, Fairbank Center, Harvard University, Cambridge, May.

Hungarian Central Statistical Office. 1959. *Statistical Yearbook, 1957.* Budapest.

Hungarian Market Research Institute. 1978. "A lakossági személygépkocsi piac egyes időszerű problémái" (Present-day problems on the private car market). Budapest. Manuscript.

Hunter, Holland. 1961. "Optimal Tautness in Development Planning," *Economic Development and Cultural Change,* July, *9* (4), part 1, pp. 561-72.

Hutchings, Raymond. 1983. *The Soviet Budget.* Albany: State University of New York Press.

Ickes, Barry W. 1986. "Cyclical Fluctuations in Centrally Planned Economies: A Critique of the Literature," *Soviet Studies,* January, *38* (1), pp. 36-52.

———. 1990. "Do Socialist Countries Suffer a Common Business Cycle?" *The Review of Economics and Statistics,* August, *72* (3), pp. 397-405.

Illyés, Gyula. 1986. *Menet a ködben* (March in the fog). Budapest: Szépirodalmi Kiadó.

International Communications Union. 1988. *Yearbook of Common Carrier Telecommunication Statistics.* Geneva: Union Internationale des Télécommunications.

International Currency Analysis, Inc. 1990. *World Currency Handbook.* Brooklyn, N.Y.

International Labour Office. 1987. *Economically Active Population, 1950-2025.* Geneva.

International Monetary Fund. 1984. *International Financial Statistics. Supplement on Output Statistics.* Supplement series, no. 8, Washington, D.C.

———. 1987. *Government Finance Statistical Yearbook, 1987.* Washington, D.C.

International Monetary Fund, IBRD, OECD, EBRD. 1990. "The Economy of the USSR: Summary and Recommendations," a study undertaken in response to a request by the Houston Summit, Washington, D.C.

Ismael, Tareq Y., and Jacqueline S. Ismael. 1986. *The People's Democratic Republic of Yemen: Politics, Economics and Society.* London: Frances Pinter.

Jánossy, Ferenc. 1963. *A gazdasági fejlettség mérhetősége és új mérési módszere* (The measurability of the economic development level and a new method for its measurement). Budapest: Közgazdasági és Jogi Könyvkiadó.

Jasay, Anthony de. 1990. *Market Socialism: A Scrutiny. 'This Square Circle'.* London: Institute of Economic Affairs.

Jeffries, Ian, and Manfred Melzer, eds. 1987. *The East German Economy.* London: Croom Helm.

Joint Economic Committee, Congress of the United States. 1989. *Pressures for Reform in the East European Economies.* 2 vols. Washington, D.C.: Government Printing Office.

Jones, Derek C., and Mieke Meurs. 1991. "On Entry of New Firms in Socialist Economies: Evidence from Bulgaria," *Soviet Studies, 43* (2), pp. 311–27.

Judith, Rudolf, ed. 1986. *40 Jahre Mitbestimmung: Erfahrungen, Probleme, Perspektiven.* Cologne: Bund Verlag.

Judy, R., and R. Clough. 1989. "Soviet Computer Software and Applications in the 1980s." Bloomington: Hudson Institute, Working Paper HI-4090-P.

Kagalovsky, Konstantin. 1989. "The Pressing Problems of State Financies in the USSR," *Communist Economies,* (4), pp. 447–54.

Kahan, Arcadius, and Blair Ruble, eds. 1979. *Industrial Labor in the USSR.* New York: Pergamon Press.

Kalecki, Michal. 1970. "Theories of Growth in Different Social Systems," *Scientia,* December, *105* (5–6), pp. 311–16.

———. 1972. *Selected Essays on the Economic Growth of the Socialist and Mixed Economies.* Cambridge: Cambridge University Press.

Kaminski, Bartlomiej. 1989. "The Economic System and Forms of Government Controls in Poland in the 1980s," in *Pressures for Reform in the East European Economies.* Vol. 2. Joint Economic Committee, Congress of the United States. Washington, D.C.: Government Printing Office, pp. 84–101.

Kant, Immanuel. [1793] 1970. "On the Common Saying: 'This May Be True in Theory, but It Does Not Apply in Practice'," in *Kant's Political Writings,* edited by Hans Reiss. Cambridge: Cambridge University Press, pp. 61–92.

Kantorovich, Leonid V. [1937] 1960. "Mathematical Methods of Planning and Organizing Production," *Management Science, 6* (4), pp. 366–422.

———. 1965. *The Best Use of Economic Resources.* Cambridge: Harvard University Press.

Kapitány, Zsuzsa. 1989a. "Kereslet és kinálat a 80-as évek autópiacán" (Demand and supply on the Hungarian car market in the 1980s), *Közgazdasági Szemle,* June, *36* (6), pp. 592–611.

———. 1989b. "Elosztási mechanizmusok Kelet-Európa autópiacain" (Allocative mechanisms on the Eastern European car markets). Budapest: Institute of Economics. Manuscript.

Kapitány, Zsuzsa, and László Kállay. 1989. *The East European Motor Industry: Prospects and Developments.* London: The Economic Intelligence Unit.
———. 1991. *The Motor Industry of Eastern Europe: Prospects to 2000 and Beyond.* London: The Economic Intelligence Unit.
Kapitány, Zsuzsa, János Kornai, and Judit Szabó. 1984. "Reproduction of Shortage on the Hungarian Car Market," *Soviet Studies,* April, *36* (2), pp. 236–56.
Kaser, Michael. 1965. *Comecon. Integration Problems of the Planned Economies.* London: Oxford University Press.
Katsenelinboigen, Aron. 1977. "Coloured Markets in the Soviet Union," *Soviet Studies,* January, *29* (1), pp. 62–85.
Katz, Barbara G., and Joel Owen. 1984. "Disequilibrium Theory, Waiting Costs and Saving Behavior in Centrally Planned Economies: A Queueing-Theoretic Approach," *Journal of Comparative Economics,* September, *8* (3), pp. 301–21.
Kautsky, Karl. 1910. *The Social Revolution.* Chicago: Charles H. Kerr.
Kendrick, John W. 1981. "International Comparisons of Recent Productivity Trends," in *Essays in Contemporary Economic Problems. Demand, Productivity and Population,* edited by William Fellner. Washington, D.C.: American Enterprise Institute for Public Policy Research, pp. 125–70.
Kenedi, János. 1981. *Do It Yourself.* London: Pluto Press.
Keren, Michael. 1972. "On the Tautness of Plans," *Review of Economic Studies, 39* (4), pp. 469–86.
———. 1973. "The New Economic System: An Obituary," *Soviet Studies,* April, *24* (4), pp. 554–87.
Keren, Michael, Jeffrey Miller, and James R. Thornton. 1983. "The Ratchet: A Dynamic Managerial Incentive Model of the Soviet Enterprise," *Journal of Comparative Economics,* December, *7* (4), pp. 347–67.
Keynes, John Maynard. 1936. *The General Theory of Employment, Interest and Money.* London: Macmillan.
Khanin, Grigorii. 1988. "Ekonomicheskii rost: al'ternativnaia otsenka" (Economic growth: An alternative assessment), *Kommunist,* November, (17), pp. 83–90.
Khrushchev, Nikita S. 1959. *Let Us Live in Peace and Friendship. The Visit of N. S. Khrushchev to the USA.* Moscow: Foreign Languages Publishing House.
———. 1960. "Report to the Congress," in *Current Soviet Politics: The Documentary Record of the Extraordinary 21th Congress of the CPSU,* edited by Leo Gruliow and the Staff of the Current Digest of the Soviet Press. New York: Columbia University Press, pp. 41–72.
Kidric, Boris. 1985. *Sabrana Dela* (Collected works). Belgrade: Izdavacki Centar Komunist.
Kis, János. 1989. *L'Egale Dignité.* Paris: Seuil.
Klacek, Jan, and Alena Nesporová. 1984. "Economic Growth in Czechoslovakia—Application of the CES Production Function," *Czechoslovak Economic Papers, 22,* pp. 83–100.

Klaus, Václav. 1989. "Socialist Economies, Economic Reforms, and Economists: Reflections of a Czechoslovak Economist," *Communist Economies, 1* (1), pp. 89-96.

———. 1990. "Policy Positions Towards the International Monetary Fund and the World Bank by Centrally Planned Economies that Are Not Members of Those Organizations," in *Economic Reforms in Centrally Planned Economies and Their Impact on the Global Economy,* edited by Jozef M. van Brabant. New York: United Nations, Department of International and Social Affairs, pp. 315-27.

Knight, Frank. [1921] 1965. *Risk, Uncertainty, and Profit.* New York: Harper and Row.

Knight, Peter T. 1984. "Financial Discipline and Structural Adjustment in Yugoslavia: Rehabilitation and Bankruptcy of Loss-Making Enterprises," *World Bank Staff Working Papers,* no. 705.

Kolakowski, Leszek. 1978. *Main Currents of Marxism.* 3 vols. Oxford: Oxford University Press.

Kolodko, Grzegorz W. 1989. "Stabilization Policy in Poland—Challenges and Constraints," *Working Papers*, no. 3. Warsaw: Institute of Finance.

———. 1991. "Polish Hyperinflation and Stabilization, 1989-90," *Most, 1* (1), pp. 9-36.

Kolodko, Grzegorz W., Danuta Gotz-Kozierkiewicz, and Elzbieta Skrzeszewska-Paczek. 1990. "Hyperinflation and Stabilization in Postsocialist Economies." Warsaw: Institute of Finance. Manuscript.

Komin, A. 1988. "Perestroika tsenovogo khoziaistva" (Restructuring of pricing management), *Voprosy Ekonomiki,* March, (3), pp. 107-14.

Konovalov, V. 1989. "Yugoslav Industry: Structure, Performance, Conduct." Washington, D.C.: Industry Development Division, World Bank. Manuscript.

Konrád, György, and Iván Szelényi. 1979. *The Intellectuals on the Road to Class Power.* New York: Harcourt Brace Jovanovich.

Kontorovich, Vladimir. 1986. "Soviet Growth Slowdown: Econometric vs. Direct Evidence," *American Economic Review,* May, *76* (2), pp. 181-85.

———. 1990. "Utilization of Fixed Capital and Soviet Industrial Growth," *Economics of Planning, 23* (1), pp. 37-50.

Koopmans, Tjalling C., and John Michael Montias. 1971. "On the Description and Comparison of Economic Systems," in *Comparison of Economic Systems: Theoretical and Methodological Approaches,* edited by Alexander Eckstein. Berkeley: University of California Press, pp. 27-78.

Korbonski, Andrzej. 1981. "The Second Economy in Poland," *Journal of International Affairs,* Spring/Summer, *35* (1), pp. 1-15.

Koriagina, Tatiana I. 1990a. "Tenevaia ekonomika v SSSR (analyz, otsenki, prognozy)" (The shadow economy in the USSR: Analysis, estimates, prognoses), *Voprosy Ekonomiki,* (3), pp. 110-20.

———. 1990b. *Platnye uslugi v SSSR.* (Paid services in the USSR). Moscow: Ekonomika.

Kornai, János. [1957] 1959. *Overcentralization in Economic Administration.* Oxford: Oxford University Press.

———. 1965. "Mathematical Programming as a Tool in Drawing Up the Five-Year Economic Plan," *Economics of Planning, 5* (3), pp. 3–18.

———. 1971. *Anti-Equilibrium.* Amsterdam: North-Holland.

———. 1972. *Rush versus Harmonic Growth.* Amsterdam: North-Holland.

———. 1980. *Economics of Shortage.* Amsterdam: North-Holland.

———. 1984. "Bureaucratic and Market Coordination," *Osteuropa Wirtschaft, 29* (4), pp. 306–19.

———. 1986a. "The Soft Budget Constraint," *Kyklos, 39* (1), pp. 3–30.

———. 1986b. "The Hungarian Reform Process: Visions, Hopes and Reality," *Journal of Economic Literature,* December, *24* (4), pp. 1687–1737.

———. 1990. *The Road to a Free Economy. Shifting from a Socialist System: The Example of Hungary.* New York: W. W. Norton.

Kornai, János, and Tamás Lipták. 1965. "Two-Level Planning," *Econometrica,* January, *33* (1), pp. 141–69.

Kornai, János, and Béla Martos, eds. 1981. *Non-Price Control.* Budapest: Akadémiai Kiadó.

Kornai, János, and Ágnes Matits. 1987. *A vállalatok nyereségének bürokratikus újraelosztása* (The bureaucratic redistribution of firms' profits). Budapest: Közgazdasági és Jogi Könyvkiadó.

———. 1990. "The Bureaucratic Redistribution of the Firms' Profits," in J. Kornai, *Vision and Reality, Market and State: New Studies on the Socialist Economy and Society.* Budapest: Corvina; Hemel Hempstead: Harvester-Wheatsheaf; and New York: Routledge, pp. 54–98.

Kornai, János, and Jörgen W. Weibull. 1978. "The Normal State of the Market in a Shortage Economy: A Queue Model," *Scandinavian Journal of Economics, 80* (4), pp. 375–98.

———. 1983. "Paternalism, Buyers' and Sellers' Market," *Mathematical Social Sciences, 6* (2), pp. 153–69.

Kotlove, Barry. 1986. "Soviet Housing Expenditures: A Cross-Sectional Study of Soviet Emigrant Families." Cambridge, Mass.: Economics of Socialism Workshop, Harvard University. Manuscript.

Kovács, János Mátyás. 1988. "Compassionate Doubts about Refonomics in Hungary." Budapest: Institute of Economics, Hungarian Academy of Sciences. Manuscript.

———. 1990. "Reform Economics: The Classification Gap," *Daedalus,* Winter, *119* (1), pp. 215–48.

Köves, András. 1983. "'Implicit Subsidies' and Some Issues of Economic Relations within the CMEA; Remarks on the Analyses Made by Michael Marrese and Jan Vanous," *Acta Oeconomica, 31* (1–2), pp. 125–36.

———. 1985. *The CMEA Countries in the World Economy: Turning Inwards or Turning Outwards.* Budapest: Akadémiai Kiadó.

———. 1986. "Foreign Economic Equilibrium, Economic Development and Economic Policy in the CMEA Countries," *Acta Oeconomica, 36* (1–2), pp. 35–53.

Központi Statisztikai Hivatal (Central Statistical Office). 1965. *Nemzetközi statisztikai évkönyv, 1965* (International statistical yearbook, 1965). Budapest.

———. 1971. *Statisztikai évkönyv, 1970* (Statistical yearbook, 1970). Budapest.

———. 1973. *Statisztikai évkönyv, 1972* (Statistical yearbook, 1972). Budapest.

———. 1975. *Statisztikai évkönyv, 1974* (Statistical yearbook, 1974). Budapest.

———. 1980a. *Statisztikai évkönyv, 1979* (Statistical yearbook, 1979). Budapest.

———. 1980b. *Közlekedési és hírközlési évkönyv, 1979* (Transport and news communication yearbook, 1979). Budapest.

———. 1982. *Statisztikai évkönyv, 1981* (Statistical yearbook, 1981). Budapest.

———. 1984. *Statisztikai évkönyv, 1983* (Statistical yearbook, 1983). Budapest.

———. 1985. *Statisztikai évkönyv, 1984* (Statistical yearbook, 1984). Budapest.

———. 1986. *Statisztikai idősorok a Kinai Népköztársaságról.* (Statistical time series on the People's Republic of China). Budapest.

———. 1987. *Statisztikai évkönyv, 1986* (Statistical yearbook, 1986). Budapest.

———. 1988. *Beruházási statisztikai évkönyv, 1987* (Statistical yearbook of investments, 1987). Budapest.

———. 1989. *Nemzetközi statisztikai évkönyv* (International statistical yearbook). Budapest.

———. 1990. *Statisztikai évkönyv, 1989* (Statistical yearbook, 1989). Budapest.

Kravis, Irving B., Alan W. Heston, and Robert Summers. 1978. "Real GDP Per Capita for More Than One Hundred Countries," *Economic Journal,* June *88* (350), pp. 215–42.

———. 1982. *World Product and Income.* Baltimore: Johns Hopkins University Press.

Kritsman, L. N. 1926. *Geroicheskii period velikoi russkoi revoliutsii—opyt analiza t.n. voennogo kommunizma.* (The heroic period of the great Russian Revolution—An attempt at analysis of so-called War Communism). Moscow: Gosudarstvennoe Izdatel'stvo.

Krueger, Anne O. 1974. "The Political Economy of the Rent-Seeking Society," *American Economic Review,* June, *64* (3), pp. 291–303.

Kuron, Jacek, and Karel Modzielewski. 1968. *An Open Letter to the Party.* New York: Merit Publishers.

Kuznets, Simon. 1964. *Postwar Economic Growth.* Cambridge: Harvard University Press.

———. 1971. *Economic Growth of Nations.* Cambridge: Harvard University Press.

Kuznetsova, T. 1989. "Kooperatsiia: kakova taktika—takovo i praktika" (The cooperatives: As are the tactics, so is the practice), *Voprosy Ekonomiki,* March, (3), pp. 149–53.

Lackó, Mária. 1975. "Consumer Savings and the Supply Situation," *Acta Oeconomica,*, *15* (3–4), pp. 365–84.

———. 1980. "Cumulating and Easing of Tensions," *Acta Oeconomica, 24* (3–4), pp. 357–77.

———. 1984 "Behavioral Rules in Distribution of Sectoral Investments in Hungary, 1951–1980," *Journal of Comparative Economics,* September, *8* (3), pp. 290–300.

———. 1989. "A beruházási hitelpiac feszültségeinek újratermelődése Magyarországon" (The reproduction of tension on the investment credit market in Hungary), *Közgazdasági Szemle,* November, *36* (11), pp. 1323–41.

Ladányi, János. 1975. "A fogyasztói árak és szociálpolitika" (Consumer prices and social policy), *Valóság, 18* (2), pp. 16–29.

Laffont, Jean-Jacques. 1989. *Economics of Uncertainty and Information.* Cambridge: MIT Press.

Laki, Mihály. 1980. "End-Year Rush Work in the Hungarian Industry and Foreign Trade," *Acta Oeconomica, 25* (1–2), pp. 37–65.

Lange, Oscar. 1936, 1937. "On the Economic Theory of Socialism," *Review of Economic Studies,* October, February, *4* (1, 2), pp. 53–71, 123–42.

Lardy, Nicholas R. 1986. "Overview: Agricultural Reform and the Rural Economy," in *China Looks Towards the Year 2000. Vol. 1. The Four Modernizations.* Joint Economic Committee, Congress of the United States. Washington, D.C.: Government Printing Office, pp. 325–35.

Largentaye, Bertrand de. 1990. "The Response of Western European Countries to the Transformations in Eastern Europe," paper prepared for the colloquium for executive directors on socialist economic reform, World Bank, April 19.

Laulan, Yves M., ed. 1973. *Banking, Money and Credit in the Soviet Union and Eastern Europe.* Brussels: NATO, Directorate of Economic Affairs.

Lavoie, Don. 1985. *Rivalry and Central Planning. The Socialist Calculation Debate Reconsidered.* Cambridge: Cambridge University Press.

Lee, Peter N. 1986. "Enterprise Autonomy Policy in Post-Mao China: A Case Study of Policy-Making, 1978–83," *China Quarterly,* March, *27* (105), pp. 45–71.

Leijonhufvud, Axel. 1968. *On Keynesian Economics and the Economics of Keynes.* New York: Oxford University Press.

Lenin, Vladimir I. [1918] 1964. "Can the Bolsheviks Retain State Power?" in V. I. Lenin, *Collected Works.* Vol. 26. Moscow: Progress, pp. 87–186.

———. [1920] 1966. "Left-Wing Communism, an Infantile Disorder," in V. I. Lenin, *Collected Works.* Vol. 31. Moscow: Progress, pp. 17–118.

———. [1917] 1969a. "State and Revolution," in V. I. Lenin, *Collected Works.* Vol. 25. Moscow: Progress, pp. 381–492.

———. [1918] 1969b. "Immediate Tasks of the Soviet Government," in V. I. Lenin, *Collected Works.* Vol. 27, Moscow: Progress, pp. 235–77.

———. [1921] 1970. "To the Heads of All Central Soviet Establishments," in V. I. Lenin, *Collected Works.* Vol. 45, p. 423.

Leontief, Wassily. 1953a. *The Structure of American Economy, 1919–1939.* New York: Oxford University Press.

———, ed. 1953b. *Studies in the Structure of the American Economy, 1919–1939. Theoretical and Empirical Explanations in Input-Output Analysis.* New York: Oxford University Press.

Leptin, Gerd, and Manfred Melzer. 1978. *Economic Reform in East German Industry.* Oxford: Oxford University Press.

Levcik, Friedrich. 1986. "The Czechoslovak Economy in the 1980's," in *East European Economies: Slow Growth in the 1980's.* Vol. 3. Joint Economic Committee, Congress of the United States. Washington D.C.: Government Printing Office, March, pp. 85–108.

Levine, Herbert S. 1966. "Pressure and Planning in the Soviet Economy," in *Industrialization under Two Systems,* edited by Henry Rosovsky. New York: John Wiley, pp. 266–86.

Levy, F., et al. 1988. *China: Finance and Investment.* Washington, D.C.: World Bank Country Studies.

Lewin, Moshe. [1968] 1974. *Russian Peasants and Soviet Power.* Oxford: Oxford University Press.

Lewis, Arthur W. 1954. "Economic Development with Unlimited Supplies of Labour," *The Manchester School,* May, *22* (2), pp. 139–91.

———. 1955. *The Theory of Economic Growth.* Homewood, Ill.: Irwin.

Lewis, John W., ed. 1970. *Party Leadership and Revolutionary Power in China.* Cambridge: Cambridge University Press.

Liberman, Evsey G. [1962] 1972. "The Plan, Profit and Bonuses," in *Socialist Economics,* edited by Alec Nove and Domenico M. Nuti. Middlesex: Penguin Books, pp. 309–18.

Lichtheim, George. 1961. *Marxism: A Historical and Critical Study.* New York: Praeger.

Lieberthal, Kenneth, and Michael Oksenberg. 1988. *Policy-Making in China: Structures and Processes.* Princeton: Princeton University Press.

Lindbeck, Assar. 1971. *The Political Economy of the New Left: An Outsider's View.* New York: Harper and Row.

Lindbeck, Assar, and Jörgen W. Weibull. 1987. "Strategic Interaction with Altruism—The Economics of Fait Accompli," *Seminar Paper,*, no. 376. Stockholm: Institute for International Economic Studies.

Lindblom, Charles E. 1977. *Politics and Markets. The World's Political Economic Systems.* New York: Basic Books.

Lipinski, Edward. 1976. "An Open Letter to Comrade Gierek," *Survey, 22* (2), pp. 194–203.

Lipton, David, and Jeffrey Sachs. 1990. "Creating a Market Economy in Eastern Europe: The Case of Poland," *Brookings Papers on Economic Activity* (1), pp. 75–133.

Lisiecki, Jerzy. 1990. "Financial and Material Transfers between East and West Germany," *Soviet Studies,* July, *42* (3), pp. 513–34.

Liska, Tibor. [1964] 1988. *Ökonosztát* (Econostat). Budapest: Közgazdasági és Jogi Könyvkiadó.

Liu, Guoguan. 1986. "Price Reform Essential to Growth," *Beijing Review,* August 18, pp. 14–18.

———. 1989. "A Sweet and Sour Decade," *Beijing Review,* January 2–8, pp. 22–29.

Liu, Pak-Wai. 1986. "Moral Hazard and Incentives in a Decentralized Planning Environment," *Journal of Comparative Economics,* June, *10* (2), pp. 91–105.

Lopinski, Maciej, Marcin Moskit, and Mariusz Wilk, eds. 1990. *Konspira. Solidarity Underground.* Berkeley: University of California Press.

Los, Maria, ed. 1990. *The Second Economy in Marxist States.* Basingstoke: Macmillan.

Lucas, Robert E. 1987. *Models of Business Cycles.* Oxford: Basil Blackwell.

Lucas, Robert E., and Thomas J. Sargent. 1981. "After Keynesian Macroeconomics," in *Rational Expectations and Econometric Practice,* edited by R. E. Lucas and T. J. Sargent. Vol. 1. Minneapolis: University of Minnesota Press pp. 259–319.

Lukács, Georg. 1971. "Lukács on His Life and Work. Interview," *New Left Review* (68), pp. 49–58.

Lydall, Harold. 1984. *Yugoslav Socialism: Theory and Practice.* Oxford: Clarendon Press, and New York: Oxford University Press.

Maddison, Angus. 1989. *The World Economy in the 20th Century.* Paris: Development Centre of the OECD.

Malecki, Witold, and Grezegorz W. Kolodko. 1990. "The Indebtedness of East European Countries," *Working Papers,* no. 12. Warsaw: Institute of Finance.

Malinvaud, Edmond. 1967. "Decentralized Procedures for Planning," in *Activity Analysis in the Theory of Growth and Planning,* edited by M. O. L. Bacharach and Edmond Malinvaud. London: Macmillan, and New York: St. Martin's Press, pp. 170–208.

———. 1977. *The Theory of Unemployment Reconsidered.* Oxford: Basil Blackwell.

Mao, Zedong. [1938] 1967. "Problems of War and Strategy," in *Selected Works.* Vol. 2. Beijing: Foreign Languages Press, pp. 267–81.

———. 1977. "On the Ten Major Relationships," in *Selected Works.* Vol. 5. Beijing: Foreign Languages Press, pp. 284–307.

Marer, Paul. 1985. *Dollar GNPs of the USSR and Eastern Europe.* Baltimore: Johns Hopkins University Press, published for the World Bank.

Marer, Paul, et al. 1991. *Historically Planned Economies. A Guide to the Data* (tentative title). Washington, D.C.: World Bank.

Marer, Paul, and Wlodzimierz Siwinski, eds. 1988. *Creditworthiness and Reform in Poland. Western and Polish Perspectives.* Bloomington: Indiana University Press.

Marglin, Stephen A. 1976. "What Do Bosses Do?" in *The Division of Labor,* edited by André Gorz. Hassocks: Harvester Press, pp. 15–54.

Markish, Yuri. 1989. "Agricultural Reforms in the USSR: Intensification Programmes of the 1980s," *Communist Economies, 1* (4), pp. 421–45.

Marrese, Michael. 1981. "The Bureaucratic Response to Economic Fluctuation: An Econometric Investigation of Hungarian Investment Policy," *Journal of Policy Modelling,, 3* (2), pp. 221–43.

———. 1983. "Agricultural Policy and Performance in Hungary," *Journal of Comparative Economics,* September, *7* (3), pp 329–45.

Marrese, Michael, and Jan Vanous. 1983. *Soviet Subsidization of Trade with Eastern Europe. A Soviet Perspective.* Berkeley: Institute of International Studies.

Martos, Béla. 1990. *Economic Control Structures: A Non-Walrasian Approach.* Amsterdam: North-Holland.

Marx, Karl. [1871] 1940. *The Civil War in France.* New York: International Publishers.

———. [1875] 1966. *Critique of the Gotha Programme.* Moscow: Progress, and New York: International Publishers.

———. [1864] 1975a. "Inaugural Address of the Working Men's International Association," in K. Marx and F. Engels, *Collected Works*. Vol. 20. New York: International Publishers, pp. 5–13.

———. [1870] 1975b. "Confidential Talk," in K. Marx and F. Engels, *Collected Works*. Vol. 21. New York: International Publishers, pp. 112–25.

———. [1867–94] 1978. *Capital*. London: Penguin.

McAuley, Alistair. 1979. *Economic Welfare in the Soviet Union*. Madison: University of Wisconsin Press.

McIntyre, Robert J. 1988. *Bulgaria: Politics, Economics and Society*. London: Frances Pinter.

McKinnon, Ronald I. 1990a. "Liberalizing Foreign Trade in a Socialist Economy: The Problem of Negative Value Added." Stanford: Department of Economics, Stanford University. Manuscript.

———. 1990b. "Stabilising the Ruble," *Communist Economies, 2* (2), pp. 131–42.

McLellan, David. 1973. *Karl Marx, His Life and Thought*. New York: Macmillan.

———. 1980. *The Thought of Karl Marx*. London: Macmillan.

Meade, James E. 1972. "The Theory of Labour-Managed Firms and of Profit-Sharing," *Economic Journal,* March, *82* (325), pp. 402–28.

Medvedev, Roy A. 1989. *Let History Judge: The Origins and Consequences of Stalinism*. Oxford: Oxford University Press.

Meerson-Aksenov, M., and B. Shragin, eds. 1978. *The Political, Social and Religious Thought of Russian Samizdat. An Anthology*. Belmont, Mass.: Nordland.

Meisner, Maurice. 1986. *Mao's China and After: A History of the People's Republic*. New York: Free Press.

Mejstrik, Michal. 1984. "Economic Effects of Export and Their Dependence on the Quality of Products," *Czechoslovak Economic Papers, 22*, pp. 57–82.

———. 1991. "Transition Measures and External Shocks in Czechoslovakia in 1991." Prague: Institute of Economic Sciences, Charles University. Manuscript.

Merkur Car Trading Co. 1980. "Merkur adatgyűjtemény, 1979" (Merkur data collection, 1979). Budapest. Manuscript.

Mesa-Lago, Carmelo. 1981. *The Economy of Socialist Cuba*. Albuquerque: University of New Mexico Press.

Michels, Robert. [1911] 1962. *Political Parties; A Sociological Study of the Oligarchical Tendencies of Modern Democracy*. New York: Free Press.

Michnik, Adam. 1985. *Letters from Prison and Other Essays*. Berkeley: University of California Press.

Mihályi, Péter. 1988. "Cycles or Shocks: East European Investments, 1950–1985," *Economics of Planning, 22* (1–2), pp. 41–56.

Milanovic, Branko. 1989. *Liberalization and Entrepreneurship. Dynamics of Reform in Socialism and Capitalism*. Armonk, N.Y.: M. E. Sharpe.

Milenkovitch, Deborah D. 1971. *Plan and Market in Yugoslav Economic Thought*. New Haven: Yale University Press.

———. 1984. "Is Market Socialism Efficient?" in *Comparative Economic Systems: An Assessment of Knowledge, Theory, and Method,* edited by Andrew Zimbalist. Boston: Kluwer-Nijhoff, pp. 65–107.

Ming, Wu. 1990. "The Chinese Economy at the Crossroads," *Communist Economies, 2* (3), pp. 241–313.

Mirrlees, James A. 1974. "Notes on Welfare Economics, Information, and Uncertainty," in *Contributions to Economic Analysis. Essays on Economic Behavior under Uncertainty,* edited by Michael S. Balch, Daniel L. McFadden, and S. Wu. Amsterdam: North-Holland, pp. 243–58.

———. 1976. "The Optimal Structure of Incentives and Authority within an Organization," *Bell Journal of Economics,* Spring, *7* (1), pp. 105–31.

Mises, Ludwig von. [1920] 1935. "Economic Calculations in the Socialist Commonwealth," in *Collectivist Economic Planning,* edited by Friedrich A. Hayek. London: Routledge and Kegan Paul, pp. 87–130.

Mitchell, Janet. 1989. "Credit Rationing, Budget Constraints and Salaries in Yugoslav Firms," *Journal of Comparative Economics,* June, *13* (2), pp. 254–80.

Molotov, Viacheslav M. [1937] 1950. *A japán-német trockista ügynökök kártevésének, diverziójának és kémkedésének tanulságai. Beszámoló az SzK(b)P Központi Bizottságának 1937. február 28-i teljes ülésén* (Lessons drawn from the damaging covert and diversionary activities of Japanese-German Trotskyite agents. Report to the Central Committee of CP(b)SU on February 28, 1937). Budapest: Szikra.

Montias, John Michael. 1962. *Central Planning in Poland.* New Haven: Yale University Press.

Moore, Geoffrey H. 1983. *Business Cycles, Inflation, and Forecasting.* Cambridge: Ballinger, published for the National Bureau of Economic Research.

Moroney, John R. 1990. "Energy Consumption, Capital and Real Output: A Comparison of Market and Planned Economies," *Journal of Comparative Economics,* June, *14* (2), pp. 199–220.

Morrisson, Christian. 1984. "Income Distribution in East European and Western Countries," *Journal of Comparative Economics,* June, *8* (2), pp. 121–38.

Muellbauer, John, and Richard Portes. 1978. "Macroeconomic Models with Quantity Rationing," *Economic Journal,* December, *88* (352), pp. 788–821.

Muraközy, László. 1985. "Hazánk költségvetéséről—nemzetközi összehasonlításban" (Hungary's budget in international comparison), *Pénzügyi Szemle, 29* (10), pp. 745–54.

———. 1989. "A látható kéz" (The visible hand). Debrecen, Hungary: Kossuth Lajos Tudományegyetem. Manuscript.

Murrell, Peter. 1990a. *The Nature of Socialist Economies. Lessons from Eastern European Foreign Trade.* Princeton: Princeton University Press.

———. 1990b. "An Evolutionary Perspective on Reform of the Eastern European Economies." College Park: University of Maryland. Manuscript.

Nachtigal, Vladimir. 1989. "The Concept of National Income and Productive Labour," *Czechoslovak Economic Papers, 26,* pp. 73–97.

Nagy, András. 1979. "Methods of Structural Analysis and Projection of International Trade," *Studies,* no. 13. Budapest: Institute of Economics.

———. 1985. "Changes in the Structure and Intensity of East-West Trade," *Acta Oeconomica, 35* (3-4), pp. 359-75.

———. 1990. "Részérdekek az összeomlásban és a felemelkedésben" (Partial interests in periods of collapse and take-off), *Közgazdasági Szemle,* September, *37* (9), pp. 1012-24.

Nagy, András, and Péter Pete. 1980. "A világkereskedelem változásainak összefoglaló elemzése" (Summary of changes in the world trade), in *A világkereskedelem szerkezeti változásai 1955-1977 között, Vol. 1,* edited by András Nagy. Budapest: MTA Közgazdaságtudományi Intézet, pp. 4-57.

Nagy, Tamás. 1966. *A gazdasági mechanizmus reformja és a politikai gazdaságtan kategóriái* (Reform of the economic mechanism and the categories of political economy). Budapest: TIT kiadvány.

Naughton, Barry. 1985. "False Starts and Second Wind: Financial Reforms in the Chinese Industrial System," in *The Political Economy of Reform in Post-Mao China,* edited by Elizabeth J. Perry and Christine P. W. Wong. Cambridge: Harvard University Press, pp. 223-52.

Nee, Victor, and David Stark, eds. 1988. *Remaking the Economic Institutions of Socialism.* Stanford: Stanford University Press.

Nelson, Harold D., ed. 1985. *Mozambique: A Country Study.* Washington, D.C.: Foreign Area Studies, The American University, Government Printing Office.

Nemchinov, Vasilii S., ed. 1965. *Primenenie matematiki v ekonomicheskikh issledovaniakh Tom. 3* (Application of mathematics in economic researches. Volume 3). Moscow: Izdatel'stvo Sotsial'no-Ekonomicheskoi Literatury.

Neuberger, Egon. 1966. "Libermanism, Computopia, and Visible Hand: The Question of Informational Efficiency," *American Economic Review,* May, *56* (2), pp. 131-44.

Neumann, von John. 1956. "Probabilistic Logics and the Synthesis of Reliable Organisms from Unreliable Components," in *Automata Studies,* edited by C. E. Shannon and J. McCarthy. Princeton: Princeton University Press, pp. 43-98.

Niskanen, William. 1971. *Bureaucracy and Representative Government.* Chicago: Aldine.

Nordhaus, William D. 1990. "Soviet Economic Reform: The Longest Road," *Brookings Papers on Economic Activity,* no. 1, pp. 287-308.

Nove, Alec. 1964. *Economic Rationality and Soviet Politics or Was Stalin Really Necessary?* New York: Praeger.

———. 1969. *An Economic History of the USSR.* London: Penguin.

———. 1983. "Has Soviet Growth Ceased?" paper presented at the Manchester Statistical Society, November 15.

———. 1989. *Glasnost' in Perspective.* Boston: Unwin and Hyman.

Novozhilov, Viktor V. 1926. "Nedostatok tovarov" (Shortage of commodities), *Vestnik Finansov,* February, (2), pp. 75-96. Republished in *EKO,* 1988, (12), pp. 10-31.

Nozick, Robert. 1974. *Anarchy, State, and Utopia.* New York: Basic Books.

Nuti, Domenico Mario. 1986a. "Hidden and Repressed Inflation in Soviet-Type Economies: Definitions, Measurements and Stabilization," *Contributions to Political Economy,* March, *5,* pp. 37–82.

———. 1986b. "Political and Economic Fluctuations in the Socialist System," *Working Papers,* no. 156. Florence: European University Institute.

———. 1990. "Internal and International Aspects of Monetary Disequilibrium in Poland," in *Economic Transformation in Hungary and Poland, European Economy.* Commission of the European Communities, no. 43, March, pp. 169–82.

Nutter, Warren G. 1968. "Markets Without Property: A Grand Illusion," in *Money, the Market and the State,* edited by N. Beadles and L. Drewry. Athens: University of Georgia Press, pp. 137–45.

Odom, William. 1976. "A Dissenting View on the Group Approach to Soviet Politics," *World Politics,* July, *28* (4), pp. 543–67.

Ofer, Gur. 1987. "Soviet Economic Growth: 1928–1985," *Journal of Economic Literature,* December, *25* (4), pp. 1767–1833.

———. 1988. "Productivity, Competitiveness and the Socialist System." Jerusalem: Department of Economics, The Hebrew University of Jerusalem, and Washington, D.C.: The Brookings Institution. Manuscript.

———. 1990. "Macroeconomic Issues of Soviet Reforms," *Working Paper,* no. 222. Jerusalem: Department of Economics, The Hebrew University of Jerusalem, April.

Olson, Mancur. 1982. *The Rise and Decline of Nations. Economic Growth, Stagflation, and Social Rigidities.* New Haven: Yale University Press.

Organization for Economic Co-operation and Development. 1990. *Historical Statistics, 1960–1988.* Paris.

———. 1991. *National Accounts. Main Aggregates. Vol. 1.* Paris.

Orlov, B. P. 1988. "Illiuzii i real'nost' ekonomicheskoi informatsii" (The illusions and reality of economic information), *EKO,* 1988 (8), pp. 3–20.

Osband, Kent. 1987. "Speak Softly, but Carry a Big Stick: On Optimal Targets under Moral Hazard," *Journal of Comparative Economics,* December, *11* (4), pp. 584–95.

Pacsi, Zoltán. 1979. "A megvalósulási idő szerepe és alakulása a beruházásokban" (Construction periods of investment projects), *Pénzügyi Szemle,* August/September, *23* (8-9), pp. 628–38.

Pareto, Vilfredo. [1916] 1935. *The Mind and Society,* edited by Arthur Livingston. New York: Harcourt Brace.

Patocka, Jan. 1977. "Letter from Prague: The Philosophy of 'Charter 77'," *Encounter,* June, *48* (6), pp. 92–93.

Pavlov, V. 1987. "Vazhnaia sostavnaia chast' perestroiki" (An important constituent part of perestroika), *Kommunist,* September, (13), pp. 14–26.

Peebles, Gavin. 1990. "China's Macroeconomy in the 1980s," *China Working Paper,* no. 5, National Center for Development Studies, The Australian National University.

Perkins, Dwight. 1988. "Reforming China's Economic System," *Journal of Economic Literature,* June, *26* (2), pp. 601–45.

Perry, Elizabeth J., and Christine P. W. Wong, eds. 1985. *The Political Economy of Reform in Post-Mao China*. Cambridge: Harvard University Council on East Asian Studies.

Péter, György. 1954a. "Az egyszemélyi felelős vezetésről" (On management based on one-man responsibility), *Társadalmi Szemle,* August/September, *9* (8–9), pp. 109–24.

———. 1954b. "A gazdaságosság jelentőségéről és szerepéről a népgazdaság tervszerű irányításában" (On the importance and role of economic efficiency in the planned control of the national economy), *Közgazdasági Szemle,* December, *1* (3), pp. 300–24.

Pető, Iván, and Sándor Szakács. 1985. *A hazai gazdaság négy évtizedének története, 1945–1985* (Four-decade history of the Hungarian economy, 1945–1985). Budapest: Közgazdasági és Jogi Könyvkiadó.

Petrakov, Nikolai Iu. 1987a. "Planovaia tsena v sisteme upravleniia narodnym khoziaistvom" (The planned price in the system of administering the national economy), *Voprosy Ekonomiki,* January, (1), pp. 44–55.

———. 1987b. "Prospects for Change in the Systems of Price Formation, Finance and Credit in the USSR," *Soviet Economy,* April/June, *3* (2), pp. 135–44.

Petschnig, Mária. 1985. "Fogyasztói árindexünk—a kritika tükrében" (Our consumer price index in the mirror of the critics). Budapest and Pécs: Institute of Economics. Manuscript.

Phelps, Edmund S., et al. 1970. *Microeconomic Foundations of Employment and Inflation Theory.* New York: W. W. Norton.

Pipes, Richard. 1984a. *Survival Is Not Enough: Soviet Realities and America's Future.* New York: Simon and Schuster.

———. 1984b. "Can the Soviet Union Reform?" *Foreign Affairs,* Fall, *63* (1), pp. 47–61.

Podkaminer, Leon. 1988. "Disequilibrium in Poland's Consumer Markets: Further Evidence on Intermarket Spillovers," *Journal of Comparative Economics,* March, *12* (1), pp. 43–60.

Podolski, T. M. 1973. *Socialist Banking and Monetary Control: The Experience of Poland.* Cambridge: Cambridge University Press.

Polányi, Karl. 1944. *The Great Transformation.* New York: Farrar and Rinehart.

———. 1957. "The Economy as Instituted Process," in *Trade and Market in the Early Empires,* edited by K. Polányi, C. M. Arensberg, and H. W. Pearson. Glencoe: Free Press, pp. 243–70.

Politicheskaia Ekonomiia Sotsializma. Uchebnik (Political economy of socialism. Textbook). 1954. Moscow: Izdatel'stvo Politicheskoi Literatury.

Popov, Gavril Kh. 1987a. "S tochki zreniia ekonomista: O romane Aleksandra Beka 'Novoe Naznachenie'" (From an economist's perspective: Bek's novel "New Appointment"), *Nauka i Zhizn',* April, (4), pp. 54–68.

———. 1987b. "Fasadi i kukhnia 'velikoi reformy'" (The facade and the kitchen of the "great reform"), *EKO* (1), pp. 144–75.

———. 1988. "Perestroika upravleniia ekonomikoi" (The restructuring of economic administration), in *Inogo ne dano,* edited by Yu. Afana'siev. Moscow: Progress, pp. 621–33.

Popper, Karl. 1959. *The Logic of Scientific Discovery.* New York: Basic Books.

Porter, Gareth. 1990. "The Politics of Renovation in Vietnam," *Problems of Communism,*, May/June, *40* (3), pp. 72–88.

Portes, Richard, et al. 1987. "Macroeconomic Planning and Disequilibrium: Estimates for Poland, 1955–1980," *Econometrica,* January, *55* (1), pp. 19–41.

Portes, Richard, and David Winter. 1980. "Disequilibrium Estimates for Consumption Goods Markets in Centrally Planned Economies," *Review of Economic Studies,* January, *47* (1), pp. 137–59.

Powell, Raymond P. 1977. "Plan Execution and the Workability of Soviet Planning," *Journal of Comparative Economics,* March, *1* (1), pp. 51–76.

Poznanski, Kazimierz Z. 1987. *Technology, Competition, and the Soviet Bloc in the World Market.* Berkeley: Institute of International Studies, University of California.

———. 1988. "The CPE Aversion to Innovations: Alternative Theoretical Explanations," *Economics of Planning, 22* (3), pp. 136–45.

Prasnikar, Janez, and Jan Svejnar. 1988. "Economic Behaviour of Yugoslav Enterprises," in *Advances in the Economic Analyses of Participatory and Labor Managed Firms,* edited by Derek Jones and Jan Svejnar. Vol. 3. Lexington, Mass.: Lexington Books, pp. 237–311.

———. 1990. "Workers' Participation in Management vs. Social Ownership and Government Policies: Yugoslav Lessons for Transforming Socialist Economies," *Working Paper,* no. 264. Pittsburgh: University of Pittsburgh.

Prokopovich, Sergei N. 1918. *Opyt ischisleniia narodnogo dokhoda 50 gub. Evropeiskoi Rossii v 1900–1913gg* (An attempt at calculating the national income of the fifty provinces of European Russia from 1910–1913). Moscow: Soviet Vserossiiskikh Kooperativnykh S'ezdov.

Proudhon, Pierre J. 1867–70. *Oeuvres Complètes.* Paris: Lacroix.

Prybyla, Jan S. 1990. *Reform in China and Other Socialist Economies.* Washington, D.C.: Published for the American Enterprise Institute.

Pryor, Frederic L. 1973. *Property and Industrial Organization in Communist and Capitalist Nations.* Bloomington: Indiana University Press.

———. 1977. "Some Costs and Benefits of Markets: An Empirical Study," *Quarterly Journal of Economics, 91* (1), pp. 81–102.

———. 1985. *A Guidebook to the Comparative Study of Economic Systems.* Englewood Cliffs, N.J.: Prentice-Hall.

Qian, Yingyi. 1986. "Kornai's Soft Budget Constraint: A Neoclassical Interpretation." Cambridge: Department of Economics, Harvard University. Manuscript.

———. 1988. "Profit Levelling and Incentives in Socialist Economies." Cambridge: Department of Economics, Harvard University. Manuscript.

———. 1990. "Incentives and Control in Socialist Economies." Ph.D. dissertation, Harvard University.

Qian, Yingyi, and Chenggang Xu. 1991. "Innovation and Financial Constraints in Centralized and Decentralized Economies." Cambridge: Department of Economics, Harvard University. Manuscript.

Quandt, Richard E. 1986. "Enterprise Purchases and the Expectations of Rationing," *Economics Letters,* March, *21* (1), pp. 13–15.

Quandt, Richard E., and Dusan Triska. 1990. *Optimal Decisions in Markets and Planned Economies.* Boulder: Westview Press.

Rákosi, Mátyás. [1950] 1955. "Legyen a DISZ pártunk biztos támasza!" (Let the Democratic Youth Organization be a firm foundation of our party!), in M. Rákosi, *A békéért és a szocializmus építéséért.* Budapest: Szikra, pp. 234–46.

Reynolds, Bruce L., ed. 1988. *Economic Reform in China: Challenges and Choices.* Armonk, N.Y.: M. E. Sharpe.

Révész, Gábor. 1990. *Perestroika in Eastern Europe: Hungary's Economic Transformation, 1945–1988.* Boulder: Westview Press.

Rigby, Thomas H., and Ferenc Fehér, eds. 1982. *Political Legitimation in Communist States.* Oxford: Macmillan.

Rimler, Judit. 1986. "Economic Obsolescence and Employment (A Comparative Analysis of the Hungarian and Dutch Economies)," *Acta Oeconomica, 36* (1–2), pp. 123–40.

Riskin, Carl. 1989. "Reform and System Change in China," *WIDER Conference Paper,* Helsinki, March.

Robinson, Joan. 1933. *The Economics of Imperfect Competition.* London: Macmillan.

———. 1969. *The Cultural Revolution in China.* Harmondsworth: Penguin.

Roland, Gérard. 1987. "Investment Growth Fluctuations in the Soviet Union: An Econometric Analysis," *Journal of Comparative Economics*, June, *11* (2), pp. 192–206.

———. 1990. "On the Meaning of Aggregate Excess Supply and Demand for Consumer Goods in Soviet-Type Economies," *Cambridge Journal of Economics,* March, *14* (1), pp. 49–62.

Ronnas, Per. 1989. "Turning the Romanian Peasant into a New Socialist Man: An Assessment of Rural Development Policy in Romania," *Soviet Studies,* October, *41* (4), pp. 543–99.

———. 1990. "The Economic Legacy of Ceausescu," *Working Paper,* no. 11. Stockholm: Stockholm Institute of Soviet and East European Economics.

Rosen, Sherwin. 1982. "Authority, Control, and the Distribution of Earnings," *Bell Journal of Economics,* Autumn, *13* (2), pp. 311–23.

Ross, Stephen A. 1973. "The Economic Theory of Agency: The Principal's Problem," *American Economic Review*, May, *63* (2), pp. 134–39.

Rostowski, Jacek. 1988. "Intra-year Fluctuations in Production and Sales: East and West," in *The Soviet Economy on the Brink of Reform. Essays in Honor of Alec Nove,* edited by Peter Wiles. Boston: Unwin Hyman, pp. 82–111.

———. 1989a. "The Decay of Socialism and the Growth of Private Enterprise in Poland," *Soviet Studies,* April, *41* (2), pp. 194–214.

———. 1989b. "Market Socialism Is Not Enough: Inflation vs. Unemployment in Reformed Communist Economies," *Communist Economies, 1* (3), pp. 269–85.

Rostowski, Jacek, and Paul Auerbach. 1986. "Storming Cycles and Economic Systems," *Journal of Comparative Economics,* September, *10* (3), pp. 293–312.

Ruble, Blair, and Alex Pravda, eds. 1986. *Trade Unions in Communist States.* Boston: Allen and Unwin.

Rudneva, E. 1989. "Instrument gosudarstvennogo regulirovaniia ekonomiki" (The tool of state regulation of the economy), *Planovoe Khoziastvo,* June (6), pp. 25-34.

Rusinow, Dennison. 1977. *The Yugoslav Experiment 1948-1974.* London: C. Hurst and Company for the Royal Institute of International Affairs, and Berkeley: University of California Press.

Sacks, Stephen R. 1989. "The Yugoslav Firm," in *Comparative Economic Systems: Models and Cases,* edited by Morris Bornstein. Homewood, Ill.: Irwin, pp. 213-33.

Sakharov, Andrei D. 1968. *Progress, Coexistence, and Intellectual Freedom.* New York: W. W. Norton.

———. 1974. *Sakharov Speaks.* New York: Alfred A. Knopf.

———. 1975. *My Country and the World.* New York: Alfred A. Knopf.

———. 1979. *Alarm and Hope.* London: Collins and Harvill Press.

Sanders, Alan J. K. 1987. *Mongolia: Politics, Economics and Society.* Boulder: Lynne Rienner Publishers.

Savezni Zavod za Statistiku (Federal Statistical Office). 1988. *Statisticki godisnjak jugoslavije 1988* (Statistical yearbook of Yugoslavia, 1988). Belgrade.

Scarf, Herbert. 1973. *A Computation of Economic Equilibria.* New Haven: Yale University Press.

Schaffer, Mark E. 1989. "The 'Credible-Commitment Problem' in the Centre-Enterprise Relationship," *Journal of Comparative Economics,* September , *13* (3) , pp. 359-82.

———. 1990. "State-Owned Enterprises in Poland: Taxation, Subsidization, and Competition Policies," *Eastern Europe,* March, p. 188.

Schama, Simon. 1989. *Citizens.* New York: Alfred A. Knopf.

Schelling, Thomas C. 1978. *Micromotives and Macrobehavior.* New York: W. W. Norton.

Schnabel, Claus. 1991. "Structural Adjustment and Privatization of the East German Economy," in *Economic Aspects of German Unification,* edited by Paul Welfens. Heidelberg: Springer, forthcoming.

Schnytzer, Adi. 1982. *Stalinist Economic Strategy in Practice: The Case of Albania.* Oxford: Oxford University Press.

Schroeder, Gertrude E. 1979. "The Soviet Economy on a Treadmill of 'Reforms'," in *The Soviet Economy in a Time of Change.* Joint Economic Committee, Congress of the United States, Washington, D.C.: Government Printing Office, pp. 312-40.

———. 1983. "Consumption," in *The Soviet Economy: Toward the Year 2000,* edited by Abram Bergson and Herbert S. Levine. London: Allen and Unwin, pp. 311-49.

———. 1985. "The Slowdown in Soviet Industry, 1976-1982," *Soviet Economy,* January/March, *1* (1), pp. 42-74.

———. 1988. "Property Rights Issues in Economic Reforms in Socialist Countries," *Studies in Comparative Communism,* Summer, *21* (2), pp. 175-88.

———. 1990a. "Measuring the Size and Growth of Consumption in the Soviet Union Relative to Western Countries," University of Virginia. Manuscript.

———. 1990b. "Soviet Consumption in the 1980s: A Tale of Woe." University of Virginia. Manuscript.

Schumpeter, Joseph A. [1912] 1968. *The Theory of Economic Development. An Inquiry into Profits, Capital, Credit, Interest and Business Cycles.* Cambridge: Harvard University Press.

Schweitzer, Iván. 1982. *Vállalatnagyság* (Firm size). Budapest: Közgazdasági és Jogi Könyvkiadó.

Scitovsky, Tibor. [1951] 1971. *Welfare and Competition.* Homewood, Ill: Irwin.

———. 1985. "Pricetakers' Plenty: A Neglected Benefit of Capitalism," *Kyklos, 38* (4), pp. 517-36.

Scott, Chris. 1990. "Soft Budgets and Hard Rents: A Note on Kornai and Gomulka," *Economics of Planning, 23* (2), pp. 117-27.

Screpanti, Emilio. 1986. "A Model of the Political Economic Systems in Centrally Planned Economies," *EUI Working Paper,* no. 85/201. Florence: European University Institute.

Selden, Mark. 1988. *The Political Economy of Chinese Socialism.* Armonk, N.Y.: M. E. Sharpe.

Seliunin, Vasilii, and Grigorii Khanin. 1987. "Lukavaia tsifra" (The cunning figure), *Novyi Mir,* February, *63* (2), pp. 181-201.

Sen, Amartya. 1973. *On Economic Inequality.* Oxford: Clarendon Press.

———. 1981. "Ethical Issues in Income Distribution: National and International," in *The World Economic Order: Past and Prospects,* edited by Sven Grassman and Erik Lundberg. London: Macmillan, pp. 465-94.

Sen Gupta, Bhabani. 1986. *Afghanistan: Politics, Economics and Society.* London: Frances Pinter.

Shafir, Michael. 1985. *Romania: Politics, Economics and Society.* London: Frances Pinter, and Boulder: Lynne Rienner.

Shmelev, Nikolai P. 1988a. "Novyi trevogi" (New worries), *Novyi Mir,* April, (4), pp. 160-75.

———. 1988b. "Rethinking Price Reform in the USSR," *Soviet Economy,* October/December, *4* (4), pp. 319-27.

Shulman, Marshall D. 1966. *Beyond the Cold War.* New Haven: Yale University Press.

Sicular, Terry. 1985. "Rural Marketing and Exchange in the Wake of Recent Reforms," in *The Political Economy of Reform in Post-Mao China,* edited by Elizabeth Perry and Christine P. W. Wong. Cambridge: Harvard University Council on East Asian Studies, pp. 83-110.

———. 1990. "Plan, Market and Inflation: Potential Problems with China's Two-Track System." Cambridge: Department of Economics, Harvard University. Manuscript.

Sigg, Hans. 1981. *Grundzüge des sowjetischen Bankwesens.* Bern: Paul Haupt .

Sik, Ota. 1966. *Economic Planning and Management in Czechoslovakia.* Prague: Orbis.

Simon, András. 1977. "A lakossági fogyasztás és megtakarítás vizsgálata ökonometriai módszerrel" (Examination of the consumption and savings of the population with econometric methods), *Szigma, 10* (4), pp. 249-64.

Simonovits, András. 1981. "Maximal Convergence Speed of Decentralized Control," *Journal of Economic Dynamics and Control,* February, *3* (1), pp. 51-64.

———. 1991a. "Investment Limit Cycles in a Socialist Economy," *Economics of Planning, 24* (1), pp. 27-46.

———. 1991b. "Investment, Starts and Cycles in a Socialist Economy," *Journal of Comparative Economics, 15* (3), pp. 460-76.

Singleton, Frederick B., and Bernard Carter. 1982. *The Economy of Yugoslavia.* London: Croom Helm, and New York: St. Martin's Press.

Skilling, H. Gordon. 1966. "Interest Groups and Communist Politics," *World Politics,* April, *18* (3), pp. 435-51.

Sláma, Jiri. 1978. "A Cross-Country Regression Model of Social Inequality," in *Income Distribution and Economic Inequality,* edited by Zvi Griliches et al. Frankfurt am Main: Campus Verlag, Halsted and Eiley, pp. 306-23.

Sletsiura, V. 1989. "Kroki ekonomicheskoi reformy" (The cracks of economic reform), *Planovoe Khoziaistvo,* September, (9), pp. 23-33.

Solomon, Susan, ed. 1983. *Pluralism in the Soviet Union.* New York: St. Martin's Press.

Solow, Robert M. [1970] 1988. *Growth Theory: An Exposition.* New York: Oxford University Press.

Solzhenitsyn, Aleksandr I. 1974-78. *The Gulag Archipelago.* 3 vols. New York: Harper and Row.

Somerville, Keith. 1986. *Angola: Politics, Economics and Society.* Boulder: Lynne Rienner Publishers.

Soós, Károly Attila. 1975. "Causes of Investment Fluctuations in the Hungarian Economy," *Eastern European Economics,* Winter, *14* (2), pp. 25-36.

———. 1984. "A Propos the Explanation of Shortage Phenomena: Volume of Demand and Structural Inelasticity," *Acta Oeconomica, 33* (3-4), pp. 305-20.

———. 1986. *Terv, kampány, pénz* (Plan, campaign, and money). Budapest: Közgazdasági és Jogi Könyvkiadó.

———. 1990. "Privatization, Dogma-Free Self-Management, and Ownership Reform," *Eastern European Economics,* Summer, *28* (4), pp. 53-70.

Sorokin, V. 1985. *Ochered'* (The line). Paris: Sintaksis.

Spence, Andrew M. 1974. *Market Signalling.* Cambridge: Harvard University Press.

Staar, Richard F. 1987. "Checklist of Communist Parties in 1986," *Problems of Communism,* March/April, *36* (2), pp. 40-56.

Stahl, Dale O., and Michael Alexeev. 1985. "The Influence of Black Markets on a Queue-Rationed Centrally Planned Economy," *Journal of Economic Theory,* April, *35* (2), pp. 234-50.

Stalin, Josef V. 1947. *Problems of Leninism.* Moscow: Foreign Languages Press.

———. 1952. *Economic Problems of Socialism in the USSR.* Moscow: Foreign Languages Press, and New York: International Publishers.

———. [1927] 1954. "Political Report of the Central Committee, 15th Congress of the CPSU, Dec. 2–19, 1927," in J. V. Stalin, *Collected Works,* vol. 10. Moscow: Foreign Languages Publishing House, pp. 277–382.

Staniszkis, Jadwiga. 1989. "The Dynamics of a Breakthrough in the Socialist System: An Outline of Problems," *Soviet Studies,* October, *41* (4), pp. 560–73.

———. 1991. *The Dynamics of Breakthrough in Eastern Europe.* Berkeley: California University Press.

State Statistical Bureau, People's Republic of China. 1985. *Statistical Yearbook of China, 1985.* New York: Oxford University Press.

———. 1987. *A Statistical Survey in 1987.* Beijing: State Statistical Bureau, New World Press, and China Statistical Information and Consultancy Service Centre.

———. 1988. *China. Statistical Yearbook, 1988.* Hong Kong: International Centre for the Advancement of Science and Technology, and Beijing: China Statistical Information and Consultancy Service Centre.

Statistisches Amt der Deutschen Demokratischen Republik. 1971. *Statistisches Jahrbuch der Deutschen Demokratischen Republik.* Berlin: Staatsverlag.

———. 1990. *Statistisches Jahrbuch der Deutschen Demokratischen Republik.* Berlin: Rudolf Haufe Verlag.

Statistisches Bundesamt. 1970. *Statistisches Jahrbuch für die Bundesrepublik Deutschland.* Stuttgart: Kohlhammer.

———. 1990. *Statistisches Jahrbuch 1989 für die Bundesrepublik Deutschland.* Stuttgart: Metzger Poeschel Verlag.

Statistika. (Statistics). 1977. *Narodnoe khoziaistvo SSSR za 60 let* (The Soviet national economy for sixty years). Moscow.

Stiglitz, Joseph E. 1974. "Incentives and Risk Sharing in Sharecropping," *Review of Economic Studies,* April, *41* (2), pp. 219–55.

———. 1976. "The Efficiency Wage Hypothesis, Surplus Labor and the Distribution of Income in L.D.C.s," *Oxford Economic Papers,* July, *28* (2), pp. 185–207.

———. 1987. "Principal and Agent," in *The New Palgrave. A Dictionary of Economics,* edited by John Eatwell, Murray Milgate, and Peter Newman. Vol. 3. London: Macmillan, and New York: The Stockton Press, pp. 966–72.

Stiglitz, Joseph E., and Andrew Weiss. 1981. "Credit Rationing in Markets with Imperfect Information," *American Economic Review,* June, *71* (3), pp. 393–410.

Stojanovic, Radmila, ed. 1982. *The Functioning of the Yugoslav Economy.* Armonk, N.Y.: M. E. Sharpe, and Nottingham: Spokesman Books.

Stoneman, Colin. 1989. *Zimbabwe: Politics, Economics, and Society.* Boulder: Lynne Rienner Publishers.

Streeten, Paul. 1959. "Unbalanced Growth," *Oxford Economic Papers,* new series, June, *11* (2), pp. 167–90.

Stuart-Fox, Martin. 1986. *Laos: Politics, Economics and Society.* Boulder: Lynne Rienner Publishers.

Summers, Robert, and Alan Heston. 1984. "Improved International Comparisons of Real Product and Its Composition, 1950–1980," *Review of Income and Wealth,* June, *30* (2), pp. 207–61.

———. 1988. "A New Set of International Comparisons of Real Product and Price Levels: Estimates for 130 Countries, 1950–1985," *Review of Income and Wealth,* March, *34* (1), pp. 1–43.

Sun, Yefang. 1982. "Some Theoretical Issues in Socialistic Economics," originally published in the period 1958–1961, in *Social Needs versus Economic Efficiency in China,* edited by K. K. Fung. Armonk, N.Y.: M. E. Sharpe.

Sutela, Pekka. 1984. *Socialism, Planning and Optimality: A Study in Soviet Economic Thought.* Helsinki: The Finnish Society of Sciences and Letters.

———. 1991. *Economic Thought and Economic Reform in the Soviet Union.* Cambridge: Cambridge University Press.

Sutton, Anthony C. 1968. *Western Technology and Soviet Economic Development 1917 to 1930.* Vol. 1. Stanford: Hoover Institution.

———. 1971. *Western Technology and Soviet Economic Development 1930 to 1945.* Vol. 2. Stanford: Hoover Institution.

———. 1973. *Western Technology and Soviet Economic Development 1945 to 1965.* Vol. 3. Stanford: Hoover Institution.

Swaan, Wim. 1990. "Price Regulation in Hungary, 1968–87: A Behavioural-Institutional Explanation," *Cambridge Journal of Economics,* September, *14* (3), pp. 247–65.

Swain, Nigel. 1987. "Hungarian Agriculture in the Early 1980s: Retrenchment Followed by Reform," *Soviet Studies,* January, *39* (1), pp. 24–39.

Szabó, Judit. 1985. "Kínálati rugalmatlanság, elszaladó kereslet, készletek és hiány" (Inelasticity of supply, runaway demand, stocks, and shortage), *Közgazdasági Szemle, 32* (7–8), pp. 951–60.

———. 1989. "Book Review. T. Liska: Ökonosztát (Econostat)," *Acta Oeconomica, 41* (1–2), pp. 237–52.

Szabó, Kálmán. 1967. "A szocialista gazdaságirányítási rendszer" (The socialist system of economic administration), in *A szocializmus politikai gazdaságtana. Tankönyv,* edited by Andor Berei et al. Budapest: Kossuth Könyvkiadó, pp. 248–294.

Szalai, Erzsébet. 1982. "A reformfolyamat és a nagyvállalatok" (The reform process and the large enterprises), *Valóság, 25* (5), pp. 23–35.

———. 1989. "See-Saw: The Economic Mechanism and Large-Company Interests," *Acta Oeconomica, 41* (1–2), pp. 101–36.

Szamuely, László. 1974. *First Models of the Socialist Economic Systems. Principles and Theories.* Budapest: Akadémiai Kiadó.

———. 1982. "The First Wave of the Mechanism Debate in Hungary (1954–1957)," *Acta Oeconomica, 29* (1–2), pp. 1–24.

———. 1984. "The Second Wave of the Economic Mechanism Debate and the 1968 Reform in Hungary," *Acta Oeconomica, 33* (1–2), pp. 43–67.

Székely, István. 1990. "The Reform of the Hungarian Financial System," in *Economic Transformation in Hungary and Poland, European Economy,* Commission of the European Communities, no. 43, March, pp. 107–23.

Szelényi, Iván. 1983. *Urban Inequalities under State Socialism.* Oxford: Oxford University Press.

———. 1986. "The Prospects and Limits of the East European New Class Project: An Autocritical Reflection on 'The Intellectuals on the Road to Class Power'," *Politics and Society, 15* (2), pp. 103–44.

———. 1988. *Socialist Entrepreneurs: Embourgeoisement in Rural Hungary.* Madison: University of Wisconsin Press.

Taigner, Stefan. 1987. "Polens Second Economy," *Osteuropa-Wirtschaft,* June *32* (2), pp. 107–21.

Tallós, György. 1976. *A bankhitel szerepe gazdaságirányítási rendszerünkben* (The role of bank credit in our system of economic administration). Budapest: Kossuth.

Tanzi, Victor, ed. 1982. *The Underground Economy in the U.S. and Abroad.* Lexington, Mass.: Lexington Books.

Tardos, Márton. 1981. "The Role of Money: Economic Relations between the State and the Enterprises in Hungary," *Acta Oeconomica 25* (1–2), pp. 19–35.

———. 1986. "The Conditions of Developing a Regulated Market," *Acta Oeconomica, 36* (1–2), pp. 67–89.

———. 1989. "The Hungarian Banking Reform." Budapest: Pénzügykutató Részvénytársaság. Manuscript.

———. 1990. "Property Ownership," *Eastern European Economics,* Spring, *28* (3), pp. 4–29.

Tedstrom, John B., ed. 1990. *Socialism, Perestroika, and the Dilemmas of Soviet Economic Reform.* Boulder: Westview Press.

Temkin, Gabriel. 1989. "On Economic Reform in Socialist Countries: The Debate on Economic Calculation under Socialism Revisited," *Communist Economies, 1* (1), pp. 31–59.

Teodorescu, Alin. 1990. "The Future of a Failure: The Romanian Economy," *Working Paper,* no. 12. Stockholm: Stockholm Institute of Soviet and East European Economics.

Thimm, Alfred L. 1980. *The False Promise of Co-Determination: The Changing Nature of European Workers' Participation.* Lexington, Mass.: Lexington Books.

Thornton, James R. 1978. "The Ratchet, Price Sensitivity, and Assortment Plan," *Journal of Comparative Economics,* March, *2* (1), pp. 57–63.

Tidrick, Gene. 1987. "Planning and Supply," in *China's Industrial Reform,* edited by Gene Tidrick and Chen Jiyuan. New York: Oxford University Press, pp. 175–209.

Timár, János. 1985. "A társadalmi újratermelés időalapja" (The total of manhours available for social reproduction). Budapest: University of Economics. Manuscript.

Toranska, Teresa. 1987. *"Them": Stalin's Polish Puppets.* New York: Harper and Row.

Treml, Vladimir G. 1987. "Income from Private Services Recognized by Official Soviet Statistics," in M. Alexeev et al., *Studies on the Soviet Second Economy, Berkeley-Duke Occasional Papers on the Second Economy in the USSR,* no. 11, December, pp. 4.1–4.27.

———. 1990. "Study of Employee Theft of Materials from Places of Employment," *Berkeley-Duke Occasional Papers on the Second Economy in the USSR,* June, no. 20.

Trotsky, Leon. [1937] 1970. *A Revolution Betrayed*. New York: Pathfinder Press.

Tsapelik, V., and A. Iakovlev. 1990. "Kolichestvennye kharakteristiki monopolii" (Quantitative characteristics of monopolies), *Voprosy Ekonomiki*, June, (6), pp. 38–46.

Tucker, Robert. 1973. *Stalin as Revolutionary*. New York: W. W. Norton.

———. 1990. *Stalin in Power. The Revolution from Above 1928–1941*. New York: W. W. Norton.

Tyson, Laura D'Andrea. 1977. "Liquidity Crises in the Yugoslav Economy: An Alternative to Bankruptcy?" *Soviet Studies*, April, *29* (2), pp. 284–95.

———. 1980. *The Yugoslav Economic System and Its Performance in the 1970s*. Berkeley: Institute of International Studies, University of California.

———. 1983. "Investment Allocation: A Comparison of the Reform Experiences of Hungary and Yugoslavia," *Journal of Comparative Economics*, September, *7* (3), pp. 288–303.

Ulam, Adam. 1973. *Stalin: The Man and His Era*. Boston: Beacon Press.

Ungvárszky, Ágnes. 1989. *Gazdaságpolitikai ciklusok Magyarországon, 1948–1988* (Economic policy cycles in Hungary, 1948–1988). Budapest: Közgazdasági és Jogi Könyvkiadó.

Union Internationale des Télécommunications. 1980. *Annuaire statistique des télécommunications du secteur public*. Geneva.

———. 1982. *Annuaire statistique des télécommunications du secteur public*. Geneva.

———. 1986. *Annuaire statistique des télécommunications du secteur public*. Geneva.

United Nations. 1977. *Comparisons of the System of National Accounts and the System of Balances of the National Economy*. Part 1. Studies in Methods, series F, no. 20. New York.

———. 1981. *Annual Bulletin of Transport Statistics for Europe, 1980*. Vol. 32. New York.

———. Economic Commission for Europe. 1986a. *Human Settlements Situation in the ECE Region around 1980*. New York.

———. 1986b. *International Trade Statistical Yearbook, 1984*. New York.

———. 1986c. "Investment in the ECE Region: Long-term Trends and Policy Issues," *Economic Bulletin for Europe, 38* (2).

———. 1987. *Environment Statistics in Europe and North America. An Experimental Compendium*. New York.

———. 1989. *Economic Bulletin for Europe*. Vol. 41. New York.

———. 1990a. *Economic Survey of Europe in 1989–1990*. New York.

———. Conference on Trade and Development. 1990b. *Handbook of International Trade Statistics 1989*. New York.

Vanek, Jaroslav. 1970. *The General Theory of Labour-Managed Market Economies*. Ithaca: Cornell University Press.

———. 1971. *The Participatory Economy: An Evolutionary Hypothesis and a Strategy for Development*. Ithaca: Cornell University Press.

———. 1972. *The Economics of Workers' Management: A Yugoslav Case Study.* London: Allen and Unwin.

Várhegyi, Éva. 1987. "Hitelezési mechanizmus és hitelelosztás Magyarországon." (The mechanism of crediting and the allocation of credit in Hungary). Candidate's thesis. Budapest.

———. 1989. "Results and Failures of Monetary Restriction. Some Lessons of Hungarian Financial Policy in 1988," *Acta Oeconomica, 41* (3–4), pp. 403–20.

———. 1990a. "The Nature of the Hungarian Credit Market, Lessons of an Empirical Investigation," *Acta Oeconomica, 42* (1–2), pp. 73–86.

———. 1990b. "Pénzfolyamatok a kormányzati törekvések ellenében" (Monetary flows against government objectives), *Külgazdaság, 34* (8), pp. 30–45.

Varian, Hal R. 1978. *Microeconomic Analysis.* New York: W. W. Norton.

Vass, Henrik, ed. 1968. "Az MSZMP Központi Bizottságának irányelvei a gazdasági mechanizmus reformjára" (The directives of the central committee of the Hungarian Socialist Worker's party for the reform of the economic mechanism), in *A Magyar Szocialista Munkáspárt határozatai és dokumentumai, 1963–1966.* Budapest: Kossuth Könyvkiadó, pp. 301–450.

Vickery, Michael. 1986. *Kampuchea: Politics, Economics and Society.* Boulder: Lynne Rienner Publishers.

Voronin, L. 1989. "Razvitie optovoi torgovli" (The development of wholesale trade), *Planovoe Khoziaistvo,* March, (3), pp. 3–13.

Voronov, A. 1990. "O problemakh preodeleniia defitsita i metodakh regulirovaniia potrebitel'skogo rynka" (On the problems of eliminating shortage and methods for the regulation of the consumer market), *Voprosy Ekonomiki,* January, (1), pp. 26–32.

Voszka, Éva. 1984. *Érdek és kölcsönös függőség* (Interest and mutual interdependence). Budapest: Közgazdasági és Jogi Könyvkiadó.

———. 1988. *Reform és átszervezés a nyolcvanas években.* (Reform and reorganization in the 1980s). Budapest: Közgazdsági és Jogi Könyvkiadó.

Ward, Benjamin M. 1958. "The Firm in Illyria: Market Syndicalism," *American Economic Review,* September, *48* (4), pp. 566–89.

Wasilewski, Jacek. 1990. "The Patterns of Bureaucratic Elite Recruitment in Poland in the 1970s and 1980s," *Soviet Studies,* October, *42* (4), pp. 743–57.

Watson, James D. 1968. *The Double Helix. A Personal Account of the Discovery of the Structure of DNA.* New York: Atheneum.

Weber, Max. [1904] 1930. *The Protestant Ethic and the Spirit of Capitalism.* London: Allen & Unwin.

———. [1925] 1978. *Economy and Society: An Outline of Interpretative Sociology,* edited by Gunther Roth and Claus Wittich. New York, Bedminster Press.

Weibull, Jörgen W. 1983. "A Dynamic Model of Trade Frictions and Disequilibrium in the Housing Market," *Scandinavian Journal of Economics, 85* (3), pp. 373–92.

———. 1984. "A Stock-Flow Approach to General Equilibrium with Trade Frictions," *Applied Mathematics and Computation, 14* (1), pp. 63–76.

Weitzman, Martin L. 1970. "Soviet Postwar Economic Growth and Capital-Labor Substitution," *American Economic Review,* September, *60* (4), pp. 676–92.

———. 1976. "The New Soviet Incentive Model," *Bell Journal of Economics,* Spring, *7* (1) pp. 251–57.

———. 1980. "The 'Ratchet Principle' and Performance Incentives," *Bell Journal of Economics,* Spring, *11* (1), pp. 302–8.

———. 1983. "Industrial Production," in *The Soviet Economy: Toward the Year 2000,* edited by Abram Bergson and Herbert S. Levine. London: Allen and Unwin, pp. 178–90.

———. 1984. *The Share Economy.* Cambridge: Harvard University Press.

———. 1985. "The Simple Macroeconomics of Profit-Sharing," *American Economic Review,* December, *75* (5), pp. 937–53.

———. 1987. "On Buyers' and Sellers' Markets under Capitalism and Socialism." Cambridge: Department of Economics, Harvard University. Manuscript.

Wellisz, Stanislaw, and Ronald Findley. 1986. "Central Planning and the 'Second Economy' in Soviet-Type Systems," *The Economic Journal,* September, *96* (383), pp. 646–58.

Whitesell, Robert S. 1989–90. "Estimates of the Output Loss from Allocative Inefficiency. A Comparison of Hungary and West Germany," *Eastern European Economics,* Winter, *28* (2), pp. 95–125.

Whitney, Thomas P., ed. 1963. *Khrushchev Speaks.* Ann Arbor: University of Michigan Press.

Wiles, Peter. 1962. *The Political Economy of Communism.* Cambridge: Harvard University Press.

———. 1968. *Communist International Economics.* Oxford: Basil Blackwell.

———. 1982. "Introduction: Zero Growth and the International Nature of the Polish Disease," in *Crisis in the East European Economy. The Spread of the Polish Disease,* edited by Jan Drewnowski. London: Croom Helm, and New York: St. Martin's Press, pp. 7–17.

Williamson, Oliver E. 1967. "Hierarchical Control and Optimum Firm Size," *Journal of Political Economy,* April, *75* (2), pp. 123–38.

———. 1970. *Corporate Control and Business Behavior.* Englewood Cliffs, N.J.: Prentice-Hall.

———. 1975. *Markets and Hierarchies: Analysis and Antitrust Implications.* New York: Free Press.

Wilpert, Bernhard, and Jörg Rayley. 1983. *Anspruch und Wirklichkeit der Mitbestimmung.* Frankfurt: Campus.

Winiecki, Jan. 1984. "Central Planning and Export Orientation," *Oeconomica Polona, 10* (3–4), pp. 295–312.

———. 1986. "Are Soviet-Type Economies Entering an Era of Long-Term Decline?" *Soviet Studies,* July, *28* (3), pp. 325–48.

———. 1988. *The Distorted World of Soviet-Type Economies.* Pittsburgh: University of Pittsburgh Press.

———. 1989. "Large Industrial Enterprises in Soviet-Type Economies: The Ruling Stratum's Main Rent-seeking Area," *Communist Economies, 4* (1), pp. 363–83.

———. 1991. *Resistance to Change in the Soviet Economic System. A Property Rights Approach.* London: Routledge.

Wolf, Thomas A. 1988. *Foreign Trade in the Centrally Planned Economy.* New York: Harwood Academic Publishers.

Wong, Christine P. W. 1986. "The Economics of Shortage and Problems of Reform in Chinese Industry," *Journal of Comparative Economics*, December, *10* (4), pp. 363–87.

World Bank. 1985. *China: Long-Term Issues and Options.* Washington, D.C.

World Development Report 1986. 1986. New York: Oxford University Press, published for the World Bank.

World Development Report 1988. 1988. New York: Oxford University Press, published for the World Bank.

Wu, Jinglian, and Renwei Zhao. 1987. "The Dual Pricing System in China's Industry," *Journal of Comparative Economics,* September, *11* (3), pp. 309–18.

Wulf, Luc de. 1985. "Financial Reform in China," *Finance and Development,* December, *22* (4), pp. 19–22.

Xue, Muqiao. 1982. *Current Economic Problems in China.* Boulder: Westview Press.

Yeltsin, Boris N. 1990. *Ispoved' na zadannaiu temu.* (Confession on a given theme). Sverdlovsk: Sredne-Ural'skoe Knizhnoe Izdatel'stvo.

Zafanolli, Wojtek. 1985. "A Brief Outline of China's Second Economy," *Asian Survey,* July, *25* (7), pp. 110–32.

Zaleski, Eugene. 1980. *Stalinist Planning for Economic Growth. 1933–1952.* London: Macmillan, and Chapel Hill: University of North Carolina Press.

Zarnovitz, Victor. 1985. "Recent Work on Business Cycles in Historical Perspective: A Review of Theories and Evidence," *Journal of Economic Literature,* June, *23* (2), pp. 523–80.

Zaslavskaya, Tatiana I. 1990. *The Second Socialist Revolution.* Bloomington: Indiana University Press.

Zauberman, Alfred. 1975. *The Mathematical Revolution in Soviet Planning.* London: Royal Institute for International Affairs and Oxford: Oxford University Press.

———. 1976. *Mathematical Theory in Soviet Planning.* Oxford: Oxford University Press.

Zelkó Lajos. 1981. "A versenyárrendszer elméleti és gyakorlati problémi" (On the theoretical and practical problems of the competitive price system), *Közgazdasági Szemle,* July/August, *27* (7–8), pp. 927–40.

Zhou, Shulian. 1981. "Sanshi nianlai wouguo jingji jiegou de huigu" (Chinese economic structure in the recent thirty years: A survey), in *Zhonqquo Jingji Jiegou, vol. 1,* edited by Ma Hong and Sun Shangqing. Beijing: People's Press, pp. 23–55.

Zhou, Xiaochuan, and Li Zhu. 1987. "China's Banking System: Current Status, Perspective on Reform," *Journal of Comparative Economics,* September, *11* (3), pp. 399–409.

Zhuravlev, S. N. 1990. "Potrebitels'kie Tseny: ikh sootnoshenie s zatratami, vliianie na dokhody naseleniia i narodnokhoziaistvennye pokazateli" (Consumer prices: Their relationship to costs, influence on the income of the population, and on macroeconomic indicators), *Seriia Ekonomicheskaia,* (1), pp. 80–96.

Zimbalist, Andrew, and Claes Brundenius. 1989. *The Cuban Economy: Measurement and Analysis of Socialist Performance.* Baltimore: Johns Hopkins University Press.

Zinov'ev, Aleksandr. 1984. *Homo Sovieticus.* London: Polonia.

Zloch-Christy, Iliana. 1987. *Debt Problems of Eastern Europe.* New York: Cambridge University Press.

Zwass, Adam. 1978. *Money, Banking, and Credit in the Soviet Union and Eastern Europe.* London: Macmillan.

Appendix

Bibliography on Postsocialist Transition

THE works listed in this bibliography, with a few exceptions, are not referred to specifically in the book. Nor was it possible to compile a full list. The selection had to be an arbitrary one because the book went to press only a very short time after the political turning point of 1989-90 in Eastern Europe.

The list is confined to works in English.

Allison, G., and G. Yavlinsky, eds. 1991. "Window of Opportunity: Joint Program for Western Cooperation in the Soviet Transformation to Democracy and the Market Economy." Cambridge: Joint Working Group of Harvard University, and Moscow: Center for Economic and Political Research. Manuscript.

Berg, Andrew, and Jeffrey Sachs. 1991. "Macroeconomic Adjustment and International Trade in Eastern Europe: The Case of Poland." Cambridge: Department of Economics, Harvard University. Manuscript.

Blanchard, Olivier, et al. 1991. *Reform in Eastern Europe.* Cambridge: MIT Press.

Blue Ribbon Commission. 1990. "Action Program for Hungary in Transformation to Freedom and Prosperity." Manuscript.

Charap, Joshua, and Karel Dyba. 1991. "Transition to a Market Economy: The Case of Czechoslovakia," *European Economic Review*, April, *35* (2-3), pp. 581-90.

Collier, Irwin L., and Horst Siebert. 1991. "The Economic Integration of Post-Wall Germany," *American Economic Review*, May, *81* (2), pp. 196-201.

Collins, Susan M., and Dani Rodrik. 1991. *Eastern Europe and the Soviet Union in the World Economy.* Washington, D.C.: Institute for International Economics.

Dhanji, Farid. 1991. "Transformation Programs: Content and Sequencing," *American Economic Review*, May, *81* (2), pp. 323-28.

Dornbusch, Rudiger. 1990a. "Economic Reform in Eastern Europe and the Soviet Union: Priorities and Strategy." Cambridge: MIT, November. Manuscript.

———. 1990b. "Priorities of Economic Reform in Eastern Europe and the Soviet Union." *CEPR Occasional Paper*, no. 5. London: Centre for Economic Policy Research.

Dyba, Karel, and Jan Svejnar. "Czechoslovakia: Recent Economic Developments and Prospects," *American Economic Review*, May, *81* (2), pp. 185-90.

Fischer, Stanley. 1991. "Privatization in East European Transformation." *Working Paper* 3703. Cambridge: National Bureau of Economic Research.

Fischer, Stanley, and Alan Gelb. 1990. "Issues in Socialist Economy Reform." *Working Paper* WPS 565. Washington, D.C.: World Bank.

Freeman, Richard B. 1992. "Getting Here from There: Labor in the Transition to a Market Economy, in Bertram Silverman, Robert Vogt, and Murray Yanowitch, eds., *Labor and Democracy in the Transition to a Market Economy: U.S. and Soviet Perspectives*. White Plains, New York: M.E. Sharpe, 1992.

Frydman, R., and A. Rapaczynski. 1990. "Markets and Institutions in Large Scale Privatizations." *Economic Research Report* 90-420. New York: New York University.

Grosfeld, Irena. 1991. "Privatization of State Enterprises in Eastern Europe: The Search for a Market Environment," *East European Politics and Society*, Winter, *5* (1), pp. 142-61.

Hare, Paul, and Irena Grosfeld. 1991. "Privatization in Hungary, Poland and Czechoslovakia," *Discussion Paper Series*, no. 544. London: Centre for Economic Policy Research.

Havrylyshyn, Oleh, and David Tarr. 1991. "Trade Liberalization and the Transition to a Market Economy," *Working Paper* WPS 700. Washington, D.C.: World Bank.

Hewett, Ed. A. 1990-91. "The New Soviet Plan," *Foreign Affairs*, Winter, *70* (5), pp. 146-67.

Hinds, M. 1990. "Issues in the Introduction of Market Forces in Eastern European Socialist Countries." *Internal Discussion Paper,* Report No. IDP-0057. Washington, D.C.: World Bank.

Holzmann, Robert. 1991. "Budgetary Subsidies in Centrally Planned Economies in Transition," *Working Paper* 91/11. Washington, D.C.: International Monetary Fund.

International Monetary Fund, IBRD, OECD, EBRD. 1990. "The Economy of the USSR: Summary and Recommendations," study undertaken in response to a request by the Houston Summit, Washington, D.C.

Jasinski, Piotr. 1990. "Two Models of Privatization in Poland. A Critical Assessment," *Communist Economies*, Fall, *2* (3), pp. 373-401.

Kawalec, Stefan. 1990. "Employee Ownership, State Treasury Ownership: Dubious Solutions," *Communist Economies*, Spring, *2* (1) pp. 83-93.

Klaus, Vacláv. 1990. "A Perspective on Economic Transition in Czechoslovakia and Eastern Europe," *The World Bank Economic Review*, pp. 13-18.

Kolodko, Grzegorz W. 1991. "Transition from Socialism and Stabilization Policies: The Polish Experience," *Rivista di Economica Politica,* forthcoming.

Kopits, George. 1990. "Fiscal Reform in European Economies in Transition." *Working Paper* 91/43. Washington, D.C.: International Monetary Fund, July.

Kornai, János. 1992. "The Principles of Privatization in Eastern Europe," *De Economist, 140,* forthcoming.

———. 1990. *The Road to a Free Economy. Shifting from a Socialist System: The Example of Hungary.* New York: W. W. Norton.

Lewandowski, Janusz, and J. Szomburg. 1989. "Property Reform as a Basis for Social and Economic Reform," *Communist Economies, 1* (3), pp. 257-68.

Lipton, David, and Jeffrey Sachs. 1990. "Creating a Market Economy in Eastern Europe: The Case of Poland," *Brookings Papers on Economic Activity* (1), pp. 75–133.

———. 1990. "Privatization in Eastern Europe: The Case of Poland," *Brookings Papers on Economic Activity* (2), pp. 293–333.

McKinnon, Ronald. 1990. "Stabilising the Ruble," *Communist Economies, 2* (2), pp. 131–42.

———. 1991. *The Order of Economic Liberalization: Financial Control in the Transition to a Market Economy.* Baltimore: The Johns Hopkins University Press.

Ministry of Finance, Hungary. 1991a. "Experiences of and Further Steps in the Tax Reform," in *Public Finance in Hungary,* Budapest.

———. 1991b. "State Budget," in *Public Finance in Hungary.* Budapest.

Móra, Mária. 1990. "Changes in the Structure and Ownership Form of State Enterprises, 1987–1990," *Economic Papers.* Budapest: Economic Research Institute.

Murrel, Peter. 1990. "An Evolutionary Perspective on Reform of the Eastern European Economies." College Park: University of Maryland. Manuscript.

Murrell, Peter, and Mancur Olson. 1991. "Devolution of Centrally Planned Economies," *Journal of Comparative Economics, 15* (2), 239–65.

Nuti, Domenico Mario. 1990a. "Privatization of Socialist Economies: General Issues and the Polish Case." Verona: Association for Comparative Economic Studies, September. Manuscript.

———. 1990b. "Stabilization and Reform Sequencing in the Reform of Socialist Economies." Paper presented at EDI seminar, March.

Peck, Merton J., and Thomas J. Richardson. 1991. *What is to be Done?* New Haven: Yale University Press.

Portes, Richard. 1990. "The European Community and Eastern Europe after 1992," *CEPR Occasional Paper*, no. 3. London: Centre for Economic Policy Research.

Schaffer, Mark E. 1990. "On the Use of Pension Funds in the Privatization of Polish State-Owned Enterprises." London: London School of Economics. Manuscript.

Shiller, Robert J., Maxim Boycko, and Vladimir Korobov. 1991. "Popular Attitudes toward Free Markets: The Soviet Union and the United States Compared," *American Economic Review*, June, *81* (3), pp. 385–400.

Siebert, Horst. 1991. "The Integration of Germany," *European Economic Review*, April, *35* (2–3), pp. 591–602.

Stark, David. 1990. "Privatization in Hungary: From Plan to Market or from Plan to Clan?" *East European Politics and Societies*, 4 (3), pp. 351–92.

Tirole, Jean. 1991. "Privatization in Eastern Europe: Incentives and the Economics of Transition," *1991 NBER Macroeconomics Annual,* Cambridge: MIT Press.

Triska, Dusan. 1990. "Privatization in Post-Communist Czechoslovakia," Stockholm, October. Manuscript.

Voszka Éva. 1991. "Tulajdonreform vagy privatizáció" (Reform of ownership or privatization), *Közgazdasági Szemle*, February, *38* (2), pp. 117–33.

Williamson, John. 1991a. *The Economic Opening of Eastern Europe*. Washington, D.C.: Institute for International Economics.

———. 1991b. *Currency Convertibility in Eastern Europe*. Washington, D.C.: Institute for International Economics.

Winiecki, Jan. 1990. "Post-Soviet-Type Economies in Transition: What Have We Learned from the Polish Transition Programme in its First Year?" *Weltwirtschaftliches Archiv, 126* (4), 765–90.

Working Group formed by a joint decision of Mikhail S. Gorbachev and Boris N. Yeltsin. 1990. "Transition to the Market. Part 1. The Concept and Program" (The Shatalin Plan). Moscow, Avkhanagel'skoe: Cultural Initiative Foundation, August.

Author Index

Subject Index

Adjustment, buyers' versus sellers' market and, 246–47
Administrative consumer prices, 153–55, 273–74
Administrative price setting, 521–25
Administrative producer prices, 149–53
Affinity, 365–68
    of private ownership and market coordination, 447–50
    of public ownership and bureaucratic coordination, 497–500
Apparatus, party
    bureaucracy and, 41
    expenditure on, 540
    role of, 36, 37–38
Appointments, 325, 410–11, 482–83
Armed forces
    disposal over, 411–12
    expenditure on, 540–41
    priority of, 174

Balances, 112
    zero, 354–55
Banking, 131–34, 343–44
    credit system, 543–47
    market socialism and, 485
    private sector and, 453–54
    two-level, 544
Bargaining
    horizontal, 122
    and inner conflict, 121–24
    market socialism and, 487–88
    plan, 244, 363
    vertical, 122, 140, 217, 491
Beveridge curve, use of, 212, 213, 244
Bonds, 138
Budget, state, 134–38
    fiscal policy and, 537–43
Budgetary institution, 76
Budget constraints
    hard, 140, 143–44, 145
    market socialism and hard and soft, 489–97
    private versus state-owned firms and, 263
    soft, 140, 142–43, 144–45, 466
Budget deficit, 538
Bureaucracy
    coercion/discipline and, 43
    defining, 40–41
    difference between bureaucratic coordination and, 91–92
    ideology and, 41
    internal conflicts, 44–45
    managing production behavior of, 270–72
    power and, 41–42
    prestige and privileges and, 42–43
    private sector and, 450–55
    property rights and, 74–75
    repression and, 45–48

Bureaucratic control. *See also* Direct bureaucratic control and planning
    indirect, 488, 507
    of wages, 223–27
Bureaucratic coordination
    defining, 91–92
    description of, 97–100
    difference between bureaucracy and, 91–92
    examples of, 94, 95
    importance of, 362–63
    market socialism and public ownership and, 497–500
Buyers' versus sellers' market, 245–52

Campaigns
    perfection, 397–98, 407
    reorganization, 398–99
Capacity, national excess, 267–68
Capitalism
    defining, 90
    Marx and, 18–19, 368
    opening toward, 423–25
Capitalist economy, promise to catch up with, 53
Capitalist ownership, 87–90
Causality, 360–65, 565–70
Centrally planned/managed economy, 117
Change. *See also* Reform; Revolution
    depth of, 386–87, 565–70
    inducements for, 383–86
    market socialism and, 507–11
    radicalism of, 387, 565–70
    tendencies of, 394–95, 565–74
Churches, influence of, 420
Classical socialism
    defining, 19–20
    viability of, 378–79
CMEA. *See* Council for Mutual Economic Assistance
Coercion/discipline, 43
Coherence of classical system
    affinity, 365–68
    causality, 360–65
    notional variations, 368–72
    Soviet effect, 372–75
    verification, 375–78
Collective property, 77
Collectivization, 76–83, 204–5
Command, planning and, 113
Command economy, use of the term, 10, 114
Commanding heights, 71
Communism, use of the term, 10, 275
Communist party
    factions within, 421
    ideology and power structure and role of, 55–57, 361
    internal conflicts and, 44–45
    mass organizations and, 40
    organization of, 33–36